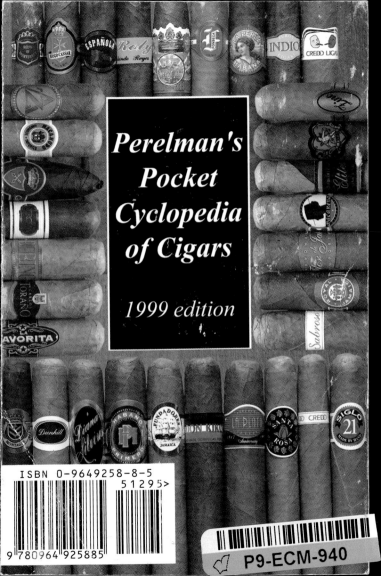

Perelman's Pocket Cyclopedia of Cigars

1999 edition

ISBN 0-9649258-8-5

51295>

9 780964 925885

P9-ECM-940

Hugo Cassar Cigars

HUGO CASSAR BUNDLES
*Great value long filler cigars from
Honduras, Mexico and Indonesia.
Average suggested retail $1.90 each.*

MYSTIQUE
*The original double-wrapped
cigar available from Dominican
Republic and Honduras.
verage suggested retail $5.75 each.*

PRIVATE COLLECTION INDONESIA
*Carribean blended tobaccos
with a Java wrapper.
Average sugg. retail $2.50 each.*

HUGO CASSAR
PETITE CORONAS
*A great small cigar with a
zesty Sumatra wrapper. Seven
cigars in a convenient pack.
Suggested retail
$3 for a pack of 7.*

Dunhill Completes The Night

DUNHILL TOBACCO OF LONDON LIMITED

AGED CIGARS

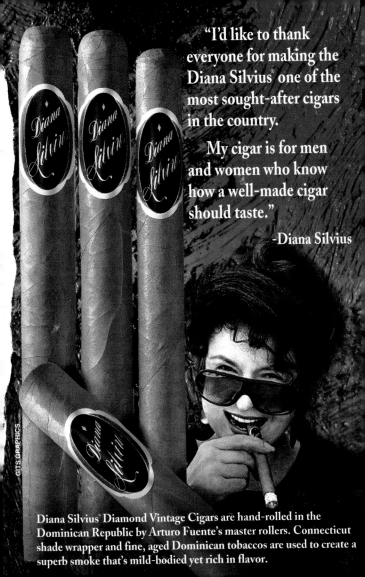

"I'd like to thank everyone for making the Diana Silvius® one of the most sought-after cigars in the country.

My cigar is for men and women who know how a well-made cigar should taste."

-Diana Silvius

Diana Silvius Diamond Vintage Cigars are hand-rolled in the Dominican Republic by Arturo Fuente's master rollers. Connecticut shade wrapper and fine, aged Dominican tobaccos are used to create a superb smoke that's mild-bodied yet rich in flavor.

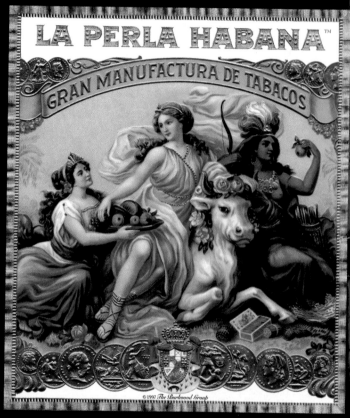

Perelman's Pocket Cyclopedia of Cigars

1999 edition

Compiled by
Richard B. Perelman

Published by
**PERELMAN
PIONEER &
COMPANY**

Los Angeles, California

$ 12.95 U.S.

ISBN 0-9649258-8-5

Published in Los Angeles, California, USA. First printing 1998. Printed by D.M. Steele of Fullerton, California. Cover photography by Long Photography, Inc. of Los Angeles, California.

Please address inquiries to:

PERELMAN PIONEER & COMPANY

POST OFFICE BOX 67B99
CENTURY CITY STATION
LOS ANGELES, CALIFORNIA 90067 USA

Things will never be
the same again.

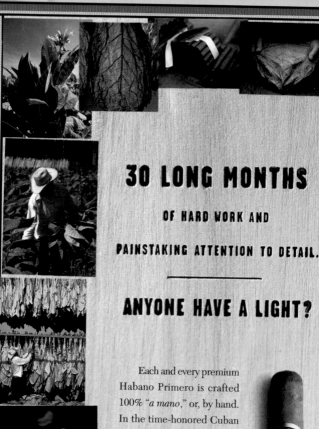

30 LONG MONTHS

OF HARD WORK AND

PAINSTAKING ATTENTION TO DETAIL.

ANYONE HAVE A LIGHT?

Each and every premium
Habano Primero is crafted
100% *"a mano,"* or, by hand.
In the time-honored Cuban
tradition. By the Dominican
Republic's most experienced
"torcedores."

HABANO
PRIMERO™

HECHO A MANO

Perelman's Pocket Cyclopedia of Cigars

1999 edition

TABLE OF CONTENTS

Introduction		1
1.	Cigar Basics	7
	1.01 About cigars	7
	1.02 Construction	7
	1.03 Shapes and sizes	9
	1.04 Enjoying cigars	12
2.	The Cigar Almanac	13
	2.01 Births and deaths	13
	2.02 Brand facts	23
	2.03 Cigars: large and small	26
	2.04 Cigars: special models	28
	2.05 Our favorite brands	35
	2.06 The Cigar Bowl	37
3.	Handmade Cigars: Listings by Brand	43
4.	Mass-Market Cigars: Listings by Brand	719
5.	Small Cigars: Listings by Brand	776

TABLE OF CONTENTS

6. International Measurement Tables 802

7. References 805

8. Ring gauge guide 808

and cigar legends:
- ▸   Victor Migenes 444
- ▸   Juan Sosa 650

Addendum

Brand information received too late to be placed
in the main listings 810

Please send comments, inquiries, questions and suggestions to
the author at:

PERELMAN, PIONEER & COMPANY
POST OFFICE BOX 67B99
CENTURY CITY STATION
LOS ANGELES, CALIFORNIA 90067 USA

Telephone: (323) 965-4905
Facsimile: (323) 965-4919
Internet: perelmanco@aol.com

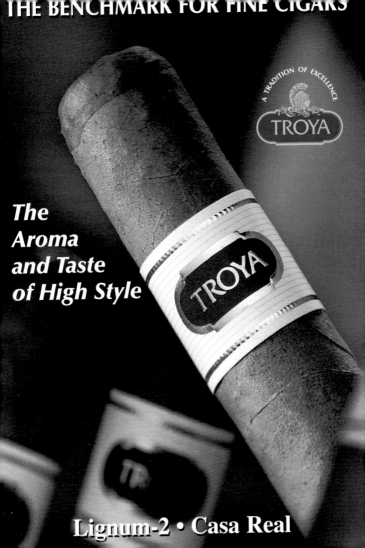

...a Worldwide Exclusive

Nowhere else in the world can you purchase these premium cigars. The Original African Camaroon wrapper along with a Dominican and Brazilian filler creates the distinguished full-bodied flavor of LOS REYES ALIADOS. Both pure Dominican classics, DON KIKO is a full bodied, rich flavored cigar of unparalleled character, while REY DE REYES draws on it's medium bodied smoothness to create a true smoking experience fit for a king.

A REYES DISTRIBUTORS EXCLUSIVE

INTRODUCTION

"Would you believe . . ."

— Don Adams as agent Maxwell Smart
in the 1960s television show *"Get Smart"*

No one in the cigar industry will believe the results of our
compilations for this edition of the *Perelman's Pocket
Cyclopedia of Cigars*. For the second year in a row, despite
continuing over-supply in many shops, new brands were
introduced at the rate of more than one a day!

In handmade cigars — the focus of most of the industry — the
number of brands in national distribution reached 1,269 by our
count. After an increase of 95 percent in 1998 from 1997, the
handmade brand total rocketed up again by another **32 percent**!
from our 1998 edition. And, of course, our tally does not count
the roughly 50-100 locally-distributed house brands of cigar
lounges and smokeshops across the nation.

All of this activity is even more amazing in the face of
continued pressure on tobacco at the legislative and regulatory
levels. Now that this year's book is completed, maybe I can
have a cigar and think about this contradiction.

Our listing is so large this year that in order to keep the sheer
size of this book in line, we had to remove the popular index
feature for the handmade and machine-made lists. We hope to
return these sections next year.

As always, our goal is to try to bring some discipline to the
classification to the 1,443 brands on the U.S. market today in
this, our fifth annual compilation.

INTRODUCTION

Here are a few tips to help users of this book, to make your exploration and research efforts more fun:

About this book:
We have provided critical details on a lot of cigars. A total of 1,443 brands are profiled, comprising more than 7,000 models. When considering the growth of the cigar trade in the U.S., compare that total to the 1,138 we listed last year, the 659 brands we profiled in the 1997 edition, 457 brands in the 1996 edition or 370 brands in our first edition in 1995.

We note that our listing represents virtually every brand marketed nationally. Readers will find some brands which are not listed here, but which are available at his or her local smokeshop. These brands are very likely:

▸ Private label, unbranded cigars offered in bundles by major manufacturers, on which store names are placed for local sale;

▸ House brands produced for individual cigar lounges or retailers, which are not generally available through wholesalers for national distribution to tobacco stores;

▸ Cigars produced in limited quantities by small, local factories and marketed regionally;

▸ New lines introduced after this book was completed;

▸ Close-outs (there are lots of these today!) or discontinued brands which are no longer available from manufacturers.

INTRODUCTION

This should not dissuade readers from trying or enjoying these cigars. We actively encourage everyone to try new cigars and refrain from the kind of "cigar snobbery" which is so easy for premium cigar smokers to fall into. **The best cigar you will ever smoke might be the next one you try.**

That's how I have discovered many of my favorite brands; I try to keep up with new products by buying one or two cigars of a new brand and note my reaction to it on a small index card. After a while, some of these "new" cigars become favorites that are integrated into the rotation of brands that I already like – an experience that would have been missed if the opportunity to try new brands was dismissed.

About the brands:
Another contradiction comes in the area of supply. Even though supplies of most brands are available, hundreds of new brands are still being introduced! As regards our listings, this situation has had an important impact in many ways:

- ▸ We have tried to list, for each handmade brand, the country of origin of the wrapper, filler and binder. While we have received wonderful cooperation from the manufacturers and distributors, more than one executive has told us something like, "This is what we would like to use, but if we can't get it, we will blend in something else."

In most cases, this should *not* be of great concern. After all, most consumers buy specific cigars based on an expectation of taste and draw, not on the ingredients. Recent history shows that master blenders have little difficulty reconfiguring brands with different tobaccos to achieve the same taste and quality of construction. But . . .

There are also brands from smaller factories which have limited access to the quality and type of tobacco that they would like to use. Their blends may change considerably, as will the taste of their brands. *Buyer beware* is the watchword for some brands, which may change considerably as they go through the seasons. We can say that the information we present here is an accurate "snapshot" of these brands in the fall of 1998.

About the shapes:
The cigar boom has changed the style and type of cigars preferred by smokers. Three obvious trends that emerged in 1997 continued during the last year:

- Cigars with larger and larger ring gauges. Where lonsdales were considered large cigars in years past, we now see robustos, churchills and double coronas as standard smokes for many. As the desire for more and more complex flavors grows, we will continue to see this trend expand.

- More and more smokers are attracted to shaped cigars, such as perfectos, torpedos and pyramids. These are hard to make and often carry a premium price, but continue to grow in popularity. Hard to find just 3-4 years ago, there are now hundreds of brands which include these shapes in their line.

- Wild mutations in size, color and flavor are on the rise. Consider the "barber pole" or "candy cane" cigar which features a double wrapper for a striped effect. Or the number of lines which offer cigars of more than 9 inches and ring gauges of 60 or more. Or the explosion of flavored cigars in every imaginable style!

A list of the brands which feature these extra large, extra long or striped-wrapper cigars is listed in section 2.04, along with a list of brands which are artificially flavored.

Cuban cigars:
Because of our concentration on cigars available in the U.S., listings of cigars produced in Cuba are not included. In response to many requests for this information, however, we have produced a companion volume, *Perelman's Pocket Cyclopedia of Havana Cigars,* available through your local tobacconist or by writing to us directly.

The future:
The "smart set" in the cigar industry predicted the demise of 1,000 brands in 1998 as consumers became more sophisticated. There will be brands which fail in 1999, but there is always room for another quality cigar. There probably won't be hundreds of new brands, but there will be some new names to replace many others which will perish for lack of interest, sales or supply of tobacco. For better or worse, these will be cataloged in our 2000 edition.

With our thanks:
This book could not have been produced without a tremendous amount of help from many people in and around the cigar industry. Representatives of most every manufacturer and distributor in the country endured many telephone calls

INTRODUCTION

requesting information, and virtually everyone we contacted was not only forthcoming, but enthusiastic about the project.

I would like to express special thanks to individuals whose efforts went far beyond the norm; without them, this book would not have been produced: Jules Abbosh, Reagan Brewer, Mark Estrin, Gaby Miller, Brad Part, Eric Workman and Rabbi Steve Nathan of Temple J.R. in Whippany, New Jersey. And the help of our editorial staff: assistant editors Chris Ralston and Bruce Tenen and associate editor Mitchel Sloan, without whom this work could not have been completed.

I hope that our readers will enjoy our work; if you have suggestions on how to make this book better, we would be pleased to hear from you; our address follows the Table of Contents.

We will also be pleased to meet our readers, either in person at our LE CIGAR NOIR festivals which we produce around the nation in cooperation with our friends at *Smoke* magazine, or via electronic mail at perelmanco@aol.com. I hope to see you in a smoke-filled room soon!

RICHARD B. PERELMAN
Los Angeles, California
November 1998

1.
CIGAR BASICS

1.01   ABOUT CIGARS

The joy of smoking rolled tobacco leaves began in the
Americas hundreds of years ago and was introduced to
Europeans after Christopher Columbus' return from his first
voyage in 1492.

In the ensuing years, the popularity and sophistication of
tobacco products has grown and the 1990s has brought a
significant increase in the popularity of cigars in the United
States. Despite much controversy, the status of cigars as a
luxury product in American culture is secure.

The important technical elements to be appreciated in cigars
include their construction and the many shapes and sizes.

1.02   CONSTRUCTION

What goes into cigars? The answer to this question is the key to
assessing the quality of a specific cigar. All but the thinnest
cigars include three elements: (1) the filler tobacco at the
center, (2) a binder leaf which holds the filler together and (3)
the outer wrapper, which is rolled around the binder.

Cigars which are made by hand use "long filler" tobacco:
leaves which run the length of a cigar. In a handmade, the
filler, binder and wrapper are combined manually to create a
cigar.

Machine-made cigars utilize high-speed machinery to combine
"short filler" tobacco - usually scraps or pieces of tobacco -

CIGAR BASICS

with a binder and wrapper. Because of the tension placed on the tobacco by the machines, the binders and wrappers are often made of a homogenized tobacco product which is stronger than natural leaves and can be produced in a variety of flavors, strengths and textures.

A few brands combine machine-bunching (using long-filler tobacco) with hand-rolled wrappers; this practice has been very properly dubbed "hand-rolled" as opposed to handmade by cigar expert Rick Hacker in *The Ultimate Cigar Book*. And some larger cigars use "mixed" or "combination" filler of long-filler and short-filler tobaccos.

The most obvious characteristic of most cigars is the color of the exterior wrapper. While not the only factor in the taste of a cigar, it is an important element and a key in many people's purchase of specific cigars. Although manufacturers have identified more than 100 different wrapper shades, six major color classifications are used herein, as noted below:

Color	Abbrev.	Description
Double Claro	*"DC"*	Also known as "American Market Selection" [AMS] or "Candela," this is a green wrapper. Once popular, it is rarely found today.
Claro	*"Cl"*	This is a very light tan color, almost beige in shade; usually from Connecticut.
Colorado Claro	*"CC"*	A medium brown found on many cigars, this category covers many descriptions. The most popular are "Natural" or "English Market Selection" [EMS]. Tobaccos in this shade are grown in many countries.

CIGAR BASICS

Color	Abbrev.	Description
Colorado	"Co"	This shade is instantly recognizable by the obvious reddish tint.
Colorado Maduro	"CM"	Darker than Colorado Claro in shade, this color is often associated with African tobacco, such as wrappers from Cameroon, or with Havana Seed tobacco grown in Honduras.
Maduro	"Ma"	Very dark brown or black; this category also includes the deep black "Oscuro" shade. Tobacco for Maduro wrappers is grown in Connecticut, Mexico, Nicaragua and Brazil.

The listing of cigar brands in this book assumes that, unless otherwise noted, handmade cigars utilize long-filler tobacco and machine-made cigars use short-filler.

1.03   SHAPES AND SIZES

There are cigars of every shape and every size for every occasion. From tiny, cigarette-like cigarillos to giant monsters resembling pool cues, there is a wide variety to choose from.

Certain sizes and shapes which have gained popularity over the years and have become widely recognized, even by non-smokers. Cigar shape names such as "corona" or "panatela" have specific meanings to the cigar industry, although there is no formally agreed-to standard for any given size.

The following table lists 20 well-known shapes, and is adapted from Paul Garmirian's explanation of sizes in *The Gourmet Guide to Cigars*. The "classical" measurements for which this shape is known are given, along with a size and girth range for each size for classification purposes:

CIGAR BASICS

Shape	Classical Lngth. x Ring	Length range	Ring range
Giant	9 x 52	8 & up	50 & up
Double Corona	7¾ x 49	6¾-7¾	49-54
Churchill	7 x 47	6¾-7⅞	46-48
Perfecto	varies	all	all
Pyramid	7 x 36⇒54	all	flared
Torpedo	6½ x 52	all	tapered
Toro	6 x 50	5⅝-6⅝	48-54
Robusto	5 x 50	4½-5½	48-54
Grand Corona	6½ x 46	5⅝-6⅝	45-47
Corona Extra	5½ x 46	4½-5½	45-47
Giant Corona	7½ x 44	7½ & up	42-45
Lonsdale	6½ x 42	6½-7¼	40-44
Long Corona	6 x 42	5⅞-6⅜	40-44
Corona	5½ x 42	5¼-5¾	40-44
Petit Corona	5 x 42	4-5	40-44
Long Panatela	7½ x 38	7 & up	35-39
Panatela	6 x 38	5½-6⅞	35-39
Short Panatela	5 x 38	4-5⅜	35-39
Slim Panatela	6 x 34	5 & up	30-34
Small Panatela	5 x 33	4-5	30-34
Cigarillos	4 x 26	6 & less	29 & less

For the purposes of classification, the cigar models of the 1,443 brands profiled have been separated into these 20 major groups. With the great increase in shaped cigars, here are our classification criteria for *figurados*:

▸ Culebras, which is made up of three small cigars twisted together. This style has returned to the U.S. market and a few manufacturers have this unique shape available.

▸ Perfecto, which has two tapered ends. Until recently, there were just a few cigars which offered Perfecto "tips" on the foot, but true Perfectos are making a big comeback. For the bold, take a look at the Puros Indios Gran Victoria (10 inches long by 60 ring) to see a true "pot-bellied" cigar.

▸ Torpedo, which was traditionally a fat cigar with two fully closed, pointed ends, but has now come to mean a cigar with an open foot and a straight body which tapers to a closed, pointed head. This "new" torpedo was popularized by the Montecristo (Havana) No. 2.

The Torpedo differs from "Pyramid"-shaped cigars, which flare continuously from the head to the foot, essentially forming a triangle.

Like the Torpedo, whose meaning has changed over time, the Royal Corona or Rothschild title is seen less and less on cigars now known as "Robustos." This change has been rapid over the past 4-5 years, but some manufacturers still label their shorter, thicker cigars as Rothschilds or even as a "Rothchild" (an incorrect spelling of the famous German banking family name). A few manufacturers use both and label their 5-5½-inch, 50-ring models as "Robustos" and reserve the "Rothschild" name for shorter, but still 50-ring, cigars of 4-4½ inches!

Many other shape names are used by manufacturers; some cigars even have multiple names. For the sake of convenience, the many types of small, very thin cigars are grouped under the "Cigarillo" title rather than distributed over a long list of names such as "Belvederes," "Demi-Tasse" and others.

1.04 ENJOYING CIGARS

The enjoyment of cigars is a personal pleasure, which is as varied as the 1,443 brands profiled. However, there are certain matters which should be considered carefully by all smokers and which require attention.

▸ Foremost among these is storage and the usefulness of a humidor in proper working condition cannot be underestimated. The death of a quality cigar due to a lack of care is a sad occurrence indeed.

▸ For those carrying cigars on the go, travel humidors or leather cigar cases are important items to keep your cigars safe and in good smoking condition.

▸ Finally, the proper tools for cutting and lighting your cigar are necessary accessories for full enjoyment.

Other authors have written extensively on these topics and references to leading books on cigars are listed in section 9. Each offers many suggestions on how to enjoy and store cigars and many details about the history and manufacture of cigars.

In addition, ***an often under-utilized resource for the smoker is your local smokeshop.*** Most are experienced, knowledgeable and have access to experts, manufacturers and the Retail Tobacco Dealers of America trade association. Use their expertise to help you!

2.
THE CIGAR ALMANAC

Here are facts, figures and a little fun about the 1,443 brands (1,269 handmades, 120 mass-market and 54 small cigars) profiled in this year's edition:

2.01 BIRTHS AND DEATHS

The cigar renaissance continued with an explosion of 506 new (or *re-introduced*) brands (496 handmades) introduced since our last edition, close to the 514 introduced in the 1998 *Cyclopedia,* but in great contrast with 170 in the 1997 edition and the 56 new handmades listed in the 1996 Cyclopedia:

Handmade (496):

A Traditional Cigar (2 blends)	Bad Frog
Aida	Balmoral
Albero	Bandolero
Alcazar	Barlovento
Alfredo's Signature Edition	BB Los Reyes
Alphonso Ortiz	Ben Miguel
Amadeus	Benedit
Amaya	Bering Dominican Hallmark
Ambassador	Big Al's
Arabian Nights	Big Bite
Arbol de Palma	Blue Parrot
Aristoff	Bogey's Stogies
Armando y Ramon	Bolero
Aroma de Cafe	Breve
Artigas	Bucanero
Arturas Felipe	Buffalo Bundles
Arzt de Los Reyes	Bullet
Astral Grand Reserve Vintage	Burt's Gold
Athenea	Burt Reynolds
Avanos	Burt's Lady
B.E.R.	Butera Vintage Maduro
Bacheche	C.A.O. Aniversario Maduro
Bad Boy	Cabañas y Carbajal

Cachita
Caiman
Campesino
Caonao
Caribu
Carl Barrister
Carmelo
Casa Anjelita
Casa de Diablo
Casa Teresa
Cataluna
Celebrity Cigars
Cesar Cigar Factory
Chateau Tamboril
Chatily's
Chavon
Che
Chocolate Rush
Cienta Azul
Cigar Trader
Cigar Trader Flavored
Ciguardians
Cisso Natural
Constantin
Corman
Costa Baja
Creme de Mint
Cristo Cubanos
Crown Classics
Cruzeros
Cuba 1800
Cubadom
Cuban Especiale
Cuban Select
Cubana Fina
Cubanacan
Cubano-A-Mano
Cubella
D&B Dominican Reserve
D&B Gold Reserve
D.G.S.

DS Bundles
Da Costa
Damn Good Dominicans
DeMarco
Dimante Nero
Discover 1492
Divino
Dolce Vita
Dominguez
Dominican Choice
Dominican Premium
Dominican Sandwiches
Dominican Segundos
Dominicana Delights
Dominion Premium
The Don
Don Alfonso
Don Angelo
Don Antonio Pellegrino Reserva Preciada
Don Antonio Reserva Preciada
Don Asa
Don Casimiro Collection
Don Claudio
Don Diego Privada Selection
Don Escobar
Don Felipe
Don Fidencio
Don Geovanni
Don Juan Urquijo
Don Macho
Don Marino
Don Miguel
Don Otilio
Don Pablo Gold Series
Don Pancho Collection
Don Primo
Don Rafael
Don Rivera
Don Rubio
Don Vidal

Don Vito
Doña Elba & Cioffi
Doña Puros
Dos Cubanitos
Dr. Funk
The Drake
Dulzura
Dunhill
Durango
E. Trinidad
El Beso
El Chico
El Colonel
El Competidor
El Cauto
Eleganté
El Gladiator
El Glorioso Dominicano
El Grande Miguel
El Guajiro
El Gusto Cubano
El Mago
El Patio
El Patron
El Piloto Cubano
El Quijote
El Rey Pescado
El Sabor a Miami
El Sabor de Miami
El Sarare
El Titan de Bronze
Emigrante
Emperor Gran Reserva
Emperor of the World
Empress of Cuba
Erté
Española Black Label
Especiales Selectos (2)
Esperanza
Essence of Vanilla
Estavan Cruz

Estela
Estelar Limited Reserve
Estelar Premium
Evel Knievel Signature Series
Evil Clown
Evita Imperial Maduro
Evita Scented
F.B. Boyd
Farina
Felipe Black
Felipe Dominicana
Ferdinand Collection
First Lady of the World
Five Star
Five Star Hondurans
Flamenco Las Palmas
Flavored Dominican
Flor de Carbonell
Flor de Gonzalez
Flor de Guarabo
Flor de Leon
Flor de Navarette
Flor de Ybor City
Flor Maria
Floribbean
Florida Pride
Flower City Special Reserve
Fonseca Vintage Collection
Francis J
Francisco Pla
French Kiss
Fresh Florida
Fuego Cubano Bronze Edition
Fuego Cubano Silver Edition
Fuego del Rey
Galardon
Galeon
Gilfranco
Golden Seal
Golden Sun
Gomez & Garcia

ALMANAC

Gourmet Dessert Cigars
Governor's
Gran Virrey
Grand Class
Grave de Peralta
Graycliff
Guanche
H. Upmann Special Selection
Habana Club
Habana Real
Habana Treasure (2)
Habano 2000 Criollo
Habano Primero
Habano 2000 Reserve
Hannibal Sensational
Havache
Havana Cigars - Don Pedro Ramos
Havana Cloud
Havana Express
Havana King Reserve
Havana Nights
Havana Republic
Havana Star
Havanilla
Henry Clay EMS
Herrera-Claverol
Hoja Cubana XXO
Hoja de Vueltabajo
Humo Blanco
Illusion
Ilona Lady Lights
Indian Dominican
Indian Habano Blend 95
Inmenso
Insignia
Islero
Jaguar of Belize
Jamaican Rum
Jamavana
James Norman
Jibarito

JM Outdoorsman
Jorge Velasquez
Jose Jimenez
Jose Paco
Joya de San Cristobal
Juan y Ramon Perfecto
Juana de Aragon
Just Number 2
Kalua Sunrise
King Cobra
King Honduran
Kiss
Kiss One
Kristian James
La Belleza
La Boca
La Brisa
La Corona
La Cuba
La Diabla
La Dolce Vita
La Exquisita
La Flor de Caño
La Flor de Tiede
La Francesca
La Gitana
La Gloria
La Gloria Boricua
La Gloria Cubana Selecion d'Oro
La Insular
La Joya Cubana
La Maria
La Marinita
La O'Paree
La Preferencia
La Rica Hoya
La Salle
La Tanita
La Tradicion Cabinet Series Perdomo
Reserve
La Trinidad

La Trinidad y Cia.
La Veleza
Lady Club
Le Bonne Cigare
The Legend
Leopoldo
Leviathan
Lew's Smokers
Little Big Man
Loaiza uNo
Long Island
Los Perez
Luis Alejandro
M.A.C.
M.C.
M.P.
Macabana
Macanudo Robust
Macbeth
Magic Flute
Manodura
Manuel
Mariachi
Mercader
Macuro
Maduros Dominicanos
Managua
Manhattan
Manhattan Cigar Co.
Maravilla
Merencigar
Meridionales
Mi Habana Unica
Miami Choice
Miavana Clasicos
Michael Angelo
Mickey Rooney's World's Greatest
  Cigar Signature Series
Miraflores
Miramonte
Miranda

Miyares
MoJo
Morejon y Cuesta
Monte Palma
Montecristo Cigare des Artes
Montecristo Habana 2000
Monteria
Mr. Luma
Mursuli Sweets
Nafilyan Signature Series
Napa Dominican Estate
Napa Dominican Reserve
Navarette
Navegante
1932 Selection
Nineteenth Hole Signature Series
Nirvana
Ño
Opium
Optimo Clasico
P & R
Paco
Paco de Cuba
Padrino
Palais Royal
Palais Royal Chateaux Reserve
Pancho Floods
Papa Arturo
Papa Juanico
Paradise Dessert Cigars
Paradise Island
Pasha Reserve Collection
Peñamil Oro
Peñamil Plata
Perique
Petrus Dominicana
Phat Boyz
Picadura
Pinar 1958
Pinnacle Reserve
Pio VI

ALMANAC

Players
Pleasant Private Stock
Pontalba
Port Royal
Premium Dominicana
Pretty Lady
Primo del Rey Club Selection
Prince Borghese
Public Enemy
Puro Venezolano
Purofino DOM
Puros 3P
Puros Morgan
Quevedo
Quintero
Quo Vadis
Rafael
Rafael de Habana
Ramondo
Rancho Dominicano
Rasputin
Rasta Rap
Rastafari
Red Head
Rare Lion
Regatta
Republica Dominicana
Rey Alphonso
Rey de Los Reyes
Reyes & Benecio
Riata
Rich & Famous
Ricos Dominicanos - Etiqueta Negra
Rio de Cuba
Roble Viejo
Rodon
Roll-X
Ruby Dooby
Rusty's
Sabana
Sabor a Miami

Sabor Cubano
Sacuba
St. Charles
Santa Cruz
Santa Maria
Santamaria
Santiago de Cuba
Santiago del Sol
Savoy
Schmokin
Scorp
Scorpion
Seleccion Royale
Señor Armando Reyes
Señor Corto
Señor San Andres
Shaman
Shaman Red
Sillem's
Sinatra
Smokin' Tiger
Soberano
Solemne
Solo Aroma
South Beach
Spirit of Cuba
Sportsman's Reserve
Stefano
Sturgis
Suarez Gran Reserve
Super Value
Sweet Lady
Sweet Millionaire
Sweet Sensation
Tabacos George
Tabacos Gran Colombia
Tabu
Tahino
Tamboril Goal
Tampa Sweetheart
Tatiana

Temptation
Teneguia
Tercera Generacion
Texana
Thompson Conserva
Tobaccos de Monterrey
Toraño
Trabucos
Trinidad y Hermano
Tropical republic
Tropical Treasure
Tropical Treats
Tsar I
Tsar II
III Trinidad
Tubano
U.S.P.A. Polo Cigars
Umo V.S.
Utopia
Valdez
Vamp
Vega Fina
Vega Vieja
Vencedora Nadal y Nadal
Victoria Pasha Boxer
Victoria Pasha Matador
Villa

Villa Havana
Villa Lobos
Vintage Aged Selection
W & D
Wall Street Smokes
Woriur
World's Best
Xcuban
Y2K
ZaldivaZamora
Zarate
Zeppelin
Ziq

Machine-made (6):
B-H
Chevere Small Cigars
Cuban Club Classics
Hula Girl
Jon Piedro
Mocambo

Small cigars: (4)
Baby
Capital
Miami Suites
Regalos Flavorillos

(A few brands which are new to this book are not shown as new in this list, since they were previously in regional or occasional distribution and not actually a "new" brand. We have listed brands which went off the market and have now returned.)

The following 231 brands were not included in this year's listings because (1) they have either been discontinued, or (2) are not currently in production for national sale – that is, they may be a regional or house brand, or (3) when we called to find out about these brands, the telephone number of the manufacturer or distributor had been disconnected or was now another business or even a residence!

Handmade (218):

Adolfo
Alpha Candela Cubana
Amoroso
Ana de Nicaragua
Anacaona
Andros
Antillas Toro Bravo
Aperitif
Armenter Reservas
Azteca Dominican Maduro
Bagatelle
Ballena Suprema
Belmondo
Bijao
Bijao Classico
Black Label
Blue Chip
Blue Label
Bravos
Bucanero
Bufido
C.C.I. Royal Satin Selection
Cammano
Caney
Carmen Gold Label
Carmen Platinum Label
Carmen White Label
Casa de Gonzalez
Casa Mayan
Cerdan
Charles Fairmorn Connshade
Cielo Umo
Clipper Gold Reserve
Confederacion Suiza

Connoisseur's Choice
Cossack
Creston
Creston "Los Montes"
Creston Prestige Cuvee
Cruzado Reserva Especial
Cruzado Reserva Grande
Cuaba
Cubana Royale Limited Reserve
Dalaly Diamantes
Dante
De Cossio
DeBerto & Martinez
Diamante
Dominican Maduro Special
Dominicana Superba
Dominico
Domino Park
Don Armando
Don Bienve
Don Cisso
Don Elegante
Don Ernesto
Don Esteban
Don Fausto
Don Fife
Don Lima
Don Mariano
Don Nilo
Don Pupo
Don Rex
Don Ricardo Honduran Selection
Don Salvador
Don Salvatore

Duarte 1884
1861
Edgar Private Reserve
El Campeon Suave
El Cid
El Coto
El Gato
El Murazo
El Noble
El Sig Ropes
Estrada y Argueta
Fantastic Flavor Cigars
Flamento Puro
Flor Cubana
Flor de Las Brenas
Flor de Manila
Flor de Nicaragua
Fortunato
Francisco Hernandez
Gitano
Gomez Lora
Habanos Hatuey
Havana 7
Havana Blaze
Havana Blends
Havana Classico
Hecho a Mano Dominicana
Hidalgos
Hugo Cassar Diamond Honduran
Hugo Signature Series
Ideal
Il Fiore d'Oro
Infiesta
J.J.
J. Maniscalco Collection
JAD
Jamaica Gem
Jamaica Heritage
John Hay
Jose Jimenez
Jose L. Piedra

Joya del Cibao
Juan Lopez
Julio Helena
Kennedy
L'Attitude 18
La Aroma Tropical
La Avida
La Bamba
La Cobra Cubana
La Damita
La Favorita
La Flor de Cuba
La Flor de Navarette
La Hoja
La Hoja Rica
La Isla
La Lunda
La Paloma
La Perla
La Prueba Flavored Cigars
La Regional
La Restina
Lancelot
Largo y Zorro
Lazarus
Legend-Ario
Leon
Leyenda
Luis Abuelo
Lusitania
Manuel Marina
Matador
Maximiliana
Montebello
Montecassino
Montoya
Morel
Mulato
Navarro
Nicaragua Especial
Nicarao

Nicole Miller
Numero Uno
O & B Dominican Reserve
Ocho Rios
Orama
Orient Express
Oro Taino
Panorea
Pantera de Oro
Pecado
Peterson Hallmark
Presidente
Presidente Caceres
Prestigio Cubano
Pueblo Dominicano
Puerto Rico
Puro Nicaragua
Real Veracruz
Reina Dominicana
Reserva del Patron
Rey del Rey
Robusto de Casa
Royal Barbados
Ronaldo Somma
Rosario
Rosato
The Rough Rider
Royal Court
Royale Gold
Royale Saludo
S P Maduro
Sabor
Sabroso
St. Tropez
San Angelo
San Fernando
San Marcos
Santiago
Santo Diego
Sebastian Reservas

Segovia
St. Christobal
660 Red
Sol y Mar
Special Jamaican
Suso
T.J.
Tabacos Universo
Tena y Vega
Tequesta
Taino
Terri Welles Signature Series
Tipo
Toro Bravo
Torquino
Universo
Van Winkle
Vega del Rey
Vega del Rey Reserva
Ventura
Victory Spirit
Villega Reales
VIP Club Collection
VSOP Vintage Reserve
Wall Street Portfolio Collection
Yulerdi
Yumuri
Yumuri 1492

Machine-made (10):
The Cigar Baron
Cima
De Herren van Ruysdael
De Olifant
Figaro
Flor de Borinquen
Le Petit Chateau
Mocha Lights
Rivaldo
Tayo

Small cigars(3):
Alternativos
Fun Little Cigars
Gesty

A handful of brands listed in the 1998 edition and not listed in this year's work are still in production, but are now house brands of their manufacturers and no longer available at wholesale.

2.02   BRAND FACTS

Here are some entertaining facts about cigar brands and where they are produced:

Ancient brands:

Some brands have been with us since the early part of the 19th Century, originating primarily in Cuba. Some of the older brand names still being produced for the U.S. market, with their original country of origin, include:

1810 Cabanas (Cuba)	1881 Calixto Lopez (Cuba)
1834 Por Larranaga (Cuba)	1882 Garcia y Vega (USA)
1837 Ramon Allones (Cuba)	1884 Cuesta-Rey (USA)
1840 Bances (Cuba)	1884 Judge's Cave (USA)
1840 Marsh Wheeling (USA)	1887 White Owl (USA)
1840 Punch (Cuba)	1888 Villiger (Germany)
1844 H. Upmann (Cuba)	1891 Fonseca (Cuba)
1845 La Corona (Cuba)	1896 Topper (USA)
1845 Partagas (Cuba)	1901 Bolivar (Cuba)
1848 El Rey del Mundo (Cuba)	1903 Leon Jimenes (Dom. Rep.)
1850 Romeo y Julieta (Cuba)	1903 Topstone (USA)
1867 Hoyo de Monterrey (Cuba)	1905 Bering (USA)
1868 Bauza (Cuba)	1912 Arturo Fuente (USA)
1868 Macanudo (Jamaica)	1912 Muniemaker (USA)
1871 Baccarat (USA)	1916 El Producto (USA)
1873 Dannemann (Brazil)	1928 Rafael Gonzalez (Cuba)
1876 Temple Hall (Jamaica)	1935 Montecristo (Cuba)

1946 Davidoff Chateau series
       of Hoyo de Monterrey
       (Cuba)

1959 Montecruz (Canary Islands)
1964 Don Diego (Canary Islands)

Bands on brands:

It is well established that in 1850, Gustave Bock of the Netherlands put bands on cigars for the first time, as a method of distinguishing his firm's Cuban-made cigars.

Brand production:

The Dominican Republic and Honduras still dominate the production origin statistics of the 1,269 handmade brands profiled, but production is up everywhere.

Some 48.2 percent of the handmade brands now come from the Dominican Republic, up from 43.6 percent in our last edition. Another 15.6 percent are from Honduras, down from 20.9 percent as Nicaragua was the big winner in terms of new production. Brands emanating from Nicaragua increased 36.4 percent to $146^{1}/_{5}$ from just over 107 last year. The number of brands bring produced was fairly steady in most other countries such as Mexico (up to 72 from 63 brands). Noteworthy increases in production are seen in Costa Rica (19 brands now), Jamaica ($13^{5}/_{6}$), Panama ($10^{1}/_{3}$) and Venezuela ($11^{1}/_{2}$).

Production increased significantly in the U.S. to 227 brands overall and 98 handmade brands, up from 61 in 1998 and $44^{1}/_{2}$ in 1997. This makes the U.S., where cigar-making was almost extinct at the beginning of this decade, the fourth-largest producer of handmade brands behind the Dominican Republic, Honduras and Nicaragua.

In classifying the origin of each brand, fractional attributions were made for cigars that are produced in more than one country (example: Padron cigars are made in both Honduras and Nicaragua). The statistics by group and country:

Country	Handmade Cigars	Machine Made	Small Cigars	Total
Bahamas	1			1
Belgium		2	2	4
Belize	1			1
Brazil	8⅓		1	9⅓
Costa Rica	19			19
Denmark			1½	1½
Dominican Republic	611½	2	2	615½
Ecuador	5			5
France			3	3
Germany	4	4	6½	14½
Guatemala	1			1
Honduras	198			198
India	2			2
Indonesia	7		1	8
Ireland		3	1	4
Jamaica	13⁵/₆			13⁵/₆
Mexico	72			72
Myanmar	1			1
Netherlands		4½	4½	9
Nicaragua	146¹/₅			146¹/₅
Panama	11⅓			11⅓

Country	Handmade Cigars	Machine Made	Small Cigars	Total
Philippines	18			18
Spain	39	1	2½	42½
Switzerland		1½	2	3½
United States	98	102	27	227
Venezuela	11½			11½

2.03 CIGARS: LARGE AND SMALL

Length:

The longest cigars? Here are the longest shapes:

19 inches	(x 60 ring)	Santa Clara Magnum
18	(x 66)	Puros Indios Chief
15	(x 125)	Hannibal Emperador
13¾	(x 49)	Mexican Emperador
13	(x 50)	Juan Clemente Gargantua
11	(x 50)	Columbus Eleven Fifty
10 inches		Cigars of this length are offered by Carbonell, Casa Blanca, Cibao, Dominican Original, King Dominican, Mendez y Lopez, Puros Indios and Royal Jamaica.

The shortest? Cigarillos of just under three inches in length are offered by:

2¾	Al-Capone	2⅞	Dannemann
2¾	Schimmelpennick	2⅞	Henri Winterman
2¾	Villiger	2⅞	Panter
2⅞	Agio	2⅞	Schimmelpennick
2⅞	Candlelight		

But for a real cigar, how about the 2¾-inch, 48-ring Celebrity Cigars "Bullet"!

Ring gauge:

The fattest of the fat? Remembering that ring gauge is measured in 64ths of the inch, there are 21 in-production cigars of an inch (64/64) or more in diameter:

125 ring	(x 15 inches)	Hannibal Emperador
70	(x 6)	Inmenso II
70	(x 5)	Inmenso I
68	(x 8)	Carbonell Piramide Gigante
68	(x 8)	Mendez y Lopez Piramide Gigante
66	(x 18)	Puros Indios Chief
66	(x 10)	Casa Blanca Jeroboam
66	(x 10)	Dominican Original Fat Tub
66	(x 10)	King Dominican No. 9
66	(x 7¼)	Don Tito Piramides
66	(x 7)	Lars Tetens Tesshu Torac Fusako
66	(x 5)	Casa Blanca Half Jeroboam
66	(x 5)	Dominican Original Gorilla
66	(x 5)	King Dominican No. 13
64	(x 9½)	Ornelas 250 mm
64	(x 9)	Royal Jamaica Goliath
64	(x 8)	Jose Benito Magnum
64	(x 7½)	Carbonell Piramide
64	(x 7½)	Cedar Joe Mega Torpedo
64	(x 7½)	Don Carlos Super Pyramid
64	(x 7½)	Evel Knievel Rocket
64	(x 7½)	Mendez y Lopez Piramide
64	(x 7½)	Regalos Especial
64	(x 7¼)	Moore & Bode Full Brass

The thinnest? There are a number of brands of small cigars which match the ring gauge of cigarettes, at 20 ring.

Shapes:

The leading brands by the number of shapes offered under one brand name:

47 Nat Sherman
28 Partagas
28 Punch
27 Lars Tetens Phat Cigars
27 Paul Garmirian
27 Rosalones
26 H. Upmann
26 Hannibal
25 Flor de Consuegra
25 Tabu
25 Te-Amo
23 Arturo Fuente
23 Don Alberto

23 Macanudo
23 Ornelas
22 Ashton
22 La Flor Dominicana
21 Davidoff
21 El Rey del Mundo
21 Miyares
21 Quintin Q-Oro
20 Avo
20 Padron
20 Roly
20 Speakeasy

Honorable mention goes to the 63 models in the 12 different series of Hugo Cassar cigars.

2.04 CIGARS: SPECIAL MODELS

Two new fashions in cigars today are flavored cigars and special double-wrapped cigars which emulate barber poles. A census of these brands:

Handmade brands with one or more flavored shapes:

	Flavor(s)
Aroma de Cafe	Coffee
Aromella	Vanilla
Bolero	Cherry, chocolate, tropical rum and vanilla
Boom Boom El Campeon	Amaretto, cafe, chocolate, cognac and vanilla
Burt's Lady	Amaretto, orange, peach, vanilla
Cachita	Amaretto, chocolate, vanilla
Carl Barrister	Vanilla
Chatily's	Amaretto, rum, vanilla
Chocolate Rush	Chocolate
Cigar Trader	Cherry, cognac, rum, vanilla, whiskey
Club Sweets	Amaretto, cherry, chocolate, mocha, rum, vanilla
Cojimar	Cinnamon, mint, Sambuca, vanilla
Creme de Mint	Mint
Cuban Cigar Factory "Vanilla Sweets"	Vanilla
Cubana Royale	Sweet Vanilla

Your Go-Anywhere humidor!

The One and Only True Portable Humidor

Humi-Pouch™ works like your professional walk-in humidor utilizing **NATURAL** humidification and daily fresh air exchanges to ensure proper aging and eliminate odor build-up, such as ammonia. The shelf life of **Humi-Pouch™** is ten months and once opened, **Humi-Pouch™** keeps cigars fresh for 60 days.

The **Humi-Pouch™** Family of Products are inexpensive, reclosable, portable and never require water.

"Safeguard your cigars with natural humidifiation"

D & B Gold Reserve	Chocolate, sugar, vanilla
Dolce Vita	Sweet
Dominicana Delights	Anisettte, chocolate, orange, rum, strawberry, vanilla
Don Armando	Sweet vanilla
Don Augusto Sabor	Vanilla
Don Geovanni	Vanilla
Don Guillermo	Chocolate, vanilla
Don Pablo	Aromatic, brandy, cognac, rum, sweet
Don Vidal Clasica	Amaretto, coffee, cognac, mint, vanilla-rum, vanilla
Doña Puros	Clove, ginger, orange
888	Cappaccino, chocolate, Guarapo, rum, vanilla
El Beso	Kaluha, rum, vanilla
El Guajiro	Chocolate, vanilla
El Emperador	Amaretto, Anise, cherry, cognac, rum
El Incomparable	Scotch
El Sabor a Miami	Amaretto, cherry, coffee, rum, vanilla
El Sabor de Miami	Bourbon, coffee, coffee/rum, cognac, vanilla, 3-Shooter
El Sublimado	Cognac
El Trofeo Habano	Pipe tobaccos
Emigrante	Amaretto, blackberry, chocolate, cognac, cinnamon, hazelnut, vanilla
Esperanza	Amaretto, cherry, cognac, vanilla
Essence of Vanilla	Vanilla
Estrella	Vanilla
Evita Scented	Amaretto, cinnamon, coconut, chocolate, mint, rum, vanilla
Famous Rum Runner	Rum
First Lady of the World	Amaretto, Vanilla
Flavored Dominicans	Amaretto, chocolate, cognac, mint, rum, vanilla, whiskey
Flor de Gurabo	Rum, vanilla
Florida Pride	Chocolate, vanilla
Francisco Pla	Amaretto, Anise, chocolate, cognac, rum, vanilla
French Kiss	Amaretto, chocolate, Gran Mariner, mint, rum, peach, vanilla
Fuego del Rey	Chocolate, cognac, pipe aroma, vanilla
Gallardo	Vanilla
Gilfranco Vanilla Bombers	Vanilla
Golden Sun	Amaretto, cherry, chocolate, cognac, rum, vanilla
Gourmet Dessert	Amaretto, Cappuccino, chocolate, rum, vanilla
Habana Treasure	Amaretto, Anise, chocolate, cognac, rum, vanilla
Habano 2000 Reserve	Sweet
Hannibal Sensational	Chocolate, coffee, rum, vanilla
Havanilla	Vanilla
Heavenly Vanilla	Vanilla

Hobo	Almond brandy, cafe latte, cherry, chocolate, cognac, expresso, Pina Colada, rum, sweet, vanilla
Illusion	Amaretto, Anisette, champagne, cherry, chocolate, chocolate mint, clove, coffee, cognac, Pina Colada, Tropical Rum, vanilla
Island Amaretto	Amaretto
Jamaican Rum	Rum
John T's	Amaretto, Brown Gold, Cafe Ole, Cappuccino, Cherry Cream Rum, sweets, vanilla
La Cuna	Cognac
La Diva	Vanilla
La Dolce Vita	Vanilla
La Francesca	Sweet
La Hoja del Sabor	Vanilla
La Maria	Amaretto, chocolate, coffee, rum, sweet, vanilla
La Tradicion Cubana	Amaretto, orange, peach, vanilla
Lady Club	Rum, sweet, vanilla
Las Vegas Cigar Co.	Maker's Mark bourbon
Maker's Mark	Rum
Manuel Casals	Amaretto, cherry, Cuban Espresso, dark rum, vanilla
Miramonte	Amaretto, cinnamon, coconut, chocolate, mint, rum, vanilla
Monte Rio	Sweet
Mursuli's	Amaretto, cherry, chocolate, coconut, coffee, raspberry, rum, vanilla
Mursuli Sweets	
Napoleon's Dream	Cognac, rum, sambuca, Southern Comfort, vanilla
Oliveros	Sweet, vanilla
Ornelas	Chocolate, vanilla
Paco	Amaretto, cherry, chocolate, cognac, mint, Pina Colada, rum, vanilla
Paradise Dessert Cigars	Amaretto, Anise, cherry, clove, chocolate, Havana rum, mint. vanilla
Penguin	Amaretto, cognac, vanilla
Picadura	Amaretto, Anise, chocolate, cognac, rum, vanilla
Pipers	Cherry, plum, vanilla
Pretty Lady	Amaretto, Anise, cherry, rum, vanilla
Prince Borghese	Amaretto, Anise, chocolate, cognac, rum, vanilla
Profesor Sila Baba	Amaretto, Bourbon, coffee, Cognac, rum, vanilla
Puros Polanco	Amaretto, rum, vanilla
Quo Vadis	Rum, vanilla
Rafael de Habana	Amaretto, Anise, chocolate, cognac, rum, vanilla
Rasputin	Amaretto, Anise, chocolate, cognac, rum, vanilla
Reyes & Benecio	Vanilla
Roll-X	Cognac, vanilla

Rum Raider	Rum
Rum Royale	Rum
Rusty's	Pipe Tobacco
St. Charles	Brandy
Sabor a Miami	Amaretto, cherry, coffee, rum, vanilla
Santiago del Sol	Amaretto, chocolate, vanilla
Scorp	Cappaccino, chocolate, Guarapo, rum, vanilla
Senor Armando Reyes	Vanilla
Smokin' Tiger	Cardamom, Clove, pineapple
Sweet Lady	Vanilla
Sweet Millionaire	Anisette, cognac, mint, pineapple, raspberry, sweet, vanilla
Sweet Sensation	Amaretto, Cafe Latte, peach, strawberry, vanilla
Tatiana	Chocolate, cinnamom, mint, rum, vanilla
Tatou	Amaretto, cherry, chocolate, coconut, coffee, cognac, hazelnut, mint, rum, vanilla
Temptation	Chocolate, mint, vanilla
Tropical Treasure	Almond Brandy, Cayman Chocolate, cognac, Jamaican Sweets, Pina Colada, spiced rum, sweet cherry, West Indies Vanilla
Tropical Treats	Chocolate, rum, vanilla
West Indies Vanilla	Vanilla
Woriur	Clove
Xotica	Amaretto, black cherry, buttered rum, coconut, Cuban coffee, mango, mint chocolate, Passion Fruit, rum and vanilla
Zaldiva	Amaretto, anise, chocolate, cognac, rum, vanilla

Machine-made brands with at one least flavored shape:	*Flavor(s):*
Al-Capone	Sweet
Arango Sportsman	Vanilla
Avanti	Anisette
Blackstone	Sweet Cherry
Dannemann	Sweet
Dutch Masters	Vanilla
Garcia y Vega Whiffs	Pipe tobacco
Hav-A-Tampa	Pipe Tobacco, sweet
Hula Girl	Coffee
Indiana Slims	Rum
King Edward	Sweet Cherry, Sweet Vanilla
Lucky Lady	Cherry
Muriel	Cherry, menthol, pipe tobacco, sweet
Nat Cicco	Almond Liquer, Cuban Cafe
Phillies	Sweet

Ramrod	Bourbon
Royal Hawaiian	Kona Coffee
Ruy Lopez	Vanilla
Schimmelpennick	Mango
Sierra Sweets	Vanilla
Swisher Sweets	Sweet
Tampa Nugget	Sweet
Tampa Resagos	Sweet
Villazon Deluxe Aromatics	Vanilla
White Owl	Sweet
William Penn	Sweet
Wolf Bros.	Rom, sweet, vanilla
X-Rated	Honey

Three brands - Black & Mild, Cherry Blend and Gold & Mild - are dedicated to the use of pipe tobacco fillers.

Please note that many brands of small cigars have one or more models which have flavoring of one type or another:

Agio	Pedroni
Al-Capone	Phillies Little Cigars
Avanti	Pipers
Baby	Prince Albert
Backwoods	Rustlers
Blackstone	St. Regis
Captain Black	Schimmelpennick
Dannemann	Super Value
Dutch Treats	Supre Sweets
Erik	Tijuana Smalls
Hav-A-Tampa Little Cigars	Tiparillo
Indiana Slims	Torino
Miami Suites	Villiger
Nativo	Winchester Little Cigars
Omega	

Brands with "barber pole"-wrapped models include:

ALMANAC

Arabian Nights
AZ
Cojimar
Crown Classics - Dominican
Da Costa
Dominican Elites
Don Alberto
Don Armando
Entrepreneur
Havache

Hugo Cassar Diamond Dominican
  Mystique
Hugo Cassar Diamond Honduran
Mystique Classic
Manuel
Miranda
Oliveros
Penguin
Santa Clara 1830

A new rage is the Culebras shape and perfectos. Makers with Culebras models include:

Handmade brands:
Aida
Caonao
Davidoff
Havache
La Flor de Cano
La Flor Dominicana

Machine-made:
Villiger

An explosion in the production of perfectos has kept the makers of these brands busy introducing new models:

Amaya
Arabian Nights
Aristoff
Ashé
Ashton
Bullet
Cacique
Caonao
Christiano Leone Director's Selection
Cibao
Colorado
Cupido
Cusano Hermanos
Dominion Premium

Don Antonio
Don Antonio Reserva Preciada
Don Diego
Don Juan
Don Juan Urquijo
Don Rafael
Dos Cubanitos
Double Happiness
El Rey de Florez
El Trofeo Habano
Entrepreneur
Fat Cat
Fighting Cock
Gilfranco Vanilla Bombers

H. Upmann
Hannibal
Havache
Havana Reserve
Herrera-Claverol
Imperio Cubano
Juan y Ramon Perfecto
La Aurora
La Concha Reserve
La Flor Dominicana
La Tradicion Cabinet Series Perdomo
Reserve
La Vieja Habana
Lady Club
Luna Azul
M.A.C.
M.P.
Macabana

Monte Real
Napa
Octavio Tavares
Oliveros
Puros Indios
Rastafari
Regatta
Roll-X
Ruby Dooby
Seleccion Royale
Senor San Andres
Tabacalera
Te-Amo
Tesoro
Umo V.S.
V Centennial
Ziq

2.05   OUR FAVORITE BRANDS

Here are some of our favorite brands, primarily from the perspective of interesting names of brands and shapes.

Themed brands:

The production of cigars is a serious business, but some manufacturers take a light-hearted - or at least a themed - approach to naming their shapes:

Brand	Theme
Alamo	6 defenders of the Alamo
Boom Boom El Campeon	2 boxing weight classes
Cacique	7 American Indian tribes
Camorra Limited Reserve	6 Italian cities
Charles the Great	6 Spanish cities
Chessman Royal Reserve	8 chess pieces and moves
Chevere	5 Jamaican cities
Double Happiness	6 states of high happiness
El Fidel	3 kinds of political status

Famous Rum Runner	3 pirate characters
Garo Maduro	4 types of singers
Jamaica Gold	5 court characters
La Fontana	8 Italian artists and scientists
Las Cabrillas	10 New World explorers
Match Play	7 famous golf courses
Nat Sherman Landmarks	5 famous New York landmarks
Nat Sherman Manhattan	5 famous New York neighborhoods
Nat Sherman VIPs	5 famous New Yorkers
New York, New York	6 famous New York streets/sites
Pleiades	10 constellations and planets
Pyramid	6 Egyptian pyramid names
Romanticos	7 great lovers and love-gods
Royal Honduras	8 royal court characters

Fun shape names:

Check out these names in the brand listings, compiled alphabetically for your amusement by our Assistant Editor, Bruce Tenen:

Shape name	*Brand*
Baguette	Dulce Diamante
Bolero	AZ
Charlemagne	La Gloria Cubana
Chocolate Sensation	La Havanita Cigar Factory
Collector's Tin	Gurkha
Ecstacy	Double Happiness
El Jefe	Big Butt
El Mambi	Don Tuto Habanos
Fat Tub	Dominican Original
Filly	Chacaro Black Stallion
Gallapagos	Penguin
Goliath	Royal Jamaica
Insurrectos	La Flor Dominicana
Jeroboam	Casa Blanca
John McKay Super Rothschilds	Bustillo
King Kong	Dominican Original
Lunchour	La Tradicion Cubana
Machine Guns	Speakeasy

Monalisa	Da Vinci
Momotomito	Flor de Farach
No. 10 Downing Street	Royal Jamaica
Pop's Choice	Lew's Smokers
Pythagoras	Credo
Rat Tail	Crown Achievement
Rough Rider	Rico Havana
Scarface	Heaven
Smokin' Lulu	Fighting Cock
Snorkys	Scarface
Sun Tzu	Heaven
Teepee	Indian
Texas Red	Fighting Cock
Wakizashi	Lars Tetens Phat Cigars
Yumbo	Tesoros de Copan
Zorro	Hamiltons Reserve

2.06   THE CIGAR BOWL

Of course there was a college football bowl game named for
cigars! The Cigar Bowl was played in the hotbed of U.S. cigar-
making: Tampa, Florida, from 1947-54, between college-
division teams. The scores:

I	1947	(Jan. 1)	Delaware 21, Rollins 7	(attendance 7,500)
II	1948	(Jan. 1)	Missouri Valley 26, West Chester 7	(10,000)
III	1949	(Jan. 1)	Missouri Valley 13, St. Thomas (Mn), 13	(11,000)
IV	1950	(Jan. 2)	Florida State 19, Wofford 6	(14,000)
V	1951	(Jan. 1)	Wisconsin-La Crosse 47, Valparaiso 14	(12,000)
VI	1951	(Dec. 29)	Brooke Army Medical 20, Camp LeJeune Marines 0	(7,500)
VII	1952	(Dec. 13)	Tampa 21, Lenoir-Rhyne 12	(7,500)
VIII	1954	(Jan. 1)	Missouri Valley 12, Wisconsin-LaCrosse 12	(5,000)
IX	1954	(Dec.)	Tampa 21, Morris Harvey 0	(unknown)

How about a bowl game in Havana? Absolutely! On January 1,
1937, Auburn and Villanova played to a 7-7 tie in the first and
only "Bacardi Bowl," held before 12,000 spectators as a part of
the Cuban National Sports Festival.

College football has also celebrated the leaf with the Smoke Bowl in 1941 (Norfolk All-Stars 16, Richmond All-Stars 2 at Richmond, Virginia) and the Tobacco Bowl in 1946 (Muhlenberg 26, St. Bonaventure 25 at Lexington, Kentucky).

ESPAÑOLA

Only One Brand Can Fill These Bands...

Red
Gold
Reserve

JM Tobacco Co.

Victor Boghossian Photography & Design

Big cigars:
Double Coronas and Giants

These are very large cigars, in fact, some of the largest available. The dimensions of these shapes include:

▸ Double Corona   6¾-7¾ inches long; 49-54 ring.
▸ Giant   8 inches and more; 50 ring and more.

Pictured opposite are:

		(shape)
▸ **FAT CAT** *Churchill*		
(Dominican Republic) 7 x 50		Double Corona
▸ **NAPA DOMINICAN RESERVE** *Gran Corona*		
(Dominican Republic) 7½ x 50		Double Corona
▸ **RAFAEL** *Double Corona*		
(United States) 7½ x 50		Double Corona
▸ **HAVANA SUNRISE** *Presidente*		
(United States) 8 x 52		Giant
▸ **JOYA DE NICARAGUA** *Viajante*		
(Nicaragua) 8½ x 52		Giant
▸ **HANNIBAL** *Emperador*		
(Indonesia) 15 x 125		Giant

And perhaps the strangest shape of all, the Culebras — three small cigars twisted together:

▸ **LA FLOR DOMINICANA** *Culebra Especial*	
(Dominican Republic) 6½ x 30	Culebras

STEWART - BECKWITH

The Humidor Maker

The Executive Entertainer Series

(408) 298-9910
Fax (408) 293-6506
E-Mail address: stewbeck@ix.netcom.com

3.
HANDMADE CIGARS:
LISTINGS BY BRAND

This section provides the details on 1,269 brands of cigars marketed nationally in the United States, a net increase of **32%** (and 308 brands) from the 1998 edition! Each brand listing includes notes on country of manufacture, the origin of the tobaccos used, shapes, names, lengths, ring gauges, wrapper color and a brief description *as supplied by the manufacturers and/or distributors of these brands.* Ring gauges for some brands of cigarillos were not available.

Please note that while a cigar may be manufactured in one country, it may contain tobaccos from many nations. The designation "handmade" indicates the use of long-filler tobacco unless otherwise noted.

Although manufacturers have recognized more than 70 shades of wrapper color, six major color groupings are used here. Their abbreviations include:

- ▸ DC = Double Claro: green, also known as American Market Selection or "AMS."
- ▸ Cl = Claro: a very light tan color.
- ▸ CC = Colorado Claro: a medium brown common to many cigars on this list.
- ▸ Co = Colorado: reddish-brown.
- ▸ CM = Colorado Maduro: dark brown.
- ▸ Ma = Maduro: very dark brown or black (also known as "double Maduro" or "Oscuro.")

HANDMADE CIGARS: BRAND LISTINGS

Many manufacturers call their wrapper colors "Natural" or "English Market Selection." These colors cover a wide range of browns and we have generally grouped them in the "CC" range. Darker wrappers such as those from Cameroon show up most often in the "CM" category.

Shape designations are based on our shape chart in section 1.03. Careful readers will note the freedom with which manufacturers attach names of shapes to cigars which do not resemble that shape at all! For easier comparison, all lengths were rounded to the shortest eighth of an inch, although some manufacturers list sizes in 16ths or even 32nds of an inch.

Although over 1,000 brands are listed, house brands of cigar lounges or individual tobacco stores do not appear. In general, all of the brands listed are available to retailers through wholesale distribution channels.

Readers who would like to see their favorite brand listed in the 2000 edition can call or write the compilers as noted after the Table of Contents.

A TRADITIONAL CIGAR
Handmade in Miami, Florida, USA.

Wrapper: USA/Connecticut   Binder: Indonesia   Filler: Dom. Rep.

Shape	Name	Lgth	Ring	Wrapper
Petit Corona	Corona	5	42	CC
Robusto	Robusto	5	50	CC
Double Corona	Churchill	7	50	CC
Double Corona	Double Corona	7½	50	CC

HANDMADE CIGARS: BRAND LISTINGS

Torpedo	Torpedo	6½	54	CC
Pyramid	Pyramid	7½	54	CC
Robusto	Robusto Gordo	5½	58	CC
Double Corona	Grandioso	7	58	CC

This red-label brand has a medium body. It debuted in 1998 and is available in your choice of box or bundle of 25.

A TRADITIONAL CIGAR
Handmade in Santiago, Dominican Republic.
Wrapper: USA/Connecticut   *Binder: Indonesia*   *Filler: Dom. Rep.*

Shape	Name	Lgth	Ring	Wrapper
Corona	Corona	5¾	42	CC-Ma
Robusto	Robusto	5	50	Ma
Churchill	Lonsdale	6¾	46	CC-Ma
Double Corona	Churchill	7	50	CC-Ma

This blue-banded brand is mild-bodied in its natural-shade wrapper and a medium-bodied taste in the maduro style. You can have your choice in either a box or bundle of 25.

A.T. COFINO
Handmade in Saõ Goncalo dos Campos, Brazil.
Wrapper: Brazil, Ecuador   *Binder: Brazil*   *Filler: Brazil*

Shape	Name	Lgth	Ring	Wrapper
Corona	Corona	5½	42	CC-Ma
Lonsdale	Lonsdale	6½	42	CC-Ma
Churchill	Churchill	7	46	CC-Ma
Robusto	Robusto	5	52	CC-Ma
Robusto	Rothschild	5½	50	CC-Ma
Double Corona	Double Corona	7½	50	CC-Ma

HANDMADE CIGARS: BRAND LISTINGS

Here is a mild-bodied cigar in the natural-shade (Ecuador) wrapper and medium-bodied (Brazil) cigar in the maduro-wrapped version produced in a small town in the Bahia state of Brazil. Introduced in 1997, it features native Brazilian interior tobaccos and is offered in boxes of 20 except for the Corona and Lonsdale sizes, which are offered in 25s.

ABSOLUTO
Handmade in Tamboril, Dominican Republic.
Wrapper: Ecuador   Binder: Dom. Rep.   Filler: Dom. Rep.

Shape	Name	Lgth	Ring	Wrapper
Double Corona	Xtra Churchill	7½	52	CC
Toro	Xtra Robusto	6	52	CC
Grand Corona	Corona Suprema	6½	46	CC

Introduced in 1997, this brand offers a medium-bodied smoke in three larger sizes, featuring an Ecuadorian-grown wrapper.

AGUILA
Handmade in Santiago, Dominican Republic.
Wrapper: USA/Connecticut   Binder: Dom. Rep.   Filler: Dom. Rep.

Shape	Name	Lgth	Ring	Wrapper
Corona	Coronita	5½	40	CC
Lonsdale	Brevas 44	7½	44	CC
Grand Corona	Brevas 46	6½	46	CC
Double Corona	Brevas 50	7½	50	CC
Robusto	Petit Gordo	4¾	50	CC

Created in 1989, this is a mild-to-medium-bodied cigar, which is hand-made in Santiago de los Caballeros, Dominican Republic. The Connecticut wrappers are aged for 5-7 years before production.

AIDA
Handmade in Guiria Ed. Sucre, Venezuela.
Wrapper: USA/Connecticut   Binder: Venezuela   Filler: Venezuela

HANDMADE CIGARS: BRAND LISTINGS

Shape	Name	Lgth	Ring	Wrapper
Churchill	Esplendido	7	48	CM
Torpedo	Torpedo	6	52	CM
Grand Corona	Sensual	6	46	CM
Small Panatela	Delicada	5	34	CM
Culebras	Culebras	7	32	CM

Introduced in 1998, this brand is aimed specifically at female smokers. It has a mild-to-medium-body, offered in individual wrapping and packed in boxes of 25.

AL-CAPONE
Handmade in Esteli, Nicaragua.

Wrapper: Brazil   Binder: Nicaragua   Filler: Nicaragua

Shape	Name	Lgth	Ring	Wrapper
Robusto	Robusto	4½	50	CM
Lonsdale	Corona Grande	6¾	43	CM
Toro	Toro	6	50	CM
Double Corona	Imperial	7	49	CM

This is a 1996 extension of the long-time cigarillo brand produced in Germany. Named for the corpulent Chicago-based gangster of the 1920s, the brand is not surprising in its medium-bodied flavor, but it also exhibits a slightly sweet taste. It is offered in boxes of 25.

ALAMO
Handmade in Danli, Honduras.

Wrapper: Ecuador   Binder: Honduras   Filler: Honduras

Shape	Name	Lgth	Ring	Wrapper
Giant	Travis	8½	52	CC
Double Corona	Crockett	7	50	CC
Churchill	Bonham	6¾	46	CC

Toro	Bowie	6	50	CC
Robusto	Esparza	5	50	CC
Lonsdale	Stockton	6½	42	CC

Named in honor of the famed mission in San Antonio, Texas where Texan freedom fighters fell in a battle against the Mexican army in 1836, this brand celebrates six members of the garrison, including well-known figures such as Col. William Barrett Travis, Jim Bowie and Davey Crockett. The cigars themselves are of medium body and slightly spicy. They are available in boxes of 25.

ALBERO
Handmade in Tenerife, Canary Islands of Spain.

Wrapper: USA/Connecticut   *Binder: Dom. Rep.*   *Filler: Brazil, Dom. Rep.*

Shape	Name	Lgth	Ring	Wrapper
Corona	No. 1	5⅝	43	CC
Cigarillo	Cigarillo	3½	21	CC

New in the U.S. in 1998, this is a mild brand offered in boxes of 25 for the Corona shape and in boxes of 20 for the cigarillos.

ALCAZAR
Handmade in Esteli, Nicaragua.

Wrapper: Nicaragua   *Binder: Nicaragua*   *Filler: Nicaragua*

Shape	Name	Lgth	Ring	Wrapper
Giant	No. 1	8	52	Ma
Double Corona	No. 2	7	50	Ma
Toro	No. 37	6	50	Ma
Robusto	No. 4	5	52	Ma
Torpedo	No. 5	6½	52	Ma

This brand is new for 1998 and features a medium body in an all-maduro line. It is offered in bundles of 20 cigars each.

HANDMADE CIGARS: BRAND LISTINGS

ALFREDO'S SIGNATURE EDITION
Handmade in Danli, Honduras.

Wrapper: Indonesia   Binder: Honduras   Filler: Dom. Rep., Nicaragua

Shape	Name	Lgth	Ring	Wrapper
Double Corona	Grande	7	54	CM
Double Corona	Churchill	7	49	CM
Toro	Toro	6	50	CM
Robusto	Robusto	4¾	52	CM
Lonsdale	Corona	6½	44	CM

Introduced in 1998, this is a full-bodied brand with a pleasant flavor and aroma. It is presented in elegant all-cedar boxes of 25.

ALHAMBRA
Handmade in Manila, the Philippines.

Wrapper: Indonesia   Binder: Philippines   Filler: Philippines

Shape	Name	Lgth	Ring	Wrapper
Robusto	Robusto	5	50	CM
Lonsdale	Corona	6½	42	CM
Churchill	Churchill	7	47	CM
Torpedo	Cortado	5½	42	CM
Short Panatela	Panatela	5	37	CM
Giant	Double Corona	8½	50	CM

Introduced in 1970, Alhambra cigars are handmade in the well-respected factories of the Philippine islands and are packed in bundles of 25 cigars each. A well-made, mild-bodied cigar with a Javan wrapper, it is modestly priced.

ALPHONSO ORTIZ
Handmade in Santiago, Dominican Republic.

Wrapper: Indonesia   Binder: Dom. Rep.   Filler: Dom. Rep.

HANDMADE CIGARS: BRAND LISTINGS

Shape	Name	Lgth	Ring	Wrapper
Giant	No. 1	8	50	CM
Double Corona	No. 2	7	49	CM
Toro	No. 3	6	50	CM
Grand Corona	No. 4	6	46	CM
Robusto	No. 5	5	50	CM
Lonsdale	No. 6	6½	44	CM
Corona	No. 7	5½	42	CM

This brand was introduced in 1997 and offers a Sumatra wrapper and a full-bodied taste. It is presented in cedar boxes of 25.

ALVARO
Handmade in Tenerife, the Canary Islands of Spain.

Wrapper: Indonesia   Binder: Indonesia   Filler: Brazil, Dom. Rep., Mexico

Shape	Name	Lgth	Ring	Wrapper
Lonsdale	Superiores	6½	42	CC
Corona	Selectos	5¼	42	CC
Cigarillo	Panatela	4¾	26	CC

Alvaro cigars are handmade in the historic Canary Islands, where the tradition of cigar making goes back for hundreds of years. This brand is very mild in body and is offered in boxes of 25.

AMADEUS
Handmade in Santiago, Dominican Republic.

Wrapper: Indonesia or USA/Connecticut   Binder: Dom. Rep.   Filler: Dom. Rep.

Shape	Name	Lgth	Ring	Wrapper
Robusto	Robusto	5	50	CC-CM
Double Corona	Double Corona	7½	50	CC-CM
Long Corona	Corona	6¼	44	CC-CM

Toro	Churchill	6½	53	CC-CM

This brand was introduced in 1997 and offers a medium-to-full-bodied taste in boxes of 25.

AMAYA
Handmade in Jalapa, Nicaragua.

Wrapper: Nicaragua　　　*Binder: Nicaragua*　　　*Filler: Nicaragua*

Shape	Name	Lgth	Ring	Wrapper
Lonsdale	Coronas	6½	44	CM
Perfecto	Perfecto	7	50	CM
Long Panatela	Panatelas	7	36	CM
Panatela	Petit Royal	5½	36	CM
Churchill	Presidente	7	46	CM
Robusto	Robusto	5	50	CM

These are medium-bodied cigars which have been produced in one form or another since 1972. They are offered in individual cellophane sleeves in boxes or bundles of 25.

AMBASSADOR
Handmade in San Andres Tuxtla, Mexico.

Wrapper: Mexico　　　*Binder: Mexico*　　　*Filler: Mexico*

Shape	Name	Lgth	Ring	Wrapper
Small Panatela	Petit Corona	4¾	34	CM
Robusto	Robusto	5	50	CM

Introduced in 1996, this is a full-bodied cigar in both sizes. It is offered in elegant cedar boxes of 25.

ANCLA Y CAZADOR
Handmade in Esteli, Nicaragua.

Wrapper: Indonesia　　　*Binder: Indonesia*　　　*Filler: Nicaragua*

HANDMADE CIGARS: BRAND LISTINGS

Shape	Name	Lgth	Ring	Wrapper
Corona	Seleccion	5½	42	CM
Robusto	Robusto	5	50	CM
Torpedo	Pincourt	6	52	CM
Double Corona	Churchill	7	49	CM

A rich, medium-to-full-bodied flavor is the reward for this brand, introduced in late 1997. Although all of the sizes are available in boxes of 25, you can carry the Seleccion with you easily in their special boxes of five.

ANDUJAR
Handmade in Santiago, Dominican Republic.
Wrapper: USA/Connecticut   Binder: Dom. Rep.   Filler: Dom. Rep.

Shape	Name	Lgth	Ring	Wrapper
Cigarillo	Romana	5	25	CC
Double Corona	Santiago	7½	50	CC
Giant	Azua	9	46	CC
Lonsdale	Macorix	6½	44	CC
Panatela	Samana	6	38	CC
Robusto	Vega	5	50	CC-Ma

Introduced in 1994, this line is the special favorite of Oscar Rodriguez, who developed the much-loved Oscar brand. Full-bodied, this line has a clean, gustatory flavor enhanced by each and every draw. The captivating aroma and exciting after-taste make this the perfect cigar for the most special moments. Andujar cigars are offered uncellophaned in all-cedar cabinets for only the truly serious smoker. An oscuro-wrapped version of the Vega debuted in 1998.

ANDULLEROS
Handmade, with short filler, in Santiago, Dominican Republic.
Wrapper: Indonesia   Binder: Dom. Rep.   Filler: Dom. Rep.

HANDMADE CIGARS: BRAND LISTINGS

Shape	Name	Lgth	Ring	Wrapper
Giant	Churchill	8	50	CM
Double Corona	Presidente	7	50	CM
Grand Corona	Doble Corona	6½	46	CM
Robusto	Robusto	5½	50	CM
Long Corona	Lonsdale	6	44	CM

Here is a short filler, handmade cigar which offers a medium-bodied smoke in an inexpensive package of 25.

ANILLO DE ORO
Handmade in Tamboril, Dominican Republic.

Wrapper: Ecuador   *Binder: Dom. Rep.*   *Filler: Dom. Rep.*

Shape	Name	Lgth	Ring	Wrapper
Double Corona	Churchill	6⅞	49	CC
Giant	President	8	50	CC
Long Corona	Corona	7	44	CC
Toro	No. 2	6	50	CC
Robusto	Torito	5	50	CC

This cigar was introduced in 1969, but the blend was changed for 1998. This new style offers a mild-to-medium taste and features a Connecticut-seed wrapper. You can try them in boxes of 25.

ANILLO DE PLATA
Handmade in Danli, Honduras.

Wrapper: Ecuador   *Binder: Honduras*
Filler: Dominican Republic, Honduras, Nicaragua

Shape	Name	Lgth	Ring	Wrapper
Torpedo	Torpedo	7	54	CC
Giant	President	8	50	CC

HANDMADE CIGARS: BRAND LISTINGS

Double Corona	Churchill	6⅞	49	CC
Toro	Toro	6	50	CC
Robusto	Robusto	5	50	CC
Lonsdale	Cetro	6¼	44	CC

This cigar was introduced in December 1996, with a mild-to-medium-bodied blend of leaves from four nations. It is presented in boxes of 25.

ANTELO
Handmade in Miami, Florida, USA.

Wrapper: USA/Connecticut   *Binder: Mexico*   *Filler: Dom. Rep.*

Shape	Name	Lgth	Ring	Wrapper
Double Corona	Presidente	7⅝	50	Cl-Ma
Churchill	Churchill	7	46	Cl-Ma
Lonsdale	No. 1	6¾	42	Cl-Ma
Corona	Cetros	5¾	42	Cl-Ma
Cigarillo	Senoritas	4⅝	28	Cl-Ma
Panatela	Panatela	6⅞	36	Cl-Ma
Corona Extra	Wavell	5⅛	46	Cl-Ma
Giant Corona	Double Corona	7½	42	Cl-Ma
Churchill	Super Cazadore	7½	46	Cl-Ma

These cigars are made by hand in a small factory in Miami, using imported leaf. The taste ranges from mild (Senoritas and Panatelas) to medium (No. 1 and Cetros) to heavy (all other shapes).

ANTONIO Y CLEOPATRA PRIVATE RESERVE
Hand-rolled in La Romana, Dominican Republic.
Wrapper: Indonesia or USA/Pennsylvania
Binder: USA/Pennsylvania   *Filler: Dom. Rep., Jamaica*

HANDMADE CIGARS: BRAND LISTINGS

Shape	Name		Lgth	Ring	Wrapper
Double Corona	Emperadore		7	50	CC
Toro	Double Corona		6¼	48	CC
Long Corona	Lonsdale		6⅛	44	CC
Grand Corona	Palma	(tubed)	6½	46	CC
Toro	Supreme	(tubed)	6¼	48	CC-Ma

The famous brand of Antonio y Cleopatra, named for the legendary Roman and Egyptian lovers of antiquity (together, more or less, from 44-31 B.C.E.), again graces a hand-rolled cigar! Introduced in late 1997, this five-shape range is machine-bunched with the Javan wrapper rolled by hand. It is mild-to-medium in body. The new maduro wrapper uses Pennsylvania broadleaf, new for 1998.

AQUA D'T
Handmade in Danli, Honduras.
Wrapper: Ecuador   *Binder: Dom. Rep.*   *Filler: Dom. Rep., Honduras, Nicaragua*

Shape	Name	Lgth	Ring	Wrapper
Double Corona	Churchill	7	50	CM
Robusto	Robusto	5	50	CM
Lonsdale	Lonsdale	6½	44	CM
Corona	Corona	5½	44	CM

Introduced in 1997, this is a mild-to-medium-bodied brand, offered in boxes of 25. Each cigar is protected in individual cellophane sleeves; you'll know it right away by the four-color, sea-serpent decoration on each box.

ARABIAN NIGHTS
Handmade in San Andres Tuxtla, Mexico.
Wrapper: Mexico   *Binder: Mexico*   *Filler: Mexico*

Shape	Name	Lgth	Ring	Wrapper
Double Corona	Giant	7	52	Stripe
Perfecto	Perfecto	7	52	Stripe

HANDMADE CIGARS: BRAND LISTINGS

Double Corona	Double Corona	7½	50	Stripe
Churchill	Churchill	7	48	Stripe
Grand Corona	Lonsdale	6½	46	Stripe
Lonsdale	Twisted Head	6¼	42	Stripe
Pyramid	Pyramid	6	48	Stripe
Torpedo	Torpedo	6	52	Stripe
Long Corona	Corona	6	42	Stripe
Robusto	Toro	5	50	Stripe

Developed in 1989 and available in the U.S. since 1995, this is an all "candy stripe" brand, wrapped with Mexican-grown maduro and Sumatra-seed leaves. The overall body is medium and the brand is offered in cedar boxes of 25 and in packages of 10, 5, 3 and 1 cigar in specific sizes.

ARANGO STATESMAN
Handmade in Danli and San Pedro Sula, Honduras.

Wrapper: Ecuador   *Binder: Dom. Rep.*   *Filler: Dom. Rep., Honduras*

Shape	Name	Lgth	Ring	Wrapper
Churchill	Barrister	7½	46	CC-Ma
Corona	Counselor	5	40	CC-Ma
Petit Corona	Executor	6	43	CC-Ma

Introduced in 1988, these are medium-bodied, handmade cigars, which should not be confused with its sister brand, the Arango Sportsman, which is a flavored machine-made cigar. The Statesman is quite aromatic, with just a hint of vanilla flavor to charm the smoker.

ARBOL DE PALMA
Handmade in San Andres Tuxtla, Mexico.

Wrapper: Mexico   *Binder: Mexico*   *Filler: Mexico*

Shape	Name	Lgth	Ring	Wrapper
Robusto	Original	5	50	CM

HANDMADE CIGARS: BRAND LISTINGS

This brand was introduced in 1996 and offers a mild-bodied taste and a value in price. It is presented without cellophane in all-cedar boxes of 25.

ARISTOFF
Handmade in San Pedro de Macoris, Dominican Republic.

Wrapper: Brazil, Cameroon, USA/Connecticut

Binder: Dominican Republic   *Filler: Dominican Republic*

Shape	Name	Lgth	Ring	Wrapper
	Special Perfecto Cigars:			
Perfecto	700S	7	52	Cl-CM
Perfecto	550S	5½	50	Cl-CM-Ma
Perfecto	450S	4½	50	Cl-CM-Ma
Perfecto	Master of the Universe	6¾	56	Cl
	Belicoso Cigars:			
Torpedo	450B	4½	50	Cl-CM-Ma
Torpedo	550B	5½	50	Cl-CM-Ma
Torpedo	700B	7	52	Cl-Ma

As much a work of art as a cigar, Aristoff was introduced in 1998 after several years of careful development. Designed to be as good as it gets, this brand is notable for its two hard-to-make shapes and medium body. It also offers the smoker the luxury of choice: a light Connecticut (offering a mild body), dark Cameroon (mild-to-medium body) or savory Brazilian maduro (medium-to-full body, slightly sweet) wrapper. The Master of the Universe blend is unique, with a Connecticut wrapper, Cameroon binder and Dominican filler.

The box? Another triumph, with a gorgeous curved shape and four bulb-style feet on African-grown Okoume wood that make it a perfect compliment to the modern living room. Oh yes, there are 24 Aristoff cigars in each box, sporting the distinctive Aristoff band designed by the Italy's Mossimo Zucchi Studio.

ARMANDO Y RAMON
Handmade, with short filler, in Esteli, Nicaragua.

Wrapper: Indonesia, Mexico   *Binder: Nicaragua*   *Filler: Dom. Rep., Nicaragua*

HANDMADE CIGARS: BRAND LISTINGS

Shape	Name	Lgth	Ring	Wrapper
Double Corona	Super Cazadore	7½	52	CM-Ma
Double Corona	Cazadore	7	50	CM-Ma
Lonsdale	Fumas	6½	44	CM-Ma

This brand was introduced in 1995 and offers a mild taste in its natural-shade wrapper and a medium-bodied taste in the maduro wrapper grown in Mexico. You can enjoy them in bundles of 25.

AROMA DE CAFE
Handmade, with mixed filler, in Santiago, Dominican Republic.
Wrapper: Dom. Rep.   Binder: Dom. Rep.   Filler: Dom. Rep.

Shape	Name	Lgth	Ring	Wrapper
Small Panatela	Eye Opener	4	34	CM
Lonsdale	Wide Awake	6½	44	CM

This is a medium-to-full-bodied, flavored brand, introduced in 1998. It is offered in boxes of 25.

AROMAS DE SAN ANDRES
Handmade in San Andres Tuxtla, Mexico.
Wrapper: Mexico   Binder: Mexico   Filler: Mexico

Shape	Name		Lgth	Ring	Wrapper
Lonsdale	Gourmet	(tubed)	6⅛	42	CM
Toro	Afficiando		6	50	CM
Double Corona	Maximillian		7½	52	CM
Robusto	Robusto		5	50	CM
Double Corona	Imperial	(tubed)	7	50	CM
Grand Corona	Crowns		6½	47	CM
Long Corona	Sceptors		6	44	CM

HANDMADE CIGARS: BRAND LISTINGS

Produced by Tabacos San Andres S.A. de C.V., this line is composed of all-Mexican tobacco of interesting origins. Although all grown in the famous San Andres Valley, the filler and binder are native seed, while the wrapper leaf is Sumatran-type tobacco which is also grown in the S.A. Valley.

AROMELLA
Handmade in San Andres Tuxtla, Mexico.

Wrapper: Mexico   Binder: Mexico   Filler: Mexico

Shape	Name	Lgth	Ring	Wrapper
Short Panatela	Petite Corona	4¾	38	CC-Ma
Long Corona	Corona Superior	6¼	42	CC-Ma

Introduced in 1994, this brand is full-bodied and flavored with vanilla. It is offered in boxes of 25.

ARTIGAS
Handmade in Mexico City, Mexico.

Wrapper: Mexico   Binder: Mexico   Filler: Mexico

Shape	Name	Lgth	Ring	Wrapper
Short Panatela	Exquisito	5	35	Ma
Long Panatela	Lancero	7½	36	Ma
Petit Corona	Petit Corona	4	42	Ma
Long Corona	Corona	6	42	Ma
Lonsdale	Tubo de Cristal (tubed)	6½	43	Ma
Lonsdale	Lonsdale	6¾	44	Ma
Giant Corona	Gran Corona	7½	44	Ma
Robusto	Rothschild	4½	50	Ma
Robusto	Robusto	5	50	Ma
Toro	Toro	6	50	Ma
Churchill	Esplendido	7	48	Ma
Double Corona	Churchill	7½	50	Ma

HANDMADE CIGARS: BRAND LISTINGS

This all-Mexican brand features a Sumatra-seed wrapper aged for two years. It is available in a medium-bodied style, or in a mild-to-medium strength for the Vintage line (same sizes, but using 1995 tobaccos). You can enjoy these cigars in boxes of 25, or in 5-packs for the Corona, Robusto and Churchill shapes.

ARTURAS FELIPE
Handmade in Esteli, Nicaragua.

Wrapper: Indonesia　　　*Binder: Indonesia*　　　*Filler: Dom. Rep.*

Shape	Name	Lgth	Ring	Wrapper
Robusto	Robusto	5½	50	CM
Lonsdale	Corona	6½	44	CM
Double Corona	Churchill	7	52	CM
Toro	Presidente	6	48	CM

Introduced in 1997, this is a medium-bodied brand featuring Sumatra-seed wrapper and binder. It is offered in boxes of 25.

ARTURO FUENTE
Handmade in Santiago, Dominican Republic.

Wrapper: Ecuador or USA/Connecticut, Cameroon
Binder: Dominican Republic　　　*Filler: Dominican Republic*

Shape	Name	Lgth	Ring	Wrapper
Corona	Brevas Royale /medium filler/	5½	42	CC-Ma
Giant	Canones	8½	52	CC-Ma
Robusto	Chateau Fuente	4½	50	CC-Ma
Churchill	Churchill	7¼	48	CC-Ma
Grand Corona	Corona Imperial	6½	46	CC-Ma
Corona Extra	Cuban Corona	5¼	45	CC-Ma
Lonsdale	Curly Head /medium filler/	6½	43	CC-Ma

Lonsdale	Curly Head Deluxe /medium filler/	6½	43	CC-Ma
Toro	Double Chateau Fuente	6¾	50	CC-Ma
Lonsdale	Fumas	7	44	CC-Ma
Long Panatela	Panatela Fina	7	38	CC-Ma
Short Panatela	Petit Corona	5	38	CC-Ma
Lonsdale	Seleccion Privada No. 1	6¾	44	CM-Ma
Robusto	Rothschild	4½	50	CC-Ma
Double Corona	Chateau Fuente Royal Salute	7⅝	54	CC-Ma
Lonsdale	Spanish Lonsdale	6½	42	CM-Ma
Grand Corona	Flor Fina 8-5-8	6	47	CM-Ma
	Hemingway Series:			*(perfecto tips)*
Robusto	Hemingway Short Story	4	48	CM
Robusto	Hemingway Best Seller	5	55	CM
Double Corona	Hemingway Untold Story	7½	53	Ma
Churchill	Hemingway Classic	7	48	CM
Grand Corona	Hemingway Signature	6	47	CM
Giant	Hemingway Masterpiece	9	52	CM

Arturo Fuente learned the art of growing and processing tobacco and the making of premium, handmade cigars in Cuba at the end of the 19th century, producing his own line in 1912. Today, his son Carlos and grandson, Carlos, Jr. oversee the more than 500 rollers who manufacture more than 24 million cigars every year. Their line offers a medium-to-full-bodied taste, with the celebrated Hemingway series a little mellower, thanks to an additional 140 days of aging. Many of the natural-wrapped cigars (including the Hemingway series) feature Cameroon leaves, with Connecticut leaf used for maduros. The Chateau Fuente, Chateau Fuente Royal Salute and Double Chateau Fuente use either Ecuadorian-grown, Connecticut-seed or Connecticut wrappers.

Figurados:
Perfectos, Pyramids and Torpedos

These shapes are the most distinctive of all, with flared ends and/or conical heads. Although the dimensions vary, the definitions remain constant:

- *Perfectos*: A cigar with a conical-shaped head *and* foot.
- *Pyramids*: A cigar whose ring gauge increases continuously from head to foot. Also known as "triangulars" or "trumpets."
- *Torpedos*: A cigar with a tapered head that flares out to straight sides. Also known as "belicosos."

Pictured opposite, from left to right:

- **LA FLOR DOMINICANA** *El Jocko Perfecto No. 1*
  (Dominican Republic) 4½ x 54   Perfecto

- **RAS TAFARI** *Afrika*
  (Jamaica)   6 x 60   Perfecto

- **EL REY DE FLOREZ** *Major Perfecto*
  (Dominican Republic) 6 x 46   Perfecto

- **FELIPE BLACK** *Belicoso*
  (Honduras)   6 x 52   Torpedo

- **HAVACHE** *Figurado*
  (Honduras)   7¼ x 54   Perfecto

- **LA VIEJA HABANA** *Torpedo No. 4*
  (Nicaragua)   7½ x 54   Torpedo

- **ARISTOFF** *700S*
  (Dominican Republic) 7 x 52   Perfecto

HANDMADE CIGARS: BRAND LISTINGS

ARTUS
Handmade in San Andres Tuxtla, Mexico.

Wrapper: Mexico   Binder: Mexico   Filler: Mexico

Shape	Name	Lgth	Ring	Wrapper
Lonsdale	Lonsdale	6¾	42	CM-Ma
Long Corona	Corona	6	42	CM-Ma
Toro	Toro	6	50	CM-Ma
Double Corona	Double Corona	7	50	CM-Ma
Robusto	Robusto	5	50	CM-Ma
Robusto	Rothschild	4½	50	CM-Ma

Mmmm, good! Here is a mild-bodied, all-Mexican cigar which is new for 1997. You can have your pick of wrappers: natural or maduro and you'll find Artus in carefully-built, all-cedar boxes of 25.

ARUBA
Handmade, with mixed filler, in Santiago, Dominican Republic.

Wrapper: Indonesia   Binder: Dom. Rep.   Filler: Dom. Rep.

Shape	Name	Lgth	Ring	Wrapper
Double Corona	Churchill	7	50	CM
Toro	Toro	6	50	CM
Robusto	Robusto	5	50	CM
Corona	Corona	5½	42	CM
Lonsdale	Lonsdale	6½	44	CM

You don't have to go there to buy it, silly . . . but Aruba will give you the medium-bodied, pleasant experience you'd enjoy if you were in Aruba . . . and you can get 25 of these 1997-introduced Arubas in a single box!

ARZT DE LOS REYES
Handmade in Santiago, Dominican Republic.

Wrapper: Dom. Rep.   Binder: Dom. Rep.   Filler: Dom. Rep.

HANDMADE CIGARS: BRAND LISTINGS

Shape	Name	Lgth	Ring	Wrapper
Churchill	Monarch	7	48	CM
Grand Corona	Regent	6	47	CM
Long Corona	Prince	6	42	CM
Toro	Duke	6	50	CM
Panatela	Earl	5½	38	CM
Robusto	Viscount	4½	50	CM

This brand was introduced in 1998 by veteran connoisseur Gary Arzt and has a medium-to-full body with aged Dominican-grown leaves. It is presented in boxes of 25.

ASHÉ
Handmade in Tamboril, Dominican Republic.
Wrapper: Indonesia, USA/Connecticut   *Binder: Dom. Rep.*   *Filler: Dom. Rep.*

Shape	Name	Lgth	Ring	Wrapper
Corona	Corona	5½	42	CM-Ma
Robusto	Robusto	5	50	CM-Ma
Grand Corona	Churchill	6	46	CM-Ma
Perfecto	Petit Perfecto	4½	46	CM-Ma
	Vintage Selection:			
Double Corona	Vintage Churchill	7	50	CM
Long Corona	Vintage Corona	6	42	CM
Robusto	Vintage Robusto	5	50	CM
Torpedo	Vintage Torpedo	6	52	CM

Here is a mild-to-medium-bodied blend, introduced in 1996, that offers a Piloto Cubano filler combined with a Connecticut wrapper and Dominican Olor binder, packed in elegant all-cedar boxes of 25. The Vintage Selection uses the same blend, but with aged leaves. The 1998-introduced Maduro line uses an Indonesian wrapper.

HANDMADE CIGARS: BRAND LISTINGS

ASHTON

Handmade in Santiago, Dominican Republic.

Wrapper: USA/Connecticut   Binder: Dom. Rep.   Filler: Dom. Rep.

Shape	Name	Lgth	Ring	Wrapper
Double Corona	Churchill	7½	52	CC
Churchill	Prime Minister	6⅞	48	CC
Lonsdale	8-9-8	6½	44	CC
Panatela	Panatela	6	36	CC
Corona	Corona	5¼	44	CC
Slim Panatela	Cordial	5	30	CC
Toro	Double Magnum	6	50	CC
Robusto	Magnum	5	50	CC
Small Panatela	Esquires	4¼	32	CC
	Aged Cabinet Selection:			
Perfecto	No. 1	9	52	CC
Perfecto	No. 2	7	48	CC
Perfecto	No. 3	6	46	CC
Robusto	No. 6	5½	52	CC
Toro	No. 7	6¼	52	CC
Double Corona	No. 8	7	49	CC
Pyramid	Pyramid	6	52	CC
	Maduro:			
Double Corona	No. 60	7½	52	Ma
Churchill	No. 50	7	48	Ma
Toro	No. 40	6	50	Ma
Lonsdale	No. 30	6¾	44	Ma
Corona	No. 20	5½	44	Ma
Robusto	No. 10	5	50	Ma

HANDMADE CIGARS: BRAND LISTINGS

Robert Levin of Holt's Tobacconist of Philadelphia, Pennsylvania set out to create a great cigar in 1985 . . . and he succeeded. Ashton cigars are manufactured without compromise, blending six tobaccos: Dominican filler and Dominican-grown, Cuban-seed binder leaves with perfect shade-grown wrapper leaves from the Connecticut Valley. The maduro wrappers are longer-aged Connecticut Broadleaf. The unique range of sizes includes three large perfecto-shaped cigars - tapered at both ends - in the Cabinet Selection series.

ASTRAL
Handmade in Danli, Honduras.

Wrapper: Ecuador   Binder: Dom. Rep.   Filler: Dom. Rep., Nicaragua

Shape	Name	Lgth	Ring	Wrapper
Lonsdale	Lujos	6½	44	CM
Double Corona	Maestro	7½	52	CM
Robusto	Besos	5	50	CM
Churchill	Favorito	7	48	CM
Torpedo	Perfeccion	7	48	CM

More than three years of planning went into the production of this brand, introduced in 1995 and made in Danli, Honduras. Mild-to-medium in body, the Connecticut-seed wrappers give this line an elegant appearance, with silky expresso and cream flavors. Special features of this line include the gentle taper of the foot of the Favorito size and the narrowed head of the Perfeccion size. Astral cigars are presented in stunning Mahogany boxes which underscore the total commitment to quality in the manufacturing process.

ASTRAL GRAND RESERVE VINTAGE
Handmade in Danli, Honduras.

Wrapper: Indonesia   Binder: Mexico   Filler: Dom. Rep., Mexico

Shape	Name		Lgth	Ring	Wrapper
Double Corona	Maestro	(tubed)	7½	52	CM
Torpedo	Perfeccion	(tubed)	7	48	CM
Lonsdale	Lujo	(tubed)	6½	44	CM
Robusto	Beso	(tubed)	5	50	CM

HANDMADE CIGARS: BRAND LISTINGS

New for 1998, this is a medium-to-full-bodied blend with notes of sweetness and a light peppery character. It is offered in elegant glass tubes in stunning all-mahogany boxes of 15.

ATHENEA

Handmade in Las Palmas, the Canary Islands of Spain.

Wrapper: USA/Connecticut   Binder: Indonesia
             Filler: Brazil, Dominican Republic, Honduras, Indonesia

Shape	Name	Lgth	Ring	Wrapper
Double Corona	Doble Corona	7½	50	CC
Toro	Toro	6	50	CC
Lonsdale	Lonsdale	6½	42	CC
Robusto	Robusto	4½	42	CC
Panatela	Panetela	6½	37	CC

This brand was introduced in 1998 and offers a mild-bodied taste in boxes of 25.

AVANOS

Handmade in the Dominican Republic and the USA.

	BLUE LABEL:	
Wrapper: Ecuador and Indonesia	Binder: Dom. Rep.	Filler: Dom. Rep.

	GOLD LABEL:	
Wrapper: Indonesia	Binder: Dom. Rep.	Filler: Dom. Rep.

Shape	Name	Lgth	Ring	Wrapper
	Blue Label, made in Tamboril, Dominican Republic:			
Robusto	Robusto	5	50	CC
	Gold Label, made in Miami, Florida, USA:			
Robusto	Robusto	5	50	CM

This brand was introduced in 1998 and is medium-bodied in both styles. The Blue Label Robusto has a double wrapper of Ecuadorian-grown, Connecticut-seed wrapper rolled over a Sumatra wrapper. Both are offered in unique, slide-top cedar boxes of 18 cigars each!

AVO

Handmade in Santiago, Dominican Republic.

Wrapper: USA/Connecticut   *Binder: Dom. Rep.*   *Filler: Dom. Rep.*

Shape	Name	Lgth	Ring	Wrapper
Lonsdale	Avo No. 1	6¾	42	Co
Toro	Avo No. 2	6	50	Co
Double Corona	Avo No. 3	7½	50	Co
Long Panatela	Avo No. 4	7	38	Co
Grand Corona	Avo No. 5	6⅞	46	Co
Panatela	Avo No. 6	6½	36	Co
Long Corona	Avo No. 7	6	44	Co
Corona	Avo No. 8	5½	40	Co
Robusto	Avo No. 9	4¾	48	Co
Pyramid	Pyramid	7	54	Co
Torpedo	Belicoso	6	48	Co
Torpedo	Petit Belicoso	5¼	46	Co
	XO Series:			
Churchill	Maestoso	7	48	CC
Robusto	Intermezzo	5½	50	CC
Long Corona	Preludio	6	40	CC
Panatela	Serenata	5¾	38	CC
Petit Corona	Notturno	5	42	CC
Small Panatela	Presto	5	31	CC
Small Panatela	Allegro	4½	34	CC
	Domaine Avo series:			
Robusto	<10>	5⅛	50	CC

HANDMADE CIGARS: BRAND LISTINGS

The perfectly-balanced marriage of five different tobaccos, mostly from the Cibao Valley of the Dominican Republic, gives the Avo line - introduced in 1987 - a rich flavor in a mild-bodied cigar. The newer XO Series offers a richer blend of six tobaccos, using a Dominican-grown, Havana-seed binder with the Connecticut Shade wrapper. The Domaine Avo series celebrates ten years of Avo cigars with a full-bodied taste in the first of what is expected to be a seven-shape line.

AZ
Handmade in San Andres Tuxtla, Mexico.

Wrapper: Mexico　　　　　　*Binder: Mexico*　　　　　　　　　*Filler: Mexico*

Shape	Name	Lgth	Ring	Wrapper
Small Panatela	Cordial	4¼	30	CM
Petit Corona	Petit Corona	5	42	CM
Long Corona	Corona	6	44	CM
Robusto	Robusto	5	50	CM
Toro	Toro	6	50	CM
Double Corona	Churchill	7	50	CM
Long Corona	Bolero	6	42	Stripe
Double Corona	Phenom	7½	52	CM

The creation of the indefatigable Andre Zabitsky, this is a well-known brand in other countries, but only introduced to the U.S. in 1996, featuring all-Mexican tobaccos and a full-bodied taste. All of the shapes use a natural wrapper, except for the Bolero, which offers a double-wrapped "barber pole" style. Maduro-wrapped versions of these shapes are also planned for this brilliantly-constructed brand.

B.E.R.
Handmade in Tamboril, Dominican Republic.

Wrapper: Indonesia　　　　　*Binder: Dom. Rep.*　　　　　　*Filler: Dom. Rep.*

Shape	Name	Lgth	Ring	Wrapper
Double Corona	Churchill	7	50	CM
Lonsdale	Lonsdale	6½	44	CM

Robusto	Rothschild	4¾	50	CM
Toro	Corona Gorda	6	50	CM

Introduced in 1997, this is a medium-bodied brand with a Sumatra wrapper, offered in boxes of 25.

BACCARAT HAVANA SELECTION
Handmade in Danli, Honduras.

Wrapper: Honduras　　　　　*Binder: Mexico*　　　　　*Filler: Honduras*

Shape	Name	Lgth	Ring	Wrapper
Small Panatela	Bonitas	4½	30	CC
Double Corona	Churchill	7	50	CC-Ma
Long Corona	Luchadore	6	43	CC
Lonsdale	No. 1	7	44	CC
Panatela	Panatela	6	38	CC
Corona	Petit Corona	5½	42	CC
Small Panatela	Platinum	4⅞	32	CC
Pyramid	Polo	7	52	CC
Robusto	Rothschild	5	50	CC-Ma
Double Corona	Double Corona	7½	50	CC
Giant	King	8½	52	CC

This fine cigar series was formally introduced in 1978, but actually dates back as far as 1871 when it was supervised by Carl Upmann. The mild body produced by the blending of the Havana-seed fillers, Mexican binder and Connecticut-seed wrapper are sweetened by the use of a special sealing gum in the cigar's cap. It is offered in boxes of 25, with four sizes also available in 10s.

BACHECHE
Handmade, with medium filler, in Tamboril, Dominican Republic.
Wrapper: Indonesia　　　　　*Binder: Dom. Rep.*　　　　　*Filler: Dom. Rep.*

HANDMADE CIGARS: BRAND LISTINGS

Shape	Name	Lgth	Ring	Wrapper
Churchill	Presidente	7	48	CM
Toro	Toro	6	50	CM
Long Corona	Lonsdale	6¼	44	CM
Robusto	Robusto	5	50	CM
Corona	Corona	5½	42	CM

New in 1998, this is a medium-filler, mild-to-medium-bodied brand available in value-priced bundles of 25.

BAD BOY
Handmade in Villa Gonzalez, Dominican Republic.
Wrapper: Indonesia or USA/Connecticut   Binder: Dom. Rep.   Filler: Dom. Rep.

Shape	Name	Lgth	Ring	Wrapper
Torpedo	Torpedo	6	56	CC-CM
Double Corona	Churchill	7	50	CC-CM
Robusto	Robusto	5	50	CC-CM

This is a mild-to-medium-bodied smoke, introduced in 1997. It features a choice of wrappers and is offered in all-cedar boxes of 10 or 25.

BAD FROG
Handmade, with medium filler, in Manila, the Philippines.
Wrapper: Philippines   Binder: Philippines   Filler: Philippines

Shape	Name	Lgth	Ring	Wrapper
Torpedo	Torpedo	5⅜	47	CM
Corona	Corona	5½	44	CM

This is a mild-to-medium-bodied blend available for the first time in 1998. It is offered in bundles of 25.

HANDMADE CIGARS: BRAND LISTINGS

BAHIA
Handmade in San Jose, Costa Rica.

Wrapper: Ecuador   Binder: Nicaragua   Filler: Nicaragua

Shape	Name	Lgth	Ring	Wrapper
Giant	Double Corona	8½	50	CC
Double Corona	Corona Gigante	7	54	CC
Torpedo	Belicoso	5½	52	CC
Toro	Esplendido	6	50	CC
Robusto	Robusto	5	50	CC
Corona	No. 4	5½	42	CC

Tony Borhani introduced the Bahia brand in December 1994, and now offers his 1992 crop vintage selection. The entire production was aged for nine months after rolling and only then released for sale. Packed uncellophaned in slide-top cabinets, Bahia is a limited production cigar of the highest quality and full bodied in taste. The prior release featured the 1989 crop selection.

BAHIA GOLD
Handmade in San Jose, Costa Rica.

Wrapper: Ecuador   Binder: Dom. Rep.   Filler: Dom. Rep.

Shape	Name	Lgth	Ring	Wrapper
Giant	A	9	48	CC
Churchill	Churchill	6⅞	48	CC
Torpedo	Belicoso	5½	52	CC
Robusto	Robusto	5	50	CC
Corona	No. 4	5½	42	CC

The Tabacalera Tambor in Costa Rica is the creation point for this 1997-introduced series of full-bodied cigars, featuring a Connecticut-seed wrapper.

BAHIA MADURO
Handmade in San Jose, Costa Rica.

Wrapper: USA/Connecticut   Binder: USA/Connecticut   Filler: Nicaragua

HANDMADE CIGARS: BRAND LISTINGS

Shape	Name	Lgth	Ring	Wrapper
Double Corona	Corona Gigantes	7	54	Ma
Torpedo	Belicosos	5½	52	Ma
Robusto	Panchos	5½	54	Ma
Robusto	Robustos	5	50	Ma

Wow! A maduro-wrapped Bahia from Tony Borhani and the Tabacalera Tambor!
Note the unusual binder, using Connecticut Broadleaf to underscore the rich
maduro taste of this full-bodied cigar introduced in late 1997.

BAHIA TRINIDAD
Handmade in San Jose, Costa Rica.

Wrapper: Ecuador   Binder: Ecuador   Filler: Dom. Rep., Nicaragua

Shape	Name	Lgth	Ring	Wrapper
Double Corona	Corona Gigantes	7	54	CC
Torpedo	Belicosos	5½	52	CC
Torpedo	Torpedo	7	54	CC
Robusto	Panchos	5½	54	CC
Robusto	Robustos	5	50	CC
Lonsdale	Elegantes	6½	42	CC

This is a medium-to-full-bodied smoke, first made available in 1997. The
Ecuadorian-grown wrapper and binder are from Sumatran seed, with Cuban-
seed Dominican and Nicaraguan-grown filler leaves. Once rolled, Bahia
Trinidads are aged for an additional 120 days to ensure perfect draw and flavor.

BALBOA
Handmade in Colon, Panama.

Wrapper: Honduras   Binder: Mexico
Filler: Dominican Republic, Honduras, Panama

Shape	Name	Lgth	Ring	Wrapper
Giant	Viajante	8½	52	CC-Ma

HANDMADE CIGARS: BRAND LISTINGS

Churchill	Churchill	7	48	CC-Ma
Lonsdale	No. 1	7	43	CC-Ma
Lonsdale	No. 2	6½	43	CC-Ma
Corona	No. 4	5½	43	CC-Ma
Long Panatela	Palma Extra	7	36	CC-Ma

This cigar is offered in bundles of 25 cigars each and is a full-bodied, even heavy, smoke.

BALI HAI
Handmade in Malan, Indonesia.

Wrapper: Indonesia *Binder: Indonesia* *Filler: Indonesia*

Shape	Name	Lgth	Ring	Wrapper
Churchill	Sultan	7	48	CC
Toro	Black Bull	6½	50	CC
Pyramid	Krakatau	6	50	CC
Robusto	Budha	5	50	CC
Long Corona	Java Special	6	42	CC

The Sumatra wrapper and Indonesian filler make this brand mild-to-medium in body. This 1997-introduced cigar is offered in spectacular, 20-count solid wood boxes from Kalimantan; the cigars are swathed in hand-woven Batik cloth.

BALMORAL
Handmade in San Pedro de Macoris, Dominican Republic.

Wrapper: Ecuador *Binder: Dom. Rep.* *Filler: Brazil, Dom. Rep.*

Shape	Name	Lgth	Ring	Wrapper
Churchill	Churchill	7	48	CC
Lonsdale	Lonsdale	6½	42	CC
Long Corona	Corona	5⅞	42	CC
Robusto	Robusto	5	48	CC

Panatela	Panatella	5½	37	CC

Already a well-known machine-made brand, this handmade version is mild in body with a Connecticut-seed wrapper. You can find it in individual cellophane sleeves in packs of 5 or boxes of 25.

BANCES
Handmade in Cofradia, Honduras.

Wrapper: Ecuador, USA/Connecticut *Binder: Honduras*
Filler: Dominican Republic, Honduras and Nicaragua

Shape	Name	Lgth	Ring	Wrapper
Churchill	Corona Immensas	6¾	48	CM-Ma
Panatela	El Prados	6¼	36	CM-Ma
Giant	Presidents	8½	52	CM-Ma
Panatela	Uniques	5½	38	CM-Ma

Bances cigars are now, for the most part, handmade in Honduras under the same supervision as the famous Hoyo de Monterrey and Punch lines. This is a true value cigar, with the same great smoking qualities of its more famous sister lines.

BANDERA
Handmade in Santiago, Dominican Republic.

Wrapper: Dom. Rep. *Binder: Dom. Rep.* *Filler: Dom. Rep.*

Shape	Name		Lgth	Ring	Wrapper
Long Corona	Petit Corona	(tubed)	6	42	CM
Long Corona	Corona	(tubed)	6	44	CM
Grand Corona	Double Corona	(tubed)	6	46	CM
Robusto	Robusto	(tubed)	5½	50	CM
Double Corona	Churchill	(tubed)	7	50	CM
Pyramid	Pyramide		6	53	CM

HANDMADE CIGARS: BRAND LISTINGS

Introduced in 1996, this brand offers a mild-to-medium body with leaves all grown in the Dominican. Each cigar is uniquely packed in cellophane sleeves and then, for most sizes, in an acrylic tube!

BANDOLERO
Handmade in Santiago, Dominican Republic.

Wrapper: Indonesia   *Binder: Dom. Rep.*   *Filler: Dom. Rep.*

Shape	Name	Lgth	Ring	Wrapper
Panatela	Panetela	6	38	Ma
Robusto	Robusto	5	50	Ma
Lonsdale	Lonsdale	6½	44	Ma
Toro	Churchill	6½	50	Ma
Pyramid	Piramide	6½	53	Ma
Double Corona	Double Corona	7½	50	Ma

Here are medium-to-full-bodied cigars introduced in 1998. They feature a maduro wrapper and are offered in cellophane-wrapped bundles of 25.

BANDOLEROS
Handmade in Santiago, Dominican Republic.

Wrapper: Dom. Rep.   *Binder: Dom. Rep.*   *Filler: Dom. Rep.*

Shape	Name	Lgth	Ring	Wrapper
Slim Panatela	4-Pack	5	30	CM

These small cigars are easy to smoke and come in handy packs for pocket or purse. The flavor is full-bodied, thanks to the all-Cuban seed construction.

BARLOVENTO
Handmade in Santiago, Dominican Republic.

Wrapper: Ecuador, Mexico   *Binder: Dom. Rep.*   *Filler: Dom. Rep.*

Shape	Name	Lgth	Ring	Wrapper
Double Corona	Churchill	7	50	CC-Ma

Giant	Presidente	8½	50	CC-Ma
Robusto	Robusto	5	50	CC-Ma
Toro	Toro	6	50	CC-Ma

This brand was introduced in 1997 and offers a medium-bodied flavor in either its natural (Ecuador) or maduro (Mexico) wrapper. You can enjoy this four-leaf filler blend in see-through boxes of 20.

BAUZA
Handmade in Santiago, Dominican Republic.

Wrapper: Ecuador   *Binder: Dom. Rep*   *Filler: Dom. Rep.*

Shape	Name	Lgth	Ring	Wrapper
Churchill	Casa Grande	6¾	48	CC
Double Corona	Fabuloso	7½	50	CC
Corona	Grecos	5½	42	CC
Lonsdale	Jaguar	6½	42	CC
Lonsdale	Medalla d'Oro No. 1	6⅞	44	CC
Short Panatela	Petit Corona	5	38	CC
Double Corona	Presidente /combination filler/	7½	50	CC
Pyramid	Pyramid	5½	55	CC
Robusto	Robusto	5½	50	CC

Introduced in 1980, these medium-to-full-bodied cigars are high in quality and high in value. Enveloped in Ecuadorian wrappers, nine sizes are offered, eight of which are in elegant wooden boxes and one in a bundle of 25 cigars with combination filler.

BB LOS REYES
Handmade in Santiago, Dominican Republic.

Wrapper: Dom. Rep.   *Binder: Dom. Rep.*   *Filler: Dom. Rep.*

HANDMADE CIGARS: BRAND LISTINGS

Shape	Name	Lgth	Ring	Wrapper
Robusto	Santo Domingo	5	50	CM
Long Corona	Santiago Corona	6	44	CM
Double Corona	Don Miguel	7	50	CM
Churchill	Don Sabri	6⅞	46	CM
Long Panatela	Gitanos Panatelas	7	36	CM
Small Panatela	Bishritos Petit	5	30	CM
Torpedo	Torpedos	6½	54	CM
Pyramid	Figuerados	6½	46	CM

The combination of aged Dominican tobaccos make this a mild-bodied brand, offered in boxes of 25, except for the Figuerados, which is offered in 20s.

BELINDA
Handmade in Cofradia, Honduras.
Wrapper: Ecuador, Honduras
Binder: Honduras   Filler: Dominican Republic, Honduras

Shape	Name	Lgth	Ring	Wrapper
Panatela	Belinda	6½	36	CM
Corona	Breva Conserva	5½	43	CM-Ma
Corona Extra	Cabinet	5⅝	45	CM
Long Corona	Corona Grande	6¼	44	CM-Ma
Churchill	Ramon	7¼	47	CM
Toro	Excellente	6	50	CM-Ma
Double Corona	Prime Minister	7½	50	CM-Ma
Robusto	Medaglia D'Oro	4½	50	CC
Robusto	Robusto	4½	50	CM-Ma
Long Corona	Spanish Twist	6¼	43	CM-Ma
Grand Corona	Vintage Corona	6¼	45	CM-Ma

Long Corona	Humidores	6	43	CM

This old Cuban brand has been successfully re-introduced in 1994 as a medium-to-heavy bodied cigar wrapped in Ecuadorian or Honduran leaves, depending on the shade. It is expertly made and presented in all-cedar boxes that continue the aging process. Of note is the new Humidores model, presented in a glass humidor containing 20 cigars, and the Vintage Corona, presented in an ammunition crate of 105 cigars!

BELLERO
Handmade in Esteli, Nicaragua.
Wrapper: Ecuador, Indonesia, Mexico   Binder: Honduras   Filler: Dom. Rep.

Shape	Name	Lgth	Ring	Wrapper
Double Corona	Churchill	7	50	CC-CM-Ma
Giant	Presidente	8	52	CC-CM-Ma
Torpedo	Torpedo	6½	52	CC-CM-Ma
Long Corona	Corona	6¼	44	CC-CM-Ma
Toro	Toro	6	52	CC-CM-Ma
Robusto	Robusto	5	50	CC-CM-Ma

Here is a mild-bodied blend with a choice of wrappers: Ecuador (Connecticut-seed), Indonesian or Mexican maduro wrappers. Introduced in 1996, it is offered in boxes of 25.

BEN MIGUEL
Handmade in Santo Domingo, Dominican Republic.
Wrapper: Ecuador   Binder: Dom. Rep.   Filler: Dom. Rep.

Shape	Name	Lgth	Ring	Wrapper
Double Corona	Presidente	7½	50	CC
Churchill	Churchill	7	48	CC
Long Panatela	Panatela	7½	38	CC
Toro	Toro	6	50	CC

Robusto	Robusto		5	50	CC
Long Corona	Corona		6	44	CC
Petit Corona	Coronita		5	44	CC
Torpedo	Torpedo		6¾	52	CC

Introduced in 1996, Ben Miguel features a Connecticut-seed wrapper grown in Ecuador. The blend with Cuban-seed filler tobaccos produces a mild-to-medium-bodied taste, offered in cellophane sleeves inside cedar boxes of 3 or 25.

BEN MIGUEL
Handmade in Santo Domingo, Dominican Republic.

Wrapper: Indonesia   *Binder: Dom. Rep.*   *Filler: Dom. Rep.*

Shape	Name	Lgth	Ring	Wrapper
Double Corona	Presidente	7½	50	CM
Churchill	Churchill	7	48	CM
Toro	Toro	5½	50	CM
Toro	Robusto	4½	50	CM
Lonsdale	Corona	6½	44	CM
Long Panatela	Panatela	7½	38	CM
Pyramid	Pyramide	6½	50	CM

This brand was introduced in 1997 by the Los Gringos Cigar Co. It offers a mild-to-medium-bodied taste, thanks to the Cuban-seed leaves in the binder and filler. It is presented in boxes of 25.

BENEDIT
Handmade in Santiago, Dominican Republic.

Wrapper: Ecuador   *Binder: Brazil*   *Filler: Dom. Rep.*

Shape	Name	Lgth	Ring	Wrapper
Double Corona	Soberanos	7½	52	CC
Double Corona	Presidentes	7	50	CC

HANDMADE CIGARS: BRAND LISTINGS

Toro	Governors	6	52	CC
Long Panatela	Palmas	8	36	CC
Lonsdale	No. 1	6⅞	44	CC
Panatela	No. 3	6⅞	38	CC
Grand Corona	Corona	6	46	CC

This is a medium-bodied brand with a three-nation blend of leaves and some unique shapes. It is available in boxes of 25.

BERING

Handmade in Cofradia and Danli, Honduras.

Wrapper: Honduras, USA/Connecticut · · · · · · · · · · · · · · · · Binder: Honduras

Filler: Dominican Republic, Honduras, Mexico, Nicaragua

Shape	Name		Lgth	Ring	Wrapper
Giant	Grande		8½	52	CC
Lonsdale	Barons		7¼	42	CC-Ma
Lonsdale	Casinos	(tubed)	7⅛	42	DC-CC
Grand Corona	Cazadores		6¼	45	CC
Grand Corona	Corona Grande		6¼	46	DC-CC
Long Corona	Corona Royale	(tubed)	6	41	CC
Corona Extra	Coronados		5⅛	45	DC-CC
Small Panatela	No. 8		4¼	32	CC
Slim Panatela	Gold No. 1		6¼	33	CC
Toro	Hispanos		6	50	CC-Ma
Corona	Imperials	(tubed)	5¼	42	CC
Lonsdale	Inmensas		7⅛	45	CC-Ma
Long Corona	Plazas		6	43	DC-CC
Pyramid	Torpedo		7	54	CC
Robusto	Robusto		4¾	50	CC

HANDMADE CIGARS: BRAND LISTINGS

Bering is a premium handmade cigar imported from Honduras. This blend of specially selected Cuban-seed, long-leaf tobaccos is the reason for the incredibly smooth draw, spicy aroma and full, rich taste. Berings are available in 15 shapes and a variety of wrappers and in a variety of packaging: 3s, 4s, 5s, 15s, 25s and 50s.

BERING DOMINICAN HALLMARK
Handmade in Villa Gonzalez, Dominican Republic.

Wrapper: USA/Connecticut   *Binder: Indonesia*   *Filler: Dom. Rep.*

Shape	Name	Lgth	Ring	Wrapper
Robusto	Robusto	4½	50	CC
Toro	Toro	6	50	CC
Churchill	Churchill	7	48	CC
Giant	Presidente	8	50	CC

Bering fans alert: here is the new Bering Dominican Hallmark Selection for 1998, a medium-bodied cigar featuring a Connecticut wrapper, in four sizes. Enjoy it in boxes of 25!

BEVERLY HILLS - VIP
Handmade in Danli, Honduras.

Wrapper: Ecuador   *Binder: Nicaragua*   *Filler: Honduras*

Shape	Name	Lgth	Ring	Wrapper
Short Panatela	No. 535	5	35	CC
Long Corona	No. 644	6	44	CC
Double Corona	No. 749	7	49	CC
Robusto	No. 550	5	50	CC
Giant	No. 854	8	54	CC

This is a handmade cigar with a Connecticut-seed wrapper and tobaccos of three different nations in the blend. The brand offers a smooth draw and mild body, and is offered in all-cedar boxes of 10 and 25 (except for nos. 749 and 854, offered only in 25s.)

HANDMADE CIGARS: BRAND LISTINGS

BIARRITZ
Handmade in Santiago, Dominican Republic.

Wrapper: Indonesia   *Binder: Dom. Rep.*   *Filler: Dom. Rep.*

Shape	Name	Lgth	Ring	Wrapper
Double Corona	Churchill	7½	50	CC
Robusto	Rothschild	4½	50	CC
Long Corona	Corona	6	44	CC

Introduced in 1997, this is a medium-bodied cigar with a Cameroon-seed wrapper and all Dominican-grown leaves. It is offered in protective cellophane sleeves inside all-cedar boxes of 25.

BIG AL'S
Handmade in Villa Gonzalez, Dominican Republic.

Wrapper: Indonesia or USA/Connecticut   Binder: Dom. Rep.   *Filler: Dom. Rep.*

Shape	Name	Lgth	Ring	Wrapper
Torpedo	Torpedo	6	56	CC-CM
Double Corona	Churchill	7	50	CC-CM
Toro	Toro	6	50	CC-CM
Robusto	Robusto	4½	50	CC-CM
Long Corona	Corona	6	44	CC-CM

Introduced in 1997, this is a mild-to-medium-bodied cigar, available in boxes of 25.

BIG BITE
Handmade in Ocotal, Nicaragua.

Wrapper: Nicaragua   *Binder: Nicaragua*   *Filler: Nicaragua*

Shape	Name	Lgth	Ring	Wrapper
Robusto	Super Robusto	4½	52	CM
Corona	Super Corona	5¾	44	CM

HANDMADE CIGARS: BRAND LISTINGS

Remarkable packaging in an air-tight can of five cigars each marks this brand as a different kind of cigar. Introduced in 1998, it is blended to team with its companion "Big Bite Beer" this is a medium-to-full-bodied cigar that uses only leaves that have been aged for 12-18 months before rolling.

BIG BUTT
Handmade in Esteli, Nicaragua.

Wrapper: Indonesia, Nicaragua   *Binder: Nicaragua*   *Filler: Nicaragua*

Shape	Name	Lgth	Ring	Wrapper
Toro	El Camaron	5¾	50	CM
Double Corona	El Jefe	7½	54	CM
Toro	Don Gordo	6	54	CM-Ma
Robusto	Gordito	4¾	54	CM

This brand honors the memory of Don Carlos Santiago, better known as "Don Gordo," a master roller who produced cigars in Cuba until the time of nationalization; he died in 1994. These big-ring cigars offer a medium-to-full body and are packed in elegant cedar cases in individual cellophane sleeves, and accompany a wide line of clothing and fashion accessories. The new maduro wrapper on the Don Gordo size is from Nicaragua.

BIG CHIEF
Handmade in Danli, Honduras.

Wrapper: USA/Connecticut   *Binder: Honduras*   *Filler: Honduras*

Shape	Name	Lgth	Ring	Wrapper
Torpedo	Torpedo	7	54	CM
Giant	Presidente	8	50	CM
Double Corona	Churchill	7	49	CM
Toro	Toro	6	50	CM
Robusto	Robusto	5	50	CM
Long Corona	Cetro	6	43	CM

HANDMADE CIGARS: BRAND LISTINGS

Here is a heavy, full-flavored cigar introduced in 1997. The natural wrapper is from Connecticut and the powerful taste comes from the all-Honduran filler.

BLAIR GOLD LABEL
Handmade in Danli, Honduras.

Wrapper: Ecuador   Binder: Honduras   Filler: Honduras

Shape	Name	Lgth	Ring	Wrapper
Giant	Presidente	8½	52	CC
Churchill	Churchill	7	48	CC
Toro	Robusto	6	50	CC
Robusto	Rothschild	4¾	50	CC
Lonsdale	Lonsdale	6½	44	CC

Introduced in 1996, this brand is offered in five handmade sizes, featuring an Ecuadorian-grown, Connecticut-seed wrapper. The taste is considered to be medium-to-full-bodied and is presented in individual cellophane sleeves and packed in boxes of 25.

BLAIR SILVER LABEL
Handmade in Las Palmas, the Canary Islands of Spain.

Wrapper: USA/Connecticut   Binder: Canary Islands   Filler: Brazil, Dom. Rep.

Shape	Name	Lgth	Ring	Wrapper
Churchill	Churchill	7	48	CC
Toro	Toro	6	50	CC
Robusto	Rothschild	5	52	CC

New in 1997, this edition of the Blair line is mild-bodied and slightly spicy. It is offered in boxes of 25.

BLUE PARROT
Handmade in Santo Domingo, Dominican Republic.

Wrapper: Indonesia   Binder: Dom. Rep.   Filler: Dom. Rep.

HANDMADE CIGARS: BRAND LISTINGS

Shape	Name	Lgth	Ring	Wrapper
Corona		5½	44	CC
Toro		6	50	CC
Churchill		6¾	46	CC
Double Corona		7	50	CC

This is a medium-bodied cigar. It is presented without shape names in four sizes in boxes of 25.

BOGAR
Handmade in Danli, Honduras.
Wrapper: Indonesia   *Binder: Honduras*   *Filler: Dom. Rep., Honduras, Mexico*

Shape	Name	Lgth	Ring	Wrapper
Corona	Corona	5½	42	CC
Corona	Toro	5½	44	CC
Robusto	Short Churchill	5	50	CC
Grand Corona	Corona Gorda I	6	46	CC
Toro	Corona Gorda II	6	50	CC
Double Corona	Churchill	7	50	CC

Introduced in 1996, this is a full-bodied cigar with a four-nation blend of leaves, featuring a Sumatra-seed wrapper. Each cigar is presented in individual cellophane sleeves, inside a vanished, all-cedar box of 25.

BOGEY'S STOGIES
Handmade in Danli, Honduras.
Wrapper: Ecuador
Binder: Indonesia   *Filler: Dom. Rep., Mexico, Nicaragua*

Shape	Name	Lgth	Ring	Wrapper
Corona	Elegante	5	42	CC
Robusto	Robusto	5	50	CC

HANDMADE CIGARS: BRAND LISTINGS

Long Corona	Corona	6¼	44	CC
Toro	Double Corona	6	50	CC
Double Corona	Churchill	7	50	CC
Giant	Presidente	8	50	CC

Designed for the golf course, this 1996-introduced brand is mild-to-medium in body. It features a Connecticut-seed wrapper and is offered in all-cedar boxes of 25.

BOHIO
Handmade in Tamboril, Dominican Republic.
Wrapper: Indonesia, USA/Connecticut
Binder: Dominican Republic   Filler: Dominican Republic

Shape	Name	Lgth	Ring	Wrapper
Double Corona	Presidentes	7½	50	CC-Ma
Churchill	Churchills	7	46	CC-Ma
Long Corona	Coronas	6	44	CC-Ma
Robusto	Robustos	5	50	CC-Ma
Corona	Petit-Coronas	5½	42	CC-Ma
Torpedo	Torpedos	7	54	CC-Ma

Introduced in 1997, this brand of the T&R Tobacco Sales Co. offers a choice of Sumatra wrapper or a Connecticut maduro wrapper, combined with Dominican-grown binder and fillers for a mild-to-medium smoke. Each cigar is sleeved in cellophane and packed in cedar boxes of 24.

BOHIO
Handmade in Santo Domingo, Dominican Republic.
Wrapper: Ecuador   Binder: Dom. Rep.   Filler: Dom. Rep.

Shape	Name	Lgth	Ring	Wrapper
Double Corona	Don Felipe	7½	50	CC
Lonsdale	Imperial	6¾	44	CC

Long Panatela	Grand Panatella	7½	38	CC
Robusto	Toro	5½	50	CC
Robusto	Robusto	4½	50	CC

A completely different brand of Bohio, this creation of the Los Gringos Cigar Company offers a mild-to-medium-bodied taste, featuring a Connecticut-seed wrapper and Piloto Cubano filler leaves. Introduced in 1997, it is offered in protective cellophane sleeves and packaged in cedar boxes of 25.

BOLERO
Handmade in Santiago, Dominican Republic.

Wrapper: Dom. Rep.   Binder: Dom. Rep.   Filler: Dom. Rep.

Shape	Name	Lgth	Ring	Wrapper
Long Corona	Long Corona	6	42	CM

This is a flavored cigar, available in cherry, chocolate, tropical rum and vanilla. It is available in bundles of 25.

BOLERO
Handmade in Navarette, Dominican Republic.

Wrapper: Ecuador   Binder: Dom. Rep.   Filler: Dom. Rep.

Shape	Name	Lgth	Ring	Wrapper
Robusto	Robusto	4¾	52	CC
Short Panatela	Petit Bolero	5	36	CC
Corona	Corona	5¾	43	CC
Long Panatela	Panatela	7	38	CC
Churchill	Churchill	7	48	CC
Double Corona	Optimus	7½	50	CC
Small Panatela	Vanilla	5	30	CC

Named for Cuba's smooth musical rhythms, this is a medium-to-full-bodied cigar. Introduced in 1998, it has a Connecticut-seed wrapper and is offered in boxes or

HANDMADE CIGARS: BRAND LISTINGS

bundles of 25. Future shapes are scheduled to include a Pyramid and Torpedo in a Connecticut Shade wrapper, packed in boxes of 10. The Vanilla shape also has a Connecticut Shade wrapper.

BOLIVAR

Handmade in Santiago, Dominican Republic.

Wrapper: USA/Connecticut   Binder: Mexico   Filler: Dom. Rep.

Shape	Name	Lgth	Ring	Wrapper
Panatela	No. 5	5¾	38	CC
Corona	No. 4	5¾	43	CC
Robusto	Robustos	5⅝	50	CC
Torpedo	Belicosos	6	52	CC
Double Corona	Coronas Gigante	7¼	49	CC
Lonsdale	Tubos No. 1	6¾	43	CC
Slim Panatela	Tubos No. 7	7	34	CC

Long a famous Cuban brand, but rarely seen in the U.S., this version of Bolivar debuted in late 1998. It offers a medium flavor with rich flavors with glorious Connecticut wrappers. There are seven sizes and the brand is offered in beautifully-dressed boxes of 20.

BOOM BOOM EL CAMPEON

Handmade in Miami, Florida, USA.

Wrapper: Mexico   Binder: Dom. Rep.   Filler: Dom. Rep.

Shape	Name	Lgth	Ring	Wrapper
Short Panatela	Bantamweight	5	38	CC
Corona	Lightweight	5½	44	CC

Ray "Boom Boom" Mancini, a charismatic lightweight boxing champion of the 1980s, is the inspiration behind this series of mild-bodied cigars. The line is offered in flavored versions, including Amaretto, cafe, chocolate, cognac and vanilla.

HANDMADE CIGARS: BRAND LISTINGS

BOQUILLA

Handmade in Union City, New Jersey, USA.

Wrapper: Dominican Republic, Mexico, USA/Connecticut

Binder: Mexico   Filler: Dominican Republic

Shape	Name	Lgth	Ring	Wrapper
Giant	Churchill	8	50	CC-Ma
Double Corona	Silverano	7	50	CC-Ma
Toro	Torito	6½	50	CC-Ma
Churchill	Imperiale	7½	46	CC-Ma
Lonsdale	Presidente	6½	44	CC-Ma
Long Corona	Senadore	6	44	CC-Ma
Long Panatela	Ninfa	7	36	CC-Ma
Lonsdale	Fuma	7	44	CC-Ma
Torpedo	Torpedo	6	54	CC-Ma
Pyramid	Pyramid	5½	46	CC-Ma
Robusto	Robusto	5	50	CC-Ma

This cigar is made by a small factory of the same name. These are medium-to-full bodied cigars, with an increased number of sizes and wrappers available for 1997.

BOSS

Handmade in Santo Domingo, Dominican Republic.

Wrapper: Indonesia   Binder: Dom. Rep.   Filler: Dom. Rep.

Shape	Name	Lgth	Ring	Wrapper
Robusto	Robusto	5½	50	CM
Lonsdale	Lonsdale	6½	42	CM
Toro	Toro	6½	50	CM
Churchill	Churchill	6⅞	47	CM

This brand debuted in 1997 and features a Sumatra wrapper around a three-leaf filler, offering a medium-bodied flavor. It is presented uncellophaned in cedar cabinets of 25.

BOYERO
Handmade in Santiago, Dominican Republic.

Wrapper: Indonesia *Binder: Dom. Rep.* *Filler: Dom. Rep.*

Shape	Name	Lgth	Ring	Wrapper
Double Corona	Churchill	7½	50	CC
Robusto	Rothschild	4½	50	CC
Corona	Petit Corona	5½	42	CC

Introduced in late 1996, this is a mild blend of leaves available in three popular shapes. The Dominican-grown interior tobaccos include Olor binders and Piloto Cubano fillers.

BOYERO PRIMERO
Handmade in Santiago, Dominican Republic.

Wrapper: Indonesia *Binder: Dom. Rep.* *Filler: Dom. Rep.*

Shape	Name	Lgth	Ring	Wrapper
Double Corona	Churchill	7½	50	CC
Robusto	Robusto	5	50	CC
Corona	Alquise	6	44	CC

Also introduced in late 1996, this version of Boyero offers a medium-bodied taste with a slightly stronger blend of Olor and Piloto Cubano binder and filler leaves, respectively.

BRAVOS
Handmade in Las Palmas, the Canary Islands of Spain.

Wrapper: Indonesia *Binder: Indonesia* *Filler: Dom. Rep., Spain*

Shape	Name	Lgth	Ring	Wrapper
Double Corona	Churchill	7¼	50	CC

HANDMADE CIGARS: BRAND LISTINGS

Toro	Toro	6	50	CC
Robusto	Robusto	5	50	CC
Lonsdale	Lonsdale	6½	43	CC

Here is a medium-bodied brand from the Canary Islands, featuring a Sumatra wrapper, Java binder and filler tobaccos from the Canary Islands and the Dominican Republic. Introduced in 1997, it is offered in boxes or bundles of 25.

BRETON LEGEND SERIES
Handmade in Santiago, Dominican Republic.

Wrapper: Indonesia   Binder: Dom. Rep.   Filler: Dom. Rep.

Shape	Name	Lgth	Ring	Wrapper
Giant	Churchill	8	50	CM
Double Corona	Presidente	7	50	CM
Grand Corona	Doble Corona	6½	46	CM
Robusto	Robusto	5½	50	CM
Long Corona	Lonsdale	6	44	CM
Long Panatela	Panatela Larga	7	36	CM
Panatela	Panetela	5½	36	CM
Pyramid	Piramide I	5½	50	CM
Torpedo	Classic No. 1	7	50	CM
Torpedo	Classic No. 2	6½	42	CM
Pyramid	Piramide II	7	50	CM

Here is a full-bodied cigar with a Sumatra wrapper, offered in boxes of 25, except for the Classic line (20 per box) and Piramide II (12 per box).

BREVE
Handmade in Santiago, Dominican Republic.

Wrapper: Dom. Rep.   Binder: Dom. Rep.   Filler: Dom. Rep.

HANDMADE CIGARS: BRAND LISTINGS

Shape	Name	Lgth	Ring	Wrapper
Petit Corona	Breve	4¼	44	CC

Long-time cigar connoisseur Gary Arzt created this brand to provide a quality cigar at a reasonable price. This is a medium-to-full-bodied brand, offered in boxes of five, 10 or 25.

BRIONES
Handmade in Danli, Honduras.

Wrapper: Ecuador　　　　　　*Binder: Nicaragua*　　　*Filler: Dom. Rep., Nicaragua*

Shape	Name	Lgth	Ring	Wrapper
Robusto	Robusto	5	50	CC
Toro	No. 1	6	52	CC
Churchill	Churchill	7	48	CC
Double Corona	Presidente	7½	50	CC
Lonsdale	Lonsdale	6½	42	CC
Torpedo	Torpedo	6½	52	CC

From the Tabacalera San Cristobal comes this blend of leaves from four nations that provides a medium-bodied flavor for this brand, introduced in 1997. It is offered in boxes of 25.

BUCANERO
Handmade in San Jose, Costa Rica.

BUCANERO WINDJAMMER:
Wrapper: Ecuador　　　　*Binder: Ecuador*　　*Filler: Dom. Rep., Nicaragua*

BUCANERO MADURO:
Wrapper: USA/Connecticut　*Binder: USA/Connecticut*　*Filler: Dom. Rep., Nicaragua*

Shape	Name	Lgth	Ring	Wrapper
	Windjammer:			
Double Corona	Corona Gigante	7	54	CC

Lonsdale	Elegante	6½	42	CC
Torpedo	Torpedo	6½	54	CC
Robusto	Robusto	5½	52	CC
	Maduro:			
Churchill	Churchill	6⅞	48	Ma
Robusto	Robusto	5½	52	Ma

Created in 1998, this is a mild-bodied brand in the Windjammer style, with a Sumatra-seed wrapper. The Maduro line is full-bodied with a Connecticut Broadleaf. Both are offered in top-hinged all-cedar boxes of 20.

BUFFALO BUNDLES
Handmade in San Jose, Costa Rica.

Wrapper: Ecuador   *Binder: Ecuador*   *Filler: Dom. Rep., Nicaragua*

Shape	*Name*	*Lgth*	*Ring*	*Wrapper*
Petit Corona	No. 100	5	42	CC
Robusto	No. 200	5	50	CC
Toro	No. 300	6	50	CC
Toro	No. 400	6	48	CC

This is a 1998-introduction, with a mild-to-medium body and excellent construction. It is presented in bundles of 20 cigars each.

BULLDOG
Handmade in Santiago, Dominican Republic.

Wrapper: USA/Connecticut   *Binder: Dom. Rep.*   *Filler: Dom. Rep.*

Shape	*Name*	*Lgth*	*Ring*	*Wrapper*
Corona	Corona	5½	44	CC
Toro	Toro	6	50	CC
Double Corona	Churchill	7	50	CC

HANDMADE CIGARS: BRAND LISTINGS

Introduced in 1996, this medium-bodied cigar will not bark or bite! It's sure to become man's best friend in bundles of 25.

BULLET
Handmade in Esteli, Nicaragua.

Wrapper: Ecuador   *Binder: Nicaragua*   *Filler: Nicaragua*

Shape	Name	Lgth	Ring	Wrapper
Perfecto	.454	4	54	CC
Perfecto	.554	5	54	CC
Perfecto	.654	6	54	CC

New for 1998, this is a mild-bodied brand from Nick Perdomo, offered in three bold shapes. It is available in value-priced boxes of 25.

BURMA
Handmade in Yangon, Myanmar.

Wrapper: Myanmar   *Binder: Myanmar*   *Filler: Myanmar*

Shape	Name	Lgth	Ring	Wrapper
Corona	Corona	5½	44	CC

Myanmar? Think Burma and you'll know that the Sittang River Valley is the origination point for the tobaccos in this brand, introduced to the U.S. market in 1997. This is a full-bodied brand and is offered in bundles of 25 or in hand-lacquered boxes of 25 or 50 with a silk liner inside.

BURT'S GOLD
Handmade in Villa Gonzalez, Dominican Republic.
Wrapper: Ecuador or USA/Connecticut

Binder: Dominican Republic   *Filler: Dominican Republic, Indonesia*

Shape	Name	Lgth	Ring	Wrapper
Robusto	Robusto	5	50	CC
Grand Corona	Lonsdale	6½	46	CC
Long Panatela	Elegancia	7	38	CC

HANDMADE CIGARS: BRAND LISTINGS

Long Panatela	Panatela	7	38	CC
Double Corona	Churchill	7½	50	CC
Torpedo	Torpedo	6½	52	CC

Introduced in 1998 with the endorsement of actor Burt Reynolds, this is a mild-to-medium-bodied cigar offered in special gold-paper wrapping in boxes of 25, or 20 for the Pyramid and Torpedo.

BURT REYNOLDS
Handmade in Villa Gonzalez, Dominican Republic.

Wrapper: Indonesia *Binder: Dom. Rep.* *Filler: Dom. Rep.*

Shape	Name	Lgth	Ring	Wrapper
Toro	Toro	6	50	CC
Grand Corona	Lonsdale	6½	46	CC
Double Corona	Churchill	7½	50	CC
Torpedo	Torpedo	6½	52	CC

Introduced in 1998, this brand — saluting the actor of the same name — is full-bodied and offered in boxes or bundles of 25, or in gift boxes of four.

BURT'S LADY
Handmade, with mixed filler,
in Villa Gonzalez, Dominican Republic.

Wrapper: Indonesia *Binder: Indonesia* *Filler: Dom. Rep.*

Shape	Name	Lgth	Ring	Wrapper
Long Panatela	Elegancia	7	38	CC

Introduced in 1998, this is a medium-bodied, flavored cigar available in Amaretto, orange, peach and vanilla flavors. It is available in boxes of 25.

BUSTILLO
Handmade in Tampa, Florida, USA.

Wrapper: Honduras *Binder: Honduras* *Filler: Honduras*

HANDMADE CIGARS: BRAND LISTINGS

Shape	Name	Lgth	Ring	Wrapper
Robusto	John McKay Super Rothschilds	4½	49	CM
Robusto	Coppola Cafe Robusto	4½	49	Ma

Here is a zesty blend of seven-year-aged Cuban-seed Honduran wrappers, offering a medium body in the John McKay Super Rothschilds and a full-bodied taste in the Coppola Cafe Robusto shape.

BUTERA ROYAL VINTAGE
Handmade in La Romana, Dominican Republic.
Wrapper: USA/Connecticut   Binder: Indonesia   Filler: Dom. Rep.

Shape	Name	Lgth	Ring	Wrapper
Robusto	Bravo Corto	4½	50	CC
Lonsdale	Cedro Fino	6½	44	CC
Toro	Dorado 652	6	52	CC
Churchill	Capo Grande	7½	48	CC
Corona	Fumo Dolce	5½	44	CC
Panatela	Mira Bella	6¾	38	CC
Toro	Cornetta No. 1	6	52	CC

Introduced in 1993, Butera Royal Vintage are true-blended, premium cigars handmade in the Dominican Republic by "first-row" cigar makers. Six distinctive whole-leaf tobaccos from three different countries are blended, including four specific types of long-filler leaves from the rarest Dominican crops. Every cigar is well-aged to maturity in cabinets of fine Spanish cedar and packaged in beautiful Mahogany chests. The spicy, flavorful blend is considered medium in body.

BUTERA VINTAGE MADURO
Handmade in La Romana, Dominican Republic.
Wrapper: USA/Connecticut   Binder: Indonesia   Filler: Brazil, Dom. Rep.

Shape	Name	Lgth	Ring	Wrapper
Robusto	No. 550	5	50	Ma

Toro	No. 650	6	50	Ma
Double Corona	No. 750	7	50	Ma
Long Corona	No. 644	6	44	Ma

This 1998-introduced brand is available only to selected dealers. It offers a smooth, medium-to-full-bodied taste in the Butera style. You can find it in elegant boxes of 20.

C.A.O.

Handmade in Danli, Honduras.

Wrapper: Costa Rica, USA/Connecticut

Binder: Honduras   Filler: Mexico, Nicaragua

Shape	Name	Lgth	Ring	Wrapper
Petit Corona	Petite Corona	5	40	CC
Long Corona	Corona	6	42	CC-Ma
Lonsdale	Lonsdale	7	44	CC
Robusto	Robusto	4½	50	CC-Ma
Toro	Corona Gorda	6	50	CC-Ma
Giant	Churchill	8	50	CC-Ma
Pyramid	Triangulare	7½	54	CC-Ma
Double Corona	Presidente	7½	54	CC-Ma

Introduced in 1995, this medium-bodied cigar line can be enjoyed at any time of the day, with its blend of Cuban-seed tobaccos in the filler and binder and a Connecticut shade wrapper. The maduro-wrapped cigars utilize Connecticut Broadleaf-seed tobaccos grown in Costa Rica. Offered in boxes of 25, with some sizes also available in four-packs.

C.A.O. ANIVERSARIO MADURO

Handmade in San Jose, Costa Rica.

Wrapper: USA/Connecticut   Binder: Ecuador   Filler: Dom. Rep., Nicaragua

HANDMADE CIGARS: BRAND LISTINGS

Shape	Name	Lgth	Ring	Wrapper
Corona	No. 4 Corona	5½	42	Ma
Robusto	Robusto	5	50	Ma
Churchill	Churchill	6⅞	48	Ma
Torpedo	Belicoso	6	54	Ma

Developed in honor of the 13th anniversary of the C.A.O. brand, this all-maduro line is offered with a medium-to-full body and exquisite construction. This brand is box-pressed and presented in boxes of 25.

C.A.O. GOLD
Handmade in Esteli, Nicaragua.
Wrapper: Ecuador   *Binder: Nicaragua*   *Filler: Nicaragua*

Shape	Name	Lgth	Ring	Wrapper
Corona	Corona	5½	42	Co
Robusto	Robusto	5	50	Co
Toro	Corona Gorda	6½	50	Co
Churchill	Churchill	7	48	Co
Torpedo	Torpedo	6¼	52	Co
Double Corona	Double Corona	7½	54	Co

Introduced in 1996, this brand features a Connecticut Shade-seed wrapper and a mild-to-medium taste. Box-pressed, these cigars are offered in boxes of 25, with some shapes also available in four-packs.

CABALLEROS
Handmade in Santiago, Dominican Republic.
Wrapper: USA/Connecticut   *Binder: Dom. Rep.*   *Filler: Dom. Rep.*

Shape	Name	Lgth	Ring	Wrapper
Double Corona	Churchill	7	50	CC
Robusto	Rothschild	5	50	CC
Churchill	Double Corona	6¾	48	CC

HANDMADE CIGARS: BRAND LISTINGS

Corona	Corona	5¾	43	CC
Corona	Petit Corona	5½	42	CC

Introduced in 1993, these are mild-to-medium bodied cigars with much flavor, produced with long filler and made completely by hand. Imported from the Dominican Republic, Caballeros cigars are offered in individual cellophane sleeves inside cedarwood boxes of 25.

CABAÑAS
Handmade in La Romana, Dominican Republic.
Wrapper: USA/Connecticut   Binder: Dom. Rep.   Filler: Dom. Rep.

Shape	Name	Lgth	Ring	Wrapper
Corona	Coronas	5½	42	Ma
Toro	Exquisitos	6½	48	Ma
Lonsdale	Premiers	6⅝	42	Ma
Grand Corona	Royales	5⅝	46	Ma

Fans of the darkest wrapper shades will not be disappointed by Cabanas, one of the oldest names in cigars; the flavorful Connecticut wrappers are essentially black. But the blend offers a mild and pleasant taste and is presented in boxes of 25.

CABAÑAS Y CARBAJAL
Handmade in La Romana, Dominican Republic.
Wrapper: Nicaragua   Binder: Dom. Rep.   Filler: Dom. Rep.

Shape	Name	Lgth	Ring	Wrapper
Churchill	Coronas Doble (glass tube)	7	46	Co
Toro	Coronas Gorda (glass tube)	6	50	Co
Lonsdale	Coronas Larga (glass tube)	6⅝	42	Co
Panatela	Palmita (glass tube)	6¾	38	Co

This is a new version of the venerable Cabañas brand, introduced in 1998. It features the Habana 2000 wrapper grown in Nicaragua, and is offered with a medium-bodied taste in cases of 20 glass tubes each.

HANDMADE CIGARS: BRAND LISTINGS

CACHITA
Handmade, with medium filler, in Tamboril, Dominican Republic.
Wrapper: Indonesia   *Binder: Dom. Rep.*   *Filler: Dom. Rep.*

Shape	Name	Lgth	Ring	Wrapper
Long Corona	Corona	6	44	CM

Introduced in 1998, this one-shape brand is flavored via a curing process. Mild and aromatic, it is available in Amaretto, chocolate and vanilla flavors in plastic containers of 12 or 25 or a wood box of 25.

CACIQUE
Handmade in Santiago, Dominican Republic.
Wrapper: Ecuador   *Binder: Dom. Rep.*   *Filler: Dom. Rep., Nicaragua*

Shape	Name	Lgth	Ring	Wrapper
Panatela	Jaraqua	6¾	36	CC
Long Corona	Tainos	6	42	CC
Lonsdale	Siboneyes	6¾	43	CC
Churchill	Caribes	6⅞	46	CC
Double Corona	Incas	7½	50	CC
Robusto	Azteca	4¾	50	CC-Ma
Toro	Apaches	6	50	CC-Ma
Torpedo	Torpedo	6	52	CC
Perfecto	Perfecto No. 1	4¾	52	CC
Perfecto	Perfecto No. 2	4	51	CC

The Cacique is handmade in the Dominican Republic. It is blended with Dominican Havana-seed "ligero" and "seco" filler. It has a Havana-seed binder and is topped off with an Ecuador-grown, Connecticut-seed wrapper. This combination of fine tobacco gives Cacique a full tobacco flavor, yet it is mild in strength.

HANDMADE CIGARS: BRAND LISTINGS

CAIMAN
Handmade in Santiago, Dominican Republic.

Wrapper: Indonesia　　　　*Binder: Dom. Rep.*　　　　*Filler: Dom. Rep.*

Shape	Name	Lgth	Ring	Wrapper
Double Corona	Churchill	7½	50	CM
Churchill	Double Corona	7	48	CM
Toro	Robusto	6	50	CM
Robusto	Rothschild	4½	50	CM

New in 1998, Caiman cigars offer a mild-bodied taste with a Sumatra wrapper. It is offered in individual cellophane sleeves in boxes of 25.

CALEYES
Handmade in Santiago, Dominican Republic.

Wrapper: Indonesia　　　　*Binder: Dom. Rep.*　　　　*Filler: Dom. Rep.*

Shape	Name	Lgth	Ring	Wrapper
Double Corona	Executive	7½	50	CC
Churchill	Churchill	7	46	CC
Robusto	Robusto	5	50	CC
Panatela	Long Panatela	7	35	CC
Torpedo	Torpedo	6	54	CC

Introduced in 1997, this is a mild blend of Cameroon-seed wrapper grown in Indonesia and Dominican binders and filler, offered in all-cedar boxes.

CALIXTO LOPEZ
Handmade in Manila, the Philippines.

Wrapper: Indonesia　　　　*Binder: Philippines*　　　　*Filler: Philippines*

Shape	Name	Lgth	Ring	Wrapper
Corona	Corona Exquisito	5⅜	43	CM
Giant Corona	Czar	8	45	CM

HANDMADE CIGARS: BRAND LISTINGS

Giant	Gigante	8½	50	CM
Lonsdale	Lonsdale Suprema	6¾	42	CM
Grand Corona	Corona No. 1	6⅜	45	CM
Toro	Nobles Extra Fino	6½	50	CM
Long Panatela	Palma Royales	7¼	36	CM
Robusto	Robustos	5	50	CM

Created in 1980 and offering a mild-bodied smoke, the Calixto Lopez line utilizes the best in Southeast Asian tobacco. The main element is home-grown Philippine tobacco from the highly-respected Isabela Valley on the northernmost Philippine island of Luzon, combined with a Java-grown wrapper. It is offered in boxes of 25, except for the Gigantes, offered in 10s.

CALLE OCHO
Handmade in Santiago, Dominican Republic.
Wrapper: USA/Connecticut   *Binder: Nicaragua*
Filler: Dominican Republic, Mexico, Nicaragua

Shape	Name		Lgth	Ring	Wrapper
Short Panatela	Coronita	(tubed)	5	38	CI
Robusto	Robusto	(tubed)	5	50	CI
Lonsdale	Corona	(tubed)	6½	42	CI
Double Corona	Churchill	(tubed)	7¼	50	CI
Torpedo	Torpedo	(tubed)	6½	52	CI

Created in 1994, this is a medium-bodied blend of leaves from five nations! Named for the epicenter of the Cuban population in Miami - 8th Street or *Calle Ocho* in Spanish - this brand is offered in glass tubes and packed in boxes of 20. The Churchill and Robusto sizes are also offered in boxes of five, while the Coronita is only available in 25s.

Please note that the limited-edition "Calle Ocho Perez Family Reunion" brand, which featured unique Candela wrappers in Churchill (7 x 50) and Corona (6½ x 42) shapes was produced in 1997 only and is no longer available.

HANDMADE CIGARS: BRAND LISTINGS

CAMACHO
Handmade in Danli, Honduras.
Wrapper: Honduras and USA/Connecticut

Binder: Honduras   Filler: Honduras

Shape	Name	Lgth	Ring	Wrapper
Giant	El Cesar	8½	52	Cl-CC-Ma
Double Corona	Executives	7½	50	Cl-CC-Ma
Churchill	Churchill	7	48	Cl-CC-Ma
Lonsdale	No. 1	7	44	Cl-CC-Ma
Robusto	Monarca	5	50	Cl-CC-Ma
Lonsdale	Cetros	6½	44	Cl-CC-Ma
Long Panatela	Pan Especial	7	36	Cl-CC-Ma
Panatela	Elegantes	6½	38	Cl-CC-Ma
Long Corona	Palmas	6	43	Cl-CC-Ma
Corona	Nacionales	5½	44	Cl-CC-Ma
Lonsdale	Cazadores	6½	44	Cl-CC-Ma
Slim Panatela	Conchitas	5½	32	Cl-CC-Ma

This outstanding full-bodied brand was originated in the 1960s and first produced in Nicaragua before moving production to Honduras. It offers connoisseurs a wide range of sizes and features tobaccos primarily from the Jamastran Valley of Honduras. Connecticut wrappers are used for the claro series when available and maduro wrappers are often in short supply for this brand.

CAMMARATA
Handmade in Tampa, Florida, USA.
See tobacco blending notes for each group.

Shape	Name	Lgth	Ring	Wrapper
I: Wrapper: Honduras Binder: Dom. Rep.				Filler: Dom. Rep.
Robusto	Rothschild	5¾	50	CM
Churchill	Lonsdale	7	46	CM

HANDMADE CIGARS: BRAND LISTINGS

Double Corona	Churchill	6¾	50	CM
Long Panatela	St. Julien Panatella	7	36	CM
II: Wrapper: Honduras Binder: Honduras				*Filler: Honduras*
Robusto	Rothschild Maduro	4	50	Ma
III: Wrapper: USA/Conn. Binder: Honduras				*Filler: Honduras*
Toro	Varsalona No. 4	6	50	CC
Double Corona	JFK	7½	49	CC
Churchill	Special Series No. 2	6¾	46	CC
Petit Corona	Special Series No. 1	5	44	CC
IV: Wrapper: Honduras Binder: Honduras				*Filler: Honduras*
Robusto	Havana 5x52	5	52	CM
Double Corona	Havava 7½x52	7½	52	CM
V: Wrapper: USA/Conn. Binder: Honduras				*Filler: Honduras*
Pyramid	Havana Pyramid	5	57	CC
VI: Wrapper: Honduras Binder: Honduras				*Filler: Honduras*
Toro	Cuban Robusto Maduro	6	54	Ma
VII: Wrapper: USA/Conn. Binder: Honduras				*Filler: Honduras*
Double Corona	Cuban Double Corona	7½	54	CC

Carmela Cammarata Varsalona is one of the few cigar rollers left from Ybor City, a West Tampa neighborhood that once hosted 300 cigar factories and 30,000 workers in the 1920s and '30s. She now rolls up to 3000 cigars per day, with blends based on Cuban-seed tobaccos from the Dominican Republic, Honduras and the USA. The all-Honduras blends are full-bodied, while the multi-nation blends offer a medium strength.

CAMORRA IMPORTED LIMITED RESERVE
Handmade in Danli, Honduras.

Wrapper: Ecuador   *Binder: Honduras*   *Filler: Honduras*

HANDMADE CIGARS: BRAND LISTINGS

Shape	Name	Lgth	Ring	Wrapper
Slim Panatela	Capri	5½	32	CM
Pyramid	Padova	5	42	CM
Robusto	Roma	5	50	CM
Corona	Genova	5½	44	CM
Lonsdale	Venezia	6½	44	CM
Churchill	San Remo	7	48	CM

Camorra Imported Limited Reserve cigars debuted in 1995 as one of the finest super-premium cigars made in Honduras. This unique blend of the finest available Honduran tobacco is blended with a smooth and oily Ecuadorian wrapper for a medium-bodied taste. Note the sweet initial taste, produced by the addition of sugar added to the vegetable gum used to seal the cap.

CAMORRA LIMITED RESERVE DOMINICAN VINTAGE
Handmade in Villa Gonzalez, Dominican Republic.

Wrapper: Indonesia   Binder: Dom. Rep.   Filler: Dom. Rep.

Shape	Name	Lgth	Ring	Wrapper
Robusto	Robusto	5	50	Ma
Torpedo	Torpedo	5¾	52	Ma
Giant	Double Corona	8	50	Ma

New for 1997, this is a medium-to-full-bodied cigar available in maduro wrapper only. It is presented in individual cellophane sleeves in an all-cedar boxes of 10, 15 or 25.

CAMPEONES
Handmade in Villa Gonzalez, Dominican Republic.

Wrapper: Cameroon or Ecuador   Binder: Indonesia   Filler: Dom. Rep., Honduras

Shape	Name	Lgth	Ring	Wrapper
Giant	Soberanos	8	52	CC-CM
Torpedo	Piramides	6¼	56	CC-CM

HANDMADE CIGARS: BRAND LISTINGS

Double Corona	Churchills	7	50	CC-CM
Lonsdale	No. 1	6⅞	44	CC-CM
Toro	Double Crown	6	50	CC-CM
Robusto	Robusto	5	50	CC-CM
Pyramid	Proprietor's Blend	7	52	CC-CM

This brand was introduced in 1995 and offers a medium-bodied smoke in a choice of Ecuadorian or Cameroon wrapper. You can find it in either boxes or bundles of 25.

CAMPESINO
Handmade, with mixed filler, in Danli, Honduras.
Wrapper: Indonesia
Binder: Dom. Rep.   Filler: Dom. Rep., Mexico, Nicaragua

Shape	Name	Lgth	Ring	Wrapper
Long Corona	Corona	6¼	44	CM
Robusto	Robusto	5	50	CM
Toro	Double Corona	6	50	CM
Churchill	Churchill	7	48	CM

This is a bundled brand made available in 1996 with mixed-filler from four nations. It is mild in body.

CANARIA D'ORO
Handmade in Santiago, Dominican Republic.
Wrapper: Mexico   Binder: Mexico   Filler: Dom. Rep., Mexico

Shape	Name	Lgth	Ring	Wrapper
Small Panatela	Babies	4⅛	32	CC
Slim Panatela	Finos	6	31	CC
Robusto	Rothschild	4½	50	Ma
Corona	Coronas	5½	43	CC

Lonsdale	Lonsdales	6½	43	CC
Robusto	Inmensos	5½	49	CC
Lonsdale	Supremos	7	45	CC

Made by hand in the Dominican Republic, this line has a creamy, medium-to-full-bodied taste with lots of aroma. Mexican tobaccos dominate the blend (including a Sumatra-seed wrapper), combined with Dominican leaf in the filler blend. It is offered in beautifully-colored boxes of 25.

CANONERO
Handmade in Saõ Goncalo dos Campos, Brazil.
Wrapper: Brazil, Ecuador, USA/Connecticut

Binder: Brazil   Filler: Brazil

Shape	Name	Lgth	Ring	Wrapper
Double Corona	No. 1: Double Corona	7½	50	CC-Ma
Robusto	No. 2: Rothschild	5½	50	CC-Ma
Robusto	No. 3: Robusto	5	52	CC-Ma
Churchill	No. 4: Churchill	7	46	CC-Ma
Lonsdale	No. 10: Lonsdale	6½	42	CC-Ma
Petit Corona	No. 20: Corona	5½	42	CC-Ma
Short Panatela	No. 30: Potra	4¼	38	CC-Ma
	25th Anniversary selection:			
Robusto	Gran Robusto	5½	50	CM
Corona	Corona	5½	42	CM

This line was first offered in the U.S. in 1995 and under the supervision of master blender Arthur Toraño and now offers a unique variety of three different wrappers combined with all-Brazilian binder and fillers. The result is a mild-bodied taste in the Connecticut-wrapped "Classico" line, a mild-to-medium-bodied flavor in the Ecuadorian-wrapped "Mediano" line and a medium-bodied, but intensely-flavored "Oscuro" line that features a Brazilian Mata Fina wrapper. The 25th Anniversary selection is new for 1998 and offers a medium-to-full-bodied taste.

HANDMADE CIGARS: BRAND LISTINGS

CAOBA
Handmade in Santiago, Dominican Republic.

Wrapper: Ecuador   *Binder: Dom. Rep.*   *Filler: Dom. Rep.*

Shape	Name	Lgth	Ring	Wrapper
Long Panatela	Panetela No. 1	7½	36	CC
Panatela	Panetela No. 2	6¾	36	CC
Robusto	Robusto	5	50	CC
Corona Extra	Pendejo	5½	46	CC
Cigarillo	Petit	4¼	26	CC
Double Corona	5-Star	7	50	CC
Churchill	4-Star	7	46	CC
Long Corona	3-Star	6¼	44	CC
Corona	2-Star	5½	42	CC
Petit Corona	1-Star	5	42	CC
Torpedo	Torpedo	6	50	CC

This brand was started under a different name in 1992, but still offers the same
mild-to-medium body. Caoba cigars are presented in individual cellophane
sleeves and packed in all-cedar cabinets.

CAOBA GOLD
Handmade in Santiago, Dominican Republic.

Wrapper: USA/Connecticut   *Binder: Dom. Rep.*   *Filler: Dom. Rep.*

Shape	Name	Lgth	Ring	Wrapper
Churchill	No. 1	7	46	CC
Long Corona	No. 2	6¼	44	CC
Corona	No. 3	5½	42	CC
Long Panatela	Panetela No. 1	7½	36	CC
Panatela	Panetela No. 2	6	36	CC

HANDMADE CIGARS: BRAND LISTINGS

Churchill	Esplendido	7	47	CC
Robusto	Robusto	5	50	CC
Double Corona	Especial	7	50	CC
Torpedo	Torpedo	6	50	CC

This brand was introduced in 1997. It offers a mild body and a Connecticut wrapper in boxes of 24, except the Especial, which is offered in boxes of 36.

CAOBA PLATINUM
Handmade in Santiago, Dominican Republic.
Wrapper: Ecuador   *Binder: Dom. Rep.*   *Filler: Dom. Rep.*

Shape	Name	Lgth	Ring	Wrapper
Churchill	No. 1	7	46	CC
Long Corona	No. 2	6¼	44	CC
Corona	No. 3	5½	42	CC
Long Panatela	Panetela No. 1	7½	36	CC
Panatela	Panetela No. 2	6	36	CC
Churchill	Esplendido	7	47	CC
Robusto	Robusto	5	50	CC
Double Corona	Especial	7	50	CC
Torpedo	Torpedo	6	50	CC

This new Caoba brand was also introduced in early 1997. It offers a mild-to-medium body and an Ecuadorian-grown wrapper in boxes of 24, except the Especial, which is offered in boxes of 36.

CAONABO
Handmade in Santiago, Dominican Republic.
Wrapper: USA/Connecticut or Cameroon
Binder: Dominican Republic   *Filler: Dominican Republic*

HANDMADE CIGARS: BRAND LISTINGS

Shape	Name	Lgth	Ring	Wrapper
Small Panatela	Helenas	5	30	CC-CM
Long Panatela	Caciques	7½	38	CC-CM
Corona	Naborias	5½	42	CC-CM
Long Panatela	Nitainos	7	36	CC-CM
Long Corona	Guanines	6	44	CC-CM
Robusto	Petit Premier	4½	50	CC-CM-Ma
Double Corona	Grand Premier	7½	50	CC-CM-Ma
Pyramid	Grand Jefe	6	54	CC-CM

This brand debuted in 1996 and is named for the chief of the Taino tribe who resisted Spanish settlement on La Española island in 1493 and 1495. It offers a mild-to-medium body and exquisite construction and is offered in cedar boxes of 25. There is a choice of wrappers on most shapes, including two maduro-wrapped shapes.

CAONAO
Handmade in Miami, Florida, USA.
Wrapper: USA/Connecticut or Mexico

Binder: Ecuador   *Filler: Dominican Republic, Honduras, Nicaragua*

Shape	Name	Lgth	Ring	Wrapper
Double Corona	Doble Corona	7¾	50	CC-Ma
Pyramid	Piramide	7¼	54	CC-Ma
Robusto	Robusto	5	50	CC-Ma
Short Panatela	Petit	5	38	CC-Ma
Slim Panatela	Lady Dolls	6	32	CC-Ma
Long Panatela	Lancero	7	38	CC-Ma
Perfecto	Diadema	9	60	CC-Ma
Double Corona	Churchill	7	50	CC-Ma
Torpedo	Torpedo	6½	54	CC-Ma

HANDMADE CIGARS: BRAND LISTINGS

Culebras	Culebras	8	48	CC & Ma

New for 1998, this is a mild-to-medium-bodied brand with a choice of wrappers: Connecticut or a Mexican maduro. The range features both a giant perfecto (the Diadema) and a Culebras. It is offered in individual cellophane sleeves in all-cedar boxes of 25.

CAPOTE
Handmade in Tenerife, the Canary Islands of Spain.

Wrapper: USA/Connecticut   *Binder: Dom. Rep.*   *Filler: Brazil, Dom. Rep.*

Shape	Name	Lgth	Ring	Wrapper
Double Corona	No. 1	7	50	CC
Toro	No. 2	6	50	CC
Lonsdale	No. 3	6½	43	CC
Panatela	No. 4	5½	39	CC

This brand was introduced in 1996, offering a mild body with a Connecticut Shade wrapper in boxes of 25.

CAPRICHO CUBANO
BY PROFESOR SILA
Handmade in Santiago, Dominican Republic.

Wrapper: Cameroon   *Binder: Indonesia*   *Filler: Dom. Rep.*

Shape	Name	Lgth	Ring	Wrapper
Corona	Corona	5½	42	CM
Grand Corona	Gran Corona	6	45	CM
Robusto	Robusto	5	52	CM
Double Corona	Double Corona	7½	50	CM

Introduced in late 1997, this is a medium-to-full-bodied blend of African, Asian and Caribbean tobaccos that features a Cameroon wrapper. Each cigar is wrapped in cedar sheets and packed into all-cedar boxes of 25.

HANDMADE CIGARS: BRAND LISTINGS

CARA MIA
Handmade in Las Palmas, the Canary Islands of Spain.

Wrapper: Ecuador   Binder: Canary Islands   Filler: Canary Islands

Shape	Name	Lgth	Ring	Wrapper
Pyramid	Pyramid	7	52	Co
Double Corona	Churchill	7	50	Co
Toro	Toro	6	50	Co
Lonsdale	Lonsdale	6½	42	Co
Corona	Corona	5½	42	Co

Cara Mia was introduced in late 1995 as a new brand from the Canary Islands of Spain, one of the world's celebrated cigar-making regions. This is a medium-bodied cigar with excellent construction, featuring a Connecticut-seed wrapper grown in Ecuador and cured to a rich Colorado shade. Cara Mia cigars are packed uncellophaned in all-cedarwood boxes of 25.

CARABANA
Handmade in Danli, Honduras.

Wrapper: USA/Connecticut   Binder: USA/Pennsylvania
Filler: Dominican Republic, Nicaragua, USA/Pennsylvania

Shape	Name	Lgth	Ring	Wrapper
Corona	Corona	5½	42	CC-Ma
Lonsdale	Lonsdale	6½	43	CC-Ma
Toro	Toro	6	49	CC-Ma
Robusto	Robusto	5	50	CC-Ma

This is a new brand for 1997, offering a mild-to-medium-bodied taste in boxes of 25. Two different Connecticut wrappers are available: shade-grown for a lighter color and flavor and Connecticut Broadleaf for a beautiful, flavorful, maduro wrapper. There is also a special "Cristal" version of the Corona shape, using a glass tube and incorporating a Sumatra-seed wrapper and Mexican binder with the brand's normal filler blend.

HANDMADE CIGARS: BRAND LISTINGS

CARBONELL
Handmade in Santiago, Dominican Republic.

Wrapper: Indonesia   *Binder: Dom. Rep.*   *Filler: Dom. Rep.*

Shape	Name	Lgth	Ring	Wrapper
Cigarillo	Palmaritos	4	28	CC
Small Panatela	Demi Tasse	5	30	CC
Panatela	Panatella	6	36	CC
Long Panatela	Panatella Grande	7½	38	CC
Corona	Palma Short	5½	42	CC
Lonsdale	Palma	6½	42	CC
Lonsdale	Palma Extra	7	42	CC
Lonsdale	Corona	6½	44	CC
Churchill	Churchill	6⅞	46	CC
Double Corona	Presidente	7½	50	CC
Robusto	Toro	5½	50	CC
Giant	Soberano	8½	52	CC
Giant	Gigante	10	56	CC
Torpedo	Piramide Breve	5½	56	CC
Torpedo	Piramide	7½	64	CC
Torpedo	Piramide Gigante	8	68	CC

Here is the largest-selling brand in the Dominican Republic, widely available in the United States in 1996. Created in 1907, it is produced in Santiago and features an Indonesian wrapper. Carbonell cigars are mild with exquisite flavor, devoid of any bitterness and are presented in boxes of 10 or 20.

CARIBU
BY RODON
Handmade, with mixed filler, in Santiago, Dominican Republic.
Wrapper: Indonesia   *Binder: Dom. Rep.*   *Filler: Dom. Rep.*

HANDMADE CIGARS: BRAND LISTINGS

Shape	Name	Lgth	Ring	Wrapper
Double Corona	No. 1	7½	50	CM
Long Corona	No. 2	6	44	CM
Corona	No. 3	5½	42	CM
Torpedo	No. 4	6	54	CM

This is a 1998-introduced brand with a mild-to-medium-bodied flavor, offered in bundles of 20.

CARL BARRISTER
Handmade in Tamboril, Dominican Republic.
Wrapper: Indonesia *Binder: Dom. Rep.* *Filler: Dom. Rep.*

Shape	Name	Lgth	Ring	Wrapper
Double Corona	Churchill	7½	50	CM
Torpedo	Torpedo	6	40	CM
Robusto	Robusto	5½	48	CM
Slim Panatela	Corona	6	32	CM
Slim Panatela	Imperial	6½	34	CM

These are mild-bodied, flavorful cigars, introduced in 1997. They are offered in individual cellophane sleeves inside boxes of 25. Vanilla flavoring on certain shapes is also available if desired.

CARLIN
Handmade in Esteli, Nicaragua.
Wrapper: Nicaragua *Binder: Nicaragua* *Filler: Nicaragua*

Shape	Name	Lgth	Ring	Wrapper
Giant	Gigante	8	52	CM
Churchill	Churchill	7	48	CM
Toro	Toro	6	50	CM
Corona	Corona	5½	43	CM

HANDMADE CIGARS: BRAND LISTINGS

Robusto	Robusto	4¾	52	CM

Introduced as a Dominican-made cigar in 1995, this brand is now made in Nicaragua and incorporates only Nicaraguan leaves. The full, robust flavor comes from the blending of three filler tobaccos, coddled by a beautiful Jalapa wrapper. Carlins are easily enjoyed, thanks to their outstanding construction.

CARLOS OLIVA
Handmade in Ocotal, Nicaragua.

Wrapper: Ecuador   Binder: Mexico   Filler: Dom. Rep., Nicaragua

Shape	Name	Lgth	Ring	Wrapper
Grand Corona	Elegante	6½	46	CC-Ma
Robusto	Toro	5	50	CC
Double Corona	Sabanero	7	50	CC-Ma
Torpedo	Torpedo	6	52	CC-Ma
Giant	Grandioso	8¼	52	CC

Here is a 1997-introduced, medium-to-full-bodied cigar of flawless construction. It features a Sumatra-seed wrapper and is available in protective cellophane sleeves inside all-cedar boxes of 25.

CARLOS TORAÑO DOMINICAN SELECTION
Handmade in Santiago, Dominican Republic.

Wrapper: USA/Connecticut   Binder: Mexico   Filler: Dom. Rep.

Shape	Name	Lgth	Ring	Wrapper
Toro	Carlos I	6	50	CM-Ma
Lonsdale	Carlos II	6¾	43	CM-Ma
Double Corona	Carlos III	7½	52	CM-Ma
Corona	Carlos IV	5¾	43	CM
Grand Corona	Carlos V	6	46	CM
Churchill	Carlos VI	7	48	CM-Ma
Robusto	Carlos VII	4¾	52	CM-Ma

HANDMADE CIGARS: BRAND LISTINGS

Panatela	Carlos VIII	6½	36	CM
Torpedo	Carlos IX	6¼	52	CM

More than two years in the making, Carlos Toraño cigars debuted in 1995. They are mild in body and are distributed in France, Germany, Great Britain and the Netherlands in addition to the United States. You can find them in elegant boxes of 25.

CARLOS TORAÑO NICARAGUAN SELECTION
Handmade in Esteli, Nicaragua.

Wrapper: Nicaragua   Binder: Nicaragua   Filler: Nicaragua

Shape	Name	Lgth	Ring	Wrapper
Toro	Double Corona	6¼	50	CM
Petit Corona	Petit Corona	5	42	CM
Churchill	Churchill	7	48	CM
Robusto	Robusto	5	50	CM
Torpedo	Torpedo	6¼	52	CM

New in 1997, this is a medium-bodied cigar with the excellent construction and perfect draw that has become a trademark of the Toraño brands. It is offered in individual cellophane sleeves in all-cedar cabinets of 25.

CARMELO
Handmade in Danli, Honduras.

Wrapper: Indonesia   Binder: Honduras   Filler: Nicaragua

Shape	Name	Lgth	Ring	Wrapper
Double Corona	Churchill	7	49	CM
Toro	Toro	6	50	CM
Robusto	Robusto	4¾	52	CM
Lonsdale	Corona	6½	44	CM

HANDMADE CIGARS: BRAND LISTINGS

Here is a new brand for 1998, with full body and a modest price! You can find it in cedar boxes of 25.

CARNIVAL HAVANA
Handmade in Segovia, Nicaragua.

Wrapper: Ecuador or Indonesia   *Binder: Nicaragua*   *Filler: Dom. Rep.*

Shape	Name	Lg:h	Ring	Wrapper
Lonsdale	No. 1	7	44	CC-Ma
Panatela	Panatela	5½	38	CC-Ma
Robusto	Robusto	5	50	CC-Ma
Toro	Double Corona	6	48	CC-Ma
Churchill	Churchill	7	48	CC-Ma
Double Corona	President	7½	52	CC-Ma
Torpedo	Torpedo	6½	54	CC-Ma

Introduced in 1997, this is a premium brand featuring a choice of wrappers: Connecticut-seed grown in Ecuador, Indonesian Sumatra or maduro. It has a mild-to-medium-bodied flavor. Enjoy it in all-cedar boxes of 25, or for those replenishing their humidors, in bundles of 25.

CARNIVAL HAVANA SUPREME
Handmade in Segovia, Nicaragua.

Wrapper: Indonesia   *Binder: Nicaragua*   *Filler: Nicaragua*

Shape	Name	Lgth	Ring	Wrapper
Churchill	Churchill	7	48	CM-Ma
Toro	Toro	6	50	CM-Ma
Robusto	Robusto	4¾	50	CM-Ma
Corona	Corona	5½	44	CM-Ma
Torpedo	Torpedo	6¾	54	CM-Ma
Pyramid	Pyramide	7	50	CM-Ma

HANDMADE CIGARS: BRAND LISTINGS

| Giant | Viajante | 8½ | 52 | CM-Ma |
| Double Corona | Presidente | 7½ | 52 | CM-Ma |

These cigars feature Cuban-seed Sumatra wrappers in a natural or maduro shade, but are mild-to-medium in body and presented either in cedar boxes or bundles of 25.

CARRINGTON
Handmade in Santo Domingo, Dominican Republic.
Wrapper: USA/Connecticut or Panama

Binder: Dominican Republic   Filler: Dominican Republic

Shape	Name	Lgth	Ring	Wrapper
Double Corona	No. 1	7½	50	DC-Cl-Ma
Long Corona	No. 2	6	42	Cl-Ma
Long Panatela	No. 3	7	36	Cl-Ma
Corona	No. 4	5½	40	Cl
Churchill	No. 5	6⅞	46	Cl
Robusto	No. 6	4½	50	Cl
Toro	No. 7	6	50	Cl
Pyramid	No. 8	6⅞	60	Cl

Introduced in 1984, Carrington cigars offer a mild to medium taste, with a solid core of spice and a nice, toasty flavor. The wrapper is Connecticut Shade tobacco or Panamanian maduro, with Dominican filler and binders. Check out the No. 8, a pyramid-shape with one of the largest ring gauges (60) of any cigar available.

CASA ANJELITA
Handmade in Santo Domingo, Dominican Republic.
Wrapper: USA/Connecticut   Binder: Dom. Rep.   Filler: Dom. Rep.

Shape	Name	Lgth	Ring	Wrapper
Corona		5½	44	CC

Toro		6	50	CC
Churchill		6¾	46	CC
Double Corona		7	50	CC

This is a mild-to-medium-bodied cigar, offered without shape names, in boxes of 25.

CASA BLANCA
Handmade in Santiago, Dominican Republic.
Wrapper: USA/Connecticut   *Binder: Mexico*   *Filler: Dom. Rep.*

Shape	*Name*	*Lgth*	*Ring*	*Wrapper*
Short Panatela	Bonita	4	36	CC
Corona	Corona	5½	42	CC
Toro	DeLuxe	6	50	CC-Ma
Robusto	Half Jeroboam	5	66	CC-Ma
Giant	Jeroboam	10	66	CC-Ma
Lonsdale	Lonsdale	6½	42	CC-Ma
Double Corona	Magnum	7	60	CC-Ma
Panatela	Panatela	6	35	CC
Double Corona	President	7½	50	CC-Ma

This line, which means "White House" in English, offers an extremely mild taste in a variety of sizes. Particularly noteworthy are the giant 66-ring Half Jeroboam and Jeroboam, the thickest straight-sided cigars offered on the U.S. market.

CASA BLANCA RESERVE
Handmade in Santiago, Dominican Republic.
Wrapper: Ecuador   *Binder: Mexico*   *Filler: Dom. Rep.*

Shape	*Name*	*Lgth*	*Ring*	*Wrapper*
Double Corona	No. 1	7½	50	CC
Toro	No. 2	6	50	CC

HANDMADE CIGARS: BRAND LISTINGS

Lonsdale	No. 3	6½	42	CC
Corona	No. 4	5½	43	CC
Robusto	No. 5	5	50	CC

"The best of the best" is the idea behind this upgraded selection of Casa Blanca, the Reserve Collection. Introduced in 1996, this elegant, mild line is offered with a Sumatra-seed wrapper in all-cedar cabinets of 25 cigars each.

CASA BUENA
Handmade in Las Palmas, the Canary Islands of Spain.
Wrapper: USA/Connecticut   Binder: Dom. Rep.   Filler: Brazil, Dom. Rep.

Shape	Name	Lgth	Ring	Wrapper
Double Corona	Especiales No. 1	7½	50	CC
Toro	Especiales No. 2	6	50	CC
Lonsdale	Especiales No. 3	6½	43	CC
Robusto	Especiales No. 4	4¾	50	CC

This brand was introduced in 1996, but refined for 1997. You'll enjoy a new blend from the Canary Islands that offers a mild-bodied smoke, with some slightly spicy interior tobaccos and Connecticut wrapper, offered in boxes of 25.

CASA DE DIABLO
Handmade in Santo Domingo, Dominican Republic.
Wrapper: Indonesia   Binder: Dom. Rep.   Filler: Dom. Rep.

Shape	Name	Lgth	Ring	Wrapper
Corona		5½	44	CC
Toro		6	50	CC
Churchill		6¾	46	CC
Double Corona		7	50	CC

The "House of the Devil" is a medium-bodied cigar with a Sumatran wrapper. It is offered without shape names, in boxes of 25.

HANDMADE CIGARS: BRAND LISTINGS

CASA DE KLAFTER
Handmade in Miami, Florida, USA.

Wrapper: Ecuador   *Binder: Ecuador*
Filler: Dominican Republic, Honduras, Mexico, Nicaragua

Shape	Name	Lgth	Ring	Wrapper
Short Panatela	Corona	5	38	CC-Co-Ma
Robusto	Robusto	5	50	CC-Co-Ma
Toro	Toro	6	50	CC-Co-Ma
Lonsdale	Lonsdale	6½	42	CC-Co-Ma
Long Panatela	Long Panatela	7½	36	CC-Co-Ma
Churchill	Churchill	7½	46	CC-Co-Ma
Double Corona	Double Corona	7½	54	CC-Co-Ma
Double Corona	Special Corona	7¼	50	CC-Co-Ma

Created in 1995, this Miami-made blend of tobaccos from five nations offers a full range of flavors from mild to full-bodied thanks to three different styles of wrappers: natural, rosado and maduro.

CASA DE NICARAGUA
Handmade in Esteli, Nicaragua.

Wrapper: Indonesia   *Binder: Nicaragua*   *Filler: Nicaragua*

Shape	Name	Lgth	Ring	Wrapper
Robusto	Rothchild	5	50	CC
Long Corona	Corona	6	43	CC-Ma
Toro	Toro	6	50	CC-Ma
Lonsdale	Double Corona	7	44	CC-Ma
Double Corona	Churchill	7	49	CC
Double Corona	Presidente	7½	52	CC
Giant	Gigante	8	54	CC-Ma
Giant	Viajante	8½	52	CC

HANDMADE CIGARS: BRAND LISTINGS

These are well-constructed cigars, offered in all-cedar boxes of 25. The body is mild, thanks to an Indonesian wrapper.

CASA MARTIN
Handmade in Las Palmas, the Canary Islands of Spain.

Wrapper: Ecuador   *Binder: Dom. Rep.*   *Filler: Brazil, Dom. Rep., Nicaragua*

Shape	Name	Lgth	Ring	Wrapper
Corona	Corona	5½	42	CC
Robusto	Robusto	4¾	48	CC
Lonsdale	Numero Uno	6⅝	43	CC
Toro	Governor	6	50	CC
Churchill	Churchill	7	46	CC
Churchill	Doble Corona	7½	48	CC

Formerly made in the Dominican Republic, this brand was remade in 1996. These cigars are mild to medium in strength, with a Ecuador-grown, Connecticut-seed wrapper and Dominican binder and blended filler tobaccos. The Casa Martin line is offered in boxes of 25 cigars.

CASA TERESA
Handmade, with mixed filler,
in Santo Domingo, Dominican Republic.

Wrapper: Indonesia   *Binder: Dom. Rep.*   *Filler: Dom. Rep.*

Shape	Name	Lgth	Ring	Wrapper
Robusto		5	50	CC
Toro		6	50	CC
Lonsdale		6¾	44	CC

This is a value-priced, mild-bodied cigar named for one of the top entertainment houses in the Dominican Republic. It is offered without shape names, in boxes of 25.

HANDMADE CIGARS: BRAND LISTINGS

CASCADA
Handmade in San Andres Tuxtla, Mexico.

Wrapper: Mexico   Binder: Mexico   Filler: Mexico

Shape	Name	Lgth	Ring	Wrapper
Robusto	IV: Robusto	5½	50	CC
Toro	II: Toro	6½	50	CC
Lonsdale	III: Lonsdale	6½	42	CC
Double Corona	I: Churchill	7½	50	CC

Here is an all-Mexican cigar, offering a medium-bodied taste. Initially introduced in 1971, it is packed in individual cellophane sleeves inside cedar boxes of 24.

CASTAÑO
Handmade in Cofradia and Danli, Honduras.

Wrapper: Ecuador, USA/Connecticut

Binder: USA/Connecticut   Filler: Honduras

Shape	Name	Lgth	Ring	Wrapper
Double Corona	Imperiales	7¼	54	CC-Ma
Churchill	Corona Immensa	7	47	CC-Ma
Robusto	Magnificos	5½	50	CC-Ma
Grand Corona	Corona Royale	6¼	45	CC-Ma
Corona	Corona Especial	5½	43	CC-Ma

Introduced in 1997, this is a full-bodied cigar with subtle flavors. It offers a Sumatra-seed wrapper in the natural shade and a Connecticut Broadleaf wrapper in the maduro shade. It is presented uncellophaned in all-cedar boxes of 25.

CATALUNA
Handmade in Santiago, Dominican Republic.

Wrapper: Indonesia   Binder: Dom. Rep.   Filler: Dom. Rep.

HANDMADE CIGARS: BRAND LISTINGS

Shape	Name	Lgth	Ring	Wrapper
Robusto	Robusto	5	50	CM
Double Corona	Double Corona	7½	50	CM
Long Corona	Corona	6¼	44	CM
Toro	Churchill	6½	53	CM

This brand was introduced in 1997 and offers a medium-bodied taste in boxes of 25.

CAVANA
Handmade in Bronx, New York, USA.

Wrapper: Mexico   *Binder: Dom. Rep.*   *Filler: Honduras, Mexico*

Shape	Name	Lgth	Ring	Wrapper
Giant	El Grande	8	50	CM-Ma
Double Corona	Churchill	7	50	CM-Ma
Lonsdale	No. 1 Imperial	7	45	CM-Ma
Slim Panatela	Panatela	6	30	CM-Ma
Toro	No. 2 Double Corona	6	50	CM-Ma
Grand Corona	No. 3 Continental	6	45	CM-Ma
Robusto	Robusto	5	50	CM-Ma
Petit Corona	No. 4 Queen	5	41	CM-Ma

Here is an all long-filler, handmade brand that offers two tastes: a mild body with the natural wrapper and a full body with the Mexican maduro wrapper. Introduced in 1996, it is in limited distribution and offered in cellophane sleeves in air-tight cases of five, or in boxes of 25.

CECIL BROOKS III
Handmade in Miami, Florida, USA.

Wrapper: Indonesia   *Binder: Indonesia*   *Filler: Mexico*

HANDMADE CIGARS: BRAND LISTINGS

Shape	Name	Lgth	Ring	Wrapper
Double Corona	Churchill	6¾	50	Ma
Double Corona	Presidente	7¼	50	Ma
Robusto	Robusto	5	50	Ma

This all-maduro brand was created in 1997, and offers a medium-to-full bodied taste available in boxes of 25.

CEDAR JOE
Handmade in Danli, Honduras.

Wrapper: Honduras   *Binder: Honduras*   *Filler: Honduras*

Shape	Name	Lgth	Ring	Wrapper
Robusto	Rothchild	4½	50	CM
Lonsdale	Corona Gorda	6½	44	CM
Double Corona	Aristo	7½	52	CM
Torpedo	Mega Torpedo	7½	64	CM
Pyramid	Club Pyramid	5½	52	CM

A 1994 creation, the Cedar Joe line offers a mild-to-medium-bodied smoke in a fine value line. The three straight-sided shapes and the two shaped styles are each offered in boxes of 10.

CEDAR JOE DULCE
Handmade in Danli, Honduras.

Wrapper: Honduras   *Binder: Honduras*   *Filler: Honduras*

Shape	Name	Lgth	Ring	Wrapper
Robusto	Rothschild	4½	50	CM
Long Corona	Corona Gorda	6¼	44	CM
Double Corona	Aristo	7½	52	CM
Double Corona	Churchill	6⅞	49	CM

HANDMADE CIGARS: BRAND LISTINGS

Here is a sweetened version of the Cedar Joe blend, mild in body and, available in ten-packs.

CEDROS
Handmade in Santiago, Dominican Republic.

Wrapper: USA/Connecticut　　　*Binder: Dom. Rep.*　　　　*Filler: Dom. Rep.*

Shape	Name	Lgth	Ring	Wrapper
Toro	Churchill	6½	50	CC
Churchill	Presidente	6⅞	46	CC
Robusto	Robusto	5	50	CC
Corona	Corona Supreme	5½	42	CC

Created by Jim and Kathi Brown-Martin in 1994, this is a mild blend of Dominican leaves with a Connecticut Shade wrapper, offered in individual cellophane sleeves presented in cedar cabinets of 25.

CELEBRITY CIGARS
Handmade in Tamboril, Dominican Republic.

Wrapper: Indonesia　　　　*Binder: Dom. Rep.*　　　　*Filler: Dom. Rep.*

Shape	Name	Lgth	Ring	Wrapper
Double Corona	Double Corona	7½	50	CM
Toro	Toro	6	50	CM
Corona	Corona	5½	44	CM
Panatela	Panatela	6	38	CM
Robusto	Bullet	2¾	48	CM

Here is a unique brand with five sizes, including the tiny Bullet at 2¾ inches. The blend is mild and all sizes are offered in cedar boxes of 25. The Bullet shape is also offered in boxes of 50.

CELESTINO VEGA
Handmade in Jaibon, Dominican Republic.

Wrapper: Indonesia　　　*Binder: Nicaragua*　　*Filler: Dom. Rep., Indonesia*

HANDMADE CIGARS: BRAND LISTINGS

Shape	Name	Lgth	Ring	Wrapper
Robusto	Robusto	5	50	CC
Lonsdale	Corona	6½	42	CC
Double Corona	Churchill	7¼	50	CC

These handmade, long-filler cigars feature Indonesian tobaccos grown on the islands of Java and Sumatra. Javan wrappers are used on all models and these cigars offer a full, flavorful taste and are uniquely packaged in boxes of five and 25.

CERVANTES
Handmade in Danli, Honduras.

Wrapper: Honduras   *Binder: Honduras*   *Filler: Honduras*

Shape	Name	Lgth	Ring	Wrapper
Lonsdale	Churchill	7¼	45	CC
Grand Corona	Corona	6¼	46	CC
Long Corona	Senadores	6	42	CC

Cervantes are handmade cigars of excellent quality, made in Honduras of all-Honduran tobacco. They are medium in taste, and presented in boxes of 25.

CESAR CIGAR FACTORY
Handmade in San Diego, California, USA.

Wrapper: Indonesia   *Binder: Dom. Rep.*   *Filler: Dom. Rep.*

Shape	Name	Lgth	Ring	Wrapper
Panatela	Panatela	5½	35	CM
Long Panatela	Panatela Larga	7	35	CM
Corona	Palma	5½	42	CM
Robusto	Robusto	5	50	CM
Lonsdale	Cetro	7	44	CM
Toro	Senador	6½	50	CM

HANDMADE CIGARS: BRAND LISTINGS

Double Corona	Churchill	7½	50	CM
Torpedo	Torpedo	6½	56	CM
Giant	Elegante	8	52	CM

Introduced in 1998, this brand is medium in body and offers a full range of sizes for every smoker to enjoy. It is presented in elegant boxes of 25.

CHACARO BLACK STALLION
Handmade in San Pedro Sula, Honduras.

Wrapper: Ecuador   Binder: Honduras   Filler: Honduras

Shape	Name	Lgth	Ring	Wrapper
Robusto	Celebration	5	50	CC
Long Corona	Classic	6¼	44	CC
Toro	Trophy	6	50	CC
Toro	Darkhan's Blue Ribbon	6	54	CC
Corona	Filly	5½	43	CC
Corona	Colt	5½	43	Ma

Here is a medium-to-full-bodied brand introduced in 1996 that celebrates Darkhan, a champion Black Arabian stallion, owned by Roy and Charlotte Ivy of Chacaro So-Black Arabians. You can salute this award-winning horse with a box of 25 of these beauties.

CHAIRMAN'S CHOICE
Handmade in Danli, Honduras.

Wrapper: Ecuador   Binder: Honduras   Filler: Honduras

Shape	Name	Lgth	Ring	Wrapper
Corona	V.P.	5½	42	CC
Robusto	Director	5	50	CC
Toro	Treasurer	6	50	CC
Churchill	President	6⅞	46	CC

HANDMADE CIGARS: BRAND LISTINGS

Double Corona	CEO	7¾	50	CC
Torpedo	Chairman	7	54	CC

Here is a medium-bodied brand introduced in 1996. The names of the shapes are common enough in big corporations, but is it proper to offer the Chairman a torpedo?

CHARLES FAIRMORN
Handmade in Danli, Honduras.

Wrapper: Honduras *Binder: Honduras* *Filler: Honduras*

Shape	Name	Lgth	Ring	Wrapper
Double Corona	Churchill	6⅞	49	CM-Ma
Long Corona	Coronas	6¼	44	CM
Robusto	Robusto	5	50	CM-Ma
Toro	Matador	6	50	CM-Ma

Sought after since their introduction in 1979, the Charles Fairmorn line from Honduras is a medium-to-full-bodied cigar which is available in four sizes. It is made by hand from selected Cuban-seed leaves and offered in boxes of 25.

CHARLES FAIRMORN BELMORE
Handmade in Santiago, Dominican Republic.

Wrapper: USA/Connecticut *Binder: Dom. Rep.* *Filler: Dom. Rep.*

Shape	Name	Lgth	Ring	Wrapper
Robusto	Robusto	4¾	50	CC
Churchill	Churchill	6⅞	46	CC
Toro	Matador	6	50	CC
Double Corona	Presidente	7½	50	CC

This series, introduced in 1991, is produced in Santiago de los Caballeros in the Dominican Republic and uses only the smoothest Connecticut wrappers. These cigars are of medium body and are offered in boxes of 25, except for the Piramide shape, offered in 20s.

HANDMADE CIGARS: BRAND LISTINGS

CHARLES THE GREAT
Handmade in Santa Rosa de Copan, Honduras.

Wrapper: USA/Connecticut   *Binder: Honduras*   *Filler: Honduras*

Shape	Name	Lgth	Ring	Wrapper
Double Corona	Madrid	7½	50	CC
Toro	Barcelona	6	50	CC
Grand Corona	Valencia	6¾	46	CC
Robusto	Granada	5	50	CC
Long Corona	Toledo	6	42	CC
Petit Corona	Cordoba	5⅛	42	CC

Charles The Great, better known as Charlemagne, was born in 742 and ruled what is now France and part of western Germany from 768-814 and through conquest and a close relationship with Pope Leo III helped to found the Holy Roman Empire, which he ruled until his death in 814. The cigars are not as old as Charlemagne, but were produced decades ago as a clear Havana, and the brand was recently resurrected by the Finck Cigar Company of San Antonio, Texas. It utilizes the brand's original box and label art and presents these medium-bodied cigars in all-wooden boxes of 25.

CHATEAU AMARETTO
Handmade, with medium filler, in Santiago, Dominican Republic.

Wrapper: Indonesia   *Binder: Dom. Rep.*   *Filler: Dom. Rep.*

Shape	Name	Lgth	Ring	Wrapper
Long Corona		6	42	CM
Long Corona		6	44	CM

This is a medium-bodied cigar, available in two sizes, and introduced in 1996. It utilizes all-Dominican filler and is offered in bundles of 25.

CHATEAU TAMBORIL
Handmade in Tamboril, Dominican Republic.

Wrapper: Dom. Rep.   *Binder: Dom. Rep.*   *Filler: Dom. Rep.*

HANDMADE CIGARS: BRAND LISTINGS

Shape	Name	Lgth	Ring	Wrapper
Long Corona	Corona	6	44	CM
Robusto	Robusto	5	52	CM
Churchill	Churchill	7	47	CM
Torpedo	Torpedo	6	54	CM
Toro	Toro	6	50	CM

This line from the Tamboril Cigar Company features a Connecticut-seed wrapper and has a medium-bodied flavor. You can try it in boxes of 25.

CHATILY'S
Handmade, with mixed filler, in Santiago, Dominican Republic.
Wrapper: Indonesia   *Binder: Dom. Rep.*   *Filler: Dom. Rep.*

Shape	Name	Lgth	Ring	Wrapper
Corona Extra	Chatily's	5½	47	CM

This brand is mild in body and debuted in 1998. Constructed with mixed filler, it is offered in glass tubes to provide peak flavors on Amaretto, rum or vanilla.

CHAVON
Handmade in Santiago, Dominican Republic.
Wrapper: Indonesia or USA/Connecticut
Binder: Dominican Republic   *Filler: Dominican Republic*

Shape	Name	Lgth	Ring	Wrapper
Corona	Corona	5½	43	CC-CM
Robusto	Robusto	5	50	CC-CM
Lonsdale	Lonsdale	6½	43	CC-CM
Toro	Toro	6	50	CC-CM
Double Corona	Churchill	7½	50	CC-CM
Pyramid	Piramide	6	52	CC-CM
Cigarillo	Purito	4	24	CC-CM

Cigarillo	Petite Panetela	5	28	CC-CM

This richly-flavored, medium-to-full-bodied cigar is handmade in the Dominican Republic and features a Dominican binder and filler with a choice or a genuine Connecticut-grown wrapper or a Sumatra-grown wrapper. It is offered in boxes of 25, except for the last three sizes above, offered in 20s. Some sizes are available in ten-packs.

CHE
Handmade in San Andres Tuxtula, Mexico.

Wrapper: Mexico   *Binder: Mexico*   *Filler: Mexico*

Shape	*Name*	*Lgth*	*Ring*	*Wrapper*
Torpedo	Torpedo	6¼	50	CM

Named and bearing the likeness of Ernesto "Che" Guevara (1928-67), the Argentine-born revolutionary who played an important role in the 1959 Cuban revolution which brought Fidel Castro to power, this cigar is medium-bodied. It is offered in individual cellophane sleeves in boxes of 25.

CHESSMAN ROYAL RESERVE
Handmade in Miami, Florida, USA.

Wrapper: Ecuador   *Binder: Ecuador*
Filler: Dominican Republic, Honduras, Nicaragua

Shape	*Name*	*Lgth*	*Ring*	*Wrapper*
Long Corona	Pawn	6	42	CC-Ma
Toro	Knight	6	52	CC-Ma
Lonsdale	Bishop	6½	44	CC-Ma
Robusto	Rook	5	52	CC-Ma
Churchill	Queen	7	47	CC-Ma
Giant	King	8	52	CC-Ma
Giant	Check Mate	6	60	CC-Ma
Torpedo	The Castle	6½	54	CC-Ma

HANDMADE CIGARS: BRAND LISTINGS

Named for chess pieces and the game-ending situation, this is a medium-bodied blend of leaves from four nations, created in 1997. The brand is offered in boxes of 25 cigars each.

CHEVERE
Handmade in Santiago, Dominican Republic.

Wrapper: USA/Connecticut   *Binder: Dom. Rep.*   *Filler: Dom. Rep.*

Shape	Name	Lgth	Ring	Wrapper
Double Corona	Kingston	7	49	CC
Grand Corona	Montego Bay	6½	45	CC
Giant	Ocho Rios	8	49	CC
Corona	Port Antonio	5½	43	CC
Lonsdale	Spanish Town	6½	42	CC

Chevere cigars are quality, hand-made products of Jamaica, offering good construction and a mild body. Introduced in 1990, the brand's shapes offer a natural wrapper, in bundles of 12 or 25 cigars each.

CHOCOLATE RUSH
Handmade, with mixed filler, in Santiago, Dominican Republic.

Wrapper: Dom. Rep.   *Binder: Dom. Rep.*   *Filler: Dom. Rep.*

Shape	Name	Lgth	Ring	Wrapper
Small Panatela	Passion	4	34	CM
Lonsdale	Addiction	6½	44	CM

This is a medium-to-full-bodied, flavored brand, introduced in 1998. It is offered in boxes of 25.

CHRISTIANO LEONÉ DIRECTOR'S SELECTION
Handmade in Santiago, Dominican Republic.

Wrapper: Indonesia   *Binder: Dom. Rep.*   *Filler: Dom. Rep.*

Shape	Name	Lgth	Ring	Wrapper
	Hollywood Series:			

HANDMADE CIGARS: BRAND LISTINGS

Long Corona	Divas	6	42	CC
Long Corona	Vanilla Divas	6	42	CC
Robusto	Vanity Fairs	5	50	CC
Toro	Glamours	6	50	CC
Grand Corona	Elegantes	6½	46	CC
Double Corona	Celebrities	7½	50	CC
	Director's Choice Series:			
Long Panatela	Agents	7½	38	CC
Perfecto	Directors	4	44	CC
Giant	Producers	8½	52	CC
Torpedo	Actors	6½	52	CC

Hooray for Hollywood! This brand celebrates the stage, film and television with shape names about performers and those that surround them. The cigars themselves are carefully made, available only in limited quantities and offer Sumatran wrappers to complement Dominican-grown fillers and binder. Medium in body, both lines were introduced in 1996 and are presented in boxes of 25.

CHURCHILL
Handmade in Esteli, Nicaragua.

Wrapper: Ecuador　　　　　　　　*Binder: Nicaragua*　　　　　　　　*Filler: Nicaragua*

Shape	Name	Lgth	Ring	Wrapper
Giant	Presidente	8	50	CM
Double Corona	Prime Minister	7¼	54	CM
Toro	Senator	6	50	CM
Corona	No. 3	5⅝	44	CM
Robusto	Robusto	4¾	50	CM

Named for the great statesman and British Prime Minister Sir Winston Churchill (1874-1965), this brand celebrates perhaps the world's most famous cigar smoker. Almost always seen with his trademark double corona — or larger —

cigar, Churchill achieved much greatness in a long life that included two stints as the leader of his beloved Great Britain (1940-45 and 1951-55). His picture adorns the box of this medium-bodied, all long-filler cigar, which is offered in boxes of 25.

CIBAO
Handmade in Tamboril, Dominican Republic.

Wrapper: Cameroon, USA/Connecticut   Binder: Dom. Rep.   Filler: Dom. Rep.

Shape	Name	Lgth	Ring	Wrapper
	Connecticut Series:			
Giant	Gigantes	10	60	CC
Torpedo	Torpedo 6	6	54	CC
Torpedo	Torpedo 7	7	54	CC
Double Corona	Presidente	7½	50	CC
Churchill	Churchill	6⅞	46	CC
Toro	Toro	6	48	CC
Long Corona	Lonsdale	6	44	CC
Robusto	Robusto	5	50	CC
Petit Corona	Petit Coronas	5	42	CC
Short Panatela	Selecto	5	38	CC
Perfecto	Pequeños Perfectos	4	51	CC
Cigarillo	Mini Puros	4	26	CC
	Maduro Series:			
Perfecto	Perfecto No. 2	5	50	Ma
Robusto	Robusto	5	50	Ma
Long Corona	Lonsdale	6	44	Ma
	Cameroon Series:			
Robustos	Robusto	5	50	CM
Long Corona	Lonsdale	6	44	CM

HANDMADE CIGARS: BRAND LISTINGS

Petit Corona	Petite Corona	5	42	CM
Short Panatela	Selectos	5	38	CM

Debuting in 1997, this is a medium-bodied brand available with a Connecticut natural-shade wrapper and a Connecticut Broadleaf maduro wrapper in three, medium-to-full-bodied sizes. The 1998-introduced Cameroon series is medium-bodied and offered in four sizes. It is presented in all-cedar boxes of 25.

CIENTA AZUL
Handmade in Danli, Honduras.

Wrapper: Indonesia *Binder: Honduras* *Filler: Honduras, Nicaragua*

Shape	Name	Lgth	Ring	Wrapper
Double Corona	No. 1	7½	52	CM
Toro	No. 2	6	50	CM
Robusto	No. 3	4¾	50	CM
Lonsdale	No. 4	6½	44	CM
Corona	No. 5	5½	42	CM

This is a bundled brand which is the successor to the "Blue Ribbon" brand. This is a medium-bodied blend with leaves from three nations, offered in bundles of 25 cigars each at modest price, accessible to all smokers.

CIFUENTES
Handmade in Kingston, Jamaica.
Wrapper: Mexico or USA/Connecticut

Binder: "Jember" *Filler: Dominican Republic*

Shape	Name	Lgth	Ring	Wrapper
Double Corona	Churchill	7¼	49	CC
Toro	Toro	6	49	CC
Lonsdale	Fancytail	6¾	42	CC
Torpedo	Belicoso	6¼	50	CC
Robusto	Maduro	4¾	49	Ma

Robusto	Rothschild	4¾	49	CC

The famous name - and face - of Ramon Cifuentes, who took over the Partagas brand in Cuba in 1889 after the death of its founder, adorn this brand, completely remade for 1997. Cigars under this brand name were produced in Havana until nationalization; today's version is mild-to-medium-bodied and beautifully constructed. The Fancytail shape has a twisted head, while the Maduro shape uses a Mexican wrapper leaf rather than the standard shade-grown Connecticut leaf. Cifuentes is available in boxes of 25 for the Churchill, Toro and Fancytail shape and in 20s for all other shapes.

CIGAR COMPADRES
Handmade in Santo Domingo, Dominican Republic.
Wrapper: Indonesia and USA/Connecticut

Binder: Dominican Republic   *Filler: Dominican Republic*

Shape	Name	Lgth	Ring	Wrapper
Torpedo	Torpedo	6	56	CC-CM
Giant	Presidente	8	50	CC-CM
Double Corona	Churchill	7	50	CC-CM
Robusto	Robusto	5	50	CC-CM
Long Corona	Lonsdale	6	44	CC-CM
Grand Corona	Grand Corona	6½	46	CC-CM
	Made with short filler:			
Torpedo	Bullet	6	56	CM

Created in 1996, this line offers a choice of Connecticut or Sumatra wrapper for a mild-to-medium or medium-bodied taste. Enjoy in wooden boxes or bundles of 25; the Grand Corona and Robusto sizes are available in cedar boxes of five.

THE CIGAR CONNECTION - NICARAGUA
Handmade in Esteli, Nicaragua.
Wrapper: Ecuador   *Binder: Nicaragua*   *Filler: Nicaragua*

HANDMADE CIGARS: BRAND LISTINGS

Shape	Name	Lgth	Ring	Wrapper
Churchill	Doble Corona	7½	48	CC
Robusto	Robusto	5½	50	CC

Introduced in 1997, this is a mild-to-medium-bodied smoke featuring Habana criollo leaves in the filler. It is offered in boxes of 25.

CIGAR TRADER
Handmade in Miami, Florida, USA.

Wrapper: Ecuador   *Binder: Ecuador*
Filler: Dominican Republic, Honduras, Mexico, Nicaragua

Shape	Name	Lgth	Ring	Wrapper
Torpedo	Torpedo	6½	54	CC
Double Corona	Double Corona	7¾	49	CC
Pyramid	Pyramides	7¼	62	CC
Robusto	Robusto	5	50	CC
Double Corona	Churchill	7	50	CC
Lonsdale	No. 1	6¼	44	CC
Toro	Oriente	6	52	CC
Cigarillo	Supremo	8½	22	CC

Introduced in 1993, this is a medium-to-full-bodied brand made in Miami with an Ecuadorian-grown, Sumatra-seed wrapper. You can find them in individual cellophane sleeves inside all-wood boxes of 25.

CIGAR TRADER FLAVORED CIGARS
Handmade in Miami, Florida, USA.

Wrapper: Ecuador   *Binder: Ecuador*   *Filler: Honduras*

Shape	Name	Lgth	Ring	Wrapper
Long Panatela	(5 flavors)	7	38	CC
Small Panatela	(5 flavors)	4½	30	CC

HANDMADE CIGARS: BRAND LISTINGS

Long Corona	(3 flavors)	6	44	CC
Short Panatela	(3 flavors)	5	38	CC
Robusto	Rum	5½	48	CC
Long Corona	Vanilla-man	6	42	CC
Slim Panatela	(2 flavors)	6	32	CC
Small Panatela	Rum Sky	4½	32	CC

Special processing of the tobacco leaf is the secret of this medium-to-full-bodied flavored line. The flavor line-up includes cherry, Cognac, rum, Rum-Cafe, Rum Sky, vanilla and Whiskey.

CIGARROS CIBAO
Handmade in Santiago, Dominican Republic.

Wrapper: Indonesia   Binder: Dom. Rep.   Filler: Dom. Rep.

Shape	Name	Lgth	Ring	Wrapper
Robusto	Gordito	4½	52	CC
Churchill	Quimosabe	6¾	46	CC
Corona	Caballero	5¼	42	CC
Petit Corona	Muchacho	4	42	CC
Slim Panatela	Flecha	5	30	CC
Double Corona	Tubano	7¾	50	CC

This mild-bodied brand debuted in 1996, offering a flavorful blend in boxes of 25. The cigars are well protected: each is paper-wrapped and each row is separated by foil sheets.

CIGUARDIANS
Handmade in Santiago, Dominican Republic.

Wrapper: Indonesia   Binder: Dom. Rep.   Filler: Dom. Rep.

Shape	Name	Lgth	Ring	Wrapper
Corona	Corona	5½	42	CM

HANDMADE CIGARS: BRAND LISTINGS

This self-proclaimed novelty cigar is brilliantly packaged, but is also a handmade, long-filler smoke with a medium-bodied flavor. It is offered in packs of three, adorned by a "ciguardian" gargoyle on the box.

CIMMARON
Handmade, with medium filler, in Tamboril, Dominican Republic.

Wrapper: Indonesia   Binder: Dom. Rep.   Filler: Dom. Rep.

Shape	Name	Lgth	Ring	Wrapper
Corona	No. I	5½	42	CM
Robusto	No. II	4¾	52	CM
Long Corona	No. III	6	44	CM
Churchill	No. IV	6⅞	46	CM
Toro	No. V	6½	50	CM
Toro	No. VI	6½	52	CM
Corona Extra	No. VII	5½	46	CM
Robusto	No. VIII	5	50	CM

Here is an value-priced, handmade cigar from the Dominican Republic. Introduced in 1997, it features a Sumatra wrapper and a mild-to-medium-bodied taste in bundles of 25.

CIMERO
Handmade in Tamboril, Dominican Republic.

Wrapper: USA/Connecticut   Binder: Dom. Rep.   Filler: Dom. Rep.

Shape	Name	Lgth	Ring	Wrapper
Double Corona	Churchill	7	50	CC
Toro	Toro	6	50	CC
Robusto	Rothchild	5	50	CC
Churchill	Lonsdale	6⅞	46	CC
Long Corona	Corona Grande	6	44	CC
Corona	Corona	5½	42	CC

HANDMADE CIGARS: BRAND LISTINGS

The brand name translates into English as "on top of the mountain." So find your favorite heights, sit a spell and light up this mild-to-medium-bodied brand re-introduced in 1995 after its original debut in the 1960s. It features a genuine Connecticut wrapper combined with Cuban-seed filler leaves packed in 5x5 all-cedar cabinets of 25.

CINCO VEGAS GRAN RESERVA
Handmade in Esteli, Nicaragua.

Wrapper: Indonesia   *Binder: Indonesia*   *Filler: Dom.Rep., Nicaragua*

Shape	Name	Lgth	Ring	Wrapper
Double Corona	Churchill	7	52	CC
Torpedo	Torpedo	6	54	CC
Torpedo	Piramide	6½	46	CC
Toro	Doble Corona	6	48	CC
Panatela	Panatela	6	38	CC
Corona	Corona	5½	44	CC
Petit Corona	Mini-Corona	4½	42	CC
Robusto	Robusto	5	50	CC
Small Panatela	Petite	5	34	CC

This brand, whose name means "five farms" in Spanish, was originally made in 1890 in Cuba. The Sumatra-grown wrapper and binder gives this new brand a rich, but mild-to-medium-bodied flavor. It is offered in boxes of 25 cigars each, except for the Piramide and Torpedo shapes, offered in 10s. Most shapes are also available in small boxes of five cigars each.

CINCO VEGAS VINTAGE SELECTION
Handmade in Esteli, Nicaragua.

Wrapper: Brazil   *Binder: Indonesia*   *Filler: Dom.Rep., Nicaragua*

Shape	Name	Lgth	Ring	Wrapper
Double Corona	Churchill	7	52	CC
Torpedo	Piramide	6½	46	CC

Toro	Doble Corona	6	48	CC
Panatela	Panatela	6	38	CC
Corona	Corona	5½	44	CC
Robusto	Robusto	5	50	CC

This is a mild-bodied version of the Cinco Vegas brand, with a Brazilian wrapper and a blend of leaves from three other nations inside. It is offered in boxes of 25.

CISSO
Handmade in Santiago, Dominican Republic and Rochester, New York, USA.

Wrapper: USA/Connecticut   *Binder: Dom. Rep.*   *Filler: Dom. Rep.*

Shape	Name	Lgth	Ring	Wrapper
Double Corona	Churchill	7	50	CC
Toro	Joven	6	50	CC
Robusto	Robusto	5	50	CC
Corona	Corona	5½	42	CC
Panatela	Panetela	6½	36	CC

Introduced in late 1996, this brand offers a medium-bodied flavor with a genuine Connecticut wrapper. It is offered in all-cedar boxes of 25. All sizes except the Churchill are made in Rochester.

CISSO NATURAL
Handmade in Santiago, Dominican Republic and Rochester, New York, USA.

Wrapper: Indonesia   *Binder: Indonesia*   *Filler: Dom. Rep.*

Shape	Name	Lgth	Ring	Wrapper
Toro	Antonio	6	50	CM
Corona	Julian	5½	42	CM
Long Corona	Alfredo	6	44	CM

HANDMADE CIGARS: BRAND LISTINGS

Torpedo	Señor Torpedo	(tubed)	6½	52	CM

This is a medium-bodied cigar introduced in late 1996. It offers a Sumatra-grown wrapper combined with Dominican leaves for a medium-bodied taste.

CLASSICO DE CONTINENTAL
Handmade in Villa Gonzalez, Dominican Republic.

Wrapper: Indonesia   *Binder: Dom. Rep.*   *Filler: Dom. Rep.*

Shape	Name	Lgth	Ring	Wrapper
Long Corona	Long Corona	6	44	CC
Robusto	Robusto	5	50	CC
Churchill	Churchill	7½	48	CC
	Machine-made with short filler:			
Long Corona	J. Barton Classico	6	42	CC

Introduced in late 1997, this line replaces an earlier Classico de Continental line of medium-bodied cigars from Nicaragua. This new line is medium-to-full bodied in flavor, thanks to its Sumatran wrapper and Dominican binder and filler. These new cigars are offered in individual cellophane sleeves in varnished cedar boxes.

CLEMENTINE
Handmade in Danli, Honduras.

Wrapper: Honduras   *Binder: Honduras*   *Filler: Honduras, Nicaragua*

Shape	Name	Lgth	Ring	Wrapper
Long Corona	Coronas	6¼	44	CM-Ma
Double Corona	Churchills	7	50	CM-Ma
Double Corona	Inmensas	7¼	54	CM
Lonsdale	No. 1	7	44	CM-Ma
Corona	No. 4	5½	44	CM-Ma
Double Corona	Presidente	7¾	50	CM-Ma
Robusto	Rothschild	5	50	CM-Ma

HANDMADE CIGARS: BRAND LISTINGS

Toro	Toro	6	50	CM-Ma
Giant	Viajante	8½	52	CM

This is a long-filler, bundle cigar which was introduced in 1991 and offers a full-bodied taste. The name of the brand supposedly came from the favorite song of the buyers who were looking for tobacco on the backroads of Central America when the brand was introduced. Please . . .

CLUB SWEETS
Handmade, with short filler, in Mexico City, Mexico.

Wrapper: Indonesia *Binder: Nicaragua* *Filler: Nicaragua*

Shape	Name	Lgth	Ring	Wrapper
Long Corona	Amaretto	6	44	CM
Long Corona	Cherry	6	44	CM
Long Corona	Chocolate	6	44	CM
Long Corona	Mocha	6	44	CM
Long Corona	Rum	6	44	CM
Long Corona	Vanilla	6	44	CM

Introduced in 1997, this series offers mild, handmade, short-filler cigars with a strong flavor. The brand is presented with bands and in bundles of 25 cigars.

COHIBA
Handmade in Santiago, Dominican Republic.

Wrapper: Cameroon *Binder: Indonesia* *Filler: Dom. Rep.*

Shape	Name	Lgth	Ring	Wrapper
Giant	A	8½	47	CM
Robusto	Robusto	5	49	CM
Double Corona	Churchill	7	49	CM
Lonsdale	Corona Especiale	6½	42	CM
Grand Corona	Lonsdale Grande	6¼	47	CM

HANDMADE CIGARS: BRAND LISTINGS

Corona Extra	Robusto Fino		4¾	47	CM
Corona	Corona		5⅛	42	CM
Petit Corona	Corona Minor		4	42	CM
Corona	Crystal Corona	(tubed)	5½	42	CM
Pyramid	Triangulo		6	54	CM

This all-new Cohiba debuted in 1997. General Cigar had produced a three-size, unbanded Cohiba for 20 years, but this new, medium-to-full-bodied blend has more of everything, including sizes and taste. The Corona Especiale is finished with a twisted head and the Crystal Corona is packaged in a glass tube. The product of five years of research, it is offered in a beautiful mahogany box.

COJIMAR
Handmade in Santo Domingo, Dominican Republic.
Wrapper: USA/Connecticut   Binder: Dom. Rep   Filler: Dom. Rep.

Shape	Name	Lgth	Ring	Wrapper
Torpedo	Torpedo	6	54	CC
Giant	Presidente	8	50	CC
Lonsdale	Coronitas	6¾	44	CC
Panatela	Laguitos	6¾	38	CC
Panatela	Cortaditos	6¾	38	Stripe
Robusto	Toro	5½	50	CC
Small Panatela	Senoritas	5	30	CC
Torpedo	Chicos	4½	43	CC

This cigar debuted in 1996. It now offers a range of popular sizes in a mild-bodied style. Note that the Senoritas shape is also available with vanilla flavoring and the Chicos shape is available in cinnamon, mint and Sambuca flavors.

COLORADO
BY DON LINO
Handmade in Santiago, Dominican Republic.
Wrapper: Indonesia   Binder: Dom. Rep.   Filler: Dom. Rep.

HANDMADE CIGARS: BRAND LISTINGS

Shape	Name	Lgth	Ring	Wrapper
Long Corona	Lonsdale	6	42	Co
Long Corona	Corona *(tube available)*	6	44	Co
Toro	Robusto *(tube available)*	6	50	Co
Double Corona	Churchill	7½	50	Co
Torpedo	Torpedo	7	54	Co
Robusto	Rothchild	4½	50	Co
Giant	Presidente	8	52	Co
Long Panatela	Panatela	7½	38	Co
Churchill	Double Corona	7	48	Co
Corona	Coffee Break *(perfecto tip)*	4	44	Co
Perfecto	Perfecto No. 2	5½	52	Co

Colorado is a medium-bodied, premium cigar originally created in 1994. Now made in the Dominican Republic, it offers an all long-filler blend which is presented in individual cellophane sleeves and in all-cedar boxes of 25 and in convenient smaller boxes of 10, 5 and 3.

COLUMBUS
Handmade in Danli, Honduras.
Wrapper: USA/Connecticut

Binder: Dominican Republic   Filler: Dominican Republic, Honduras

Shape	Name	Lgth	Ring	Wrapper
Giant	Eleven Fifty	11	50	CM
Giant	Double Corona	8½	50	CM
Churchill	Churchill *(tube available)*	7	47	CM
Long Corona	Tubos *(tubed)*	6⅛	42	CM
Grand Corona	Columbus	5¾	46	CM
Robusto	Short Churchill	5	50	CM
Petit Corona	Perfectos	5	44	CM

Small Panatela	Tina		4½	30	CM

This is a full-bodied cigar, made by hand in the Dominican Republic, and offered in boxes of 25.

COMMANDANTE

Handmade, with short filler, in Licey, Dominican Republic.

Wrapper: Indonesia　　　　　*Binder: Dom. Rep.*　　　　　*Filler: Dom. Rep.*

Shape	Name	Lgth	Ring	Wrapper
Giant	Churchill	8	48	Ma
Grand Corona	Double Corona	6½	46	Ma
Long Corona	Diplomatico	6	44	Ma
Robusto	Robusto	5	50	Ma

Well made, albeit with short filler, and offering a medium-bodied taste, Commandante featured Piloto Cubano filler tobaccos and is offered in elegant boxes of 25.

CONDAL

Handmade in Tenerife, the Canary Islands of Spain.

Wrapper: USA/Connecticut　　　　*Binder: Mexico*　　　　*Filler: Dom. Rep.*

Shape	Name	Lgth	Ring	Wrapper
Lonsdale	No. 1	6⅝	43	Cl
Corona	No. 4	5⅓	43	Cl
Churchill	No. 10	7½	47	Cl
Robusto	Robusto	5⅔	50	Cl
Double Corona	Churchill	7½	50	Cl

Condal cigars are all handmade and are medium-to-full in body; they are offered in all-cedar boxes of 25.

HANDMADE CIGARS: BRAND LISTINGS

CONQUISTADOR
Handmade in Veracruz, Mexico.

Wrapper: Mexico Binder: Mexico Filler: Mexico

Shape	Name	Lgth	Ring	Wrapper
Short Panatela	Chico	5	36	CC-Ma
Lonsdale	Lonsdale	6½	40	CC-Ma
Corona	Corona	5½	42	CC-Ma
Toro	No. 1	6½	48	CC-Ma
Robusto	Robusto	5	50	CC-Ma
Double Corona	Churchill	7	50	CC-Ma
Giant	Inmensa	8	52	CC-Ma
Pyramid	Figurado	5½	54	CC-Ma
Torpedo	Petit Belicoso	5	50	CC-Ma
Torpedo	Torpedo	6½	56	CC-Ma
	Made with mixed filler:			
Double Corona	Churchill	7	50	CC-Ma
Robusto	Robusto	5½	50	CC-Ma

This all-Mexican brand offers a full-bodied flavor in its Sumatra-seed, natural-wrapped version and full strength in the maduro-wrapped edition. Introduced in 1997, it is offered in individual cellophane sleeves in all-cedar boxes or in bundles of 25.

CONSTANTIN
Handmade in the Dominican Republic.

Wrapper: Indonesia Binder: Dom. Rep. Filler: Dom. Rep.

Shape	Name	Lgth	Ring	Wrapper
Long Corona	Corona Extra	6	44	CM
Churchill	Churchill	6⅞	46	CM
Robusto	Robusto	5	50	CM

Corona Extra	Especial No. 2	5	46	CM

Offered in 3-packs and in wood boxes of 10 and 25, this is a medium-to-full-bodied cigar with aged tobaccos. It has been available in Europe since the middle 1990s, but introduced to the U.S. market only in 1998.

CONUCOS
Handmade in Santiago, Dominican Republic.
Wrapper: USA/Connecticut   *Binder: Dom. Rep.*   *Filler: Dom. Rep., Honduras*

Shape	Name	Lgth	Ring	Wrapper
Long Corona	Panatelas	5⅞	40	CC
Corona	Coronas	5¼	42	CC
Robusto	Robustos	5	50	CC
Long Corona	Celebracion	6¼	44	CC

New for 1996, this brand offers a smooth, mild body thanks to the blending of a genuine Connecticut wrapper with a Dominican binder and Dominican and Honduran filler leaves.

COPA HAVANA
Handmade in Danli, Honduras.
Wrapper: Ecuador or USA/Connecticut

Binder: Nicaragua   *Filler: Nicaragua*

CAMEROON BLEND:

Wrapper: Cameroon   *Binder: Cameroon*
Filler: Costa Rica, Dominican Republic, Nicaragua

Shape	Name	Lgth	Ring	Wrapper
Long Corona	Corona	6	43	CC-CM-Ma
Robusto	Robusto	5	50	CC-CM-Ma
Corona Extra	Short Churchill	5½	47	CC-CM-Ma
Toro	Toro	6	54	CC-CM-Ma
Churchill	Churchill	7	47	CC-CM-Ma

HANDMADE CIGARS: BRAND LISTINGS

Torpedo	Torpedo	7	54	CC-CM-Ma
Pyramid	Pyramid	6½	52	CC-CM-Ma

Introduced in 1996, the Copa Havana brand offers a choice of wrappers: Cameroon, Ecuadorian Rosado or genuine Connecticut Broadleaf in a maduro shade. The wrappers provide a choice of strengths, from mild-to-medium (Ecuador-grown Sumatra-seed), medium (Connecticut maduro) to medium-to-full-bodied (Cameroon). It is offered in boxes of 25.

CORMAN
Handmade in Santiago, Dominican Republic.

Wrapper: Indonesia   Binder: Dom. Rep.   Filler: Dom. Rep.

Shape	Name	Lgth	Ring	Wrapper
Double Corona	Lagunas No. 1	7½	50	CM
Robusto	Lagunas No. 2	5½	50	CM
Churchill	Lagunas No. 3	7	48	CM
Grand Corona	Lagunas No. 4	6½	46	CM
Lonsdale	Lagunas No. 5	6½	42	CM
Corona	Lagunas No. 6	5½	40	CM
Cigarillo	Lagunitas	5½	28	CM

This is a mild brand, made by hand in Santiago. It is offered in boxes of 25.

COSTA BAJA
Handmade in San Andres Tuxtla, Mexico.

Wrapper: Mexico   Binder: Mexico   Filler: Mexico

Shape	Name	Lgth	Ring	Wrapper
Long Corona	No. 1	6¼	44	CM
Robusto	No. 2	5	50	CM

This is a sister brand to Veracruz, with a medium body and offered in a bundle of 25.

HANDMADE CIGARS: BRAND LISTINGS

COTICAS
Handmade in Villa Gonzalez, Dominican Republic.

Wrapper: Indonesia   Binder: Dom. Rep.   *Filler: Dom. Rep.*

Shape	Name	Lgth	Ring	Wrapper
Double Corona	Churchill	7½	50	CC
Lonsdale	Corona	6½	44	CC
Churchill	Double Corona	7	48	CC
Corona	Petit Corona	5½	42	CC
Robusto	Rothschild	4½	50	CC
Toro	Toro	6	50	CC

Named for the Coticas bird, this blend offers a medium flavor featuring a Sumatra wrapper and Piloto Cubano filler leaves. Introduced in 1995, it is presented in individual cellophane sleeves and packed in cedar boxes of 25 cigars each.

CREDO
Handmade in Santiago, Dominican Republic.

Wrapper: USA/Connecticut   Binder: Dom. Rep., Mexico   *Filler: Dom. Rep.*

Shape	Name	Lgth	Ring	Wrapper
Slim Panatela	Jubilante	5	34	CC
Corona	Anthanor	5¾	42	CC
Churchill	Magnificat	6⅞	46	CC
Robusto	Arcane	5	50	CC
Double Corona	Pythagoras	7	50	CC

The Credo cigar line has been designed by the famous Belaubre family with a French flair. Their recipe produces a medium-strength smoke that is very smooth. Only the finest ingredients are used after being meticulously cured. The Magnificat, Arcane and Pythagoras models utilize a Dominican binder, while the Jubilate and Anthanor include a Mexican binder. The finished product, created in 1993, is offered in beautiful boxes imported from France.

CREDO CIGARS AND HUMIDIFIERS

CONDITIONS OF PLEASURE

Imported exclusively by Hollco Rohr

HANDMADE CIGARS: BRAND LISTINGS

CREDO LIGAS
Handmade in Danli, Honduras.

Wrapper: Indonesia   Binder: Honduras   Filler: Honduras

Shape	Name	Lgth	Ring	Wrapper
Slim Panatela	No. 1 Demi-Tasse	5½	32	CC
Robusto	No. 2 Robusto	5	50	CC
Corona	No. 3 Corona	5¾	43	CC
Churchill	No. 4 Churchill	7	48	CC
Giant	No. 5 Double Corona	8	52	CC

This newer line of the Credo brand was introduced in mid-1997. It offers a medium-to-full-bodied flavor in five popular shapes, and is offered in cellophane sleeves in a colorfully-adorned box that features the masks of comedy and tragedy.

CREME DE MINT
Handmade, with mixed filler, in Santiago, Dominican Republic.

Wrapper: Dom. Rep.   Binder: Dom. Rep.   Filler: Dom. Rep.

Shape	Name	Lgth	Ring	Wrapper
Small Panatela	Menthol Mood	4	34	CM
Lonsdale	Menthol Madness	6½	44	CM

This is a medium-to-full-bodied, flavored brand, introduced in 1998. It is offered in boxes of 25.

CREMOSA CUBANOS
Handmade in Santiago, Dominican Republic.

Wrapper: USA/Connecticut   Binder: Dom. Rep.   Filler: Dom. Rep.

Shape	Name	Lgth	Ring	Wrapper
Robusto	Robusto	5	50	CC
Corona	Corona	5½	42	CC
Lonsdale	Lonsdale	6¾	44	CC

HANDMADE CIGARS: BRAND LISTINGS

Toro	Toro	6	50	CC
Torpedo	Torpedo	6	52	CC
Double Corona	Churchill	7	50	CC

Introduced in 1997, this is a medium-bodied brand, which mixes Dominican leaves with a Connecticut Shade wrapper for a flavorful taste. You can experience it in boxes of 25.

CRISPIN PATIÑO
Handmade in Cumana, Venezuela.

Wrapper: Honduras   *Binder: Venezuela*   *Filler: Venezuela*

Shape	Name	Lgth	Ring	Wrapper
Grand Corona	No. 3	6	46	CM
Corona Extra	No. 2	5½	46	CM
Petit Corona	No. 1	5	42	CM
Robusto	Robusto	5	50	CM
Double Corona	Double Corona	7	50	CM

Introduced to the U.S. market in 1996, this has been a popular Venezuelan brand since 1928. Full-bodied and made of Venezuelan filler and binder with seven-year-old Honduran wrapper, it is produced with pride by the Patiño family, which started making cigars in 1900.

CRISTAL DE LEON
Handmade in Danli, Honduras.
Wrapper: Honduras or USA/Connecticut

Binder: Costa Rica   *Filler: Dominican Republic, Honduras*

Shape	Name		Lgth	Ring	Wrapper
Corona	Cristals	(tubed)	5½	43	CC

Introduced in 1996, this is a handmade, all long-filler cigar from Honduras, featuring either a Sumatra-seed wrapper grown in Honduras for a medium-bodied taste or a Connecticut wrapper, which gives a mild-to-medium bodied flavor. The packaging lives up to the brand's name: each cigar is presented in an air-tight glass tube.

HANDMADE CIGARS: BRAND LISTINGS

CRISTAL DE VENEZUELA
Handmade in Cumana, Venezuela.

Wrapper: Venezuela　　　　*Binder: Venezuela*　　　　*Filler: Venezuela*

Shape	Name	Lgth	Ring	Wrapper
	Reserva Privada 1893:			
Giant	Inmensa	8	52	CM
Double Corona	Churchill Signature	7½	52	CM
Double Corona	Churchill	7	50	CM
Torpedo	Torpedo	6½	54	CM
Toro	Presidente	6¼	48	CM
Robusto	Robusto Primero	5½	52	CM
Robusto	Robusto	5¾	50	CM
Robusto	Corona	5½	48	CM
Corona Extra	Purito	4¾	46	CM
Slim Panatela	Purito Panatella	5	34	CM
	Cumana 1893:			
Corona	Corona Especial No. 3	5¾	46	CM
Corona	Corona No. 2	5½	42	CM
Double Corona	Churchill	7	50	CM
Robusto	Robusto	5½	50	CM

This brand has been around, in one form or another, since 1893 and even today is only available in limited quantities and in a limited number of the shapes listed above at any one time. Made of all-Venezuelan tobacco, it offers a medium-bodied taste in the Reserva Privada blend and mild-to-medium strength in the Cumana 1893 style. It is presented in boxes of 25 except for the Purito Panatella, which is packed in 50s.

CRISTO CUBANOS
Handmade in Santiago, Dominican Republic.

Wrapper: USA/Connecticut　　　*Binder: Dom. Rep.*　　　*Filler: Dom. Rep.*

HANDMADE CIGARS: BRAND LISTINGS

Shape	Name	Lgth	Ring	Wrapper
Double Corona	Churchill	7	49	CC
Petit Corona	Corona	5	42	CC
Lonsdale	Lonsdale	6½	44	CC
Pyramid	Piramid	6½	54	CC
Robusto	Robusto	5	52	CC
Toro	Toro	6	50	CC

Here is a new brand in 1998, with excellent construction and a mild-to-medium-bodied taste that offers a marvelous flavor.

CROWN ACHIEVEMENT
Handmade in Danli, Honduras.
Wrapper: Ecuador

Binder: Dominican Republic *Filler: Costa Rica, Honduras, Nicaragua*

Shape	Name	Lgth	Ring	Wrapper
Giant	Churchill	8	50	CI
Corona	Corona	5½	42	CI
Churchill	Double Corona	7	48	CI
Grand Corona	Grand Corona	6	46	CI
Lonsdale	Lonsdale	6½	42	CI
Torpedo	Rat Tail	6	54	CI
Robusto	Robusto	4½	50	CI

Here is a new, medium-bodied brand for 1997. It is blessed with excellent construction and aged leaves from five nations, offered in cedar boxes of 25.

CROWN CLASSICS – DOMINICAN
Handmade in La Romana, Dominican Republic.
Wrapper: Ecuador or Indonesia *Binder: Dom. Rep.* *Filler: Dom. Rep.*

P L É I A D E S

HAND-ROLLED TO MEET THE HIGHEST EXPECTATIONS

OF CONNOISSEURS. MADE FROM THE CHOICEST LEAF

AND LONG FILLER IN THE DOMINICAN REPUBLIC.

THEY ARE HAND SELECTED FOR WRAPPER COLOR

AND PACKED IN FLAVOR-ENHANCING CEDAR BOXES.

Imported by Swisher International, Inc.

Robustos and Toros

These are very popular sizes as enthusiasts look for the flavor of a larger ring gauge of a Churchill or Double Corona combined with shorter lengths for a shorter smoke. The dimensions of these shapes include:

‣ Robusto	4½-5½ inches long; 48-54 ring.
‣ Toro	5⅝-6⅝ inches long; 48-54 ring.

Pictured opposite, from left to right:

		(shape)
‣ **DON JIVAN CLASICO** *Rothschild* (Dominican Republic) 4½ x 52		Robusto
‣ **ESTAVAN CRUZ** *Robusto* (Costa Rica)	5 x 50	Robusto
‣ **SAVOY** *Robusto* (Ecuador)	5 x 50	Robusto
‣ **CAONAO** *Robusto* (United States)	5 x 50	Robusto
‣ **ZIQ** *Robusto* (Honduras)	6 x 48	Toro
‣ **ROBALI** *Corona* (Costa Rica)	6 x 50	Toro
‣ **BURT REYNOLDS** *Toro* (Dominican Republic)	6 x 50	Toro
‣ **PLASENCIA** *Toro* (Nicaragua)	6 x 50	Toro

HANDMADE CIGARS: BRAND LISTINGS

Shape	Name	Lgth	Ring	Wrapper
Double Corona	Crown Classics	6¾	50	Stripe

This very well made, double-wrapped, mild-bodied brand was introduced in 1997 and is offered in a favorite size in convenient packs of five.

CROWN CLASSICS – HONDURAN
Handmade in Danli, Honduras.

Wrapper: Honduras   *Binder: Honduras*   *Filler: Honduras*

Shape	Name	Lgth	Ring	Wrapper
Lonsdale		6⅝	44	CM
Robusto		4¾	50	CM-Ma
Toro		6¼	50	CM
Double Corona		7½	50	CM
Giant		8	52	CM
Torpedo		6⅝	54	CM
Long Corona		6	42	CM

This is an respected old brand, without shape names, introduced about 1990. It is medium-bodied and features all-Honduran tobaccos, offered in bundles of 25.

CRUZ REAL
Handmade in Vera Cruz, Mexico.

Wrapper: Mexico   *Binder: Mexico*   *Filler: Mexico*

Shape	Name	Lgth	Ring	Wrapper
Lonsdale	No. 1	6⅝	42	CC-Ma
Long Corona	No. 2	6	42	CC-Ma
Panatela	No. 3	6⅝	35	CC-Ma
Double Corona	No. 14	7½	50	CC-Ma
Toro	No. 19	6	50	CC-Ma
Robusto	No. 24	4½	50	CC-Ma

Robusto	No. 25	5½	52	CC-Ma
Giant	No. 28	8½	54	CC-Ma

Cruz Real is a true "puro" using wrapper, binder and filler from Mexico. The fine combination of Mexican-grown Sumatra-seed wrappers (Cuban-seed for maduro) and San Andres binder and fillers are the perfect union for this lightly spicy, mild-to-medium-bodied cigar, which was introduced in 1994. You can enjoy them in boxes of 10 or 25, or in a hand-carved humidor filled with 60 of these great cigars!

CRUZ REAL SPECIAL EDITION
Handmade in Vera Cruz, Mexico.

Wrapper: Mexico　　　　*Binder: Mexico*　　　　*Filler: Mexico*

Shape	Name	Lgth	Ring	Wrapper
Double Corona	Emperador	7½	50	CC
Toro	Canciller	6	50	CC
Long Corona	Ministro	6	42	CC

This superb, specially-made cigar offers tobaccos from Mexico blended to provide a mild-to-medium-bodied taste, offered in boxes of 25.

CRUZEROS
Handmade in Santiago, Dominican Republic.

Wrapper: USA/Connecticut　　　*Binder: Dom. Rep.*　　　*Filler: Dom. Rep.*

Shape	Name	Lgth	Ring	Wrapper
Giant	Grand Corona	8½	50	CC
Petit Corona	Petit Corona	5½	40	CC
Lonsdale	Lonsdale	7½	40	CC
Corona	Corona	5¾	42	CC
Small Panatela	Demi Tasse	5	34	CC
Robusto	Robusto	5	50	CC
Churchill	Churchill	6⅞	46	CC

HANDMADE CIGARS: BRAND LISTINGS

Here is a 1998-introduced brand which is elegantly made and offers, by size, tastes from medium up to full body. Try these out in boxes of 25!

CU-AVANA
Handmade in Tamboril, Dominican Republic.

Wrapper: Indonesia   *Binder: Dom. Rep.*   *Filler: Dom. Rep.*

Shape	Name	Lgth	Ring	Wrapper
Robusto	Robusto	5	50	CC
Long Corona	Cu-Abano Lite	6	42	CC
Double Corona	Cu-Abano Churchill	7	50	CC
Churchill	Gentleman's Day	7	46	CC
Short Panatela	Lady's Night	5	36	CC

The shapes vary in strength from mild (Lady's Night, Cu-Abano Lite) to medium (Gentleman's Day) to full-bodied (Cu-Abano, Robusto). It was introduced in 1997. The wrapper is genuine Sumatra-grown and you can enjoy Cu-Avana in cedar boxes of 25.

CUBA 1800
Handmade in Miami, Florida, USA.

Wrapper: Indonesia   *Binder: Indonesia*   *Filler: Dom. Rep., Indonesia, Mexico*

Shape	Name	Lgth	Ring	Wrapper
Cigarillo	Finos	5	28	CM-Ma
Torpedo	Torpedos	6½	54	CM-Ma
Robusto	Robustos	5	50	CM-Ma
Long Panatela	Lanceros	7½	38	CM-Ma
Long Corona	Panetelas	6	42	CM-Ma
Double Corona	Churchills	7	50	CM-Ma
Double Corona	Presidente	7½	52	CM-Ma

This is a mild cigar in the natural-wrapped version and full-bodied in the maduro-wrapped style. It features a Sumatra-grown wrapper and is presented in your choice of box or bundle of 25.

HANDMADE CIGARS: BRAND LISTINGS

CUBADOM
Handmade, with mixed filler, in Las Vegas, Nevada, USA.

Wrapper: Mexico   Binder: Dom. Rep.   Filler: Colombia, Dom. Rep., Mexico

Shape	Name	Lgth	Ring	Wrapper
Double Corona	Palma Real	7½	50	Ma
Churchill	Cazador	7	46	Ma
Lonsdale	Cervantes	6½	44	Ma
Corona	Breva	5¼	42	Ma

This is a full-bodied brand that debuted in 1998. It is available only with a Mexican maduro wrapper, in boxes of 25.

CUBAN CIGAR FACTORY "MAESTROS"
Handmade in San Diego, California, USA

Wrapper: Ecuador   Binder: Ecuador   Filler: Honduras, Mexico

Shape	Name	Lgth	Ring	Wrapper
Torpedo	No. 1	6	54	Ma
Toro	No. 2	6½	50	Ma
Robusto	No. 3	4¾	52	Ma
Grand Corona	No. 4	5¾	46	Ma

California, here I come! Experienced Cuban hands direct the making of these cigars in the lively Cuban Cigar Factory in the Gaslamp District of San Diego. You can see them rolling, then try the finished result — a full-bodied, all-maduro series with a rich flavor, offered in boxes of 25.

CUBAN CIGAR FACTORY "TRADICIONALES"
Handmade in San Diego, California, USA.

Wrapper: Ecuador   Binder: Indonesia   Filler: Dom. Rep., Honduras, Mexico

Shape	Name	Lgth	Ring	Wrapper
Slim Panatela	Fino	5¾	32	CM-Ma
Corona	Corona	5¾	42	CM-Ma

HANDMADE CIGARS: BRAND LISTINGS

Lonsdale	El Cubano	6¾	44	CM-Ma
Panatela	Panatela	6¾	36	CM-Ma
Robusto	Robusto	5	50	CM-Ma
Grand Corona	Havana	6	46	CM-Ma
Toro	Monterico	5½	52	CM-Ma
Double Corona	Cuban Round Largo	7¼	50	CM-Ma
Double Corona	Presidente	7¾	52	CM-Ma
Torpedo	Torpedo	7	56	CM-Ma

Here is a mild-to-medium-bodied cigar that you can see being made by hand by the Cuban Cigar Factory in San Diego's Gaslamp District! It features a Sumatra-seed wrapper and Java wrapper and is offered in boxes of 25.

CUBAN CIGAR FACTORY "VANILLA SWEETS"
Handmade in San Diego, California, USA.
Wrapper: Ecuador   *Binder: Ecuador*   *Filler: Honduras, Mexico*

Shape	Name	Lgth	Ring	Wrapper
Slim Panatela	Coronita	5¾	32	CM
Lonsdale	Especial	6½	40	CM
Petit Corona	Petit Corona	5	42	CM
Corona Extra	Emperador	5½	46	CM
Toro	Corona Grande	6	50	CM

Here is a carefully-made, all-long-filler, flavored cigar that starts with Cuban-seed filler leaves and cures them with pure vanilla and a taste of honey. The quality of the result is obvious and you can try them in boxes of 25.

CUBAN ESPECIALE
Handmade in Santo Domingo, Dominican Republic.
Wrapper: Indonesia   *Binder: Dom. Rep.*   *Filler: Dom. Rep.*

HANDMADE CIGARS: BRAND LISTINGS

Shape	Name	Lgth	Ring	Wrapper
Corona		5½	44	CC
Toro		6	50	CC
Churhill		6¾	46	CC
Double Corona		7	50	CC

This is a mild-to-medium-bodied brand, offered without shape names, in boxes of 25.

CUBAN SANDWICH

Handmade, with short filler, in Santiago, Dominican Republic.

Wrapper: USA/Connecticut   Binder: Dom. Rep.   Filler: Dom. Rep.

Shape	Name	Lgth	Ring	Wrapper
Corona	Breva	5½	44	CC-Ma
Lonsdale	Cetros	6¾	44	CC-Ma
Double Corona	Churchill	7	50	CC-Ma
Toro	Toro	6	50	CC-Ma

Here is a modestly-priced, short-filler cigar from one of the Dominican Republic's finest factories. The short filler is the center of the "sandwich" formed by the binder and results in a pleasant, mild-to-medium-bodied smoke. It if offered in natural and maduro wrapper shades in boxes or bundles of 25.

CUBAN SELECT

Handmade in Santiago, Dominican Republic.

Wrapper: Cameroon, Indonesia   Binder: Dom. Rep.   Filler: Dom. Rep.

Shape	Name	Lgth	Ring	Wrapper
Churchill	Hemingway Classico	7	46	CM-Ma
Pyramid	Pyramid	6½	44	CM-Ma
Torpedo	Torpedo	6½	52	CM-Ma
Toro	Toro	6	52	CM-Ma

HANDMADE CIGARS: BRAND LISTINGS

Giant	Double Corona	8	50	CM-Ma
Double Corona	Churchill	7½	50	CM-Ma
Toro	Robusto	6	50	CM-Ma
Robusto	Belicoso	5	50	CM-Ma
Grand Corona	Corona I	6	46	CM-Ma
Corona	Corona II	5¾	44	CM-Ma
Petit Corona	Petit Hemingway	4	44	CM-Ma
Lonsdale	Lonsdale	6½	42	CM-Ma
Long Panatela	Lancero	7½	38	CM-Ma
Slim Panatela	Long Panatela	5¾	30	CM-Ma
Small Panatela	Panatela	4¾	30	CM-Ma

This is a full-bodied brand that is available in a natural-shade (Java) wrapper and Cameroon-grown maduro wrapper. It is offered in a box of 25.

CUBANA FINA
Handmade, with short filler, in Miami, Florida, USA.
Wrapper: Indonesia   *Binder: Dom. Rep.*   *Filler: Dom. Rep.*

Shape	Name	Lgth	Ring	Wrapper
Lonsdale	Small Fumas	6½	44	CM
Churchill	Imperiales	7½	46	CM

This mild-blend, short-filler blend was introduced in 1997 by the King Richard Cigar Co. of Indianapolis. You can find it in 25-count boxes or in plastic canisters that are easy to use and easy on the wallet.

CUBANA ROYALE
Handmade in Los Angeles, California, USA.
Wrapper: Brazil, Ecuador   *Binder: Honduras*   *Filler: Honduras, Nicaragua*

Shape	Name	Lgth	Ring	Wrapper
Corona	Corona	5¾	42	CC-Ma

HANDMADE CIGARS: BRAND LISTINGS

Lonsdale	El Cubano	6¾	44	CC-Ma
Robusto	Robusto	5	50	CC-Ma
Double Corona	Presidente	7¾	52	CC-Ma
Pyramid	Pyramid	6¾	56	CC-Ma
Panatela	Panatela	6¾	36	CC

Made by hand in a small factory in Southern California, these are quality, hard-to-find cigars with a full body and a choice of natural-shade wrappers from Brazil (Sumatra-seed) or maduro wrapper from Ecuador. Cubana Royale cigars are available in boxes of 25, wrapped in raw tobacco leaves!

CUBANACAN
Handmade in Esteli, Nicaragua.

Wrapper: Indonesia   *Binder: Nicaragua*   *Filler: Nicaragua*

Shape	Name	Lgth	Ring	Wrapper
Robusto	Robusto	5	50	CM
Long Corona	Corona	6	44	CM
Toro	Double Corona	6	48	CM
Double Corona	Churchill	7	52	CM
Giant	Presidente	8	54	CM

Introduced in 1996, this is a mild-bodied brand which is available in boxes of 25.

CUBANO-A-MANO
Handmade in Manila, the Philippines.

Wrapper: Indonesia   *Binder: Philippines*   *Filler: Philippines*

Shape	Name	Lgth	Ring	Wrapper
Double Corona		7	52	CM
Churchill		7	47	CM
Robusto		5	52	CM
Torpedo		7	52	CM

Petit Corona		5	44	CM

Although there are no shape names, this is a mild blend introduced in 1998. It offers a Java wrapper in five popular sizes, available in boxes of 25.

CUBELLA
Handmade in Santiago, Dominican Republic.

Wrapper: Dom. Rep.   Binder: Dom. Rep.   Filler: Dom. Rep.

Shape	Name	Lgth	Ring	Wrapper
Robusto	Robusto	5	50	CM
Toro	Lonsdale	6	50	CM
Double Corona	Churchill	7	50	CM

This mild--to-medium-bodied brand was introduced in 1997. It is offered in protective cellophane sleeves in your choice of boxes or bundles of 25.

CUBITA
Handmade in Santiago, Dominican Republic.

Wrapper: USA/Connecticut   Binder: Dom. Rep.   Filler: Dom. Rep.

Shape	Name	Lgth	Ring	Wrapper
Double Corona	No. 2000	7	50	CC
Corona	No. 500	5½	43	CC
Lonsdale	No. 8-9-8	6¾	43	CC
Panatela	No. 2	6¼	38	CC
Toro	No. 700	6	50	CC
Small Panatela	Delicias	5⅛	30	CC

Introduced in 1986, this is a medium-to-heavy bodied cigar, with excellent construction. The six-shape brand uses only aged tobaccos and offers these cigars in beautiful cedar cases of 25 cigars each.

CUESTA-REY
Handmade in Santiago, Dominican Republic.
Wrapper: Cameroon and USA/Connecticut

Binder: Dominican Republic   *Filler: Dominican Republic*

Shape	Name		Lgth	Ring	Wrapper
	Cabinet Selection:				
Giant	No. 1		8½	52	CC-Ma
Long Panatela	No. 2		7	36	CC-Ma
Lonsdale	No. 95		6¼	42	CC-Ma
Double Corona	No. 898		7	49	CC-Ma
Lonsdale	No. 1884		6¾	44	CC-Ma
	Centennial Collection:				
Giant	Dominican No. 1		8½	52	CC-Ma
Churchill	Dominican No. 2		7¼	48	CC-Ma
Long Panatela	Dominican No. 3		7	36	CC-Ma
Lonsdale	Dominican No. 4		6½	42	CC-Ma
Corona	Dominican No. 5		5½	43	CC-Ma
Toro	Dominican No. 60		6	50	CC-Ma
Churchill	Aristocrat	*(tubed)*	7¼	48	CC-Ma
Long Corona	Captiva	*(tubed)*	6⅛	42	CC-Ma
Long Panatela	Rivera	*(tubed)*	7	35	CC-Ma
Small Panatela	Cameo		4¼	32	CC-Ma
Robusto	Robusto No. 7		4½	50	CC-Ma
Pyramid	Pyramid No. 9		6¼	52	CC-Ma
Giant	Individual	*(boxed)*	8½	52	CC-Ma

Backed by more than a century of experience in the manufacture of handmade cigars since 1884, the Cuesta-Rey selection offers both mild-to-medium (Cabinet) and medium-bodied (Centennial) cigars. Connecticut Shade wrappers are used for all models except Cabinet Selection No. 95, which uses a

HANDMADE CIGARS: BRAND LISTINGS

Cameroon wrapper. Connecticut Broadleaf tobacco is used for all of the maduro wrappers.

CUPIDO
Handmade in Esteli, Nicaragua.

Wrapper: Indonesia   *Binder: Nicaragua*   *Filler: Nicaragua*

Shape	Name	Lgth	Ring	Wrapper
Churchill	Churchill	7	48	CM
Robusto	Robusto	5½	50	CM
Perfecto	Torpito	4½	54	CM

There are only three sizes, but what a cigar! Mild-to-medium in body, but without a trace of bitterness, the secret is in the blending of Cuban-seed ligero leaves in the filler, combined with the Sumatran-grown wrapper. Production is limited; where available, Cupido cigars are offered in elegant all-cedar boxes of 25.

CUSANO ESTATE RESERVE
Handmade in Villa Gonzalez, Dominican Republic.

Wrapper: Indonesia, USA/Connecticut   *Binder: Dom. Rep.*   *Filler: Dom. Rep.*

Shape	Name	Lgth	Ring	Wrapper
Toro	Toro Grande	6	52	Ma
Giant	Double Robusto	8	52	Ma
Torpedo	Belicoso	6	54	CC

A product of careful blending, this special reserve selection offers a medium-to-full bodied taste with two-year aged Cuban-seed leaves in the filler. Two of the shapes utilize an Indonesian maduro wrap while the Belicoso uses a Connecticut Shade wrapper. It is presented in boxes of 20.

CUSANO HERMANOS
Handmade in Santiago, Dominican Republic.

Wrapper: USA/Connecticut, Dominican Republic

Binder: Dominican Republic   *Filler: Dominican Republic*

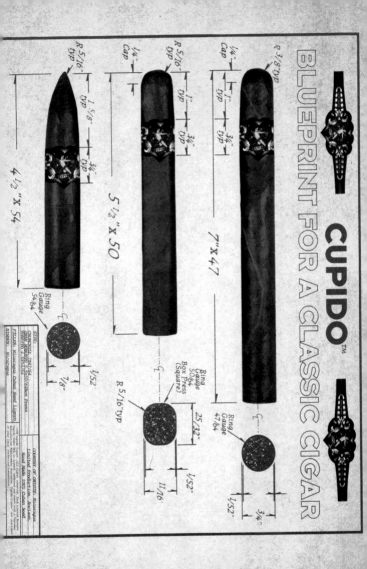

CUPIDO™

BLUEPRINT FOR A CLASSIC CIGAR

R 3/8" typ

1/4" Cap

7" typ

3/4" typ

R 5/16" typ

7" x 47

Ring
Gauge
47/64

R 5/16" typ

1/52"

1/52"

3/4"

1/4" Cap

R 5/16" typ

1" typ

3/4" typ

3/4"

5 1/2" x 50

Ring
Gauge
50/64
Box Press
(Square)

25/32"

R 5/16" typ

11/16"

1/52"

R 5/16" typ

1 5/8" typ

3/4"

4 1/2" x 54

Ring
Gauge
54/64

7/8"

1/52"

FILLER: Nicaragua Cuban Seed Ligero

BINDER: Nicaragua

SIZES:
CHURCHILL 7X47/64
TORO 5.5X50/64/Box Press
BELICOSO 4.5X54/64

COUNTRY OF ORIGIN: Nicaragua
Limited Production. Aciano.
Hand Made 100% Cuban Seed

HANDMADE CIGARS: BRAND LISTINGS

Shape	Name	Lgth	Ring	Wrapper
Robusto	Bullet	4	50	CC-Ma
Robusto	Robusto	5	50	CC-Ma
Long Corona	Corona	6	44	CC-Ma
Churchill	Churchill	7	46	CC-Ma
Pyramid	Pyramid	6	54	CC-Ma
Perfecto	Perfecto	7	56	CC-Ma

This brand debuted in 1996, with a full-bodied taste and a smooth draw based on a blend of five tobaccos. The Dominican-grown maduro wrapper adds a spicy finish compared to the Connecticut Shade-wrapped models. It is offered in boxes of 20, except for the Perfecto, available in 10s.

CUSANO ROMANI
Handmade in Santiago, Dominican Republic.
Wrapper: USA/Connecticut   Binder: Dom. Rep.   Filler: Dom. Rep.

Shape	Name	Lgth	Ring	Wrapper
Pyramid	Pyramid	6	54	CC

A single roller is specially appointed to create this pyramid shape, introduced in 1996. Five tobaccos - two Dominican-seed and two Cuban-seed - are combined with the elegant Connecticut Shade wrappers to create a smooth smoke with medium-to-full body and a pleasant aroma.

CUSANO SELECTION
Handmade in Santiago, Dominican Republic.
Wrapper: Indonesia or USA/Connecticut
Binder: Dominican Republic   Filler: Dominican Republic

Shape	Name	Lgth	Ring	Wrapper
Torpedo	Torpedo	6½	53	CM-Ma
Toro	Toro	6½	50	Ma
Robusto	Robusto	5	50	CM-Ma

HANDMADE CIGARS: BRAND LISTINGS

This all-maduro line debuted in 1996, with Indonesian wrappers and a medium-to-full-bodied taste. The Connecticut-wrapped version was added later, with a medium body. The Cusano Selection is offered in individual cellophane sleeves and packed in boxes of 20.

D & B DOMINICAN RESERVE
Handmade in Villa Gonzalez, Dominican Republic.

Wrapper: Indonesia   *Binder: Dom. Rep.*   *Filler: Dom. Rep.*

Shape	Name	Lgth	Ring	Wrapper
Giant	Presidente	8	52	CM
Churchill	Churchill	7½	49	CM
Torpedo	Torpedo	6	52	CM
Long Corona	Corona	6	44	CM
Robusto	Robusto	5	50	CM

This series offers a medium-bodied taste in the distinctive D & B multi-colored box. You can enjoy the cigars and the box 25 at a time.

D & B GOLD RESERVE
Handmade in Villa Gonzalez, Dominican Republic.

Wrapper: Ecuador   *Binder: Dom. Rep.*   *Filler: Dom. Rep.*

Shape	Name	Lgth	Ring	Wrapper
Torpedo	Torpedo	6¾	52	CC
Double Corona	Churchill	7½	50	CC
Toro	Robusto	6	50	CC
Long Corona	Corona	6	44	CC
Small Panatela	Petit	4	30	CC

Introduced in 1997, this is a mild-to-medium-bodied blend featuring a Connecticut-seed wrapper grown in Ecuador. You can find it in boxes of 25. The Petit is a flavored shape available in chocolate, sugar and vanilla.

HANDMADE CIGARS: BRAND LISTINGS

D.G.S.
Handmade in San Goncalo de Campos, Brazil.

Wrapper: Brazil   Binder: Brazil   Filler: Brazil

Shape	Name	Lgth	Ring	Wrapper
Toro	Churchill	6½	48	CM
Corona Extra	Corona Extra	5½	46	CM

The abbreviated title stands for "Damn Good Smoke" and this brand features all Mata Fina tobaccos from Brazil. It is medium in body and offered in all-cedar boxes of 25.

DS BUNDLES
Handmade, with mixed filler, in Santiago, Dominican Republic.

Wrapper: USA/Connecticut   Binder: Dom. Rep.   Filler: Dom. Rep.

Shape	Name	Lgth	Ring	Wrapper
Double Corona	Churchill	7	50	CC-Ma
Toro	Toro	6	50	CC-Ma
Lonsdale	Fuma	6⅞	43	CC-Ma
Corona	Breva	5½	43	CC-Ma

Here is a modestly-priced, high-quality bundled cigar from the Dominican Republic. Introduced in 1996, it offers a mild taste with a Connecticut Broadleaf wrapper. The filler is a sandwich of long-filler surrounding a short-filler core

DA COSTA
Handmade in San Andres Tuxtla, Mexico.

Wrapper: Mexico   Binder: Mexico   Filler: Mexico

Shape	Name	Lgth	Ring	Wrapper
Double Corona	Presidente	7½	50	CC
Double Corona	Churchill	7	50	CC
Toro	Toro	6	50	CC
Robusto	Robusto	5	50	CC

Lonsdale	Lonsdale	6½	42	CC
Long Corona	Corona	6	42	CC
Long Corona	Corona Especial	6	44	CC
Long Panatela	Panatela	7	38	CC
Pyramid	Piramide	6	52	Stripe
Lonsdale	Divino	6½	42	Stripe
Toro	Dominante	6	50	Stripe
Torpedo	Maximiliano	6½	52	Stripe
Lonsdale	Da Costa De Lux	6½	42	CC

This is a medium-bodied brand which was introduced in 1998. It is offered in boxes of 5, 10, 20 or 25 cigars.

DANIEL MARSHALL ARTIST DOMINICAN RESERVE
Handmade in Santiago, Dominican Republic.

Wrapper: USA/Connecticut   *Binder: Mexico*   *Filler: Dom. Rep.*

Shape	Name	Lgth	Ring	Wrapper
Robusto	Robusto	5	50	CC
Long Corona	Corona	6	44	CC
Churchill	Churchill	7	48	CC

This brand is a special selection, aged for an additional 12 months, of the standard D. Marshall Signature cigars. Personally picked by Daniel Marshall himself, these are truly the "cream of the crop" and available only by special request.

DANIEL MARSHALL SIGNATURE/DOMINICAN RESERVE
Handmade in Santiago, Dominican Republic.

Wrapper: USA/Connecticut   *Binder: Mexico*   *Filler: Dom. Rep.*

Shape	Name	Lgth	Ring	Wrapper
Robusto	Robusto	5	50	CC

HANDMADE CIGARS: BRAND LISTINGS

| Long Corona | Corona | 6 | 44 | CC |
| Churchill | Churchill | 7 | 48 | CC |

A perfect complement to the famous D.Marshall humidors, this 1996-introduced brand was developed to Mr. Marshall's personal standards. It offers a medium-to-full body and consists entirely of three to four-year-old tobaccos.

DANIEL MARSHALL SIGNATURE/HONDURAN RESERVE
Handmade in Danli, Honduras.
Wrapper: USA/Connecticut   Binder: Honduras   Filler: Honduras, Nicaragua

Shape	Name	Lgth	Ring	Wrapper
Robusto	Robusto	5	50	CC
Long Corona	Corona	6½	44	CC
Double Corona	Churchill	7½	50	CC

Created in 1996, this cigar exhibits none of the harshness which sometimes accompanies Honduran-made cigars. It boasts a Connecticut Shade wrapper and has a medium-to-full body; it is presented in all-cedar boxes of 25.

DANIEL MARSHALL SIGNATURE/SUMATRA LIMITED RESERVE
Handmade in Santiago, Dominican Republic.
Wrapper: Indonesia   Binder: Dom. Rep.   Filler: Dom. Rep.

Shape	Name	Lgth	Ring	Wrapper
Robusto	Robusto	5	50	CC
Long Corona	Corona	6	44	CC
Churchill	Churchill	7	48	CC

You cannot stop the expanding cigar empire of the energetic Daniel Marshall, you can only hope to contain him! Introduced in 1997, this line offers a medium-bodied smoke in three popular sizes, offered in all-cedar boxes of 25.

DANLYS
Handmade in Danli, Honduras.
Wrapper: Honduras   Binder: Mexico   Filler: Honduras, Mexico

HANDMADE CIGARS: BRAND LISTINGS

Shape	Name	Lgth	Ring	Wrapper
Double Corona	Churchill	7	50	CM
Short Panatela	Petit	4¼	38	CM
Panatela	Panatella	6	38	CM
Churchill	President	6¾	48	CM
Toro	Toro	6⅛	50	CM
Lonsdale	No. 1	7	42	CM
Petit Corona	No. 4	5	42	CM

This is a fairly old brand, dating from 1972. It is medium-to-full in body and is offered in natural wrapper shades, in economical bundles of 25.

DAVIDOFF
Handmade in Santiago, Dominican Republic.
Wrapper: USA/Connecticut   Binder: Dom. Rep.   Filler: Dom. Rep.

Shape	Name	Lgth	Ring	Wrapper
Long Panatela	No. 1	7½	38	CC
Panatela	No. 2	6	38	CC
Slim Panatela	No. 3	5⅛	30	CC
Panatela	Tubos	6	38	CC
Cigarillo	Ambassadrice	4½	26	CC
	Aniversario Series:			
Giant	Aniversario No. 1	8⅔	48	CC
Churchill	Aniversario No. 2	7	48	CC
	Grand Cru Series:			
Lonsdale	Grand Cru No. 1	6⅛	43	CC
Corona	Grand Cru No. 2	5⅝	43	CC
Petit Corona	Grand Cru No. 3	5	43	CC
Petit Corona	Grand Cru No. 4	4⅝	41	CC

Petit Corona	Grand Cru No. 5	4	41	CC
	Special Series:			
Culebras	Special "C"	6½	33	CC
Double Corona	Double "R"	7½	50	CC
Robusto	Special "R"	4⅞	50	CC
Pyramid	Special "T"	6	52	CC
	Thousand Series:			
Small Panatela	1000	4⅝	34	CC
Petit Corona	2000	5	43	CC
Slim Panatela	3000	7	33	CC
Long Corona	4000	6⅛	42	CC
Grand Corona	5000	5⅝	46	CC

A carefully controlled series of events leads to the production of a Davidoff cigar. This celebrated brand, first created in Cuba in 1946, requires tobaccos which have been aged up to four years and only the finest leaves are used in a factory which is solely dedicated to the creation of this brand. Four different blends are used to create the five different series: the large-sized, but mild and light Anniversarios; the mild, delicate and aromatic Nos. 1-2-3, Tubos and Ambassadrice; the fuller-bodied, but still mild "Thousand" series; and the fullest-bodied Grand Cru and Special ranges, which share the same blend.

To celebrate the 10th anniversary of its flagship U.S. store at 535 Madison Avenue in New York, Davidoff produced a limited-edition "535" cigar in late 1997. Only 10,000 of the 6 x 50-ring cigars were made, offering a medium-bodied taste in special wooden boxes of 10. If you've found them, you're looking at a collector's item!

DA VINCI
Handmade in Danli, Honduras.

Wrapper: Ecuador   *Binder: Dominican Republic*
Filler: Dominican Republic, Honduras, Nicaragua

HANDMADE CIGARS: BRAND LISTINGS

Shape	Name	Lgth	Ring	Wrapper
Pyramid	Renaissance	7	54	CC
Giant	Leonardo	8½	52	CC
Churchill	Ginerva de Benci	7	48	CC
Toro	Monalisa	6	50	CC
Long Corona	Cecilia Gallerani	6	43	CC
Robusto	Madonna	5	50	CC

These masterpieces seek to reach the level of achievement of its namesake, the brilliant Italian artist and scientist who lived from 1452-1519. A full line of personal and smoking accessories is topped by the Connecticut Shade-seed wrapped cigar line, each of which offers a mild-to-medium body. The all-cedar boxes each feature a different Da Vinci painting (except for the Renaissance model), including a notebook self-portrait for the Leonardo model. Besides the boxes of 25, Da Vincis are also available in handy four-packs.

DA VINCI
Handmade in Esteli, Nicaragua.

Wrapper: Ecuador   Binder: Nicaragua   Filler: Dom. Rep., Nicaragua

Shape	Name	Lgth	Ring	Wrapper
Pyramid	Figurado	7	54	CC
Giant	Maestro	8½	52	CC
Churchill	Mezzanote	7	48	CC
Toro	Dolce Vita	6	50	CC
Long Corona	Bambina	6	43	CC
Robusto	Quadro	5	50	CC

New in 1997, this second Da Vinci line offers a medium body and is offered in boxes of 25 or in packages of four for cigar lovers who need their masterpieces with them on the go!

HANDMADE CIGARS: BRAND LISTINGS

DAMN GOOD DOMINICANS
Handmade in Santo Domingo, Dominican Republic.

Wrapper: Indonesia   *Binder: Dom. Rep.*   *Filler: Dom. Rep.*

Shape	Name	Lgth	Ring	Wrapper
	Gold Label:			
Toro	Toro	6	50	CM
Grand Corona	Double Corona	6½	46	CM
Churchill	Churchill	7	48	CM
	Silver Label:			
Toro	Toro	6	50	CM
Grand Corona	Double Corona	6½	46	CM
Churchill	Churchill	7	48	CM

This series is medium in body and is offered in bundles of 24.

DEMARCO
Handmade in Esteli, Nicaragua.

Wrapper: Nicaragua   *Binder: Indonesia*   *Filler: Nicaragua*

Shape	Name	Lgth	Ring	Wrapper
Churchill	Churchill	7	48	Ma
Corona	Corona	5½	43	Ma
Lonsdale	Lonsdale	7	44	Ma
Robusto	Robusto	4¾	52	Ma
Short Panatela	Short Panatela	5½	38	Ma
Toro	Toro	6	50	Ma

This is an all-maduro-wrapped line that offers a full-bodied flavor and aroma. Try it in boxes of 25.

HANDMADE CIGARS: BRAND LISTINGS

DE ORTEGA
Handmade in Tamboril, Dominican Republic.
Wrapper: Indonesia or USA/Connecticut

Binder: Dominican Republic   Filler: Dominican Republic

Shape	Name	Lgth	Ring	Wrapper
	Emperador de Ortega:			
Torpedo	Torpedo	6½	52	CC-CM
Double Corona	Churchill	7	50	CC-CM
Robusto	Robusto	5	50	CC-CM
Small Panatela	Panetela	5	30	CC
Toro	Hemingway	6½	48	CC-CM
	Reserva 21:			
Double Corona	Churchill	7	50	CC-CM
Torpedo	Torpedo	6½	52	CC-CM
Robusto	Robusto	5	50	CC-CM
Grand Corona	Corona	6	46	CC-CM
Toro	Hemingway	6½	48	CC-CM
Small Panatela	Panetela	5	30	CM
	Reserva 21 Lights:			
Panatela	Regular	6	36	CM

This brand group was introduced in 1997, offering a variety of flavors. The Emperador line is full-bodied, the Reserva 21 line is medium-bodied and the Lights style is mild in flavor. All are offered in boxes of 25.

DE SOL
Handmade, with short filler, in Santiago, Dominican Republic.
Wrapper: Indonesia   Binder: Dom. Rep.   Filler: Dom. Rep.

Shape	Name	Lgth	Ring	Wrapper
Double Corona	Churchill	7½	50	CM

Robusto	Robusto	5	50	CM

Introduced in 1998, this is a short-fill, mild brand from the respected Puros Don Rico, offered in bundles of 25.

DEFIANT
Handmade in Santiago, Dominican Republic.
Wrapper: Ecuador, Mexico   *Binder: Nicaragua*   *Filler: Honduras, Nicaragua*

Shape	Name	Lgth	Ring	Wrapper
Robusto	Robusto	4¾	50	CC-Ma
Long Corona	Corona	6	44	CC-Ma
Toro	Toro	6	50	CC-Ma
Double Corona	Presidente	7½	52	CC
Torpedo	Belicoso	6½	52	CC-Ma
Torpedo	Belicoso Fino	5	52	CC-Ma
Pyramid	Petit Bouquet	4	50	CC-Ma

This brand was introduced in 1996 and offers a smooth, medium-bodied taste. Now produced in the Dominican Republic (originally in Honduras), it is presented in boxes of 25 cigars. The new maduro-wrapped line utilizes a Mexican wrapper leaf.

DEL VALLE
Handmade in Danli, Honduras.
Wrapper: Ecuador   *Binder: Nicaragua*   *Filler: Costa Rica, Honduras*

Shape	Name	Lgth	Ring	Wrapper
Petit Corona	Corona	5	44	CC
Robusto	Robusto	5	50	CC
Double Corona	Churchill	7	49	CC
Torpedo	Torpedo	6	52	CC
Giant	Presidente	8	50	CC

HANDMADE CIGARS: BRAND LISTINGS

Introduced in 1996, this is a medium-to-full-bodied cigar with a blend of four nations in the blend. It is presented in individual cellophane sleeves in boxes of 25.

DIAMOND CROWN
Handmade in Santiago, Dominican Republic.

Wrapper: USA/Connecticut   *Binder: Dom. Rep.*   *Filler: Dom. Rep.*

Shape	Name	Lgth	Ring	Wrapper
Giant	No. 1	8½	54	CC
Double Corona	No. 2	7½	54	CC
Toro	No. 3	6½	54	CC
Robusto	No. 4	5½	54	CC
Robusto	No. 5	4½	54	CC

This mild-bodied, all-54 ring series is an impossible-to-find, 1996-introduced product of the Tabacalera A. Fuente y Cia., made for the J.C. Newman Cigar Co. of Tampa, Florida. You can find these cigars in elegantly-appointed boxes of 15.

DIANA SILVIUS
Handmade in Santiago, Dominican Republic.

Wrapper: USA/Connecticut   *Binder: Dom. Rep.*   *Filler: Dom. Rep.*

Shape	Name	Lgth	Ring	Wrapper
Double Corona	Diana Churchill	7	50	CC
Robusto	Diana Robusto	4⅞	52	CC
Churchill	Diana 2000	6¾	46	CC
Lonsdale	Diana Corona	6½	42	CC

Introduced in 1990, this is a superb smoke which is medium in body and rich in flavor. Diana Silvius cigars strike a subtle balance between taste and aroma. The blend of four filler tobaccos, predominantly Cuban-seed leaves grown in the Dominican Republic, produces a smooth finish that leaves a hint of sweetness on the palate. Every one of these cigars is handmade by the master rollers of Tabacalera A. Fuente y Cia.

HANDMADE CIGARS: BRAND LISTINGS

DIEGO DE OCAMPO
Handmade in Santiago, Dominican Republic.

Wrapper: Indonesia   *Binder: Dom. Rep.*   *Filler: Dom. Rep.*

Shape	Name	Lgth	Ring	Wrapper
Corona	Corona	5½	43	CM
Robusto	Robusto	5	50	CM
Lonsdale	Lonsdale	6½	43	CM
Toro	Toro	6	50	CM
Double Corona	Churchill	7½	50	CM

Introduced in 1997, Diego de Ocampo offers a medium-bodied taste, well-balanced between the delicate Indonesian wrapper and Dominican-grown binder and filler leaves. It is presented in boxes of 25.

DIEGO SILANG
Handmade in Manila, the Philippines.

Wrapper: Philippines   *Binder: Philippines*   *Filler: Philippines*

Shape	Name	Lgth	Ring	Wrapper
Double Corona	El Presidente	7½	52	CC
Churchill	Churchill	7	47	CC
Lonsdale	Diego Primo	7	44	CC
Corona	Corona	5½	44	CC
Robusto	Diego Quinto	5	52	CC
Short Panatela	Gabriela	5	35	CC

This brand, one of the latest in the long and storied history of cigar-making in the Philippines, debuted in 1996. All of the leaves are grown in the Ilocos Valley of the Philippines, with Sumatra seeds used for the wrappers and Cuban seeds for the binder and filler. The result is a mild-to-medium bodied smoke, packed in boxes of 25.

HANDMADE CIGARS: BRAND LISTINGS

DIGNITY
Handmade in Santiago, Dominican Republic.
Wrapper: USA/Connecticut   Binder: Dom. Rep.   *Filler: Dom. Rep.*

Shape	Name	Lgth	Ring	Wrapper
Corona	Corona	5½	44	CC
Toro	Toro	6	50	CC
Double Corona	Churchill	7	50	CC

Here is a medium-bodied, exceptionally smooth cigar with an elegant Connecticut wrapper, offered in bundles of 25.

DIMANTE NERO
Handmade in Santiago, Dominican Republic.
Wrapper: USA/Connecticut   Binder: Dom. Rep.   *Filler: Dom. Rep.*

Shape	Name	Lgth	Ring	Wrapper
Robusto	Robusto	5	50	CC
Corona	Petite Corona	5½	42	CC
Lonsdale	Corona	6¾	44	CC
Long Corona	Lonsdale	6¼	44	CC
Churchill	Churchill	7	48	CC

Introduced in 1997, the "Black Diamond" is a mild-bodied cigar which is dipped in white wine to add a special touch of flavor. It is offered in all-cedar boxes of 25.

DISCOVER 1492
Handmade in Miami, Florida, USA.
Wrapper: Ecuador   Binder: Dom. Rep.   *Filler: Colombia, Dom. Rep., Honduras*

Shape	Name	Lgth	Ring	Wrapper
Pyramid	Pyramid	7¼	54	CC
Torpedo	Torpedo	6½	54	CC
Double Corona	Double Corona	7¾	50	CC

HANDMADE CIGARS: BRAND LISTINGS

Churchill	Churchill	7	48	CC
Toro	Toro	6	50	CC
Toro	Corona	6	48	CC
Robusto	Robusto	5	50	CC

This salute to Columbus was introduced in 1997 and is made in Little Havana in Miami, Florida. It offers a mild-to-medium body and is available in boxes or bundles of 25.

DIVINO
Handmade in Santiago, Dominican Republic.

Wrapper: Indonesia   *Binder: Dom. Rep.*   *Filler: Dom. Rep.*

Shape	Name	Lgth	Ring	Wrapper
Robusto	No. 552	5	52	CM
Toro	No. 652	6	52	CM
Double Corona	No. 752	7	52	CM

There is no doubt when you have a Divino. This is the only brand which offers a heat-sensitive label that reacts to the heat produced by the cigar between 90-120 degrees (F), going from black through the color spectrum and back to black when the internal temperature reaches more than 120 degrees. This medium-bodied brand thus monitors your intervals between puffs and drives your friends crazy as they try to figure out why you are holding a rainbow in your hand! Divino is available in boxes of 25.

DOLCE VITA
Handmade in Danli, Honduras.

Wrapper: Indonesia   *Binder: Honduras*   *Filler: Honduras, Nicaragua*

Shape	Name	Lgth	Ring	Wrapper
Churchill	Sweet Churchill	7	48	CM
Lonsdale	Sweet Lonsdale	7	44	CM
Robusto	Sweet Robusto	5	50	CM

HANDMADE CIGARS: BRAND LISTINGS

Toro	Sweet Toro	6	50	CM

Introduced in 1997, this is a sweetened cigar to celebrate the "sweet life" ("dolce vita" in Italian). It is well constructed and elegantly presented in varnished, 5x5-packed boxes of 25.

DOMINGOLD
Handmade in Santiago, Dominican Republic.
Wrapper: Cameroon   Binder: USA/Connecticut   Filler: Brazil, Dom. Rep.

Shape	Name	Lgth	Ring	Wrapper
Toro	Toro	6	50	CC
Long Corona	Lonsdale	6¼	42	CC
Robusto	Robusto	5	50	CC
Corona	Corona	5½	42	CC
Double Corona	Churchill	7	50	CC

These bundles of 20 cigars are seconds of one of the finest cigar factories in the Dominican Republic. You'll be hard-pressed to tell the difference between these medium-strength cigars and their more-famous siblings.

DOMINGUEZ
Handmade in Navarette, Dominican Republic.
Wrapper: Cameroon   Binder: Dom. Rep.   Filler: Dom. Rep.

Shape	Name	Lgth	Ring	Wrapper
Double Corona	Double Corona	7½	50	CM
Robusto	Robusto	4½	50	CM
Long Corona	Cetros	6	44	CM
Corona	Petit Cetros	5½	42	CM
Pyramid	Pyramid	6	54	CM
Long Panatela	Long Panatela	7½	38	CM

HANDMADE CIGARS: BRAND LISTINGS

Here is a 1997-introduced brand, offering a full-bodied flavor from Manolo
Dominguez, the maker of Caonabo cigars. It features a Dominican-grown Olor
binder and Piloto Cubano-seed filler. It is presented in individual cellophane
sleeves in boxes or bundles of 25.

DOMINICAN CHOICE
Handmade in Santiago, Dominican Republic.
Wrapper: USA/Connecticut   Binder: Dom. Rep.   Filler: Dom. Rep.

Shape	Name	Lgth	Ring	Wrapper
Torpedo	Torpedeo	6¼	52	CC

This is a medium-bodied brand, offered in one shape. Offered only in limited
distribution, it is available in boxes of 25.

DOMINICAN DELICIAS
Handmade in Santiago, Dominican Republic.
Wrapper: Indonesia   Binder: Dominican Republic
Filler: Dom. Rep., Honduras, Indonesia, Nicaragua

Shape	Name	Lgth	Ring	Wrapper
Robusto	Selection 701	5	50	CM
Double Corona	Selection 702	7¼	50	CM
Lonsdale	Selection 703	6½	42	CM
Long Corona	Selection 704	6	42	CM
Corona	Selection 705	5½	42	CM
Toro	Selection 706	6	50	CM

Sometimes also identified as "Dominican Escudo," this is a medium-to-full-
bodied cigar offered in bundles of 10 or boxes of 25.

DOMINICAN ELITES
Handmade in Tamboril, Dominican Republic.
Wrapper: Indonesia   Binder: Dom. Rep.   Filler: Dom. Rep.

Dominican

Elites

e•lite, i•lēt´, a•lēt´, *n.* {FR. lit. elected or select.} Those who are choice or select; the best; a superior cigar made by skilled craftsmen from aged Cuban seed and Dominican tobacco with an aged Sumatran wrapper.

HANDMADE CIGARS: BRAND LISTINGS

Shape	Name	Lgth	Ring	Wrapper
Robusto	Robusto	5½	50	CM
Lonsdale	Lonsdale	6½	42	CM-Stripe
Churchill	Churchill	7	47	CM
Double Corona	President	7½	50	CM
Torpedo	Torpedo	6	54	CM

These elegant cigars offer medium strength in flavor from leaves aged for three or more years, including a Sumatran-grown wrapper. The "Barber Pole"-wrapped Lonsdale shape incorporates a genuine Connecticut wrapper with the Sumatra wrapper. Introduced in 1997, this line is presented in all-cedar chest-style boxes, with each cigar protected in an individual cellophane sleeve.

DOMINICAN ESTATES
Handmade in the Dominican Republic.
Wrapper: USA/Connecticut   Binder: Mexico   Filler: Dom. Rep.

Shape	Name	Lgth	Ring	Wrapper
Toro	Corona Gorda	6	50	CC
Double Corona	Double Corona	7	50	CC
Corona	Full Corona	5½	43	CC
Lonsdale	Lonsdale	6½	43	CC
Robusto	Robusto	4½	50	CC

These cigars are mild to the taste, thanks to their Connecticut wrappers, and very well constructed for an easy draw.

DOMINICAN ORIGINAL
Handmade in Santiago, Dominican Republic.
Wrapper: USA/Connecticut   Binder: Dom. Rep.   Filler: Dom. Rep.

Shape	Name	Lgth	Ring	Wrapper
Long Corona	Cetros	6	44	CC
Churchill	Churchill	6⅞	46	CC-Ma

HANDMADE CIGARS: BRAND LISTINGS

Giant	Fat Tub	10	66	CC-Ma
Robusto	Gorilla	5	66	CC-Ma
Giant	King Kong	8½	52	CC-Ma
Small Panatela	Miniatures	4¼	32	CC
Double Corona	Monster	7	60	CC-Ma
Lonsdale	No. 1	6¾	43	CC-Ma
Corona	No. 2	5¾	43	CC-Ma
Long Panatela	Palma Fina	7	37	CC-Ma
Pyramid	Piramide	6½	56	CC-Ma
Double Corona	Presidente	7½	50	CC-Ma
Robusto	Robusto	4½	50	CC-Ma
Toro	Toro	6	50	CC-Ma
Torpedo	Torpedo	7	50	CC-Ma

Talk about sizes! Here is the brand for the lover of unusual, especially large sizes. The Connecticut wrapper and Dominican filler give these cigars a mild taste, and they are offered in bundle packs.

DOMINICAN PREMIUM
Handmade in Santiago, Dominican Republic.
Wrapper: Ecuador or USA/Connecticut

Binder: Mexico   *Filler: Dominican Republic*

Shape	Name	Lgth	Ring	Wrapper
Giant	Presidente	8	50	CC
Double Corona	El Grande	7	60	CC
Double Corona	Churchill	7	49	CC
Toro	Regulares	6	50	CC
Lonsdale	No. 1	6¾	43	CC
Panatela	No. 3	6¾	38	CC

HANDMADE CIGARS: BRAND LISTINGS

Corona	No. 4	5½	43	CC
Robusto	Rothschilds	5	50	CC
Panatela	Super Fino	6	35	CC

Take your choice of a Connecticut or a Sumatra-seed, Ecuadorian-grown wrapper in this medium-bodied blend. Aged for six months, they are offered in bundles of 25.

DOMINICAN SANDWICHES
Handmade, with mixed filler, in Santiago, Dominican Republic.

Wrapper: Indonesia   Binder: Dom. Rep.   Filler: Dom. Rep.

Shape	Name	Lgth	Ring	Wrapper
Robusto	Robusto	5	50	CM
Churchill	Churchill	7	48	CM
Toro	Toro	6	48	CM
Torpedo	Torpedo	6	52	CM
Long Corona	Corona	6	44	CM

Light one of these up with a beer and a submarine sandwich and you're ready to go! This is a modestly-priced bundled brand, with a mixed filler of long and short pieces cradled by the Dominican-grown binder in the "sandwich" style. It is medium-bodied and offered in bundles of 25.

DOMINICAN SEGUNDOS
Handmade in Santiago, Dominican Republic.

Wrapper: USA/Connecticut   Binder: Mexico   Filler: Dom. Rep.

Shape	Name	Lgth	Ring	Wrapper
Toro	Toro	6	50	CC
Robusto	Wavell	5	50	CC
Lonsdale	No. 1	6¾	44	CC
Corona	No. 4	5½	43	CC

HANDMADE CIGARS: BRAND LISTINGS

These are medium-bodied cigars, mostly seconds of well-known and respected brands. They are offered in boxes of 25.

DOMINICAN SELECTION
Handmade in Santiago, Dominican Republic.

Wrapper: Ecuador, USA/Connecticut   *Binder: Dom. Rep.*   *Filler: Dom. Rep.*

Shape	Name	Lgth	Ring	Wrapper
Giant	Presidente	8	50	CC-CM
Double Corona	El Grande	7	60	CC-CM
Double Corona	Churchill	7	49	CC-CM
Toro	Regulares	6	50	CC-CM
Lonsdale	No. 1	6¾	43	CC-CM
Panatela	No. 3	6¾	38	CC-CM
Corona	No. 4	5½	43	CC-CM
Robusto	Rothschilds	5	50	CC-CM
Panatela	Super Fino	6	35	CC-CM

If you're looking for excellent value in a beautifully-made cigar, this is your brand! It features a choice of either a genuine Connecticut wrapper or an Ecuadorian-grown, Sumatra-seed wrapper and a medium-bodied flavor, offered in bundles of 25 cigars each.

DOMINICANA DELIGHTS
Handmade, with short filler, in the Dominican Republic.

Wrapper: Indonesia   *Binder: Dom. Rep.*   *Filler: Dom. Rep.*

Shape	Name	Lgth	Ring	Wrapper
Panatela		5½	38	CC

This is a mild, flavored brand, using short fillers. You can try Anisette, chocolate, orange, rum, strawberry and vanilla, in boxes of 25.

HANDMADE CIGARS: BRAND LISTINGS

DOMINION PREMIUM
Handmade in Santiago, Dominican Republic.
Wrapper: Dom. Rep.   Binder: Dom. Rep.   Filler: Dom. Rep.

Shape	Name	Lgth	Ring	Wrapper
Double Corona	Churchill	7	50	CM
Toro	Short Churchill	6	50	CM
Pyramid	Pyramid	6	52	CM-Ma
Long Corona	Double Corona	6	44	CM
Robusto	Robusto	5	50	CM-Ma
Perfecto	Perfecto	5	44	Ma

Introduced in 1997, this is a mild brand in the natural-shade wrapper, but medium-bodied in the maduro-wrapped version. It is available in cedar boxes of 25 cigars each.

DOMINIQUE
Handmade in Santiago, Dominican Republic.
Wrapper: USA/Connecticut   Binder: Dom. Rep.   Filler: Dom. Rep.

Shape	Name	Lgth	Ring	Wrapper
Giant	No. 52	8½	52	CI-CC-Ma
Lonsdale	No. 74	7	43	CI-CC-Ma
Grand Corona	Madison	6	46	CI-CC-Ma
Corona	Nacionales	5½	42	CC
Double Corona	Pierce	6⅞	49	CI-CC-Ma
Robusto	Toro	4½	50	CC-Ma

These bundles are made by the famous Tabacalera A. Fuente in the Dominican Republic. They of high quality and moderate pricing, offering a mild flavor in packages of 25 cigars each.

HANDMADE CIGARS: BRAND LISTINGS

THE DON
Handmade in Esteli, Nicaragua and Belize City, Belize.

Wrapper: Nicaragua   Binder: Nicaragua   Filler: Nicaragua

Shape	Name	Lgth	Ring	Wrapper
Corona	Corona	5½	42	CM
Robusto	Robusto	4½	50	CM

Introduced in 1998, this is a medium-bodied brand, offered in a cedar box of 25 cigars. It is rolled in Esteli and then finished in Belize City before shipping.

DON ALBERTO
Handmade in Licey, Dominican Republic.

CLASSICO DOMINICAN SERIES:

Wrapper: Dom. Rep.   Binder: Dom. Rep.   Filler: Dom. Rep.

ORO DE HABANA SERIES:

Wrapper: USA/Connecticut   Binder: Dom. Rep.   Filler: Dom. Rep.

ROYAL SERIES:

Wrapper: Dominican Republic and USA/Connecticut

Binder: Dominican Republic   Filler: Dominican Republic

SUPERIOR HABANA:

Wrapper: USA/Connecticut   Binder: Dom. Rep.   Filler: Dom. Rep.

Shape	Name	Lgth	Ring	Wrapper
	Superior Habana series:			
Pyramid	Piramid	6½	53	CC
Robusto	Robusto	5	50	CC
Giant	Churchill	8	48	CC
Grand Corona	Double Corona	6½	46	CC
Lonsdale	Corona	7	44	CC
Long Panatela	Panatela	7½	38	CC

HANDMADE CIGARS: BRAND LISTINGS

Small Panetela	Reina	5	30	CC
	Oro de Habana series:			
Pyramid	Piramid	6½	53	CC
Robusto	Robusto	5	50	CC
Giant	Churchill	8	48	CC
Grand Corona	Double Corona	6½	46	CC
Lonsdale	Corona	7	44	CC
	Classico Dominican series:			
Pyramid	Piramid	6½	53	Ma
Robusto	Robusto	5	50	Ma
Giant	Churchill	8	48	Ma
Grand Corona	Double Corona	6½	46	Ma
Lonsdale	Corona	7	44	Ma
Long Panetela	Panatela	7½	38	Ma
Small Panatela	Reina	5	30	Ma
	Royal series:			
Pyramid	Piramid	6½	53	Stripe
Giant	Presidential	8	48	Stripe
Lonsdale	Corona	7	44	Stripe
Robusto	Robusto	5	50	Stripe

Created in 1996, here is a series offering different blends and tastes, all within the mild-to-medium range. All feature binder and filler tobaccos from the Dominican Republic, with genuine Connecticut wrappers used on the Oro de Havana (mild-to-medium-bodied) and Superior Habana (medium bodied) series. The Royal series offers the "barber pole" double wrapper style, utilizing Connecticut and Dominican leaves for a medium-bodied taste. The Classico Dominican uses a Dominican-grown maduro wrapper and a mild-bodied flavor.

HANDMADE CIGARS: BRAND LISTINGS

DON ALFONSO
Handmade in the Dominican Republic.

Wrapper: USA/Connecticut   *Binder: Dom. Rep.*   *Filler: Dom. Rep.*

Shape	Name	Lgth	Ring	Wrapper
Double Corona	Churchill	7½	49	CC
Grand Corona	Grande Corona	6	46	CC
Robusto	Robusto	5	50	CC
Toro	Toro	6½	52	CC

Introduced in 1998, this is a special offer from G.A. Andron & Co., offering a medium-bodied taste in all-cedar boxes of 25.

DON ANGELO
Handmade in Vera Cruz, Mexico.

Wrapper: Mexico   *Binder: Mexico*   *Filler: Mexico*

Shape	Name	Lgth	Ring	Wrapper
Double Corona	Churchill	7	50	CM-Ma
Robusto	Robusto	5	50	CM-Ma
Lonsdale	Toro	6½	42	CM-Ma

Here is an all-Mexican, mild but slightly sweet brand which was introduced in 1998. It is offered in boxes of 25.

DON ANTONIO
Handmade in Dingelstadt, Germany.

Wrapper: USA/Connecticut   *Binder: Honduras*   *Filler: Brazil, Honduras, Indonesia*

Shape	Name		Lgth	Ring	Wrapper
Double Corona	Churchill	*(tube available)*	6⅞	49	CC
Lonsdale	Lonsdale	*(tube available)*	6¼	44	CC
Perfecto	Perfecto Grande		6¾	45	CC
Panatela	Panatela Larga		6	38	CC

HANDMADE CIGARS: BRAND LISTINGS

Robusto	Robusto	(tube available)	5	50	CC
Corona Extra	Torpelito		4⅞	46	CC
Perfecto	Perfecto		5⅛	45	CC

Here is a three-country blend of tobaccos that produces a mild-bodied flavor in this 1997-introduced brand. Handmade with all long-filler leaves, it is presented in individual cellophane sleeves in wood boxes of 20.

DON ANTONIO
Handmade in Dingelstadt, Germany.
Wrapper: Brazil, Indonesia   *Binder: Indonesia*
Filler: Brazil, Dominican Republic, Honduras, Indonesia

Shape	Name	Lgth	Ring	Wrapper
Slim Panatela	El Gusto (tubes available)	6⅛	33	CC-CM
Panatela	La Verdad (tubes available)	5½	35	CC-CM

Here is a rarity: a handmade, 100% tobacco, dry-cure cigar from Germany. Other shapes in the Don Antonio line are machine-produced, but these are made by hand and offer a mild to medium flavor depending on your choice of wrapper: mild Indonesian leaf grown in Sumatra, or the strong Brazilian leaf from the Bahia region.

DON ANTONIO PELLEGRINO RESERVA PRECIADA
Handmade in Santiago, Dominican Republic.
Wrapper: Ecuador   *Binder: Dom. Rep.*   *Filler: Dom. Rep.*

Shape	Name	Lgth	Ring	Wrapper
Robusto		5	50	CC-CM
Corona		5½	42	CC-CM
Long Corona		6	42	CC-CM
Long Corona		6	44	CC-CM
Toro		6	50	CC-CM
Lonsdale		6½	42	CC-CM

Grand Corona		6½	46	CC-CM
Torpedo		6½	52	CC-CM
Pyramid		6½	52	CC-CM
Churchill		6¾	46	CC-CM
Churchill		7	48	CC-CM
Double Corona		7	50	CC-CM
Churchill		7½	48	CC-CM
Double Corona		7½	50	CC-CM

Although it has no shape names, this is a medium-bodied blend with a choice of Connecticut-seed or Sumatra-seed wrappers. Introduced in 1997, it is offered in boxes or bundles of 25.

DON ANTONIO RESERVA PRECIADA
Handmade in Villa Gonzalez, Dominican Republic.
Wrapper: Ecuador or USA/Connecticut
Binder: Dominican Republic   *Filler: Dominican Republic, Indonesia*

Shape	Name	Lgth	Ring	Wrapper
Perfecto		3¾	44	CC
Small Panatela		5	30	CC
Short Panatela		5	38	CC
Robusto		5	50	CC
Long Corona		6	44	CC
Toro		6	50	CC
Lonsdale		6½	42	CC
Lonsdale		6½	44	CC
Grand Corona		6½	46	CC
Torpedo		6½	52	CC
Pyramid		6½	52	CC

Long Panatela		7	38	CC
Churchill		7	48	CC
Double Corona		7½	50	CC

Although it has no shape names, this is a mild-bodied blend with a Connecticut-seed wrapper. It is offered in boxes or bundles of 25.

DON ARMANDO
Handmade in Tamboril, Dominican Republic.

Wrapper: USA/Connecticut   Binder: Dom. Rep.   Filler: Dom. Rep.

Shape	Name	Lgth	Ring	Wrapper
	Premium Series:			
Double Corona	Churchill	7	50	CC
Long Panatela	Mirage	7	38	Stripe
Lonsdale	Lonsdale	6¾	44	CC
Robusto	Toros	5	50	CC
Corona Extra	Corona Extra	5½	44	CC
Small Panatela	Illusion	5	30	CC
	Classic Series:			
Double Corona	Churchill	7	50	CM
Lonsdale	Lonsdale	6¾	44	CM
Robusto	Robusto	5	50	CM
Corona	Corona Extra	5½	44	CM

This version of Don Armando debuted in the U.S. in 1995, offering a mild-to-medium-bodied flavor and two-year aging. It is presented in individual cellophane sleeves and packed in boxes of five and in all-cedar boxes of 25. Note the Mirage shape has a double wrapper of Connecticut and Sumatra leaves and the Illusion has a vanilla-flavored, sweet tip.

HANDMADE CIGARS: BRAND LISTINGS

DON ASA
Handmade in Danli, Honduras.

Wrapper: Indonesia   Binder: Mexico   Filler: Dom. Rep., Mexico

Shape	Name	Lgth	Ring	Wrapper
Double Corona	Churchill	7½	50	CM
Lonsdale	Lonsdale	6½	44	CM
Robusto	Robusto	5	50	CM

This brand has been around — more or less — since 1963. In its present incarnation, it offers a medium-to-full-bodied taste. You can find it in all-wooden boxes of 25.

DON AUGUSTO
Handmade in Tamboril, Dominican Republic.

Wrapper: Indonesia or USA/Connecticut   Binder: Dom. Rep.   Filler: Dom. Rep.

Shape	Name	Lgth	Ring	Wrapper
Corona	Petit Corona	5½	42	CC
Robusto	Robusto	5	50	CC-CM
Toro	Toro	6½	50	CC-CM
Grand Corona	Corona Gorda	6	46	CC-CM
Giant	Churchill	8	50	CC-CM
Robusto	Colossus Jr.	4¾	60	CC-CM
Double Corona	Double Corona	7½	52	CC-CM
Lonsdale	Corona	6½	44	CC
Giant	Colossus	9½	60	CC-CM

Introduced in 1997, this brand now offers two wrapper shades for your consideration: a U.S.-grown Connecticut wrapper and a genuine Sumatra wrapper. In either case, this is a mild-to-medium-bodied cigar, offered in boxes of 25. Eight shapes are available with a Sumatra wrapper, packaged in bundles of 25.

HANDMADE CIGARS: BRAND LISTINGS

DON AUGUSTO SABOR
Handmade, with mixed filler, in Santiago, Dominican Republic.
Wrapper: USA/Connecticut   *Binder: Dom. Rep.*   *Filler: Dom. Rep.*

Shape	Name	Lgth	Ring	Wrapper
Short Panatela	Junior	5	34	CC
Panatela	Panatela	6	36	CC
Corona	Petit Corona	5½	42	CC

This is a flavored cigar, introduced in 1998. It is offered with vanilla flavoring in bundles of 25.

DON BARCO
Handmade in Santiago, Dominican Republic.
Wrapper: Indonesia   *Binder: Dom. Rep.*   *Filler: Dom. Rep.*

Shape	Name	Lgth	Ring	Wrapper
Double Corona	Galeon	7¾	50	CC
Toro	Admiral	6	50	CC
Robusto	Capitan	5	50	CC
Churchill	Marinero	6¾	46	CC

Introduced in 1996, this is a medium-bodied cigar from the Dominican Republic, offered in boxes of 20 cigars each.

DON BARTOLO
Handmade in Manila, the Philippines.
Wrapper: Indonesia   *Binder: Philippines*   *Filler: Philippines*

Shape	Name	Lgth	Ring	Wrapper
	Gold Series:			
Corona	Corona	5½	44	CC
Robusto	Robusto	5	52	CC
Churchill	Churchill	7	47	CC

HANDMADE CIGARS: BRAND LISTINGS

Double Corona	Double Corona	7	52	CC
	Miguelon Series:			
Corona	Corona	5½	44	CC
Robusto	Robusto	5	52	CC
Churchill	Churchill	7	47	CC
Double Corona	Double Corona	7	52	CC

Philippine tobacco is the core of the Miguelon series, first offered in 1996. This group has Sumatran wrappers on all sizes except for the Corona, which features a Javan wrapper. The result is a mild to medium-bodied smoke, offered in boxes of 25. The Gold Series is new for 1998 and is also mild-to-medium in body with a slightly different flavor.

DON CARLOS
Handmade in Santiago, Dominican Republic.

Wrapper: Cameroon *Binder: Dom. Rep.* *Filler: Dom. Rep.*

Shape	Name	Lgth	Ring	Wrapper
Torpedo	No. 2	6	55	CM
Corona	No. 3	5½	44	CM
Petit Corona	No. 4	5⅛	43	CM
Robusto	Robusto	5¼	50	CM
Robusto	Double Robusto	5¾	52	CM
Toro	Presidente	6½	50	CM

Here is the result of careful planning and brilliant execution in the making of a new brand from the workshops of Tabacalera A. Fuente. The flawless construction and smooth taste of this medium-bodied cigar make it a rewarding experience from the beginning.

DON CARLOS
Handmade in Danli, Honduras.

Wrapper: Ecuador *Binder: Nicaragua* *Filler: Mexico, Nicaragua*

- 205 -

HANDMADE CIGARS: BRAND LISTINGS

Shape	Name	Lgth	Ring	Wrapper
Double Corona	Churchill	7	49	CC
Robusto	Rothchild	5	50	CC
Corona	Corona	5½	42	CC
Pyramid	Pyramid	5½	52	CC
Pyramid	Super Pyramid	7½	64	CC

Introduced in 1997, this brand has a mild body and a blend that features a
Sumatra-seed wrapper grown in Ecuador. It is offered in boxes of 25.

DON CASIMIRO COLLECTION
Handmade in Tampa, Florida, USA.
Wrapper: Ecuador or Indonesia   Binder: Dom. Rep.   Filler: Dom. Rep., Indonesia

Shape	Name	Lgth	Ring	Wrapper
Robusto	Robusto	5	50	CC-CM
Toro	Robusto Largo	6	50	CC-CM
Corona	Coronita	5½	42	CC-CM
Long Panatela	Lancero	7	38	CC-CM
Double Corona	Churchill	7	50	CC-CM
Torpedo	Torpedo	5½	54	CC-CM

Introduced in 1998, this is a mild-bodied brand available in a choice of Sumatra
or Ecuador-grown, Connecticut-seed wrappers. Named for the founder of a
Tampa restaurant in 1905 (!), you can find it in packs of 5 or boxes of 25.

DON CISSO
Handmade, with short filler, in Santiago, Dominican Republic.
Wrapper: Indonesia   Binder: Indonesia   Filler: Dom. Rep.

Shape	Name	Lgth	Ring	Wrapper
Long Corona	No. 1	6	44	CM
Corona	No. 2	5½	42	CM

HANDMADE CIGARS: BRAND LISTINGS

This is a medium-bodied brand made with short filler tobaccos in the Dominican Republic. It is offered in packs of 25.

DON CLAUDIO
Handmade in Tamboril, Dominican Republic.

Wrapper: USA/Connecticut   *Binder: Dom. Rep.*   *Filler: Dom. Rep.*

Shape	Name	Lgth	Ring	Wrapper
	Green Label and Black Label Vintage Reserve:			
Robusto	Robusto	5	50	CC
Lonsdale	Lonsdale	6¼	44	CC
Double Corona	Churchill	7½	50	CC
	Red Label XO:			
Robusto	Robusto Grande	5½	50	CC
Grand Corona	Lonsdale Exquisite	6	46	CC

Introduced in 1997, this is a medium-bodied brand available in three styles. The Green Label group is aged for six months, the Black Label Vintage Reserve is aged for 18 months and the Red Label is aged up to three years. It is available in boxes of 25.

DON CORLEONE
Handmade in Danli, Honduras.

Wrapper: Ecuador   *Binder: Honduras*   *Filler: Dom. Rep., Honduras*

Shape	Name	Lgth	Ring	Wrapper
Torpedo	Torpedo	7	54	CC
Giant	Presidente	8	50	CC
Double Corona	Churchill	6⅞	49	CC
Toro	Toro	6	50	CC
Robusto	Robusto	5	50	CC
Long Corona	Cetro	6¼	44	CC

HANDMADE CIGARS: BRAND LISTINGS

A cigar you can't refuse? Why not! It's a mild cigar with a rich flavor that salutes the famous Mario Puzo character from his novel *The Godfather*. It is offered in boxes of 25.

DON DIEGO
Handmade in La Romana, Dominican Republic.
Wrapper: USA/Connecticut or Mexico

Binder: Dom. Rep.   Filler: Brazil, Dom. Rep.

Shape	Name		Lgth	Ring	Wrapper
Small Panatela	Babies		5	33	CM
Toro	Coronas Bravas		6½	48	CC-Ma
Petit Corona	Coronas Major	(tubed)	5	42	CC
Corona	Coronas		5⅝	42	DC-CC
Toro	Grandes		6	50	CC-Ma
Panatela	Grecos		6½	38	CC
Lonsdale	Lonsdales		6⅝	42	DC-CC
Churchill	Monarchs	(tubed)	7¼	46	CC
Petit Corona	Petit Coronas		5⅛	42	DC-CC
Panatela	Royal Palms	(tubed)	6⅛	36	CC
Perfecto	Figurado		5¾	48	CC
Robusto	Robusto		4½	50	CC-Ma
Torpedo	Torpedo		6	50	CC-Ma
Toro	Toro	(tubed)	6	50	CC
	Machine-made, with short filler:				
Cigarillo	Preludes		4	28	CC

Well-known for its mild taste, Don Diego cigars have earned a wide following, thanks to their consistency of construction, accessible strength and excellent value for the money. Fans of rarely-seen Candela wrappers on handmade cigars will find three major shapes available. This brand originated in 1964 in the Canary Islands, but production was moved to the Dominican Republic in 1982. Maduro-wrapped shapes, using Mexican leaves, were introduced in 1998 and offers a full-bodied taste.

HANDMADE CIGARS: BRAND LISTINGS

DON DIEGO PRIVADA SELECTION
Handmade in La Romana, Dominican Republic.

Wrapper: USA/Connecticut   Binder: Dom. Rep.   *Filler: Brazil, Dom. Rep.*

Shape	Name	Lgth	Ring	Wrapper
Lonsdale	Privada No. 1	6⅝	43	CC
Toro	Privada No. 2	6⅝	50	CC
Panatela	Privada No. 3	6½	38	CC
Corona	Privada No. 4	5⅝	42	CC

Introduced in 1998, this is a new version of the Don Diego brand with a mild body and a smooth flavor. Each cigar is wrapped in aromatic cedar and then packed in boxes of 25.

DON DOMINGUEZ
Handmade in Santiago, Dominican Republic

Wrapper: Indonesia   Binder: Dom. Rep.   *Filler: Dom. Rep.*

Shape	Name	Lgth	Ring	Wrapper
Double Corona	Churchill	7½	50	CC
Robusto	Robusto	5	50	CC
Corona	Corona Gorda	6	44	CC
Grand Corona	Lonsdale	6½	46	CC

The Don Dominguez "Signature Series" is a full-bodied, no-holds-barred cigar from the Dominican Republic. All of the leaves are of Cuban-seed origin and the brand is produced in limited quantities. The finished product is presented in all-cedar boxes of 25.

DON ESCOBAR
Handmade, with medium filler, in Manila, the Philippines.

Wrapper: Indonesia   Binder: Philippines   *Filler: Philippines*

Shape	Name	Lgth	Ring	Wrapper
Double Corona		7	52	CM

Churchill			7	47	CM
Robusto			5	52	CM
Petit Corona			5	44	CM
Pyramid			5	50	CM

This is a medium-filler, medium-bodied blend that features a Sumatra wrapper. It is offered in bundles of 25.

DON FELIPE
Handmade in Santiago, Dominican Republic.

Wrapper: USA/Connecticut   *Binder: Dom. Rep.*   *Filler: Dom. Rep.*

Shape	*Name*	*Lgth*	*Ring*	*Wrapper*
Corona	Corona	5¾	42	CC
Robusto	Robusto	5	50	CC
Churchill	Lonsdale	6¾	46	CC
Double Corona	Churchill	7	50	CC

Here is a mild-bodied brand available in either bundles or boxes of 25.

DON FIDENCIO
Handmade, with short filler, in Santiago, Dominican Republic.

Wrapper: Indonesia   *Binder: Dom. Rep.*   *Filler: Dom. Rep.*

Shape	*Name*	*Lgth*	*Ring*	*Wrapper*
Double Corona		7¼	50	CM
Toro		5¾	50	CM
Churchill		7¼	48	CM
Grand Corona		6¼	46	CM

Although this brand has no shape names, it is mild in body. It is offered in four sizes in bundles of 25.

HANDMADE CIGARS: BRAND LISTINGS

DON FRANCISCO
Handmade in San Andres Tuxtla, Mexico.

Wrapper: Indonesia or USA/Connecticut   *Binder:* Mexico   *Filler:* Mexico

Shape	Name	Lgth	Ring	Wrapper
Robusto	Robusto	5	50	CC
Double Corona	Churchill	7	50	CC
Lonsdale	Lonsdale	6½	42	CC

San Andres Tuxtla is the closest point on the Mexican peninsula to Cuba. So it's no wonder that Cuban-seed tobaccos power this full-bodied cigar, introduced in 1996 and offered in boxes of 25.

DON FRANCISCO RESERVE
Handmade in El Paraiso, Honduras.
Wrapper: Honduras or USA/Connecticut

Binder: Honduras   *Filler:* Ecuador, Honduras

Shape	Name	Lgth	Ring	Wrapper
Robusto	Robusto	5	50	CM-Ma
Double Corona	Churchill	7	50	CM-Ma
Lonsdale	Lonsdale	6½	42	CM-Ma

Here is a 1996-introduced brand, offering a medium-bodied flavor thanks to its blend of Honduran tobaccos with wrapper leaf from Honduras or Connecticut. Although in limited production, it offers a welcome aroma and mellow taste to those who are able to enjoy it.

DON GEOVANNI
Handmade in Santo Domingo, Dominican Republic.
Wrapper: Indonesia   *Binder:* Dom. Rep.   *Filler:* Dom. Rep.

Shape	Name	Lgth	Ring	Wrapper
Double Corona	Churchill I	7	50	CM
Torpedo	Torpedo	6	52	CM

Churchill	Churchill II	7	48	CM
Robusto	Robusto	5½	50	CM
Churchill	Corona Grande	7	46	CM
Grand Corona	Corona	6	46	CM
Lonsdale	Imperial	7	44	CM
Lonsdale	Lonsdale	6½	42	CM

Introduced in 1998, this brand offers a mild-to-medium-bodied taste. Both boxes of 25 and bundles of 25 are available. All shapes are also available with vanilla flavoring.

DON GUILLERMO
Handmade in Santiago, Dominican Republic.

Wrapper: USA/Connecticut   Binder: Dom. Rep.   Filler: Dom. Rep.

Shape	Name	Lgth	Ring	Wrapper
Churchill	No. I	6⅞	46	CC-CM-Ma
Robusto	Compa	5	50	CC-CM-Ma
Giant	Don Guillermo	8	50	CC-CM-Ma
Long Panatela	No. II	7	36	CC-CM-Ma
Long Corona	No. IV	6	44	CC-CM-Ma
Pyramid	Figurado	5½	48	CC-CM-Ma
Small Panatela	Guillermito	5	30	CC-CM-Ma
Torpedo	Torpedo	6½	54	CC-CM-Ma
Pyramid	Piramide	6½	52	CC
Robusto	No. VI	4	50	CC-CM-Ma
Small Panatela	Lady Pilar	5	30	CC

First offered in 1993, this is a mild-bodied cigar with its Connecticut and Indonesian wrapper shades and medium-to-full in maduro. Depth in the taste of the cigar is provided by the use of Cuban-seed tobaccos in the filler. The brand is offered with vanilla flavoring in the Guillermito size and chocolate in the Lady Pilar size.

DON JIVAN CLASSICO
Handmade in Santiago, Dominican Republic.

Wrapper: USA/Connecticut   *Binder: Dom. Rep.*   *Filler: Dom. Rep.*

Shape	Name	Lgth	Ring	Wrapper
Slim Panatela	Slim Panatela	5¼	30	CC
Long Corona	Corona	6	44	CC
Churchill	Grand Corona	6¾	46	CC
Robusto	Robusto	5½	50	CC
Double Corona	Double Corona	7½	52	CC
Petit Corona	Petit Corona	4	42	Ma
Robusto	Rothschild	4½	52	Ma

Inspired by Jivan Tabibian, the gregarious owner of famous Remi restaurant in Santa Monica, California, this is a 1996-introduced, medium-bodied smoke. Noteworthy for its label artwork by artist Milton Glazer, Don Jivan is offered without cellophane in all-cedar boxes of 25.

DON JOSE
Handmade in Danli, Honduras.

Wrapper: Honduras   *Binder: Honduras*   *Filler: Honduras*

Shape	Name	Lgth	Ring	Wrapper
Giant	El Grandee	8½	52	CC-Ma
Double Corona	San Marco	7	50	CC-Ma
Toro	Turbo	6	50	CC-Ma
Long Corona	Granada	6	43	CC-Ma
Robusto	Valrico	4½	50	CC-Ma

These Honduran handmades provide a rich taste in both a natural and maduro wrapper. The tobaccos are all grown in Honduras of Cuban-seed origin and are offered in bundles of 20 cigars each.

HANDMADE CIGARS: BRAND LISTINGS

DON JUAN
Handmade in Ocotal, Nicaragua.

Wrapper: Ecuador   Binder: Dom. Rep.   Filler: Dom. Rep., Nicaragua

Shape	Name	Lgth	Ring	Wrapper
Panatela	Lindas	5½	38	CM
Long Corona	Cetros	6	43	CM
Panatela	Palma Fina	6⅞	36	CM
Robusto	Robusto	5	50	CM
Lonsdale	No. 1	6⅝	44	CM
Toro	Matador	6	50	CM
Churchill	Churchill	7	48	CM
Giant	Presidente	8½	50	CM
Torpedo	Torpedo	6	52	CM
Perfecto	Perfecto No. 1	4¾	52	CM
Perfecto	Perfecto No. 2	4	51	CM

Introduced in 1992, Don Juan is a handmade cigar from Nicaragua. The filler is
Nicaraguan, with a Dominican Havana-seed binder and a Connecticut Shade
wrapper. Cigar connoisseurs consider this a medium-strength cigar.

DON JUAN PLATINUM
Handmade in Santiago, Dominican Republic.

Wrapper: USA/Connecticut   Binder: Dominican Republic
Filler: Dominican Republic, Honduras, Nicaragua

Shape	Name	Lgth	Ring	Wrapper
Long Corona	Cetro	6	43	CC
Robusto	Robusto	5	50	CC
Lonsdale	No. 1	6⅝	44	CC
Double Corona	Churchill	7	48	CC
Torpedo	Torpedo	6	52	CC

HANDMADE CIGARS: BRAND LISTINGS

Introduced in 1997, here is the work of Pedro Martin, who blended this medium-bodied masterpiece. You can find it in individual cellophane sleeves inside all-cedar boxes of 25.

DON JUAN URQUIJO
Handmade in Manila, the Philippines.

Wrapper: Ecuador   *Binder: Brazil, Dom. Rep.*   *Filler: Philippines*

Shape	Name	Lgth	Ring	Wrapper
Giant Corona	Churchill	7½	45	CC
Robusto	Robusto	5	50	CC
Corona	Corona	5½	42	CC
Short Panatela	Panatela	5	37	CC
Perfecto	Figurado	5	42	CC
Pyramid	Pyramid	6	50	CC

This product of the Philippines is mild-to-medium, but with plenty of character thanks to its double binder of Brazilian and Dominican leaves. You can enjoy them in slide-top cedar boxes of 25.

DON JULIAN
Handmade in Esteli, Nicaragua.

Wrapper: Ecuador, Indonesia, Mexico   *Binder: Nicaragua*   *Filler: Dom. Rep.*

Shape	Name	Lgth	Ring	Wrapper
Long Corona	Corona	6¼	44	CC-CM-Ma
Torpedo	Torpedo	6½	52	CC-CM-Ma
Robusto	Robusto	5	50	CC-CM-Ma
Double Corona	Churchill	7	50	CC-CM-Ma
Toro	Toro	6	52	CC-CM-Ma
Giant	Presidente	8	52	CC-CM-Ma

Made in Nicaragua, this brand offers a mild-to-medium bodied smoke with a choice of Ecuador-grown, Connecticut-seed, Indonesian or Mexican maduro wrappers in boxes of 25.

HANDMADE CIGARS: BRAND LISTINGS

DON JULIO

Handmade in Santiago, Domincan Republic.

Wrapper: USA/Connecticut   Binder: Dom. Rep.   Filler: Dom. Rep.

Shape	Name	Lgth	Ring	Wrapper
Lonsdale	Corona Deluxe	7	44	CC
Toro	Fabulosos	6	50	CC
Corona	Miramar	5¾	43	CC
Robusto	Private Stock No. 1	4½	50	CC
Giant	Supremos	8½	52	CC

Don Julio cigars are handmade, bundled cigars produced in the Dominican Republic. These cigars are mild-bodied, easy to draw, yet exceptionally flavorful. The composition of select Cuban-seed tobaccos took several months to develop, giving Don Julio its delicate taste. Enjoy them in bundles of 20.

DON LEO

Handmade in Villa Gonzalez, Dominican Republic.

Wrapper: Ecuador   Binder: Dom. Rep.   Filler: Dom. Rep.

Shape	Name	Lgth	Ring	Wrapper
Double Corona	Churchill	7½	50	CC
Lonsdale	Corona	6½	44	CC
Churchill	Double Corona	7	48	CC
Long Panatela	Panatela	7	36	CC
Corona	Petite Corona	5½	42	CC
Torpedo	Torpedo	6¾	52	CC
Giant	Presidente	8	52	CC
Toro	Robusto	6	50	CC
Robusto	Rothschild	4½	50	CC
Toro	Toro	6	52	CC

HANDMADE CIGARS: BRAND LISTINGS

Don Leo is a handmade, long-filler cigar introduced in 1995 from the Puros de Villa Gonzalez factory near Santiago. The blend of leaves from the Dominican and the Connecticut wrapper provide a mild body in boxes of 25 cigars.

DON LINO
BY LEON JIMENES
Handmade in Santiago, Dominican Republic.

Wrapper: USA/Connecticut   Binder: Dom. Rep.   Filler: Dom. Rep.

Shape	Name		Lgth	Ring	Wrapper
Double Corona	Churchill		7½	50	CC
Lonsdale	No. 1	(tube available)	6½	42	CC
Corona Extra	Toros		5½	46	CC
Robusto	Robusto		5½	50	CC
Torpedo	Belicoso		6¼	52	CC
Torpedo	Petit Belicoso		5	52	CC
Robusto	Rothschild		4½	50	CC

Don Lino is now made in the Dominican Republic, having been previously produced in Honduras in 1990 and later in Nicaragua. For 1998, this new blend is mild-bodied in taste and has consistent smooth flavors. It is available in boxes of 25, except for the tubed style of the No. 1, offered in 10s.

DON LINO ORO
Handmade in Santiago, Dominican Republic.

Wrapper: Dom. Rep.   Binder: Dom. Rep.   Filler: Dom. Rep.

Shape	Name	Lgth	Ring	Wrapper
Long Corona	Lonsdale	6	42	CM
Churchill	Churchill	6⅞	46	CM
Long Corona	Corona	6	44	CM
Robusto	Robusto	5	50	CM
Robusto	Rothchild	4½	50	CM

Torpedo	Torpedo	6	53	CM

Introduced in 1991, but now produced in the Dominican Republic, this is a full-bodied version of the Don Lino line with 100% Dominican leaf from Corojo seeds that originated in Cuba. You can enjoy these gems in boxes of 25, or in special packages of 5 for the Corona and Torpedo shapes.

DON MACHO
Handmade in Danli, Honduras.

Wrapper: Honduras *Binder: Honduras* *Filler: Honduras*

Shape	Name	Lgth	Ring	Wrapper
Double Corona	Presidente	7½	50	CM
Churchill	Churchill	7	48	CM
Lonsdale	No. 1	7	44	CM
Toro	Toro	6	50	CM
Robusto	Rothschild	5	50	CM
Lonsdale	Lonsdale	6	43	CM
Corona	Corona	5½	44	CM
Panatela	Panatela	6	38	CM

New for 1998, this is a mild-to-medium blend that features a Ecuador-seed wrapper. It is offered in boxes of 25.

DON MANOLO COLLECTION
Handmade in Santiago, Dominican Republic.
Wrapper: Indonesia, USA/Connecticut
Binder: Dominican Republic *Filler: Dominican Republic*

Shape	Name	Lgth	Ring	Wrapper
	Series 1–Maduro, has been discontinued			
	Series 2–Connecticut:			
Long Corona	Lonsdale	6	44	CC
Robusto	Robusto	5	50	CC

Double Corona	Churchill	7½	52	CC
Long Panatela	Panatela	7	38	CC
	Series 3–Sumatra:			
Robusto	Robusto	5	50	CM
Long Corona	Lonsdale	6	44	CM
Double Corona	Churchill	7	50	CM
Pyramid	Pyramid	6	54	CM

This brand made its debut in 1996, with a medium-to-full-bodied maduro group that has been discontinued for 1999, a mild-to-medium-bodied Connecticut-wrapped line and a medium-bodied, Sumatra-wrapped series. All are available in boxes of 25 except for the Pyramid shape, offered in bundles of 10.

DON MARCOS
Handmade in La Romana, Dominican Republic.

Wrapper: USA/Connecticut   *Binder: Dom. Rep.*   *Filler: Dom. Rep.*

Shape	Name		Lgth	Ring	Wrapper
Slim Panatela	Baby		5¼	33	CM
Corona	Coronas		5½	42	CC
Toro	Toros		6	50	CC
Torpedo	Torpedos		6	50	CC
Panatela	Naturals	*(tubed)*	6	38	CC
Lonsdale	Cetros		6½	42	CC
Toro	Double Corona		6½	48	CC
Churchill	Monarchs		7	46	CC

This brand was one of the best-sellers in the western U.S. during the 1960s and 1970s and was re-introduced in a big way in 1995. Well made and easy to smoke, the Don Marcos line has a mild to medium body and an inviting Connecticut Shade wrapper.

HANDMADE CIGARS: BRAND LISTINGS

DON MARINO
Handmade in Santiago, Dominican Republic.

Wrapper: Indonesia *Binder: Dom. Rep.* *Filler: Dom. Rep.*

Shape	Name	Lgth	Ring	Wrapper
Corona	Corona	5¾	42	CM
Robusto	Robusto	5	50	CM
Churchill	Lonsdale	6¾	46	CM
Double Corona	Churchill	7	50	CM

Here is a mild-to-medium-bodied cigar, available in boxes of bundles of 25.

DON MATEO
Handmade in Danli, Honduras.

Wrapper: Mexico *Binder: Mexico* *Filler: Nicaragua*

Shape	Name	Lgth	Ring	Wrapper
Slim Panatela	No. 1	7	30	CC
Panatela	No. 2	6⅞	35	CC
Long Corona	No. 3	6	42	CC
Corona	No. 4	5½	44	CC
Lonsdale	No. 5	6⅝	44	CC
Churchill	No. 6	6⅞	48	CC
Robusto	No. 7	4¾	50	CC-Ma
Toro	No. 8	6¼	50	CC-Ma
Double Corona	No. 9	7½	50	CC-Ma
Giant	No. 10	8	52	CC-Ma
Toro	No. 11	6⅝	54	CC-Ma

A medium-bodied taste in a banded, bundled cigar is the promise of the well-made and modestly-priced Don Mateo line. The Mexican wrapper is available in both natural and maduro wrappers for most sizes.

HANDMADE CIGARS: BRAND LISTINGS

DON MELO
Handmade in Santa Rosa de Copan, Honduras.

Wrapper: Honduras   Binder: Honduras   Filler: Honduras

Shape	Name	Lgth	Ring	Wrapper
Giant	Presidente	8½	50	Ma
Double Corona	Churchill	7	49	Ma
Long Corona	Corona Gorda	6¼	44	Ma
Long Corona	No. 2	6	42	Ma
Corona Extra	Corona Extra	5½	46	Ma
Corona	Petit Corona	5½	42	Ma
Robusto	Nom Plus	4¾	50	Ma
Petit Corona	Cremas	4½	42	Ma

This line honors the father of the Honduran cigar trade, who was the first
Honduran national to open a cigar factory in that country in 1896. From humble
origins in 1789, the cigar trade has grown considerably in the town of Santa
Rosa de Copan and this medium-to-full-bodied smoke, wrapped in all-black leaf,
salutes that success.

DON MELO CENTENARIO
Handmade in Santa Rosa de Copan, Honduras.

Wrapper: Honduras   Binder: Honduras   Filler: Honduras

Shape	Name	Lgth	Ring	Wrapper
Churchill	Liga A	7	48	CM
Toro	Liga B	6	55	CM
Long Corona	Liga C	6	44	CM
Robusto	Liga D	5	52	CM
Torpedo	Liga T	6⅛	54	CM

Here is a limited edition, centennial salute to the man (Don Melo Bueso) who
help found the modern Honduran cigar industry. Only 2,000 boxes of each size
will be made of this medium-bodied smoke. Even the boxes will be special:
hand-crafted in Caoba wood with a removable tray of Spanish cedarwood.

HANDMADE CIGARS: BRAND LISTINGS

DON MIGUEL
Handmade in Villa Gonzalez, Dominican Republic.

Wrapper: Brazil, Indonesia   *Binder: Dom. Rep.*   *Filler: Brazil, Dom. Rep.*

Shape	Name	Lgth	Ring	Wrapper
Robusto	Robusto	5	50	Ma
Long Corona	Corona	6	42	Ma
Lonsdale	Imperial Corona	7	44	Ma
Giant	Big Duke	9½	50	CC

This brand was introduced in 1910 and offers a mild-to-medium taste in a Brazilian maduro wrapper. The Big Duke size has a Indonesian wrapper. It is offered in boxes of 10 or boxes or bundles of 25.

DON NORBERTO
Handmade in Ocotal, Nicaragua.

Wrapper: Indonesia   *Binder: Nicaragua*   *Filler: Honduras*

Shape	Name	Lgth	Ring	Wrapper
Double Corona	Churchill	7½	50	CC
Petit Corona	Petit Corona	5	42	CC
Robusto	Corona	5	48	CC
Churchill	Double Corona	7	48	CC
Toro	Robusto	6	50	CC
Long Panatela	Panatela	7	36	CC
Robusto	Torito	5	52	CC

This blend changed in 1997, and now offers a mild-to-medium-bodied flavor, offered in boxes of 25.

DON OTILIO
Handmade in Santiago, Dominican Republic.

Wrapper: Ecuador   *Binder: Dom. Rep.*   *Filler: Dom. Rep., Honduras*

HANDMADE CIGARS: BRAND LISTINGS

Shape	Name	Lgth	Ring	Wrapper
Robusto	Robusto	5	50	CC-Ma
Giant	Presidente	8	50	CC-Ma
Churchill	Churchill	7½	49	CC-Ma
Torpedo	Toro	6½	53	CC-Ma
Long Corona	Cetro	6	44	CC-Ma
Pyramid	Pyramide	6⅞	52	CC-Ma

Introduced in 1996, this brand is named for a long-time tobacco grower in the Dominican Republic. Don Otilio is a mild-to-medium-bodied blend of Dominican and Honduran filler, Cuban-seed binder and an Ecuadorian-grown wrapper.

DON OTILIO
Handmade in Santiago, Dominican Republic.
Wrapper: Indonesia   *Binder: Dom. Rep.*   *Filler: Dom. Rep.*

Shape	Name	Lgth	Ring	Wrapper
Giant	Churchill	8	50	CM
Double Corona	Presidente	7	50	CM
Grand Corona	Doble Corona	6½	46	CM
Robusto	Robusto	5½	50	CM
Long Corona	Lonsdale	6	44	CM

This is a mild-bodied cigar, available in an elegant up-right box of 25.

DON PABLO
Handmade in Las Vegas, Nevada, USA.
Wrapper: USA/Connecticut   *Binder: Dominican Republic*
Filler: Brazil, Dominican Republic, Ecuador, Mexico

Shape	Name	Lgth	Ring	Wrapper
Slim Panatela	Pencil	7	32	CC
Slim Panatela	Panatela	7	34	CC

Lonsdale	Panatela Especial	7	40	CC-Ma
Corona	Corona	5¾	42	CC
Toro	Monterico	5¾	52	CC-Ma
Toro	Cuban Round	6	48	CC-Ma
Churchill	Imperial	6¾	46	CC-Ma
Double Corona	Cuban Round Largo	7½	50	CC-Ma
Torpedo	Torpedo	6¾	58	CC-Ma
Double Corona	Largo Cognac	7½	50	CC
Toro	Monterico Cognac	5¾	52	CC

These are mild to medium-bodied cigars of good quality, handmade in a storefront on the Las Vegas strip. Fully in keeping with its location, this small factory offers some gaudy specialties, including the Largo and Monterico sizes made with five-year-aged tobaccos cured with 20-year-old cognac. You can also have cigars cured with rum or brandy or sweetened for a modest charge!

DON PABLO GOLD SERIES
Handmade in Las Vegas, Nevada, USA.
Wrapper: Indonesia   *Binder: Ecuador*   *Filler: Honduras*

Shape	Name	Lgth	Ring	Wrapper
Toro	Monterico	5¾	52	CC-Ma
Churchill	Imperial	6¾	46	CC-Ma
Double Corona	Largo	7½	50	CC

This new brand from the Don Pablo Cigar Co. has a medium body and is new for 1998. Go to the store and see your smokes made in front of your eyes!

DON PANCHO COLLECTION
Handmade in Danli, Honduras.
Wrapper: Indonesia   *Binder: Honduras*   *Filler: Dom. Rep., Ecuador*

Shape	Name	Lgth	Ring	Wrapper
Robusto	Robusto	5	50	CM

Long Corona	Corona	6	43	CM
Double Corona	Churchill	7½	50	CM

Introduced in 1998, this is a mild blend, with a Sumatra wrapper, available in boxes of 25.

DON PATRICIO
Handmade in Managua, Nicaragua.

Wrapper: Nicaragua   *Binder: Nicaragua*   *Filler: Nicaragua*

Shape	Name	Lgth	Ring	Wrapper
Double Corona	Presidente	7	50	Ma
Toro	Toro	6	50	Ma
Lonsdale	Lonsdale	6¼	44	Ma
Robusto	Robusto	5	50	Ma
Corona	Corona	5½	42	Ma

Here is a mild-bodied cigar with excellent construction from 18-month-aged leaves, available in slide-top, all-cedar boxes of 25 cigars each.

DON PEPE
Handmade in Cruz des Almas, Brazil.

Wrapper: Brazil   *Binder: Brazil*   *Filler: Brazil*

Shape	Name	Lgth	Ring	Wrapper
Double Corona	Double Corona	7½	50	CM
Robusto	Robusto	5	50	CM
Short Panatela	Half Corona	4⅜	35	CM
Slim Panatela	Slim Panatela	5⅛	30	CM
Long Corona	Petit Lonsdale	6	40	CM
Churchill	Churchill	7	47	CM

Introduced in 1994, this brand is produced by the famed Suerdieck factory in Brazil. The wrapper is a Sumatran-seed tobacco, with native Brazilian leaves used for the binder and filler to blend into a mild-bodied cigar.

HANDMADE CIGARS: BRAND LISTINGS

DON PRIAMO
Handmade in Navarette, Dominican Republic.

Wrapper: Indonesia   Binder: Dom. Rep.   Filler: Dom. Rep.

Shape	Name	Lgth	Ring	Wrapper
Double Corona	Churchill	7½	50	CC
Robusto	Robusto	5	50	CC

Don Priamo cigars were introduced in early 1997 and named in honor of Priamo Reyes, patriarch of the Reyes tobacco family. These cigars offer a mild taste, packaged in all-cedar, slide-top boxes of 25.

DON PRIMO
Handmade in Santiago, Dominican Republic.

Wrapper: Indonesia   Binder: Dom. Rep.   Filler: Dom. Rep.

Shape	Name	Lgth	Ring	Wrapper
Corona	Corona Classico (tube available)	5½	42	CC
Robusto	Robusto	5½	50	CC
Churchill	Churchill	6⅞	46	CC

Named for the Primo Pipe Company of Vashon, Washington, founded in 1975. The cigar was introduced in 1998 and is mild-bodied long-filler leaves. It has a sweet tip and is offered in individual glass tubes or in cedar-lined boxes of 25.

DON QUIJOTE
Handmade in Cumana, Venezuela.

Wrapper: Honduras   Binder: Venezula   Filler: Venezuela

Shape	Name	Lgth	Ring	Wrapper
Churchill	Churchill	6⅝	47	CC
Corona	No. 5	5½	42	CC
Panatela	Carolinas	6½	38	CC

HANDMADE CIGARS: BRAND LISTINGS

Introduced in 1996, this unique, mild brand from Venezuela is made under the supervision of master cigar maker Vladimir Perez and offered in boxes of 25.

DON QUIXOTE
Handmade in Santa Rosa de Copan, Honduras.

Wrapper: Ecuador *Binder: Honduras* *Filler: Honduras*

Shape	Name	Lgth	Ring	Wrapper
Double Corona	Churchill	7	50	CM
Robusto	Nom Plus	4¾	50	CM
Lonsdale	Corona Gorda	6½	44	CM
Toro	Toro	6	50	CM
Small Panatela	Muneca/Princess	4	30	CM
Panatela	Panatela	6¾	35	CM

Here is a medium-to-full-bodied cigar introduced in 1997. It features a Sumatra-seed wrapper and binder and filler leaves that are aged at least 1½ years. It is offered in boxes of 25.

DON RAFAEL
Handmade in Santiago, Dominican Republic.

Wrapper: Indonesia, USA/Connecticut *Binder: Dom. Rep.* *Filler: Dom. Rep.*

Shape	Name	Lgth	Ring	Wrapper
Long Corona	No. 17 Petite Corona	6	42	CC-Ma
Long Corona	No. 27 Lonsdale	6	44	CC-Ma
Long Corona	No. 37 Corona	6	46	CC-Ma
Robusto	No. 47 Robusto	4½	50	CC-Ma
Robusto	No. 57 Robusto	5½	50	CC-Ma
Double Corona	No. 67 Churchill	7½	50	CC-Ma
Toro	No. 77 Toro	6	54	CC-Ma

HANDMADE CIGARS: BRAND LISTINGS

This Victor Sinclair-produced brand has a mild body but lots of flavor. You can take your choice from Connecticut-grown, natural-shade wrappers or Indonesian-grown maduro wrappers in boxes of 25.

DON RAFAEL
Handmade in Villa Gonzalez, Dominican Republic.

Wrapper: Ecuador, Indonesia   Binder: Dom. Rep.   Filler: Dom. Rep.

Shape	Name	Lgth	Ring	Wrapper
Perfecto		3¾	44	CM-Ma
Small Panatela		5	30	CM-Ma
Short Panatela		5	38	CM-Ma
Robusto		5	50	CM-Ma
Long Corona		6	44	CM-Ma
Toro		6	50	CM-Ma
Lonsdale		6½	42	CM-Ma
Lonsdale		6½	44	CM-Ma
Grand Corona		6½	46	CM-Ma
Long Panatela		7	38	CM-Ma
Churchill		7	48	CM-Ma
Double Corona		7½	50	CM-Ma
Torpedo		6½	52	CM-Ma
Pyramid		6½	52	CM-Ma

This cigar (which does not have shape names) offers a mild-a-medium-bodied taste, featuring Ecuadorian-grown Connecticut-seed wrappers and medium-bodied maduro wrappers from Sumatra. Introduced in 1997, it is presented in boxes or bundles of 25.

DON RENE
Handmade in Miami, Florida, USA.

Wrapper: Ecuador   Binder: Honduras   Filler: Dom. Rep., Nicaragua

HANDMADE CIGARS: BRAND LISTINGS

Shape	Name	Lgth	Ring	Wrapper
Torpedo	Torpedo	6½	54	CC-Ma
Corona Extra	Toro	5½	46	CC-Ma
Double Corona	Churchill	7¼	50	CC
Lonsdale	Corona	6½	44	CC
Corona	Coronita	5½	42	CC-Ma
Robusto	Robusto	5½	50	CC-Ma
Long Panatela	Lancero	7	38	CC
Small Panatela	Senoritas	5	30	CC

This brand debuted in 1996. It offers a mild-to-medium-bodied flavor, with each cigar protected in individual cellophane sleeves. Each shape is presented in all-cedar boxes of 25. The Senoritas and Coronita shapes are also available in a handy five-pack, while the Robusto shape is available in a four-pack.

DON RENE VINTAGE
Handmade in Santiago, Dominican Republic.
Wrapper: Indonesia   Binder: Dom. Rep.   Filler: Dom. Rep.

Shape	Name	Lgth	Ring	Wrapper
Double Corona	Churchill	7½	50	CC
Robusto	Rothschild	4½	50	CC
Long Corona	Corona	6	44	CC

This vintage selection is mild-to-medium in flavor and offered in all-cedar boxes of 25.

DON RIVERA
Handmade in Santiago, Dominican Republic.
Wrapper: USA/Connecticut   Binder: Dom. Rep.   Filler: Dom. Rep.

Shape	Name	Lgth	Ring	Wrapper
Double Corona	Churchill	7½	50	CC

Robusto	Robusto	4½	50	CC
Long Panatela	Panetela	7½	38	CC
Slim Panatela	Josefina	6	30	CC
Corona	Corona	5½	42	CC

Introduced in 1998, this is a mild-bodied brand, available in all-cedar boxes of 25.

DON RUBIO
Handmade in Santa Rosa de Copan, Honduras.

Wrapper: Ecuador   Binder: Honduras   Filler: Honduras

Shape	Name	Lgth	Ring	Wrapper
Corona Extra	Corona Extra	5½	46	CM
Robusto	Nom Plus	5	50	CM
Petit Corona	Petit Corona	5⅛	42	CM

This is a medium-bodied bundled brand offered in 25s.

DON SIXTO
Handmade in Danli, Honduras.

Wrapper: Ecuador   Binder: Honduras   Filler: Honduras, Nicaragua

Shape	Name	Lgth	Ring	Wrapper
Double Corona	Presidente	7	52	CC
Double Corona	Churchill	6⅞	49	CC
Toro	Toro	6	50	CC
Robusto	Robusto	4½	50	CC
Long Corona	Corona	6	43	CC
Panatela	Panatela	6½	38	CC
Small Panatela	Senorita	4½	30	CC
Pyramid	Torpedo	7	54	CC

HANDMADE CIGARS: BRAND LISTINGS

Introduced in 1997, this is a medium-bodied brand with a Connecticut-seed wrapper and a blend of binder and filler leaves from three nations. A tribute to Sixto Plasencia Juarez, one of the patriarchs of the Cuban cigar industry, Don Sixto cigars are offered in individual cellophane sleeves packed in all-cedar boxes 25.

DON SUERTE
Handmade in Tamboril, Dominican Republic.

Wrapper: Dom. Rep. or Indonesia   *Binder: Dom. Rep.*   *Filler: Dom. Rep.*

Shape	Name	Lgth	Ring	Wrapper
Double Corona	Presidente	7½	50	CM
Robusto	Robusto	5	50	CM
Grand Corona	Suave	6½	46	CM
Long Panatela	Panatela	7	38	CM
Long Corona	Corona Extra	6	42	CM
Torpedo	Torpedo	6½	54	CM

Take your choice of Dominican-grown or Indonesian wrappers on this mild-to-medium-bodied brand, offered in boxes of 25.

DON TITO
Handmade in Miami, Florida, USA.

Wrapper: Ecuador   *Binder: Nicaragua*
Filler: Dominican Republic, Honduras, Nicaragua

Shape	Name	Lgth	Ring	Wrapper
Double Corona	Churchill	7	50	CC-Ma
Double Corona	Double Corona	7¾	49	CC-Ma
Lonsdale	No. 1	6¾	43	CC-Ma
Lonsdale	No. 2	6½	43	CC-Ma
Long Panatela	Panatela	7	38	CC
Pyramid	Piramides	7¼	66	CC-Ma

Robusto	Robusto	5	50	CC-Ma
Grand Corona	Taino	6¼	46	CC-Ma
Torpedo	Torpedo	6½	60	CC-Ma

Don Tito was a new brand in 1996, from the "Little Havana" area of Miami, sporting a balanced blend that provides a rich, full-bodied taste. The brand has some of the largest sizes you can find anywhere and is presented in boxes of 25.

DON TOMAS
Handmade in Danli, Honduras.
Wrapper: Indonesia   *Binder: Mexico*   *Filler: Dom. Rep., Mexico, Nicaragua*

Shape	Name		Lgth	Ring	Wrapper
Double Corona	Presidentes		7½	50	CM-Ma
Lonsdale	Corona Grandes	(tubed)	6½	44	CM
Lonsdale	Cetros No. 2		6½	44	CM-Ma
Toro	Corona Gordas		6	52	CM
Robusto	Coronas		5½	50	CM-Ma
Corona Extra	Toros		5½	46	CM
Petit Corona	Blunts		5	42	CM
Robusto	Rothschild		4½	50	CM-Ma

Don Tomas cigars are justly famous for their mild-to-medium-bodied taste and silky construction. Havana-seed tobaccos are gathered from four nations, eventually ending as the top-quality cigars which are so well known to smokers worldwide. The new blend has natural wrappers from Indonesia and a blended filler surrounded by a Mexican binder.

DON TOMAS INTERNATIONAL SELECTION
Handmade in Danli, Honduras.
Wrapper: Indonesia   *Binder: Dom.Rep.*   *Filler: Dom.Rep., Mexico, Nicaragua*

Shape	Name	Lgth	Ring	Wrapper
Lonsdale	No. 1	6½	44	CM

Robusto	No. 2	5½	50	CM
Corona	No. 3	5½	42	CM
Toro	No. 5	6	52	CM

The International Selection is newly blended in 1997 and combines leaves from four nations to produce an effortless draw filled with rich flavors for a medium-bodied smoke. You can find it in boxes of 10.

DON TOMAS SPECIAL EDITION
Handmade in Danli, Honduras.

Wrapper: Indonesia   Binder: Mexico   Filler: Dom. Rep., Mexico, Nicaragua

Shape	Name	Lgth	Ring	Wrapper
Double Corona	No. 100	7½	50	CC
Lonsdale	No. 200	6½	44	CC
Robusto	No. 300	5	50	CC
Long Panatela	No. 400	7	36	CC
Corona Extra	No. 500	5½	46	CC
Toro	No. 600	6	52	CC

Distinctive, smooth drawing and opulent is the Don Tomas Special Edition. This is a new blend that is medium-to-full-bodied but slightly spicy, offered in boxes of 25.

DON TUTO HABANOS
Handmade in Llano Bonito, Costa Rica.

Wrapper: Indonesia   Binder: Costa Rica   Filler: Costa Rica, Nicaragua

Shape	Name	Lgth	Ring	Wrapper
Lonsdale	Presidente	6½	44	CC-CM
Long Corona	Coronas	6	42	CC-CM
Robusto	Robusto	5	50	CC-CM
Toro	Toro	6	50	CC-CM

Double Corona	El Mambi	7	50	CC-CM

Introduced in 1996, this namesake brand of the family-owned Factory Don Tuto in Costa Rica offers a medium-to-full-bodied taste. The Indonesian-grown wrapper comes from Cameroon-seed or from Cuban-seed. The brand is presented in boxes of 2, 5, 10 and 25, with each cigar individually packed in a cellophane sleeve.

DON VIDAL
Handmade in Villa Gonzalez, Dominican Republic.

Wrapper: Indonesia   Binder: Dom. Rep.   Filler: Dom. Rep.

Shape	Name	Lgth	Ring	Wrapper
	Selecto Series:			
Double Corona	Churchill	7½	50	CM
Churchill	Gran Corona	7	48	CM
Robusto	Robusto	5	50	CM
Torpedo	Torpedo	7	52	CM
Short Panatela	No. 5	5	36	CM
Long Corona	No. 6	6	43	CM
	Clasica Series, made with short filler:			
Double Corona	Churchill	7½	50	Ma
Churchill	Gran Corona	7	48	Ma
Toro	Corona Gorda	6¼	50	Ma
Robusto	Robusto	5	50	Ma
Short Panatela	No. 5	5	36	Ma
Long Corona	No. 6	6	43	Ma
Torpedo	Torpedo	7	52	Ma

This is a full-bodied cigar in either style. The Sumatra-seed wrappers and Dominican interior leaves are carefully-blended for flavor and presented in boxes or bundles of 25. The No. 6 and 7 sizes in the Clasica Series is also available in Amaretto, coffee, cognac, mint, vanilla-rum and vanilla flavors.

DON VITO
Handmade in Las Palmas, the Canary Islands of Spain.

Wrapper: USA/Connecticut   *Binder: Indonesia*   *Filler: Dom. Rep., Spain*

Shape	Name	Lgth	Ring	Wrapper
Giant	Padrino	8	50	CC
Churchill	Capo	7	46	CC
Robusto	Alfonso	5	50	CC
Long Corona	Napolitano	6	44	CC
Corona	Siciliano	5½	42	CC

This is a mild-to-medium-bodied cigar back in production after a hiatus in 1997. It is attractively packaged in cedar boxes of 25.

DON XAVIER
Handmade in Las Palmas, the Canary Islands of Spain.

Wrapper: USA/Connecticut   *Binder: Canary Islands*
Filler: Brazil, Canary Islands, Dominican Republic

Shape	Name	Lgth	Ring	Wrapper
Long Panatela	Panatela	7½	39	CC
Panatela	Petit Panatela	5⅝	39	CC
Lonsdale	Lonsdale	6⅝	42	CC
Corona	Petit Lonsdale	5⅝	42	CC
Churchill	Gran Corona	7	46	CC
Corona Extra	Corona	5⅝	46	CC
Double Corona	Churchill	7½	50	CC
Robusto	Robusto	4⅝	50	CC
Pyramid	Pyramid	7	52	CC

HANDMADE CIGARS: BRAND LISTINGS

The flagship of the Marcos Miguel line, this is a mild blend of tobaccos of four nations in a variety of shapes. Introduced in the current range in 1996, Don Xavier cigars are offered in boxes of 5, 10 and 25 cigars each.

DON YÀNES
Handmade in Cumana, Venezuela.

Wrapper: USA/Connecticut   *Binder: Venezuela*   *Filler: Venezuela*

Shape	Name	Lgth	Ring	Wrapper
Double Corona	Churchill	7	50	CM
Robusto	Robusto	5	50	CM
Long Corona	No. 1	6¼	42	CM

Here is an old Venezuelan standard, introduced to the U.S. market in 1996. This is an all long-filler cigar which is made by hand and is considered medium-bodied.

DOÑA ELBA & CIOFFI
Handmade in Esteli, Nicaragua.

Wrapper: Indonesia   *Binder: Nicaragua*   *Filler: Nicaragua*

Shape	Name	Lgth	Ring	Wrapper
Torpedo	Mombacho	5½	54	CM-Ma
Double Corona	Cordova	7	52	CM-Ma
Churchill	Revolver	7	48	CM-Ma
Toro	Cana	6	50	CM-Ma
Robusto	Burro	4¾	50	CM-Ma

Introduced in 1996, this is a mild-to-medium-bodied brand available in both natural and maduro-shade wrappers. It is offered in boxes of 25.

DOÑA PUROS
Handmade in Santa Rosa de Copan, Honduras.

Wrapper: Honduras   *Binder: Nicaragua*   *Filler: Honduras*

HANDMADE CIGARS: BRAND LISTINGS

Shape	Name	Lgth	Ring	Wrapper
Torpedo	Torpedo	6½	54	CM
Torpedo	Torpedo Campanela	5	54	CM
Giant	Presidente	8½	50	CM
Double Corona	Churchill	7	50	CM
Robusto	Robusto	5½	50	CM
Robusto	Rothchild	4½	50	CM
Lonsdale	Corona No. 1	6½	44	CM
Petit Corona	Petit Corona	5	44	CM
Lonsdale	Banana	6½	42	CM
Cigarillo	Mistinguett	8	28	CM
Cigarillo	Senoritas	4	28	CM
	Flavored series:			
Giant Corona	Ginger Double Corona	8	44	CM
Petit Corona	Ginger Petit Corona	5	44	CM
Robusto	Ginger Robusto	5½	50	CM
Lonsdale	Orange Robusto	6½	44	CM
Lonsdale	Clove Robusto	6½	44	CM

Well made and medium-to-full in body, this brand debuted in 1998 and is available in boxes or bundles of 25, except for the Torpedo (20s) and Senoritas (50s).

DOS CUBANITOS
Handmade in Miami, Florida, USA.

Wrapper: Indonesia   Binder: Indonesia   Filler: Dom. Rep., Indonesia, Mexico

Shape	Name	Lgth	Ring	Wrapper
Perfecto	Figurado	5	52	CM-Ma

Torpedo	Torpedo	6½	54	CM-Ma
Double Corona	Churchill	7	50	CM-Ma
Double Corona	Presidente	7½	52	CM-Ma
Robusto	Robusto	5	50	CM-Ma
Long Corona	Corona	6	44	CM-Ma
Panatela	Panetela	6	42	CM-Ma
Long Panatela	Lanceros	7½	38	CM-Ma
Cigarillo	Finos	5	28	CM-Ma

Designed to mirror the blend of the original Cohiba line from Havana, this is a full-bodied cigar. The "two little Cubans" is offered in boxes of 25.

DOS REINAS
Handmade in Esteli, Nicaragua.

Wrapper: Indonesia   *Binder: Dom. Rep.*   *Filler: Mexico, Nicaragua*

Shape	Name	Lgth	Ring	Wrapper
Corona	Corona	5¾	42	CC
Toro	Toro	6	50	CC
Robusto	Robusto	5	50	CC
Torpedo	Torpedo	6⅞	54	CC
Churchill	Churchill	6⅞	48	CC
Pyramid	Piramide	6⅞	54	CC

This brand was introduced in 1997 and features Cuban-seed filler leaves, combined with an Indonesian wrapper for a medium-to-full-bodied smoke. Each cigar is wrapped in cellophane and then packed into all-cedar boxes of 25.

DOS RIOS
Handmade in Esteli, Nicaragua.

Wrapper: Ecuador   *Binder: Nicaragua*   *Filler: Dom. Rep., Nicaragua*

HANDMADE CIGARS: BRAND LISTINGS

Shape	Name	Lgth	Ring	Wrapper
Long Corona	Especial	6	44	CC
Grand Corona	Rios Extra	6½	46	CC
Robusto	Robusto	4⅞	50	CC
Toro	Toro	6	50	CC
Double Corona	Esplendido	7	50	CC
Pyramid	Pyramid	6½	52	CC

New for 1997, this is a full-bodied cigar from Nick's Cigar Company of Miami. It features a Sumatra-seed wrapper grown in Ecuador an is presented in slide-top cedar cabinets of 25.

DOUBLE HAPPINESS
Handmade in Manila, the Philippines.

Wrapper: Brazil *Binder: Philippines* *Filler: Philippines*

Shape	Name		Lgth	Ring	Wrapper
Pyramid	Nirvana I		6	52	CC
Toro	Nirvana II		6	54	CC
Toro	Euphoria		6½	53	CC
Robusto	Bliss		5¼	48	CC
Perfecto	Rapture		5	53	CC
Churchill	Ecstacy		7	47	CC
Corona	Sublime	(tubed)	5½	44	CC

This brand is debuted in 1995 and handmade in Manila, the Philippines, with a Brazil-grown, Sumatra-seed wrapper and an Isabela binder and filler, grown in the Philippines. Each shape is presented in bundles of 25, or in a magnificent varnished Narra wood box of 26 (really!, except for the Sublime, offered in 20s), including a hand-sewn crushed velvet liner!

HANDMADE CIGARS: BRAND LISTINGS

DR. FUNK
Handmade in Navarette, Dominican Republic.

Wrapper: Indonesia · *Binder: Dom. Rep.* · *Filler: Dom. Rep.*

Shape	Name	Lgth	Ring	Wrapper
Torpedo	Torpedo	6	54	CM
Giant	Churchill	8½	50	CM

This is a medium-bodied brand which debuted in 1998. It is offered in bundles of 25.

THE DRAKE
Handmade in Esteli, Nicaragua.

Wrapper: Nicaragua · *Binder: Nicaragua* · *Filler: Nicaragua*

Shape	Name	Lgth	Ring	Wrapper
Robusto	Robusto	4½	52	Ma
Toro	Corona	6	50	Ma
Double Corona	Churchill	7	52	Ma
Giant	Presidente	8½	50	Ma

This all-maduro-wrapped brand from the Texana Cigar Co. has a medium-bodied flavor. Introduced in 1997, it is offered in wood boxes of 25.

DULCE DIAMANTE
Handmade in Danli, Honduras.

Wrapper: Honduras or Indonesia
Binder: Honduras or Nicaragua · *Filler: Honduras or Nicaragua*

Shape	Name	Lgth	Ring	Wrapper
	Wrapper: Indonesia Binder: Honduras			*Filler: Honduras*
Small Panatela	Baguette	4½	30	CC
	Wrapper: Honduras Binder: Nicaragua			*Filler: Honduras*
Petit Corona	Heart	5	42	CM

HANDMADE CIGARS: BRAND LISTINGS

	Wrapper: Honduras Binder: Honduras			Filler: Honduras
Double Corona	Marquise	7	49	Ma
	Wrapper: Honduras Binder: Nicaragua			Filler: Nicaragua
Robusto	Brilliant	5½	50	CM
	Wrapper: Indonesia Binder: Honduras			Filler: Nicaragua
Toro	Emerald	6	50	CC

Introduced in 1996, this unusual brand utilizes a different blend for each shape! The overall effect is a medium-bodied smoke for all shapes except the Baguette, which is mild-bodied. It is presented in boxes of 25.

DULCE MARIA
Handmade in Navarette, Dominican Republic.

Wrapper: Indonesia   *Binder: Dom. Rep.*   *Filler: Dom. Rep.*

Shape	Name	Lgth	Ring	Wrapper
Churchill	Churchill	7	48	CC
Robusto	Robusto	5	50	CC
Lonsdale	Corona Grande	6½	46	CC
Long Corona	Corona	6	44	CC
Pyramid	Pyramid	6	50	CC

Here is a 1997-introduced cigar that offers a mild-to-medium-bodied flavor and is offered at a modest price for excellent value. "Sweet Mary" is presented in bundles of 25.

DULZURA
Handmade in Las Palmas, the Canary Islands of Spain.

Wrapper: USA/Connecticut   *Binder: Spain*   *Filler: Brazil, Dom. Rep.*

Shape	Name	Lgth	Ring	Wrapper
Toro	No. 1	6¼	48	CC
Robusto	No. 2	5½	48	CC

HANDMADE CIGARS: BRAND LISTINGS

Here is a mild cigar with a Canary Islands binder and offered in boxes of 25.

DUNHILL
Handmade in Tenerife, the Canary Islands of Spain.

Wrapper: USA/Connecticut   Binder: Dom. Rep.   Filler: Dom. Rep.

Shape	Name	Lgth	Ring	Wrapper
Robusto	Coronas Extra	5½	50	CC
Lonsdale	Corona Grandes	6½	43	CC
Corona	Coronas	5½	43	CC
Lonsdale	Lonsdale Grandes	7½	42	CC
Slim Panatela	Panatelas	6	30	CC

This hand-rolled cigar debuted in 1986 and is mild enough for the casual smoker, yet its distinctive taste will satisfy the connoisseur. The tobacco blend and binder are now grown in the Dominican Republic and finished with a genuine Connecticut wrapper.

DUNHILL
Handmade in La Romana, Dominican Republic.

Wrapper: USA/Connecticut   Binder: Dom. Rep.   Filler: Brazil, Dom. Rep.

Shape	Name		Lgth	Ring	Wrapper
Double Corona	Peravias		7	50	CI
Toro	Condados		6	48	CI
Lonsdale	Diamantes		6⅝	42	CI
Panatela	Samanas		6½	38	CI
Corona	Valverdes		5½	42	CI
Robusto	Altamiras	(tubed)	5	48	CI
Churchill	Cabreras	(tubed)	7	48	CI

Introduced in 1989, Dunhill's master cigar makers roll a special selection of Piloto Cubano and Olor tobaccos from the Cibao Valley of the Dominican Republic. Wrapping the blend in a Dominican binder, the bunch is then finished with the finest quality Connecticut shade-grown leaf from the Windsor Valley. Prior to final packaging, these cigars are aged in cedar-lined rooms to provide the final mellowing of their mild-to-medium-bodied flavor.

DUNHILL
Handmade in Danli, Honduras.

Wrapper: Indonesia *Binder: Mexico* *Filler: Brazil, Dom. Rep., Mexico*

Shape	Name		Lgth	Ring	Wrapper
Churchill	Churchill	(tube available)	7	48	CM
Corona	Corona	(tube available)	5½	41	CM
Lonsdale	Lonsdale		6½	42	CM
Robusto	Robusto		4½	50	CM
Toro	Toro		6	50	CM

A new tradition is in the making with the 1998 introduction of these medium-bodied, well-balanced Honduran-made cigars, the first from that country to bear the Dunhill marque! The filler leaves include a tempting mix of Brazilian, Mexican and Dominican Piloto Cubano for a spicy start, complemented by the Indonesian wrapper. You can find this new treasure in elegantly-decorated boxes of 25.

DUO
Handmade in Tamboril, Dominican Republic.
Wrapper: Dominican Republic and USA/Connecticut
Binder: Dominican Republic *Filler: Dominican Republic*

Shape	Name	Lgth	Ring	Wrapper
Lonsdale	Lonsdale	7	44	Dual
Double Corona	Churchill	7½	50	Dual

Like both natural and maduro wrappers? Here's your chance to enjoy both in the same cigar! The Duo, which debuted in 1997, offers the top half of the cigar wrapped in a Colorado Claro-shade Connecticut wrapper and the bottom in a maduro shade Dominican-grown wrapper. The result? A mild-to-medium-bodied smoke whose flavor is "renewed" halfway through! It is offered in boxes of 25.

HANDMADE CIGARS: BRAND LISTINGS

DURANGO
Handmade in Santiago, Dominican Republic.

Wrapper: Indonesia   *Binder: Indonesia*   *Filler: Indonesia, Pipe Tobacco*

Shape	Name	Lgth	Ring	Wrapper
Grand Corona	Grand Corona	6	46	CM
Robusto	Robusto	5	50	CM

Here is a full-bodied brand with a choice of blends: either the Traditional, with Virginia Cavendish pipe tobacco filler or a Colombian Mocha with a combination of Black Cavendish and Virginia pipe tobaccos, both mixed with long-filler Indonesian leaves. You can enjoy either in pack of four, ten-packs and in bundles of 20 cigars each.

E. TRINIDAD
Handmade in Miami, Florida, USA.

Wrapper: Ecuador   *Binder: Indonesia*   *Filler: Dom. Rep.*

Shape	Name	Lgth	Ring	Wrapper
Lonsdale	Lonsdale	6¾	43	CC
Robusto	Robusto	5	50	CC
Toro	Toro	6	50	CC
Churchill	Churchill	6¾	48	CC
Torpedo	Torpedo	6¼	54	CC

Developed by the Sosa and Trinidad families, this is a full-bodied cigar first offered in 1998. It is presented in wooden boxes of 25.

888
Handmade, with short filler, in Mexico City, Mexico.

Wrapper: Mexico   *Binder: Mexico*   *Filler: Mexico*

Shape	Name	Lgth	Ring	Wrapper
Corona	No. 1	5¼	40	CM
Toro	No. 2	6¼	50	CM

HANDMADE CIGARS: BRAND LISTINGS

Here is a five-flavor cigar: Guarapo (a traditional Cuban sugar-cane drink), Gold Label Vanilla, Chocolate, rum and Cappuccino, with a light-to-medium body introduced in 1997. The flavor is added through the curing process and the cigars are available in bundles of 25.

898 COLLECTION
Handmade in Kingston, Jamaica.

Wrapper: USA/Connecticut   *Binder: Dom. Rep.*   *Filler: Dom. Rep.*

Shape	Name	Lgth	Ring	Wrapper
Double Corona	Churchill	7½	49	CC
Corona	Corona	5½	42	CC
Lonsdale	Lonsdale	6½	42	CC
Lonsdale	Monarch	6¾	45	CC
Robusto	Robusto	5½	49	CC

Introduced in 1991 and made completely by hand in Kingston, Jamaica, the 898 Collection is uncompromising in its commitment to quality of construction and ease of smoking. These are mild-bodied cigars, offered in boxes of 25 cigars each.

1876
Handmade in Santiago, Dominican Republic.

Wrapper: USA/Connecticut   *Binder: Dom. Rep.*   *Filler: Dom.Rep.*

Shape	Name	Lgth	Ring	Wrapper
Slim Panatela	Kelly's	5	30	CC
Long Panatela	Panatela	7	36	CC
Corona	Corona	5½	42	CC
Long Corona	Corona Grande	6	44	CC
Robusto	Robusto	5	50	CC
Churchill	Churchill	7	46	CC
Double Corona	Presidente	7½	50	CC
Pyramid	Piramide	7	54	CC

HANDMADE CIGARS: BRAND LISTINGS

Introduced in 1995, this is a mild-to-medium blend of leaves, available in bundles or tins of 25 cigars.

1881
Handmade in Manila, the Philippines.

Wrapper: Indonesia   *Binder: Brazil*   *Filler: Philippines*

Shape	Name	Lgth	Ring	Wrapper
Corona	Corona	5½	44	CM
Robusto	Robusto	5	50	CM
Lonsdale	Conde de Guell	6¾	44	CM
Torpedo	Torpedo	6	52	CM
Giant	Double Corona	8½	50	CM

The Philippine cigar industry is hundreds of years old and La Flor de la Isabella was formally incorporated in 1881 - hence the name of this brand. It offers excellent craftsmanship and a medium-bodied taste with a Javan wrapper in boxes of 25.

EDGAR
Handmade in Santiago, Dominican Republic.

Wrapper: Indonesia, USA/Connecticut   *Binder: Dom. Rep.*   *Filler: Dom. Rep.*

Shape	Name	Lgth	Ring	Wrapper
Double Corona	Churchill	7½	50	CC-Ma
Grand Corona	Corona	6	46	CC-Ma
Long Corona	Lonsdale	6	44	CC-Ma
Robusto	Robusto	5½	50	CC-Ma
Corona	Duke	5½	43	CC

Here is a medium-bodied smoke, introduced in 1997 and offered in your choice of a Connecticut-grown natural-shade wrapper or an Indonesian-grown maduro-shade wrapper. You can find it in boxes of 25.

HANDMADE CIGARS: BRAND LISTINGS

EL BESO
Handmade in Anaheim, California, USA.

Wrapper: Indonesia   *Binder: Indonesia*   *Filler: Dom. Rep.*

Shape	Name	Lgth	Ring	Wrapper
Robusto	Robusto	5	52	CM-Ma
Long Corona	Leon	6	44	CM
Toro	Segovia	6½	52	CM-Ma
Churchill	Double Corona	7	46	CM-Ma
Torpedo	Torpedo	6	54	CM-Ma
Long Corona	Cache Corona	6	44	CM
Robusto	Cache Robusto	5	50	CM
Robusto	Vanilla Kiss Robusto	5	50	CM
Long Corona	Vanilla Kiss Corona	6	44	CM

Introduced in 1998, this is a mild-bodied brand that is available in a variety of sizes. It is available in boxes of 25. Rum flavoring is available on the Robusto size, along with Kahlua or vanilla on two other sizes each.

EL CANELO
Handmade in Miami, Florida, USA.
Origin of wrapper, binder and filler leaves varies, depending on availability.

Shape	Name	Lgth	Ring	Wrapper
Giant	Viajantes	8½	52	CC-Ma
Giant	Embajadores	8	50	CC
Churchill	Sargentos	7½	46	CC
Churchill	Churchills	7	48	CC-Ma
Long Corona	Smokers	7	43	CC-Ma
Toro	Toros	6	50	CC
Robusto	Nom-Plus	4¾	50	CC-Ma

Lonsdale	Infiesta No. 1	7	43	CC-Ma
Long Corona	San Marcos	6	44	CC-Ma
Long Panatela	Elegante	7	36	CC
Small Panatela	Princess	4½	30	CC
Long Panatela	Canelitas Largas	7½	38	CC-Ma
Slim Panatela	St. Georges	7	30	CC-Ma
Slim Panatela	St. Augustine	5½	30	CC-Ma
Corona	Corona	5½	42	CC-Ma
Robusto	Robusto	5½	50	CC
Torpedo	Torpedo	5½	52	CC

These are mild-to-medium cigars with Connecticut wrappers, made in a small factory in the Little Havana section of Miami.

EL CHICO
Handmade, with medium filler, in Tamboril, Dominican Republic.
Wrapper: Indonesia   *Binder: Dom. Rep.*   *Filler: Dom. Rep.*

Shape	Name	Lgth	Ring	Wrapper
Cigarillo	Cigarillo	4	28	CM
Long Corona	Corona	6	44	CM
Robusto	Robusto	5½	50	CM
Panatela	Lonsdale	6	38	CM

This is a mild-to-medium-bodied cigar, made with medium filler and introduced in 1998. It is available in four sizes in humidified containers.

EL COLONEL
Handmade in Tamboril, Dominican Republic.
Wrapper: USA/Connecticut   *Binder: Dom. Rep.*   *Filler: Dom. Rep.*

HANDMADE CIGARS: BRAND LISTINGS

Shape	Name	Lgth	Ring	Wrapper
Robusto	Robusto	5	50	CM
Toro	Corona Gorda	6	50	CM
Double Corona	Double Corona	7¾	50	CM
Churchill	Churchill	7	47	CM
Lonsdale	Lonsdale	6½	42	CM
Long Panatela	Panatela Larga	7½	38	CM
Grand Corona	Corona Grande	6½	47	CM
Petit Corona	Petit Corona	5	42	CM
Corona	Corona	5½	42	CM
Long Corona	Corona Larga	6	42	CM
Corona Extra	Corona Extra	5½	47	CM
Panatela	Panatela	6	38	CM
Pyramid	Pyramid	6	54	CM

This brand was introduced in 1996 and is mild-to-medium-bodied in strength. It is available with or without cellophane sleeves in all-cedar boxes of 5, 10 or 25.

EL COMPETIDOR
Handmade in San Andres Tuxtla, Mexico.

Wrapper: Cameroon   Binder: Mexico   Filler: Mexico

Shape	Name	Lgth	Ring	Wrapper
Robusto	Ejecutivos Premium	5	50	CM
Robusto	Aromaticos Premium	5½	54	CM
Lonsdale	Emisarios Premium	7	42	CM
Pyramid	Piramyd Premium	6¼	52	CM
Double Corona	Deliciosos Premium	6¾	52	CM
Double Corona	Ideales Premium	7½	50	CM

Double Corona	Perfectos Special Premium	7	52	CM
Torpedo	Figurados Special Premium	7½	52	CM
Torpedo	Super Torpedo Premium	7¾	58	CM
Giant	Exclusivo Special Premium	8¼	54	CM
Pyramid	Pyramid Extra	8¼	56	CM

Here is a medium-bodied brand, introduced in 1998 and offered in either boxes of bundles of 25.

EL CAUTO
Handmade in Santiago, Dominican Republic.

Wrapper: Honduras   Binder: Honduras   Filler: Dom. Rep.

Shape	Name	Lgth	Ring	Wrapper
Corona	No. 4	5½	42	CM
Double Corona	Churchill	6¾	54	CM
Lonsdale	Corona	6½	43	CM
Lonsdale	Lonsdale	6½	40	CM
Corona Extra	No. 400	4	45	CM
Slim Panatela	Panetela	5¾	34	CM
Grand Corona	Toro	5¾	45	CM
Robusto	Wavell	4¾	49	CM

New for 1998, this is a nice, medium-bodied brand with just a hint of spice on the finish. You can enjoy it in value-priced bundles of 20.

EL CREDITO
Handmade in Miami, Florida, USA.

Wrapper: Ecuador   Binder: Nicaragua   Filler: Dom. Rep., Nicaragua

Shape	Name	Lgth	Ring	Wrapper
Giant	Gigantes	9	49	CC-Ma

Giant	Senadores	8	52	CC-Ma
Double Corona	Monarchs	7¼	54	CC-Ma
Double Corona	Imperiales	7¾	49	CC-Ma
Double Corona	Churchill	7	50	CC-Ma
Churchill	Supremos	7½	48	CC-Ma
Toro	Small Churchill	6	52	CC-Ma
Robusto	Rothchild	5	50	CC-Ma
Grand Corona	Corona Extra	6¼	46	CC-Ma
Giant Corona	Corona Grande	7¾	44	CC-Ma
Lonsdale	No. 1	6¾	43	CC-Ma
Long Corona	Cetros	6¼	43	CC-Ma
Corona	Nacionales	5½	43	CC-Ma
Small Panatela	Small Corona	4½	40	CC-Ma
Long Panatela	Panetelas	7	37	CC-Ma
	Made with short filler:			
Churchill	Super Habanero	7½	46	CC-Ma
Lonsdale	Fumas	6¾	44	CC-Ma

This is a medium-bodied smoke, made in the famous El Credito factory in Miami and offered in bundles of 25 cigars each.

EL DIABLO
Handmade in Santiago, Dominican Republic.

Wrapper: Dom. Rep.   *Binder: Dom. Rep.*   *Filler: Dom. Rep.*

Shape	*Name*	*Lgth*	*Ring*	*Wrapper*
Torpedo	Torpedo	6	52	CM
Corona Extra	Corona	5½	46	CM

Ready for "The Devil"? This is a medium-to-full-bodied cigar with all-Dominican tobacco and a balanced flavor. Introduced in 1996, it is offered in boxes of 25, except for the Torpedo, available in boxes of 10.

HANDMADE CIGARS: BRAND LISTINGS

EL DIAMANTE
Handmade in Jalapa, Nicaragua.

Wrapper: Ecuador, Indonesia   *Binder: Indonesia*   *Filler: Dom. Rep., Nicaragua*

Shape	Name	Lgth	Ring	Wrapper
Double Corona	Churchill	7	50	CC
Toro	Toro	6	49	CC
Lonsdale	Palma	6½	44	CC
Robusto	Rothchild	5½	50	CC
Corona	Corona	5½	43	CC

This blend debuted way back in 1975 and has been around in various forms since then. You can have your choice of a Connecticut-seed-wrapped version that offers mild body, or a Sumatra wrapper that offers a mild-to-medium taste. Either way, you can enjoy these beauties in either boxes or bundles of 25.

EL DORADO GOLD RESERVE
Handmade in Danli, Honduras.
Wrapper: Indonesia or Mexico

Binder: Costa Rica   *Filler: Brazil, Dominican Republic, Mexico*

Shape	Name		Lgth	Ring	Wrapper
Robusto	Robusto		4¾	50	CM
Lonsdale	Lonsdale		6⅝	44	CM
Churchill	Churchill		7	48	CM
Giant	Presidente		8	52	CM
Churchill	Premier	(tubed)	7	48	CM-Ma

Not your sister's cigar! Here is a 1997-introduced, *full-bodied* cigar that celebrates the legend of El Dorado (literally, "the gilded"), a king of a fabulously wealthy city located by early explorers of the Amazon regions in South America. While the cigar is not covered in gold, it does offer strong flavor in boxes of 25. The new maduro wrapper uses a Mexican leaf.

HANDMADE CIGARS: BRAND LISTINGS

EL EMPERADOR
Handmade in Santiago, Dominican Republic.

Wrapper: Indonesia   *Binder: Dom. Rep.*   *Filler: Dom. Rep.*

Shape	Name	Lgth	Ring	Wrapper
Double Corona	Churchill	7	50	Ma
Torpedo	Torpedo	6	52	Ma
Robusto	Robusto	5½	50	Ma
Churchill	Double Corona	6¾	48	Ma
Double Corona	Esplendidos	7	50	Ma
Panatela	Panatela	6	38	CM

This is a medium-to-full-bodied line, introduced in 1996. It features a maduro-shade Sumatra wrapper and a Dominican-grown Olor binder. It is available in handcrafted, Spanish Cedar boxes of 25. The Panatela is flavored and available in Amaretto, Anise, cherry, cognac and rum.

ELEGANTE
Handmade in Danli, Honduras.

Wrapper: Ecuador   *Binder: Honduras*   *Filler: Dom. Rep., Honduras*

Shape	Name	Lgth	Ring	Wrapper
Double Corona	Grande	7½	50	CC
Churchill	Especial	7	48	CC
Lonsdale	Centimo	7	44	CC
Robusto	Queen	5	50	CC

Originally made in Tampa beginning in 1985 and now made in Honduras, this is a medium-bodied combination of Cuban seed, Dominican long filler, wrapped in a light Ecuadorian-grown leaf, and offered in boxes of 25.

ELEGANTÉ
Handmade in Navarette, Dominican Republic.

Wrapper: Indonesia   *Binder: Dom. Rep.*   *Filler: Dom. Rep.*

HANDMADE CIGARS: BRAND LISTINGS

Shape	Name	Lgth	Ring	Wrapper
Double Corona	Churchill	7	50	CM
Grand Corona	Corona	6½	46	CM
Robusto	Robusto	5	50	CM

This is a new brand in late 1998, with a mild-to-medium body, offered in modestly-priced bundles of 25.

EL ESENCIAL
Handmade in Tamboril, Dominican Republic.
Wrapper: Indonesia   Binder: Dom. Rep.   Filler: Dom. Rep.

Shape	Name	Lgth	Ring	Wrapper
Corona	Corona	5½	42	CM
Churchill	Lonsdale	6¾	46	CM
Toro	Robusto	6	50	CM
Double Corona	Churchill	7½	50	CM

Here is a full-bodied brand introduced in 1996. The wrapper is from Sumatra and the filler in all Piloto Cubano tobacco. You can find it in cellophane sleeves in either bundles or boxes of 25.

EL ESENCIAL WHITE LABEL
Handmade, with mixed filler, in Tamboril, Dominican Republic.
Wrapper: Indonesia   Binder: Dom. Rep.   Filler: Dom. Rep.

Shape	Name	Lgth	Ring	Wrapper
Corona	Corona	5½	42	CM
Churchill	Lonsdale	6¾	46	CM
Toro	Robusto	6	50	CM
Double Corona	Churchill	7½	50	CM

This blend is medium-to-full-bodied, introduced in 1996. The filler is a mixed "sandwich" of long-filler and cut leaves and is offered in bundles of 25.

HANDMADE CIGARS: BRAND LISTINGS

EL FARO
Handmade in Santiago, Dominican Republic.

Wrapper: Indonesia   *Binder: Dom. Rep.*   *Filler: Dom. Rep.*

Shape	Name	Lgth	Ring	Wrapper
Double Corona	Churchill	7½	50	CC
Toro	Robusto	6	50	CC
Robusto	Rothschild	4½	50	CC
Long Corona	Lonsdale	6	42	CC
Long Corona	Corona	6	44	CC

Named for the El Faro Lighthouse near Santo Domingo, this cigar presents a medium-bodied taste. This blend debuted in 1998, offered in bundles of 25.

EL FIDEL
Handmade in Villa Gonzalez, Dominican Republic.

Wrapper: Indonesia   *Binder: Dom. Rep.*   *Filler: Dom. Rep.*

Shape	Name	Lgth	Ring	Wrapper
Robusto	Peasant	5	50	CC
Long Corona	Revolutionary	6	44	CC
Double Corona	Dictator	7	50	CC

Here is a not too subtle salute to Fidel Castro, leader of the Cuban Revolution in 1959 and the head of the Cuban state since that time. In seeming contrast to the fiery Castro, this blend is rather mild and is offered in slide-top cedar boxes of 25.

EL GAUCHO
Handmade in Danli, Honduras.

Wrapper: Honduras   *Binder: Honduras*   *Filler: Honduras*

Shape	Name	Lgth	Ring	Wrapper
Giant	Ganza	8	54	CM
Churchill	Pampas	7¼	46	CM

HANDMADE CIGARS: BRAND LISTINGS

Double Corona	Bolas	6¾	50	CM
Long Corona	Corral	6	44	CM
Robusto	Ponchos	4½	52	CM

Introduced in 1997, this brand offers a heavy-bodied cigar in an all-Honduran blend with a Sumatra-seed wrapper. Each shape is presented in all-cedar cabinets.

EL GLADIATOR
Handmade in Esteli, Nicaragua.

Wrapper: Ecuador, Mexico   Binder: Indonesia   Filler: Dom. Rep.

Shape	Name	Lgth	Ring	Wrapper
Double Corona	Viajante	7¾	52	CC-Ma
Toro	Toro	6½	50	CC-Ma
Robusto	Robusto	4¾	50	CC-Ma
Long Corona	Corona	6	44	CC-Ma
Panatela	No. 4	5½	38	CC-Ma

This brand was introduced in 1995, with a mild body in the natural (Ecuador) wrapper and a medium body with the Mexican maduro wrapper. It is offered in boxes of 25.

EL GLORIOSO DOMINICANO
Handmade in Santiago, Dominican Republic.

Wrapper: USA/Connecticut   Binder: Dom. Rep.   Filler: Dom. Rep.

Shape	Name	Lgth	Ring	Wrapper
Corona Extra	No. 100	4½	46	CC
Robusto	No. 200	5	50	CC
Corona	No. 300	5½	43	CC
Toro	No. 400	6	52	CC
Lonsdale	No. 500	6½	44	CC

Double Corona	No. 600	7	50	CC

A product of the much-respected MATASA factory, this is a mild-to-medium-bodied cigar introduced in 1998. You can find it in elegant cedar boxes of 25 in the classic 8-9-8 layered presentation.

EL GRANDE MIGUEL
Handmade in Santo Domingo, Dominican Republic.
Wrapper: Ecuador *Binder: Dom. Rep.* *Filler: Dom. Rep.*

Shape	Name	Lgth	Ring	Wrapper
Corona		5½	44	CC
Toro		6	50	CC
Churchill		6¾	46	CC
Double Corona		7	50	CC

"The Big Mike" is well-named for the owner of Big Mike's Premium Cigars in South Plainfield, New Jersey. The brand, which has no shape names, is mild and available in boxes of 25.

EL GUAJIRO
Handmade in Tenerife, the Canary Islands of Spain.
Wrapper: USA/Connecticut *Binder: Spain* *Filler: Spain*

Shape	Name	Lgth	Ring	Wrapper
Toro	Doble Coronas	6¼	49	CC
Robusto	Robustos	5¼	50	CC
Corona	Brevas	5¾	43	CC
Short Panatela	Palmeros	4½	39	CC
Small Panatela	Trompetas	4⅛	33	CC
Small Panatela	Senoritas	4	33	CC
Corona Extra	Grand Cedro	6	43	CC
Petit Corona	No. 5	5	42	CC

HANDMADE CIGARS: BRAND LISTINGS

	Machine-made:			
Cigarillo	Aromas	3½	23	CC
Cigarillo	Palmeritos	3¾	24	CC

This is a full-bodied brand from the Canary Islands, using locally-grown binder and filler and offered in packs of five and 10, in cellophaned bundles of 20 and in cedar boxes of 25. The machine-made small cigars are available in chocolate and vanilla-flavored styles.

EL GUSTO CUBANO
Handmade in Tamboril, Dominican Republic.
Wrapper: USA/Connecticut Binder: Dom. Rep.   Filler: Dom. Rep.

Shape	Name	Lgth	Ring	Wrapper
Churchill	Churchill	7	47	CC
Long Corona	Corona	6	44	CC
Robusto	Robusto	5	50	CC

The Tamboril Cigar Company developed this brand in 1998 to provide a Connecticut-wrapped version of its Cordova Collection blend. It is a mild-to-medium-bodied smoke and is offered in unique "Uni-Freshpaks" of five cigars each.

EL INCOMPARABLE
Handmade in Danli, Honduras.
Wrapper: Ecuador Binder: Nicaragua Filler: Dom. Rep., Mexico, Nicaragua

Shape	Name	Lgth	Ring	Wrapper
Long Corona	Corona	6	44	CC
Robusto	Robusto	4½	50	CC
Double Corona	Churchill	7	49	CC
Torpedo	Torpedo	7	56	CC
	Made with short filler:			
Small Panatela	Wilds	4¼	30	CM

HANDMADE CIGARS: BRAND LISTINGS

This is a fairly new brand, introduced in 1996, which is unique for its process that imbues the tobacco with 21-year-old Glenfarclas single malt scotch whisky. These full-bodied and spicy cigars are offered in equally stunning packaging, in a five-pack of aluminum tubes (except for the Wild shape) to ensure absolute, perfect freshness.

EL MAGO
Handmade in Las Palmas, Canary Islands of Spain.

Wrapper: Spain   Binder: Spain   Filler: Spain

Shape	Name	Lgth	Ring	Wrapper
Long Corona	Panatelas	6¼	40	CC
Toro	Nuncios	6¼	48	CC

This is a mild brand made up of Canary Islands-grown tobaccos, available without cellophane in a wood box of 25.

EL PARAISO
Handmade in Danli, Honduras.

Wrapper: Ecuador   Binder: Mexico   Filler: Costa Rica, Honduras, Nicaragua

Shape	Name	Lgth	Ring	Wrapper
Giant	Grande	8½	52	CC-Ma
Double Corona	Presidente	7½	50	CC
Torpedo	Torpedo	7	54	CC-Ma
Churchill	Double Corona	7	46	CC
Panatela	Panatelas Extra	6½	36	CC
Toro	Toro	6	50	CC-Ma
Corona	Corona	5¾	43	CC
Robusto	Robustos	4¾	52	CC-Ma
Slim Panatela	Pequenos	5	30	CC

Tobaccos from five nations go into the creation of El Paraiso, which results in a medium-bodied blend and excellent construction. Packed in cedar boxes of 18, 25 or 50 - depending on size - this brand is also modestly priced.

HANDMADE CIGARS: BRAND LISTINGS

EL PATIO
Handmade in Saõ Goncalo de Campos, Brazil.

Wrapper: USA/Connecticut   Binder: Brazil   Filler: Brazil

Shape	Name	Lgth	Ring	Wrapper
Corona	Corona	5½	42	CC
Toro	Toro	6	50	CC

New for 1998, this is a mild-boded brand available in value-priced bundles of 25.

EL PATRON
Handmade in Esteli, Nicaragua.

Wrapper: Nicaragua   Binder: Nicaragua   Filler: Nicaragua

Shape	Name	Lgth	Ring	Wrapper
Double Corona	Churchill	7	50	CM
Robusto	Robusto	5	50	CM
Long Corona	Corona	6	44	CM

This is a medium-bodied cigar, which debuted in 1998. It has a dark Nicaraguan wrapper and is offered in boxes of 10 or 25.

EL PILOTO CUBANO
Handmade in Santiago, Dominican Republic.

Wrapper: Dom. Rep.   Binder: Dom. Rep.   Filler: Dom. Rep.

Shape	Name	Lgth	Ring	Wrapper
Toro	Toro	5¾	50	CM

Introduced in 1998, this is a slightly sweet cigar, with all-Dominican leaves and a mild-to-medium body. It is available in bundles of 60 or in a plastic humidor with 120 cigars inside!

EL QUIJOTE
Handmade in San Andres Tuxtula, Mexico.

Wrapper: Mexico   Binder: Mexico   Filler: Mexico

HANDMADE CIGARS: BRAND LISTINGS

Shape	Name	Lgth	Ring	Wrapper
Petit Corona	Bronce	5	40	CM
Lonsdale	Plata	6¼	44	CM
Churchill	Oro	7	48	CM

This all-Mexican, mild-bodied brand was introduced in late 1997. The presentation is cedar boxes is unique, as the Bronce is offered in boxes of 15, the Plata in boxes of 16 and the Oro in boxes of boxes of 14 . . . or one! A clear-top box is also available.

EL REY DEL MUNDO
Handmade in Cofradia, Honduras.
Wrapper: Ecuador, USA/Connecticut

Binder: Honduras   *Filler: Dominican Republic, Honduras*

Shape	Name	Lgth	Ring	Wrapper
Robusto	Robusto	5	54	Ma
Toro	Robusto Larga	6	54	Ma
Double Corona	Robusto Suprema	7¼	54	Ma
Robusto	Robusto Zavalla	5	54	CM
Robusto	Rothschilde	5	50	CM
Grand Corona	Rectangulares	5⅝	45	CM
Panatela	Tino	5½	38	CM
Lonsdale	Cedars	7	43	CM
Toro	Choix Supreme	6⅛	49	CM
Grand Corona	Corona	5⅝	45	CM
Giant	Coronation	8½	52	CM
Double Corona	Double Corona	7	49	CM
Torpedo	Flor de Llaneza	6½	54	CM
Pyramid	Flor de LaVonda	6½	52	CM
Double Corona	Flor del Mundo	7¼	54	CM

HANDMADE CIGARS: BRAND LISTINGS

Petit Corona	Petit Lonsdale	4⅝	43	CM
Churchill	Corona Inmensa	7¼	47	CM-Ma
Slim Panatela	Plantations	6½	30	CC
Cigarillo	Elegantes	5⅜	29	CC
Short Panatela	Reynitas	5	38	CC
Small Panatela	Cafe au Lait	4½	35	CC

This name means "The King of the World" in Spanish and it lives up to its name
with its excellent construction and strong flavor from the Honduran filler and
binder and Sumatran-seed Ecuadorian wrapper. Launched in its current form in
1994, a total of 47 sizes are planned, of which 21 are currently in production.
The "Lights" group is mild in strength, with a Connecticut wrapper, Honduran
binder and filler tobacco from the Dominican Republic.

EL REY DE FLOREZ
Handmade in Tamboril, Dominican Republic.

Wrapper: Dom. Rep., Indonesia   Binder: Dom. Rep.   Filler: Dom. Rep.

Shape	Name	Lgth	Ring	Wrapper
Double Corona	Presidente	7½	50	CM-Ma
Grand Corona	Suave	6½	46	CM-Ma
Lonsdale	Panatella	7	40	CM-Ma
Robusto	Robusto	5	50	CM-Ma
Long Corona	Corona Extra	6	42	CM-Ma
Perfecto	Petite Perfecto	4½	42	CM-Ma
Perfecto	Minor Perfecto	5	46	CM-Ma
Perfecto	Major Perfecto	6	46	CM-Ma

"The King of Florez" was crowned in 1997 and offers a smooth, full-bodied flavor
with a choice of natural-shade wrappers from Sumatra or maduro wrappers from
the Dominican Republic. These outstanding cigars are presented without
cellophane in elegant, all-cedar boxes.

HANDMADE CIGARS: BRAND LISTINGS

EL REY PESCADO
Handmade in Santo Domingo, Dominican Republic.

Wrapper: Indonesia *Binder: Dom. Rep.* *Filler: Dom. Rep.*

Shape	Name	Lgth	Ring	Wrapper
Corona		5½	44	CC
Toro		6	50	CC
Churchill		6¾	46	CC
Double Corona		7	50	CC

Here is the "Kingfish." This is a mild cigar, without shape names, offered in four sizes in boxes of 25.

EL RICO HABANO
Handmade in Miami, Florida, USA and
Villa Gonzalez, Dominican Republic.

Wrapper: Ecuador *Binder: Nicaragua* *Filler: Honduras, Nicaragua*

Shape	Name	Lgth	Ring	Wrapper
Double Corona	Gran Habanero Deluxe	7¾	50	CM
Churchill	Double Coronas	7	47	CM
Corona Extra	Gran Coronas	5¾	46	CM
Long Corona	Lonsdale Extra	6¼	44	CM
Corona	Coronas	5¾	42	CM
Petit Corona	Petit Habanos	5	40	CM
Robusto	Habano Club	5	48	CM
Long Panatela	No. 1	7½	38	CM

This is a heavy-bodied cigar produced with imported Havana-seed tobaccos and made by hand in Ernesto Carrillo's famous El Credito cigar factory in Miami and the new El Credito facility in Villa Gonzalez, Dominican Republic. They are the most robust of the family of brands which includes La Hoja Selecta (mild) and La Gloria Cubana (medium-bodied).

HANDMADE CIGARS: BRAND LISTINGS

EL SABINAR
Handmade in Villa Gonzalez, Dominican Republic.

Wrapper: Indonesia   Binder: Dom. Rep.   Filler: Dom. Rep.

Shape	Name	Lgth	Ring	Wrapper
Churchill	1492	6¾	46	CC
Robusto	No. 3	4½	52	CC
Corona	No. 4	5¼	42	CC
Corona Extra	No. 5	5½	46	CC

This is a new brand for 1996, offering a medium-bodied blend. The wrapper is a
Sumatra-seed leaf grown in Ecuador. El Sabinar cigars are offered in cellophane
sleeves inside cedar cabinets of 25, with the No. 3 also offered in boxes of 10.

EL SABOR A MIAMI
Handmade, with short filler, in Miami, Florida, USA.

Wrapper: Indonesia   Binder: Indonesia   Filler: Dom. Rep.

Shape	Name	Lgth	Ring	Wrapper
Long Corona	Corona	6	44	CM

Introduced in 1997, here is a flavored brand, available in Amaretto, cherry,
coffee, rum and vanilla flavors. It is mild-to-medium in body and available in
boxes of 25.

EL SABOR DE MIAMI
Handmade in Miami, Florida, USA.

Wrapper: Indonesia   Binder: Cameroon   Filler: Dom. Rep., Nicaragua

Shape	Name	Lgth	Ring	Wrapper
Corona	El Cubanito	5½	44	CM
Cigarillo	Señorita	5	28	CM

This flavored, hand-made cigar is offered without cellophane wrapping in
humidor (glass) jars of 20 or 40 cigars. There are six flavors: rum, coffee/rum,
cognac, bourbon, vanilla and 3-Shooter (cognac, Frangelico, rum) which are
blended into a medium-bodied taste.

HANDMADE CIGARS: BRAND LISTINGS

El Sarare
Handmade in Cumana, Venezuela.

Wrapper: Ecuador   Binder: Venezuela   Filler: Venezuela

Shape	Name	Lgth	Ring	Wrapper
Toro	Toro	6¼	50	CC
Robusto	Robusto	5	50	CC

Mild in body, this brand was introduced in 1997 and is offered in boxes of 25.

El Sol
Handmade in Santiago, Dominican Republic and Tampa, Florida, USA

Wrapper: USA/Connecticut   Binder: Dom. Rep.   Filler: Dom. Rep.

Shape	Name	Lgth	Ring	Wrapper
Corona	Brevas	5½	42	CC-Co-Ma
Lonsdale	Corona Imperial	6¼	43	DC-CC-Co-Ma
Grand Corona	Palma Imperial	6½	46	CC-Co-Ma
Double Corona	Churchill	7	50	CC-Co-Ma
Double Corona	Emperador	7¾	50	CC-Co-Ma
Robusto	Rothschild	4½	50	CC-Co-Ma
Lonsdale	Londres Deluxe *(short filler)*	6½	43	CC-Ma
Long Corona	Dominicana 742	6¼	43	CC
Toro	Dominicana 852	6	50	CC-Ma
Double Corona	Dominicana 952	7	50	CC-Ma

This brand dates back all the way to 1928! In its current form, it offers a mild smoke and is made both in Tampa and in the Dominican Republic.

El Sublimado
Handmade in Danli, Honduras.

Wrapper: Ecuador   Binder: Dom. Rep.   Filler: Dom. Rep.

HANDMADE CIGARS: BRAND LISTINGS

Shape	Name	Lgth	Ring	Wrapper
Long Corona	Corona	6	44	CC
Robusto	Robusto	4½	50	CC
Torpedo	Torpedo	7	56	CC
Double Corona	Churchill	7	49	CC
	Made with short filler:			
Small Panatela	Wilds	4¼	30	CM

With its mild-to-medium body and totally unique flavor, El Sublimado cigars have earned a place in the hearts of discriminating smokers. Three-year-old leaves from the Cibao Valley of the Dominican Republic are mellowed with 50-year-old Noces d'Or cognac following a secret (and patented) method which enhances the flavor as combined with Connecticut-seed wrappers grown in Ecuador. The unusual packaging of this 1993-inaugurated brand offers these cigars in boxes of five aluminum tubes (except for the Wild shape) to ensure absolute freshness and peak of flavor.

EL TIGRE
Handmade in Danli, Honduras.

Wrapper: Indonesia   *Binder: Nicaragua*   *Filler: Honduras, Mexico*

Shape	Name	Lgth	Ring	Wrapper
Long Corona	Lonsdale	6	42	CM
Robusto	Robusto	5	50	CM
Double Corona	Churchill	7	49	CM
Giant	Double Corona	8½	52	CM
Torpedo	Pyramid	6	52	CM

"The Tiger" roars with a medium-to-full-bodied flavor and features a Sumatra wrapper. Introduced in 1996, El Tigre is offered in elegant, all-cedar boxes of 25 cigars each.

EL TIGRE
Handmade in Ocotal, Nicaragua.

Wrapper: Ecuador   *Binder: Nicaragua*   *Filler: Nicaragua*

HANDMADE CIGARS: BRAND LISTINGS

Shape	Name	Lgth	Ring	Wrapper
Robusto	Robusto	4¾	50	CM
Giant	Churchill	8½	42	CM
Corona	Corona	5½	42	CM
Toro	Toro	6	50	CM

More roar! This shade of The Tiger has only a mild bite, thanks to its Sumatra-seed wrapper grown in Ecuador and Nicargauan binder and filler. It is presented in all-cedar boxes of 25.

EL TITAN DE BRONZE
Handmade in Miami, Florida USA.
Wrapper: Ecuador or Indonesia   Binder: Cameroon   Filler: Dom. Rep., Nicaragua

Shape	Name	Lgth	Ring	Wrapper
Double Corona	Churchill	7½	50	CM
Torpedo	Torpedo	6½	54	CM
Lonsdale	No. 1	6½	44	CM
Grand Corona	Gloria Habano	6¼	46	CM
Toro	Corona	5¾	48	CM
Robusto	Robusto	5	50	CM
Corona	El Cubanito	5½	44	CM
	Made with short filler:			
Grand Corona	El Titan	6½	46	Ma

This medium-bodied brand is offered in cellophane sleeves in boxes of 25. The natural-shade wrapper features an Ecuadorian-grown leaf; Indonesian leaves are used for the maduro-wrapped shape.

EL TROFEO HABANO
Handmade in Folsom, California, USA,
Lake Tahoe, Nevada, USA and Tamboril, Dominican Republic.
Wrapper: Indonesia   Binder: Dom. Rep.   Filler: Dom. Rep.

HANDMADE CIGARS: BRAND LISTINGS

Shape	Name	Lgth	Ring	Wrapper
Small Panatela	Petit	4½	32	CC-CM-Ma
Petit Corona	Corona	5	44	CC-CM-Ma
Lonsdale	Corona Grande	6½	44	CC-CM-Ma
Robusto	Robusto	5	50	CC-CM-Ma
Double Corona	Churchill	7	50	CC-CM-Ma
Robusto	Monte Rico	5½	52	CC-CM-Ma
Perfecto	Perfecto No. 3	4¼	52	CC-CM-Ma
Perfecto	Perfecto No. 2	5¾	52	CC-CM-Ma
Perfecto	Perfecto No. 1	6¾	52	CC-CM-Ma
Toro	El Gordo	6½	54	CC-CM-Ma
Torpedo	Torpedo No. 1	5	54	CC-CM-Ma
Torpedo	Torpedo No. 2	6½	54	CC-CM-Ma
Torpedo	Super Torpedo	8½	56	CC-CM-Ma
	Flavored shapes:			
Petit Corona	Corona	5	40	CC-CM
Lonsdale	Corona Grande	6½	44	CC-CM
Robusto	Robusto	5	50	CC-CM

Introduced in 1996, this is a mild cigar in the Connecticut wrapper, medium-bodied with an Indonesian wrapper and medium-to-full-bodied in the maduro shade. The flavored versions are blended with short filler pipe tobaccos. You can try these treats in bundles or boxes of 25.

EL TURQUITO
Handmade in Danli, Honduras.

Wrapper: Ecuador   *Binder: Honduras*   *Filler: Nicaragua*

Shape	Name	Lgth	Ring	Wrapper
Long Corona	Corona	6	44	CC

Giant	Presidente	8	52	CC
Robusto	Robusto	5	50	CC
Double Corona	Churchill	7	50	CC

New in 1997, this is a medium-bodied blend that features a Connecticut-seed wrapper. It is offered in boxes of 25.

EL UNICORNIO
Handmade in Antigua, Guatemala.

Wrapper: Ecuador   Binder: Honduras   Filler: Costa Rica, Dom. Rep., Nicaragua

Shape	Name	Lgth	Ring	Wrapper
Robusto	Rothchild	4½	50	CC
Toro	Toro	6	50	CC
Giant	Viajante	8½	52	CC
Lonsdale	Corona	6½	44	CC
Giant	Presidente	8½	52	CC

Here is "the Unicorn," an all-long filler, handmade cigar from Guatemala, offering a medium-to-full-bodied taste in boxes of 25.

EL VALLE DORADO
Handmade in Esteli, Nicaragua.

Wrapper: Indonesia   Binder: Nicaragua   Filler: Honduras, Nicaragua

Shape	Name	Lgth	Ring	Wrapper
Long Corona	Cetro	6¼	44	CC
Churchill	Churchill	7	48	CC
Double Corona	Presidente	7½	50	CC
Robusto	Robusto	5	50	CC
Toro	Toro	6	50	CC

Introduced in 1997, this brand has a mild-to-medium body, offered in 25s.

HANDMADE CIGARS: BRAND LISTINGS

EMIGRANTE
Handmade in Santiago, Dominican Republic.

Wrapper: Indonesia   *Binder: Dom. Rep.*   *Filler: Dom. Rep.*

Shape	Name	Lgth	Ring	Wrapper
Churchill	Hemingway Classico	7	46	CM-Ma
Pyramid	Pyramid	6½	44	CM-Ma
Torpedo	Torpedo	6½	52	CM-Ma
Toro	Toro	6	52	CM-Ma
Giant	Double Corona	8	50	CM-Ma
Double Corona	Churchill	7½	50	CM-Ma
Toro	Robusto	6	50	CM-Ma
Robusto	Belicoso	5	50	CM-Ma
Grand Corona	Corona I	6	46	CM-Ma
Corona	Corona II	5¾	44	CM-Ma
Petit Corona	Petit Hemingway	4	44	CM-Ma
Lonsdale	Lonsdale	6½	42	CM-Ma
Long Panatela	Lancero	7½	38	CM-Ma
Slim Panatela	Long Panatela	5¾	30	CM-Ma
Small Panatela	Panatela	4¾	30	CM-Ma

This mild-to-medium-bodied brand was introduced in 1998. It is available in all-cedar boxes of 25. The Lonsdale and Panatela shapes are available in medium-to-full-bodied, mixed-filler flavored versions including Amaretto-brandy, blackberry, chocolate, cognac, cinnamon, hazelnut and vanilla.

EMPEROR GRAN RESERVA
Handmade in Santo Domingo, Dominican Republic.

Wrapper: Ecuador   *Binder: Dom. Rep.*   *Filler: Dom. Rep.*

HANDMADE CIGARS: BRAND LISTINGS

Shape	Name	Lgth	Ring	Wrapper
Long Corona	Corona	6	43	CC
Robusto	Robusto	5	52	CC
Churchill	Churchill	7	48	CC
Giant	Presidente	8	50	CC
Toro	Churchill	6	54	CC

Here is a 1997-introduced brand with a mild-to-medium body and a Connecticut-seed wrapper. It is offered in boxes of 20.

EMPEROR OF THE WORLD
Handmade in Santo Domingo, Dominican Republic.

Wrapper: Indonesia   Binder: Dom. Rep.   Filler: Dom. Rep.

Shape	Name	Lgth	Ring	Wrapper
Toro	Toro	5¾	50	CM
Churchill	Churchill	6¾	48	CM

Introduced in 1996, this is a medium-bodied blend with a Sumatra wrapper and offered in bundles of 25.

EMPRESS OF CUBA
Handmade in Danli, Honduras.

Wrapper: Indonesia   Binder: Honduras   Filler: Honduras, Nicaragua

Shape	Name	Lgth	Ring	Wrapper
Double Corona	Churchill	7	50	CM
Giant	Presidente	8½	50	CM
Robusto	Robusto	5	50	CM
Toro	Toro	6	50	CM

This brand debuted in 1997 and offers a medium-bodied taste. You can find it in see-through-top boxes of 20.

HANDMADE CIGARS: BRAND LISTINGS

ENCANTO
Handmade in Santa Rosa de Copan, Honduras.

Wrapper: Honduras   Binder: Honduras   Filler: Honduras

Shape	Name	Lgth	Ring	Wrapper
Giant	Grandioso	8	60	CM
Giant	Viajante	8½	52	CM
Double Corona	Churchill Claro	6⅞	49	CM-Ma
Lonsdale	Elegante	7	44	CM
Toro	Toro	6	50	CM-Ma
Lonsdale	Corona Larga	6¼	44	CM
Long Corona	Cetro Claro	6	42	CM-Ma
Robusto	Rothschild	4½	50	CM-Ma
Corona	Petit Corona	5½	42	CM
Panatela	Palma Fina	6¾	36	CM

This is a very well made cigar, introduced in 1977, offering a medium-to-heavy bodied taste in a variety of sizes and wrappers. It is offered in boxes of 25.

ENTRE RIOS
Handmade in Santiago, Dominican Republic.

Wrapper: Indonesia   Binder: Dom. Rep.   Filler: Dom. Rep.

Shape	Name	Lgth	Ring	Wrapper
Toro	Toro	6½	50	CC
Corona	Corona	5½	42	CC

Here is a new brand, introduced in 1997 and made in Santiago, the Dominican Republic. It features a Sumatra wrapper, Olor binder and filler and a mild-to-medium-bodied taste.

ENTREPRENEUR
Handmade in Santiago, Dominican Republic.

Wrapper: Ecuador, Indonesia   Binder: Dom. Rep.   Filler: Dom. Rep.

HANDMADE CIGARS: BRAND LISTINGS

Shape	Name	Lgth	Ring	Wrapper
Double Corona	Churchill	7½	50	CC-Stripe
Churchill	Gran Corona	6¾	45	CC-Stripe
Toro	Toro	6	50	CC-Stripe
Lonsdale	Lonsdale	6½	44	CC-Stripe
Robusto	Robusto	5	50	CC-Stripe
Corona	Corona	5½	42	CC-Stripe
Torpedo	Torpedo	6	52	CC-Stripe
Pyramid	Piramide	6	52	CC-Stripe
Perfecto	Short Cut	4	52	CC-Stripe

This is a mild-to-medium-bodied smoke, featuring a Sumatra wrapper or a striped double-wrapped version using Ecuador and Sumatra wrapper leaves. Introduced in 1997, it is offered in individual cellophane sleeves and packed in boxes of 25.

ERTÉ
Handmade in San Jose, Costa Rica.

Wrapper: Indonesia   Binder: Ecuador   Filler: Dom. Rep., Mexico, Nicaragua

Shape	Name	Lgth	Ring	Wrapper
Double Corona	Churchill	7¾	50	CM
Lonsdale	Lonsdale	6½	42	CM
Corona	Corona	5½	42	CM
Robusto	Robusto	5	52	CM

This salute to the noted artist debuted in 1998 and is reflected in both elegant bands and beautiful humidors. The medium-bodied cigars, which incirporate seven specific types of tobacco, are offered in gorgeously-decorated boxes of 20.

HANDMADE CIGARS: BRAND LISTINGS

ESCUDO CUBANO
Handmade in Villa Gonzalez, Dominican Republic.

Wrapper: Indonesia   Binder: Dom. Rep.   Filler: Dom. Rep.

Shape	Name	Lgth	Ring	Wrapper
Double Corona	Churchill	7	50	CC
Torpedo	Torpedo	5½	52	CC
Lonsdale	No. 1	6½	44	CC
Corona Extra	Gran Corona	5¾	46	CC
Long Panatela	Lancero	7¾	38	CC
Robusto	Robusto	5	50	CC

This line of Escudo Cubano was introduced in early 1997, and offers a mild-to-medium-bodied taste in boxes of 25.

ESCUDO CUBANO
Handmade in Esteli, Nicaragua.

Wrapper: Ecuador   Binder: Nicaragua   Filler: Nicaragua

Shape	Name	Lgth	Ring	Wrapper
Giant	Presidente	8½	52	CC
Double Corona	Churchill	7	50	CC
Lonsdale	No. 1	6½	44	CC
Torpedo	Torpedo	7½	54	CC
Pyramid	Piramide	7	50	CC
Long Panatela	Lancero	7	38	CC
Robusto	Robusto	5	50	CC

Introduced in 1996, this is a mild blend of tobaccos, including a Connecticut-seed wrapper grown in Ecuador and binder grown in the Jalapa Valley. These cigars are presented in unique cedar boxes of 25, featuring a plexiglass top!

HANDMADE CIGARS: BRAND LISTINGS

ESPADA DE ORO
Handmade in Danli, Honduras.

Wrapper: Indonesia   *Binder: Honduras*   *Filler: Honduras*

Shape	Name	Lgth	Ring	Wrapper
Double Corona	Monarch	7	52	Ma
Long Corona	Corona Gorda	6¼	44	Ma
Robusto	Rothschild	5	50	Ma

Created in 1992, this is a Honduran and Indonesian brand that offers a medium-bodied taste, thanks to a specially-selected blend of Cuban-seed tobaccos grown in Honduras. It is offered in specially-constructed boxes of 10 or 20 cigars each.

ESPANOLA BLACK LABEL
Handmade in Santiago, Dominican Republic.

Wrapper: Indonesia   *Binder: Dom. Rep.*   *Filler: Dom. Rep.*

Shape	Name	Lgth	Ring	Wrapper
Corona	Corona	5½	42	CM
Robusto	Robusto	5	50	CM
Toro	Sassoun	6	50	CM
Churchill	Excellente	6⅞	46	CM
Double Corona	Presidente	7	50	CM
Torpedo	Belicoso	5½	52	CM

Introduced in 1998, this is a medium-bodied brand with a Sumatra wrapper, offered in a value-priced bundle of 25.

ESPANOLA GOLD LABEL
Handmade in Santiago, Dominican Republic.

Wrapper: USA/Connecticut   *Binder: Dom. Rep.*   *Filler: Dom. Rep.*

Shape	Name	Lgth	Ring	Wrapper
Panatela	Torito	6	36	CC

Corona	Corona	5½	42	CC
Churchill	Excellente	6⅞	46	CC
Robusto	Robusto	5	50	CC
Lonsdale	Lonsdale	7	44	CC
Toro	Sassoun	6	50	CC
Torpedo	Belicoso	5½	52	CC
Double Corona	Churchill	6¾	50	CC
Double Corona	Presidente	7	50	CC

Silky smooth Connecticut shade-grown wrappers encase this mild blend from the Dominican Republic. Debuting in 1996, the eight shapes of this original Espanola series are presented without cellophane in cedar cabinets of 25 cigars.

ESPANOLA GREEN LABEL
Handmade in Santiago, Dominican Republic.

Wrapper: USA/Connecticut   *Binder: Dom. Rep.*   *Filler: Dom. Rep.*

Shape	Name	Lgth	Ring	Wrapper
Panatela	Torito	6	36	CC
Corona	Corona	5½	42	CC
Lonsdale	Lonsdale	7	44	CC
Churchill	Excellente	6⅞	46	CC
Long Corona	Corona Grande	6	44	CC
Churchill	Churchill	6¾	50	CC
Robusto	Robusto	5	50	CC
Toro	Sassoun	6	50	CC
Double Corona	Double Corona	7½	50	CC
Torpedo	Belicoso	5½	52	CC
Giant	Fabuloso	8	52	CC

HANDMADE CIGARS: BRAND LISTINGS

Formerly known as the Reserve Series, this line was introduced in 1996 and offers a more robust taste, generally judged to be medium in strength. It is presented in 5x5 packaging in all-cedar cabinet boxes of 25.

ESPANOLA RED LABEL
Handmade in Santiago, Dominican Republic.

Wrapper: Indonesia   *Binder: Dom. Rep.*   *Filler: Dom. Rep.*

Shape	Name	Lgth	Ring	Wrapper
Panatela	Torito	6	36	CM
Corona	Corona	5½	42	CM
Churchill	Excellente	6⅞	46	CM
Robusto	Robusto	5	50	CM
Lonsdale	Lonsdale	7	44	CM
Torpedo	Belicoso	5½	52	CM
Toro	Sassoun	6	50	CM
Double Corona	Churchill	6¾	50	CM
Double Corona	Presidente	7	50	CM
Giant	Fabuloso	8	52	CM

With a Sumatra wrapper and the fullest body of the entire Espanola line, this cigar — introduced in 1997 — offers every conceivable size for the convenience of all smokers. Like its siblings, it is presented nude in five-row packaging inside all-cedar cabinet boxes.

ESPECIALES SELECTOS-DOMINICAN
Handmade in Santiago, Dominican Republic.

Wrapper: USA/Connecticut   *Binder: Dom. Rep.*   *Filler: Dom. Rep.*

Shape	Name	Lgth	Ring	Wrapper
Churchill	Churchill	6⅞	48	CC
Toro	Toro	6	50	CC
Lonsdale	Lonsdale	6¾	44	CC

Robusto	Robusto	5	50	CC
Petit Corona	Palmita	5	40	CC
Corona	No. 4	5½	43	CC

New in 1998, this is a mild-to-medium-bodied blend from Juan Sosa's Antillian Cigar Company. This blend of U.S. and Dominican tobaccos is offered in open-faced cedar boxes of 25.

ESPECIALES SELECTOS - NICARAGUAN
Handmade in Esteli, Nicaragua.

Wrapper: Nicaragua *Binder: Nicaragua* *Filler: Nicaragua*

Shape	Name	Lgth	Ring	Wrapper
Giant	Gigantes	8	54	CM
Double Corona	Presidentes	7	52	CM
Churchill	Churchill	6⅞	48	CM
Toro	Double Corona	5⅝	48	CM
Robusto	Robusto	4½	52	CM

This brand was introduced by Juan Sosa in 1998. It offers a mild body in value-priced bundles of 25.

ESPERANZA
Handmade in Santiago, Dominican Republic.

Wrapper: Indonesia, USA/Connecticut *Binder: Dom. Rep.* *Filler: Dom. Rep.*

Shape	Name	Lgth	Ring	Wrapper
Pyramid	Piramide	5¾	54	CC-CM
Torpedo	Torpedo	6½	53	CC-CM
Double Corona	Churchill	7½	50	CC-CM
Double Corona	Hemingway Churchill	7½	50	CC-CM
Torpedo	Torpedo Short	5	50	CC-CM
Robusto	Robusto	5	50	CC-CM

HANDMADE CIGARS: BRAND LISTINGS

Robusto	Robusto Short	4	50	CC-CM
Corona	Petit Corona	5½	42	CC-CM
Short Panatela	Panatela	5	36	CC-CM
Small Panatela	Petit	4½	30	CC-CM

This is a mild blend, introduced in 1998 and offered in cellophane sleeves in packs of five or in boxes of 25. It is also available in special flavored versions in the Panatela and Petit shapes in Amaretto, cherry, cognac and vanilla.

ESPINOSA CLASSICO
Handmade in Tegucigalpa, Honduras.
Wrapper: Ecuador or Indonesia   *Binder: Dominican Republic*
Filler: Dominican Republic, Indonesia, Nicaragua

Shape	Name	Lgth	Ring	Wrapper
Corona	Corona	5½	44	CC-CM
Long Corona	Lonsdale	6	44	CC
Robusto	Robusto	5	50	CC-CM
Churchill	Churchill	7	48	CC-CM
Long Panatela	Lancero	7½	38	CC
Pyramid	Piramide	7	54	CC
Double Corona	Presidente	7	50	CC

Introduced in 1997, this is a medium-to-full-bodied brand that features a Connecticut-seed wrapper and Dominican, Indonesian and Nicaraguan-grown filler leaves. In 1998, an Indonesian wrapper is available on three sizes. It is attractively presented in all-cedar cabinets of 25 cigars each.

ESPINOSA GOLD
Handmade in Santiago, Dominican Republic.
Wrapper: Ecuador or Indonesia   *Binder: Dom. Rep.*   *Filler: Dom. Rep.*

Shape	Name	Lgth	Ring	Wrapper
Corona	Corona	5½	44	CC-CM

Long Corona	Lonsdale	6	44	CC
Robusto	Robusto	5	50	CC-CM
Double Corona	Churchill	7½	50	CC-CM
Pyramid	Piramide	7	52	CC-CM

This brand was introduced in 1997, with a mild-to-medium-bodied flavor and wrapper from Sumatra. New for 1998 is the Ecuadorian-grown, Connecticut-seed wrapped version. It is offered in an all-cedar box of 25.

ESSENCE OF VANILLA
Handmade, with mixed filler, in Santiago, Dominican Republic.
Wrapper: Dom. Rep.   *Binder: Dom. Rep.*   *Filler: Dom. Rep.*

Shape	Name	Lgth	Ring	Wrapper
Small Panatela	Cat Nap	4	34	CM
Lonsdale	Siesta	6½	44	CM

This is a flavored, medium-to-full-bodied brand, introduced in 1998. It is offered in boxes of 25.

ESTAVAN CRUZ
Handmade in San Jose, Costa Rica.
Wrapper: Ecuador   *Binder: Ecuador*   *Filler: Dom. Rep., Nicaragua*

Shape	Name	Lgth	Ring	Wrapper
Torpedo	Belicoso	6	54	CM-Ma
Double Corona	Corona Gigante	7	54	CM-Ma
Robusto	Ponchos	5½	52	CM-Ma
Robusto	Robusto	5	50	CM-Ma

Medium-bodied, but full of flavor and brilliantly constructed, this Sumatra-seed-wrapped brand was introduced in 1996 but exploded onto the market in 1998. The maduro-wrapped style is full-bodied. It is offered in the most popular shapes and smartly packaged in 3s, 10s, 20s and in flip-up boxes of 25.

HANDMADE CIGARS: BRAND LISTINGS

ESTELA
Handmade in Santiago, Dominican Republic.

Wrapper: Indonesia   Binder: Dom. Rep.   Filler: Dom. Rep.

Shape	Name	Lgth	Ring	Wrapper
Toro	Don Aurelio	6½	50	CM
Churchill	Churchill	6⅞	47	CM
Robusto	Robusto	5½	50	CM
Lonsdale	Lonsdale	6½	42	CM

Introduced in 1997, this is a mild but spicy cigar. It is offered in individual cellophane sleeves in packs of four and in cedar boxes of 25.

ESTELAR LIMITED RESERVE
Handmade in Miami, Florida, USA.
Wrapper: Indonesia or USA/Connecticut

Binder: Ecuador   Filler: Dom. Rep., Honduras, Nicaragua

Shape	Name	Lgth	Ring	Wrapper
Double Corona	Churchill	7	50	CC-CM
Torpedo	Torpedo	6½	54	CC-CM
Lonsdale	Lonsdale	6½	42	CC-CM
Toro	Toro	6	50	CC-CM
Long Corona	Corona	6	44	CC-CM
Robusto	Robusto	5	50	CC-CM

Introduced in 1997, this is a full-bodied cigar with a choice of a Sumatra-grown or Connecticut wrapper. It is available in individual cellophane sleeves in all-cedar boxes of 25.

ESTELAR PREMIUM
Handmade in Santo Domingo, Dominican Republic.
Wrapper: Indonesia or USA/Connecticut

Binder: Honduras   Filler: Dominican Republic

HANDMADE CIGARS: BRAND LISTINGS

Shape	Name	Lgth	Ring	Wrapper
Double Corona	Double Corona	7½	50	CC-CM
Churchill	Churchill	6¾	48	CC-CM
Lonsdale	Lonsdale	6½	44	CC-CM
Toro	Toro	6	50	CC-CM
Robusto	Robusto	5	50	CC-CM

Made by hand in Santo Domingo, this is a medium-bodied cigar with a choice of Sumatran or Connecticut wrapper. It is presented in all-cedar cabinets of 25.

ESTEVAN REY CABINET SELECTION
Handmade in Tamboril, Dominican Republic.

Wrapper: Ecuador   Binder: Dom. Rep.   Filler: Dom. Rep.

Shape	Name	Lgth	Ring	Wrapper
Long Corona	Corona	6	42	CC
Robusto	Robusto	5	50	CC
Double Corona	Churchill	7½	50	CC

Introduced in 1997, this is a medium-bodied cigar with Piloto Cubano filler leaves and an Ecuadorian wrapper. Each cigar is protected in an individual cellophane sleeve and packed in boxes of 25.

ESTEVAN REY PREMIUM SELECTION
Handmade in Tamboril, Dominican Republic.

Wrapper: Dom. Rep.   Binder: Dom. Rep.   Filler: Dom. Rep.

Shape	Name	Lgth	Ring	Wrapper
Long Corona	Corona	6	42	CC
Robusto	Robusto	5	50	CC
Double Corona	Churchill	7½	50	CC

Here is a mild-to-medium bodied, all-Dominican leaf cigar, also introduced in 1997. Slightly milder than the Cabinet Selection of this brand, it is also offered in cellophane sleeves and packed in boxes of 25.

HANDMADE CIGARS: BRAND LISTINGS

ESTRELLA
Handmade in San Andres Tuxtla, Mexico.

Wrapper: Indonesia   *Binder: Mexico*   *Filler: Mexico*

Shape	Name	Lgth	Ring	Wrapper
Lonsdale	Lonsdale	6½	42	CC
Toro	Toro	6	50	CC
Panatela	Coronita	5½	38	CC

Here is a mild cigar with vanilla flavoring in all shapes and a Sumatra wrapper, introduced in 1997. It is offered in individual cellophane sleeves in boxes of 25.

ESTRELLA BLANCA
Handmade, with short filler, in San Andres Tuxtla, Mexico.

Wrapper: Mexico   *Binder: Mexico*   *Filler: Mexico*

Shape	Name	Lgth	Ring	Wrapper
Robusto	Robusto	5	50	CC
Long Corona	Lonsdale	6	42	CC
Toro	Corona Gorda	6	50	CC

New for 1997, this is a mild-bodied brand offered in value-priced boxes of 25.

EVELIO
Handmade in Danli, Honduras.

Wrapper: Ecuador   *Binder: Nicaragua*
Filler: Honduras, Mexico, Nicaragua

Shape	Name	Lgth	Ring	Wrapper
Corona	Corona	5¾	42	CC
Churchill	Double Corona	7⅝	47	CC
Lonsdale	No. 1	7	44	CC
Robusto	Robusto	4¾	54	CC-Ma
Toro	Robusto Larga	6	54	CC-Ma

Pyramid	Torpedo	7	54	CC

The lifetime of expertise which resides in master roller Evelio Oviedo is the secret behind this brand, introduced in 1996. This is a full-bodied but smooth smoke in six of the most popular sizes, prepared in the same all-by-hand method that Oviedo knew from his days in Cuba at the H. Upmann factory in Havana. Evelio cigars are presented in all-cedar boxes of 25.

EVEL KNIEVEL SIGNATURE SERIES
Handmade in Santiago, Dominican Republic.
Wrapper: Indonesia *Binder: Dom. Rep.* *Filler: Dom. Rep.*

Shape	Name	Lgth	Ring	Wrapper
Pyramid	Rocket	7½	64	CM

Only in America would you find these unique cigars, shaped like the rocket that sent the legendary daredevil Evel Knievel over the Snake River. They are medium in body and are offered in a special commemorative box of 20.

EVIL CLOWN
Handmade in Santiago, Dominican Republic.
Wrapper: Indonesia *Binder: Nicaragua* *Filler: Dom. Rep., Nicaragua*

Shape	Name	Lgth	Ring	Wrapper
Churchill	Churchill	7¼	48	CM

Don't be scared! The Evil Clown brand was introduced in 1998 and has a mild body to go with its stunning packaging. It is offered in boxes of 20.

EVITA
Handmade in Santiago, Dominican Republic.
Wrapper: Indonesia *Binder: Dom. Rep.* *Filler: Dom. Rep.*

Shape	Name	Lgth	Ring	Wrapper
Long Corona	Corona	6	44	CC
Grand Corona	Extra Corona	6	46	CC
Giant	Double Corona	8½	52	CC

Robusto	Robusto	5	50	CC
Churchill	Churchill	7½	48	CC
Torpedo	Torpedo	6½	52	CC
Double Corona	Presidente	7½	50	CC
Churchill	Lancero	7	46	CC
Long Panatela	Panatella	7	36	CC

Don't cry for this brand, Argentina! A 1997 tribute to the former first lady of Argentina, Evita Peron (1919-52), this is a mild-to-medium-bodied brand offered in boxes of 25.

EVITA IMPERIAL MADURO
Handmade in Santiago, Dominican Republic.

Wrapper: Dom. Rep.   *Binder: Dom. Rep.*   *Filler: Dom. Rep.*

Shape	Name	Lgth	Ring	Wrapper
Long Corona	Corona	6	44	Ma
Robusto	Robusto	5	50	Ma
Double Corona	Presidente	7½	50	Ma
Torpedo	Belicoso	5	52	Ma

A sister to the Evita brand, this is a medium-bodied cigar introduced in 1998. It is available in a flip-top cedar box of 25.

EVITA SCENTED
Handmade, with mixed filler, in Santiago, Dominican Republic.

Wrapper: Indonesia   *Binder: Dom. Rep.*   *Filler: Dom. Rep.*

Shape	Name	Lgth	Ring	Wrapper
Short Panatela	Small	5	36	CM
Long Corona	Large	6	42	CM

Available in bundles of 25 and in glass-topped boxes of 10 or 25, this is a mild cigar available in Amaretto, cinnamon, coconut, chocolate, mint, rum and vanilla. The flavoring is applied in a painstaking process which includes soaking of the leaves for up to two weeks and then a special drying process for the same period.

EXCALIBUR
BY HOYO DE MONTERREY
Handmade in Cofradia, Honduras.

Wrapper: USA/Connecticut   *Binder: Honduras*
Filler: Dominican Republic, Honduras and Nicaragua

Shape	Name		Lgth	Ring	Wrapper
Double Corona	No. I		7¼	54	CC-Ma
Churchill	No. II		6¾	47	CC-Ma
Toro	No. III		6⅛	48	CC-Ma
Grand Corona	No. IV		5⅝	46	CC-Ma
Grand Corona	No. V		6¼	45	CC-Ma
Panatela	No. VI		5½	38	CC-Ma
Petit Corona	No. VII		5	43	CC-Ma
Cigarillo	No. VIII		5¼	29	CC-Ma
Churchill	Banquets	(tubed)	6¾	48	CC
Giant	Emperor		8½	52	CC-Ma
Robusto	Epicures		5¼	50	CC-Ma
Cigarillo	Miniatures		3	22	CC
Cigarillo	Cigarillo		4	24	CC

Excalibur cigars are handmade in Honduras and are the choicest cigars picked from the famous Hoyo de Monterrey line of fine cigars. All of the shapes are wrapped in beautiful Connecticut Shade wrappers, which gives each and every Excalibur cigar a robust, but exquisitely smooth taste. Shapes 1-8 are available in boxes of 20, as are the Epicures, Minis and Cigarillos; the Minis, Cigarillos, Banquets and Emperors are packed in 10s.

HANDMADE CIGARS: BRAND LISTINGS

EXCELSIOR
Handmade in San Andres Tuxtla, Mexico.

Wrapper: USA/Connecticut   Binder: Mexico   *Filler: Dom. Rep., Mexico*

Shape	Name	Lgth	Ring	Wrapper
Long Corona	No. 1	6¼	42	CC
Lonsdale	No. 2	6¾	44	CC
Robusto	No. 3	5½	52	CC
Churchill	No. 4	7	48	CC
Giant	No. 5	8	50	CC
Giant	Individuale	8½	52	CC

This brand was introduced in 1996, offering a blend of tobaccos and a medium-bodied flavor in boxes of 25 cigars each, except for the Individuale, which is offered in boxes of 10.

EXPRESS IMPORTS
Handmade in Danli, Honduras.

Wrapper: Mexico   Binder: Mexico   *Filler: Nicaragua*

Shape	Name	Lgth	Ring	Wrapper
Slim Panatela	No. 1	7	30	CC-Ma
Panatela	No. 2	6⅞	35	CC-Ma
Long Corona	No. 3	6	42	CC-Ma
Corona	No. 4	5½	42	CC-Ma
Lonsdale	No. 5	6⅝	44	CC-Ma
Churchill	No. 6	6⅞	48	CC-Ma
Robusto	No. 7	4¾	50	CC-Ma
Toro	No. 8	6¼	50	CC-Ma
Double Corona	No. 9	7½	50	CC-Ma
Giant	No. 10	8	52	CC-Ma
Torpedo	No. 11	6⅝	54	CC-Ma

HANDMADE CIGARS: BRAND LISTINGS

This is a medium-bodied cigar, available in both natural and maduro wrappers, since 1992. It is offered in bundles of 25.

F.B. BOYD
Handmade in Tamboril, Dominican Republic.

Wrapper: Indonesia, USA/Connecticut   Binder: Dom. Rep.   Filler: Dom. Rep.

Shape	Name	Lgth	Ring	Wrapper
Double Corona	Churchill	7½	50	CC-Ma
Toro	Short Churchill	6½	50	CC-Ma
Torpedo	Figurado	6½	53	CC
Grand Corona	Grand Corona	6	46	CC-Ma
Robusto	Rothschild	5	50	CC-Ma

Developed in honor of textile magnate L.M. Boyd, a devoted cigar smoker and distributed by his successors, this is a mild cigar for the new smoker. Introduced in 1998, it is offered in a choice of Connecticut natural or Indonesian maduro wrappers and presented in cellophane sleeves inside all-cedar chests of 25.

F.D. GRAVE
Handmade in Danli, Honduras.

Wrapper: USA/Connecticut   Binder: USA/Connecticut   Filler: Honduras, Indonesia

Shape	Name	Lgth	Ring	Wrapper
Double Corona	Churchill	7¾	50	CM
Double Corona	Corona Grande	7	52	CM
Long Corona	Lonsdale	6¼	44	CM
Robusto	Robusto	5	50	CM

One of the most respected names in U.S. cigar history is back with an all-handmade line of exceptional quality, made in Honduras. Introduced in late 1995, the four-shape line is full-bodied in taste and offers a Connecticut Broadleaf wrapper and filler, to complement the Honduran and Indonesian fillers. The F.D. Grave series are presented in individual cellophane sleeves inside an all-wood cabinet box.

HANDMADE CIGARS: BRAND LISTINGS

FAMOUS PRIVATE SELECTION
Handmade in Santiago, Dominican Republic.
Wrapper: USA/Connecticut   *Binder: Dom. Rep.*   *Filler: Dom. Rep.*

Shape	Name	Lgth	Ring	Wrapper
Double Corona	Presidente	7½	50	CC-Ma
Torpedo	Torpedo	6½	50	CC-Ma
Grand Corona	Suave	6½	46	CC-Ma
Long Corona	Corona Extra	6	42	CC-Ma
Toro	Toro	6	50	CC-Ma
Robusto	Robusto	5	50	CC-Ma

First available in 1997, this mild-to-medium-bodied brand offers a rich flavor and excellent construction at a very agreeable price. You'll find it presented in cedar cabinets of 25 cigars each. The maduro-wrapped version debuted in 1998.

THE FAMOUS RUM RUNNER
Handmade, with medium filler, in Jaibon, Dominican Republic.
Wrapper: Indonesia   *Binder: Indonesia*
Filler: Columbia, Dominican Republic, Indonesia

Shape	Name	Lgth	Ring	Wrapper
Short Panatela	Wench	4½	36	CM
Petit Corona	Bucaneer	4¾	42	CM
Lonsdale	Pirate	6½	42	CM

This is a flavored cigar produced by the Caribbean Cigar Company and introduced in 1994. Made by hand, it uses medium filler and offers a medium-to-full body and sweet flavor. Not surprisingly, the black and gold band features the skull-and-crossbones emblem of pirate ships of yore!

FARINA
Handmade in San Andres Tuxtla, Mexico.
Wrapper: Mexico   *Binder: Mexico*   *Filler: Mexico*

HANDMADE CIGARS: BRAND LISTINGS

Shape	Name	Lgth	Ring	Wrapper
Robusto	Robusto	5	50	CM
Long Corona	Corona	6	42	CM
Toro	Toro	6	50	CM
Lonsdale	Lonsdale	6½	42	CM
Giant Corona	Lonsdale Extra	7½	42	CM
Double Corona	Churchill	7	50	CM
Double Corona	Presidente	7½	50	CM

This is a 1998-introduced, mild-bodied cigar — unusual for an all-Mexican-grown *puro*. You can try it in bundles or boxes of 25.

FAT CAT
BY DON RICO
Handmade in Santiago, Dominican Republic.
Wrapper: Dom. Rep., Indonesia   Binder: Dom. Rep.   Filler: Dom. Rep.

Shape	Name	Lgth	Ring	Wrapper
Robusto	Robusto	5	50	CC
Long Corona	Corona	6	44	CC
Double Corona	Churchill	7	50	CC-Ma
Toro	Toro	6	50	Ma
Perfecto	Shorty	4	51	CC
Torpedo	Torpedo	6	52	CC-Ma

These are "fat" cigars indeed, as all but one has a ring gauge of 50 or more. A product of the Puros Don Rico factory, these are mild-to-medium-bodied cigars in the Indonesian-grown natural wrapper and medium-bodied in the Dominican-grown maduro shade. It is offered in cedar boxes of 25.

FELIPE BLACK
Handmade in Santa Rosa de Copan, Honduras.
Wrapper: Honduras   Binder: Honduras   Filler: Honduras

HANDMADE CIGARS: BRAND LISTINGS

Shape	Name	Lgth	Ring	Wrapper
Double Corona	Glorioso	7¾	50	Ma
Churchill	Suntuoso	7	48	Ma
Torpedo	Belicoso	6	52	Ma
Robusto	Robusto	5	52	Ma
Corona	Sereno	5¾	42	Ma
Petit Corona	Nino	4¼	44	Ma

Introduced in 1998, this is an oscuro-wrapped brand with an extra-full-bodied taste. It is presented without cellophane in boxes of 25 except for the Belicoso shape, offered in 20s.

FELIPE DOMINICANA
Handmade in Tamboril, Dominican Republic.

Wrapper: USA/Connecticut   *Binder: Dom. Rep.*   *Filler: Nicaragua*

Shape	Name	Lgth	Ring	Wrapper
Double Corona	Double Corona	7½	50	CC
Toro	Don Felipe	6⅛	54	CC
Panatela	Panatela	6	38	CC
Pyramid	Boa	4½	Tpr	CC
Robusto	Superbo	4¾	54	CC
Corona	Corona	5⅓	42	CC

Finally a Dominican-produced from Felipe Gregorio! This is a medium-bodied, spicy blend, developed in 1998. It is presented in cellophane sleeves in boxes of 20.

FELIPE GREGORIO
Handmade in Danli, Honduras.

Wrapper: Honduras   *Binder: Honduras*   *Filler: Honduras*

HANDMADE CIGARS: BRAND LISTINGS

Shape	Name	Lgth	Ring	Wrapper
Double Corona	Glorioso	7¾	50	CM
Churchill	Suntouso	7	48	CM
Torpedo	Belicoso	6	54	CM
Corona	Sereno	5¾	42	CM
Robusto	Robusto	5	52	CM
Petit Corona	Nino	4¼	44	CM

Introduced in 1992, this brand shows off the efforts of a single plantation in Honduras - Jamastram - in the famous valley of the same name. Their Havana-seed tobaccos offer full-bodied, but mellow flavor with an elegant, sweet aroma.

FELIPE II
Handmade in Danli, Honduras.

Wrapper: Indonesia   Binder: Honduras   Filler: Honduras

Shape	Name	Lgth	Ring	Wrapper
Double Corona	Reserva A	7¾	50	CM
Torpedo	Reserva B	6	52	CM
Churchill	Reserva X	7	48	CM
Toro	Reserva D	6	50	CM
Robusto	Reserva R	5	52	CM
Corona	Reserva C	5½	42	CM
Petit Corona	Reserva N	4¼	44	CM

Introduced in 1997, this is a medium-to-full-bodied cigar with peppery highlights and offered in a fabulous cabinet-style box. The Sumatra-grown wrapper complements the Cuban-seed binder and filler and the perfect construction for an enjoyable experience every time you light one up.

FERDINAND COLLECTION
Handmade in Esteli, Nicaragua.

Wrapper: Nicaragua   Binder: Nicaragua   Filler: Nicaragua

HANDMADE CIGARS: BRAND LISTINGS

Shape	Name	Lgth	Ring	Wrapper
Giant	Pantera Grande	8	48	Co-Ma
Churchill	Churchill	7	48	Co-Ma
Torpedo	Torpedo	5½	54	Co-Ma
Pyramid	Pyramid	6¾	48	Co-Ma
Robusto	Rothschild	5½	50	Co-Ma
Robusto	Robusto	4½	48	Co-Ma
Corona	Corona	5½	42	Co-Ma

Introduced in 1997, these all-Nicaraguan cigars are mild-to-medium in body in either wrapper shade. You can find them in boxes of 25 in slide-top, all-cedar cabinets.

FIGHTING COCK
Handmade in Manila, the Philippines.

Wrapper: Indonesia   Binder: Philippines   Filler: Philippines

Shape	Name		Lgth	Ring	Wrapper
Pyramid	Sidewinder I		6	52	CM
Toro	Sidewinder II		6	54	CM
Toro	Texas Red		6½	53	CM
Robusto	Smokin' Lulu		5¼	48	CM
Perfecto	Rooster Arturo		5	53	CM
Churchill	C.O.D.		7	47	CM
Corona	Fly Boy	(tubed)	5½	44	CM

Introduced in 1995, these hand-made, Manila-manufactured cigars offer a medium-bodied taste, combining a Javan sun-grown wrapper with Philippine Isabela binder and filler. The brand is presented in stunning varnished wooden boxes of 25, each equipped with a hand-sewn, crushed velvet liner (except for the Fly Boy shape, offered in 20s), or in bundles of 25. The shapes are named after actual champion roosters!

HANDMADE CIGARS: BRAND LISTINGS

FIRST LADY OF THE WORLD
Handmade in Santo Domingo, Dominican Republic.
Wrapper: Ecuador or Indonesia   Binder: Dom. Rep.   Filler: Dom. Rep.

Shape	Name	Lgth	Ring	Wrapper
Short Panatela	Petite	5	36	CC

This brand was introduced in 1996 and is made with long-filler leaves. It is mild-to-medium in body and presented in boxes of 25. It is available in Amaretto and vanilla flavors.

FIRST PRIMING
Handmade in Danli, Honduras.
Wrapper: Honduras   Binder: Honduras   Filler: Honduras

Shape	Name	Lgth	Ring	Wrapper
Giant	Grandees	8½	52	CC-Ma
Double Corona	Largos	7½	50	CC-Ma

This is a medium-bodied cigar, made of all Honduran tobacco. An excellent value, it is offered in modestly-priced bundles of 25.

FITTIPALDI
Handmade in Santiago, Dominican Republic.
Wrapper: Dom. Rep.   Binder: Dom. Rep.   Filler: Dom. Rep.

Shape	Name	Lgth	Ring	Wrapper
Giant	Presidente	8	50	CM
Torpedo	Torpedo	6¾	54	CM
Toro	Toro	6	50	CM
Robusto	Robusto	4½	50	CM
Churchill	Churchill	7	48	CM
Lonsdale	Lonsdale	6½	42	CM
Long Corona	Corona	6	44	CM

HANDMADE CIGARS: BRAND LISTINGS

Yes, this brand is owned by famous Brazilian racer Emerson Fittipaldi, winner of Formula 1 world championships in 1972 and 1974 and the Indianapolis 500 in 1989 and 1993. The band features the checkered flag, symbol of victory in racing and the cigars themselves are produced in conjunction with the much-respected Reyes family. The blend of the currently-offered 1993 Vintage is medium-to-full in strength, featuring a Cameroon-seed wrapper. Fittipaldi cigars are presented in cellophane sleeves and packed in all-cedar cabinets of 25.

FIVE STAR
Handmade in Santiago, Dominican Republic.

Wrapper: USA/Connecticut   Binder: Mexico   Filler: Dom. Rep.

Shape	Name	Lgth	Ring	Wrapper
Lonsdale	No. 100	6½	44	CC
Long Corona	No. 200	6	44	CC
Corona	No. 300	5½	44	CC
Double Corona	No. 400	7	50	CC
Toro	No. 500	6	50	CC
Slim Panatela	No. 600	6	34	CC
Robusto	No. 700	5	50	CC
Giant	No. 800	8½	52	CC
Slim Panatela	No. 900	6¾	34	CC

Introduced in 1998, this is a quality, bundled cigar with a mild body and a smooth finish. An excellent value, this brand is offered in bundles of 20.

FIVE STAR HONDURANS
Handmade in Danli, Honduras.

Wrapper: Ecuador or Indonesia   Binder: Nicaragua   Filler: Mexico, Nicaragua

Shape	Name	Lgth	Ring	Wrapper
Double Corona	Churchill	7	50	CC-CM
Long Corona	Corona	6	44	CC-CM
Robusto	Robusto	5	50	CC-CM

HANDMADE CIGARS: BRAND LISTINGS

Introduced in 1997, this is a medium-bodied brand with a choice of Ecuadorian or Sumatran wrappers. It is available in bundles of 20.

FLAMENCO LAS PALMAS
Handmade in La Romana, Dominican Republic.

Wrapper: Mexico, Nicaragua   *Binder: Dom. Rep.*   *Filler: Dom. Rep.*

Shape	Name	Lgth	Ring	Wrapper
	The Habanos:			
Corona	Coronas	5⅝	42	Co
Lonsdale	Palmas	6⅝	42	Co
Grand Corona	Gordas	5⅝	47	Co
Robusto	Robustos	5	50	Co
Toro	Corona Doble	6½	50	Co
	The Traditionals:			
Lonsdale	Corona Cristal	6⅝	40	Co
Toro	Gloria Dominicana	6	50	Co
	The Oscuros:			
Robusto	No. 5	5	50	Ma
Toro	No. 6	6½	50	Ma

This brand, familiar to long-time smokers, re-emerged in 1998. It features a Nicaraguan-grown Habana 2000 wrapper for the natural-shade shapes and a Mexican-grown oscuro wrapper. The result is a medium-bodied smoke, offered in brightly-colored boxes of 20.

FLAVORED DOMINICAN
Handmade in Santiago, Dominican Republic.

Wrapper: Indonesia   *Binder: Dom. Rep.*   *Filler: Dom. Rep.*

Shape	Name	Lgth	Ring	Wrapper
Small Panatela	Flavored	5	30	CM

HANDMADE CIGARS: BRAND LISTINGS

The name says it all. Introduced in 1998, this is a mild-bodied, flavored, Dominican-made brand available in bundles of 25 in Amaretto, chocolate, cognac, mint, vanilla and whiskey.

FLOR DE AMOR
Handmade in Esteli, Nicaragua.

Wrapper: Indonesia   *Binder: Indonesia*   *Filler: Mexico, Nicaragua*

Shape	Name	Lgth	Ring	Wrapper
Toro	Corona	5¾	52	CC
Toro	Corona Extra	6	52	CC
Robusto	Robusto	5	52	CC
Torpedo	Torpedo	5¾	54	CC
Churchill	Churchill	7	48	CC

Introduced in 1997, this is a mild-bodied cigar featuring Cuban-seed filler tobaccos, offered in protective cellophane sleeves and packed in all-cedar boxes of 25.

FLOR DE CARBONELL
Handmade in Santiago, Dominican Republic.

Wrapper: Dom. Rep.   *Binder: Dom. Rep.*   *Filler: Dom. Rep.*

Shape	Name	Lgth	Ring	Wrapper
Lonsdale		7	44	CM

Although it has no shape name, this is a medium-to-full-bodied blend offered in one size. Introduced in 1998, it is offered in all-cedar boxes of 25.

FLOR DE CONSUEGRA
Handmade in Cofradia, Honduras.
Wrapper: Ecuador or Honduras

Binder: Honduras   *Filler: Dom. Rep., Honduras, Nicaragua*

Shape	Name	Lgth	Ring	Wrapper
Lonsdale	No. 1	6½	44	CM-Ma

Petit Corona	No. 10	5	41	CM-Ma
Grand Corona	No. 15	6¼	45	CM-Ma
Toro	No. 16	6	48	CM-Ma
Churchill	No. 18	7¼	46	CM-Ma
Panatela	No. 22	6⅞	36	CM-Ma
Churchill	No. 23	7	46	CM-Ma
Churchill	No. 25	6¾	48	CM-Ma
Double Corona	Double Corona	6⅞	49	CM-Ma
Corona	Corona	5½	42	CM-Ma
Churchill	No. 27	7¾	46	CM-Ma
Giant	No. 28	8½	52	CM-Ma
Grand Corona	Cuban Corona	5⅝	45	CM-Ma
Corona	Petites	5½	43	CM-Ma
Robusto	No. 30	5¼	50	CM-Ma
Grand Corona	No. 31	6½	47	CM-Ma
Corona	No. 32	5½	44	CM-Ma
Petit Corona	No. 45	4¼	44	CM-Ma
Short Panatela	Panatela	5⅜	38	CM-Ma
Double Corona	No. 50	7½	50	CM-Ma
Panatela	No. 67	6¾	39	CM-Ma
Panatela	No. 85	6¼	35	CM-Ma
Robusto	Robustos	4½	50	CM-Ma
Long Corona	No. 90	6	44	CM-Ma
Giant	Presidentes	8½	49	CM-Ma

This cigar is essentially a seconds line for well-known brands such as Belinda and El Rey del Mundo. In these sizes, it is mostly a medium-to-full-bodied smoke, offered in two wrapper shades and in bundles of 25.

HANDMADE CIGARS: BRAND LISTINGS

FLOR DE DIOS
Handmade in Esteli, Nicaragua.

Wrapper: Nicaragua *Binder: Nicaragua* *Filler: Nicaragua*

Shape	Name	Lgth	Ring	Wrapper
Double Corona	Churchill	7	50	CM
Petit Corona	Corona	5	42	CM
Lonsdale	Lonsdale	6½	44	CM
Pyramid	Pyramid	6½	50	CM
Toro	Toro	6	50	CM
Robusto	Robusto	5	50	CM

Here is an all-Nicaraguan brand offering a medium-bodied smoke in three of the most popular sizes. Introduced in 1997, it is offered in boxes of 25.

FLOR DE FARACH
Handmade in Esteli, Nicaragua.

Wrapper: Ecuador *Binder: Honduran*
Filler: Dominican Republic, Honduras, Nicaragua

Shape	Name	Lgth	Ring	Wrapper
Double Corona	Francisco	7¼	54	CC
Churchill	Churchill	7	48	CC
Torpedo	Momotombo	6¾	54	CC
Pyramid	Momotomito	7	52	CC
Pyramid	Lonsdale	6½	43	CC
Corona	Corona	5½	44	CC
Robusto	Robusto	4½	54	CC
Short Panatela	Petit Lancero	4¼	39	CC

Here is the revival of an ancient Cuban brand which dates from 1903, much appreciated until it disappeared in 1960. In 1996, a Nicaraguan version of the Flor de Farach was introduced. It's a medium-to-full-bodied cigar, with a beautiful Sumatra-seed wrapper grown in Ecuador and a rich flavor.

HANDMADE CIGARS: BRAND LISTINGS

FLOR DE FILIPINAS
Handmade in Manila, the Philippines.

Wrapper: Philippines   *Binder: Philippines*   *Filler: Philippines*

Shape	Name	Lgth	Ring	Wrapper
Pyramid	Cortado	5⅜	50	CC
Churchill	Churchill	6¾	47	CC
Lonsdale	Coronas Largas	6¾	44	CC
Corona	Coronas	5½	44	CC
Panatela	Cetros	5⅞	39	CC
Short Panatela	Half Corona	4	39	CC
Short Panatela	Panatellas	4⅞	35	CC
Pyramid	Pyramide	6	52	CC
Robusto	Robusto	5	53	CC

Introduced in 1996, this is an inexpensive, medium-bodied but handmade brand
from the Philippines. Made from Philippine Isabela tobacco in the binder and
filler, it is covered in a Philippine Cagayan Valley wrapper and offered in boxes
or bundles of 25.

FLOR DE FLOREZ
Handmade in Danli, Honduras.

Wrapper: USA/Connecticut   *Binder: Honduras*   *Filler: Honduras*

Shape	Name	Lgth	Ring	Wrapper
Double Corona	Presidente	7	49	CC
Lonsdale	Cetros No. 2	6½	44	CC
Toro	Corona	6	49	CC
Robusto	Rothchild	4⅞	47	CC
Petit Corona	Blunt	5	42	CC

Essentially a family secret, American smokers discovered Flor de Florez in 1995.
Now produced in Honduras, these cigars are medium-to-full in body, using an
all-Honduran blend, including a Connecticut Shade wrapper.

HANDMADE CIGARS: BRAND LISTINGS

FLOR DE FLOREZ CABINET SELECTION
Handmade in Managua, Nicaragua.

Wrapper: Nicaragua *Binder: Nicaragua* *Filler: Nicaragua*

Shape	Name	Lgth	Ring	Wrapper
Double Corona	Gigantes	7½	49	CM
Churchill	Sir Winston	7	47	CM
Long Panatela	Gran Panatela	7	38	CM
Corona Extra	Florez-Florez	5½	46	CM
Robusto	Robusto	5	50	CM
Petit Corona	Coronita	5	42	CM

This is a fairly new line from Flor de Florez, introduced in 1996. This is an all-Nicaraguan cigar, offering a medium-to-full-bodied flavor with rich spices in the taste, offered in boxes of 25.

FLOR DE FLOREZ MIAMI BLEND
Handmade in Miami, Florida, USA.

Wrapper: Ecuador *Binder: Mexico* *Filler: Brazil, Honduras, Nicaragua*

Shape	Name	Lgth	Ring	Wrapper
Double Corona	Double Corona	7½	49	CC
Churchill	Churchill	7	47	CC
Torpedo	Torpedo	6	52	CC
Toro	Toro	6	50	CC
Long Panatela	Panatela	7	38	CC
Grand Corona	Corona	6½	46	CC
Robusto	Robusto	5	50	CC
Torpedo	Double Torpedo	7	54	CC

Viva Miami! This new blend, offered for the first time in 1997, offers a medium-to-full-bodied taste, perfect for evenings on the *Calle Ocho*. It is presented without cellophane in all-cedar, slide-top cabinets of 25.

HANDMADE CIGARS: BRAND LISTINGS

FLOR DE GONZALEZ
Handmade in Miami, Florida, USA.
Wrapper: Ecuador
Binder: Dom. Rep. or Honduras   Filler: Dom. Rep., Honduras, Nicaragua

Shape	Name	Lgth	Ring	Wrapper
Double Corona	Churchill	7	50	CC-Ma
Toro	Extra Corona	6	50	CC-Ma
Double Corona	Magnum	7	60	CC-Ma
Lonsdale	No. 1	6¾	44	CC-Ma
Corona	No. 4	5½	44	CC-Ma
Pyramid	Piramide No. 2	7	62	CC-Ma
Double Corona	Presidente	7½	50	CC-Ma
Torpedo	Torpedo	6¼	62	CC-Ma
Robusto	Wavell	5	50	CC-Ma
Giant	Monster	9	60	CC-Ma
Panatela	Panatela	6¾	38	CC-Ma

This brand was introduced in 1996, made in the Miami area and offering a wide range, including some really, really big ring gauges. Available in both natural and maduro wrappers, the body is mild and all shapes are offered in boxes of 25.

FLOR DE GURABO
Handmade in Cibao, Dominican Republic.
Wrapper: Indonesia   Binder: Dom. Rep.   Filler: Dom. Rep.

Shape	Name	Lgth	Ring	Wrapper
Double Corona	Churchill	7½	50	CM
Robusto	Robusto	5	50	CM
Long Corona	Corona	6	42	CM
Long Corona	Lonsdale	6	44	CM
Panatela	Panatela	6	38	CM

HANDMADE CIGARS: BRAND LISTINGS

This brand was introduced in late 1997. It offers a mild-to-medium body and is presented in boxes of bundles of 25. The robusto shape is also available with short filler and in flavored versions featuring rum or vanilla.

FLOR DE HONDURAS
Handmade in Danli, Honduras.

Wrapper: Honduras   *Binder: Honduras*   *Filler: Honduras*

Shape	Name	Lgth	Ring	Wrapper
Giant	Viajantes	8½	52	CM-Ma
Torpedo	Torpedo	7	54	CM-Ma
Double Corona	Churchill	7	49	CM-Ma
Toro	Toro	6	50	CM-Ma
Lonsdale	Corona	6¾	43	CM
Robusto	Robustos	4¾	52	CM-Ma

This brand was introduced in 1996. It offers a mild-bodied taste and is conveniently packaged in triangular bundles of 25.

FLOR DE JALAPA
Handmade in Esteli, Nicaragua.

Wrapper: Ecuador   *Binder: Nicaragua*   *Filler: Nicaragua*

Shape	Name	Lgth	Ring	Wrapper
Giant	Presidente	8½	52	CM
Toro	Toro	6	50	CM
Long Corona	Gran Corona	6	44	CM
Churchill	Churchill	7	48	CM
Robusto	Robusto	4¾	50	CM

This brand was introduced in January 1996. It is light to medium in strength and uses a Havana-seed wrapper, grown in Ecuador. These cigars are offered in boxes of 25.

HANDMADE CIGARS: BRAND LISTINGS

FLOR DE LEON
Handmade in Esteli, Nicaragua.

Wrapper: Indonesia   *Binder: Nicaragua*   *Filler: Nicaragua*

Shape	Name	Lgth	Ring	Wrapper
Robusto	Robusto	4¾	50	CM
Corona	Corona	5½	42	CM
Churchill	Churchill	7	48	CM

Introduced in 1998, this is a mild-to-medium-bodied cigar offered in glass tubes in boxes of 12 cigars each.

FLOR DE LOS REYES
Handmade in Navarette, Dominican Republic.

Wrapper: Indonesia   *Binder: Dom. Rep.*   *Filler: Dom. Rep.*

Shape	Name	Lgth	Ring	Wrapper
Giant	Emilio	8½	52	CM
Double Corona	Churchill	7½	50	CM
Robusto	Robusto	5	50	CM
Grand Corona	Lonsdale	6	46	CM
Torpedo	Torpedo	6¼	52	CM

Introduced in 1997 by the Blue Springs, Missouri-based Grand Cigar Company, this is a medium-bodied cigar with a hint of spice on the finish. The Sumatra wrapper is combined with Cuban-seed tobaccos in the binder and filler. Flor de Los Reyes cigars are offered in individual cellophane sleeves inside all-cedar boxes of 25. A Connecticut-wrapped version, mild-to-medium in strength, is also planned.

FLOR DE MEXICO
Handmade in San Andres Tuxtla, Mexico.

Wrapper: Mexico   *Binder: Mexico*   *Filler: Mexico*

Shape	Name	Lgth	Ring	Wrapper
Toro	Churchill	6	52	CM-Ma

HANDMADE CIGARS: BRAND LISTINGS

Toro	Toro	6⅛	50	CM-Ma
Lonsdale	No. 1	6½	46	CM-Ma
Churchill	No. 2	6¾	48	CM
Short Panatela	No. 3	4¼	38	CM
Corona	No. 4	5½	44	CM-Ma

Created in 1979, this is a full-bodied cigar made in Mexico and offered in bundles of 25 cigars each.

FLOR DE NAVARETTE
Handmade in Navarette, Dominican Republic.

Wrapper: Indonesia   Binder: Dom. Rep.   Filler: Dom. Rep.

Shape	Name	Lgth	Ring	Wrapper
Long Corona	Lonsdale	6	44	CM
Robusto	Robusto	5	50	CM
Double Corona	Churchill	7	50	CM

This is a 1996-introduced, medium-bodied brand. You can find "the flower of Navarette" in all-cedar boxes, or in bundles, of 25.

FLOR DE NICARAGUA
Handmade in Esteli, Nicaragua.

Wrapper: USA/Connecticut   Binder: Indonesia   Filler: Nicaragua

Shape	Name	Lgth	Ring	Wrapper
Churchill	Churchill	6⅞	48	CC
Robusto	Consul	4½	52	CC
Corona	Corona	5½	42	CC

This brand debuted in 1995 and has a medium-bodied taste. It is available in boxes of 25.

HANDMADE CIGARS: BRAND LISTINGS

FLOR DE ORO
Handmade in Esteli, Nicaragua.

Wrapper: Indonesia   *Binder: Indonesia*   *Filler: Nicaragua*

Shape	Name	Lgth	Ring	Wrapper
Lonsdale	No. 1	6½	44	CC
Giant	Presidente	8½	52	CC
Robusto	Robusto	5	50	CC
Torpedo	Torpedo	6½	54	CC
Double Corona	Churchill	7	50	CC

This is a new cigar in 1997, with a mild-to-medium-bodied taste and offered in cellophane sleeves in all-cedar boxes of 25.

FLOR DE PALICIO
Handmade in Cofradia, Honduras.

Wrapper: Ecuador, Indonesia   *Binder: Honduras*
Filler: Dominican Republic, Honduras and Nicaragua

Shape	Name	Lgth	Ring	Wrapper
Lonsdale	No. 1	7	40	CM
Long Corona	No. 2	6	42	CM-Ma
Churchill	Corona	6¾	48	CM-Ma

This is a handmade, medium-bodied cigar, created under the supervision of the master cigar makers who manufacture Hoyo de Monterrey and Punch. This elegant brand is offered in equally elegant boxes of 25 each.

FLOR DE SELVA
Handmade in Danli, Honduras.

Wrapper: Ecuador   *Binder: Honduras*   *Filler: Honduras*

Shape	Name	Lgth	Ring	Wrapper
Small Panatela	Panatela	4½	30	CC
Robusto	Robusto	4¾	50	CC

HANDMADE CIGARS: BRAND LISTINGS

Long Corona	Fino	6	44	CC
Robusto	Corona	5½	48	CC
Churchill	Churchill	7	49	CC
Double Corona	Double Corona	7½	52	CC

This brand debuted in Europe in 1994 and in the U.S. in 1997. It offers a medium body, featuring a Connecticut-seed wrapper grown in Ecuador. It is presented in cellophane and packed in all-cedar boxes of 25, with the Corona and Robusto sizes available in sevens.

FLOR DE YBOR CITY
Handmade in Santiago, Dominican Republic.
Wrapper: USA/Connecticut   *Binder: Dom. Rep.*   *Filler: Dom. Rep.*

Shape	Name	Lgth	Ring	Wrapper
Corona Extra	Ybor Corona	5¼	45	CC-Ma
Lonsdale	Ybor No. 1	6½	43	CC-Ma
Toro	Ybor No. 80	6	50	CC-Ma
Grand Corona	Ybor No. 85	6	47	CC-Ma
Churchill	Ybor Pierce	7¼	48	CC-Ma
Giant	Ybor Presidente	8½	52	CC-Ma
Robusto	Ybor Toro	4½	50	CC-Ma

This bundles brand is produced in one of the world's most famous factories. It was introduced in 1995 and is medium-to-heavy in body.

FLOR DEL CARIBE
Handmade in Danli, Honduras.
Wrapper: Ecuador and Indonesia   *Binder: Honduras*
Filler: Dominican Republic, Honduras and Nicaragua

Shape	Name	Lgth	Ring	Wrapper
Corona	Duques	5½	43	CM-Ma

HANDMADE CIGARS: BRAND LISTINGS

| Churchill | Super Cetro | 7 | 46 | CM-Ma |
| Double Corona | Sovereign | 7½ | 54 | CM-Ma |

This brand is offered in elegant boxes of 25 cigars each. The medium-to-full-bodied range was reduced from six to three sizes in 1996, with a maduro wrapper now available for all sizes.

FLOR DEL TODO
Handmade in Esteli, Nicaragua.

Wrapper: Indonesia, Nicaragua   Binder: Indonesia   Filler: Dom. Rep., Nicaragua

Shape	Name	Lgth	Ring	Wrapper
Toro	Doble Corona	6	48	CC-Ma
Toro	Gran Corona	5⅞	48	CC-Ma
Petit Corona	Corona	5	42	CC-Ma
Robusto	Robusto	5	50	CC-Ma

This brand was introduced in 1997, offered in either bundles or boxes of 25. It has a full-bodied flavor and a modest price. Check it out!

FLOR MARIA
Handmade in Miami, Florida, USA.

Wrapper: Mexico or USA/Connecticut
Binder: Dominican Republic   Filler: Dominican Republic, Honduras, Nicaragua

Shape	Name	Lgth	Ring	Wrapper
Double Corona	Presidente	7½	50	CC-Ma
Double Corona	Churchill	7	50	CC-Ma
Toro	Extra Corona	6	50	CC-Ma
Torpedo	Torpedo	6¼	52	CC-Ma
Robusto	Wavell	5	50	CC-Ma
Lonsdale	No. 1	6½	44	CC-Ma
Corona	No. 4	5½	44	CC-Ma

Panatela	Panetela	6¾	38	CC-Ma
Slim Panatela	Pencil	6¾	32	CC-Ma

Introduced in 1997, this is a mild-bodied cigar in its Connecticut-wrapped version and medium-bodied in its Mexican-grown, maduro-wrapped edition. It is offered in cellophane sleeves in boxes or bundles of 25.

FLORIBBEAN
Handmade in Danli, Honduras.

Wrapper: Indonesia *Binder: USA/Pennsylvania* *Filler: Dom. Rep., Nicaragua*

Shape	Name	Lgth	Ring	Wrapper
Petit Corona	Elegante	5	42	CM
Robusto	Robusto	5	50	CM
Long Corona	Corona	6¼	44	CM
Toro	Double Corona	6	50	CM
Churchill	Churchill	7	48	CM
Giant	Presidente	8	50	CM

A Sumatra wrapper is featured in this 1996-introduced, medium-bodied brand. It is offered in an all-cedar box of 25.

FLORIDA PRIDE
Handmade in Santiago, Dominican Republic.

Wrapper: Ecuador *Binder: Dom. Rep.* *Filler: Dom. Rep.*

Shape	Name	Lgth	Ring	Wrapper
Robusto	Robusto	5½	50	CC
Double Corona	Churchill	7¼	50	CC
Panatela	Lonsdale	6	38	CC

This brand debuted in 1997 and is mild-to-medium on body. The Lonsdale shape is available in chocolate and vanilla-flavored versions and all of the sizes are offered in see-through-top boxes of 25.

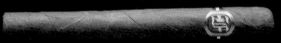

HANDMADE CIGARS: BRAND LISTINGS

FLOWER CITY SPECIAL RESERVE
Handmade in Rochester, New York, USA.

Wrapper: Indonesia   Binder: Indonesia   Filler: Dom. Rep., Mexico

Shape	Name	Lgth	Ring	Wrapper
Toro	State Street	6¼	50	CM
Robusto	Dewey Avenue	5	50	CM
Long Corona	Main Street	6	44	CM
Corona	Park Avenue	5½	42	CM
Long Panatela	East Avenue	7	35	CM
Short Panatela	Monroe Avenue	5	35	CM

This brand debuted in 1998 and is full-bodied. It is offered in boxes of 20.

FONSECA
Handmade in Santiago, Dominican Republic.

Wrapper: USA/Connecticut   Binder: Mexico   Filler: Dom. Rep.

Shape	Name	Lgth	Ring	Wrapper
Long Corona	8-9-8	6	43	Co
Grand Corona	7-9-9	6½	46	Co-Ma
Double Corona	10-10	7	50	Co-Ma
Robusto	5-50	5	50	Co-Ma
Petit Corona	2-2	4¼	40	Co-Ma
Pyramid	Triangular	5½	56	Co

One of the world's most famous names in Port is also a respected name in cigars. Medium in body, this refined, cabinet-selection brand debuted in 1962 and was re-introduced in its current blend in 1991. It is blended from the choicest tobaccos grown in the Cibao Valley of the Dominican Republic. The wrapper is outstanding Connecticut Shade (natural) or Connecticut Broadleaf (maduro) leaf. The Triangular shape is one of the hardest to make and offers a rich flavor, concentrated by its conical shape.

HANDMADE CIGARS: BRAND LISTINGS

FONSECA VINTAGE COLLECTION
Handmade in Santiago, Dominican Republic.

Wrapper: Ecuador   Binder: Dom. Rep.   Filler: Dom. Rep.

Shape	Name	Lgth	Ring	Wrapper
Double Corona	Churchill	7	50	CC
Long Corona	Cetros	6	43	CC
Robusto	Robusto	5	50	CC

This is a new brand for 1998 and offers a Connecticut-seed wrapper and a medium-to-full-bodied taste. You can find this exquisitely-made range in three sizes and in packs of four and boxes of 24.

FONTICIELLA
Handmade in Miami, Florida, USA.

Wrapper: Ecuador   Binder: Indonesia   Filler: Dom. Rep., Honduras, Mexico

Shape	Name	Lgth	Ring	Wrapper
Robusto	Acendados	5	50	CC
Lonsdale	Corona Classico	6½	44	CC
Toro	Imperial	6½	52	CC
Double Corona	Embajador	7	50	CC
Torpedo	Imperial Torpedo	6½	54	CC
Giant	Executivo	8	50	CC

These are mild cigars, featuring an Ecuadorian wrapper and a four-nation blend inside. Created in 1996 under the direction of Don Fernando Fonticiella and grandson Carlos Fonticiella, Jr., you can find it in boxes of 25.

FRANCIS J
Handmade in Santiago, Dominican Republic.

Wrapper: Indonesia   Binder: Dom. Rep.   Filler: Dom. Rep.

Shape	Name	Lgth	Ring	Wrapper
Torpedo	Torpedo Vintage	7	54	CM

HANDMADE CIGARS: BRAND LISTINGS

Torpedo	Torpedo Reserve	7	54	CM
Double Corona	Churchill	7½	50	CM
Toro	Robusto	6	48	CM
Grand Corona	Corona Reserve	6	46	CM
Grand Corona	Corona Cognac	6	46	CM

Introduced in 1997, this is a mild-to-medium-bodied and very smooth brand presented in walnut boxes, in which the cigars are aged for six months. Francis J are offered in boxes of 10 or 20.

FRANCISCO PLA
Handmade in Esteli, Nicaragua.

Wrapper: Cameroon   Binder: Cameroon   Filler: Dominican Republic

Shape	Name	Lgth	Ring	Wrapper
Torpedo	Torpedo	7	52	CM
Double Corona	Presidente	7½	50	CM
Double Corona	Churchill	7	50	CM
Toro	Corona Gorda	6	50	CM
Robusto	Robusto	5	50	CM
Churchill	Corona	7	46	CM
Grand Corona	Petite Corona	6	46	CM
Lonsdale	Palma	7	42	CM
Long Panatela	Lanceros	7½	38	CM
Slim Panatela	Panetela	6½	32	CM
Cigarillo	Pencil	6	28	CM

Here is a full-bodied blend from a five-brand family. It is available in either bundles, boxes or glass jar humidors of 25 each. The Pencil shape is available in six flavors: Amaretto, Anise, chocolate, cognac, rum and vanilla.

HANDMADE CIGARS: BRAND LISTINGS

FREE CUBA
Handmade in Santiago, Dominican Republic.
Wrapper: Indonesia   Binder: Nicaragua   Filler: Dom. Rep., Indonesia, Nicaragua

Shape	Name	Lgth	Ring	Wrapper
Robusto	Robusto	5	50	CM
Lonsdale	Corona	6½	42	CM
Double Corona	Churchill	7¼	50	CM
Torpedo	Torpedo	6½	52	CM

This brand was introduced in 1996 by the Caribbean Cigar Company. Thanks to its Java wrapper and blended filler, Free Cuba belies its fiery name with a full-bodied flavor, offered in all-cedar box of 25 in an 8-9-8 format.

FRENCH KISS
Handmade in Villa Gonzalez, Dominican Republic.
Wrapper: USA/Connecticut   Binder: Dom. Rep.   Filler: Dom. Rep.

Shape	Name	Lgth	Ring	Wrapper
Small Panatela	Chica	5	30	CC
Long Corona	Chico Corona	6	42	CC
Torpedo	Guapo	6	52	CC
Grand Corona	Lonsdale	6½	46	CC
Pyramid	Pyramid	6½	52	CC
Long Panatela	Panetela	7	38	CC
Robusto	Robusto	5	50	CC
Double Corona	Churchill	7	50	CC

This is a flavored brand which debuted in 1998. It has a medium body and is available in Amaretto, chocolate, Gran Mariner, mint, rum, peach and vanilla. It is presented in boxes of 25.

HANDMADE CIGARS: BRAND LISTINGS

FRESH FLORIDA
Handmade in Tamboril, Dominican Republic.

Wrapper: Ecuador Binder: Dom. Rep. Filler: Dom. Rep.

Shape	Name	Lgth	Ring	Wrapper
Lonsdale	Corona	6¼	44	CC
Toro	Robusto Superior	6	50	CC
Robusto	Robusto	5	50	CC
Long Panatela	Lanceros	7½	38	CC
Pyramid	Pyramide Largo	7	48	CC
Pyramid	Pyramide	6	48	CC
Long Corona	Onyx	6	44	CC-Ma
Short Panatela	Palmita	4¾	38	CC
Churchill	Churchill	7	48	CC
Giant	Presidente	8	52	CC

Introduced in 1998, this is a mild-to-medium-bodied cigar with a Connecticut-seed wrapper grown in Ecuador except for the Onyx shape which is offered in a maduro-wrapped, medium-bodied shade. All shapes are available in either boxes or bundles of 25 cigars each.

FUEGO CUBANO
Handmade in Chiriqui, Panama.

Wrapper: Cameroon Binder: Dom. Rep. Filler: Dom. Rep.

Shape	Name	Lgth	Ring	Wrapper
Slim Panatela	Palmita	6	34	CC
Petit Corona	Panetella	5	40	CC
Robusto	Cuba Libre	5	48	CC
Corona	Corona	5½	42	CC
Robusto	Robusto	5	50	CC

Grand Corona	Toro	6	46	CC
Lonsdale	Lonsdale	6½	44	CC
Toro	Double Corona	6½	48	CC
Double Corona	Churchill	7	50	CC
Toro	Corona Grande	6	52	CC
Torpedo	Torpedo	6	52	CC
Giant	Presidente	8	50	CC
Corona Extra	Companion	3½	46	CC
	Made with short filler:			
Grand Corona	Fuma	6½	46	CC

"Cuban Fire" is the name of this brand, with offers a medium-bodied smoke thanks to Cuba-seed filler leaves and a Sumatra-seed Cameroon wrapper. Introduced in 1997, it is presented in an all-cedar box.

FUEGO CUBANO BRONZE EDITION
Handmade in Chiriqui, Panama.

Wrapper: Cameroon   Binder: Dom. Rep.   Filler: Dom. Rep.

Shape	Name	Lgth	Ring	Wrapper
Panatela	Petite Palmita	5½	36	CM
Panatela	Palmita	6½	36	CM
Corona	Corona	5½	42	CM
Robusto	Robusto	5½	49	CM
Corona Extra	Toro	5½	46	CM
Grand Corona	Lonsdale	6½	46	CM
Double Corona	Churchill	7	49	CM

Introduced in 1998, this blend is full-bodied with a Sumatra-seed wrapper and rich flavor. It is offered in all-cedar boxes of 25.

HANDMADE CIGARS: BRAND LISTINGS

FUEGO CUBANO GOLD EDITION
Handmade in Chiriqui, Panama.

Wrapper: Ecuador　　　　　*Binder: Ecuador*　　　　　*Filler: Dom. Rep.*

Shape	Name	Lgth	Ring	Wrapper
Slim Panatela	Palmita	6	34	CC
Petit Corona	Panetella	5	40	CC
Robusto	Cuba Libre	5	48	CC
Corona	Corona	5½	42	CC
Robusto	Robusto	5	50	CC
Grand Corona	Toro	6	46	CC
Lonsdale	Lonsdale	6½	44	CC
Toro	Double Corona	6½	48	CC
Double Corona	Churchill	7	50	CC
Toro	Corona Grande	6	52	CC
Torpedo	Torpedo	6	52	CC
Giant	Presidente	8	50	CC

First available in 1997, this is a mild-to-medium-bodied cigar with Cuban-seed filler tobaccos grown in the Dominican Republic and a golden Ecuador-grown wrapper. It is offered in all-cedar boxes of 25.

FUEGO CUBANO SILVER EDITION
Handmade in Chiriqui, Panama.

Wrapper: Cameroon　　　　　*Binder: Dom. Rep.*　　　　　*Filler: Dom. Rep.*

Shape	Name	Lgth	Ring	Wrapper
Small Panatela	Petite Palmita	4½	34	CC
Panatela	Palmita	6	36	CC
Corona	Corona	5½	42	CC
Robusto	Robusto	5	49	CC

Corona Extra	Toro	5½	46	CC
Long Corona	Lonsdale	6	42	CC
Toro	Double Corona	6½	48	CC
Double Corona	Churchill	7	49	CC
Torpedo	Torpedo	6	52	CC
Corona Extra	Companion	3½	46	CC

This is a medium-to-full-bodied smoke that debuted in 1997. It is also presented in boxes of 25, except for the Companion shape, offered in 50s.

FUEGO DEL REY
Handmade in Jember, Indonesia.

Wrapper: Brazil or Indonesia   *Binder: Indonesia*   *Filler: Indonesia*

Shape	Name	Lgth	Ring	Wrapper
Robusto	Robusto	5	50	CM-Ma
Robusto	Pipe Aroma	5	50	CM
Robusto	Vanilla	5	50	CM
Robusto	Chocolate	5	50	CM
Robusto	Cognac	5	50	CM
Torpedo	Torpedo	6	50	CM-Ma
Toro	Corona Grande	6	50	CM
Double Corona	Churchill	7	50	CM

Introduced in 1997, this popularly-priced, mild-bodied brand is offered in four sizes, including five styles of robusto: standard, chocolate, cognac, vanilla-flavored and with pipe aroma. The two maduro-wrapped shapes use a Brazilian wrapper leaf. It is available in elegantly-designed 3-packs, 1-packs or in flip-top boxes of 20. It's a perfect cigar to enjoy every day.

HANDMADE CIGARS: BRAND LISTINGS

FUENTE FUENTE OPUS X
Handmade in Santiago, Dominican Republic.

Wrapper: Dom. Rep.   *Binder: Dom. Rep.*   *Filler: Dom. Rep.*

Shape	Name	Lgth	Ring	Wrapper
Toro	Perfecxion No. 2	6⅜	52	CM
Double Corona	Double Corona	7⅝	49	CM
Grand Corona	Fuente Fuente	5⅝	40	CM
Churchill	Reserva d'Chateau	7	48	CM
Petit Corona	Perfecxion No. 5	4⅞	40	CM
Toro	Perfecxion X	6¼	48	CM
Panatela	Petit Lancero	6¼	39	CM
Robusto	Robusto	5¼	50	CM
Lonsdale	No. 1	6½	42	CM
Giant	A	9¼	47	CM

This full-bodied brand was introduced in 1996 and is scarcely available anywhere. A project of the Tabacalera A. Fuente y Cia., this brand features all-Dominican tobacco, including the new rosado wrapper leaf grown on the Fuente's own farm.

FUNDADORES JAMAICA
Handmade in Kingston, Jamaica.

Wrapper: Ecuador, USA/Connecticut   *Binder: Mexico*
Filler: Dominican Republic, Jamaica, Mexico

Shape	Name	Lgth	Ring	Wrapper
Double Corona	Churchill	7½	49	CC-Ma
Toro	Robusto Gorda	6	50	CC-Ma
Lonsdale	Lonsdale	6½	42	CC-Ma
Corona	Corona	5½	42	CC-Ma
Robusto	Petit Robusto	4	50	CC-Ma

Fundadores
Pride of Jamaica

Santa Cruz
Jamaican Heritage

Barrington House
Premium Cigars, Ltd.

Kingston 5, Jamaica W.I.

Home of Award Winning Cigars

1980 - Prague
1980 - Buenos Aires   1981 - London
1982 - Lisbon   1982 - Brussels
1983 - Rome   1984 - Madrid

The quality of aged and matured tobacco used,
the skill and experience in choosing the blend, and
the craft that has been expressed in their production by
hand for four decades are your assurance that these
exquisite cigars are unsurpassed in richness, aroma
and smoking satisfaction.

We are also the creators & manufacturers of private
label super premium cigars for world renowned resorts,
cigar bars, exclusive golf clubs and championship
sporting events.

George Campbell
Factory Manager

Barrington G. Adams
C.E.O.

HANDMADE CIGARS: BRAND LISTINGS

This brand is produced by the Barrington House of Kingston, Jamaica and offers mild, rich flavors. Offered in wood boxes of 25, Connecticut Shade or Connecticut-seed (grown in Ecuador) wrappers are offered in both a natural and maduro style. Fundadores Jamaica is available in a Gold Label Cabinet Series that features vintage leaf and a Red Label with aged leaf.

GALANTE CLASE
Handmade in Danli, Honduras.

Wrapper: Ecuador   Binder: Dom. Rep.   Filler: Honduras, Nicaragua

Shape	Name	Lgth	Ring	Wrapper
Double Corona	Churchill	7	49	CC
Robusto	Rothchild	5	50	CC
Toro	Toro	6	50	CC
Giant	Soberano	8	50	CC
Corona	No. 4	5½	42	CC
Slim Panatela	Muneca/Petit	5⅜	34	CC
Small Panatela	Muneca/Tico	4½	30	CC

Here is a mild-to-medium-bodied brand with Sumatra-seed wrappers grown in Ecuador. Introduced in 1997, it is offered in bundles of 25.

GALARDON
Handmade in San Andres Tuxtla, Mexico.

Wrapper: Mexico   Binder: Mexico   Filler: Mexico

Shape	Name	Lgth	Ring	Wrapper
Long Corona	Corona	6¼	42	CM

This is a new cigar in 1998 and available only in limited quantities. It is offered in boxes of 25 and has a full-bodied taste.

GALEON
Handmade in Villa Gonzalez, Dominican Republic.

Wrapper: Indonesia   Binder: Indonesia   Filler: Dom. Rep.

HANDMADE CIGARS: BRAND LISTINGS

Shape	Name	Lgth	Ring	Wrapper
Toro	Robusto	6	50	CM
Robusto	Rothschild	4½	50	CM
Churchill	Double Corona	7	48	CM

This is a value-priced brand from the Puros de Villa Gonzalez factory. Introduced in 1998, it is mild in body and available in boxes of 25.

GALIANO
Handmade in Santiago, Dominican Republic.
Wrapper: USA/Connecticut   Binder: Dom. Rep.   Filler: Dom. Rep.

Shape	Name	Lgth	Ring	Wrapper
Double Corona	Presidente	7½	50	CC
Corona	Corona	5¾	43	CC
Churchill	Churchill	7	48	CC
Toro	Toro	6	50	CC
Lonsdale	No. 1	7	43	CC
Robusto	Robusto	4¾	52	CC
Short Panatela	Petit Corona	5	36	CC
Long Panatela	Panatela	7	36	CC

Originally introduced in 1994, this is a mild-to-medium-bodied brand which is in national distribution in the U.S. for the first time in 1996. Very well constructed, it features a genuine Connecticut Shade wrapper and is packed in all-cedar cabinets of 25.

GALIANOS
Handmade in Santo Domingo, Dominican Republic.
Wrapper: Ecuador, Mexico   Binder: Dom. Rep.   Filler: Dom. Rep.

Shape	Name	Lgth	Ring	Wrapper
Double Corona	President	7½	50	CC-Ma

HANDMADE CIGARS: BRAND LISTINGS

Churchill	Churchill	7	48	CC-Ma
Lonsdale	No. 1	7	43	CC-Ma
Long Panatela	Panetela	7	36	CC-Ma
Torpedo	Torpedo	6	52	CC-Ma
Toro	Toro	6	50	CC-Ma
Corona	Corona	5¾	43	CC-Ma
Robusto	Robusto	4¾	52	CC-Ma

This brand was introduced in 1992 and offers a medium-to-full-bodied flavor in either its natural Ecuadorian wrapper or in a Mexican-grown maduro wrapper. You can find it in boxes of 25.

GALLARDO
Handmade in Danli, Honduras.

Wrapper: Ecuador, Indonesia   Binder: Honduras   Filler: Honduras, Nicaragua

Shape	Name	Lgth	Ring	Wrapper
Toro	Missles	6	54	CC-CM
Giant	Soberano	8	50	CC-CM
Double Corona	Churchill	7	49	CC-CM
Toro	Toro	6	50	CC-CM
Robusto	Rothschild	5	50	CC-CM
Corona	No. 4	5½	42	CC-CM
Long Panatela	Palma Fina	7	38	CC-CM
Small Panatela	Pygmeos	4½	30	CC-CM
	Made with medium filler:			
Petit Corona	Vanilla	4	42	CM

Introduced in 1997, this is a medium-bodied cigar offered in a choice of wrappers and presented in all-cedar cabinets of 25 cigars. The Rothschild and No. 4 shapes are also available in gift packs of five. A portion of the sales price of each box is used to support an experimental organic tree farm on the north coast of Honduras.

GARGOYLE
Handmade in Manila, Philippines.

Wrapper: Philippines   *Binder: Philippines*   *Filler: Philippines*

Shape	Name	Lgth	Ring	Wrapper
Double Corona	Bacchus	7¼	50	CM
Robusto	Florentine	5	50	CM
Corona	Parisian	5¾	42	CM

This all-Philippine brand debuted in 1995 and offers a mild flavor in three popular sizes. Each is available in boxes of 25, with each cigar protected in cellophane sleeves.

GARMEISTER
Handmade in Eureka Springs, Arkansas, USA.

Wrapper: Ecuador   *Binder: Indonesia*   *Filler: Dom. Rep., Indonesia*

Shape	Name	Lgth	Ring	Wrapper
Robusto	Robusto	5	50	CC
Toro	Corona Grande	6	48	CC
Torpedo	Torpedo	6½	52	CC
Double Corona	Garmeister	7	58	CC

Here is the story of some folks who learned how to roll cigars on the kitchen table and are now developing a growing following in the mid-South area. Introduced in 1995, Garmeister cigars utilize a flavorful Connecticut-seed wrapper and blend it with leaves from the Dominican Republic and Indonesia for a mild taste, offered in bundles of 25.

GARO
Handmade in Santiago, Dominican Republic.

Wrapper: USA/Connecticut   *Binder: Dom. Rep.*   *Filler: Dom. Rep.*

HANDMADE CIGARS: BRAND LISTINGS

Shape	Name	Lgth	Ring	Wrapper
Double Corona	Presidente	7½	50	CC
Churchill	Churchill	7	48	CC
Toro	Opus	6	50	CC
Lonsdale	Numero Uno	7	43	CC
Robusto	Robusto	4¾	52	CC
Torpedo	Torpedo	6½	52	CC
Corona	Corona	5¾	43	CC
Long Panatela	Panatela	7	36	CC

First available in 1996, the Garo line is made by hand in the Dominican Republic, offering a mild-to-medium body. It uses only Cuban-seed long filler, combined with a Dominican Olor binder and genuine Connecticut Shade-grown wrapper leaves. Even the band is elegant, employing the famous "Fleur de Lis" design.

GARO MADURO
Handmade in Santiago, Dominican Republic.
Wrapper: Brazil   *Binder: Dom. Rep.*   *Filler: Dom. Rep.*

Shape	Name	Lgth	Ring	Wrapper
Torpedo	Baritone	4½	52	Ma
Robusto	Alto	5	50	Ma
Torpedo	Tenor	5½	52	Ma
Torpedo	Soprano	6½	52	Ma

Here is a 1997-introduced, all-maduro line which offers a full-bodied smoke, thanks to its Brazilian wrapper, which is aged for more than three years. It is offered in boxes of 25.

GARO VERDE
Handmade in Santiago, Dominican Republic.
Wrapper: Indonesia   *Binder: Dom. Rep.*   *Filler: Dom. Rep.*

HANDMADE CIGARS: BRAND LISTINGS

Shape	Name	Lgth	Ring	Wrapper
Double Corona	Verde 1	7½	50	CC
Toro	Verde 2	6½	50	CC
Robusto	Verde 3	5	50	CC
Corona	Verde 4	5½	42	CC

The Garo "green" line offers a medium-to-full-bodied taste featuring a Sumatra wrapper and Cuban-seed filler leaves grown in the Dominican Republic. Introduced in 1997, it offers four popular sizes and is available in boxes of 25.

GARCIA Y VEGA
Handmade in Kingston, Jamaica.

Wrapper: USA/Connecticut　　　*Binder: Mexico*　　　*Filler: Dom. Rep., Mexico*

Shape	Name	Lgth	Ring	Wrapper
Churchill	Churchill	7	45	CC
Lonsdale	Lonsdale	6½	42	CC
Panatela	Corona	5½	38	CC

Garcia y Vega has been a famous name in cigars since it was introduced in 1882. In 1996, a new handmade series was introduced to complement the existing machine-made line with a Connecticut Shade wrapper and offering a medium body.

GATO
Handmade in Santiago, Dominican Republic.

Wrapper: Indonesia　　　*Binder: Dom. Rep.*　　　*Filler: Dom. Rep.*

Shape	Name	Lgth	Ring	Wrapper
Corona	Corona	5½	42	CC
Long Corona	Corona Grande	6	44	CC
Robusto	Robusto	5	50	CC
Double Corona	Presidente	7½	50	CC

HANDMADE CIGARS: BRAND LISTINGS

This is a medium-bodied blend, available in a choice of packaging: bundles, boxes or amatista jars.

GEOFFREY
Handmade in Santiago, Dominican Republic.

Wrapper: Dom. Rep. *Binder: Dom. Rep.* *Filler: Dom. Rep.*

Shape	Name	Lgth	Ring	Wrapper
Long Corona	Corona	6	44	CC
Robusto	Robusto	5	50	CC
Double Corona	Churchill	7	50	CC

Geoffrey made its debut in 1997 as a medium-bodied and slight sweet-tasting smoke. It is offered in individual cellophane sleeves in either boxes or bundles of 25.

GILBERTO OLIVA
Handmade in Ocotal, Nicaragua.

Wrapper: Costa Rica, USA/Connecticut
Binder: Dominican Republic *Filler: Dominican Republic, Nicaragua*

Shape	Name	Lgth	Ring	Wrapper
Lonsdale	No. 1	6½	44	CC
Robusto	Robusto	5½	50	CC-Ma
Double Corona	Churchill	7	50	CC-Ma
Toro	Viajante	6	52	CC
Torpedo	Torpedo	6	52	CC-Ma

Although this brand was new in 1996, it has already established a reputation for quality. Here is a medium-bodied, richly flavored cigar in both a natural (Connecticut) and maduro-shade (Costa Rican) wrapper in the most popular sizes. The line is complemented by the elegant, all-cedar boxes in which 25 cigars are held.

HANDMADE CIGARS: BRAND LISTINGS

GILFRANCO
Handmade in Esteli, Nicaragua.

Wrapper: Indonesia *Binder: Nicaragua* *Filler: Nicaragua*

Shape	Name	Lgth	Ring	Wrapper
Torpedo	Torpedo No. 2	6½	54	CM
Churchill	Churchill	7	48	CM
Toro	Double Corona	6	50	CM
Robusto	Robusto	5	50	CM

This is a medium-bodied cigar made with great care in Nicaragua and offered in this brand in value-priced packs of 25.

GILFRANCO VANILLA BOMBERS
Handmade, with short filler, in San Juan, Puerto Rico.

Wrapper: Puerto Rico *Binder: Homogenized tobacco leaf* *Filler: Puerto Rico*

Shape	Name	Lgth	Ring	Wrapper
Perfecto	Perfecto	4¾	44	CM

Here is a medium-bodied flavored cigar that is imbued with vanilla and walnut oil and offer a brightly-flavored taste in boxes of 100.

GIOCONDA
Handmade in Danli, Honduras.

Wrapper: USA/Connecticut *Binder: Honduras*
Filler: Dominican Republic, Honduras, Nicaragua

Shape	Name	Lgth	Ring	Wrapper
Double Corona	President	7¼	54	CC
Long Corona	Lonsdale	6¼	44	CC
Churchill	Churchill	6¾	48	CC
Robusto	Robusto	4½	50	CC
	Bundle group:			

HANDMADE CIGARS: BRAND LISTINGS

Lonsdale	Cazadores	6½	44	CC
Churchill	Churchill No. 1	7	48	CC
Torpedo	Aristocrats	6	52	CC
Toro	Diplomats	6	54	CC

New life was given to this brand by Vincent & Tampa Cigar Co.'s Mario Garrido. It is now made in Honduras and offers a medium-bodied blend, presented in boxes of 25. The bundle group features a Connecticut Broadleaf wrapper.

GISPERT
Handmade in Danli, Honduras.
Wrapper: Ecuador　　　　　　　　　　　*Binder: Dominican Republic*
Filler: Dominican Republic, Honduras, Nicaragua

Shape	Name	Lgth	Ring	Wrapper
Double Corona	Churchill	7½	50	CM
Toro	Toro	6	50	CM
Robusto	Robusto	5	52	CM
Lonsdale	Lonsdale	6½	44	CM

Introduced in 1996, this is a Honduran version of an old Cuban brand with excellent construction and a mild-to-medium-bodied taste. The wrapper is Connecticut-seed grown in Ecuador and each box of 25 is packed in cedar. The brand is only available in limited distribution to members of the Tobacconists' Association of America (TAA).

GLORIA PALMERA
Handmade in Las Palmas, Canary Islands of Spain.
Wrapper: USA/Connecticut　　　　　　　　*Binder: Indonesia*
Filler: Brazil, Dominican Republic, Spain

Shape	Name	Lgth	Ring	Wrapper
Double Corona	Doble Corona	7½	50	CC
Toro	Toro	6	50	CC

HANDMADE CIGARS: BRAND LISTINGS

Robusto	Robusto	5	50	CC
Lonsdale	Lonsdale	6½	43	CC

Introduced in 1996, this is a mild-bodied cigar which offers a genuine Connecticut wrapper, presented in boxes or bundles of 25.

GOLDEN SEAL
Handmade in Miami, Florida, USA.

Wrapper: Brazil   *Binder: Indonesia*   *Filler: Dom. Rep., Indonesia, Mexico*

Shape	*Name*	*Lgth*	*Ring*	*Wrapper*
Cigarillo	Finos	5	28	CM-Ma
Torpedo	Torpedo	6½	54	CM-Ma
Robusto	Robusto	5	50	CM-Ma
Long Panatela	Lancero	7½	38	CM-Ma
Long Corona	Panatela	6	42	CM-Ma
Double Corona	Churchill	7	50	CM-Ma
Double Corona	Presidente	7½	52	CM-Ma

Here is a mild-to-medium-bodied blend with a yummy Brazil wrapper. It is offered in packs of 25.

GOLDEN SUN
Handmade in Esteli, Nicaragua.

Wrapper: Ecuador or Indonesia   *Binder: Nicaragua*   *Filler: Nicaragua*

Shape	*Name*	*Lgth*	*Ring*	*Wrapper*
Cigarillo	Cigarillos	4½	28	CM
Panatela	Panatela	6½	38	CC
Grand Corona	Corona	6	46	CC

Available in six flavors: Amaretto, cherry, chocolate, cognac, rum and vanilla, this is a mild-bodied blend. Introduced in 1997, the Cigarillo size has a Sumatra wrapper, while the others utilize Connecticut-seed wrappers grown in Ecuador.

HANDMADE CIGARS: BRAND LISTINGS

GOMEZ & GARCIA
Handmade, with medium filler, in San Andres Tuxtla, Mexico.

Wrapper: Mexico   *Binder: Mexico*   *Filler: Mexico*

Shape	Name	Lgth	Ring	Wrapper
Panatela	Delicados	6	36	CM
Long Corona	Deliciosos	6	42	CM
Robusto	Ideales	5	50	CM
Robusto	Aromaticos	5½	54	CM

Sumatra-seed wrapper and binder surround Mexican-grown Corojo tobaccos in this medium-fill, mild-to-medium-bodied brand, It is offered in boxes of 10.

GOURMET DESSERT CIGARS
Handmade, with mixed filler, in Danli, Honduras.

Wrapper: Indonesia   *Binder: Indonesia*   *Filler: Caribbean blend*

Shape	Name	Lgth	Ring	Wrapper
Panatela	Chocolate	6	38	CM
Panatela	Vanilla	6	38	CM
Panatela	Cappuccino	6	38	CM
Panatela	Rum	6	38	CM
Panatela	Amaretto	6	38	CM

This brand debuted in 1998 and offers one shape in five flavors. The flavors are imbued into the tobacco prior to rolling and the finished product is offered in bundles of 25.

GOVERNOR'S
Handmade in La Romana, Dominican Republic.

Wrapper: USA/Connecticut   *Binder: Dom. Rep.*   *Filler: Dom. Rep.*

Shape	Name	Lgth	Ring	Wrapper
Petit Corona	Pequeños	4½	42	CC

Torpedo	Torpedo	6	52	CC
Corona	Corona	5½	44	CC
Robusto	Robusto	4¾	50	CC
Lonsdale	Lonsdale	6½	44	CC
Toro	Toro	6½	50	CC
Panatela	Panatela	5¾	39	CC
Churchill	Churchill	7	48	CC

This is a well-made, medium-to-full-bodied cigar with excellent construction. It is offered in value-priced bundles of 25.

GRAN HABANO
Handmade in Canca la Piedra, Dominican Republic.

Wrapper: Indonesia   Binder: Dom. Rep.   Filler: Dom. Rep.

Shape	Name	Lgth	Ring	Wrapper
Double Corona	Churchill	7	50	CC
Toro	Toro	6	50	CC
Robusto	Robusto	5	50	CC
Long Corona	Corona	6	44	CC
Corona	Petit Corona	5½	42	CC

New in 1997, this is a medium-to-full-bodied cigar which features a Sumatra wrapper, Olor binder and Piloto Cubano filler leaves. It is presented in cellophane sleeves and packed in all-cedar cabinets.

GRAN RESERVE SUAREZ
Handmade in the Dominican Republic.
Wrapper: Indonesia, USA/Connecticut

Binder: Dominican Republic   Filler: Dominican Republic

Shape	Name	Lgth	Ring	Wrapper
Robusto	Robusto	5	50	CC-CM

HANDMADE CIGARS: BRAND LISTINGS

Double Corona	Presidente	7½	52	CC-CM
Grand Corona	Royal Corona	6½	46	CC-CM
Long Panatela	Lonsdale	7	36	CC-CM
Pyramid	Torpedo Royale	7	50	CC-CM
Torpedo	Especial No. 1	7	50	CC-CM

Take your choice of Connecticut or Sumatra wrappers in this medium (Connecticut) to full (Sumatra)-bodied line, available in boxes of 25 except for the Torpedo Royale (12 to the box) and Especial No. 1 (20 per box).

GRAN VIRREY
Handmade in San Andres Tuxtla, Mexico.

Wrapper: Mexico   Binder: Mexico   Filler: Mexico

Shape	Name	Lgth	Ring	Wrapper
Toro	Toro	6¼	52	CM

Introduced in 1998, this is a mild-to-medium-bodied cigar, offered only in limited quantities.

GRAND CLASS
Handmade in Santo Domingo, Dominican Republic.

Wrapper: Dom. Rep.   Binder: Dom. Rep.   Filler: Dom. Rep.

Shape	Name	Lgth	Ring	Wrapper
Panatela	Panatela	5½	38	CM
Long Corona	Corona	6	42	CM
Robusto	Robusto	5	50	CM
Churchill	Churchill	7	48	CM
Double Corona	Presidente	7	50	CM

These are Dominican *puros* with tobaccos from the 1995 harvest. Medium in body, they are presented in cellophane sleeves, inside boxes of 25.

HANDMADE CIGARS: BRAND LISTINGS

GRAND CRUZ
Handmade in Licey, Dominican Republic.

Wrapper: Indonesia *Binder: Dom. Rep.* *Filler: Dom. Rep.*

Shape	Name	Lgth	Ring	Wrapper
Giant	Presidente	8	50	Ma
Lonsdale	Corona	7	44	Ma
Grand Corona	Double Corona	6½	46	Ma
Pyramid	Piramid	6½	53	Ma
Robusto	Robusto	5	50	Ma
Long Corona	Diplomatico	6	44	Ma

Here is an all-maduro line with a medium-to-full body. The Indonesian maduro wrapper is complemented by Cuban-seed, Dominican-grown binder and fillers. The line is presented is boxes of 25.

GRAND NICA
Handmade in Esteli, Nicaragua.

Wrapper: Brazil *Binder: Nicaragua* *Filler: Nicaragua*

Shape	Name	Lgth	Ring	Wrapper
Toro	Toro	6	50	CM
Petit Corona	Petit Corona	5	42	CM
Double Corona	Churchill	7	52	CM
Robusto	Robusto	5	52	CM
Torpedo	Torpedo	6¼	52	CM

Introduced in 1996, this line features all-Cuban seed tobaccos and offers a medium-bodied taste. It is offered in all-cedar cabinets of 25 cigars, each protected by cellophane sleeves.

HANDMADE CIGARS: BRAND LISTINGS

GRAVE DE PERALTA
Handmade in Cibao, Dominican Republic.
Wrapper: Cameroon or USA/Connecticut

Binder: Dominican Republic　　　　　　　　　　　　　*Filler: Dominican Republic*

Shape	Name	Lgth	Ring	Wrapper
	Azul:			
Robusto	Robusto	5	50	CM
Long Corona	Lonsdale	6	44	CM
Double Corona	Churchill	7	50	CM
	Rojo:			
Robusto	Robusto	5	50	CC
Corona	Corona	5½	42	CC
Double Corona	Churchill	7	50	CC
Long Corona	Lonsdale	6	44	CC

Adorned by the Peralta family crest, these two styles offer a medium-to-full-bodied flavor in the Azul (Blue Crest) series with Cameroon wrappers. The Rojo (Red Crest) series presents a mild-to-medium taste with a Connecticut wrapper. Introduced in 1998, both series are offered in boxes of 25.

GRAYCLIFF
Handmade in Nassau, the Bahamas.
Wrapper: Indonesia　　　*Binder: Indonesia*　　　*Filler: Brazil, Honduras, Nicaragua*

Shape	Name	Lgth	Ring	Wrapper
Double Corona	Chairman	7¾	50	CM
Long Panatela	Elegante	7¼	38	CM
Churchill	Presidente	7	48	CM
Torpedo	Pirate	6	52	CM
Panatela	Corona Especiale	6	38	CM
Robusto	P.G.	5¼	50	CM

Short Panatela	Grande Dame	5	35	CM

Enrico Garzaroli, the elegant owner of Graycliff — the first five-star restaurant in the Caribbean — wanted a great cigar to complement his cuisine. Now, with the help of Avelino Lara, supervisor of the Cohiba brand in Havana for many years, he has it. Under his supervision, there are 12 rollers producing these medium-to-full-bodied cigars with gorgeous wrappers and a rich, satisfying flavor.

THE GRIFFIN'S
Handmade in Santiago, Dominican Republic.

Wrapper: USA/Connecticut   *Binder: Dom. Rep.*   *Filler: Dom. Rep.*

Shape	Name	Lgth	Ring	Wrapper
Long Panatela	No. 100	7	38	CC
Lonsdale	No. 200	7	44	CC
Long Corona	No. 300	6¼	44	CC
Panatela	No. 400	6	38	CC
Corona	No. 500	5	42	CC
Slim Panatela	Privilege	5	31	CC
Double Corona	Prestige	7½	50	CC
Robusto	Robusto	5	50	CC

While the mythical character of the Griffin gives this brand its name, the effort which gives the cigars their high quality is very real. The filler includes three different Cibao Valley tobaccos combined with a Dominican binder and Connecticut wrapper to give it a mildly spicy, flavorful taste.

GUANCHE
Handmade, with mixed filler, in Cumana, Venezuela.

Wrapper: Indonesia   *Binder: Venezuela*   *Filler: Venezuela*

Shape	Name	Lgth	Ring	Wrapper
Lonsdale	Ejecutivo	7¼	42	CM
Long Corona	Corona Grande	6	44	CM

HANDMADE CIGARS: BRAND LISTINGS

Corona	Corona	5½	42	CM

This value-priced brand is new for 1998 and is mild-to-medium in body. It is offered in boxes of 25.

GUARANTEED JAMAICA
Handmade in Kingston, Jamaica.

FOUNDER'S SERIES:
Wrapper: USA/Connecticut   *Binder: Mexico*
Filler: Dominican Republic, Jamaica, Mexico

HERITAGE SERIES:
Wrapper: USA/Connecticut   *Binder: Ecuador*
Filler: Dominican Republic, Jamaica, Mexico

Shape	Name	Lgth	Ring	Wrapper
	Founder's Series:			
Toro	Windsor Supreme	6	50	CC
Corona	Devon Corona	5½	42	CC
Robusto	Hyde Park Short Story	4	50	CC
	Heritage Series:			
Grand Corona	No. 1	6	45	CC
Petit Corona	No. 4 Corona	5	40	CC
Toro	Aristocrat	6	50	CC
Robusto	Naturales	5	50	CC

These are well-made, high-quality cigars from the Combined Tobacco Co. factory in Kingston, Jamaica. The Connecticut wrapper surrounds either an Ecuadorian or Mexican binder and a combination of leaves from three nations to give this brand a rich flavor in boxes of 25. The Founder's Series features Jimmy Chang's original, mild blend for Macanudo prior to its acquisition by General Cigar Company in the 1980s. The Heritage Series is mild-to-medium in body and was formerly known as Jamaica Heritage.

HANDMADE CIGARS: BRAND LISTINGS

GURKHA
Handmade in Tamboril, Dominican Republic.

Wrapper: USA/Connecticut   Binder: Dom. Rep.   Filler: Dom. Rep.

Shape	Name		Lgth	Ring	Wrapper
	Grand Reserve Selection:				
Double Corona	Churchill	*(tubed)*	7½	50	CC
Robusto	Robusto	*(tubed)*	5	50	CC
Torpedo	Torpedo	*(tubed)*	6½	53	CC
	Vintage Selection:				
Double Corona	Double Corona		7½	52	CC
Robusto	Robusto		5	50	CC
Double Corona	Churchill		7	50	CC
Long Corona	Corona		6	44	CC
Torpedo	Torpedo		6¼	53	CC
Lonsdale	Lonsdale		7	42	CC
Petit Corona	Petit Corona		5	42	CC
Double Corona	Presidente		7½	54	CC
	His Majesty's Reserve:				
Double Corona	Churchill		7½	50	CC
Toro	Robusto		6	50	CC
Double Corona	Double Corona		7	53	CC

The Gurkha brand has been around, in one form or another, since 1887. That's as long as the Gurkhas, a Nepalese tribe who fought for the British in World Wars I and II, have been around. This edition offers three versions: the Grand Reserve shows a mild-to-medium body in wax-sealed glass tubes, with a Connecticut wrapper and a light finish thanks to a touch of Louis XIII Cognac; the Vintage Selection offers a medium-to-full taste, as does the His Majesty's Reserve edition. The His Majesty's Reserve are offered in humidor boxes with a combination of sizes included, at a majestic price of $5,000 per box!

HANDMADE CIGARS: BRAND LISTINGS

H M
Handmade in Manila, the Philippines.

Wrapper: Indonesia *Binder: Indonesia* *Filler: Philippines*

Shape	Name	Lgth	Ring	Wrapper
Robusto	Robusto	5	52	CM
Torpedo	Torpedo	6½	52	CM
Lonsdale	Lonsdale	7	44	CM
Double Corona	Presidente	7½	52	CM
Robusto	Rothchild	4¼	52	CM
Toro	Toro	6	52	CM
Long Panatela	Panatela	7	39	CM
Double Corona	Churchill	7	52	CM

H M stands for Humberto Mendoza and this tribute to the late Cuban farmer is a mild blend of tobaccos featuring an Indonesian wrapper grown in Java and offered in beautiful Narra wood boxes, or in bundles of 25.

H. UPMANN
Handmade in the La Romana, Dominican Republic.

Wrapper: Indonesia, Mexico *Binder: Dom. Rep.* *Filler: Dom. Rep.*

Shape	Name	Lgth	Ring	Wrapper
Grand Corona	Churchills	5⅝	46	CM
Churchill	Corona Imperiales	7	46	CM-Ma
Petit Corona	Corona Major (tubed)	5	42	CM
Corona	Coronas	5½	42	CM
Corona	Corona Cristals (glass tube)	5½	42	CM
Toro	Coronas Bravas	6½	48	CM-Ma
Long Panatela	El Prado	7	36	CM
Lonsdale	Lonsdales	6⅝	42	CM

Churchill	Monarch _(tubed)_	7	46	CM
Panatela	Naturales _(tubed)_	6⅛	36	CM
Lonsdale	No. 2000	7	42	CM
Panatela	Panatela Cristal _(glass tube)_	6¾	36	CM
Robusto	Pequenos No. 100	4½	50	CM
Corona Extra	Pequenos No. 200	4½	46	CM
Petit Corona	Pequenos No. 300	4½	42	CM
Petit Corona	Petit Coronas	5	42	CM
Panatela	Extra Finos Gold _(tubed)_	6¾	38	CM
Panatela	Finos Gold _(tubed)_	6⅛	36	CM
Petit Corona	Tubos Gold _(tubed)_	5	42	CM
Perfecto	Figurado	5¾	48	CM-Ma
Torpedo	Torpedo	6	50	CM-Ma
Toro	Toro	6	50	CM-Ma
Toro	Grande Maduro	6½	48	Ma
Double Corona	Premier	7	50	CM
	Machine-made with short-filler:			
Cigarillo	Aperitif	4	28	CM
Small Panatela	Demi Tasse	4½	33	CM

Legendary is the only way to describe the H. Upmann brand, originated in Cuba in 1844. Today's Dominican-produced Upmann appeared in the U.S. for the first time in 1975 and combines a medium-bodied taste with first-class construction and a consistency – even through a change in wrapper tobacco from Cameroon to Indonesia – which makes this brand a dependable favorite of smokers everywhere. The maduro-shade wrapper was introduced in this brand in 1998, using a dark Mexican-grown leaf.

HANDMADE CIGARS: BRAND LISTINGS

H. Upmann Cabinet Selection
Handmade in La Romana, Dominican Republic.
Wrapper: Indonesia　　　　*Binder: Dom. Rep.*　　　　*Filler: Dom. Rep.*

Shape	Name	Lgth	Ring	Wrapper
Giant	Columbo	8	50	CM
Robusto	Corsario	5½	50	CM
Robusto	Robusto	4½	50	CM-Ma

The larger girth of these marvelous cigars affords the smoker a full volume of smoke and a richness of taste and aroma that smaller-ring cigars cannot provide. The enthusiast will appreciate the "boite nature" packaging of 50 cigars per box, except for the Columbo size, offered in 10s.

H. Upmann Chairman's Reserve
Handmade in La Romana, Dominican Republic.
Wrapper: USA/Connecticut　　*Binder: Dom. Rep.*　　*Filler: Brazil, Dom. Rep.*

Shape	Name	Lgth	Ring	Wrapper
Long Panatela	Chairman's Reserve	7½	38	CC
Churchill	Churchill	6¾	48	CC
Double Corona	Double Corona	7	50	CC
Robusto	Robusto	5	50	CC
Torpedo	Torpedo	6	50	CC

This new brand, introduced in 1996, offers smokers a chance to sample the blend made for Consolidated Cigar Corporation's owner, Ron Perelman. It is medium-bodied and elegantly made; the Chairman's Reserve is individually boxed in a mahogany slide-top case inside packs of five! The other shapes are available in 20s.

H. Upmann Special Selection
Handmade in La Romana, Dominican Republic.
Wrapper: Indonesia, Mexico　　*Binder: Dom. Rep.*　　*Filler: Dom. Rep.*

HANDMADE CIGARS: BRAND LISTINGS

Shape	Name	Lgth	Ring	Wrapper
Churchill	Crown Imperial	7⅛	46	CM
Lonsdale	Special Polo	6¾	42	CM
Toro	Souvenir	6	50	CM
Grand Corona	After Dinner	5⅝	46	CM
Robusto	Rothschild	4½	50	CM-Ma
Corona	New Yorker	5⅝	42	CM

This is special! It's more Upmann magic, this time with medium body with Indonesian wrappers on all shapes and a Mexican maduro wrapper on one size. Each cigar is wrapped in aromatic cedar sleeves and then packed in boxes of 25.

HABANA CLUB
Handmade in Esteli, Nicaragua.

Wrapper: Ecuador, Mexico   Binder: Nicaragua   Filler: Dom. Rep., Nicaragua

Shape	Name	Lgth	Ring	Wrapper
Double Corona	President	7½	52	CC-Ma
Robusto	Robusto	5	50	CC-Ma
Churchill	Churchill	7	48	CC-Ma
Lonsdale	No. 1	7	43	CC-Ma
Panatela	Corona Especial	6	38	CC-Ma
Torpedo	Torpedo	6½	54	CC-Ma

Named for the famous rum of Cuba, Habana Club was introduced in 1996. It offers a mild flavor in the Ecuadorian-grown natural wrapper and a medium-bodied flavor in the Mexican-grown maduro version. It is offered in boxes of 25 plus a Churchill four-pack.

HANDMADE CIGARS: BRAND LISTINGS

HABANA GOLD
Handmade in San Pedro Sula, Honduras.
Wrappers: Black Label—Indonesia; White Label—Nicaragua
Binder: Nicaragua   Filler: Nicaragua

Shape	Name	Lgth	Ring	Wrapper
Petit Corona	Petite Corona	5	42	CC-CM
Long Corona	Corona	6	44	CC-CM
Robusto	Robusto	5	50	CC-CM
Pyramid	Torpedo	6	52	CC-CM
Double Corona	Churchill	7	52	CC-CM
Churchill	Double Corona	7½	46	CC-CM
Giant	Presidente	8½	52	CC-CM
Torpedo	No. 2	6⅛	52	CC-CM

Cuban-seed tobaccos are married with wrappers from Nicaragua (White Label)
or Sumatra-grown leaves (Black Label) to create a distinctive new brand:
Habana Gold. Medium (White Label) to medium-to-full (Black Label) in body,
these cigars continue to age as they are offered in cellophane sleeves inside
beautiful cedar boxes.

HABANA GOLD STERLING VINTAGE
Handmade in San Pedro Sula, Honduras.
Wrapper: Ecuador   Binder: Ecuador   Filler: Nicaragua

Shape	Name	Lgth	Ring	Wrapper
Petit Corona	Petite Corona	5	42	CM
Long Corona	Corona	6	44	CM
Robusto	Robusto	5	50	CM
Pyramid	Torpedo	6	52	CM
Double Corona	Churchill	7	52	CM
Churchill	Double Corona	7½	46	CM
Giant	Presidente	8½	52	CM

Torpedo	No. 2	6⅛	52	CM

This new blend includes an Ecuador-grown wrapper and binder, offering dark, full flavor, thanks to the specially aged wrapper leaf. The taste is nothing less than "sterling."

HABANA REAL
Handmade in Miami, Florida, USA.

Wrapper: Ecuador, Indonesia   Binder: Indonesia   Filler: Dom. Rep.

Shape	Name	Lgth	Ring	Wrapper
Double Corona	Churchill	7	50	CC-CM-Ma
Robusto	Robusto	5	50	CC-CM-Ma
Torpedo	Torpedo	6	52	CC-CM-Ma
Lonsdale	Corona	6½	42	CC-CM-Ma
Grand Corona	Double Corona	6½	46	CC-CM-Ma
Panatela	Panatela	6¾	36	CC-CM-Ma

Introduced in 1996, this is a mild cigar with a choice of Ecuador-grown, Connecticut-seed wrapper or a Sumatra wrapper. You can enjoy either of them in wood boxes of 25.

HABANA TREASURE
Handmade in Tamboril, Dominican Republic.

Wrapper: Ecuador   Binder: Dom. Rep.   Filler: Dom. Rep.

Shape	Name	Lgth	Ring	Wrapper
Double Corona	Churchill	7	50	CC
Toro	Corona Gorda	6	50	CC
Double Corona	President	7½	50	CC
Lonsdale	Palma	7	42	CC
Churchill	Corona	7	46	CC
Robusto	Robusto	5	50	CC

Torpedo	Torpedo	7	52	CC

This medium-bodied blend debuted in 1997 and is offered with a Connecticut-seed wrapper. It is available in elegant glass jars of 25, or in "refill" bundles of 25.

HABANA TREASURE
Handmade in Esteli, Nicaragua.

Wrapper: Cameroon　　　*Binder: Cameroon*　　　*Filler: Dominican Republic*

Shape	Name	Lgth	Ring	Wrapper
Torpedo	Torpedo	7	52	CM
Double Corona	Presidente	7½	50	CM
Double Corona	Churchill	7	50	CM
Toro	Corona Gorda	6	50	CM
Robusto	Robusto	5	50	CM
Churchill	Corona	7	46	CM
Grand Corona	Petite Corona	6	46	CM
Lonsdale	Palma	7	42	CM
Long Panatela	Lanceros	7½	38	CM
Slim Panatela	Panetela	6½	32	CM
Cigarillo	Pencil	6	28	CM

Here is a mild-bodied blend from a five-brand family. It is available in either bundles or boxes of 25 each. The Pencil shape is available in six flavors: Amaretto, Anise, chocolate, cognac, rum and vanilla.

HABANA 2000 CRIOLLO
Handmade in Esteli, Nicaragua.

Wrapper: Nicaragua　　　*Binder: Nicaragua*　　　*Filler: Nicaragua*

Shape	Name	Lgth	Ring	Wrapper
Robusto	Robusto	5	50	CM

Long Corona	Corona	6	42	CM

This is an all-Nicaraguan, full-bodied cigar that salutes Cuba's engineered "Habana 2000" criollo type of tobacco. Introduced in 1998, this brand is offered in slide-top boxes of 25.

HABANICA
Handmade in Condega, Nicaragua.

Wrapper: Nicaragua   Binder: Nicaragua   Filler: Nicaragua

Shape	Name	Lgth	Ring	Wrapper
Churchill	Serie 747	7	47	CM
Grand Corona	Serie 646	6	46	CM
Panatela	Serie 638	6	38	CM
Corona Extra	Serie 546	5¼	46	CM
Robusto	Serie 550	5	50	CM
Torpedo	Serie T	6	52	CM

Created in 1995, this is a medium-bodied smoke that is smooth and non-acidic. Made in Condega, Nicaragua, it combines choice Havana-seed tobaccos grown in nearby Jalapa to create a pleasant, rich taste.

HABANO PRIMERO
Handmade in Santiago, Dominican Republic.

Wrapper: Indonesia   Binder: Mexico   Filler: Brazil, Dom. Rep., Mexico

Shape	Name	Lgth	Ring	Wrapper
Churchill	Churchill	7	48	CM
Lonsdale	Lonsdale	6½	44	CM
Toro	Corona Gorda	6	52	CM
Robusto	Robusto	5	50	CM
Pyramid	Pyramid	6	52	CM

HANDMADE CIGARS: BRAND LISTINGS

New for 1998, this is a medium-to-full-bodied blend with a smooth draw and complex taste that has a hint of spice. It is presented in a colorful box of 25.

HABANO 2000 RESERVE
Handmade in Santo Domingo, Dominican Republic.

Wrapper: Ecuador *Binder: Indonesia* *Filler: Dom. Rep., Nicaragua*

Shape	Name	Lgth	Ring	Wrapper
Short Panatela	Sweet Panatella	5	38	CC
Long Corona	Sweet Corona	6	42	CC
Robusto	Robusto	5	50	CC
Toro	Churchill	6½	52	CC

Introduced in 1998, two of the shapes are sweetened and all are medium-bodied. It is presented in boxes of five and 25.

HAMILTONS
Handmade in La Romana, Dominican Republic.

Wrapper: Indonesia *Binder: Dom. Rep.* *Filler: Dom. Rep.*

Shape	Name	Lgth	Ring	Wrapper
Churchill	George I	7⅛	48	CC
Robusto	George II	5	50	CC
Torpedo	George III	6	50	CC
Lonsdale	George IV	6½	44	CC
Corona	George V	5½	42	CC
Long Panatela	George VI	7½	38	CC
Cigarillo	George VII	4½	28	CC
Panatela	George VIII	6¾	38	CC

This brand debuted in 1996, established by the noted actor and celebrity George Hamilton, a man who is never without his trademark tan. These eight sizes are made in the Consolidated Cigar Company factory in the Dominican Republic, and differ from the separate series produced by Tabacos Dominicanos. This is a medium-bodied blend and is available only at selected retailers.

HANDMADE CIGARS: BRAND LISTINGS

HAMILTONS HOUSE
Handmade in Tamboril, Dominican Republic.
Wrapper: Indonesia   Binder: Dom. Rep.   Filler: Dom. Rep.

Shape	Name	Lgth	Ring	Wrapper
Robusto	Robusto	5	52	CC
Long Corona	Corona	6	44	CC
Toro	Toro	6	50	CC
Double Corona	Double Corona	7	50	CC
Torpedo	Torpedo	6	54	CC

Beautifully made, but not quite as deeply tanned as George Hamilton himself, this is a medium-to-full-bodied range introduced in late 1997. You can enjoy them in elegant boxes of 25.

HAMILTONS RESERVE
Handmade in Santiago, Dominican Republic.
Wrapper: USA/Connecticut   Binder: Dom. Rep.   Filler: Dom. Rep.

Shape	Name	Lgth	Ring	Wrapper
Cigarillo	Lady H	5	26	CC
Long Panatela	Zorro	7½	38	CC
Corona	Corona	5½	42	CC
Robusto	Robusto	5	50	CC
Double Corona	King George	7½	50	CC
Pyramid	Torpedo	6⅛	52	CC

A 1996 companion brand to the Hamiltons brand above, this line is produced at the Tabadom factory in Santiago. This is a medium-bodied blend with a smooth Connecticut wrapper.

HANNIBAL
Handmade in Mission Escuba, Indonesia.
Wrapper: Indonesia   Binder: Indonesia   Filler: Indonesia

HANDMADE CIGARS: BRAND LISTINGS

Shape	Name	Lgth	Ring	Wrapper
Churchill	El Supremo	7	47	CC
Lonsdale	Excelsior	7	44	Ma
Petit Corona	Excelencia Suma Corona	5	44	CC
Pyramid	El Jumbo	5½	44	CC
Corona	Imperiales Corona	5½	44	CC
Double Corona	Premo del Premo	7½	52	CC
Pyramid	Obelisco	5½	52	CC
Robusto	Poco de Paz	5	52	CC
Perfecto	Barracuda	5	52	CC
Panatela	La Fortuna	6	35	CC
Short Panatela	Excelencia Infanta	4	39	CC
Panatela	Contessa	6	39	CC
Long Panatela	Prima Donna	7½	39	CC
Robusto	Poca Dulce	5	52	CC
Double Corona	Premo del Mundo	7	52	CC
Corona	Premo Corona	5½	44	CC
	Handmade with short filler:			
Giant	Emperador	15	125	CC
Lonsdale	Sensacionales	6¾	44	CC
Cigarillo	Duquesa	4½	20	CC
Short Panatela	Valentino Casanova	5	35	CC
Corona	Christobal Colon	5¼	44	CC
	Hannibal Gold Vintage:			*(aged six years)*
Corona	Premo Corona	5½	44	CC
Robusto	Poco de Paz	5	52	CC

HANDMADE CIGARS: BRAND LISTINGS

Double Corona	Premo del Premo	7½	52	CC
Perfecto	Barracuda	5	52	CC
Panatela	La Fortuna	6	35	CC

Available in the U.S. in 1997, the foundations of this brand go back to 1586 when Havana seeds and cuttings were planted at the Mission Escuba in Indonesia. These are medium and medium-to-full bodied cigars, handmade in some unusual shapes including the trumpet-style El Jumbo and the perfecto-tipped Barracuda, which also has a pigtail head. For a test of patience, try the gigantic Emperador with a ring gauge of 125, the largest available anywhere. The Poca Dulce and Premo del Mundo sizes are blended for a fuller-bodied flavor. All of the tobaccos are aged for at least two years. The Hannibal Gold Vintage line features tobaccos aged for four years, then rolled and aged for two more years in the box!

HANNIBAL SENSATIONAL
Handmade in Ocotal, Nicaragua.

Wrapper: Nicaragua	Binder: Nicaragua			Filler: Nicaragua
Shape	Name	Lgth	Ring	Wrapper
Grand Corona	Flavor Tubes (tubed)	6	46	CM
Corona	Flavor Suites	5⅝	44	CM

These flavored cigars debuted in 1998 and have a mild-to-medium body. They are offered in chocolate, coffee, rum and vanilla flavors. You can find them in unique packaging, with four cigars per pack, in jars of 32 or in humidified dispensers of 44!

HASA REY
Handmade in Danli, Honduras.

Wrapper: Honduras	Binder: Honduras			Filler: Honduras
Shape	Name	Lgth	Ring	Wrapper
Toro	Churchill	6½	52	CM
Short Panatela	Petit	4¼	38	CM
Toro	Toro	6⅛	50	CM

Lonsdale	No. 1	6½	44	CM
Corona	No. 4	5½	44	CM

The name is a phonetic version of the Yiddish word "chazarai," (pronounced HAAS-a-RYE) originally referring to junk or trash, but now in use as a general reference to goods or "stuff." This cigar stuff dates from 1969 and is a full-bodied bundle of 25 cigars. Stuff one in your mouth and light up!

HAVACHE
Handmade in Danli, Honduras.

Wrapper: Indonesia   Binder: Mexico   Filler: Honduras

Shape	Name	Lgth	Ring	Wrapper
Culebras	Culebra	7	38	CM
Torpedo	Torpedo Series 100	7¼	54	CM
Perfecto	Figurado	7¼	54	CM
Pyramid	Piramide	7	54	CM
Perfecto	Figurado Series 100	7	60	CM
Perfecto	Perfecto	6½	52	CM
Torpedo	Torpedo Series 200	6¼	52	CM
Toro	El Casino	6	48	Stripe
Torpedo	Stocky Torpedo	5¾	60	CM
Perfecto	Cubanito	5¼	50	CM
Robusto	Robusto	5	50	CM
Torpedo	Baril	6½	56	CM
Perfecto	Emperadoro	9	60	CM

This stunning brand is a virtual display of the cigarmaker's art! These are full-bodied cigars introduced in 1998 and offered in boxes of 25.

HANDMADE CIGARS: BRAND LISTINGS

HAVANA
Handmade in Union City, New Jersey, USA.
Wrapper: Dominican Republic, Mexico, USA/Connecticut
Binder: Mexico, USA/Connecticut   *Filler: Dominican Republic, Honduras*

Shape	Name	Lgth	Ring	Wrapper
Giant	Churchill	8	50	CC-Ma
Double Corona	Silverano	7	50	CC-Ma
Toro	Torito	6½	50	CC-Ma
Churchill	Imperiale	7½	46	CC-Ma
Lonsdale	Presidente	6½	44	CC-Ma
Long Corona	Senadore	6	44	CC-Ma
Long Panatela	Ninfa	7	36	CC-Ma
Lonsdale	Fuma	7	44	CC-Ma
Torpedo	Torpedo	6	54	CC-Ma
Pyramid	Pyramid	5½	46	CC-Ma
Robusto	Robusto	5	50	CC-Ma

This cigar is made by the Boquilla cigar factory in Union City. These are medium-to-full bodied cigars – now banded – with a wider range of shapes and wrappers available.

HAVANA CIGARS - DON PEDRO RAMOS
Handmade in Esteli, Nicaragua.
Wrapper: Ecuador, Mexico   *Binder: Nicaragua*   *Filler: Dom. Rep.*

Shape	Name	Lgth	Ring	Wrapper
Torpedo	Torpedo	6½	54	CC-Ma
Double Corona	Presidente	7½	52	CC-Ma
Churchill	Churchill	7	48	CC-Ma
Robusto	Robusto	5	50	CC-Ma
Toro	Double Corona	6	48	CC-Ma

HANDMADE CIGARS: BRAND LISTINGS

Panatela	Panatela	5½	38	CC-Ma

Named for, and produced under the direction of, former major league pitcher Pedro Ramos, this is a medium-to-full-bodied blend available in boxes of 25. The natural-shade wrapper is from Ecuador (Connecticut-seed) and the maduro-shade wrapper is from Mexico.

HAVANA CLASE
Handmade in San Pedro Sula, Honduras.

Wrapper: Ecuador   Binder: Honduras, Nicaragua   Filler: Nicaragua

Shape	Name	Lgth	Ring	Wrapper
Double Corona	Churchill	7	50	CC
Robusto	Rothchild	5½	50	CC-Ma
Lonsdale	Corona Gorda	6½	44	CC
Corona	Corona	5½	42	CC-Ma

Introduced in 1997, this is a medium-bodied cigar that features Cuban-seed filler leaves and Sumatra-seed wrappers. The new Maduro-wrapped series debuted in 1998 and uses a Honduran binder and produce a full-bodied taste. The natural-wrapped cigars are offered in boxes of 25, while the maduros are available in bundles of 25.

HAVANA CLOUD
Handmade in Quayaquil, Ecuador.

Wrapper: Ecuador   Binder: Ecuador   Filler: Dom. Rep.

Shape	Name	Lgth	Ring	Wrapper
Robusto	Robusto	5	50	CC
Lonsdale	Churchill	6½	44	CC

Introduced in 1998, this bundle brand is offered with either long or short filler. It presents a medium body with a Sumatra-grown wrapper, Ecuadorian binder and Piloto Cubano-seed filler.

HANDMADE CIGARS: BRAND LISTINGS

HAVANA COOL
Handmade, with short filler, in Esteli, Nicaragua.
Wrapper: Nicaragua   *Binder: Nicaragua*   *Filler: Nicaragua*

Shape	Name	Lgth	Ring	Wrapper
Long Corona	Alhambra	6	44	CM
Robusto	Granada	5	50	CM
Churchill	Riviera	7	48	CM
Short Panatela	Salamanca	4	38	CM

This is a medium-to-full bodied smoke introduced in 1996 and made with all-Nicaraguan tobacco and offered in boxes of 25.

HAVANA EXPRESS
Handmade in Santiago, Dominican Republic.
Wrapper: Indonesia   *Binder: Dom. Rep.*   *Filler: Dom. Rep.*

Shape	Name	Lgth	Ring	Wrapper
Double Corona	Churchill	7	50	CM
Torpedo	Torpedo	6¼	54	CM
Corona	Corona	5¾	42	CM
Robusto	Robusto	4½	50	CM
Lonsdale	Lancero	7	44	CM

This brand was introduced in 1998 and has a mild body. It is available in all-cedar boxes of 25.

HAVANA KING
Handmade in Tamboril, Dominican Republic.
Wrapper: Indonesia   *Binder: Dom. Rep.*   *Filler: Dom. Rep.*

Shape	Name	Lgth	Ring	Wrapper
Double Corona	Presidente	7½	50	CM
Churchill	Churchill	6⅞	46	CM

Long Corona	Corona	6	44	CM
Torpedo	Torpedo	6	52	CM
Robusto	Robusto	5	50	CM

Introduced in 1996, this is a medium-to-full-bodied brand featuring all-Dominican filler and a Sumatra wrapper and offered in protective cellophane sleeves inside boxes or bundles of 25. There is also a special Torpedo shape with a double wrapper of Ecuadorian and Indonesian leaves, also medium-to-full in body.

HAVANA KING RESERVE
Handmade in Tamboril, Dominican Republic.
Wrapper: Ecuador   Binder: Dom. Rep.   Filler: Dom. Rep.

Shape	Name	Lgth	Ring	Wrapper
Double Corona	Presidente	7½	50	CC
Churchill	Churchill	6⅞	46	CC
Long Corona	Corona	6	44	CC
Torpedo	Torpedo	6	52	CC
Robusto	Robusto	5	50	CC
Small Panatela	Rosas	5	30	CC

This brand is a little milder than its sibling above, with a mild-to-medium-bodied blend of Dominican-grown Piloto Cubano filler tobaccos with Connecticut-seed wrappers offered in protective cellophane sleeves inside boxes of 25. The Rosas shape is offered only in bundles of 25.

HAVANA NIGHTS
Handmade, with short filler, in Tamboril, Dominican Republic.
Wrapper: Indonesia, USA/Connecticut   Binder: Dom. Rep.   Filler: Dom. Rep.

Shape	Name	Lgth	Ring	Wrapper
	Havana Nights:			
Panatela	Panatella	6	38	CM
Corona	Corona	5½	42	CM

HANDMADE CIGARS: BRAND LISTINGS

	Havana Nights Reserve:			
Panatela	Panatela	6	38	CC
Corona	Corona	5½	42	CC

Formerly known as Acapa Sweets, this blend was introduced in 1997. It is mild-bodied with a Connecticut wrapper in the "Reserve" line and medium-bodied in the Sumatra-wrapped standard version. All are available in Amaretto, cognac, butter rum and vanilla in boxes of 25. The cigarillo size is offered in boxes of 50.

HAVANA REPUBLIC
Handmade in Jalapa, Nicaragua.
Wrapper: Ecuador or Indonesia
Binder: Nicaragua   Filler: Dominican Republic, Nicaragua

Shape	Name	Lgth	Ring	Wrapper
	Epicurean Series:			
Corona	Royal Corona	5½	44	CC
Robusto	Robusto	5	50	CC
Lonsdale	No. 1	7	44	CC
Grand Corona	Medal d'Ore	6	46	CC
Churchill	Churchill D'Churchill	7	48	CC
Double Corona	Lusitania	7½	50	CC
Giant	Series A	8½	52	CC
	Grand Havana Series:			
Corona	Royal Corona	5½	44	CM
Robusto	Robusto	5	50	CM
Lonsdale	No. 1	7	44	CM
Grand Corona	Medal d'Ore	6	46	CM
Churchill	Churchill D'Churchill	7	48	CM
Double Corona	Lusitania	7½	50	CM

Giant	Series A	8½	52	CM

Introduced in 1997, here is a unique, two-series blend with a mild-bodied flavor in the Epicurean Series and a medium-bodied flavor in the Grand Havana Series. In either case, you can find them in boxes of 25.

HAVANA RESERVE
BY DON LINO
Handmade in Santiago, Dominican Republic.

Wrapper: Mexico, USA/Connecticut   Binder: Dom. Rep.   Filler: Dom. Rep.

Shape	Name		Lgth	Ring	Wrapper
Lonsdale	No. 1		6½	42	CC-Ma
Grand Corona	Toros		6½	46	CC-Ma
Long Panatela	Panatela		6	36	CC
Double Corona	Churchill		7½	50	CC-Ma
Lonsdale	Petit Corona		6¾	40	CC
Robusto	Rothschild		4½	50	CC
Robusto	Robustos		5½	50	CC-Ma
Torpedo	Torpedo		6	53	CC-Ma
Perfecto	Don Nestor		4¼	46	CC
Perfecto	Perfecto No. 2		5½	52	CC
Long Corona	Corona Tubos	*(tubed)*	6	44	CC
Robusto	Robusto Tubos	*(tubed)*	5	50	CC
Churchill	Supremo Clasico		7	47	CC
Churchill	Doble Corona		7	48	Ma

Introduced in 1993, Havana Reserve was made in Honduras through 1996. In 1997, production was moved to the Dominican Republic. It is a handmade cigar with Dominican long filler and binder that assures consistent, mild-bodied taste and burning qualities. The wrapper is selected from only the finest Connecticut leaf for the unique taste that is only found in Havana Reserve. All shapes are

HANDMADE CIGARS: BRAND LISTINGS

available in boxes of 25, except for the Tubos and Supremo Clasico which are available in 10s. The Maduro-wrapped shapes are medium-to-full in body.

HAVANA ROYALE
Handmade in Santiago, Dominican Republic.

Wrapper: Indonesia   *Binder: Dom. Rep.*   *Filler: Dom. Rep.*

Shape	Name	Lgth	Ring	Wrapper
Torpedo	Torpedo	6	54	CC
Giant	Presidente	8	50	CC
Churchill	Churchill	7	48	CC
Toro	Royale	6	50	CC
Long Corona	Gran Corona	6	44	CC
Robusto	Robusto	4½	50	CC

Sumatra wrapper? Cuban-seed binder and filler? Mild-to-medium-bodied taste! Olé! New in 1997, Havana Royales are presented in elegant, cedar-chest-style boxes of 25 cigars each, individually protected by cellophane sleeves. The Gran Corona shape is also available in a short-filler, flavored style if desired.

HAVANA SELECT
Handmade in Miami, Florida, USA.

Wrapper: Indonesia   *Binder: Nicaragua*   *Filler: Dom. Rep.*

Shape	Name	Lgth	Ring	Wrapper
Robusto	Robusto	5	50	CM
Robusto	Corona Gorda	5½	48	CM
Torpedo	Torpedo	6	54	CM
Long Corona	Corona	6	44	CM
Robusto	Capone	5½	54	CM
Toro	Toro	6½	50	CM
Double Corona	Churchill	7½	50	CM
Giant	Presidente	8	52	CM

HANDMADE CIGARS: BRAND LISTINGS

Here is a full-bodied brand introduced in 1997 and offering a Sumatra wrapper and Piloto Cubano filler in a variety of shapes. Check out the fat Capone shape, or any of the others in boxes of 25.

HAVANA STAR
Handmade in Ojo de Agua, Honduras.

Wrapper: Indonesia   Binder: Honduras   Filler: Honduras, Nicaragua

Shape	Name	Lgth	Ring	Wrapper
Cigarillo	Chico	4½	28	CM
Double Corona	Churchill	7	50	CM
Robusto	Rothschild	5	50	CM

This brand debuted in 1998 and offers a medium-bodied taste in three sizes. You can enjoy it in bundles of 25 for the larger sizes, or in boxes of five or 30 for the Chico size.

HAVANA SUNRISE
Handmade in Miami, Florida, USA.
Wrapper: Ecuador or USA/Connecticut

Binder: Dom. Rep.   Filler: Dom. Rep., Honduras, Indonesia, Nicaragua

Shape	Name	Lgth	Ring	Wrapper
Cigarillo	Panatela - Cache	5	28	Co
Robusto	Robusto	5	50	Co
Torpedo	Torpedo	6	54	Co
Long Corona	Corona	6	44	Co
Toro	Double Corona	6	48	Co
Toro	Emperador	6¼	54	Co
Churchill	Havana	6¾	46	Co
Torpedo	Pyramid	7	60	Co
Long Panatela	Lancero	7½	38	Co
Double Corona	Churchill	7½	50	Co

Giant	Presidente	8	52	Co

Created in the heart of "Little Havana" in Miami, Florida, Havana Sunrise cigars were introduced in 1996. Offering a medium-to-full-bodied flavor, they are presented in handsome cedar boxes of 25, where the cigars continue to age and obtain an even more elegant finish. The Churchill, Lancero and Panatela-Cache sizes are offered in boxes of 15.

HAVANA VERDE
Handmade in Danli, Honduras.

Wrapper: Indonesia *Binder: Honduras* *Filler: Dom. Rep., Honduras*

Shape	Name	Lgth	Ring	Wrapper
Robusto	Robusto	5	50	CC
Double Corona	Churchill	7	50	CC
Double Corona	Double Corona	7½	52	CC
Grand Corona	Corona Gorda	6	46	CC

This brand debuted in late 1996, offering a medium-to-full body that features a Sumatra-seed wrapper. It is presented in varnished, all-cedar boxes of 25.

HAVANILLA
Handmade in Tamboril, Dominican Republic.

Wrapper: USA/Connecticut *Binder: Dom. Rep.* *Filler: Dom. Rep.*

Shape	Name	Lgth	Ring	Wrapper
Small Panatela	Cigarillo	5	30	CC

This is a very mild brand with a savory vanilla flavor. It is offered in boxes of 25.

HEAVEN
Handmade in Santiago, Dominican Republic.

Wrapper: Ecuador *Binder: Dom. Rep.* *Filler: Dom. Rep.*

Shape	Name	Lgth	Ring	Wrapper
Double Corona	Scarface	7⅝	50	CC-Ma

HANDMADE CIGARS: BRAND LISTINGS

Torpedo	Machiavelli	6	54	CC-Ma
Long Corona	Bugsy	6	44	CC-Ma
Robusto	Sun Tzu	5	50	CC-Ma

Introduced in 1996, this is two lines within one brand: the Cloud Nine series offers a natural-shade wrapper with a medium-bodied flavor, while the Private Reserve has a Ecuadorian-grown maduro wrapper, which is medium-to-full in body. Either way, you can enjoy these cigars in boxes of 25.

HEAVENLY VANILLA
Handmade in Santiago, Dominican Republic.
Wrapper: USA/Connecticut   Binder: Dom. Rep.   Filler: Dom. Rep.

Shape	Name	Lgth	Ring	Wrapper
Long Corona	Corona	6	42	CC
Small Panatela	Petite	5½	30	CC

This is a 1997-introduced, all-vanilla flavored cigar with a sweet tip, offered in boxes of 25.

HENRY CLAY
Handmade in La Romana, Dominican Republic.
Wrapper: USA/Connecticut   Binder: Dom. Rep.   Filler: Dom. Rep.

Shape	Name		Lgth	Ring	Wrapper
Corona	Brevas		5½	42	Ma
Corona Extra	Brevas a la Conserva		5⅝	46	Ma
Churchill	Brevas Finas		6½	48	Ma
Toro	Grande	(tube)	6½	48	Ma
Toro	Toro		6	50	Ma

There are two new sizes in this line in 1998 and this will please its devoted followers, who are lovers of its medium-bodied taste and Connecticut Broadleaf maduro wrappers. Undoubtedly named for the famous American politician of the same name (U.S. senator from Kentucky 1806-07, 1810-11, 1831-42, 1849-52; U.S. representative and Speaker of the House 1811-14, 1815-21, 1823-25; U.S.

secretary of state 1825-29), this brand originated in Cuba and the Henry Clay factory in Havana is still pictured on the brand's box.

HENRY CLAY EMS
Handmade in La Romana, Dominican Republic.

Wrapper: Nicaragua   Binder: Dom. Rep.   *Filler: Dom. Rep.*

Shape	Name		Lgth	Ring	Wrapper
Lonsdale	Cedro Deluxe		6⅝	42	CM
Toro	Souvenir		6½	50	CM
Torpedo	Obelisk		6	50	CM
Corona Extra	Corona Gorda		5⅝	47	CM
Corona	Fantasia	*(glass tube)*	5⅝	40	CM
Robusto	Mirabelle		5	50	CM

Hey Henry! How about a new series with a Habano 2000 wrapper and a medium-to-full body. Here it is, offered in boxes of 20.

HENRY GEORGE
Handmade in Santiago, Dominican Republic.

Wrapper: USA/Connecticut   Binder: Dom. Rep.   *Filler: Dom. Rep.*

Shape	Name	Lgth	Ring	Wrapper
Double Corona	Double Corona	7½	49	CC
Lonsdale	Lonsdale	7	44	CC
Toro	Toro	6½	50	CC

Created in 1997, this is a medium-to-full-bodied brand, named after the famous American economist and New York mayoral candidate Henry George (1839-1897). If you prefer his cigar to his economic theories, you'll find it in bundles of 25.

HERMOSA FLOR
Handmade in the Jalapa Valley, Nicaragua.

Wrapper: Indonesia   Binder: Nicaragua   *Filler: Nicaragua*

HANDMADE CIGARS: BRAND LISTINGS

Shape	Name	Lgth	Ring	Wrapper
Double Corona	Viajante	7	54	CC-Ma
Double Corona	Presidente	7½	50	CC-Ma
Toro	Toro	6	50	CC-Ma
Lonsdale	No. 3	6½	44	CC-Ma
Robusto	Corona	5½	48	CC-Ma
Robusto	Robusto	4½	52	CC-Ma

Created in 1995, this medium-bodied cigar is offered with a Sumatra-grown wrapper in either shade and binder and filler leaves from Nicaragua. You can find it in all-cedar cabinets of 25 cigars each.

HERRERA-CLAVEROL
Handmade in Miami, Florida, USA.
Wrapper: Ecuador and Indonesia or Mexico   *Binder: Mexico or Nicaragua*
Filler: Dominican Republic, Mexico, Nicaragua

Shape	Name	Lgth	Ring	Wrapper
Perfecto	Rubio	9	58	CC
Perfecto	Mulato	9	58	Ma

This unique brand was introduced in 1998 and is made by hand without molds! It features a double wrapper of Connecticut-seed over Sumatra leaves and Mexican maduro binder in the Rubio for a medium-to-full-bodied taste. In the full-bodied Mulato, a Mexican maduro wrapper is used with a Nicaraguan binder. Each is offered in an individual wood box.

HIDALGO
Handmade, with mixed filler, in Colon, Panama.
Wrapper: Ecuador   *Binder: Mexico*
Filler: Dominican Republic, Honduras, Panama

Shape	Name	Lgth	Ring	Wrapper
Lonsdale	Cazadore	7	44	CC
Lonsdale	Fuma	7	44	Ma

Corona	Corona	5½	42	CC-Ma
Churchill	Double Corona	7	48	CC-Ma
Giant	Monarch	8½	52	CC-Ma

These medium-bodied cigars use mixed filler (long and short) and are offered in bundles of 20 cigars each.

HOBO
Handmade in Santiago, Dominican Republic.
Wrapper: Ecuador or Indonesia   Binder: Indonesia   *Filler: Dom. Rep.*

Shape	Name	Lgth	Ring	Wrapper
Short Panatela	Compadre	5	38	CC
Petit Corona	El Rey	5	42	CC
Grand Corona	Amigo	6	46	CC
Robusto	Matador	5	50	CC
Double Corona	Patron	7	50	CC

This is a flavored brand, available in almond brandy, cafe latte, cherry, chocolate, cognac, expresso, Pina Colada, rum, vanilla and sweet styles. It's a medium-bodied smoke, available with a continuous flavoring process in "Flavor-Mate" platforms.

HOJA CUBANA
Handmade in Esteli, Nicaragua.

YELLOWBAND:
Wrapper: Ecuador   Binder: Nicaragua   Filler: Dom. Rep., Nicaragua

CUBA 1965:
Wrapper: Ecuador
Binder: Dom. Rep.   Filler: Dom. Rep., Honduras, Nicaragua

Shape	Name	Lgth	Ring	Wrapper
	Yellowband:			
Petit Corona	Cubito	4	44	CC

Long Corona	Corona	6	44	CC-Ma
Robusto	Robusto	5	50	CC-Ma
Toro	Epicure	6	50	CC-Ma
Toro	Tainos	6	54	CC
Double Corona	Churchill	7	50	CC-Ma
Double Corona	Gigante	7	54	CC
Torpedo	Torpedo	6½	54	CC-Ma
	Cuba 1965:			
Petit Corona	Punch	4	44	CC
Robusto	Rothschild	5	50	CC
Toro	Especial 650	6	50	CC
Double Corona	Monarcas	7	49	CC
Torpedo	Belicoso	5½	54	CC

This limited-production brand debuted in 1994. The Cuba 1965 style offers a mild-to-medium body, while the Yellowband blends are medium in strength. Created by master blender Carlos Gutierrez, "the leaf of Cuba" offers a smooth draw and features an Ecuadorian-grown Rosado wrapper. It is presented in all-cedar, slide-top cabinet-style boxes of 25.

HOJA CUBANA XXO
BY TONY BOHANI
Handmade in San Jose, Costa Rica.

Wrapper: Ecuador   *Binder: Ecuador*   *Filler: Dom. Rep., Nicaragua*

Shape	Name	Lgth	Ring	Wrapper
Lonsdale	Lonsdale	6½	42	CC
Robusto	Series R	5	50	CC
Toro	Reserva 650	6	50	CC
Double Corona	Series C	7	50	CC

HANDMADE CIGARS: BRAND LISTINGS

Here is the newest of the Hoja Cubana line, a sensational, limited-production line from Tony Borhani and the Tabacalera Tambor. Introduced in 1998, this range has a mild-to-medium body and is offered in elegant boxes of 20.

HOJA DE HONDURAS
Handmade in Danli, Honduras.

Wrapper: Ecuador   *Binder: Honduras*   *Filler: Honduras*

Shape	Name	Lgth	Ring	Wrapper
Double Corona	Churchill	7	50	CC
Giant	General	8½	52	CC
Giant	Inmensas	8	54	CC
Lonsdale	Number 1	7	43	CC
Long Panatela	Palma Extra	7	36	CC
Corona	Reyes	5½	42	CC
Toro	Toro	6	50	CC

These are medium-to-full bodied cigars, well constructed and offered in boxes of 25.

HOJA DE MEXICALI
Handmade in San Andres Tuxtla, Mexico.

Wrapper: Mexico   *Binder: Mexico*   *Filler: Mexico*

Shape	Name	Lgth	Ring	Wrapper
Lonsdale	Lonsdale	6⅝	42	CM
Long Corona	Royal Corona	6	42	CM
Double Corona	Soberano	7½	50	CM
Toro	Toro	6	50	CM-Ma
Giant	Viajante	8½	52	CM

This Mexican "puro" is a heavy-bodied cigar created in 1985 with all-San Andres Valley tobaccos, offered in convenient bundles of 25 cigars each.

HANDMADE CIGARS: BRAND LISTINGS

HOJA DE NICARAGUA
Handmade in Esteli, Nicaragua.

Wrapper: Nicaragua   *Binder: Nicaragua*   *Filler: Nicaragua*

Shape	Name	Lgth	Ring	Wrapper
Double Corona	Churchill	7	49	CM-Ma
Robusto	Consul	4½	52	CM-Ma
Toro	Corona Nacio	5⅝	48	CM-Ma
Long Corona	No. 3	6	44	CM-Ma
Long Corona	No. 6	6	42	CM-Ma
Double Corona	Presidente	7½	50	CM-Ma
Giant	Viajante	8½	52	CM-Ma
Double Corona	Diplomatico	7	54	CC-Ma
Panatela	Petite	5½	38	CC-Ma

Here is an all-Nicaraguan cigar offered in elegant boxes of 25, offering a spicy, medium-bodied taste thanks to a blend of Cuban-seed tobaccos.

HOJA DE ORO
Handmade in San Andres Tuxtla, Mexico.

Wrapper: Mexico   *Binder: Mexico*   *Filler: Mexico*

Shape	Name	Lgth	Ring	Wrapper
Double Corona	No. 100	7	50	CC-Ma
Double Corona	No. 101	7½	50	CC-Ma
Toro	No. 103	6	50	CC-Ma
Lonsdale	No. 104	6¾	45	CC-Ma
Robusto	No. 105	4½	50	CC-Ma
Grand Corona	No. 106	6	45	CC-Ma
Corona Extra	No. 107	5	45	CC-Ma

HANDMADE CIGARS: BRAND LISTINGS

Another product of the famous San Andres Valley in Mexico, the Hoja de Oro line utilizes all-Mexican tobacco, including filler tobacco from San Andres mixed with Cuban-seed leaf grown in the northern part of the Mexican state of Veracruz. The binder is San Andres-grown while the wrapper is Sumatran-seed, also grown in the San Andres Valley.

HOJA DE VUELTABAJO
Handmade in Santiago, Dominican Republic.

Wrapper: Indonesia   Binder: Dom. Rep.   Filler: Dom. Rep.

Shape	Name	Lgth	Ring	Wrapper
Panatela	Panetela	6	38	Ma
Robusto	Robusto	5	50	Ma
Lonsdale	Lonsdale	6½	44	Ma
Toro	Churchill	6½	50	Ma
Pyramid	Piramide	6½	53	Ma
Double Corona	Double Corona	7½	50	Ma

Introduced in 1998, this brand offers all-maduro, medium-to-full-bodied taste in bundles of 25.

HOJA REAL
Handmade in San Andres Tuxtla, Mexico.

Wrapper: Mexico   Binder: Mexico   Filler: Mexico

Shape	Name	Lgth	Ring	Wrapper
Double Corona	Churchill	7½	50	CC
Robusto	Robusto	5½	50	CC
Long Corona	No. 1	6¼	44	CC

This brand has been around since about 1992, but available in the U.S. beginning in 1997. It combines a Sumatra-seed wrapper with Mexican binder and filler tobaccos for a medium-bodied flavor. Each all-cedar box is numbered and personally signed by the master blender as proof of its quality.

HANDMADE CIGARS: BRAND LISTINGS

HOMBRE DE ORO
Handmade in Villa Gonzalez, Dominican Republic.

Wrapper: Ecuador   Binder: Mexico   Filler: Dom. Rep.

Shape	Name	Lgth	Ring	Wrapper
Double Corona	Churchills	7½	50	CC
Lonsdale	Corona	6½	44	CC
Churchill	Double Corona	7	48	CC
Corona	Petit Corona	5½	42	CC
Robusto	Rothschild	4½	50	CC
Toro	Toro	6	50	CC

This is a new cigar in 1997 offering a mild-bodied flavor that features Cuban-seed filler leaves grown in the Dominican Republic. It is presented in individual cellophane sleeves in cedar boxes of 25.

HONDURAS SPECIAL
Handmade in Danli, Honduras.

Wrapper: Honduras   Binder: Honduras   Filler: Honduras

Shape	Name	Lgth	Ring	Wrapper
Giant	No. 201	8½	52	CM
Short Panatela	No. 202	4½	36	CM
Double Corona	No. 203	7½	50	CM
Toro	No. 204	6	50	CM
Robusto	No. 205	4½	50	CM
Lonsdale	No. 206	6⅝	43	CM
Corona	No. 207	5½	42	CM
Panatela	No. 208	6⅞	35	CM
Panatela	No. 209	6	36	CM
Corona Extra	No. 210	5½	46	CM

This hard-to-find brand is full-bodied and sells quickly, thanks to its packaging in bundles of just 10 cigars, which keeps the modest price within reach of every smoker.

HOYO DE CORTEZ CORTO
Handmade, with medium filler, in Santiago, Dominican Republic.
Wrapper: Indonesia   *Binder: Dom. Rep.*   *Filler: Dom. Rep.*

Shape	Name	Lgth	Ring	Wrapper
Double Corona	Churchill	7½	52	CC
Churchill	Corona Gorda	7	48	CC
Robusto	Robusto	5	50	CC
Lonsdale	Panatela	6½	44	CC

Introduced in 1997, this is a value-priced cigar with a medium-bodied flavor and a Sumatra wrapper.

HOYO DE CORTEZ ESCOGIDO
Handmade in Santiago, Dominican Republic.
Wrapper: Indonesia   *Binder: Dom. Rep.*   *Filler: Dom. Rep.*

Shape	Name	Lgth	Ring	Wrapper
Double Corona	Churchill	7½	52	CC
Churchill	Gran Corona	7	48	CC
Robusto	Robusto	5	50	CC
Lonsdale	Panatela	6½	42	CC
Torpedo	Torpedo	7	54	CC

This brand debuted in 1997 and offers a medium body, featuring a Sumatra-grown wrapper. It is presented in individual cellophane sleeves in all-cedar boxes of 25.

HOYO DE CORTEZ PREMERA CALIDAD
Handmade in Santiago, Dominican Republic.
Wrapper: Ecuador   *Binder: Dom. Rep.*   *Filler: Dom. Rep.*

HANDMADE CIGARS: BRAND LISTINGS

Shape	Name	Lgth	Ring	Wrapper
Double Corona	Churchill	7½	52	CC
Churchill	Gran Corona	7	48	CC
Robusto	Robusto	5	50	CC
Torpedo	Torpedo	7	54	CC

Here is a 1997-introduced brand with a medium body and a Connecticut-seed wrapper grown in Ecuador. It is offered in protective cellophane sleeves and packed in all-cedar boxes of 25.

HOYO DE HONDURAS
Handmade in Danli, Honduras.

Wrapper: Honduras　　　　*Binder: Honduras*　　　　*Filler: Honduras*

Shape	Name	Lgth	Ring	Wrapper
Grand Corona	No. 1	6½	46	CM
Corona	No. 4	5½	44	CM
Toro	Churchill	6½	52	CM
Short Panatela	Petit	4¼	38	CM
Churchill	Presidente	6¾	48	CM
Robusto	Robusto	5	50	CM
Toro	Toro	6	50	CM

Created in 1985, this is an all-Honduran, full-bodied cigar, offered in economical bundles of 25.

HOYO DE MONTERREY
Handmade in Cofradia, Honduras.

Wrapper: Ecuador or USA/Connecticut　　　　*Binder: Honduras*
Filler: Dominican Republic, Honduras and Nicaragua

Shape	Name	Lgth	Ring	Wrapper
Giant	Presidents	8½	52	CC-Ma

© 1998 VILLAZON & CO., INC.

En la manera de los Indios

Cofradia, Honduras. Where the temperature of tobacco is measured by the palm of the hand -- "the Indian way."

HOYO DE MONTERREY®
THE AUTHENTIC HONDURAN

HANDMADE CIGARS: BRAND LISTINGS

Double Corona	Sultans		7¼	54	CC-Ma
Churchill	Double Coronas		6¾	48	CC-Ma
Toro	Governors		6⅛	50	CC-Ma
Corona	Cafe Royales	(tubed)	5⅝	43	CC-Ma
Long Corona	Crystals	(glass jar)	6	43	CC-Ma
Small Panatela	Petit		4¾	31	CC-Ma
Grand Corona	Churchills		6¼	45	CC-Ma
Corona Extra	Coronas		5⅝	46	CC-Ma
Robusto	Rothschilds		4½	50	CC-Ma
Corona	Super Hoyos		5½	44	CC-Ma
Long Corona	Ambassadors		6¼	44	CC-Ma
Slim Panatela	Largo Elegantes		7¼	34	CC-Ma
Cigarillo	Margaritas		5¼	29	CC-Ma
Short Panatela	Demitasse		4	39	CC-Ma
Petit Corona	Sabrosos		5	40	CC-Ma

This ancient brand began in Cuba but first appeared in a Honduran-manufactured blend in 1969. Hoyo de Monterrey cigars are medium-to-heavy in flavor. Handmade in Honduras, these are truly quality cigars with a large variety of sizes to give exceptional satisfaction to the smoker. The tobaccos are blended from four nations, including the Cuban-seed Honduran binder and Sumatra-seed wrappers from Ecuador. The maduro wrappers use only the finest Connecticut broadleaf available.

HUGO CASSAR
Handmade in Danli, Honduras.

Wrapper: Indonesia   Binder: Honduras   Filler: Honduras, Mexico

Shape	Name	Lgth	Ring	Wrapper
Robusto	No. 1 Rothschild	4¾	50	CC
Corona Extra	No. 2 Corona	5½	46	CC

Lonsdale	No. 3 Lonsdale	6¾	44	CC
Churchill	No. 4 Toro	7	48	CC
Double Corona	No. 5 Double Corona	6¾	54	CC
Double Corona	No. 6 Churchill	7½	50	CC
Giant	No. 7 Giant	8	52	CC

A careful blend and smooth draw is the mark of these cigars, which are expertly crafted, medium in body and packaged in bundles of 25 cigars. An excellent value.

HUGO CASSAR
Handmade in San Andres Tuxtla, Mexico.
Wrapper: Mexico   *Binder: Mexico*   *Filler: Mexico*

Shape	Name	Lgth	Ring	Wrapper
Robusto	Rothschild	4½	50	CC
Robusto	Robusto	5½	52	CC
Long Corona	Corona	6	42	CC
Toro	Toro	6½	50	CC
Double Corona	Churchill	7½	50	CC

Here is an all-Mexican brand with a Sumatra-seed, natural-shade, full-bodied wrapper grown in Mexico, offering a medium-bodied taste. You can find these modestly-priced line in all-cedar boxes of 25.

HUGO CASSAR
Handmade in San Andres Tuxtla, Mexico.
Wrapper: Mexico   *Binder: Mexico*   *Filler: Mexico*

Shape	Name	Lgth	Ring	Wrapper
Robusto	Tulum	4¾	50	CC-Ma
Long Corona	Monterey	6	42	CC-Ma
Panatela	Durango	6¾	36	CC-Ma

Double Corona	Veracruz	7	54	CC-Ma
Double Corona	Yucatan	7½	50	CC-Ma
Giant	Sierra Madre	8	52	CC-Ma

These cigars are Mexican puros, offered in both a natural and maduro wrapper. They offer a spicy, sweet flavor, with medium body, and are packaged in bundles of 25 cigars each.

HUGO CASSAR DIAMOND DOMINICAN
Handmade in Villa Gonzalez, Dominican Republic.
Wrapper: USA/Connecticut   *Binder: Dom. Rep.*   *Filler: Dom. Rep.*

Shape	Name	Lgth	Ring	Wrapper
Robusto	Robusto	4¾	50	CC
Corona	Corona	5½	42	CC
Grand Corona	Grand Corona	6	46	CC
Toro	Toro	6½	52	CC
Lonsdale	Lonsdale	7	44	CC
Giant	El Presidente	8	50	CC

This careful blend of aged tobaccos, introduced in 1996, produces a cigar which is filled with a rich spiciness, with cocoa flavors and a mild-to-medium body, and offered in specially-constructed cedar boxes of 20 (except for El Presidente, available in 10s).

HUGO CASSAR DIAMOND DOMINICAN MYSTIQUE
Handmade in Villa Gonzalez, Dominican Republic.
Wrapper: Dominican Republic and USA/Connecticut
Binder: Dominican Republic   *Filler: Dominican Republic*

Shape	Name	Lgth	Ring	Wrapper
Torpedo	Torpedo	6	53	Stripe
Toro	Toro	6¼	50	Stripe
Lonsdale	Lonsdale	7	44	Stripe

HANDMADE CIGARS: BRAND LISTINGS

Giant	Churchill	8	50	Stripe

Talk about unique! Here is a "barber pole" of a cigar with a double wrapper: Connecticut Shade and a Dominican brewleaf, surrounding Dominican binder and filler tobaccos, for a medium body. Introduced in 1996, there's no doubting the popularity of this new concept in cigar making, which is presented in bundles of 24 or all-cedar boxes of 10 (except for the Torpedo, also available in boxes of 24).

HUGO CASSAR DIAMOND HONDURAN MYSTIQUE CLASSIC
Handmade in Danli, Honduras.
Wrapper: Costa Rica and Ecuador

Binder: Dominican Republic   *Filler: Nicaragua*

Shape	Name	Lgth	Ring	Wrapper
Long Corona	Corona	6	44	CM
Toro	Toro	6½	52	CM
Torpedo	Torpedo	6	53	CM
Churchill	Churchill	7¾	47	CM

Introduced in 1996, this is a deeply-colored, beautifully-prepared "barber pole" cigar. It is a medium-bodied smoke with a double wrapper from Costa Rica (maduro shade) and Ecuador (natural shade). These cigars are elegantly presented in perfectly-fitted, all-cedar boxes of 20 cigars each.

HUGO CASSAR PRIVATE COLLECTION
Handmade in Tamboril, Dominican Republic.
Wrapper: Dom. Rep.   *Binder: Dom. Rep.*   *Filler: Dom. Rep.*

Shape	Name	Lgth	Ring	Wrapper
Robusto	Robusto	5	50	CC
Long Corona	Corona	6	42	CC
Torpedo	Torpedo	6	48	CC
Toro	Toro	6½	52	CC
Double Corona	Presidente	7½	49	CC

HANDMADE CIGARS: BRAND LISTINGS

Here is a mild cigar introduced in 1996. It features all Dominican tobacco, is elegantly prepared and presented in stunning all-cedar boxes of 25 cigars. The Corona, Robusto and Presidente shapes are also offered in boxes of 25.

HUGO CASSAR PRIVATE COLLECTION
Handmade in Danli, Honduras.

Wrapper: Ecuador   *Binder: Dom. Rep.*   *Filler: Mexico, Nicaragua*

Shape	Name	Lgth	Ring	Wrapper
Robusto	Robusto	4¾	52	CC
Long Corona	Matador	6	42	CC
Toro	Elegantes	6	50	CC
Lonsdale	Imperial	7	44	CC
Double Corona	Emperador	7¾	47	CC

Beautifully finished, this is a medium-bodied smoke with tobaccos from four nations. The cigars are presented in precisely-finished cedar boxes of 25 cigars each.

HUGO CASSAR PRIVATE COLLECTION
Handmade in Kudus, Indonesia.

Wrapper: Indonesia   *Binder: Indonesia*   *Filler: Brazil, Dom. Rep., Jamaica*

Shape	Name	Lgth	Ring	Wrapper
Toro	Toros	6	50	CC
Churchill	Churchill	7½	46	CC
Small Panatela	Petite Corona	4½	34	CC
Cigarillo	Mini	3¾	26	CC

Introduced in 1997, this is a mild-bodied cigar. The Toro and Churchill shapes have a Javan wrapper and filler from the Dominican Republic and Jamaica only, while the Petite Corona and Mini shapes add a Brazilian leaf in the filler and feature a Sumatran wrapper.

HANDMADE CIGARS: BRAND LISTINGS

HUGO CASSAR PRIVATE COLLECTION
Handmade in San Andres Tuxtla, Mexico.

Wrapper: Mexico *Binder: Mexico* *Filler: Mexico*

Shape	Name	Lgth	Ring	Wrapper
Robusto	Rothschild	4½	50	Ma
Long Corona	Corona	6	42	Ma
Toro	Toro	6½	50	Ma
Robusto	Robusto	5½	52	Ma
Double Corona	Churchill	7½	50	Ma

From the fertile San Andres Valley comes the Hugo Cassar Private Collection. These are medium-bodied cigars with all-Mexican tobacco, packed in cedar boxes to maintain them at the peak of flavor. The maduro wrappers are Mexican-grown, Cuban-seed leaves.

HUGO GOLD
Handmade in Esteli, Nicaragua.

Wrapper: Nicaragua *Binder: Nicaragua* *Filler: Nicaragua*

Shape	Name	Lgth	Ring	Wrapper
Long Corona	Corona	6	44	CM
Robusto	Robusto	5	52	CM
Toro	Toro	6	50	CM
Churchill	Churchill	6⅞	48	CM
Giant	Gigante	8	54	CM

This is the gold standard in Nicaraguan cigars, with a medium body and all-Nicaraguan tobaccos. The wrapper is Cuban-seed and you can find this elegant cigar in all-cedar boxes of 24.

HUGO SIGNATURE SERIES
Handmade in Villa Gonzalez, Dominican Republic.

Wrapper: Indonesia or Mexico *Binder: Dom. Rep.* *Filler: Dom. Rep.*

HANDMADE CIGARS: BRAND LISTINGS

Shape	Name	Lgth	Ring	Wrapper
	Natural wrapper:			
Toro	Toro	6¼	50	CC
Lonsdale	Lonsdale	7	44	CC
Giant	Churchill	8	50	CC
	Maduro wrapper:			
Robusto	Robusto	5	52	Ma
Toro	Toro	6	50	Ma
Churchill	Lonsdale	7	48	Ma
Giant	Churchill	8	54	Ma

This cigar was introduced in 1997. You can have your choice of a natural wrapper grown in Indonesia (mild-bodied blend), or a yummy maduro wrapper from Mexico (mild-to-medium body). In either case, these well-made cigars are offered in boxes of 24.

HUMO BLANCO
Handmade in Managua, Nicaragua.

Wrapper: Indonesia   Binder: Costa Rica   Filler: Costa Rica, Nicaragua

Shape	Name	Lgth	Ring	Wrapper
Robusto	Robusto	5	50	CM
Long Corona	Lonsdale	6	44	CM
Churchill	Churchill	7	50	CM

The "White Smoke" cigar presents a medium-bodied taste, utilizing leaves from three nations. Each is offered in a cellophane sleeve and the brand is presented in a slide-top cedar box of 25 cigars each.

HURRICANOS
Handmade in Danli, Honduras.

Wrapper: Ecuador   Binder: Honduras   Filler: Honduras, Nicaragua

HANDMADE CIGARS: BRAND LISTINGS

Shape	Name	Lgth	Ring	Wrapper
Double Corona	Churchill	7	49	CM
Toro	Short Churchill	6	50	CM
Lonsdale	Lonsdale	7	43	CM
Robusto	Robusto	5	50	CM
Corona	Corona	5½	42	CM

It's a hurricane! This brand, new in 1997, stormed its way to popular acclaim when first introduced and is now delighting smokers with a medium-bodied taste. It is presented in cellophane sleeves, packed in cedar boxes of 25.

ILLUSION
Handmade in Granada, Nicaragua.

Wrapper: Ecuador *Binder: Nicaragua* *Filler: Nicaragua*

Shape	Name	Lgth	Ring	Wrapper
Long Corona	Heavenly Flavors	6	42	CC

Here is a flavored cigar that is cured for 21 days and available in Amaretto, Anisette, champagne, cherry, chocolate, chocolate mint, clove, coffee, cognac, Pina Colada, Tropical Rum and vanilla.

ILONA LADY LIGHTS
Handmade in Santiago, Dominican Republic.

Wrapper: USA/Connecticut *Binder: Dom. Rep.* *Filler: Dom. Rep.*

Shape	Name	Lgth	Ring	Wrapper
Long Panatela	Ilona Lady Lights	7½	38	CC

Introduced by Ilona Garafola in 1996, this is a mild-bodied cigar designed to appeal to women. It has a sweet flavor with a hint of vanilla and is offered in boxes of 25.

IMPERIO CUBANO
Handmade in Miami, Florida, USA.

Wrapper: Ecuador *Binder: Mexico* *Filler: Dom. Rep.*

HANDMADE CIGARS: BRAND LISTINGS

Shape	Name	Lgth	Ring	Wrapper
Torpedo	Gran Torpedo	7	54	CC
Torpedo	Torpedo	6¼	54	CC
Churchill	Churchill	6¾	48	CC
Toro	Toro	6	50	CC
Robusto	Robusto	5	50	CC
Lonsdale	Lonsdale	6¾	43	CC
Corona	Corona	5½	43	CC
Double Corona	Presidente	7½	50	CC
Perfecto	Perfecto	5	41	CC
Perfecto	Mini Perfecto	4	40	CC

From Little Havana in Miami comes this brand, introduced in 1996, available only in limited distribution and with limited production. Master cigar maker Juan Sosa offers a mild-to-medium-bodied flavor in this brand, thanks in part to a Connecticut-seed wrapper grown in Ecuador.

INDIAN ANNIVERSARY LIMITED RESERVE SERIES A
Handmade in Danli, Honduras.

Wrapper: Ecuador   *Binder: Mexico*   *Filler: Honduras, Nicaragua*

Shape	Name	Lgth	Ring	Wrapper
Robusto	The Bear	5	50	CM
Pyramid	The Bison	6½	54	CM
Churchill	The Buffalo	7	47	CM

Introduced in 1997, here is a specially-aged brand with exquisite construction and a full-bodied flavor. It features a Sumatra-seed wrapper and is offered in boxes of 25.

HANDMADE CIGARS: BRAND LISTINGS

INDIAN CLASSIC
Handmade in Danli, Honduras.
Wrapper: Ecuador, USA/Connecticut

Binder: Mexico   Filler: Honduras, Nicaragua

Shape	Name	Lgth	Ring	Wrapper
Double Corona	Chief	7½	52	CM
Robusto	Boxer	4½	50	CM-Ma
Pyramid	Teepee	5½	52	CM-Ma
Toro	Tomahawk	6	52	CM-Ma

Here is a much-celebrated 1995 addition to the cigar scene, offering a medium-bodied taste in an exquisitely-crafted cigar. The brand features an Ecuadorian-grown, Sumatra-seed wrapper and Mexican Morron binder and is offered in all-cedar boxes of 25. The glorious maduro series debuted in 1997 and features a Connecticut Broadleaf wrapper and a medium-to-full-bodied taste

INDIAN DOMINICAN
Handmade in Santiago, Dominican Republic.
Wrapper: Cameroon   Binder: Dom. Rep.   Filler: Dom. Rep.

Shape	Name	Lgth	Ring	Wrapper
Torpedo	Hawk	6	53	CM
Pyramid	Scout	4½	52	CM

New for 1998, this is a full-bodied, peppery blend with a Cameroon wrapper and lots of flavor. You can enjoy them in magnificently-adorned cedar boxes of 25.

INDIAN HABANO BLEND 95
Handmade in Danli, Honduras.
Wrapper: Indonesia   Binder: Mexico   Filler: Nicaragua

Shape	Name	Lgth	Ring	Wrapper
Robusto	Robusto	5	50	CM
Grand Corona	Churchill	6½	47	CM

HANDMADE CIGARS: BRAND LISTINGS

Long Corona	Corona	6	42	CM

This is a bundled brand, offered in value-priced, cello-wrapped groupings of 25. Introduced in 1998, these cigars have a medium-to-full body thanks to their Sumatra wrappers and Mexican Morron fillers.

INDIAN HEAD
Handmade in Danli, Honduras.

Wrapper: Ecuador *Binder: Honduras* *Filler: Dom. Rep., Honduras*

Shape	Name	Lgth	Ring	Wrapper
Panatela	Lindas	5½	38	CC-Ma
Corona	No. 4	5½	42	CC-Ma
Long Corona	No. 2	6	43	CC-Ma
Panatela	Palma Fina	6⅞	36	CC-Ma
Long Corona	Corona Gorda	6¼	44	CC-Ma
Robusto	Rothschild	5	50	CC-Ma
Lonsdale	No. 1	7	42	CC
Toro	Toros	6	50	CC
Churchill	Corona Grande	7½	46	CC-Ma
Double Corona	Churchills	7	49	CC-Ma
Giant	Viajantes	8½	52	CC
Giant	Gigantes	8	54	CC

Indian Head cigars are mild-to-medium in strength using Honduran filler and binder tobaccos combined with a Ecuador-grown, Connecticut-seed wrapper (natural and maduro). They are presented in bundles of 25 cigars each.

INDIAN PRINCESS
Handmade in Danli, Honduras.

Wrapper: Ecuador *Binder: Honduras* *Filler: Honduras*

HANDMADE CIGARS: BRAND LISTINGS

Shape	Name	Lgth	Ring	Wrapper
Giant	Chief	8	52	CC
Churchill	Churchill	6⅞	48	CC
Corona	Corona	5½	43	CC
Corona Extra	Corona Extra	5½	46	CC
Long Corona	Long Corona	6	42	CC
Double Corona	Presidente	7½	50	CC
Robusto	Rothschild	4¾	50	CC
Toro	Toro	6¼	50	CC

This is a medium-bodied brand introduced in 1996. It is offered in value-priced bundles of 25.

INDIGO
Handmade in Tamboril, Dominican Republic.

Wrapper: Indonesia   Binder: Dom. Rep.   Filler: Dom. Rep.

Shape	Name	Lgth	Ring	Wrapper
	Cabinet Selection:			
Corona	Corona	5½	42	CM
Long Corona	Corona Grande	6	42	CM
Grand Corona	Gran Corona	6	46	CM
Robusto	Robusto	5	48	CM
Robusto	Robusto Gordo	5	50	CM
Churchill	Churchill	7	47	CM
Toro	Toro	6	50	CM
	Box pressed:			
Corona	Corona	5½	42	CM
Lonsdale	Lonsdale	6½	42	CM

Robusto	Robusto	5	48	CM
Grand Corona	Gran Corona	6	46	CM
Churchill	Churchill	7	47	CM
Torpedo	Torpedo	6	52	CM
Toro	Humidor No. 1	6	60	CM

Introduced in 1997, Indigo offers two series of shapes. The blend is medium-to-full-bodied and the brand is offered in two groups: Cabinet Selection (round-shaped) and box-pressed. It is presented without cellophane in boxes of 25.

INMENSO
Handmade in Esteli, Nicaragua.

Wrapper: Ecuador   Binder: Nicaragua   Filler: Honduras, Nicaragua

Shape	Name	Lgth	Ring	Wrapper
Robusto	Inmenso I	5	70	CM-Ma
Toro	Inmenso II	6	70	CM-Ma

Want a really big cigar? How about one that can double as a billy club? Then here's your brand, introduced in 1998. With its huge 70 ring gauge, this appears to be an overpowering smoke, but it is medium-bodied. You can try it — if you dare — in all-cedar boxes of 10.

INSIGNIA
Handmade in Santiago, Dominican Republic.

Wrapper: Indonesia   Binder: Nicaragua   Filler: Dom. Rep., Nicaragua

Shape	Name	Lgth	Ring	Wrapper
Toro	Toro	6	50	CM

Here is a mild, but slightly spicy cigar, introduced in 1998. It is offered in individual boxes and in boxes of 20.

HANDMADE CIGARS: BRAND LISTINGS

INSURGENTES
Handmade, with short filler, in San Andres Tuxtla, Mexico.

Wrapper: Mexico   Binder: Mexico   Filler: Mexico

Shape	Name	Lgth	Ring	Wrapper
Corona	Petite Corona	5½	41	CM

Here is a single size, short-filler brand which offers a medium-bodied, somewhat earthy flavor at a modest price.

INTERNATIONAL
Handmade in Santiago, Dominican Republic.

Wrapper: Ecuador, Mexico   Binder: Dom. Rep.   Filler: Nicaragua

Shape	Name	Lgth	Ring	Wrapper
Robusto	Robusto	4¾	50	CC-Ma
Long Corona	Corona	6	44	CC-Ma
Toro	Toro	6	50	CC-Ma
Double Corona	Presidente	7½	52	CC
Torpedo	Belicoso	6¼	52	CC-Ma
Torpedo	Belicoso Fino	5	52	CC-Ma
Pyramid	Petit Bouquet	4	50	CC-Ma

Introduced in 1996 and formerly known as Alta Gracia, this Miami-based brand offers a medium-bodied taste in a slightly sweet blend, presented in boxes of 25. The newer maduro-wrapped versions utilize a Mexican wrapper.

IRACEMA
Handmade in Cruz des Almas, Brazil.

Wrapper: Brazil   Binder: Brazil   Filler: Brazil

Shape	Name	Lgth	Ring	Wrapper
Lonsdale	Macumba	6½	42	CM
Corona	Mata Fina Especial	5¼	44	CM

HANDMADE CIGARS: BRAND LISTINGS

	Machine-made:			
Cigarillo	Cigarrilhas	3⅛	28	CM

Introduced about 1960, this cigar is a product of the famous Suerdieck Charutos e Cigarrilhas Ltda. factory in Brazil. The range offers a medium-bodied flavor in four shapes. The tobaccos are all Brazilian grown, including Mata Fina leaf for the wrappers of the Macumba and Mata Fina shapes offering up a seductive, tropical aroma.

ISABELLA
Handmade, with mixed filler, in Santiago, Dominican Republic.
Wrapper: Indonesia   *Binder: Dom. Rep.*   *Filler: Dom. Rep.*

Shape	Name	Lgth	Ring	Wrapper
Double Corona	Churchill	7	50	CM
Toro	Toro	6	50	CM
Robusto	Robusto	5	50	CM
Corona	Corona	5½	42	CM
Lonsdale	Lonsdale	6½	44	CM

New for 1997, this is a medium-bodied cigar . . . but with character, thanks to its Sumatra wrapper. You can guess which character it is after enjoying a box of 25!

ISLAND AMARETTO
Handmade, with medium filler, in Jaibon, Dominican Republic.
Wrapper: Indonesia   *Binder: Indonesia*
Filler: Colombia, Dominican Republic, Indonesia

Shape	Name	Lgth	Ring	Wrapper
Short Panatela	Bellissima	4½	36	CM
Petit Corona	Bella	4¾	42	CM
Lonsdale	Grand Bella	7	42	CM

This is a flavored cigar produced by the Caribbean Cigar Company and introduced in 1995. It is handmade using 100% tobacco, but with medium filler instead of long filler leaves. It has a medium-to-full-bodied taste and is offered in boxes of 25 cigars each.

ISLANDS
Handmade in Malan, Indonesia.

Wrapper: Indonesia   *Binder: Indonesia*   *Filler: Indonesia*

Shape	Name	Lgth	Ring	Wrapper
Churchill	Lombok	7	48	CC
Toro	Sumbawa	6½	50	CC
Pyramid	Komodo	6	50	CC
Robusto	Borneo	5	50	CC
Long Corona	Sumatra	6	42	CC

If the green-skinned, red-lipped, moustache-bearing mascot isn't enough to draw your attention, check out the Rattan-patterned bamboo boxes and hand-woven Batik cloth in which the cigars are packed. Oh, yes, this 1997-introduced brand is mild in flavor thanks to its all-Indonesian leaves.

ISLERO
Handmade in San Andres Tuxtula, Mexico.

Wrapper: Mexico   *Binder: Mexico*   *Filler: Mexico*

Shape	Name	Lgth	Ring	Wrapper
Robusto	Robusto	5¼	50	CM
Panatela	Panetela	6¼	39	CM
Toro	Toro	6	50	CM
Double Corona	Presidente	7½	50	CM
Giant	Emperador	9	50	CM
Robusto	Maduro	5¼	50	Ma
Torpedo	Belicoso	6	50	CM
Pyramid	Piramide	6	50	CM

HANDMADE CIGARS: BRAND LISTINGS

Introduced in 1997, this is a medium-bodied brand in its natural wrapper and full-bodied in its maduro wrapper. It is offered in boxes of 25.

J. CORTES
Handmade in Santo Domingo, Dominican Republic.
Wrapper: USA/Connecticut

Binder: Dominican Republic   *Filler: Brazil, Dominican Republic, Indonesia*

Shape	Name	Lgth	Ring	Wrapper
Slim Panatela	No. 2	5	32	CC
Corona	No. 3	5½	40	CC
Robusto	No. 5	5	50	CC
Grand Corona	No. 6	6½	46	CC
Churchill	No. 7	7	48	CC

J. Cortes is an old Belgian brand famous for its machine-made cigars, which started in 1926 and for long-filler cigars for the European market (which contain some Cuban tobacco). In 1996, J. Cortes launched a new series of hand-made cigars for the U.S. market made in the Dominican Republic. The five shapes offer a mild-to-medium-bodied taste and then carefully aged for 9-12 months in Belgium for the smoothest possible smoke. This is an excellent choice for those seeking a milder premium cigar. All of the handmade shapes are presented uncellophaned in all-cedar boxes of 25.

J. L. FERRER 1891
Handmade in Santiago, Dominican Republic.

Wrapper: USA/Connecticut   *Binder: Dom. Rep.*   *Filler: Dom. Rep.*

Shape	Name	Lgth	Ring	Wrapper
Torpedo	Torpedo	6½	54	CC
Toro	Super Robusto	6	50	CC
Lonsdale	Churchill	7	44	CC
Robusto	Robusto	5	50	CC
Corona	Corona Petite	5½	42	CC

HANDMADE CIGARS: BRAND LISTINGS

Introduced in 1995, this is a medium-bodied cigar with Dominican Olor and Piloto Cubano filler leaves, offered in boxes of 25 or in special plexi-topped display cases of 20.

JAGUAR OF BELIZE
Handmade in Esteli, Nicaragua and Belize City, Belize.

Wrapper: Indonesia   *Binder: Indonesia*   *Filler: Indonesia & Nicaragua*

Shape	Name	Lgth	Ring	Wrapper
Double Corona	Churchill	7	50	CC

You'll find this 1998-introduced brand in an elegant cedar box in 8-9-8 packaging. Rolled in Esteli, Nicaragua and finished in Belize City, Belize, this is a mild-to-medium-bodied, slightly spicy blend offered in a single size.

JAMAICA BAY
Hand-rolled in Kingston, Jamaica.

Wrapper: USA/Connecticut   *Binder: Mexico*   *Filler: Dom. Rep., Mexico*

Shape	Name	Lgth	Ring	Wrapper
Double Corona	No. 100	7½	49	CC
Toro	No. 200	6	50	CC
Lonsdale	No. 300	6¾	45	CC
Lonsdale	No. 400	6½	42	CC
Panatela	No. 500	6¾	38	CC
Corona	No. 600	5½	42	CC

These are mild cigars, machine-bunched and then hand-wrapped with Connecticut Shade leaves. They are offered only in limited distribution, in bundles of 20 cigars each.

JAMAICA GOLD
Handmade in Santa Rosa de Copan, Honduras.

Wrapper: Honduras   *Binder: Honduras*   *Filler: Honduras*

HANDMADE CIGARS: BRAND LISTINGS

Shape	Name	Lgth	Ring	Wrapper
Double Corona	Prince	7¾	50	CM
Lonsdale	Baron	6½	44	CM
Panatela	Count	5½	38	CM
Corona	Duke	5½	42	CM
Torpedo	Torpedo	7	52	CM

Created in 1982, this is a mild-to-medium-bodied cigar, with a Connecticut-seed wrapper. The brand is offered in all-wooden boxes of 25 cigars, plus a ten-pack for the Prince size and five-packs for the Baron and Duke sizes.

JAMAICAN RUM
Handmade, with mixed filler, in Santiago, Dominican Republic.
Wrapper: Dom. Rep.   *Binder: Dom. Rep.*   *Filler: Dom. Rep.*

Shape	Name	Lgth	Ring	Wrapper
Small Panatela	Single Shot	4	34	CM
Lonsdale	Double Shot	6½	44	CM

This is a medium-to-full-bodied, flavored brand, introduced in 1998. It is offered in boxes of 25.

JAMAVANA
Handmade in Maypen, Jamaica.
Wrapper: Indonesia   *Binder: Indonesia*   *Filler: Dom. Rep., Indonesia*

Shape	Name		Lgth	Ring	Wrapper
Grand Corona	No. 1 Tube	(tubed)	5⅞	45	CM
Double Corona	Churchill		7⅞	51	CM
Corona	Corona		5½	40	CM
Lonsdale	Corona Grande		6⅜	42	CM
Lonsdale	Double Corona		6⅞	45	CM
Double Corona	Giant Corona		7½	49	CM

Robusto	Robusto	4⅜	49	CM

This is a mild-bodied cigar, made in the famous Royal Jamaica factory and offered in modestly-priced bundles of ten.

JAMES NORMAN
Handmade in Santiago, Dominican Republic.

Wrapper: Indonesia   *Binder: Dom. Rep.*   *Filler: Dom. Rep.*

Shape	Name	Lgth	Ring	Wrapper
Double Corona	Churchill	7	50	CM
Toro	Robusto Largo	6	50	CM
Robusto	Robusto	5	50	CM
Corona	Corona	5½	42	CM

Here is a mild-bodied cigar, first offered in 1998. It features a Javan wrapper and is available in four shapes in boxes of 25.

JIBARITO
Handmade in Santiago, Dominican Republic.

Wrapper: Ecuador   *Binder: Dom. Rep.*   *Filler: Dom. Rep.*

Shape	Name	Lgth	Ring	Wrapper
Corona	Quatro	5½	42	CC
Panatela	Princesa	6	38	CC
Lonsdale	Lonsdale	6½	44	CC
Robusto	Robusto	5	50	CC
Toro	Gran Corona	6¼	50	CC
Double Corona	Vegiagante	7⅞	52	CC

This brand debuted in 1997 and offers a medium-to-full-bodied taste. You can find it in slide-top, all-cedar boxes of 25.

HANDMADE CIGARS: BRAND LISTINGS

JIMENEZ
Handmade in Bronx, New York, USA.
Wrapper: Cameroon or USA/Connecticut

Binder: Indonesia   Filler: Colombia, Dom. Rep.

Shape	Name	Lgth	Ring	Wrapper
Long Corona	Corona	6	44	CC
Toro	Toro	6	54	CC
Cigarillo	Masterpiece	7	28	Ma
Robusto	Robusto	5	50	CC
Torpedo	Torpedo	6½	52	CC
Petit Corona	Petite Corona	5	42	CC
Lonsdale	No. 1	6½	42	CC
Churchill	Churchill	7	47	CC-CM
Double Corona	Fabuloso	7	54	CM

Introduced in 1997, this is a medium-bodied brand with a choice of wrappers in the larger sizes, offered in packs of 25. Pick one up on your way to see the Bronx Bombers at Yankee Stadium!

JM OUTDOORSMAN
Handmade, with mixed filler, in
Santo Domingo, Dominican Republic.

Wrapper: Indonesia   Binder: Dom. Rep.   Filler: Dom. Rep.

Shape	Name	Lgth	Ring	Wrapper
Corona	Corona	5½	42	CM
Robusto	Robusto	5	50	CM
Toro	Toro	6	50	CM
Double Corona	Churchill	6¾	50	CM
Double Corona	Presidente	7	50	CM
Torpedo	Torpedo	6¾	52	CM

HANDMADE CIGARS: BRAND LISTINGS

Here is a value-priced, medium-to-full-bodied cigar offered in bundles of 25. It features a Sumatra-grown wrapper around a sandwich filler of long leaves surrounding shorter filler tobaccos.

JOHN AYLESBURY
Handmade in Danli, Honduras.

Wrapper: Honduras, Mexico   *Binder: Honduras*   *Filler: Honduras*

Shape	Name	Lgth	Ring	Wrapper
Toro	Churchill	6⅝	49	CC-Ma
Lonsdale	Pinceles	7	43	CC
Long Corona	Puritos	6	43	CC
Panatela	Morning	5½	39	CC
Panatela	Panatela Larga	6¾	36	CC
Small Panatela	Picos	4½	32	CC
Toro	Rothschild	6	50	CC-Ma

Introduced in 1978, the John Aylesbury Honduran series has a medium body and a subtle aroma. All seven sizes are offered with a Honduran-grown wrapper, while the maduro-wrapped shapes feature a Mexican leaf.

JOHN AYLESBURY PREMIUM
Handmade in La Romana, Dominican Republic.

Wrapper: USA/Connecticut   *Binder: Dom. Rep.*   *Filler: Dom. Rep.*

Shape	Name	Lgth	Ring	Wrapper
Slim Panatela	Panatela	6	32	CC
Lonsdale	Lonsdale	6⅝	42	CC
Corona	Corona	5½	42	CC
Panatela	Elegante	6¾	38	CC
Churchill	Churchill	7	46	CC
Robusto	Rothschild	4½	50	CC

HANDMADE CIGARS: BRAND LISTINGS

The John Aylesbury Premium line offers a mild-bodied smoke in a beautifully-constructed cigar that debuted in 1991. These cigars are matured and then offered in graceful, solid mahogany boxes.

JOHN T'S CROWDPLEASER
Handmade in Santiago, Dominican Republic.

Wrapper: Dom. Rep.   Binder: Dom. Rep.   Filler: Pipe tobaccos

Shape	Name		Lgth	Ring	Wrapper
Panatela	Brown Gold	(tubed)	5½	38	CC
Panatela	Cherry Cream	(tubed)	5½	38	CC
Panatela	Cappuccino	(tubed)	5½	38	CC
Panatela	Cafe Ole	(tubed)	5½	38	CC
Panatela	Amaretto	(tubed)	5½	38	CC

Nicknamed "The Crowdpleaser," this brand has been created to offer a more pleasant, sweeter aroma than most cigars. The result is a mild smoke with considerable flavor (take your pick!) in a panatela shape packed in bundles of 20 tubes. Unusual to say the least!

JORGE VELASQUEZ
Handmade in Santiago, Dominican Republic.

Wrapper: Ecuador   Binder: Dom. Rep.   Filler: Dom. Rep.

Shape	Name	Lgth	Ring	Wrapper
Toro	I	6	52	CC-Ma
Churchill	II	7	48	CC-Ma
Double Corona	III	7½	50	CC-Ma
Lonsdale	IV	6¾	43	CC-Ma
Corona	V	5½	42	CC-Ma
Robusto	VI	5	50	CC-Ma
Long Corona	VII	6	42	CC-Ma
Long Panatela	VIII	7	38	CC-Ma

HANDMADE CIGARS: BRAND LISTINGS

Yes, this is the cigar named for the Hall of Fame jockey who has won thousands of thoroughbred races. Introduced in 1998, it is mild in body, reasonably priced and is offered in boxes of 25.

JOSE BENITO
Handmade in Santiago, Dominican Republic.

Wrapper: Ecuador   *Binder: Dom. Rep.*   *Filler: Dom. Rep.*

Shape	Name	Lgth	Ring	Wrapper
Double Corona	Presidente	7¾	50	CM
Double Corona	Churchill	7	50	CM
Lonsdale	Corona	6¾	43	CM
Panatela	Panatela	6¾	38	CM
Long Corona	Palma	6	43	CM
Panatela	Petite	5½	38	CM
Robusto	Rothschild	4¾	50	CM
Small Panatela	Chico	4¼	34	CM
Small Panatela	Havanitos	5	32	CM
Giant	Magnum	8	64	CM

Since its introduction in the 1970s, every Jose Benito cigar is the result of individually-chosen long-filler tobacco blended from the finest Dominican farms and specially selected Sumatra-seed wrapper leaves. They result in a medium-bodied smoke, upholding the family's tradition of excellence in tobacco which began in the mid-1800s.

JOSÉ GIRBÉS
Handmade in Santiago, Dominican Republic.
Wrapper: Indonesia or USA/Connecticut

Binder: Dominican Republic   *Filler: Dominican Republic*

Shape	Name	Lgth	Ring	Wrapper
Corona	Corona	5½	43	CC
Robusto	Robusto	5	50	CC

HANDMADE CIGARS: BRAND LISTINGS

Lonsdale	Lonsdale	6½	43	CC
Toro	Toro	6	50	CC
Double Corona	Churchill	7½	50	CC
Pyramid	Piramide	6	52	CC
Cigarillo	Purito	4	24	CC
Cigarillo	Petite Panetela	5	28	CC

This richly-flavored, medium-bodied cigar is handmade in the Doninican Republic and features a Dominican binder and filler with a choice or a genuine Connecticut-grown wrapper or a Sumatra-grown wrapper. It is offered in boxes of 25, except for the last three sizes above, offered in 20s. Some sizes are available in ten-packs.

JOSE JIMENEZ
Handmade in San Andres Tuxtla, Mexico.

Wrapper: Mexico or USA/Connecticut   Binder: Mexico   Filler: Mexico

Shape	Name	Lgth	Ring	Wrapper
Robusto	Robusto	5	50	CC-CM
Toro	Toro	6	50	CC-CM
Churchill	Churchill	7	47	CC-CM
Torpedo	Torpedo	6½	52	CC-CM

No, this is not a salute to Bill Dana's comic alter ego; the brand is named agter one of the Jimenez brothers who own the plantation where the leaves for this brand are grown. Introduced in 1998, it is medium in body and offered in boxes of 25. These first four sizes are only a small sample of future sizes to be included in this brand. But Jose won't mind if you buy some and tell your friends: "My cigar . . . Jose Jimenez!"

JOSE LLOPIS
Handmade in Colon, Panama.

Wrapper: Ecuador   Binder: Mexico
                    Filler: Dominican Republic, Honduras, Panama

HANDMADE CIGARS: BRAND LISTINGS

Shape	Name	Lgth	Ring	Wrapper
Giant	Viajante	8½	52	CC-Ma
Churchill	Churchill	7	48	CC-Ma
Lonsdale	No. 1	7	43	CC-Ma
Lonsdale	No. 2	6½	43	CC-Ma
Corona	No. 4	5½	43	CC-Ma
Long Panatela	Palma Extra	7	36	CC-Ma
Robusto	Rothschild	4¾	50	CC-Ma
Double Corona	Soberano	7¼	52	CC-Ma

Introduced in 1984, this cigar is offered in bundles of 20 and is medium in strength; it should not be confused with its milder sibling brand, Jose Llopis Gold.

JOSE LLOPIS GOLD
Handmade in Colon, Panama.

Wrapper: USA/Connecticut   *Binder: Mexico*
Filler: Dominican Republic, Honduras, Panama

Shape	Name	Lgth	Ring	Wrapper
Giant	Viajante	8½	52	CC-Ma
Churchill	Churchill	7	48	CC-Ma
Lonsdale	No. 1	7	43	CC-Ma
Lonsdale	No. 2	6½	43	CC-Ma
Long Panatela	Palma Extra	7	36	CC-Ma
Corona	No. 4	5½	43	CC-Ma
Robusto	Rothschild	4½	50	CC-Ma
Pyramid	Pyramid	7	50	CC-Ma

Created in 1989, this well-respected brand is all handmade and wrapped in Connecticut shade-grown leaves (natural) or Connecticut Broadleaf (maduro). All of its sizes are offered in cedar boxes. This mild-bodied cigar is distinctive for its gold band.

HANDMADE CIGARS: BRAND LISTINGS

JOSE MARTI
Handmade in Santiago, Dominican Republic.
Wrapper: USA/Connecticut *Binder: Dom. Rep.* *Filler: Dom. Rep.*

Shape	Name	Lgth	Ring	Wrapper
Panatela	Creme	6	36	CC
Corona	Corona	5½	42	CC
Lonsdale	Palma	7	42	CC
Lonsdale	Maceo	6⅞	44	CC
Robusto	Robusto	5½	50	CC
Double Corona	Jose Marti	7½	50	CC

Introduced in 1994, Jose Marti is a very mild, sweet cigar with a golden brown Connecticut wrapper. It offers excellent draw, a silky, smooth taste and a wonderful aroma. Offered in boxes of 20.

JOSE MARTI
Handmade in Esteli, Nicaragua.
Wrapper: Ecuador *Binder: Honduras*
Filler: Dominican Republic, Honduras, Nicaragua

Shape	Name	Lgth	Ring	Wrapper
Double Corona	Don Juan	7¼	54	CC
Lonsdale	Lonsdale	6½	44	CC
Churchill	Valentino	7	48	CC
Torpedo	Masaya Figurado	6¾	54	CC
Pyramid	Trinidad Piramide	7	48	CC
Short Panatela	Petite Lancero	4½	38	CC
Corona	Remedios	5½	44	CC
Robusto	Robusto	4½	52	CC
Giant	Rey del Rey	8½	52	CC
Toro	Robusto Extra	6½	52	CC

HANDMADE CIGARS: BRAND LISTINGS

This is a new, 1996 blend for the Jose Marti brand, offering a spicy, full-bodied taste and showing off an Ecuadorian-grown, Sumatra-seed wrapper. The brand has an excellent array of shapes and sizes, including two shaped cigars.

JOSÉ PACO
Handmade in Esteli, Nicaragua.

Wrapper: Nicaragua *Binder: Nicaragua* *Filler: Nicaragua*

Shape	Name	Lgth	Ring	Wrapper
Robusto	Robusto	5	52	CM
Lonsdale	Lonsdale	6½	42	CM
Toro	Corona	6	50	CM
Double Corona	Churchill	7	52	CM

This brand was introduced in 1997 and offers a mild-to-medium flavor and gentle aroma. It is offered in boxes of 25.

JOSE R. OLIVA
Handmade in Ocotal, Nicaragua.

Wrapper: Indonesia *Binder: Nicaragua* *Filler: Nicaragua*

Shape	Name	Lgth	Ring	Wrapper
Giant	Presidente	8	52	CC
Double Corona	Churchill	7	50	CC-Ma
Robusto	Rothschild	5	50	CC-Ma
Torpedo	Belicoso	6	52	CC-Ma
Toro	Double Corona	6½	48	CC
Corona	Lonsdale	5¾	43	CC

From the famous house of Oliva comes this "JRO" cigar, a mild-to-medium-bodied beauty which features a Sumatra wrapper. You can find them in cellophane sleeves inside all-cedar boxes of 25.

HANDMADE CIGARS: BRAND LISTINGS

JOYA DE HONDURAS
Handmade in Ojo de Agua, Honduras.

Wrapper: Ecuador   Binder: Nicaragua   Filler: Honduras, Nicaragua

Shape	Name	Lgth	Ring	Wrapper
Corona	Cuatro	5½	42	CM
Double Corona	Churchill	7	49	CM
Long Panatela	Palma Fina	7	38	CM
Toro	Toro	6	50	CM
Small Panatela	Pigmeo	4½	30	CM
Robusto	Rothschild	5	50	CM
Torpedo	Misiles	6	54	CM

This is an old brand which has now been revived in a mild-to-medium-bodied range and offering a size of interest to almost every smoker. Made by hand in Honduras, these cigars are offered in all-wood boxes of 25.

JOYA DEL REY
Handmade in Danli, Honduras.

Wrapper: Indonesia   Binder: Honduras   Filler: Dom. Rep., Nicaragua

Shape	Name		Lgth	Ring	Wrapper
Robusto	Robusto Grande	(tubed)	4¾	50	CC
Corona	Corona Grande	(tubed)	5½	42	CC
Toro	Toro Grande	(tubed)	6	50	CC
Double Corona	Churchill Grande	(tubed)	7	49	CC
Corona	No. 42		5½	42	CC
Lonsdale	No. 43		7	43	CC
Double Corona	No. 49		7	49	CC
Toro	No. 50		6	50	CC
Giant	No. 52		8½	52	CC

HANDMADE CIGARS: BRAND LISTINGS

The translation of this brand name means "Gems of the King." This is a medium-bodied brand using Cuban-seed tobaccos for the binder and filler. Joya del Rey cigars are offered in all-cedar boxes of 12 for the tubed shapes and in boxes of 25 for all other shapes.

JOYA DE NICARAGUA
Handmade in Esteli, Nicaragua.

Wrapper: Ecuador, Costa Rica　　　*Binder: Nicaragua*　　　*Filler: Nicaragua*

Shape	Name	Lgth	Ring	Wrapper
Giant	Viajante	8½	52	CC
Churchill	Churchill	6⅞	48	CC
Toro	Toro	6	50	CC
Slim Panatela	Senorita	5½	34	CC
Small Panatela	Piccolino	4½	30	CC
Panatela	Petit	5½	38	CC
Robusto	Consul	4½	52	CC
Lonsdale	No. 1	6⅝	44	CC
Panatela	No. 5	6⅞	35	CC
Long Corona	No. 6	6	42	CC
	Maduro Deluxe:			
Churchill	Churchill	6⅞	48	Ma
Toro	Toro	6	50	Ma
Robusto	Robusto	4¾	52	Ma
Lonsdale	No. 1	6⅝	44	Ma

Always popular since its introduction in the 1970s, this cigar was newly blended in 1996. The standard series now sports a mild taste thanks to an Ecuadorian-grown, Connecticut-seed wrapper, while the Costa Rica-grown maduro line is a full-bodied smoke. These cigars are meticulously cured and skillfully rolled which makes them truly the "Jewel of Nicaragua."

HANDMADE CIGARS: BRAND LISTINGS

JOYA DE SAN CRISTOBAL
Handmade in Danli, Honduras.

Wrapper: Ecuador   Binder: Honduras   Filler: Mexico, Nicaragua

Shape	Name	Lgth	Ring	Wrapper
Double Corona	Grande	7	54	CC
Double Corona	Churchill	7	49	CC
Toro	Toro	6	50	CC
Robusto	Robusto	4¾	52	CC
Lonsdale	Corona	6½	44	CC

A quality, spicy cigar which debuted in 1998, this is a mild-bodied brand available in five sizes. It is presented in cedar boxes of 25.

J-R ULTIMATE
Handmade in Cofradia, Honduras.

Wrapper: Honduras   Binder: Honduras   Filler: Honduras

Shape	Name	Lgth	Ring	Wrapper
Lonsdale	Cetro	7	42	DC-CC-CM-Ma
Grand Corona	Corona	5⅝	45	DC-CC-CM-Ma
Grand Corona	Corona Tubos (tubed)	5⅝	45	CC
Churchill	Double Corona	6¾	48	DC-CC-CM-Ma
Giant	Estelo Individuel	8½	52	CM
Cigarillo	Habanellas	5	28	CC
Double Corona	No. 1	7¼	54	CC-CM-Ma
Long Corona	No. 5	6⅛	44	DC-CC-CM-Ma
Toro	Padron	6	54	CC-Ma
Panatela	Petit Cetro	5½	38	CC-CM-Ma
Petit Corona	Petit Corona	4⅝	43	CC-CM-Ma
Giant	President	8½	52	CC-CM-Ma

Robusto	Rothschild	4½	50	CC-CM-Ma
Toro	Toro	6	50	DC-CC-CM-Ma

This is a full-bodied cigar with Havana-seed wrappers in multiple shades. Made in Cofradia, Honduras, these cigars are carefully aged for at least one year and packed uncellophaned in thick cedar cases.

JUAN CLEMENTE
Handmade in Santiago, Dominican Republic.
Wrapper: USA/Connecticut   Binder: Dom.Rep.   Filler: Dom.Rep.

Shape	Name	Lgth	Ring	Wrapper
	Classic:			
Petit Corona	Corona	5	42	Co
Long Corona	Grand Corona	6	42	Co
Panatela	Panatela	6½	34	Co
Long Panatela	Especiale	7½	38	Co
Churchill	Churchill	6⅞	46	Co
Cigarillo	Demi Tasse	3⅝	34	Co
Small Panatela	"530"	5	30	Co
Petit Corona	Demi-Corona	4	40	Co
Robusto	Rothschild	4⅞	50	Co
Giant	Gigante	9	50	Co
Giant	Gargantua	13	50	Co
Cigarillo	Mini	4⅛	22	Co
Panatela	Especiale No. 2	6	38	Co
	Club Selection:			
Toro	No. 1	6	50	Co
Corona Extra	No. 2	4½	46	Co
Lonsdale	No. 3	7	44	Co

Corona	No. 4	5¾	42	Co
Torpedo	Obelisco	6	54	Co

Sought after since 1982, this is the product of a small cigar factory that has only one, ultra-demanding client. The Juan Clemente Classic line offers a full, round, medium-bodied smoke with complex flavors and spices. The vintage "Club Selection" line is a more robust blend, with four years of aging that creates a rich, smooth character for an exquisite cigar for the connoisseur.

JUAN DOLIO
Handmade in the Dominican Republic.

Wrapper: Indonesia *Binder: Dom. Rep.* *Filler: Dom. Rep.*

Shape	Name	Lgth	Ring	Wrapper
Double Corona	Senator	7	50	CM
Lonsdale	Elegante	6½	44	CM
Robusto	Principe	5	50	CM
Petit Corona	Corona	5	44	CM

Juan Dolio has been sold in the Dominican Republic as a domestic cigar as far back as 1876. Now exported to the United States, it features a Sumatra wrapper, Dominican-grown Olor binder and Dominican-grown Olor and Piloto Cubano leaves in the filler. It is considered medium-bodied.

JUAN GUILLERMO DE ROBLES
Handmade in Dingelstadt, Germany.

Wrapper: Dom. Rep. *Binder: Dom. Rep.* *Filler: Dom. Rep.*

Shape	Name	Lgth	Ring	Wrapper
Double Corona	Churchill	7	49	CC
Toro	Lonsdale	6½	49	CC
Panatela	Panatella Larga	6	38	CC
Robusto	Robusto	5	50	CC

This is a handmade cigar from Germany, with a mild taste and all-Dominican leaves. It is offered in slide-top cedar boxes of 10 or 25.

JUAN Y RAMON
Handmade in Villa Gonzalez, Dominican Republic.
Wrapper: Dominican Republic or USA/Connecticut
Binder: Dominican Republic   *Filler: Dominican Republic*

Shape	Name	Lgth	Ring	Wrapper
Toro	Short Churchill	6½	50	CC-Ma
Pyramid	Figurado	6¼	53	CC-Ma
Double Corona	Churchill	7½	50	CC-Ma
Corona	Corona	5½	42	CC
Long Corona	Grand Corona	6	44	CC-Ma
Panatela	Panatela	6	38	CC
Robusto	Rothschild	5	50	CC-Ma

Introduced in 1996, this is a medium-bodied blend of Piloto Cubano and Olor leaves in the filler surrounded by a Connecticut Shade-grown wrapper (maduros are Dominican-grown). Elegantly packaged, Juan y Ramon cigars are available in all-cedar boxes of 20, except for the Figurado, offered in 24s.

JUAN Y RAMON PERFECTO
Handmade in Tamboril, Dominican Republic.
Wrapper: Nicaragua   *Binder: Dom. Rep.*   *Filler: Dom. Rep.*

Shape	Name	Lgth	Ring	Wrapper
Perfecto	Perfecto 4	4	44	CM
Perfecto	Perfecto 5	5	46	CM

Introduced in 1998, this is a medium-to-full-bodied blend in two perfecto shapes. It is offered in individual cellophane sleeves in all-cedar boxes of 24.

JUANA DE ARAGON
Handmade, with short filler, in Esteli, Nicaragua.
Wrapper: Indonesia   *Binder: Nicaragua*   *Filler: Nicaragua*

Shape	Name	Lgth	Ring	Wrapper
Long Corona	Corona	6	44	CM

HANDMADE CIGARS: BRAND LISTINGS

Talk about value! This is a 1998-introduced cigar with a medium body, available in cellophane sleeves in all-cedar boxes of 25 and a price that will make you smile.

JUST NUMBER 2
Handmade in Santiago, Dominican Republic.

Wrapper: Indonesia   *Binder: Dom. Rep.*   *Filler: Dom. Rep.*

Shape	Name	Lgth	Ring	Wrapper
Double Corona	Churchill	7	50	CM
Lonsdale	Lonsdale	7	44	CM
Slim Panatela	Panatela	6	30	CM
Corona	Corona	5½	44	CM
Robusto	Toro	5	50	CM

There are five shapes, not two. This brand was introduced in 1997 and offers a medium-to-full body in cedar boxes of 25.

JUSTINO
Handmade in Santiago, Dominican Republic.

Wrapper: USA/Connecticut   *Binder: Dom. Rep.*   *Filler: Dom. Rep.*

Shape	Name	Lgth	Ring	Wrapper
Robusto	Ponton	5	50	CC
Corona	Candelones	5¾	43	CC
Torpedo	Navarette	6¼	52	CC
Churchill	Mejia	7	48	CC
Small Panatela	Justino Jr.	4¾	30	CC

Here is a mild-to-medium-bodied cigar in four popular shapes. The Connecticut wrapper is combined with Olor binders and Piloto Cubano filler leaves for a smooth draw and presented in boxes of ten or 20.

HANDMADE CIGARS: BRAND LISTINGS

KALUA SUNRISE
Handmade, with mixed filler, in Santiago, Dominican Republic.

Wrapper: Indonesia   Binder: Dom. Rep.   Filler: Dom. Rep.

Shape	Name	Lgth	Ring	Wrapper
Long Corona	Corona	6	42	CM
Small Panatela	Minis	4¾	30	CM

Introduced in 1988, this is a mild cigar offered in bundles of 25, with the Mini size also available in bundles of ten.

KEY WEST HAVANA GOLD LABEL
Handmade in Santiago, Dominican Republic.

Wrapper: USA/Connecticut   Binder: Dom. Rep.   Wrapper: Dom. Rep.

Shape	Name	Lgth	Ring	Wrapper
Slim Panatela	Amelia	5	30	CC
Long Panatela	Marti	7	38	CC
Long Corona	Estella	6	44	CC
Robusto	Cortez	5	50	CC
Double Corona	Sanchez	7½	50	CC
Pyramid	Piramide	7	54	CC

Introduced in 1994, this brand has become a Key West tradition! It offers a mild-to-medium-bodied flavor, packed in bundles or tins of 25 cigars each.

KING COBRA
Handmade in Santiago, Dominican Republic.

Wrapper: Ecuador   Binder: Indonesia   Filler: Dom. Rep.

Shape	Name	Lgth	Ring	Wrapper
Robusto	Robusto	5	50	CC
Grand Corona	Corona Extra	6	46	CC
Double Corona	Churchill	7½	50	CC

HANDMADE CIGARS: BRAND LISTINGS

Lonsdale	Lonsdale	7	42	CC

This is a vaccum-packed brand, good for a full year, with a Connecticut-seed wrapper. Introduced in 1997, it has a full-bodied taste that is available in boxes of 25.

KING DOMINICAN
Handmade in Santiago, Dominican Republic.
Wrapper: USA/Connecticut   *Binder: Honduras*
Wrapper: Brazil, Dominican Republic

Shape	Name	Lgth	Ring	Wrapper
Lonsdale	No. 1	6½	42	CC-Ma
Corona	No. 2	5½	42	CC-Ma
Robusto	No. 6	4¾	50	CC-Ma
Giant	No. 7	8½	52	CC-Ma
Double Corona	No. 8	7	60	CC-Ma
Giant	No. 9	10	66	CC-Ma
Double Corona	No. 10	7½	49	CC-Ma
Robusto	No. 13	5	66	CC-Ma

A full, yet deliciously mild bundled cigar, introduced in 1989. The natural-wrapped version has a smooth herbal character, while the maduro wrapper offers a rich earthiness to the palate. These delicate flavors and the line's smooth draw are truly unique, as are its range in some of the largest available ring gauges.

KING HONDURAN
Handmade in Santa Rosa de Copan, Honduras.
Wrapper: Honduras   *Binder: Honduras*   *Filler: Honduras*

Shape	Name	Lgth	Ring	Wrapper
Lonsdale	No. 1	6½	42	CM-Ma
Corona	No. 2	5½	42	CM-Ma
Toro	No. 3	6	50	CM-Ma

Robusto	No. 6	4¾	50	CM-Ma
Giant	No. 7	8½	52	CM-Ma
Double Corona	No. 10	7½	49	CM-Ma

Introduced in 1998, this is a medium-bodied blend of all-Honduran-grown tobaccos. It is available in either natural or maduro wrapper in bundles of 25.

KING RICHARD
Handmade in Miami, Florida, USA.
Wrapper: USA/Connecticut or Indonesia
Binder: USA/Connecticut or Dom. Rep.   *Filler: Dom. Rep.*

Shape	Name	Lgth	Ring	Wrapper
Double Corona	Royal Tycoon	7⅝	50	CM-Ma
Churchill	Royal Churchill	6⅞	46	CM-Ma
Lonsdale	Royal Duke	6¾	42	CM-Ma
Torpedo	Royal Stud	6	52	CM-Ma
Robusto	Royal Knight	5	50	CM-Ma
Panatela	Royal Madame	6⅞	36	CM
	Made with short filler:			
Lonsdale	Royal Trucker	6½	44	CM

Take your choice of natural or maduro wrappers in this brand, created in 1996 in Little Havana. The taste varies between mild-to-medium (Stud, Madame), medium (Duke, Knight) and full-bodied (Tycoon, Churchill, Royal Trucker). All of the long-fill shapes use Connecticut wrappers and binders, while the Royal Trucker has an Indonesian wrapper and Dominican binder.

KINGS CLUB
Handmade in Danli, Honduras.
Wrapper: Ecuador   *Binder: Honduras*   *Filler: Dom. Rep.*

Shape	Name	Lgth	Ring	Wrapper
Pyramid	Alfonso XII	7	54	CC-Ma

HANDMADE CIGARS: BRAND LISTINGS

Giant	King Ferdinand	8½	52	CC-Ma
Robusto	Henry VIII	4½	50	CC-Ma
Lonsdale	King Philip	6¼	44	CC-Ma
Toro	Louis XIV	6	50	CC-Ma
Churchill	King Arthur	7	48	CC-Ma

Introduced in 1997, this brand is named after great royals of the past. Cigar history buffs will not be surprised that the largest cigar is named after Ferdinand of Spain, one of the most important monarchs in the promotion of tobacco after its discovery by Columbus. The cigars themselves are medium-bodied and feature a blend of Dominican-grown Piloto Cubano filler leaves. The Kings Club is offered in all-cedar boxes of 25.

KINGSTON
Handmade in San Andres Tuxtla, Mexico.

Wrapper: Mexico　　　　*Binder: Mexico*　　　　*Filler: Mexico*

Shape	Name	Lgth	Ring	Wrapper
Lonsdale	Corona Grande	6⅝	42	CC-Ma
Double Corona	Giant Corona	7½	50	CC-Ma
Panatela	Panatela Extra	6½	35	CC-Ma
Long Corona	Royal Corona	6	42	CC-Ma
Toro	Toro	6	50	CC-Ma
Robusto	Rothschild	4½	50	CC-Ma
Giant	Viajante	8½	50	CC-Ma

All of the tobacco in this brand is grown in Mexico, with the wrapper grown from Sumatran seeds. It is full-bodied and offered in bundles of 25.

KISKEYA
Handmade, with mixed filler, in Santiago, Dominican Republic.

Wrapper: Ecuador　　　　*Binder: Dom. Rep.*　　　　*Filler: Dom. Rep.*

Shape	Name	Lgth	Ring	Wrapper

Corona	Corona	5½	42	CC
Lonsdale	Lonsdale	6½	43	CC
Robusto	Robusto	5	50	CC
Churchill	Churchills	7	48	CC

These cigars are handmade with sandwich filler, with natural wrappers of Ecuador-grown, Connecticut-seed tobacco. Medium in body, they are packed in boxes of 25 cigars.

KISS

Handmade in Santo Domingo, Dominican Republic.

Wrapper: Ecuador   *Binder: Dom. Rep.*   *Filler: Dom. Rep.*

Shape	Name	Lgth	Ring	Wrapper
	Vanilla:			
Small Panatela	Chica	5	30	CC
Corona	Chico	5½	42	CC
Torpedo	Torpedo	6	54	CC
	Cognac:			
Long Corona	Paco	6	44	CC
Robusto	Pancho	4½	50	CC
Double Corona	Macho	7½	50	CC

Introduced in 1998, this brand offers a medium-to-full-bodied taste. The two flavors are presented in wood boxes of five or 25.

KISS ONE

Handmade in Navarrete, Dominican Republic.

Wrapper: Indonesia   *Binder: Dom. Rep.*   *Filler: Dom. Rep.*

Shape	Name	Lgth	Ring	Wrapper
Torpedo	Torpedo	6	54	CM
Giant	Churchill	8½	50	CM

HANDMADE CIGARS: BRAND LISTINGS

This is a medium-bodied brand which debuted in 1998. It is offered in bundles of 25.

KRISTIAN JAMES
Handmade in Ojo de Agua, Honduras.

Wrapper: Indonesia   Binder: Honduras   Filler: Honduras, Nicaragua

Shape	Name	Lgth	Ring	Wrapper
Double Corona	Churchill	7	50	CM
Corona	Cuatro	5½	42	CM
Robusto	Rothschild	5	50	CM
Torpedo	Misiles	6	54	CM
Long Panatela	Palma Fina	7	38	CM
Giant	Soberano	8	52	CM

This brand debuted in 1997 and offers a mild blend of tobaccos from three nations. It is offered in boxes of 25.

LA AURORA
Handmade in Santiago, Dominican Republic.

Wrapper: Cameroon   Binder: Dom. Rep.   Filler: Dom. Rep.

Shape	Name		Lgth	Ring	Wrapper
Short Panatela	Petit Coronas		4½	37	CM
Corona	Aurora No. 4		5¼	43	CM
Short Panatela	Coronas		5	38	CM
Long Corona	Cetros		6⅜	41	CM
Toro	Bristol Especiales		6⅜	48	CM
Panatela	Palmas Extra		6¾	35	CM
Short Panatela	Sublimes	(tubed)	5	38	CM
Robusto	Robusto		5	50	CM
Double Corona	Double Corona		7½	50	CM

Small Panatela	Finos	4	30	CM
Toro	Gran Corona	6½	50	CM
Torpedo	Belicoso	6¼	52	CM
Torpedo	Petit Belicoso	5	52	CM
	Aurora Preferidos 1903 Edition:			
Perfecto	No. 1	4	50	CM
Perfecto	No. 2	4½	54	CM
Perfecto	No. 3	6	58	CM

Respected since its introduction in 1903, La Aurora is a medium-bodied cigar offering a unique blend of Dominican fillers and binder, completed with a rare Cameroon wrapper for a soft, accessible taste. Take your choice of sizes in boxes of 25, or in five-packs in the Cetro, Corona or Double Corona shapes.

The spectacular Preferidos 1903 Edition is a series of three perfectos which reprises the shapes made by Don Eduardo Leon Jimenes at the opening of the La Aurora in 1903. These are medium-to-full-bodied cigars in the old perfecto shape that truly brings a little bit of the start of the 20th Century to smokers at the dawn of the 21st Century.

LA BELLEZA
Handmade in Tenerife, Canary Islands of Spain.
Wrapper: USA/Connecticut   Binder: Dom. Rep.   Filler: Brazil, Dom. Rep.

Shape	Name	Lgth	Ring	Wrapper
Double Corona	Imperiales	7½	50	CC
Robusto	Especiales	4¾	50	CC
Lonsdale	Reserva	6½	43	CC
Panatela	Dianas	5½	39	CC

This brand was introduced to the U.S. market in 1998, offering a mild-to-medium body. It is presented in all-cedar boxes of 25.

HANDMADE CIGARS: BRAND LISTINGS

LA BOCA
Handmade in Tamboril, Dominican Republic.

Wrapper: Indonesia   Binder: Dom. Rep.   Filler: Dom. Rep.

Shape	Name	Lgth	Ring	Wrapper
Double Corona	Churchill	7	50	CM
Lonsdale	Lonsdale	7	44	CM
Slim Panatela	Panatela	6	30	CM
Corona	Corona	5½	44	CM
Robusto	Toro	5	50	CM

Introduced in 1996, "The Mouth" is filled with mild-to-medium-bodied flavors and is offered in cedar boxes of 25.

LA BRISA
Handmade in San Andres Tuxtula, Mexico.

Wrapper: Mexico   Binder: Mexico   Filler: Mexico

Shape	Name	Lgth	Ring	Wrapper
Robusto	Robusto	5	50	CM-Ma
Robusto	Robusto Extra	5	52	CM-Ma
Toro	Toro	6½	52	CM-Ma
Long Corona	Corona	6	42	CM-Ma
Double Corona	Churchill	7½	50	CM-Ma

Here is a 1997-introduced, mild-to-medium (natural) or medium (maduro)-bodied brand of all Mexican-grown tobaccos. All are available in boxes of 24.

LA CONCHA RESERVE
Handmade in Santiago, Dominican Republic.

Wrapper: Indonesia   Binder: Dom. Rep.   Filler: Dom. Rep.

Shape	Name	Lgth	Ring	Wrapper
Long Corona	Dionesa Fina	6	44	CC

Double Corona	Desadario	7½	50	CC
Churchill	Ernesto Especial	7	46	CC
Pyramid	Cubana Pyramides	7	54	CC
Robusto	Everisto	5½	50	CC
Torpedo	El Tigre	6	52	CC
Perfecto	Belisimo	4	42	CC

Introduced in 1997, this is a mild-to-medium-bodied brand which combines a Sumatra wrapper with Dominican-grown Olor and Piloto Cubano leaves. It is offered in boxes or bundles of 25.

LA CORONA
Handmade in La Romana, Dominican Republic.

Wrapper: Indonesia — — *Binder: Dom. Rep.* — — *Filler: Dom. Rep.*

Shape	Name		Lgth	Ring	Wrapper
Corona	Corona		5½	42	CM
Toro	Tubulares	*(tubed)*	6½	48	CM
Robusto	Robusto		5	50	CM
Torpedo	Torpedo		6	50	CM
Double Corona	Double Corona		7¾	50	CM

Here is a famous, ancient brand originally produced in Cuba and now made by hand once again in the Dominican Republic. This is a medium-bodied blend, offered in boxes of 25.

LA COSECHA
Handmade in Esteli, Nicaragua.

Wrapper: Indonesia — — *Binder: Nicaragua* — — *Filler: Nicaragua*

Shape	Name	Lgth	Ring	Wrapper
Robusto	Robusto	4¾	50	CC
Corona	Corona	5½	42	CC

Toro	Toro	6	50	CC
Double Corona	Churchill	7	50	CC

Here is a 1997-introduced, mild-bodied cigar that features a Cameroon-seed wrapper, available in boxes of 25.

LA CUNA
Handmade, with short filler, in Esteli, Nicaragua.

Wrapper: Indonesia　　　*Binder: Nicaragua*　　*Filler: Dom. Rep., Nicaragua*

Shape	Name	Lgth	Ring	Wrapper
Small Panatela	Flavors	5	34	CM

This short-fill brand is available in three flavored versions: rum, sweets and vanilla, in bundles of 25 or packs of five.

LA DIABLA
Handmade in Santiago, Dominican Republic.

Wrapper: Indonesia　　　*Binder: Dom. Rep.*　　　*Filler: Dom. Rep.*

Shape	Name	Lgth	Ring	Wrapper
Long Corona	Corona	6	44	CM
Robusto	Robusto	5	50	CM

There's just a touch of vanilla flavoring in this brand to complement its mild-bodied taste. Introduced in 1998, it is presented in boxes of 25.

LA DILIGENCIA
Handmade in Danli, Honduras.

Wrapper: USA/Connecticut　　　　　*Binder: Dominican Republic*
Filler: Dominican Republic, Honduras, Nicaragua

Shape	Name	Lgth	Ring	Wrapper
Giant	Presidente	8½	52	CC
Toro	Toro	6	50	CC
Long Corona	Grand Corona	6	44	CC

HANDMADE CIGARS: BRAND LISTINGS

| Churchill | Churchill | 7 | 48 | CC |
| Robusto | Robusto | 4¾ | 50 | CC |

This brand was introduced in 1996 and offers a light to medium body, thanks to a blend of tobaccos from four nations. La Diligencia offers lots of flavor and is packaged in boxes of 25 cigars each.

LA DIVA
Handmade in Villa Gonzalez, Dominican Republic.

Wrapper: USA/Connecticut   *Binder: Dom. Rep.*   *Filler: Dom. Rep.*

Shape	Name	Lgth	Ring	Wrapper
Long Corona	Corona	6	44	CC
Robusto	Robusto	4½	50	CC
Giant	Churchill	8	50	CC
Torpedo	Torpedo	7	54	CC
Double Corona	Golden Giant	7	60	CC

This cigar was introduced in 1996 and is unique for the process which imbues the leaves with the essence of the marvelous Cognac Pierre Ferrand "Selection des Anges." Combined with Connecticut Shade wrappers and Dominican leaves in the interior of the cigar, the blend has a medium body and is offered in glass tubes, elegant wooden boxes or individually cellophaned in bundles of 25.

LA DOLCE VITA
Handmade in Miami, Florida, USA.

Wrapper: Indonesia   *Binder: Indonesia*   *Filler: Dom. Rep.*

Shape	Name	Lgth	Ring	Wrapper
Small Panatela	Petite	5	30	CM

Introduced in 1997, this is a mild-to-medium-bodied cigar with a vanilla flavor and a sugar tip. It is available in boxes of 20.

LA EMINENCIA
Handmade in Danli, Honduras.

HANDMADE CIGARS: BRAND LISTINGS

Wrapper: Ecuador   *Binder: Honduras*
Filler: Brazil, Dominican Republic, Honduras, Nicaragua

Shape	Name	Lgth	Ring	Wrapper
Giant	Supreme	8½	52	CC
Toro	After Dinner	6	50	CC
Robusto	Rothschild	4½	50	CC
Churchill	Corona Inmensa	7¼	46	CC
Grand Corona	Fumas No. 1 /mixed filler/	6½	46	CC
Corona Extra	Robusto	5⅝	46	CC
Corona	Cubanitas /mixed filler/	5½	44	CC
Long Panatela	Palmas	7	38	CC
Torpedo	Torpedo	6¾	54	CC
Pyramid	Pyramid	7	54	CC

Back in distribution in 1996 after a short absence, La Eminencia is made by
hand in Honduras and by machine in Tampa, Florida. The handmade blend is
mild to medium-bodied, with both natural and maduro wrappers available in all
sizes.

LA ESTRELLA CUBANA
Handmade in Esteli, Nicaragua.

Wrapper: Nicaragua   *Binder: Nicaragua*   *Filler: Nicaragua*

Shape	Name	Lgth	Ring	Wrapper
Double Corona	Churchill	7	52	CM-Ma
Toro	Torpedo	6	54	CM-Ma
Toro	Gran Corona	6	48	CM-Ma
Panatela	Panetela	6	38	CM-Ma
Corona	Corona	5½	44	CM-Ma
Robusto	Robusto	5	50	CM-Ma

HANDMADE CIGARS: BRAND LISTINGS

Here is the "Cuban Star." Fans of full-bodied cigars will enjoy this all-Nicaraguan brand, which is offered in natural and maduro (actually, oscuro!) shade wrappers in boxes of 25.

LA EXQUISITA
Handmade in Tenerife, the Canary Islands of Spain.

Wrapper: USA/Connecticut   *Binder: Spain*   *Filler: Spain*

Shape	Name	Lgth	Ring	Wrapper
Robusto	Robustos	5¼	50	CC
Toro	No. 1	6¼	49	CC
Long Corona	No. 2	6	43	CC
Petit Corona	No. 3	5	42	CC

This is a medium-bodied blend from the Canary Islands, using locally-grown binders and fillers. It is offered in all-cedar boxes of 25.

LA FABULOSO
Handmade in Danli, Honduras.

Wrapper: Honduras   *Binder: Honduras*   *Filler: Honduras*

Shape	Name	Lgth	Ring	Wrapper
Grand Corona	No. 1	6½	46	CM
Corona	No. 4	5½	44	CM
Toro	Churchill	6½	52	CM
Long Panatela	Panatela	7	36	CM
Short Panatela	Petit	4½	38	CM
Churchill	Presidente	6¾	48	CM
Robusto	Robusto	5	50	CM
Toro	Toro	6⅛	50	CM

Created in the early 1970s, this is a mild-to-medium-bodied cigar, offered in economical bundles of 25.

HANDMADE CIGARS: BRAND LISTINGS

LA FAMA
Handmade in Tenerife, the Canary Islands of Spain.

Wrapper: USA/Connecticut   Binder: Dom. Rep.   Filler: Brazil, Dom. Rep.

Shape	Name	Lgth	Ring	Wrapper
Panatela	Solera	5½	39	CC
Long Corona	Royal	6¼	43	CC
Grand Corona	Cedros	6½	47	CC
Double Corona	Churchill	7	50	CC

This brand is very mild in body and is made by hand in the Canary Islands. It is offered in elegant boxes of 25 cigars each.

LA FAVORITA
Handmade in Tenerife, the Canary Islands of Spain.

Wrapper: USA/Connecticut   Binder: Mexico   Filler: Brazil, Dom. Rep.

Shape	Name	Lgth	Ring	Wrapper
Double Corona	Doble Corona	7½	50	CC
Toro	Toro	6	50	CC
Robusto	Robusto	5	50	CC
Lonsdale	Lonsdale	6½	43	CC

Here is a new brand for 1997, with a mild body and offered in beautifully-appointed cedar boxes of 25.

LA FINCA
Handmade in Esteli, Nicaragua.

Wrapper: Ecuador   Binder: Nicaragua   Filler: Dom. Rep., Honduras, Nicaragua

Shape	Name	Lgth	Ring	Wrapper
Double Corona	Bolivares	7½	50	CM
Grand Corona	Cazadore	6½	45	CM
Corona	Corona	5½	42	CM

Corona	Crystales	5⅝	44	CM
Grand Corona	Fuma	6½	46	CM
Corona Extra	Fuma Corta	5½	46	CM
Pyramid	Figurado	6¾	54	CM
Giant	Gran Finca	8½	52	CM
Toro	Joya	6	50	CM
Pyramid	Pyramides	7	48	CM
Robusto	Robusto	4½	50	CM
Lonsdale	Romeo	6½	42	CM
Churchill	Valentino	6¾	48	CM

This is a heavy-bodied cigar, La Finca shapes are offered in boxes of 25 cigars each.

LA FLOR DE ARMANDO MENDEZ
Handmade in Tampa, Florida, USA.

Wrapper: USA/Connecticut   Binder: Honduras   Filler: Honduras

Shape	Name	Lgth	Ring	Wrapper
Toro	La Flor de A. Mendez	6	50	CM

This is a medium-bodied blend, offered in six-packs from the respected Cammarata Cigar Factory in the Ybor City section of Tampa, Florida.

LA FLOR DE CANO
Handmade in Santiago, Dominican Republic.

Wrapper: Cameroon   Binder: Mexico   Filler: Dom. Rep., Nicaragua

Shape	Name	Lgth	Ring	Wrapper
Torpedo	Belicoso	6	52	CM
Pyramid	Bouqets	4½	54	CM
Grand Corona	Churchill	6¼	47	CM
Corona	Corona	5½	43	CM

Culebras	Culebras		6	31	CM
Toro	Diademas	(tubed)	6¼	49	CM
Cigarillo	Miniatures		3¾	24	CM
Robusto	Robusto		4½	49	CM
Lonsdale	Selectos		6½	43	CM

New for 1998 is this Dominican version of a famous — and still produced — Cuban brand. This version has some of the most unusual shapes available in the line — the Culebras for example — and offers a medium-bodied taste. Most shapes are available in boxes of 25, but the Diademas is offered in 20s and the Miniatures in 8-packs.

LA FLOR DEL TEIDE
Handmade in Tenerife, the Canary Islands of Spain.

Wrapper: Indonesia, USA/Connecticut   *Binder: Spain*   *Filler: Spain*

Shape	Name	Lgth	Ring	Wrapper
Double Corona	Churchill	7½	50	CM
Churchill	Nuncios	7	46	CM
Lonsdale	Imperials	6½	42	CM
Corona	Coronas	5⅝	42	CM
Panatela	Panatelas	6½	35	CM
Torpedo	Figurado	6	50	CM
Robusto	Robusto	5	50	CM
Toro	Toro	6	50	CM

This is a medium-bodied cigar introduced to the U.S. market in 1998, It is offered with a choice of Connecticut or Sumatra wrapper and Canary Islands binder and filler. It is packed with cellophane in boxes of 10, 25, 40 or 60s!

LA FLOR DOMINICANA
Handmade in Santiago, Dominican Republic.

HANDMADE CIGARS: BRAND LISTINGS

PREMIUM AND RESERVA ESPECIAL SERIES:
Wrapper: USA/Connecticut   Binder: Dom. Rep.   Filler: Dom. Rep.

MADURO SERIES:
Wrapper: Mexico   Binder: Dom. Rep.   Filler: Dom. Rep.

COLORADO SERIES:
Wrapper: USA/Connecticut   Binder: Dom. Rep.   Filler: Dom. Rep., Nicaragua

2000 SERIES:
Wrapper: Cameroon   Binder: Dom. Rep.   Filler: Brazil, Dom. Rep.

EL JOCKO SERIES:
Wrapper: USA/Connecticut   Binder: Dom. Rep.   Filler: Dom. Rep., Nicaragua

CULEBRA ESPECIAL:
Wrapper: Mexico, USA/Connecticut   Binder: Dom. Rep.   Filler: Dom. Rep.

Shape	Name	Lgth	Ring	Wrapper
	Premium:			
Churchill	Mambises	6⅞	48	CC
Robusto	Maceo	5	48	CC
Lonsdale	Alcalde	6½	44	CC
Corona	Insurrectos	5½	42	CC
Petit Corona	Macheteros	4	40	CC
Slim Panatela	Demi-Tasse	5	30	CC
	Reserva Especial:			
Double Corona	Churchill	6⅞	49	CC
Robusto	Robusto	5	48	CC
Robusto	Belicoso	5½	52	CC
Torpedo	Figurado	6½	52	CC
	Maduro Especiales:			
Lonsdale	No. 1	6½	44	Ma
Torpedo	No. 2	6½	52	Ma

Robusto	No. 3	5	48	Ma
	2000 Series:			
Lonsdale	No. 1	6½	44	CM
Robusto	No. 2	4¾	50	CM
Robusto	No. 3	4⅝	40	CM
	Colorado Series:			
Robusto	Robustos	5	48	CM
Lonsdale	Lonsdales	6½	42	CM
Corona	Coronas	5½	42	CM
	El Jocko Series:			
Perfecto	Perfecto No. 1	4½	54	CM
Perfecto	Perfecto No. 2	4½	54	CC
	Culebra Especial:			
Culebras	Culebra Especial	6½	30	CC-Ma

Introduced in 1994, Cuban-seed tobaccos from the Cibao Valley of the Dominican Republic are the stuff of which La Flor Dominicana cigars are founded . . . but in an amazing variety of shapes and sizes from the endlessly inventive Litto Gomez. These leaves are wrapped with Connecticut Shade leaves to produce a mild-to-medium bodied blend in the Premium line and a medium-to-full-bodied taste in the Reserva Especial group. The Mexican maduro-wrapped line is new for 1997 and offers a medium-bodied taste. The Colorado Series presents a medium-to-full-bodied taste with a Connecticut Broadleaf wrapper, while the Colorado series uses a Cameroon wrapper and both Brazilian and Dominican filler tobaccos to produce a full-bodied experience. The amazing artistry of the El Jocko group perfectos overshadows the rich, full-bodied taste using Connecticut Broadleaf wrappers and the unique Culebras has both a maduro-shade and two natural-shade wrappers in its three-cigar twist!

LA FONTANA VINTAGE
Handmade in Danli, Honduras.

Wrapper: USA/Connecticut　　　*Binder: Mexico*　　　*Filler: Honduras*

HANDMADE CIGARS: BRAND LISTINGS

Shape	Name	Lgth	Ring	Wrapper
Corona	Verdi	5½	44	CC
Robusto	Galileo	5	50	CC
Lonsdale	Puccini	6½	44	CC
Churchill	Da Vinci	6⅞	48	CC
Double Corona	Michelangelo	7½	52	CC
Slim Panatela	Rossini	5½	33	CC
Pyramid	Mona Lisa	4¾	46	CC
Torpedo	Belicoso	6	54	CC
Panatela	Dante	5½	38	CC

This is a mild blend which debuted in 1993. It is constructed of Honduran-grown tobaccos in the binder and a light Connecticut wrapper. This creation of master blender Tino Argudin includes two new, shaped sizes for 1997 and is offered in elegant 25-cigar boxes.

LA FRANCESCA
Handmade in Tamboril, Dominican Republic.

Wrapper: USA/Connecticut   Binder: Dom. Rep.   Filler: Dom. Rep.

Shape	Name	Lgth	Ring	Wrapper
Small Panatela	Dulce Vanilla	5	30	CC

This long-filler, flavored brand is available in vanilla and debuted in 1998. It is presented in cellophane sleeves in boxes of 10.

LA GIANNA HAVANA
Handmade in Esteli, Nicaragua.

Wrapper: Nicaragua   Binder: Nicaragua   Filler: Nicaragua

Shape	Name	Lgth	Ring	Wrapper
	Classic Series:			
Long Corona	Lonsdale	6¼	44	CC
Double Corona	Churchill	7	49	CC

Robusto	Robusto	5	50	CC
Torpedo	Torpedo	6	54	CC
Torpedo	Bellabusto	5	52	CC
	Angelic Series:			
Long Corona	Lonsdale	6¼	44	CM
Double Corona	Churchill	7	49	CM
Robusto	Robusto	5	50	CM
Torpedo	Torpedo	6	54	CM
Torpedo	Bellabusto	5	52	CM
	Ebony Selection:			
Long Corona	Lonsdale	6¼	44	Ma
Double Corona	Churchill	7	49	Ma
Robusto	Robusto	5	50	Ma
Torpedo	Torpedo	6	54	Ma
Torpedo	Bellabusto	5	52	Ma

The Classic line was introduced in 1996, with the Angelic (formerly Graciella) and Ebony series debuting in 1997. The brand offers a mild-bodied taste in the Classic line, and medium-bodied flavor in the other lines in five popular shapes. The aging process continues in the elegant cedar boxes in which La Gianna cigars are presented.

LA GITANA
Handmade in Tamboril, Dominican Republic.

Wrapper: USA/Connecticut   Binder: Dom. Rep.   Filler: Dom. Rep.

Shape	Name	Lgth	Ring	Wrapper
Double Corona	Churchill	7½	50	CC
Churchill	Corona Grande	6¾	46	CC
Long Corona	Lonsdale	6¼	44	CC
Robusto	Robusto	5	50	CC

Corona	La Linda	5½	42	CC

This is a medium-bodied brand introduced in 1998 and offered in boxes of 25.

LA GLORIA

Handmade in Santiago, Dominican Republic.

Wrapper: Indonesia or USA/Connecticut

Binder: Brazil   *Filler: Dominican Republic*

Shape	Name	Lgth	Ring	Wrapper
Pyramid	Piramides	6½	58	CC-CM-Ma
Double Corona	Churchills	7	50	CC-CM-Ma
Lonsdale	Medaille No. 1	6⅞	44	CC-CM-Ma
Toro	Double Coronas	6	52	CC-CM-Ma
Robusto	Wavells	5	50	CC-CM-Ma
Corona	Gloria No. 4	5½	44	CC-CM-Ma

Originally produced outside of Cuba in 1962, this old brand name now adorns a versatile cigar, offered in three wrapper shades: a mild-bodied Connecticut wrapper, a medium-bodied Indonesian wrapper or a full-bodied, maduro-shade Connecticut Broadleaf. It is presented in boxes of 25.

LA GLORIA BORICUA

Handmade in Santiago, Dominican Republic.

Wrapper: Indonesia   *Binder: Dom. Rep.*   *Filler: Dom. Rep.*

Shape	Name	Lgth	Ring	Wrapper
Corona	Equisito	5¼	42	CM
Panatela	Maravilloso	6	38	CM
Lonsdale	Magnifico	6½	44	CM
Robusto	Formidable	5	50	CM
Double Corona	Glorioso	7⅜	52	CM

HANDMADE CIGARS: BRAND LISTINGS

This brand debuted in 1997 and presents a medium-to-full-bodied taste. It is offered in all-cedar boxes of 25.

LA GLORIA CUBANA
Handmade in Miami, Florida, USA and
Villa Gonzalez, Dominican Republic.

Wrapper: Ecuador   Binder: Nicaragua   Filler: Dom.Rep., Nicaragua

Shape	Name	Lgth	Ring	Wrapper
Giant	Crown Imperial	9	49	DC-CC-Ma
Giant	Soberano	8	52	DC-CC-Ma
Double Corona	Charlemagne	7¼	54	DC-CC-Ma
Double Corona	Double Corona	7¾	49	DC-CC-Ma
Double Corona	Churchill	7	50	DC-CC-Ma
Toro	Corona Gorda	6	52	DC-CC-Ma
Robusto	Wavell	5	50	DC-CC-Ma
Grand Corona	Glorias Extra	6¼	46	DC-CC-Ma
Giant Corona	Coronas Extra Larga	7¾	44	DC-CC-Ma
Lonsdale	Medaille D'Or No. 1	6¾	43	DC-CC-Ma
Long Corona	Medaille D'Or No. 2	6¼	43	DC-CC-Ma
Corona	Glorias	5½	43	DC-CC-Ma
Small Panatela	Minutos	4½	40	DC-CC-Ma
Long Panatela	Panatela De'Luxe	7	37	DC-CC-Ma
Panatela	Medaille D'Or No. 4	6	32	DC-CC-Ma
Torpedo	Torpedo No. 1	6½	Tpr	DC-CC-Ma
Pyramid	Piramides	7¼	Tpr	DC-CC-Ma

This is a medium-bodied smoke of absolutely exquisite quality made in the El Credito factory in Miami, Florida (primarily for local sale only) and in a new facility in Villa Gonzalez, Dominican Republic. All sizes are offered in boxes of 25, except for the Crown Imperial and the Piramides, which are offered in boxes of 10.

HANDMADE CIGARS: BRAND LISTINGS

LA GLORIA CUBANA SELECION D'ORO
Handmade in Santiago, Dominican Republic.

Wrapper: *USA/Connecticut*   Binder: *Dom. Rep.*   Filler: *Dom. Rep.*

Shape	Name	Lgth	Ring	Wrapper
Lonsdale	No. 1	6¾	44	CC
Toro	No. 2	6½	52	CC
Robusto	No. 5	5	50	CC
Toro	No. 6	6	52	CC
Double Corona	No. 10	7¼	54	CC

Go Ernesto! This is a 1998-introduced special version of the La Gloria Cubana line. It is mild-to-medium in body and is offered in boxes of 25.

LA HABANERA
Handmade in Santiago, Dominican Republic.

Wrapper: *USA/Connecticut*   Binder: *Dom. Rep.*   Filler: *Dom. Rep.*

Shape	Name	Lgth	Ring	Wrapper
Churchill	Churchill	6⅞	46	CI
Long Corona	Diplomaticos	6	44	CI
Lonsdale	Elegante	6¾	42	CI
Toro	Emperadores	6	50	CI
Small Panatela	Especiale	5	30	CI
Double Corona	Presidente	7½	50	CI
Corona	Puritanos	5¾	42	CI
Long Panatela	Selectos	7	36	CI

This is an old brand name from 1902 that now combines a genuine Connecticut wrapper with Dominican-grown binder and fillers for a mild-to-medium-bodied taste. La Habanera is presented in colorful boxes of 25, with the Churchill and Puritanos shapes available in four-packs.

HANDMADE CIGARS: BRAND LISTINGS

LA HABANITA CIGAR FACTORY
Handmade in Chicago, Illinois, USA.

Wrapper: Dom. Rep.   Binder: Dom. Rep.   Filler: Dom. Rep.

Shape	Name	Lgth	Ring	Wrapper
Slim Panatela	Petit	5	32	CM
Corona	Fino	5½	42	CM
Panatela	Panatella	6	36	CM
Panatela	Chocolate Sensation	6	36	CM
Robusto	Santiago	5	50	CM
Robusto	Señor Julio	5½	52	CM
Grand Corona	Fuma	6	46	CM
Grand Corona	Monte Rico	6	46	CM
Toro	Cueste de Oro	6	50	CM
Double Corona	Favorito	7	50	CM
Double Corona	Maestro	7¾	52	CM
Torpedo	Torpedo	6	54	CM
Torpedo	Gran Torpedo	7	54	CM

From the Windy City comes this brand, whose history dates back to the tobacco fields of Cuba in 1938. Today's version uses all Dominican tobacco and offers a medium-bodied blend of leaves.

LA HOJA DEL SABOR
Handmade in Tamboril, Dominican Republic.

Wrapper: Indonesia   Binder: Dom. Rep.   Filler: Dom. Rep.

Shape	Name	Lgth	Ring	Wrapper
	Sweetness added:			
Corona	Corona	5½	44	CC-Ma
Slim Panatela	Petite	5	34	CC-Ma

HANDMADE CIGARS: BRAND LISTINGS

Introduced in 1997, this brand now concentrates on two sweetened sizes, featuring a Sumatra wrapper in a natural shade. The result is a mild and sweet cigar, presented in individual cellophane sleeves in a colorful, paper-wrapped box.

LA HOJA RICA
Handmade in Santiago, Dominican Republic.

Wrapper: Indonesia　　　　　*Binder: Indonesia*　　　　*Filler: Dominican Republic*

Shape	Name	Lgth	Ring	Wrapper
Churchill	Churchill	6¾	48	CM
Toro	Toro	6	50	CM
Corona Extra	Corona	5½	46	CM
Robusto	Robusto	4½	52	CM

New in 1997, this hand-made line offers a medium-to-full-bodied smoke with Dominican-grown Olor and Piloto Cubano leaves powering the filler. Each cigar is wrapped in cellophane and each size is offered in all-cedar boxes of 25.

LA HOJA SELECTA
Handmade in Miami, Florida, USA.

Wrapper: USA/Connecticut　　　*Binder: Ecuador*　　　*Filler: Dom.Rep., Nicaragua*

Shape	Name	Lgth	Ring	Wrapper
Double Corona	Chateau Sovereign	7½	52	CI
Churchill	Cosiac	7	48	CI
Toro	Choix Supreme	6	50	CI
Robusto	Palais Royals	4¾	50	CI
Lonsdale	Selectos No. 1	6½	42	CI
Corona	Cetros de Oro	5¾	43	CI
Panatela	Bel Aires	6¾	38	CI

These are the mildest cigars produced by the El Credito factory in Miami, Florida, thanks to their Connecticut Shade wrappers and filler tobaccos from the Dominican Republic.

HANDMADE CIGARS: BRAND LISTINGS

LA INSULAR

Handmade in La Romana, Dominican Republic.

Wrapper: Indonesia

Binder: USA/Pennsylvania *Filler: Costa Rica, Indonesia, USA/Connecticut*

Shape	Name	Lgth	Ring	Wrapper
Petit Corona	No. 442	4½	42	CM
Robusto	No. 450	4½	50	CM
Corona	No. 5542	5½	42	CM
Petit Corona	No. 542	5⅛	42	CM
Panatela	No. 539	5¾	39	CM
Grand Corona	No. 546	5⅝	46	CM
Robusto	No. 550	5	50	CM
Toro	No. 650	6	50	CM
Torpedo	Torpedo	6	50	CM

Here is a new, quietly-introduced brand for 1998 that offers a medium-bodied taste and an excellent value. It is medium in body and offered in bundles of 25.

LA ISLA

Handmade in Union City, New Jersey, USA.

Wrapper: USA/Connecticut *Binder: Dominican Republic*

Filler: Costa Rica, Dominican Republic, Honduras, Mexico

Shape	Name	Lgth	Ring	Wrapper
Churchill	Churchill	7⅛	46	CC-Ma
Robusto	Soberanos Cortos	5½	50	CC-Ma
Giant	Soberanos	8	50	CC-Ma
Giant	Presidente	8	50	CC-Ma
Churchill	Especiale	7	46	CC-Ma
Churchill	Corona	7	46	CC-Ma
Panatela	Panatela	6¼	35	CC-Ma

Long Panatela	Palmas	7	35	CC-Ma
Lonsdale	Fumas	6¾	44	CC-Ma
Lonsdale	No. 1	7⅛	42	CC-Ma
Long Corona	No. 2	6¼	40	CC-Ma
Corona	No. 4	5½	40	CC-Ma

These medium-to-full-bodied cigars are handmade in a small store in Union City, New Jersey. The wide variety of sizes – 12 in all – are enveloped in Connecticut-grown leaves, including Connecticut Broadleaf tobaccos for the maduro wrappers.

LA JOYA CUBANA
Handmade in Miami, Florida, USA.
Wrapper: Ecuador or Indonesia   Binder: Dom. Rep.   *Filler: Dom. Rep.*

Shape	Name	Lgth	Ring	Wrapper
Robusto	Robusto	5	50	CC-Ma
Toro	Corona Gorda	6	48	CC-Ma
Long Corona	Corona	6	44	CC-Ma
Churchill	Cubana	6¾	46	CC-Ma
Double Corona	Churchill	7½	50	CC-Ma

Introduced in 1998, this is a medium-to-full-bodied smoke offered with a choice of a Connecticut-seed wrapper grown in Ecuador or a Sumatra-grown maduro wrapper. It is presented in individual cellophane sleeves inside boxes of 25, except for the Churchill shape, which is offered in boxes of 15.

LA LUNA
Handmade in Miami, Florida, USA.

CASJUCA BLEND:
Wrapper: Ecuador   Binder: Ecuador   Filler: Dom. Rep., Ecuador, Honduras

HANDMADE CIGARS: BRAND LISTINGS

LITTLE HAVANA BLEND:
Wrapper: Indonesia
Binder: Ecuador   *Filler: Dom. Rep., Ecuador, Honduras, Indonesia*

SELECCION DOMINICANA:
Wrapper: Indonesia   *Binder: Ecuador*   *Filler: Dom. Rep., Indonesia*

Shape	Name	Lgth	Ring	Wrapper
	Casjuca Blend:			
Robusto	Robusto	5	50	CC
Double Corona	Churchill	7	50	CC
Lonsdale	Corona	6¾	44	CC
Lonsdale	Especiale No. 1	6½	42	CC
Pyramid	Pyramides No. 2	6¼	52	CC
Petit Corona	Colada	4	44	CC
	Little Havana Blend:			
Robusto	Robusto	5	50	CC-Ma
Double Corona	Churchill	7	50	CC
Lonsdale	Corona	6¾	44	CC
Lonsdale	Especiale No. 1	6½	42	CC
Pyramid	Pyramides No. 2	6½	52	CC-Ma
Petit Corona	Colada	4	44	CC-Ma
	Seleccion Dominicana:			
Robusto	Robusto	5	50	CM
Double Corona	Churchill	7	50	CM
Lonsdale	Corona	6¾	44	CM
Lonsdale	Especiale No. 1	6½	42	CM
Pyramid	Pyramides No. 2	6¼	52	CM
Petit Corona	Colada	4	44	CM

HANDMADE CIGARS: BRAND LISTINGS

This is a complicated brand because it is offered in three separate versions. The Casjuca blend is medium-to-full-bodied, as is the 1998-introduced Seleccion Dominicana. The Little Havana Blend is full-bodied. These are beautifully-made cigars which are offered in boxes of 25, except for the Colada size, offered in 24s.

LA LUNDA DE SANTA MARIA
Handmade in Santa Maria, Panama.

Wrapper: Panama   *Binder: Panama*   *Filler: Panama*

Shape	Name	Lgth	Ring	Wrapper
Toro	Presidente	6¼	48	Ma
Robusto	Robusto	5	50	Ma
Toro	Toro	6	50	Ma
Double Corona	Churchill	7	50	Ma

This brand, which was first produced back in 1922, is offered today in four shapes. The flavor is full-bodied and the cigars are presented in boxes of 25.

LA MARIA
Handmade, with short filler, in Tamboril, Dominican Republic.

Wrapper: USA/Connecticut   *Binder: Dom. Rep.*   *Filler: Dom. Rep.*

Shape	Name	Lgth	Ring	Wrapper
Panatela	Petit Corona	5½	38	CC

This brand debuted in 1997 and is available in a standard and in a vanilla-flavored version. It is mild in body and offered in cedar boxes of 20.

LA MARINITA
Handmade in Villa Gonzalez, Dominican Republic.

Wrapper: Indonesia   *Binder: Dom. Rep.*   *Filler: Dom. Rep.*

Shape	Name	Lgth	Ring	Wrapper
Torpedo	Torpedo	6	56	CM
Double Corona	Churchill	7	50	CM

HANDMADE CIGARS: BRAND LISTINGS

Toro	Toro	6	50	CM
Robusto	Robusto	4½	50	CM
Churchill	Corona Larga	7	46	CM

This brand was introduced in 1996 and offers a mild taste. It is presented in elegant all-cedar boxes of 25.

LA MAXIMILIANA
Handmade in Danli, Honduras.

Wrapper: Indonesia   *Binder: Honduras*   *Filler: Nicaragua*

Shape	Name	Lgth	Ring	Wrapper
Double Corona	Perfectus	7	50	CC
Lonsdale	Fumas	7	44	CC
Toro	Optimus	6	48	CC
Long Corona	Luxus	6	43	CC
Corona	Dulcis	5½	42	CC

Introduced in 1996, this brand offers a medium body and a spicy taste, thanks to its Sumatra-grown wrapper, combined with Honduran and Nicaraguan leaves inside. La Maximiliana cigars are presented in a traditional box-pressed format in individual cellophane sleeves.

LA NATIVE
Handmade in Danli, Honduras.

Wrapper: Nicaragua   *Binder: Honduras*   *Filler: Honduras, Nicaragua*

Shape	Name	Lgth	Ring	Wrapper
Giant	Gigantes	8	52	CM
Churchill	Corona Grande	7½	46	CM
Churchill	Churchill	6⅞	49	CM
Robusto	Rothchild	5	50	CM
Toro	Toro	6	50	CM

HANDMADE CIGARS: BRAND LISTINGS

Long Corona	Cetros	6	43	CM
Small Panatela	Super Fino	4½	30	CM
Long Corona	Petits	6	42	CM

These Honduran-made cigars were introduced in 1994 and offer a very smooth draw with a medium-bodied taste and excellent construction. La Native is offered in boxes of 10 and 20.

LA NUBIA
Handmade in Las Palmas, the Canary Islands of Spain.

Wrapper: USA/Connecticut *Binder: Indonesia*
Filler: Brazil, Dominican Republic

Shape	Name	Lgth	Ring	Wrapper
Short Panatela	Viuditas	4	35	CC
Small Panatela	Panatelas	4¾	32	CC
Small Panatela	Senoritas	4	32	CC
Petit Corona	Petit	4½	40	CC
Corona	No. 13	5⅛	42	CC
Lonsdale	No. 15	5⅞	43	CC
Lonsdale	No. 17	6½	44	CC
Robusto	Robusto	4¾	50	CC
Double Corona	Churchill	7½	50	CC

First manufactured way back in 1925, this is a mild-bodied blend of tobaccos from four nations. La Nubia cigars are offered in boxes of 25 except for the Viuditas and Panatelas shapes (20) and Senoritas (30).

LA O'PAREE
Handmade, with medium filler, in Manila, the Philippines.

Wrapper: Indonesia *Binder: Philippines* *Filler: Philippines*

Shape	Name	Lgth	Ring	Wrapper
Double Corona		7	52	CM

HANDMADE CIGARS: BRAND LISTINGS

Churchill		7	47	CM
Robusto		5	52	CM
Petit Corona		5	44	CM
Pyramid		5	50	CM

Although it has no shape names, this is a medium-bodied, medium-filler cigar with a Sumatra wrapper. It is offered in bundles of 25.

LA PALMA DE ORO
Handmade in Las Palmas, the Canary Islands of Spain.
Wrapper: Indonesia or USA/Connecticut   *Binder: Brazil*
Filler: Dominican Republic, Spain

Shape	Name	Lgth	Ring	Wrapper
Corona	Cafe	5½	44	CC
Robusto	Robusto	5	50	CC
Double Corona	Double Corona	6¾	50	CC
Toro	Don Jorge	6¼	54	CC
Double Corona	Superior	7½	54	CC

These cigars, available in the U.S. beginning in 1997, offer a mild body with a hint of spice on the finish. Depending on availability, you have your choice of either Connecticut-grown or Java-grown wrappers in boxes of 10.

LA PANTERA DIAMOND COLLECTION
Handmade in Ojo de Agua, Honduras.
Wrapper: Indonesia   *Binder: Honduras*   *Filler: Costa Rica, Honduras, Nicaragua*

Shape	Name	Lgth	Ring	Wrapper
Double Corona	Churchill	7	50	CM
Corona	No. 4	5½	42	CM
Long Panatela	Palma Fina	7	38	CM
Pyramid	Pyramid	5½	52	CM

Robusto	Rothchild	5	50	CM
Toro	Toro	6	50	CM
Torpedo	Torpedo	7	54	CM
Pyramid	Misiles	6	54	CM
Giant	Gigante	8	52	CM

Known simply as "La Pantera" since introduction in 1996, the Diamond Collection is a mellow, mild-to-medium bodied cigar, thanks to its Sumatra-seed wrapper, offered in wooden boxes of 25.

LA PANTERA PREDATOR EMERALD COLLECTION
Handmade in Esteli, Nicaragua.

Wrapper: Indonesia   *Binder: Nicaragua*   *Filler: Dom. Rep., Nicaragua*

Shape	Name	Lgth	Ring	Wrapper
Double Corona	Churchill	7	50	CM
Robusto	Robusto	5	50	CM
Torpedo	Torpedo	7	54	CM
Grand Corona	Lancero No. 1	6½	45	CM

Here is the strongest of the Predator blends, the green-banded, full-bodied Emerald Collection. The Sumatra wrapper is well-matched with the Nicaraguan and Dominican tobaccos for a powerful flavor, available in boxes of 25.

LA PANTERA SAPPHIRE COLLECTION
Handmade in Ojo de Agua, Honduras.

Wrapper: Indonesia   *Binder: Honduras*   *Filler: Honduras, Nicaragua*

Shape	Name	Lgth	Ring	Wrapper
Double Corona	Churchill	7	50	CM
Corona	No. 4	5½	42	CM
Long Panatela	Palma Fina	7	38	CM
Robusto	Rothchild	5	50	CM

| Torpedo | Misile | 6 | 54 | CM |
| Giant | Soberano | 8 | 52 | CM |

This is a stronger blend than its sister brand, the Diamond Collection. Spicier and more robust, this is a medium-bodied cigar which features aged tobaccos and is offered in cedar cabinets of 25.

LA PERLA HABANA
Handmade in Santiago, Dominican Republic.

Wrapper: Indonesia   *Binder: Indonesia*   *Filler: Dom. Rep.*

Shape	Name	Lgth	Ring	Wrapper
Petit Corona	Perlas	4	40	CC
Corona	Coronas	5¾	43	CC
Lonsdale	Lonsdales	6¾	43	CC
Robusto	Robustos	4¾	52	CC
Toro	Toros	6	50	CC
Double Corona	Double Coronas	7½	52	CC
Torpedo	Figurados	6¼	52	CC

Here is a new brand in 1997, with a medium body and a famous old Cuban name. This reincarnation of the "Pearl of Havana" is presented in cellophane sleeves and packed in cedar boxes of 25.

LA PLATA
Handmade in Los Angeles, California, USA; Cofradia, Honduras and Villa Gonzalez, Dominican Republic.

CLASSIC SELECTION:
Wrapper: USA/Connecticut   *Binder: Honduras*   *Filler: Dom.Rep., Honduras*

ANNIVERSARY DOMINICAN SELECTION:
Wrapper: Indonesia   *Binder: Dom. Rep.*   *Filler: Dom. Rep.*

Cigar Legends: Victor Migenes

It's a long way from the tobacco fields of Puerto Rico to downtown Los Angeles, but that's the story of the Migenes family and the "silver" cigar, La Plata.

Victor Migenes, Sr. literally grew up in the tobacco fields of his native Puerto Rico, but soon he was hand-rolling cigars in a Manhattan cigar store. Then he left to see if life on the West Coast was better. By 1951, he had taken over an old cigar shop and founded the La Plata Cigar Company at 804 South Broadway in Los Angeles.

Migenes rolled cigars and sold them on the spot. From vaudevillians to business tycoons, his customer list expanded and so did his store, at two locations on Hill Street and finally, in 1971, at 1026 South Grand Avenue.

With 15 rollers and expanding demand, Migenes's son, Victor Jr. helped when not playing drums for studio bands or even for the Bay City Rollers on occasion. In 1984, when his father took ill, 20-something Victor took over.

Ever the promoter from his rock 'n roll days, Victor Jr. was one of the first to hold monthly cigar dinners at the dawn of the cigar boom in 1991. Sell-out after sell-out ensued and the quiet La Plata brand became a well-known name in California. More demand led to production in Honduras and Los Angeles and then to the Dominican Republic in 1997 to celebrate La Plata's first half-century.

The distinctive La Plata band debuted in 1995 and the brand's continuing expansion is a tribute to its quality and value. Today, most of the production is in Honduras and the Dominican Republic; the Los Angeles showroom is a laboratory for new blends and new sizes to keep La Plata growing into the 21st Century. . . a continuing story of turning "silver" into gold! *(Photograph courtesy Tom Ellis)*

HANDMADE CIGARS: BRAND LISTINGS

Shape	Name	Lgth	Ring	Wrapper
	La Plata Selection: a continuously-changing line-up of shapes, made by hand in Los Angeles.			
	Classic Selection:			
Giant	Prime Minister	8	50	Ma
Double Corona	Royal Wilshire	7	52	Ma
Robusto	Robusto Uno	4½	52	Ma
Long Corona	Magnificos	6	44	Ma
Robusto	Hercules	5½	54	Cl
Panatela	Ashford Classic	6	34	Cl
Short Panatela	Dessert Specials	5	36	Cl
Long Corona	Grand Classic	6	44	Cl
Double Corona	Enterprise Classic	7	52	Cl
	Dominican Selection:			
Petit Corona	Petit Corona	4¾	40	CM
Robusto	Robusto	4¾	52	CM
Torpedo	Torpedo	6	50	CM
Toro	Toro	6	50	CM
Double Corona	Double Corona	7	52	CM

Founded in 1947, the popular La Plata line is now focused on its production with Villazon's master cigar makers in Honduras to help meet the demand of this charismatic line. The original La Plata Selection is still made in Los Angeles, but is continuously changing in sizes, shapes and tobaccos available. The newer Classic Selection offers either Connecticut wrappers in either claro (mild to medium body) or maduro (full body) shades. The Dominican Selection was introduced to celebrate La Plata's 50th anniversary in 1997 and offers a medium-to-full-bodied smoke with a delicious Indonesian wrapper and a glamorous red band.

HANDMADE CIGARS: BRAND LISTINGS

LA PREFERENCIA
Handmade in Santiago, Dominican Republic.
Wrapper: Ecuador, Indonesia or USA/Connecticut

Binder: Dominican Republic

Filler: Dominican Republic

Shape	Name	Lgth	Ring	Wrapper
Torpedo	Torpedo	7	54	CC-CM
Long Corona	Corona	6	44	CM
Long Corona	Petit Corona	6	42	CM
Robusto	Rothschild	4½	50	CM
Double Corona	Imperial	7½	52	CM
Churchill	Churchill	6⅞	47	CM
Toro	Toro	6½	50	CM

This cigar appeared in 1997 and offers a choice of wrappers and strengths. The Torpedo, Corona, Petit Corona and Rothschild are offered in a medium-bodied, Ecuadorian-grown, Connecticut-seed wrapper, while the Torpedo is also offered in a Connecticut-grown wrapper. The Imperial, Churchill and Toro are available in a medium-to-full-bodied Indonesian wrapper.

LA PRIMADORA
Handmade in Danli, Honduras.
Wrapper: Ecuador or Mexico   Binder: Indonesia   Filler: Honduras, Nicaragua

Shape	Name	Lgth	Ring	Wrapper
Giant	Emperor	8½	50	CC-Ma
Toro	Solitaire	6	50	CC-Ma
Robusto	Starbrite	4½	50	CC-Ma
Panatela	Falcon	6½	34	CC-Ma
Lonsdale	Excellentes	6½	42	CC-Ma
Corona	Petite Cetros	5½	42	CC-Ma

La Primadora is a mild-bodied cigar with a unique and slightly spicy blend of long-filler tobaccos. These imported cigars are well constructed, with a

HANDMADE CIGARS: BRAND LISTINGS

consistent finish and offered in bundles of 25 cigars each.

LA PRIMERA
Handmade in Santiago, Dominican Republic.

Wrapper: Ecuador *Binder: Nicaragua* *Filler: Dom.Rep., Nicaragua*

Shape	Name	Lgth	Ring	Wrapper
Giant	Presidente	8½	52	CC
Double Corona	Churchill	7	50	CC
Toro	Toro	6	50	CC
Lonsdale	No. 1	6¾	44	CC
Robusto	Wavell	5	50	CC
Corona	No. 4	5¾	43	CC

This brand was introduced in 1996 from one of the most respected factories in the Dominican Republic. It offers a medium-flavored blend with considerable smoothness and is offered in wooden boxes of 25.

LA REAL
Handmade in Condega, Nicaragua.

Wrapper: Nicaragua *Binder: Nicaragua* *Filler: Nicaragua*

Shape	Name	Lgth	Ring	Wrapper
Double Corona	Imperiales	7	50	CM
Robusto	Baron	5	50	CM

"The Royal" is an all-Nicaraguan, full-bodied smoke which debuted in 1995. It's for the serious smoker, though: packed without cellophane and in boxes of 50. Light 'em up!

LA REGENTA
Handmade in Las Palmas, the Canary Islands of Spain.
Wrapper: USA/Connecticut
Binder: Dominican Republic *Filler: Brazil, Canary Islands, Dominican Republic*

HANDMADE CIGARS: BRAND LISTINGS

Shape	Name	Lgth	Ring	Wrapper
Giant	Individual	8	50	CI
Double Corona	Premiers	7½	50	CI
Churchill	Gran Corona	7¼	46	CI
Pyramid	Piramide	7	52	CI
Lonsdale	No. 1	6¾	42	CI
Robusto	Especial No. 2	4¾	50	CI
Corona	No. 3	5¾	42	CI
Petit Corona	No. 4	5⅛	42	CI
Petit Corona	No. 5	4½	42	CI

One of the famous brands from the Canary Islands, the La Regenta line is famous for its perfect construction, easy draw and mild taste in every shape. A very old brand that had been out of sight for several years, it was returned to the U.S. market by the Marcos Miguel Tobacco Corp. in late 1996. You can find it today in elegant boxes of 25; the No. 1 shape is also available in a 5-pack.

LA RICA HOYA
Handmade in Las Palmas, the Canary Islands of Spain.

Wrapper: Indonesia   Binder: Brazil   Filler: Brazil, Dom. Rep.

Shape	Name	Lgth	Ring	Wrapper
Corona	Corona No. 2	5¼	44	CM
Corona	Yaguas	5¼	42	CM

This is a mild-bodied cigar, offered in boxes of 25.

LA SALLE
Handmade in Santiago, Dominican Republic.

Wrapper: Indonesia   Binder: Dom. Rep.   Filler: Dom. Rep.

Shape	Name	Lgth	Ring	Wrapper
Long Corona	Lonsdale	6	44	CM

Double Corona	Presidente	7½	50	CM
Robusto	Robusto	5	50	CM
Toro	Toro	6	50	CM

This is a medium-bodied cigar, introduced in 1997. It is offered in double-bundles of 20.

LA TANITA
Handmade in Las Palmas, the Canary Islands of Spain.
Wrapper: USA/Connecticut   Binder: Spain   Filler: Brazil, Dom. Rep., Spain

Shape	Name	Lgth	Ring	Wrapper
Lonsdale	No. 1	6¼	43	CC
Corona	No. 2	5½	43	CC
Toro	Especial	6¼	48	CC
Double Corona	Churchill	7½	49	CC
Robusto	Robusto	5¼	50	CC

Here is a mild brand that has been around for more than 50 years, available in cedar boxes of 25.

LA TRADICION CABINET SELECTION
Handmade in Miami, Florida, USA and Esteli, Nicaragua.
Wrapper: Ecuador or USA/Connecticut   Binder: Ecuador
Filler: Dominican Republic, Honduras, Nicaragua

Shape	Name	Lgth	Ring	Wrapper
Long Panatela	Lanceros	7¼	38	CC-CM-Ma
Long Corona	Coronas	6	44	CC-CM-Ma
Robusto	Robustos	5	50	CC-CM-Ma
Double Corona	Churchills	7	49	CC-CM-Ma
Double Corona	Double Coronas	7⅝	50	CC-CM-Ma
Torpedo	Torpedoes	6½	54	CC-CM-Ma

HANDMADE CIGARS: BRAND LISTINGS

Torpedo	Gran Torpedo	7½	60	CC-CM-Ma
Toro	Elite	6	60	CC-CM-Ma

Introduced in 1995, this is a medium-to-full-bodied series from Nick's Cigar Company of Miami, Florida. You can take your choice of wrappers from Connecticut or Ecuador in natural, rosado or maduro wrappers and enjoy them from slide-top, all-cedar boxes of 25.

LA TRADICION CABINET SERIES PERDOMO RESERVE
Handmade in Esteli, Nicaragua.

Wrapper: Ecuador   *Binder: Nicaragua*   *Filler: Nicaragua*

Shape	Name	Lgth	Ring	Wrapper
Torpedo	No. 1	4	55	CM
Perfecto	No. 2	5	55	CM
Perfecto	No. 3	5½	55	CM
Torpedo	X	7	54	CM
Giant	A	9¼	47	CM

Wow! Here's Nick Perdomo's ultimate expression of the cigar maker's art, with gorgeous Rosado wrappers around Cuban-seed filler leaves. Introduced in 1998, the result is a full-bodied taste presented in box-pressed all-mahogany cabinets of 25. Light one up and be somebody!

LA TRADICION CUBANA
Handmade in Miami, Florida, USA.
Wrapper: Ecuador, Indonesia, Mexico
Filler: Dominican Republic, Nicaragua
Binder: Honduras

Shape	Name	Lgth	Ring	Wrapper
Double Corona	Churchill	7	50	CC-CM-Ma
Long Corona	Corona	6	44	CC-CM-Ma
Double Corona	Double Corona	7¼	50	CC-CM-Ma
Long Panatela	Lanceros	7	38	CC-CM-Ma

HANDMADE CIGARS: BRAND LISTINGS

Robusto	Robusto	5	50	CC-CM-Ma
Torpedo	Torpedo	6½	54	CC-CM-Ma
	Made with short filler:			
Short Panatela	Lunchour	5	38	CC

Introduced in 1995, this brand is made under the supervision of the ever-vigilant Luis Sanchez in a small factory which prizes quality above all else. Offered in boxes of 25, the blend has a medium-to-full body in an Ecuadorian or Indonesian natural-shade wrapper or in a full-bodied Mexican maduro wrapper. The Indonesian-wrapped Lunchour shape is available in Amaretto, chocolate, coffee, rum, sweet or vanilla flavors, if desired.

LA TRINIDAD
Handmade in Villa Gonzalez, Dominican Republic.

Wrapper: Indonesia   Binder: Dom. Rep.   Filler: Dom. Rep.

Shape	Name	Lgth	Ring	Wrapper
Robusto	Robusto	5	50	CM
Double Corona	Churchill	7	50	CM
Toro	Toro	6½	50	CM
Torpedo	Torpedo	6	52	CM
Giant Corona	Corona Grande	7¾	44	CM
Giant	Presidente	8	52	CM
Toro	Double Corona	6½	52	CM
Giant Corona	Lonsdale	7½	42	CM
Toro	Corona Extra	6	52	CM
Long Corona	Corona	6	44	CM

This 1997-introduced brand offer a smooth draw and excellent construction. It is a mild-to-medium-bodied cigar and offered in all-cedar boxes of 25.

HANDMADE CIGARS: BRAND LISTINGS

LA TRINIDAD Y CIA.
Handmade in Santiago, Dominican Republic.
Wrapper: Indonesia   Binder: Honduras   Filler: Dom. Rep., Honduras, Nicaragua

Shape	Name	Lgth	Ring	Wrapper
Double Corona	Double Magnum	7	54	CM
Grand Corona	Regalia	6½	46	CM
Lonsdale	Lonsdale	6½	43	CM
Panatela	Panatela Superfino	6	35	CM
Toro	Magnum	5¾	50	CM
Corona	Corona	5½	43	CM
Petit Corona	Half Corona	4¼	40	CM
Robusto	Wavell	5	50	CM

This is a new brand for 1998 and is medium in body with a rich flavor. It is offered in bundles of 20.

LA UNICA
Handmade in Santiago, Dominican Republic.
Wrapper: USA/Connecticut   Binder: Dom. Rep.   Filler: Dom. Rep.

Shape	Name	Lgth	Ring	Wrapper
Giant	No. 100	8½	52	Cl-Ma
Double Corona	No. 200	7	49	Cl-Ma
Lonsdale	No. 300	6¾	44	Cl-Ma
Robusto	No. 400	4½	50	Cl-Ma
Corona	No. 500	5½	42	Cl-Ma

Introduced in 1986, this brand has a mild flavor and aroma in a well-constructed cigar, with a natural or maduro wrapper. An excellent value, these long-filler cigars are packaged in bundles of 20 cigars each.

HANDMADE CIGARS: BRAND LISTINGS

LA VELEZA
Handmade in Tamboril, Dominican Republic.

Wrapper: Indonesia   Binder: Dom. Rep.   Filler: Dom. Rep.

Shape	Name	Lgth	Ring	Wrapper
Robusto	Robusto	5	50	CC
Long Corona	Lonsdale	6	44	CC
Toro	Presidente	6	50	CC
Churchill	Churchill	7	46	CC
Double Corona	Presidente	7½	50	CC
Torpedo	Torpedo	7	54	CC

First marketed in 1997, this brand features a tasty Sumatran wrapper for a mild-to-medium-bodied flavor. It is offered in value-priced bundles of 10 or 25 cigars, except for the Torpedo shape, offered in bundles of 10 or 20.

LA VELEZA
Handmade in Santiago, Dominican Republic.

Wrapper: Dom. Rep.   Binder: Dom. Rep.   Filler: Dom. Rep.

Shape	Name	Lgth	Ring	Wrapper
Robusto	Robusto	5	50	CM
Toro	Lonsdale	6	50	CM
Double Corona	Churchill	7	50	CM

Made of all-Dominican leaves, these are medium in strength and offered in boxes of 25.

LA VENGA
Handmade in Honduras.

Wrapper: Ecuador, Indonesia   Binder: Honduras
Filler: Dominican Republic, Honduras and Nicaragua

Shape	Name	Lgth	Ring	Wrapper
Corona	No. 10	5½	43	CC

Robusto	No. 37	4½	50	CC-Ma
Double Corona	No. 59	7¼	54	CC-Ma
Long Corona	No. 60	6¼	44	CC-Ma
Toro	No. 61	6¼	50	CC-Ma
Corona Extra	No. 62	5½	47	CC-Ma
Churchill	No. 63	7¼	46	CC-Ma
Churchill	No. 70	6¾	48	CC-Ma
Giant	No. 80	8½	52	CC-Ma
	Short-filler tobacco:			
Corona	Fuma	5½	44	CC-Ma

The complex blend of this cigar provides a medium-to-full bodied taste and is offered in economically-priced bundles of 25.

LA VIEJA HABANA
Handmade in Esteli, Nicaragua.

SERIES A:

Wrapper: Ecuador   *Binder: Cameroon*   *Filler: Dom. Rep., Honduras, Nicaragua*

SERIES B:

Wrapper: Cameroon   *Binder: Cameroon*   *Filler: Nicaragua*

Shape	Name	Lgth	Ring	Wrapper
	Series A:			
Torpedo	Bullet	4½	54	CM-Ma
Torpedo	Torpedo no. 1	5½	54	CM-Ma
Torpedo	Torpedo no. 2	6	54	CM-Ma
Torpedo	Torpedo no. 3	6½	54	CM-Ma
Torpedo	Torpedo no. 4	7½	54	CM-Ma
Robusto	Habanos 54	5	54	CM-Ma
	Series B:			

Perfecto	Half Chicago	4½	46	CM
Perfecto	Chicago	5½	50	CM
Perfecto	Full Chicago	6½	52	CM

Named for the old city of Havana — "La Vieja Habana" — this brand offers a medium-to-full-bodied taste with plenty of large shapes in the line. Introduced in 1994, the Series A blend includes a choice of Ecuador-grown rosado or oscuro wrappers. The Series B (Chicago) group was introduced in 1998 and offers a full-bodied taste with Cameroon binder and wrapper. Each cigar is tissue-wrapped and presented in boxes of 25.

LADY CLUB

Handmade, with mixed filler, in Santiago, Dominican Republic.

Wrapper: Indonesia   *Binder: Indonesia*   *Filler: Dom. Rep.*

Shape	Name	Lgth	Ring	Wrapper
Perfecto		3¾	44	CC
Small Panatela		5	30	CC
Short Panatela		5	38	CC
Robusto		5	50	CC
Long Corona		6	44	CC
Toro		6	50	CC
Lonsdale		6½	42	CC
Lonsdale		6½	44	CC
Grand Corona		6½	46	CC
Long Panatela		7	38	CC
Churchill		7	48	CC
Double Corona		7½	50	CC

Introduced in 1998, this is a medium-bodied flavored cigar, made with mixed filler. It has a Sumatra-seed wrapper and is available in bundles of 25. There are no shape names.

HANDMADE CIGARS: BRAND LISTINGS

LADY JANE
Handmade in Danli, Honduras.

Wrapper: Indonesia   *Binder: Honduras*   *Filler: Honduras, Mexico*

Shape	Name	Lgth	Ring	Wrapper
Long Corona	Princesa	6¼	44	CC
Corona	Petit Corona	5½	42	CC

There are just two shapes in this brand, but they offer a pleasant, mild-bodied flavor with a Sumatra wrapper. Lady Jane cigars are presented in cellophane sleeves in boxes of 25.

LAMBS CLUB
Handmade in Santiago, Dominican Republic.

Wrapper: Ecuador   *Binder: Honduras*   *Filler: Brazil, Dom. Rep.*

Shape	Name	Lgth	Ring	Wrapper
Double Corona	Churchill	7	50	CC
Long Corona	Corona Extra	6½	43	CC
Toro	Toro	6	50	CC
Robusto	Rothschild	4¾	50	CC
Petit Corona	Chico	4¾	40	CC

Lambs Club is a super-premium Dominican cigar, handmade by one of the most respected manufacturers in that country. Its rich, flavorful character is derived from the finest Dominican Olor and Piloto tobaccos, which together with a smooth Ecuadorian wrapper, develops a spicy, medium-bodied taste.

LARS TETENS PHAT CIGARS
Handmade in New York, New York, USA.

EL NIÑO:

Wrapper: Cameroon   *Binder: Venezuela*   *Filler: Venezuela*

GOLF:

Wrapper: Ecuador   *Binder: Dom. Rep.*   *Filler: Dom. Rep. Venezuela*

HANDMADE CIGARS: BRAND LISTINGS

GRASS:
Wrapper: Cameroon or USA/Connecticut
Binder: Dominican Republic   *Filler: Dominican Republic*

HAPPY CUBA:
Wrapper: Ecuador   *Binder: Dom. Rep.*   *Filler: Dom. Rep.*

MUSASHI:
Wrapper: Cameroon and USA/Connecticut
Binder: Dominican Republic   *Filler: Dominican Republic, Venezuela*

PHAT CIGARS:
Wrapper: Cameroon and USA/Connecticut
Binder: Dominican Republic   *Filler: Dominican Republic*

PHAT PHREE:
Wrapper: Cameroon   *Binder and Filler: international blend*

TESSHU TOBAC:
Wrapper: Cameroon or USA/Connecticut
Binder: Dom. Rep. or Venezuela   *Filler: Dom. Rep., Venezuela*

T.G.S.:
Wrapper: Cameroon   *Binder: Dom. Rep.*   *Filler: Dom. Rep., Venezuela*

Shape	Name	Lgth	Ring	Wrapper
	El Niño:			
Robusto	El Nino	5	50	CM
	Golf:			
Double Corona	Brassie	7	50	CC
Corona	Niblick	5½	42	CC
Robusto	Mashie	5	50	CC
	Happy Cuba:			
Double Corona	No. 1	7½	50	CM
Long Corona	No. 2	6	44	CM
Robusto	No. 3	5¼	50	CM

HANDMADE CIGARS: BRAND LISTINGS

	Phat Cigars:			
Double Corona	Churchill	7½	50	CI
Pyramid	Asadachi	6	60	CI
Toro	Brief XTC	6	50	CI
Lonsdale	Sun Fook Ka	6½	44	CI
Long Corona	Royal	6	44	CI
Robusto	Shorty	5¼	50	CI
Panatela	Slim	5¼	36	CI
	Phat Phree, made with short filler:			
Petit Corona	Big Tone	4½	42	CM
Small Panatela	Aircatcher *(machine-made)*	4	30	CM
	Musashi:			
Double Corona	Two Skies	7½	52	CM
Robusto	5 Rings	5¼	50	CI
Corona Extra	Sport	3	45	CI
	Tesshu Tobac:			
Double Corona	Fusako	7	66	CC
Toro	Seizan	6	50	CC
Robusto	Yamaoka	5	50	CC
	T.G.S. Series:			
Double Corona	T.G.S.	7	50	CM
	Grass:			
Small Panatela	Da Joint	4½	34	CM
Pyramid	Medium	4	50	CM
Pyramid	Big	5	62	CM
Pyramid	Bigger	6	62	CM

HANDMADE CIGARS: BRAND LISTINGS

This mysterious, 1995-introduced brand is hard to find, expensive and utterly impossible to explain. The cigars are rolled in New York with constantly changing shapes, names, sizes and blend; this listing is a snapshot of the brand at the time of publication. The relative strengths of the series include El Niño, mild; Phat Phree and Tesshu: mild to medium; Phat: medium; Golf, medium through full, depending on size; Happy Cuba and Musashi: medium to full, and Grass and T.G.S.: full-bodied. Some of the lines are treated with special oils; there are also two free-form lines: "Evolving" with constantly changing shapes and blends and "Rare and Expensive," reportedly made with pre-embargo Cuban tobacco. Some people like these cigars, some do not. They are, however, unique. And no other brand can claim any bands that rival this one for size, color or the quality of artwork, perhaps a collector's item in the making.

LAS CABRILLAS
Handmade in Danli, Honduras.

Wrapper: USA/Connecticut   Binder: Mexico   Filler: Nicaragua

Shape	Name	Lgth	Ring	Wrapper
Small Panatela	Pizarro	5½	32	CC
Double Corona	Maximilian	7	56	CC-Ma
Giant	Columbus	8¼	52	CC-Ma
Double Corona	Balboa	7½	54	CC-Ma
Double Corona	De Soto	6⅞	50	CC-Ma
Robusto	Cortez	4¾	50	CC-Ma
Lonsdale	Ponce de Leon	6¾	44	CC-Ma
Churchill	Vasco de Gama	7	48	CC-Ma
Long Corona	Magellan	6	42	CC
Panatela	Coronado	6⅞	35	CC

The explorers of the "New World" are saluted in this brand, which debuted in 1993 and which offers a medium-bodied taste. New in 1997 is the Maximilian, a double corona, which will be offered in boxes of 20, and the Vasco de Gama, which like the rest of the brand – except Columbus (10s) and Pizarro (60s) – is available in boxes of 25.

HANDMADE CIGARS: BRAND LISTINGS

LAS VEGAS CIGAR CO.
Handmade in Las Vegas, Nevada, USA.

Wrapper: Ecuador, Mexico   Binder: Dom. Rep.   Filler: Dom. Rep., Mexico

Shape	Name		Lgth	Ring	Wrapper
Robusto	Rothchild		4½	52	Cl-Ma
Small Panatela	Nix		5	30	Cl
Corona	Corona		5¾	42	Cl-Ma
Lonsdale	Corona Largo		6¾	44	Cl
Corona	Montefino		5¾	52	Cl-Ma
Grand Corona	Fuma	(short filler)	6¾	46	Cl
Panatela	Panatela		6¾	36	Cl
Double Corona	Churchill		7½	50	Cl-Ma
Giant	Excalibur		8¾	52	Cl-Ma
Toro	El Rey Corto		5	62	Cl-Ma
Torpedo	Torpedo		7	60	Cl-Ma
Lonsdale	Rum		6¾	44	Cl-Ma

You'll find this small factory in a storefront on the famous Las Vegas Strip. The body varies from mild (Corona, Corona Largo) to heavy (Excalibur, El Rey), with the majority of the sizes rated as medium. Note the large number of shapes with big ring gauges. All of the shapes are available sweetened, and vanilla flavoring is available in the Nix size only.

LE BONNE CIGARE
Handmade in Santiago, Dominican Republic.

Wrapper: Indonesia   Binder: Dom. Rep.   Filler: Dom. Rep.

Shape	Name	Lgth	Ring	Wrapper
Lonsdale	Corona	6½	44	CM
Lonsdale	Lonsdale	7	44	CM
Double Corona	Churchill	7½	49	CM

HANDMADE CIGARS: BRAND LISTINGS

Toro	Robusto	6	50	CM

This is a mild cigar which debuted in 1997. It is offered in economical bundles of 25.

LEGACY
Handmade in Danli, Honduras.

Wrapper: Ecuador *Binder: Honduras* *Filler: Honduras*

Shape	Name	Lgth	Ring	Wrapper
Giant	No. 6 Napoleon	8½	52	CC
Double Corona	No. 5 Monarch	7	52	CC
Churchill	No. 4 Corona Grande	7½	46	CC
Lonsdale	No. 3 Elegante	7	43	CC
Robusto	No. 2 Rothchild	5	50	CC
Long Corona	No. 1 Super Cetro	6	43	CC

This is a premium, imported cigar offered in unique 18-pack bundles. Made entirely by hand with high-quality, long-filler tobaccos, the price is just as captivating as the medium-bodied taste.

THE LEGEND
Handmade in Esteli, Nicaragua.

Wrapper: Nicaragua *Binder: Nicaragua* *Filler: Nicaragua*

Shape	Name	Lgth	Ring	Wrapper
Robusto	Robusto	4½	52	CC
Toro	Corona	6	50	CC
Double Corona	Churchill	7	52	CC

The Connecticut-seed wrappers gives this 1997-introduced brand from the Texana Cigar Co. a mild-to-medium-bodied taste. Try them in boxes of 25!

HANDMADE CIGARS: BRAND LISTINGS

LEGION
Handmade in Esteli, Nicaragua.

Wrapper: Ecuador   Binder: Nicaragua   Filler: Nicaragua

Shape	Name	Lgth	Ring	Wrapper
Giant	No. 852	8	52	CI
Churchill	No. 748	7	48	CI
Toro	No. 650	6	50	CI
Robusto	No. 450	4¾	50	CI
Lonsdale	No. 644	6½	44	CI
Corona	No. 544	5½	44	CI
Toro	No. 654	6	54	CI
Double Corona	No. 752	7	52	CI

New in 1997, this is a medium-bodied brand with an elegant aroma, offered in boxes of 25.

LEMPIRA
Handmade in Danli, Honduras.

Wrapper: Ecuador   Binder: Costa Rica.   Filler: Costa Rica, Honduras, Nicaragua

Shape	Name	Lgth	Ring	Wrapper
Corona	Coronas	5½	42	Co
Robusto	Robusto	5	50	Co
Lonsdale	Lonsdale	6½	44	Co
Long Panatela	Lanceros	7½	38	Co
Toro	Toro	6	50	Co
Churchill	Churchills	7	48	Co
Double Corona	Presidents	7¾	50	Co

The Lempira is manufactured in Honduras using a blended filler from Costa Rica, Honduras and Nicaragua, adding a binder from Costa Rica for extra flavor.

HANDMADE CIGARS: BRAND LISTINGS

The wrapper is Ecuadorian-grown, Connecticut Shade. This is a medium-strength cigar with lots of flavor. It is offered in boxes of 20.

LEON
Handmade in Los Angeles, California, USA.

Wrapper: Ecuador   Binder & Filler: Central American blend

Shape	Name	Lgth	Ring	Wrapper
Lonsdale	Cazadores	7	44	Ma
Lonsdale	Cetro	6½	44	CC
Churchill	Cubarro	7	46	CC
Lonsdale	Fuma	7	44	Ma
Long Panatela	Panetelas	7	36	CC
Double Corona	Presidentes	7½	50	CC-Ma
Lonsdale	Numero 4	6½	44	Ma
Toro	Tronquito	5¾	50	CC-Ma
Giant	Gigante	8	52	Ma

In a nondescript shop on 6th Street in midtown Los Angeles is Roberto Leon, putting together handmade, medium-bodied cigars that are favored by enthusiasts who appreciate quality and value. One common sight: motorcycle-mounted police lighting up a Presidentes for the road!

LEON JIMENES
Handmade in the Santiago, Dominican Republic.

Wrapper: USA/Connecticut   Binder: Dom. Rep.   Filler: Dom. Rep.

Shape	Name	Lgth	Ring	Wrapper
Double Corona	No. 1	7½	50	CM
Churchill	No. 2	7	47	CM
Lonsdale	No. 3	6½	42	CM
Corona	No. 4	5⅝	42	CM
Short Panatela	No. 5	5	38	CM

Robusto	Robusto		5½	50	CM
Pyramid	Torpedo		6	58	CM
Torpedo	Gran Corona		6½	50	CM
Torpedo	Belicoso		6¼	52	CM
Robusto	Petit Belicoso		5	52	CM
Churchill	Churchill De Luxe		7	47	CM
Lonsdale	Cristal	(tubed)	6½	42	CM
Small Panatela	Petites		4	30	CM

Introduced in the 1970s, Leon Jimenes is a hand-made, medium-bodied cigar with Dominican fillers and binder, encased in a Connecticut wrapper that provides excellent balance and an exquisite aroma. The brand is presented in individual cellophane sleeves, packed in elegant all-cedar boxes of 5, 10 or 25 in most shapes.

LEOPOLDO
Handmade in Santiago, Dominican Republic.
Wrapper: Indonesia   *Binder: Dom. Rep.*   *Filler: Dom. Rep.*

Shape	Name	Lgth	Ring	Wrapper
Robusto	Robusto	5	50	CM
Double Corona	Double Corona	7½	50	CM
Long Corona	Corona	6¼	44	CM
Toro	Churchill	6½	53	CM

This brand was introduced in 1997 and offers a mild taste in boxes of 25.

LEROY NEIMAN
BY DON DIEGO
Handmade in La Romana, Dominican Republic.
Wrapper: USA/Connecticut   *Binder: Dom. Rep.*   *Filler: Brazil, Dom. Rep.*

HANDMADE CIGARS: BRAND LISTINGS

Shape	Name	Lgth	Ring	Wrapper
Lonsdale	LeRoy Nieman Selection	6¾	44	CC

This unique one-size brand was introduced in 1997 and features a striking artwork on the box to go along with the medium-bodied flavor. A limited number of boxes are signed by the artist.

LEVIATHAN
Handmade in Santiago, Dominican Republic.
Wrapper: Ecuador, Mexico   Binder: Dom. Rep.   Filler: Dom. Rep.

Shape	Name	Lgth	Ring	Wrapper
Toro	Toro	6	60	CC-Ma
Double Corona	Churchill	7	60	CC-Ma
Giant	Presidente	8	60	CC-Ma

Supersize me! These all-60-ring cigars are medium in body and are offered in a choice of natural (Ecuador) or Mexican maduro wrappers in elegant boxes of 20.

LEW'S SMOKERS
Handmade in Cofradia, Honduras.
Wrapper: Honduras   Binder: Mexico   Filler: Honduras

Shape	Name	Lgth	Ring	Wrapper
Churchill	Sunday Special	7	48	CM
Long Corona	Pop's Choice	6	44	CM

This brand debuted in 1996, created by the endlessly creative Lew Rothman, who puts his name on a medium-bodied blend of Havana seed fillers, Mexican binder and Connecticut-seed wrappers grown in Honduras. The gimmick? A special sweetening of the gum used to seal the cap, to give a sweet taste upon lighting!

LEW'S SMOKERS
Handmade in Esteli, Nicaragua.
Wrapper: Nicaragua   Binder: Nicaragua   Filler: Dom. Rep., Honduras, Nicaragua

HANDMADE CIGARS: BRAND LISTINGS

Shape	Name	Lgth	Ring	Wrapper
Lonsdale	No. 100	6½	43	CM
Corona	No. 200	5½	43	CM
Grand Corona	No. 300	5⅝	45	CM
Robusto	No. 400	4½	50	CM
Toro	No. 500	6	50	CM
Churchill	No. 600	6⅞	48	CM

This is a 1998-introduced, medium-bodied cigar with all-long filler tobaccos. It is an excellent value, offered in packs of 10.

LICENCIADOS
Handmade in Santiago, Dominican Republic.
Wrapper: USA/Connecticut   Binder: Dom. Rep.   Filler: Dom. Rep.

Shape	Name	Lgth	Ring	Wrapper
Double Corona	Churchill	7	50	CM
Long Corona	Excellentes	6¾	43	CM
Small Panatela	Expreso	4½	35	CM
Torpedo	Figurado	6	56	CM
Corona	No. 4	5¾	43	CM
Long Panatela	Panatela Linda	7	38	CM
Giant	Presidentes	8	50	CM
Giant	Soberanos	8½	52	CM
Toro	Toro	6	50	CM
Robusto	Wavell	5	50	CC-Ma
Corona	No. 200	5¾	43	Ma
Lonsdale	No. 300	6¾	43	Ma
Toro	No. 400	6	50	Ma
Giant	No. 500	8	50	Ma

HANDMADE CIGARS: BRAND LISTINGS

Introduced in 1988, this veteran handmade brand has earned a reputation for excellence in taste, construction and value. The wide range of shapes and medium-bodied flavor makes it accessible to many smokers. It is offered in colorful boxes of 25.

LICEY
Handmade in Licey, Dominican Republic.

Wrapper: Indonesia   *Binder: Dom. Rep.*   *Filler: Dom. Rep.*

Shape	Name	Lgth	Ring	Wrapper
Giant	Churchill	8	48	Ma
Long Corona	Diplomatico	6	44	Ma
Pyramid	Piramid	6½	53	Ma
Robusto	Robusto	5	50	Ma
Grand Corona	Double Corona	6½	46	Ma

Named for the city of its birth, this cigar offers a mild-bodied flavor in an all-maduro line. Look for it in elegant cedar cabinets of 25.

LITTLE BIG MAN
Handmade in San Andres Tuxtla, Mexico.

Wrapper: Mexico   *Binder: Mexico*   *Filler: Mexico*

Shape	Name	Lgth	Ring	Wrapper
Giant	Double Corona	8	50	CC
Double Corona	Giant	7¼	52	CC
Churchill	Grand Corona	7	46	CC
Churchill	Churchill	7	48	CC
Toro	Robusto Extra	6	52	CC
Lonsdale	Lonsdale	6½	42	CC
Slim Panatela	Slim Panatela	6	33	CC
Toro	Toro Extra	6¼	50	CC
Robusto	Robusto	5½	48	CC

Small Panatela	Short Panatela	4¾	33	CC
Robusto	Toro	5	50	CC

Created in 1989 and introduced to the U.S. in 1995, the Sumatra-seed wrapper helps to give this brand a medium-to-full-bodied flavor. Introduced in 1998, it is offered in cellophane sleeves in cedar boxes of 25.

LOAIZA UNO
Handmade in Quevedo, Ecuador.

Wrapper: Ecuador   *Binder: Ecuador*   *Filler: Ecuador*

Shape	Name	Lgth	Ring	Wrapper
Robusto	Uno	4½	48	CM

This one-size brand was introduced in 1997. It offers a mild-bodied taste and is offered in cedar boxes of 25.

LONE WOLF
Handmade in Santiago, Dominican Republic.

                 LOBO ROJO:

Wrapper: Indonesia   *Binder: Dom. Rep.*   *Filler: Dom. Rep.*

            SIGNATURE SELECT:

Wrapper: USA/Connecticut   *Binder: Dom. Rep.*   *Filler: Dom. Rep.*

             VINTAGE SERIES:

Wrapper: Indonesia   *Binder: Dom. Rep.*   *Filler: Dom. Rep.*

Shape	Name	Lgth	Ring	Wrapper
	Lobo Rojo:			
Robusto	Robusto	5	50	Co
Short Panatela	Petit Corona	5	38	Co
Lonsdale	Lonsdale	6⅜	44	Co
Torpedo	Belicoso	6¼	52	Co
Churchill	Churchill	6⅜	48	Co

HANDMADE CIGARS: BRAND LISTINGS

Double Corona	Double Corona	7½	50	Co
	Signature Select:			
Robusto	Robusto	5	50	CC
Corona	Corona	5½	44	CC
Toro	Toro	6	50	CC
Torpedo	Triangular	6	52	CC
Double Corona	Churchill	7	50	CC
	Vintage Series:			
Robusto	Robusto	4½	50	CC
Corona	Corona	5½	42	CC
Toro	Toro	6	50	CC
Torpedo	Torpedo	6	52	CC
Churchill	Churchill	6¾	48	CC
Double Corona	Double Corona	7½	50	CC
	Machine-made:			
Small Panatela	Lobitos	4	30	CC

Lone Wolf is a 1996-created brand developed by well-known film and television stars Jim Belushi and Chuck Norris. Three different Dominican manufacturers are involved in the making of these cigars, which offer a taste for every palate. Belushi's Lobo Rojo ("Red Wolf") series features a Cameroon-seed wrapper and is considered medium-bodied in strength. The Signature Select blend is chosen by Norris for its mild-to-medium-bodied taste and complex blend of flavors. It is offered in traditional 8-9-8 varnished boxes. The Vintage Series also has a mild-to-medium strength of flavor using two-year aged Dominican filler and an Indonesian wrapper. The Lobitos, introduced in 1998, has a Connecticut wrapper, Dominican filler and Dominican short filler. It is mild in flavor.

LONG ISLAND
Handmade in Tamboril, Dominican Republic and Esteli, Nicaragua.

HANDMADE CIGARS: BRAND LISTINGS

Wrapper: Indonesia	*DOMINICAN SELECTION:* *Binder: Dom. Rep.*				*Filler: Dom. Rep.*

Wrapper: Nicaragua	*NICARAGUAN SELECTION:* *Binder: Nicaragua*				*Filler: Nicaragua*

Shape	Name	Lgth	Ring	Wrapper
	Dominican Selection:			
Toro	East Hampton	6	50	CM
Robusto	Gold Coast	5	50	CM
Grand Corona	North Fork	6	46	CM
Robusto	South Fork	5	50	CM
Double Corona	West Hampton	7	50	CM
	Nicaraguan Selection:			
Double Corona	No. 1	7	50	CM
Toro	No. 2	6	50	CM
Lonsdale	No. 3	6½	44	CM
Robusto	No. 4	5	50	CM

Take your choice of these medium-bodied blends, from either the Dominican Republic or Nicaragua. The Dominican style is offered in all-cedar boxes of 25, while the Nicaraguan line is presented in bundles of 25.

LOS NICAS
Handmade in Esteli, Nicaragua.

Wrapper: Nicaragua	*Binder: Nicaragua*				*Filler: Nicaragua*

Shape	Name	Lgth	Ring	Wrapper
Robusto	Robusto	5	50	CC
Corona	Corona	5½	42	CC
Toro	Grande Robusto	6	50	CC
Double Corona	Presidente	7	50	CC

HANDMADE CIGARS: BRAND LISTINGS

Here is a new cigar in 1997, with a medium body. It is available in today's most popular shapes (look at those 50-ring sizes!) and offered in bundles of 25 or in boxes of 5 or 25.

LOS PEREZ
Handmade in Tamboril, Dominican Republic.

Wrapper: Indonesia   Binder: Dom. Rep.   Filler: Dom. Rep.

Shape	Name	Lgth	Ring	Wrapper
Torpedo	Torpedo	6½	54	CM
Double Corona	Churchill	7½	50	CM
Toro	Toro	6¼	50	CM
Lonsdale	Lonsdale	6¼	44	CM
Robusto	Robusto	5	50	CM
Corona	Corona	5½	42	CM

This is a new brand for 1998, mild-to-medium in body and offered in your choice of bundles, boxes or even a humidified jar of 25!

LUIS ALEJANDRO
Handmade in Miami, Florida, USA.
Wrapper: Ecuador or USA/Connecticut

Binder: Ecuador   Filler: Dominican Republic, Honduras

Shape	Name	Lgth	Ring	Wrapper
Corona	Corona	5½	42	Co-Ma
Long Panatela	Lancero	7¼	38	Co-Ma
Robusto	Robusto	4⅞	50	Co-Ma
Toro	Toro	6	50	Co-Ma
Churchill	Churchill	7	47	Co-Ma
Double Corona	Double Corona	7⅝	50	Co-Ma
Giant	Presidente	8	52	Co-Ma
Torpedo	Torpedo	6½	54	Co-Ma

HANDMADE CIGARS: BRAND LISTINGS

This brand debuted in 1997 and is produced in a small factory in Miami. Two different wrappers are available: rosado or maduro. Each is offered in a slide-top box of 25 cellophane-wrapped cigars each.

LUNA AZUL
Handmade in Navarette, Dominican Republic.
Wrapper: Dominican Republic, Indonesia or USA/Connecticut

Binder: Dominican Republic   *Filler: Dominican Republic*

Shape	Name	Lgth	Ring	Wrapper
Double Corona	Churchill	7½	50	CC-CM
Robusto	Robusto	5½	50	CC-CM-Ma
Grand Corona	Corona Grande	6¾	46	CM
Lonsdale	Corona	6¼	44	CM
Corona	Petite Corona	5½	42	CM
Churchill	Double Corona	6¾	48	CC-CM
Giant	Full Moon	9½	50	CM
Pyramid	Pyramid	6	52	CC-CM
Perfecto	Perfecto	4½	50	CM

The idea behind the name? "Cigars this good come only once in a blue moon!" This is a medium-bodied blend, offered in cedar boxes of 25, in bundles of 25 or in special cedar carry cases of three cigars in the Corona Grande and Churchill sizes. The Full Moon comes as a single, only. The 1998-introduced maduro wrapper makes that style a medium-to-full-bodied smoke.

M.A.C.
Handmade in Tamboril, Dominican Republic.
Wrapper: Indonesia or USA/Connecticut

Binder: Dominican Republic   *Filler: Dominican Republic*

Shape	Name	Lgth	Ring	Wrapper
	Indonesian wrapper:			
Robusto	Robusto	5	50	CM

Long Corona	Rothchild	6¼	42	CM
Double Corona	Churchill	7½	50	CM
Torpedo	Figurado	6½	53	CM
Perfecto	Petit Perfecto	4½	53	CM
Toro	Toro	6	54	CM
	Connecticut wrapper:			
Robusto	Robusto	5	50	CC
Torpedo	Figurado	6½	53	CC
Petit Corona	Baby MAC	4½	42	CC
Toro	Toro	6	54	CC
Perfecto	Perfecto	5½	43	CC

Here is a medium-bodied brand from the Morgan Alexander Cigar Company, aged for at least 45 days after rolling. It is presented in wood boxes of 25.

M.C.
Handmade in Santiago, Dominican Republic.

Wrapper: Indonesia   *Binder: Dom. Rep.*   *Filler: Dom. Rep.*

Shape	Name	Lgth	Ring	Wrapper
Double Corona	Churchill	7	50	CM
Torpedo	Torpedo	6	52	CM
Robusto	Robusto	5	50	CM
Corona	Corona	5½	42	CM

This is a medium-bodied cigar first offered in 1998 with a Sumatra wrapper and Piloto Cubano filler. It has a rich flavor and is offered in bundles of 25.

M.P.
Handmade in Jalapa, Nicaragua.

Wrapper: Nicaragua   *Binder: Nicaragua*   *Filler: Nicaragua*

HANDMADE CIGARS: BRAND LISTINGS

Shape	Name	Lgth	Ring	Wrapper
Lonsdale	Coronas	6½	44	CM
Perfecto	Hemingway Perfecto	7	50	CM
Long Panatela	Panatelas	7	36	CM
Panatela	Petit Royal	5½	36	CM
Churchill	Presidente	7	46	CM
Robusto	Robusto	5	50	CM

These are medium-bodied cigars which have been produced in one form or another since 1972. They are offered in individual cellophane sleeves in boxes of bundles of 25.

MACABANA
Handmade in San Andres Tuxtla, Mexico.

Wrapper: Mexico   Binder: Mexico   Filler: Mexico

Shape	Name	Lgth	Ring	Wrapper
Perfecto	Antiguo	5	54	CM

Introduced in 1996, this is a mild-bodied blend in a perfecto shape, offered without cellophane in boxes of 25.

MACABI
Handmade in Santiago, Dominican Republic.

Wrapper: USA/Connecticut   Binder: Mexico   Filler: Dom. Rep.

Shape	Name	Lgth	Ring	Wrapper
Double Corona	Super Corona	7¾	52	Co
Double Corona	Double Corona	6⅞	49	Co
Lonsdale	No. 1	6¾	44	Co
Torpedo	Belicoso Fino	6¼	52	Co
Toro	Corona Extra	6	50	Co
Corona	Media Corona	5½	43	Co

Robusto	Royal Corona	5	50	Co

Introduced in 1995, this brand – launched as the "pride of Miami" – has been made in Santiago, Dominican Republic beginning in 1997. Handmade in the centuries-old tradition and under the watchful eye of master cigar maker Juan Sosa, Macabi brings a mild-bodied flavor to connoisseurs of fine cigars. Very smooth and slightly spicy, these gems are offered uncellophaned in slide-top cedar boxes.

MACANUDO
Handmade in Santiago, Dominican Republic
and in Kingston, Jamaica.

Wrapper: USA/Connecticut   Binder: Mexico   Filler: Dom. Rep., Jamaica, Mexico

Shape	Name	Lgth	Ring	Wrapper
	Handmade in Jamaica:			
Small Panatela	Ascot	4⅛	32	Cl
Short Panatela	Caviar	4	36	Cl
Slim Panatela	Claybourne	6	31	DC-Cl
Short Panatela	Petit Corona	5	38	Cl
Corona	Duke of Devon	5½	42	DC-Cl-Ma
Long Panatela	Portofino *(tubed)*	7	34	Cl
Corona	Hampton Court *(tubed)*	5¾	43	Cl
Robusto	Hyde Park	5½	49	Cl-Ma
Lonsdale	Baron de Rothschild	6½	42	DC-Cl-Ma
Robusto	Crystal *(tubed)*	5½	50	Cl
Torpedo	Duke of Windsor	6	50	Cl
Giant	Prince of Wales	8	52	Cl
Cigarillo	Miniature	3¾	24	Cl
	Handmade in the Dominican Republic:			
Double Corona	Prince Philip	7½	49	DC-Cl-Ma
	Vintage Cabinet Selection, handmade in Jamaica:			

MACANUDO.®
True cigar taste. Every time.

© 1998 Montego y Cia

HANDMADE CIGARS: BRAND LISTINGS

Double Corona	I		7½	49	CM
Lonsdale	II		6½	43	CM
Corona	III		5½	43	CM
Corona Extra	IV		4½	47	CM
Robusto	V		5½	49	CM
Torpedo	VI		6	52	CM
Long Panatela	VII		7½	38	CM
Robusto	VIII	(tubed)	5½	50	CM
Churchill	XX		7	47	CM

An exceptionally consistent cigar, made with Connecticut Shade wrappers that have been aged for at least three years. The cigar has a silky feel to the hand and has a taste which is only found in a Macanudo. The Vintage Cabinet Selection cigars are each more than four years in the making and include filler leaves from the Dominican Republic and Mexico. Vintage Cabinet cigars have been offered only in the following years: 1979, 1984, 1988 and 1993.

MACANUDO ROBUST
Handmade in Santiago, Dominican Republic.
Wrapper: USA/Connecticut   Binder: USA/Connecticut   Filler: Dom. Rep.

Shape	Name		Lgth	Ring	Wrapper
Double Corona	Prince Philip		7½	49	CM
Lonsdale	Baron de Rothschild		6½	42	CM
Corona	Duke of Devon		5½	42	CM
Robusto	Hyde Park		5½	49	CM
Corona	Hampton Court	(tubed)	5¾	43	CM
Short Panatela	Petit Corona		5	38	CM

Introduced in 1998, this was the "buzz" of the Retail Tobacco Dealers of America trade show. Can Macanudo Robust succeed where New Coke failed? As a medium-to-full-bodied brand, can it find fans where its older sibling became the top-selling handmade brand in America by being so mild? You can find it in

MACARENA Cigars

A cigar hand made with delicacy
and care which only Spanish
women are capable of putting
into such a task.

Due to this, Macarena cigars are
quite unique, and can be set
aside for connoisseurs.

When you think of a great cigar,
think of Macarena.

What CAN YOU EXPECT
from the hands
of a Spanish WOMAN?

Always a MASTERPIECE

THE GREEN BOX

HANDMADE CIGARS: BRAND LISTINGS

boxes of 25, except for the Prince Philip size, offered in 10s.

MACARENA
Handmade in Las Palmas, the Canary Islands of Spain.
Wrapper: USA/Connecticut   Binder: Indonesia   Filler: Brazil, Dom. Rep., Indonesia

Shape	Name	Lgth	Ring	Wrapper
Double Corona	Doble Corona	7½	50	CC
Toro	Toro	6	50	CC
Robusto	Robusto	5	50	CC
Lonsdale	Lonsdale	6½	43	CC

Yes, it's a cigar inspired by the dance craze of the mid-90s, the "macarena." Although smoking this brand might not make you a better dancer, it will certainly mark you as a keen observer of pop culture! The blend is mild and this 1997-introduced brand is offered in boxes of 25 cigars each.

MACBETH
Handmade in Santiago, Dominican Republic.
Wrapper: USA/Connecticut   Binder: Mexico   Filler: Dom. Rep., Mexico

Shape	Name	Lgth	Ring	Wrapper
Giant	Duncan	8	50	CC
Churchill	Malcolm	7	48	CC
Long Corona	Macduff	6	43	CC
Robusto	Banquo	4½	50	CC

Shakespeare would be proud. Here is a full-bodied cigar that was introduced in 1998 and offered in boxes of 25, except for the Duncan shape, offered in 16s.

MACURO
Handmade in Guiria Ed. Sucre, Venezuela.
Wrapper: Venezuela   Binder: Venezuela   Filler: Venezuela

Shape	Name	Lgth	Ring	Wrapper
Double Corona	Trinidad	7	52	CM

HANDMADE CIGARS: BRAND LISTINGS

Grand Corona	Colon	6	46	CM
Robusto	Orinoco	5	52	CM
Small Panatela	Niño	5	34	CM
Pyramid	Piramide No. 1	6½	54	CM
Pyramid	Piramide No. 2	3½	50	CM
Torpedo	Torpedo No. 1	6½	52	CM
Torpedo	Torpedo No. 2	3½	52	CM
Petit Corona	Tatu	3½	44	CM

This all-Venezuelan brand offers a full-bodied taste. It is offered in individual cellophane sleeves in cedar boxes of 25, except for the Tatu shape that is available in 24s.

MADAME MARSHALL
BY DANIEL MARSHALL
Handmade in Santiago, Dominican Republic.

Wrapper: Cameroon   *Filler: Dominican Republic*

Shape	Name	Lgth	Ring	Wrapper
Small Panatela	Madame Marshall	4	30	CC

New for 1997, this is a small but very well made cigar from the Dominican Republic. It has a medium-bodied taste thanks to the Cameroon wrapper and is offered in elegant, all-cedar boxes.

MADRIGAL HABANA
Handmade in San Andres Tuxtla, Mexico.

Wrapper: Mexico   Binder: Mexico   *Filler: Mexico*

Shape	Name	Lgth	Ring	Wrapper
Giant	Monarch	8	54	CC-Ma
Double Corona	Imperial	7½	52	CC-Ma
Robusto	Robusto	5	52	CC-Ma

HANDMADE CIGARS: BRAND LISTINGS

Toro	Governor	6	50	CC-Ma
Lonsdale	Classic Corona	7	44	CC-Ma
Corona	Petit Corona	5½	42	CC-Ma

Re-introduced in 1996, this is an old Havana brand which had been kicked around by several cigar manufacturers since the 1970s and was produced primarily in Honduras. In 1985, Brick-Hanauer acquired the brand and found the right formula for a new, mild smoke featuring all-Mexican tobacco. The blend includes Connecticut Shade-seed tobacco for the natural wrappers and Jaltepec leaves for the maduro wrappers. Even the box speaks elegance: it is an exact copy of a 1927 box of Madrigal, then made in Havana.

MADUROS DOMINICANOS
Handmade in Santiago, Dominican Republic.
Wrapper: Dom. Rep.   *Binder: Dom. Rep.*   *Filler: Dom. Rep.*

Shape	Name	Lgth	Ring	Wrapper
Robusto	Amistad	5	50	Ma
Long Corona	El Niño	6	44	Ma
Double Corona	Tornado	7	50	Ma

Here is an all-maduro blend that features all-Dominican aged leaves. It is fairly mild in taste and offered in cedar boxes of 25.

MAESTRO CUBANO
Handmade in Danli, Honduras.
Wrapper: Indonesia   *Binder: Honduras*   *Filler: Honduras, Mexico*

Shape	Name	Lgth	Ring	Wrapper
Robusto	Robusto	5	50	CC
Double Corona	Churchill Original Label	7½	52	CC
Torpedo	Torpido Figurado	6	52	CC
Long Corona	Lonsdale	6¼	44	CC

HANDMADE CIGARS: BRAND LISTINGS

This brand debuted in late 1996 and offers a medium-bodied taste. It features a Sumatra-seed wrapper and a two-nation interior blend that is presented in varnished, all-cedar boxes of 25.

MAESTRO DE LA PALMA
Handmade in Las Palmas, the Canary Islands of Spain.
Wrapper: Indonesia or USA/Connecticut

Binder: Canary Islands   *Filler: Canary Islands*

Shape	Name	Lgth	Ring	Wrapper
Robusto	Santa Cruz	4¾	50	CM-Ma
Corona Extra	Urbano	5½	46	CM-Ma
Grand Corona	Punta Gorda	6½	46	CM
Double Corona	El Paso	7¼	50	CM

Here is a 1997-introduced, mild-bodied cigar available in English Market Selection (Connecticut) or maduro leaf (Indonesia). You can find it in boxes of 25.

MAGIC FLUTE
Handmade in San Andres Tuxtla, Mexico.

Wrapper: Mexico   *Binder: Mexico*   *Filler: Mexico*

Shape	Name	Lgth	Ring	Wrapper
Double Corona	Churchill	7½	50	CM-Ma
Long Corona	Lonsdale	6	44	CM-Ma
Robusto	Robusto	5	50	CM-Ma
Toro	Toro	6	50	CM-Ma

This is a mild-to-medium-bodied cigar introduced in 1997. You can enjoy them in a choice of Sumatra-seed or maduro wrapper is elegantly-finished boxes of 20.

MAKER'S MARK
Handmade in Navarette, Dominican Republic.

Wrapper: Indonesia   *Binder: Dom. Rep.*   *Filler: Dom. Rep.*

HANDMADE CIGARS: BRAND LISTINGS

Shape	Name	Lgth	Ring	Wrapper
Toro	Robusto	6	50	CM

The famous bourbon, frozen into a cigar?!? Not quite . . . this is a medium-to-full-bodied, long-filler, quality cigar which is imbued with the luscious taste of famous Maker's Mark bourbon over a 5-7 day process. It features a Sumatra wrapper and is offered in individual glass tubes, in "Amatista"-style glass jars or in re-supply boxes of 25.

MANAGUA
Handmade in Esteli, Nicaragua.

Wrapper: Indonesia   Binder: Nicaragua   Filler: Nicaragua

Shape	Name	Lgth	Ring	Wrapper
Panatela	Petits	5½	36	Ma
Long Panatela	Senoritas	7	36	Ma
Corona	Habanas	5½	42	Ma
Robusto	Consul	5	50	Ma
Long Corona	Corona	6	44	Ma
Long Panatela	Lanceros	7½	38	Ma
Churchill	Presidente	7	46	Ma
Double Corona	Churchill	7	50	Ma
Torpedo	Torpedo	6	54	Ma
Pyramid	Piramides	7	50	Ma
Giant	Magnum	8	52	Ma

Introduced in 1998, this is a medium-bodied brand with a maduro wrapper. It is available in either boxes of bundles of 25.

MANHATTAN
Handmade in Tamboril, Dominican Republic.

Wrapper: Indonesia   Binder: Indonesia   Filler: Dom. Rep.

HANDMADE CIGARS: BRAND LISTINGS

Shape	Name	Lgth	Ring	Wrapper
Robusto	Brooklyn Blunt	5	60	Ma
Pyramid	City Lights	4½	52	Ma
Torpedo	High Rise	6	62	Ma

From the imagination of Hugo Cassar comes this a new brand for 1998, with all-maduro wrapped shapes and a full-bodied flavor. You can try them in all-cedar boxes of 15.

MANHATTAN CIGAR COMPANY
Handmade in Santiago, Dominican Republic.
Wrapper: Ecuador or USA/Connecticut
Binder: Dominican Republic   Filler: Dominican Republic

Shape	Name	Lgth	Ring	Wrapper
	Classic Red Label:			
Robusto	Robusto	5	50	CC
Grand Corona	Corona Elegante	6½	46	CC
Toro	Churchill	6½	49	CC
Torpedo	Torpedo	6	53	CC
	Limited Edition:			
Robusto	Robusto	5	50	CC
Toro	Toro	6	52	CC
Torpedo	Torpedo	6	53	CC

The "Classic Red Label" series was introduced in 1996 and offers a mild-bodied smoke with a Ecuadorian-grown, Connecticut-seed wrapper. The "Limited Edition" debuted in 1997 with a medium body and a Connecticut-grown wrapper. Both are offered in individual cellophane sleeves inside boxes of 25.

MANIFIESTO
Handmade in Villa Gonzalez, Dominican Republic.
Wrapper: Indonesia   Binder: Dom. Rep.   Filler: Dom. Rep.

HANDMADE CIGARS: BRAND LISTINGS

Shape	Name	Lgth	Ring	Wrapper
Giant	Presidente	8	52	CC
Torpedo	Torpedo	6	52	CC
Toro	Toro	6	54	CC
Double Corona	Churchill	7½	50	CC
Toro	Robusto	6	50	CC
Robusto	Rothschild	4½	50	CC
Churchill	Double Corona	7	48	CC
Lonsdale	Corona	6½	44	CC
Corona	Petit Corona	5½	42	CC
Long Panatela	Panetela	7	36	CC

Here is a new brand for 1997, with a medium-bodied flavor and a Sumatra wrapper. It is offered in all-cedar boxes of 10 in five shapes and in 25s in all shapes.

MANODURA
Handmade in Villa Gonzalez, Dominican Republic.

Wrapper: Brazil, USA/Connecticut   *Binder: Dom. Rep.*   *Filler: Dom. Rep.*

Shape	Name	Lgth	Ring	Wrapper
Robusto	Robusto	5	50	CC-Ma
Long Corona	Corona	6	42	CC-Ma
Lonsdale	Double Corona	7	44	CC-Ma

Introduced in 1997, this "strong hand" cigar is a medium-to-full-bodied blend available in either a Connecticut-grown natural wrapper or Brazilian maduro wrapper.

MANUEL
Handmade in Tamboril, Dominican Republic.

Wrapper: Indonesia   *Binder: Dom. Rep.*   *Filler: Dom. Rep.*

HANDMADE CIGARS: BRAND LISTINGS

Shape	Name	Lgth	Ring	Wrapper
Robusto	Robusto	5	50	CM
Lonsdale	Royal Corona	6¾	44	CM
Double Corona	Churchill	7½	50	Stripe

Here is a full-bodied brand which debuted in 1997. It is offered in all-cedar boxes of 25.

MANUEL CASALS
Handmade in Santo Domingo, Dominican Republic.
Wrapper: Indonesia   *Binder: Dom. Rep.*   *Filler: Dom. Rep.*

Shape	Name	Lgth	Ring	Wrapper
Double Corona	Churchill	7½	52	CM
Long Corona	No. 1	6	44	CM
Robusto	No. 3	5½	50	CM
Robusto	Short Tails	4½	50	CM

Here is a medium-bodied cigar introduced in 1997. Formerly made in Mexico, it features a Sumatra wrapper and Dominican interior tobaccos and is presented in boxes of 25. The Short Tails are rum flavored.

MARAVILLA
Handmade in Honduras.
Wrapper: Ecuador   *Binder: Honduras*   *Filler: Costa Rica, Honduras, Nicaragua*

Shape	Name	Lgth	Ring	Wrapper
Corona	Corona	5¾	44	CC
Giant	Gigante	8	52	CC
Lonsdale	Lonsdale	7	44	CC
Robusto	Robusto	4¾	52	CC
Toro	Toro	6	50	CC

HANDMADE CIGARS: BRAND LISTINGS

This is a new brand for 1998 and offers a blend of tobaccos from four nations. The taste is medium-bodied and the brand is presented in boxes of 25.

MARIA MANCINI
Handmade in Cofradia, Honduras.

Wrapper: Nicaragua *Binder: Honduras* *Filler: Honduras*

Shape	Name	Lgth	Ring	Wrapper
Double Corona	Clemenceau	7½	50	CM
Corona	Corona Classico	5½	44	CM
Toro	Robusto Larga	6	50	CM
Robusto	De Gaulle	4¾	50	CM
Lonsdale	Grandee	6¾	44	CM
Lonsdale	Palma Delgado	6½	40	CM

This is a heavy-bodied, square-pressed blend, featuring Cuban-seed tobaccos that produce a full-flavored taste with an easy draw. It is offered in uncellophaned in cedar trunks of 40.

MARIACHI
Handmade in San Andres Tuxtla, Mexico.

Wrapper: Mexico *Binder: Mexico* *Filler: Mexico*

Shape	Name	Lgth	Ring	Wrapper
Giant	Presidente	8½	54	CM-Ma
Robusto	Robusto	5½	50	CM-Ma
Double Corona	Churchill	7	50	CM-Ma
Toro	Toro	6	50	CM-Ma

Olé! Here is a 1997-introduced, mild-to-medium-bodied brand which celebrates the energy and joy of Mexican music at its finest. The wrapper is Sumatra-seed and the binder and filler are genuine Mexican Morron leaves. You can enjoy these in humidor-style boxes of 20!

HANDMADE CIGARS: BRAND LISTINGS

MARIO PALOMINO
Handmade in Kingston, Jamaica.

Wrapper: USA/Connecticut   Binder: Mexico   Filler: Jamaica

Shape	Name	Lgth	Ring	Wrapper
Slim Panatela	Buccaneers	5½	32	CC
Petit Corona	Petit Corona	5	41	CC
Slim Panatela	Rapier	6	32	CC
Long Corona	Festivale	6	41	CC
Lonsdale	Cetro	6½	42	CC
Grand Corona	Corona Immensa	6	47	CC
Lonsdale	Caballero	7½	45	CC
Double Corona	Presidente	7½	49	CC
Giant	Churchill	8	52	CC

These cigars are manufactured by The Palomino Brothers Tobacco Co. in Jamaica. The blend features Jamaican filler and in combination with the Mexican binder and Connecticut Shade wrapper produce a heavy, full-bodied flavor.

MARQUEZ MENDOZA
Handmade in Villa Gonzalez, Dominican Republic.

Wrapper: Ecuador   Binder: Dom. Rep.   Filler: Dom. Rep.

Shape	Name	Lgth	Ring	Wrapper
Double Corona	Marquez I	7½	50	CC
Toro	Marquez II	6	50	CC
Robusto	Marquez III	5	52	CC
Long Panatela	Marquez IV	7	36	CC

Introduced in 1997, this brand offers a mild-bodied smoke with a Connecticut-seed wrapper, offered in boxes of 25.

HANDMADE CIGARS: BRAND LISTINGS

MARSH 1840
Handmade in Danli, Honduras.

Wrapper: USA/Connecticut   *Binder: USA/Pennsylvania*
Filler: Dominican Republic, Nicaragua, USA/Pennsylvania

Shape	Name	Lgth	Ring	Wrapper
Lonsdale	Lonsdale	6½	43	CC-Ma

A grand old name in U.S. cigar making – M. Marsh & Son – again adorns a handmade cigar for the first time in more than 70 years! This new handmade cigar is offered in one classic size only and presents a mild-to-medium taste with its blend of U.S.-grown, Dominican and Nicaraguan tobaccos. The available wrappers include shade-grown Connecticut and Connecticut Broadleaf for the maduro version. You can find it boxes of 25.

MASTER BRADLEY'S PREMIUM DOMINICAN
Handmade in Santiago, Dominican Republic.

Wrapper: Indonesia   *Binder: Dom. Rep.*   *Filler: Dom. Rep.*

Shape	Name	Lgth	Ring	Wrapper
Long Corona	Breva	6	44	CC
Robusto	Toro	5	50	CC
Churchill	Churchill	7	48	CC

Introduced in 1997, here is a mild-to-medium-bodied, value-priced bundle of 20 cigars, each protected in an individual cellophane sleeve. The wrapper is genuine Sumatra, with a blend of Dominican-grown leaves inside.

MATACAN
Handmade in San Andres Tuxtla, Mexico.

Wrapper: Mexico   *Binder: Mexico*   *Filler: Mexico, Nicaragua*

Shape	Name	Lgth	Ring	Wrapper
Double Corona	No. 1	7½	50	CC-Ma
Toro	No. 2	6	50	CC-Ma
Grand Corona	No. 3	6⅝	46	CC-Ma

Lonsdale	No. 4	6⅝	42	CC-Ma
Long Corona	No. 5	6	42	CC-Ma
Panatela	No. 6	6⅝	35	CC-Ma
Robusto	No. 7	4¾	50	CC-Ma
Giant	No. 8	8	52	CC-Ma
Small Panatela	No. 9	5	32	CC-Ma
Double Corona	No. 10	6⅞	54	CC-Ma

Good value, good quality and a medium-bodied taste led by San Andres Valley tobaccos is the promise of Matacan. These cigars are offered in bundles of 20.

M.A.T.A.S.A. SECONDS
Handmade in Santiago, Dominican Republic.

Wrapper: USA/Connecticut   Binder: Mexico   Filler: Dom. Rep.

Shape	Name	Lgth	Ring	Wrapper
Short Panatela	Chico	4	36	CC
Double Corona	Churchill	7	50	CC
Long Corona	Corona	6	43	CC
Giant	King Kong	8½	52	CC
Lonsdale	No. 2	6½	43	CC
Lonsdale	No. 3	6¾	44	CC
Corona	No. 4	5½	42	CC
Short Panatela	No. 5	5	35	CC
Panatela	No. 21	5½	38	CC
Grand Corona	No. 505	6½	45	CC
Long Panatela	Palma Fina	6⅞	36	CC
Toro	Regulare	6	50	CC
Short Panatela	Palmita	5	38	CC
Grand Corona	Seniors	6	46	CC

Panatela	Super Fino	6	36	CC
Long Panatela	Largo Delgado	6⅞	38	CC
Long Panatela	Taino	7½	38	CC
Robusto	Wavell	4½	50	CC

``MATASA" is a highly-respected name in the cigar trade as it is the name of one of the Dominican Republic's finest cigar manufacturing groups. These seconds are overruns of some of the factory's "big name" cigars, and are very mild with a beautiful Connecticut wrapper.

MATCH PLAY
Handmade in the Santiago, Dominican Republic.

Wrapper: Ecuador   Binder: Dom. Rep.   Filler: Dom. Rep.

Shape	Name	Lgth	Ring	Wrapper
Robusto	Cypress	4¾	50	CC
Petit Corona	Inverness	5	43	CC
Long Corona	St. Andrews	6¼	44	CC
Toro	Turnberry	6	50	CC
Churchill	Prestwick	6⅞	46	CC
Double Corona	Olympic	7½	50	CC
Pyramid	Troon	7	54	CC

This brand was introduced in 1995; it is a handmade, medium-bodied cigar that is the product of a balanced blend from four distinctly different tobaccos. It is enhanced by a Connecticut Seed wrapper that has a unique growing cycle and final processing procedure. Its golf-themed band is further reflected in the shape names taken from some of the world's great golf courses.

MATCH PLAY SERIE MEDALLISTA
Handmade in Santiago, Dominican Republic.

Wrapper: USA/Connecticut   Binder: Dom. Rep.   Filler: Dom. Rep.

HANDMADE CIGARS: BRAND LISTINGS

Shape	Name	Lgth	Ring	Wrapper
Torpedo	No. 18	5¾	44	CC
Torpedo	No. 36	6	46	CC
Torpedo	No. 54	5½	48	CC
Torpedo	No. 72	6	52	CC

No, the heads of the cigars aren't shaped like golf clubs, but they might as well be! Here's a totally unique, all-torpedo line which celebrates the number of holes completed after one (18), two (36), three (54) or four (72) rounds of a golf tournament. The line offers a medium-to-full flavor and is offered in slide-top boxes of 25.

MAXIM'S
Handmade in Santiago, Dominican Republic.

Wrapper: Dom. Rep.   Binder: Dom. Rep.   Filler: Dom. Rep.

Shape	Name	Lgth	Ring	Wrapper
Torpedo	Omnibus	7	52	CC
Long Panatela	Royale	7	38	CC
Toro	Bistrot	6	50	CC
Double Corona	Imperial	7½	52	CC
Corona	Belle Epoque	5½	44	CC
Slim Panatela	Sem	5	30	CC

Elegant is the word for this brand, introduced in 1997. It is medium-bodied and features a Dominican-grown wrapper. Maxim's is presented in protective cellophane sleeves and packaged in all-cedar boxes of 25.

MAXIUS
Handmade in Santiago, Dominican Republic.
Wrapper: Indonesia or USA/Connecticut

Binder: Dominican Republic   Filler: Dominican Republic

HANDMADE CIGARS: BRAND LISTINGS

Shape	Name	Lgth	Ring	Wrapper
	Sumatra line:			
Robusto	Robusto	5	50	CM
Lonsdale	Lonsdale	6½	44	CM
Churchill	Churchill	6⅞	48	CM
Double Corona	Double Corona	7½	50	CM
Torpedo	Belicoso	6¼	52	CM
	Connecticut line:			
Long Corona	Corona	6	44	CC
Robusto	Robusto	5	50	CC
Slim Panatela	Panatella	7	32	CC
Churchill	Churchill	6⅞	48	CC
Torpedo	Torpedo	6¼	52	CC

This brand was new in 1996 and offers two different styles: the Sumatra line, which is medium-to-full in body and has a spicy finish, and the Connecticut line, which is mild-to-medium in body and slightly sweet. Both are products of the finest manufacturing facilities in the Dominican Republic.

MAYA
Handmade in Danli, Honduras.

Wrapper: Ecuador   *Binder: Honduras*   *Filler: Honduras, Nicaragua*

Shape	Name	Lgth	Ring	Wrapper
Slim Panatela	Petit	5½	34	CI
Robusto	Robusto	5	50	CI-Ma
Torpedo	Torpedo	7	54	CI
Double Corona	Executives	7¾	50	CI-Ma
Churchill	Churchills	6⅞	49	CI-Ma
Lonsdale	Elegantes	7	43	CI
Long Corona	Corona	6¼	44	CI-Ma

HANDMADE CIGARS: BRAND LISTINGS

Long Corona	Cetros	6	43	Cl
Panatela	Palma Fina	6⅞	36	Cl
Corona	Petit Coronas	5½	42	Cl
Toro	Matador	6	50	Cl-Ma
Giant	Viajantes	8½	52	Cl

Introduced in the mid-1980s, the Maya brand is a Honduran, handmade, long-filler cigar with predominantly Honduran filler blended with Dominican Havana seed tobaccos. Maya's Havana-seed binder and Ecuadorian-grown, Connecticut-seed wrapper complete this mild-to-medium strength cigar.

MAYORGA
Handmade in Esteli, Nicaragua.

Wrapper: Costa Rica, Nicaragua Binder: Nicaragua   *Filler: Nicaragua*

Shape	Name	Lgth	Ring	Wrapper
	de Segovia blend:			
Robusto	Robusto	4¾	50	CC
Corona	Corona	5½	44	CC
Toro	Toro	6	50	CC
Churchill	Churchill	7	48	CC
Torpedo	Torpedo	6¾	54	CC
	Maduro blend:			
Robusto	Robusto	4¾	50	Ma
Toro	Toro	6	50	Ma

Get ready for unbounded pleasure in this brand, introduced in 1997. It offers a Nicaraguan shade-grown wrapper and Nicaraguan-grown, Cuban-seed binder and filler leaves. It has a medium body and rich, sometimes spicy flavors. You can find it carefully packaged in all-cedar boxes of 25. The newer Maduro blend features a Costa Rican wrapper and presents a full-bodied flavor.

HANDMADE CIGARS: BRAND LISTINGS

MEDAL OF HONOR
Handmade in Esteli, Nicaragua.

Wrapper: Nicaragua *Binder: Nicaragua* *Filler: Nicaragua*

Shape	Name	Lgth	Ring	Wrapper
Robusto	No. 100	4¾	50	CC-Ma
Toro	No. 200	6	50	CC-Ma
Lonsdale	No. 300	6½	42	CC-Ma
Double Corona	No. 500	7½	50	CC-Ma
Giant	No. 700	8½	52	CC-Ma

A new standard for value, this premium bundle was introduced in 1995 and moved in 1998 to Nicaragua, using excellent-quality, long-filler tobaccos and distinctive packaging. These cigars are available in a choice of wrapper shades, with a medium body in bundles of 20.

MEMPHIS BLUE
Handmade in Veracruz, Mexico.

Wrapper: Indonesia *Binder: Mexico* *Filler: Dom. Rep., Honduras, Mexico*

Shape	Name	Lgth	Ring	Wrapper
Double Corona	Churchill	7	50	CM
Double Corona	Double Corona	7¼	50	CM
Robusto	Robusto	5	50	CM
Long Corona	Corona	6	42	CM

Introduced in 1997, this Mexican-made, medium-bodied brand features a Sumatra wrapper and a three-nation interior blend. You can find it in boxes of 25.

MENDEZ Y LOPEZ
Handmade in Santiago, Dominican Republic.

Wrapper: Indonesia *Binder: Dom. Rep.* *Filler: Dom. Rep.*

Shape	Name	Lgth	Ring	Wrapper
Cigarillo	Palmaritos	4	28	CM

HANDMADE CIGARS: BRAND LISTINGS

Small Panetela	Finos	5	30	CM
Corona	Favorito	5½	42	CM
Robusto	Robusto	5½	50	CM
Panatela	Panetela	6	36	CM
Lonsdale	Latinos	6½	42	CM
Lonsdale	Exclusivos	6½	44	CM
Churchill	Churchill	6⅞	46	CM
Lonsdale	Palma de Mayorca	7	42	CM
Long Panatela	Panetelas Extra	7½	38	CM
Double Corona	Presidentes	7½	50	CM
Giant	Soberanos	8½	52	CM
Giant	Viajante	10	56	CM
Pyramid	Piramide Breve	5½	56	CM
Pyramid	Piramide	7½	64	CM
Torpedo	Piramide Gigante	8	68	CM

This is a very old Cuban brand, now re-constituted as a mild-bodied brand with 16 different shapes, including the stunning Piramide Gigante with its 68-ring diameter at the foot! It debuted in its present form in 1997 and is presented in boxes of 10 or 20 cigars each.

MERCADER

Handmade, with short filler, in Santiago, Dominican Republic.

Wrapper: Indonesia   Binder: Dom. Rep.   Filler: Dom. Rep.

Shape	Name	Lgth	Ring	Wrapper
Toro	Toro	6½	50	CM
Robusto	Robusto	4½	50	CM

New in 1998, this short-fill brand is medium-to-full-bodied with a Sumatra-seed wrapper. It is offered in boxes of 25.

HANDMADE CIGARS: BRAND LISTINGS

MERCEDES
Handmade in Santo Domingo, Dominican Republic.
Wrapper: Indonesia, USA/Connecticut
Binder: Dominican Republic   *Filler: Dominican Republic*

Shape	Name	Lgth	Ring	Wrapper
Torpedo	No. 1 Torpedo	7	60	CC-Ma
Double Corona	No. 2 Double Corona	7½	52	CC-Ma
Long Panatela	No. 3 Lonsdale	7	38	CC-Ma
Corona	No. 4 Corona	5½	44	CC-Ma
Robusto	No. 5 Robusto	5	50	CC-Ma
Toro	No. 6 Toro	6	50	CC-Ma
Pyramid	No. 7 Pyramid	6	52	CC-Ma
Small Panatela	No. 9 Cordial	5	30	CC

Here is an easy-to-draw, medium-bodied (in Connecticut-grown natural) or
medium-to-full-bodied (in Indonesian-grown maduro) cigar introduced into the
U.S. in 1996. Available previously in France and the Caribbean, it is presented
uncellophaned in all-cedar boxes of 25.

MERENCIGAR
Handmade in Santiago, Dominican Republic.
Wrapper: Indonesia   *Binder: Dom. Rep.*   *Filler: Dom. Rep.*

Shape	Name	Lgth	Ring	Wrapper
Long Corona	Corona	6¼	44	CM
Robusto	Robusto	5¼	50	CM

Here is a 1997-introduced brand, with a mild body and a Sumatra wrapper. It is
slightly spicy and offered in boxes of 25.

MERIDIONALES
Handmade, with medium filler,
in Villa Gonzalez, Dominican Republic.
Wrapper: Indonesia   *Binder: Dom. Rep.*   *Filler: Dom. Rep.*

HANDMADE CIGARS: BRAND LISTINGS

Shape	Name	Lgth	Ring	Wrapper
Robusto	Robusto	5	50	CM
Churchill	Lonsdale	6¾	46	CM
Double Corona	Presidente	7¾	50	CM

Introduced in 1996, this medium-fill brand has a medium-bodied taste and is offered in boxes of bundles of 25.

MEXICAN EMPERADOR
Handmade in San Andres Tuxtla, Mexico.

Wrapper: Mexico *Binder: Mexico* *Filler: Mexico*

Shape	Name	Lgth	Ring	Wrapper
Giant	Emperador	13¾	49	CC

The size says it all! This is a unique product of the famous San Andres Valley region of Mexico, the birthplace of many great brands. Despite its immense length, the 49-ring width makes it an accessible smoke, albeit a time-consuming one. The Emperador is individually packaged in an elegant, slide-top cedar box.

MI FLOR
Handmade in Danli, Honduras.

Wrapper: Ecuador *Binder: Dom. Rep.* *Filler: Dom. Rep., Honduras*

Shape	Name	Lgth	Ring	Wrapper
Double Corona	Presidente	7½	50	CM
Churchill	Churchill	7	48	CM
Toro	Toro	6	50	CM
Long Corona	Cetro	6¼	44	CM
Robusto	Robusto	5	50	CM
Corona	Corona	5½	42	CM

Introduced in 1997, this is a mild-to-medium-bodied cigar with a blend of three nations giving it a distinctive flavor. You will find "my flower" in cellophane sleeves inside all-cedar boxes of 25.

HANDMADE CIGARS: BRAND LISTINGS

MI HABANA UNICA
Handmade in Santiago, Dominican Republic.

Wrapper: Indonesia *Binder: Dom. Rep.* *Filler: Dom. Rep.*

Shape	Name	Lgth	Ring	Wrapper
Robusto	Robusto	5	50	CM
Churchill	Churchill	7	48	CM

This is a mild-to-medium brand aged for two years with a Sumatra wrapper and Piloto Cubano filler leaves. It is presented in an specially-edged box in 25s.

MIAMI CHOICE
Handmade in Miami, Florida, USA.

Wrapper: Ecuador *Binder: Mexico* *Filler: Mexico*

Shape	Name	Lgth	Ring	Wrapper
Lonsdale	Lonsdales	6¾	43	CC

This is a medium-bodied blend offered in limited distribution. It has a Connecticut-seed wrapper and is offered in boxes of 25.

MIAVANA CLASICOS
Handmade in San Andres Tuxtla, Mexico.

Wrapper: Mexico *Binder: Mexico* *Filler: Mexico*

Shape	Name	Lgth	Ring	Wrapper
Robusto	Robusto	5½	52	CM
Double Corona	Churchill	7½	52	CM

This is a medium-bodied brand, offered in boxes of 25 with a dark, flavorful blend of tobaccos grown in Mexico.

MICHAEL ANGELO
Handmade in Santiago, Dominican Republic.

Wrapper: USA/Connecticut *Binder: Dom. Rep.* *Filler: Dom. Rep.*

HANDMADE CIGARS: BRAND LISTINGS

Shape	Name	Lgth	Ring	Wrapper
Torpedo	Torpedo	6½	52	CC
Robusto	Robusto	5	50	CC
Double Corona	Churchill	7	49	CC
Double Corona	Presidente	7	52	CC
Long Corona	Corona	6	44	CC

Introduced in 1997, this is a medium-bodied brand offered in boxes of 25. The bands show the works of the great Italian painter and sculptor Michelangelo and the vintage tobaccos have been aged for years prior to rolling.

MICKEY ROONEY'S WORLD'S GREATEST CIGAR
SIGNATURE SERIES
Handmade in Esteli, Nicaragua.

Wrapper: Nicaragua   Binder: Nicaragua   Filler: Nicaragua

Shape	Name	Lgth	Ring	Wrapper
Corona	Corona	5½	44	CM
Robusto	Robusto	4¾	50	CM
Churchill	Churchill	7	48	CM
Double Corona	Presidente	7½	52	CM
Torpedo	Torpedo	6¾	54	CM

Introduced in 1998, here is a cigar backed by one of Hollywood's most celebrated performers, Mickey Rooney. It is a mild-to-medium-bodied blend, offered in boxes of 25. It is also presented in a special rosewood humidor of 36 Churchill-sized cigars.

MICUBANO
Handmade in Esteli, Nicaragua.

Wrapper: Nicaragua   Binder: Nicaragua   Filler: Nicaragua

Shape	Name	Lgth	Ring	Wrapper
Robusto	No. 450	4¾	50	CM

HANDMADE CIGARS: BRAND LISTINGS

Corona	No. 542		5½	42	CM
Toro	No. 650		6	50	CM
Lonsdale	No. 644		6½	44	CM
Churchill	No. 748		7	48	CM
Giant	No. 852		8½	52	CM
Toro	Tubo No. 1	*(tubed)*	6	50	CM

Here, at long last, is a cigar made up of 100 percent Cuban-seed tobacco, which debuted in 1995. Grown in Nicaragua, the filler, binder and wrapper combine for a rich, uninhibited, full-bodied taste that is offered uncellophaned in beautiful all-cedar boxes of 25 cigars each.

MILLENNIUM
Handmade in Santiago, Dominican Republic.
Wrapper: USA/Connecticut   *Binder: Nicaragua*   *Filler: Dom. Rep.*

Shape	*Name*	*Lgth*	*Ring*	*Wrapper*
Torpedo	M	4½	52	CM
Torpedo	MM	5½	52	CM
Torpedo	MMM	6½	52	CM

This brand was introduced in 1997, but has a new blend in 1998. This style is mild-to-medium in body with a unique peppery flavor, available in boxes of 25.

MIRAFLORES
Handmade in Cumana, Venezuela.
Wrapper: Indonesia   *Binder: Venezuela*   *Filler: Venezuela*

Shape	*Name*	*Lgth*	*Ring*	*Wrapper*
Torpedo	Torpedo	6½	52	CM
Double Corona	Double Corona	7	50	CM
Robusto	Robusto	5	50	CM
Long Corona	No. 3	6	44	CM

HANDMADE CIGARS: BRAND LISTINGS

Corona	Corona	5½	42	CM
Panatela	Conchitas	5½	36	CM

Introduced in 1997, this is a medium-bodied blend. It is presented in cellophane sleeves inside cedar boxes of 5 (robustos only) and 25, The Torpedo shape is available in 3s or 20s.

MIRAMONTE
Handmade, with short filler, in Miami, Florida, USA.

Wrapper: Indonesia   Binder: Dom. Rep.   Filler: Dom. Rep.

Shape	Name	Lgth	Ring	Wrapper
Corona	Flavors	5½	44	CM

Introduced in 1996, this is a mild-to-medium-bodied cigar available in five flavors: Amaretto, Cuban Espresso, dark rum, vanilla and cherry. It is offered in wood boxes of 25.

MIRANDA
Handmade in San Andres Tuxtla, Mexico.

Wrapper: Mexico   Binder: Mexico   Filler: Mexico

Shape	Name		Lgth	Ring	Wrapper
Double Corona	Churchill		7	50	CC
Toro	Toro		6	50	CC
Robusto	Robusto		5	50	CC
Lonsdale	Lonsdale		6½	42	CC
Torpedo	Maximiliano		6½	52	Stripe
Lonsdale	Cristal	(tubed)	6½	42	CC

This is a medium-bodied brand which was introduced in 1998. It is offered in boxes of 5, 10, 20 or 25 cigars.

MIYARES
Handmade in Miami, Florida, USA.

HANDMADE CIGARS: BRAND LISTINGS

Wrapper: Ecuador

CORONA MIYARES:
Binder: Indonesia *Filler: Dom. Rep., Indonesia*

Wrapper: Dom. Rep.

HABANA MIYARES:
Binder: Indonesia *Filler: Dom. Rep., Indonesia*

Wrapper: Indonesia

SOL DE CUBA:
Binder: Mexico *Filler: Dom. Rep., Indonesia*

FREEDOM:
Wrapper: Ecuador *Binder: Indonesia* *Filler: Dom. Rep., Indonesia*

Shape	Name	Lgth	Ring	Wrapper
	Corona Miyares:			
Torpedo	Torpedo	6½	54	CC
Torpedo	Torpedo Corto	5½	54	CC
Double Corona	Churchill	7	50	CC
Robusto	Robusto	5	50	CC
Churchill	Double Corona	7	48	CC
Long Corona	Corona	6	42	CC
Long Panatela	Lancero	7¼	38	CC
	Habana Miyares:			
Torpedo	Torpedo	6½	54	Ma
Torpedo	Torpedo Corto	5½	54	Ma
Double Corona	Churchill	7	50	Ma
Robusto	Robusto	5	50	Ma
Churchill	Double Corona	7	48	Ma
Long Corona	Corona	6	42	Ma
	Sol de Cuba:			
Torpedo	Torpedo	6½	54	CM
Torpedo	Torpedo Corto	5½	54	CM

HANDMADE CIGARS: BRAND LISTINGS

Double Corona	Churchill	7	50	CM
Robusto	Robusto	5	50	CM
Churchill	Double Corona	7	48	CM
Long Corona	Corona	6	42	CM
Long Panatela	Lancero	7¼	38	CM
	Freedom:			
Giant	Freedom	8	54	CC-Ma

This 1998-introduced brand offers three distinct series and a noteworthy specialty cigar. The gold-banded Corona Miyares group is mild-bodied, the red-banded Habana Miyares line is medium-to-full in body and the yellow-banded Sol de Cuba is medium-bodied. The Freedom cigar is a totally unique star-spangled with a medium-bodied taste in both a maduro and "claro" shade showing off both stars and stripes in a salute to the American flag! All of these lines are available in boxes of 25, except for the Freedom cigar, which is available individually.

MOCAMBO
Handmade in San Andres Tuxtla, Mexico.

Wrapper: Mexico   Binder: Mexico   Filler: Mexico

Shape	Name	Lgth	Ring	Wrapper
Double Corona	Churchill	7	50	CC-Ma
Toro	Double Corona	6	51	CC-Ma
Panatela	Empire	6½	39	CC
Giant	Inmensa	8½	50	CC-Ma
Lonsdale	Premier	6⅝	43	CC-Ma
Robusto	Robusto	4½	50	CC-Ma
Long Corona	Royal Corona	6	42	CC-Ma
Churchill	S/L	6¾	48	CC-Ma
	Made with short filler:			
Long Corona	Corona	6	42	CC

HANDMADE CIGARS: BRAND LISTINGS

Toro	Toro	6	50	CC
Robusto	Robusto	4½	50	CC

This is a heavy-bodied cigar, offered with a choice of a natural-colored wrapper or a sweeter, maduro-shade wrapper.

MOJO
Handmade in Navarette, Dominican Republic.
Wrapper: Indonesia　　　　　*Binder: Dom. Rep.*　　　　　*Filler: Dom. Rep.*

Shape	Name	Lgth	Ring	Wrapper
Torpedo	Torpedo	6	54	CM
Giant	Churchill	8½	50	CM

This is a medium-bodied brand which debuted in 1998. It is offered in bundles of 25.

MONTAGUE
Handmade in Pandaan, Indonesia.
Wrapper: Brazil, Indonesia　　　　　　　　　*Binder: Indonesia*
　　　　　　Filler: Brazil, Indonesia

Shape	Name	Lgth	Ring	Wrapper
Double Corona	No. 1	7¼	50	Cl-Ma
Grand Corona	No. 2	6⅝	45	Cl-Ma
Long Corona	No. 3	6	40	Cl-Ma
Robusto	Robustos	5	50	Cl-Ma
Lonsdale	Lanceros	7½	40	Cl-Ma

Introduced in 1997, this brand earns high marks from both cigar lovers and industry observers. Brought to the U.S. by the world's second-largest cigar maker, Montague is saluted as "The Consistently Perfect Cigar." The natural Claro wrapper provides a smooth, mild smoking experience, while the maduro wrapper offers a spicy, more flavorful medium-bodied taste. You can enjoy this brand in elegant, hinged cedar boxes of 25.

THE CONSISTENTLY PERFECT CIGAR.™

Every Leaf.
Every Roll.
Every Draw.
Every Montague.®
Only Montague.™

"Every Montague cigar is draw tested to provide a consistently smooth draw."

Montague Maduro Robusto rated 90
by Cigar Aficionado's Cigar Insider! (April '98)

Montague Claro #1 rated 4.4 (5 pt. Scale)
by SMOKE magazine! (Fall '98)

© 1998 Swedish Match North America Inc.

HANDMADE CIGARS: BRAND LISTINGS

MONTE CANARIO
Handmade in Las Palmas, the Canary Islands of Spain.

Wrapper: USA/Connecticut   *Binder: Dominican Republic*
Filler: Brazil, Canary Islands, Dominican Republic

Shape	Name	Lgth	Ring	Wrapper
Lonsdale	Nuncios	6¾	44	CI
Lonsdale	Imperiales	6½	42	CI
Corona	No. 3	5¾	42	CI
Panatela	Panatela	6	38	CI
Robusto	Robustos	4¾	50	CI
Double Corona	Churchill	7	50	CI
Torpedo	Figurados	6	50	CI

Part of the long history of cigar-making in the Canary Islands, the Monte Canario brand has been around in one form or another since the 1920s. It's a mild smoke, featuring a Connecticut wrapper and a blend of leaves from three nations on the interior. It is presented uncellophaned in boxes of 25.

MONTE CARLO
Handmade in Danli, Honduras.

Wrapper: Honduras   *Binder: Honduras*   *Filler: Honduras*

Shape	Name	Lgth	Ring	Wrapper
Churchill	Churchill	7	48	CM
Lonsdale	No. 1	7	44	CM
Robusto	Rothschild	5	50	CM
Long Corona	Lonsdale	6	43	CM
Panatela	Panetela	6	38	CM
Corona	Corona	5½	44	CM

Named for the famed gambling resort, this is a mild-to-medium blend which was introduced to the U.S. market in 1998. It has a Connecticut-seed wrapper and is offered in boxes of 25.

HANDMADE CIGARS: BRAND LISTINGS

MONTE PALMA
Handmade in Las Palmas, the Canary Islands of Spain.

Wrapper: Spain　　　　　*Binder: Dom. Rep.*　　　　*Filler: Brazil, Dom. Rep.*

Shape	Name	Lgth	Ring	Wrapper
Double Corona	No. 1 Churchill	7½	50	CC
Toro	No. 2 Toro	6	50	CC
Robusto	No. 3 Robusto	4¾	50	CC
Churchill	No. 4 Presidentes	6¾	46	CC
Lonsdale	No. 5 Lonsdale	6½	42	CC
Grand Corona	No. 6 Senadores	5¾	46	CC
Panatela	No. 7 Panetelas	6	38	CC
Corona	No. 8 Capitolios	5¼	42	CC
Petit Corona	No. 9 Cremas	4¾	41	CC
	Made with medium filler:			
Petit Corona	Coronas	5	42	CC

With its Sumatra-seed, Canary Islands-grown wrapper and Brazil and Dominican blend, this is a medium-to-full-bodied cigar that has been around since 1925. It is offered in all-cedar boxes of 25.

MONTE REAL
Handmade in Santiago, Dominican Republic.

Wrapper: Ecuador, Mexico　　　*Binder: Dom. Rep.*　　　　　*Filler: Dom. Rep.*

Shape	Name	Lgth	Ring	Wrapper
Double Corona	Churchill	7½	50	CC-Ma
Churchill	Grand Corona	6¾	45	CC-Ma
Lonsdale	Lonsdale	6½	44	CC-Ma
Toro	Toro	6	50	CC-Ma
Corona	Corona	5½	42	CC-Ma

HANDMADE CIGARS: BRAND LISTINGS

Robusto	Robusto	5	50	CC-Ma
Torpedo	Torpedo	6	52	CC-Ma
Pyramid	Piramide	6	52	CC-Ma
Perfecto	Short Cut	4	52	CC-Ma

Here is a 1997-introduced brand, with a shiny Ecuador-grown, Connecticut-seed wrapper and a mild body and a Mexican maduro wrapper and a medium body. It is offered in cellophane sleeves inside boxes or bundles of 25.

MONTE RIO
Handmade in Santiago, Dominican Republic.

Wrapper: Ecuador   *Binder: Dom. Rep.*   *Filler: Dom. Rep.*

Shape	Name	Lgth	Ring	Wrapper
Long Corona	Corona	6	44	CC
Grand Corona	Extra Corona	6	46	CC
Giant	Double Corona	8½	52	CC
Robusto	Robusto	5	50	CC
Churchill	Churchill	7½	48	CC
Torpedo	Torpedo	6½	52	CC
	Scented Cigars:			
Long Corona		6	42	CC
Short Panatela		5	36	CC
Robusto		5	50	CC

Introduced in 1997, here is a medium-bodied brand offered in seven popular sizes in boxes of 25. The Scented Series has no shape names, but is available in seven flavors, in bundles of 25: Amaretto, cinnamon, coconut, chocolate, mint, rum and vanilla.

MONTECRISTO
Handmade in La Romana, Dominican Republic.

Wrapper: USA/Connecticut   *Binder: Dom. Rep.*   *Filler: Dom. Rep.*

HANDMADE CIGARS: BRAND LISTINGS

Shape	Name		Lgth	Ring	Wrapper
Churchill	Churchill		7	48	CC
Lonsdale	No. 1		6½	44	CC
Torpedo	No. 2		6	50	CC
Corona	No. 3		5½	44	CC
Robusto	Robustos		4¾	50	CC
Long Corona	Tubos	*(tubed)*	6	42	CC
Toro	Double Corona		6¼	50	CC
Corona Extra	Corona Grande		5¾	46	CC

This famous name in cigars is relatively young, as the brand was originated in 1935 in Cuba. Today's Dominican version, introduced in 1995, offers outstanding craftsmanship and a slow-burning, medium-to-heavy-bodied smoke whose obvious quality is the lasting impression.

MONTECRISTO CIGARE DES ARTES
Handmade in La Romana, Dominican Republic.
Wrapper: Indonesia   Binder: Dom. Rep.   Filler: Brazil, Dom. Rep., USA/Connecticut

Shape	Name		Lgth	Ring	Wrapper
Giant	A		9¼	47	CM
Churchill	Delacroix	*(tubed)*	7	46	CM
Torpedo	Belicosos Largas		7	52	CM
Toro	Coronas Gigantes		6½	52	CM

Introduced in 1998, this is a carefully-produced, full-bodied cigar designed to be as good as the craft allows. Limited in availability, it is offered in boxes of 25 for the Belicosos Largas and Corona Gigante, in 20s for the Delacroix and in boxes of 10 for the "A". Each is adorned with a Impressionist-style illustration of Paris in the 1920s, a haven for artists, entertainers, writers . . . and cigars!

MONTECRISTO HABANA 2000
Handmade in La Romana, Dominican Republic.
Wrapper: Nicaragua   *Binder: Dom. Rep.*   *Filler: Dom. Rep.*

HANDMADE CIGARS: BRAND LISTINGS

Shape	Name		Lgth	Ring	Wrapper
Panatela	Fancytail		6¾	39	CM
Churchill	Kilimanjaro	(glass tube)	7	46	CM
Toro	Magnum	(glass tube)	6	50	CM

Introduced in 1998, this is a more powerful version of the Montecristo blend, featuring the Habana 2000 wrapper leaf grown in Nicaragua. This is a full-bodied cigar available in boxes of 25.

MONTECRUZ
Handmade in La Romana, Dominican Republic.
Wrapper: Indonesia, USA/Connecticut
Binder: Dominican Republic   Filler: Brazil, Dominican Republic

Shape	Name		Lgth	Ring	Wrapper
Churchill	No. 200		7¼	46	CI-CM
Lonsdale	No. 210		6½	42	DC-CI-CM
Corona	No. 220		5½	42	DC-CI-CM
Long Panatela	No. 255		7	36	CI-CM
Short Panatela	No. 270		4¾	36	CM
Slim Panatela	No. 276		6	32	CM
Cigarillo	No. 281		6	28	CM
Petit Corona	Cedar Aged		5	42	CI-CM
Robusto	Robusto		4½	49	CM
Giant	Individuales		8	46	CM
Toro	Colossus		6½	50	CM
Long Corona	Tubos	(tubed)	6	42	CM
Panatela	Tubulares	(tubed)	6⅛	36	CI-CM
	Machine-made small cigars:				
Cigarillo	Chicos		4	28	CI-CM
Slim Panatela	Juniors		5¼	33	CI-CM

HANDMADE CIGARS: BRAND LISTINGS

Originated in 1959 in the Canary Islands of Spain, Montecruz Sun Grown cigars have been hand crafted in La Romana in the Dominican Republic since 1977. The filler is a blend of Dominican-grown Piloto Cubano, Olor and Brazilian tobaccos, while the binder is a Santo Domingo leaf. The cigar is then finished with a Java wrapper known for its silky feel and rich taste. The Natural Claro line, which debuted in 1988, delivers the rich flavor that Montecruz is famous for, but with a milder taste due to the use of a Connecticut Shade wrapper, from the famous Windsor Valley. The number of sizes in production for 1998 has been reduced to increase availability of the more popular shapes.

MONTENEGRO
Handmade in San Andres Tuxtla, Mexico.

Wrapper: Mexico   Binder: Mexico   *Filler: Mexico*

Shape	Name	Lgth	Ring	Wrapper
Long Corona	No. 2 *(tube available)*	6¼	42	CM-Ma
Long Corona	Cedar Lonsdale	6¼	42	CM-Ma
Double Corona	Churchill	7½	50	CM

This brand was initially introduced in 1971, this is a mild-bodied cigar featuring a Sumatra-seed wrapper grown in Mexico. It is presented in individual cellophane sleeves, or a glass tube for the No. 2 shape, packed in all-cedar boxes of 25.

MONTERIA
Handmade in Esteli, Nicaragua.

Wrapper: Indonesia   Binder: Nicaragua   *Filler: Dom. Rep.*

Shape	Name	Lgth	Ring	Wrapper
Churchill	Venado	7	48	CM
Robusto	Jabali	5	50	CM
Torpedo	Puma	6½	54	CM
Double Corona	Oso	7½	52	CM
Long Corona	Zorra	6	44	CM

Here is a new cigar for 1998, aimed at the outdoors enthusiast, with a mild-to-medium body and offered in boxes of 10 or 25.

HANDMADE CIGARS: BRAND LISTINGS

MONTERO
Handmade in Santiago, Dominican Republic.

Wrapper: Ecuador   Binder: Dom. Rep.   Filler: Dom. Rep.

Shape	Name	Lgth	Ring	Wrapper
Torpedo	Torpedo No. 2	6¼	52	CI
Double Corona	Presidente	7½	50	CI
Churchill	Churchill	6⅞	46	CI
Toro	Toro	6	50	CI
Long Corona	Cetro	6	44	CI
Robusto	Robusto	5	50	CI
Panatela	Petit Panatella	5½	38	CI

The Montero is a premium cigar from the Dominican Republic, introduced in 1995. It is hand made with the long filler and binder from the Dominican Republic and a Connecticut-seed wrapper from Ecuador. Available only in a natural wrapper, the Montero is a medium-bodied cigar.

MONTES DE OCA
Handmade in San Ramon, Costa Rica.

Wrapper: Nicaragua   Binder: Costa Rica   Filler: Costa Rica

Shape	Name	Lgth	Ring	Wrapper
Corona	No. 3	5½	42	CC
Long Corona	No. 2	6	44	CC-Ma
Toro	Esplindido	6	50	Ma
Churchill	Churchill	7½	48	CC-Ma

This cigar was introduced in 1989, but is only in limited distribution. If you can find it, you'll enjoy a rich, medium-to-full-bodied taste, presented uncellophaned in all-cedar boxes of 25.

MONTES DE ORO
Handmade in San Ramon, Costa Rica.

Wrapper: Nicaragua   Binder: Costa Rica   Filler: Costa Rica

HANDMADE CIGARS: BRAND LISTINGS

Shape	Name	Lgth	Ring	Wrapper
Long Corona	No. 2	6	44	Ma
Churchill	Churchill	7¾	48	Ma
Toro	Esplendido	6	50	CC-Ma
Robusto	Robusto	5	49	CC-Ma

This is a medium-bodied blend of tobaccos introduced in 1996. It is offered in bundles of 25 cigars with two new natural-wrapped shapes for 1998.

MONTESINO
Handmade in Santiago, Dominican Republic.
Wrapper: USA/Connecticut   *Binder: Dom. Rep.*   *Filler: Dom. Rep.*

Shape	Name	Lgth	Ring	Wrapper
Churchill	Gran Corona	6¾	48	CM
Lonsdale	No. 1	6⅞	43	CM
Long Corona	No. 2	6¼	44	CM
Corona	Diplomatico	5½	42	CM
Churchill	Napoleon Grande	7½	46	CM
Toro	Toro	6	50	CM
Torpedo	Belicoso No. 2	6	49	CM
Torpedo	Super Belicoso	6¾	54	CM
Torpedo	Belicoso Magnum	5¼	52	CM
Robusto	Robusto	5	50	CM

This well-known brand debuted in its current format in 1981 and is handmade in Santiago, Dominican Republic. Its quality of construction and taste, combined with its modest cost, makes it an excellent value.

MOORE & BODE
Handmade in Miami, Florida, USA.
Wrapper: USA/Connecticut   *Binder and Filler: Central & South American*

HANDMADE CIGARS: BRAND LISTINGS

Shape	Name	Lgth	Ring	Wrapper
	Miami blend:			
Corona	Bishop	5	41	Cl
Grand Corona	Corona	6	46	Cl
Lonsdale	Corona Largo	7	44	Cl
Slim Panatela	34's	6¾	34	Cl
Robusto	Salvadore	5	50	Cl
Toro	North Greenway	6¾	50	Cl
Double Corona	Number Ten	7½	50	Cl
Pyramid	Brass	5½	58	Cl
Pyramid	Full Brass	7¼	64	Cl
	Flamboyan blend:			
Corona	Bishop	5	41	Cl
Grand Corona	Corona	6	46	Cl
Lonsdale	Corona Largo	7	44	Cl
Slim Panatela	34's	6¾	34	Cl
Robusto	Salvadore	5	50	Cl
Toro	North Greenway	6¾	50	Cl
Double Corona	Number Ten	7½	50	Cl
Pyramid	Brass	5½	58	Cl
Pyramid	Full Brass	7¼	64	Cl

There are cigars, and there is the art of the cigar. Moore & Bode cigars are among the foremost expositions of the roller's art, expressed in the highest possible quality of construction. Two series of identical shapes are made; the Miami Blend (introduced 1991) is a mild-to-medium bodied cigar, while the Flamboyan Blend (1995) is medium to heavy.

MORAN

Handmade in Santiago, Dominican Republic.

Wrapper: Indonesia, USA/Connecticut   Binder: Dom. Rep.   Filler: Dom. Rep.

HANDMADE CIGARS: BRAND LISTINGS

Shape	Name	Lgth	Ring	Wrapper
Petit Corona	Baroness	5	42	CC-Ma
Churchill	Czarina	6¾	48	CC-Ma
Robusto	Duchess	5½	50	CC-Ma
Double Corona	Grand Dame	7½	50	CC-Ma
Lonsdale	Princess	6¼	44	CC-Ma

We didn't know that a Duchess could be so "robusto" until we saw this brand! Introduced in 1995, each shape in this brand is named for a female member of a royal or feudal court. The cigars are pretty good, too, with a mild-to-medium bodied flavor and a choice of Connecticut-grown natural or Indonesian-grown maduro wrapper.

MOREJON Y CUESTA
Handmade in Miami, Florida, USA.

Wrapper: Brazil   Binder: Indonesia   Filler: Dom. Rep., Indonesia, Mexico

Shape	Name	Lgth	Ring	Wrapper
Cigarillo	Finos	5	28	CM-Ma
Torpedo	Torpedos	6½	54	CM-Ma
Robusto	Robustos	5	50	CM-Ma
Long Panatela	Lanceros	7½	38	CM-Ma
Long Corona	Panetelas	6	42	CM-Ma
Double Corona	Churchills	7	50	CM-Ma
Double Corona	Presidente	7½	52	CM-Ma

This is a mild-to-medium-bodied cigar in the natural-wrapped version and full-bodied in the maduro-wrapped style. It features a Brazilian wrapper and is presented in your choice of box or bundle of 25.

MORENO MADURO
Handmade in La Romana, Dominican Republic.

Wrapper: Mexico   Binder: Dom. Rep.   Filler: Brazil, Dom. Rep.

HANDMADE CIGARS: BRAND LISTINGS

Shape	Name	Lgth	Ring	Wrapper
Corona	No. 445	5½	44	Ma
Slim Panatela	No. 326	6	32	Ma
Lonsdale	No. 426	6½	42	Ma
Churchill	No. 467	7¼	46	Ma
Toro	No. 486	6	48	Ma
Double Corona	No. 507	7	50	Ma
Giant	No. 528	8½	52	Ma

These are mild to medium-bodied cigars, wrapped in dark maduro wrappers and featuring a pleasant blend of tobacco from three nations.

MOTTA
Handmade in San Andres Tuxtla, Mexico.

Wrapper: Mexico   Binder: Mexico   Filler: Mexico, Nicaragua

Shape	Name	Lgth	Ring	Wrapper
Toro	Toro	6	50	CC
Robusto	Robusto	5	50	CC
Long Corona	Corona Especial	6	44	CC
Double Corona	Churchill	7	50	CC

Introduced in 1996, this is a mild-to-medium-bodied cigar with a Sumatra-seed wrapper and Mexican and Cuban-seed/Nicaraguan-grown leaves in the filler. You can find it in cedar boxes of 25.

MR. LUMA
Handmade in Villa Gonzalez, Dominican Republic.

Wrapper: Dom. Rep., Indonesia   Binder: Dom. Rep.   Filler: Dom. Rep.

Shape	Name	Lgth	Ring	Wrapper
Double Corona	Presidente	7½	50	CC-CM
Robusto	Robusto	5	50	CC-CM

Pyramid	Pyramid	6	53	CM
Robusto	Robusto	5	50	CM
Churchill	Churchill	6⅞	46	CM
Long Corona	Corona	6	44	CM
Long Panatela	Panatella	7½	38	CM
Small Panatela	Especial	5	30	CM

This brand debuted in 1998 with a medium body and a choice of wrappers: Dominican-grown or Indonesian. It is available in all-cedar boxes of 3, 10 or 25.

MURSULI'S
Handmade in Los Angeles, California, USA.

Wrapper: Ecuador or USA/Connecticut   *Binder: Honduras*
Filler: Dominican Republic, Honduras

Shape	Name	Lgth	Ring	Wrapper
Torpedo	Torpedo Grande	7¼	56	CC-Ma
Torpedo	Torpedo	6	56	CC-Ma
Toro	Churchill	6½	52	CC-Ma
Robusto	Robusto	5	52	CC-Ma
Churchill	Double Corona	7	46	CC
Panatela	Sweet Panatela	6	36	CC
Long Corona	Corona	6	43	CC-Ma
Corona	Sweet Corona	6	43	CC
Toro	Oscar No. 1	6	50	CC
Giant	Cubano	8	50	CC
Double Corona	Presidente	7	50	CC-Ma
Slim Panatela	Sweet Linda	5	32	CC
Short Panatela	Petite Corona	5	36	CC

HANDMADE CIGARS: BRAND LISTINGS

Blended by veteran cigar maker Oscar Mursuli, these handmade smokes offer a choice of natural wrappers from Connecticut (natural) or maduro-wrapped shapes featuring leaves from Ecuador. In either shade, this is a medium-to-full-bodied cigar, offered in boxes or bundles of 25 cigars each. The Sweet Panatela is dipped in sugar syrup at the end only, while the Corona and Linda are also available in a sweetened style.

MURSULI SWEETS
Handmade, with short filler, in Los Angeles, California, USA.

Wrapper: Indonesia *Binder: Honduras* *Filler: Dom. Rep.*

Shape	Name	Lgth	Ring	Wrapper
Slim Panatela	Panatela	6	32	CM

New for 1998, this is a one-size, flavored line available in Amaretto, cherry, chocolate, coffee, coconut, raspberry, rum and vanilla. It has a medium body and is offered in bundles of 25.

NAFILYAN SIGNATURE SERIES
Handmade in Villa Gonzalez, Dominican Republic.

Wrapper: Ecuador *Binder: Dom. Rep.* *Filler: Dom. Rep.*

Shape	Name	Lgth	Ring	Wrapper
Double Corona	Churchill	7½	50	CC
Churchill	Gran Corona	7	48	CC
Robusto	Robusto	5	50	CC
Torpedo	Torpedo	7	52	CC

First available in 1996, this is a mild-to-medium-bodied blend, with a Connecticut-seed wrapper. It is available in either boxes or bundles of 25.

NAPA
Handmade in Santa Rosa de Copan, Honduras.

Wrapper: Nicaragua *Binder: Nicaragua* *Filler: Nicaragua*

Shape	Name	Lgth	Ring	Wrapper
Petit Corona	Petite Corona	5	42	CM

HANDMADE CIGARS: BRAND LISTINGS

Robusto	Rothschild	4¾	50	CM
Toro	Toro	6	50	CM
Perfecto	Perfecto	5¾	50	CM
Churchill	Churchill	7½	48	CM

Originally introduced in late 1996, this is a full-bodied blend that debuted in 1998. Very well made, this line is offered in all-cedar boxes of 25.

NAPA DOMINICAN ESTATE
BY DON DIEGO
Handmade in La Romana, Dominican Republic.

Wrapper: Indonesia   *Binder: Dom. Rep.*   *Filler: Dom. Rep.*

Shape	Name	Lgth	Ring	Wrapper
Robusto	Robusto	4½	50	CM
Long Corona	Lonsdale	6	44	CM
Toro	Toro	6	50	CM
Churchill	Churchill	7	48	CM
Pyramid	Pyramid	6	50	CM

With a new blend for 1998 and a new manufacturing agreement with Consolidated Cigar Corp., this is a medium-bodied blend that will impress you with its quality. The wrapper is from Java and each cigar is individually cellophaned in a beautiful, artistic box of 25.

NAPA DOMINICAN RESERVE
BY H. UPMANN
Handmade in La Romana, Dominican Republic.

Wrapper: Indonesia   *Binder: Dom. Rep.*   *Filler: Brazil, Dom. Rep.*

Shape	Name	Lgth	Ring	Wrapper
Corona	Petite Corona	5½	42	CM
Robusto	Robusto	5	50	CM
Toro	Toro	6	50	CM

HANDMADE CIGARS: BRAND LISTINGS

| Double Corona | Gran Corona | 7½ | 50 | CM |
| Pyramid | Pyramid | 6 | 50 | CM |

You'll recognize this brand instantly from the gorgeous ultramarine blue box that radiates quality. This is a new blend for 1998, with a Connecticut-seed wrapper and a medium-to-full-bodied taste. You can enjoy it in boxes of 25.

NAPA RESERVE
Handmade in Las Palmas, the Canary Islands of Spain.

Wrapper: USA/Connecticut   Binder: Dom. Rep.   Filler: Brazil, Dom. Rep., Spain

Shape	Name	Lgth	Ring	Wrapper
Corona	Corona	5¾	42	CC
Robusto	Robusto	4¾	50	CC

This line first appeared in early 1997 and with a new blend for 1998, it offers a mild-to-medium-bodied smoke, available in all-cedar boxes of 25.

NAPOLEON'S DREAM
Handmade in Danli, Honduras.

Wrapper: Honduras   Binder: Honduras   Filler: Honduras

Shape	Name	Lgth	Ring	Wrapper
Lonsdale	Cognac	6½	44	CM
Lonsdale	Rum	6½	44	CM
Lonsdale	Southern Comfort	6½	44	CM
Lonsdale	Vanilla	6½	44	CM
Lonsdale	Sambuca	6½	44	CM

You want flavored? Forget it . . . you really want *cured* tobacco which is thoroughly imbued with flavors such as cognac, rum, sambuca, vanilla and Southern Comfort. That's the secret of this 1997-introduced, all-flavored brand with a mild-to-medium body. The 18-24 month process of introducing these flavors into the tobaccos make this a flavored experience unlike any other available. Napoleon's Dream are also presented properly: in the famous "Cigar Jar" that keeps these flavored smokes from affecting the taste of other, non-flavored cigars. Look for it in tubes of one cigar, gift packs of 12 or full packs of 25 or 75.

NAT SHERMAN
Handmade in the Dominican Republic, Honduras and Jamaica.

EXCHANGE SELECTION:
Wrapper: USA/Connecticut • Binder: Mexico • Filler: Dom. Rep.

LANDMARK SELECTION:
Wrapper: Cameroon • Binder: Mexico • Filler: Dom. Rep.

MANHATTAN SELECTION:
Wrapper: Mexico • Binder: Mexico • Filler: Dom. Rep.

GOTHAM SELECTION:
Wrapper: USA/Connecticut • Binder: Dom. Rep. • Filler: Dom. Rep.

VIP SELECTION:
Wrapper: USA/Connecticut • Binder: Dom. Rep. • Filler: Brazil, Dom. Rep.

CITY DESK SELECTION:
Wrapper: Mexico • Binder: Dom. Rep. • Filler: Dom. Rep., Mexico

HOST SELECTION:
Wrapper: USA/Connecticut • Binder: Honduras • Filler: Honduras

METROPOLITAN SELECTION:
Wrapper: USA/Connecticut • Binder: Dom. Rep. • Filler: Dom. Rep.

LSN SELECTION:
Wrapper: USA/Connecticut • Binder: Mexico • Filler: Dom. Rep.

Shape	Name	Lgth	Ring	Wrapper
	Exchange Selection, made in the Dominican Republic:			
Small Panatela	Academy No. 2	5	31	CC
Panatela	Murray Hill No. 7	6	38	CC
Lonsdale	Butterfield No. 8	6½	42	CC

HANDMADE CIGARS: BRAND LISTINGS

Grand Corona	Trafalgar No. 4	6	47	CC
Double Corona	Oxford No. 5	7	49	CC
Lonsdale	Carpe Diem	6¾	43	CC
	Landmark Selection, made in the Dominican Republic:			
Panatela	Metropole	6	34	CM
Corona	Hampshire	5½	42	CM
Lonsdale	Algonquin	6¾	43	CM
Robusto	Vanderbilt	5	47	CM
Double Corona	Dakota	7½	49	CM
	Manhattan Selection, made in the Dominican Republic:			
Cigarillo	Beekman	5¼	28	CM
Slim Panatela	Tribeca	6	31	CM
Panatela	Chelsea	6½	38	CM
Lonsdale	Gramercy	6¾	43	CM
Robusto	Sutton	5½	49	CM
	Gotham Selection, made in the Dominican Republic:			
Slim Panatela	No. 65	6	32	CC
Long Corona	No. 1400	6¼	44	CC
Toro	No. 711	6	50	CC
Double Corona	No. 500	7	50	CC
	VIP Selection, made in the Dominican Republic:			
Panatela	Zigfield " Fancytale"	6¾	38	CC
Corona	Barnum (tubed)	5½	42	CC
Lonsdale	Morgan	7	42	CC
Robusto	Astor	4½	50	CC
Toro	Carnegie	6	48	CC
	City Desk Selection, made in the Dominican Republic:			

Long Corona	Gazette	6	42	Ma
Grand Corona	Dispatch	6½	46	Ma
Toro	Telegraph	6	50	Ma
Double Corona	Tribune	7½	50	Ma
	Host Selection, made in Honduras:			
Small Panatela	Hudson	4⅝	32	CM
Corona	Hamilton	5½	42	CM
Lonsdale	Hunter	6	43	CM
Grand Corona	Harrington	6	46	CM
Robusto	Hobart	5	50	CM
Double Corona	Hampton	7	50	CM
Giant Corona	Halstead	8	40	CM
Pyramid	Hanover	5½	56	CM
Pyramid	Huron	4½	44	CM
	Metropolitan Selection, made in the Dominican Republic:			
Corona	Anglers	5½	43	CC
Pyramid	Nautical	7	48	CC
Toro	University	6	50	CC
Pyramid	Explorers	5½	56	CC
Pyramid	Metropolitan	7	60	CC
	LSN Selection, made in Jamaica:			
Slim Panatela	A2	5	31	CC
Lonsdale	A4	6¾	43	CC
Robusto	A6	5½	49	CC
Double Corona	A8	7½	49	CC

Nat Sherman, "tobacconist to the world" for more than six decades, offers enough variety in its series to keep the serious smoker trying new sizes and blends for several months. The Exchange Selection provides a mild, smooth and polished flavor thanks to its Connecticut wrapper; the Landmark Selection is more intensely flavorful and full-bodied due to its Cameroon wrapper; the Manhattan Selection is a lean and racy blend of medium body and a nut-like flavor, finished with a soft, light-tasting Mexican wrapper; the Gotham Selection is the most delicate and mild of the group, finished in a mellow Connecticut wrapper; the VIP Selection offers a rich, crisp aroma along with buttery smoothness in the draw and mild taste; the City Desk Selection uses a dark maduro wrapper to give a full, hearty flavor, but without harshness; and the Host Selection matches a sweet Connecticut wrapper with Cuban-seed filler and binders to provide a solid flavor of medium strength and a rustic aroma.

Newer selections include the Metropolitan (introduced in 1995), which offers a medium-to-full-bodied smoke and three shaped sizes, and the LSN Selection (1996), which is also medium-to-full in body, but more spicy.

NATIONAL BRAND
Handmade in Danli, Honduras.

Wrapper: Honduras   *Binder: Mexico*   *Filler: Honduras*

Shape	Name	Lgth	Ring	Wrapper
Giant	Imperial	8½	52	CC-Ma
Churchill	Churchill	7	48	CC-Ma
Long Corona	Lonsdale	6	43	CC-Ma
Corona	Corona	5½	42	CC
Robusto	Rothschild	5	50	CC-Ma
Churchill	Soberanos	6⅞	46	CC
Panatela	Royal Palm	6⅛	36	CC

First offered in 1978, this is a Honduran-produced cigar with all Honduran-grown tobacco, including a Connecticut-seed wrapper, offered in bundles of 25 cigars each. It is considered mild-to-medium in strength.

NATIVO
Handmade in Mayaguez, Puerto Rico.

Wrapper: Indonesia   *Binder: Dom. Rep.*   *Filler: Dom. Rep., Puerto Rico*

Shape	Name	Lgth	Ring	Wrapper

HANDMADE CIGARS: BRAND LISTINGS

Robusto	Robusto	5½	50	CC
Grand Corona	Gran Corona	6	46	CC
Toro	Toro	6	50	CC
Lonsdale	Longsdale	6¼	44	CC
Giant	Churchill	8	50	CC
Cigarillo	Le Petit Chateau	4	28	CC

This is a mild-to-medium-bodied blend of Caribbean binder and filler leaves, enveloped by an Indonesian-grown wrapper. Introduced in 1997, it is offered in an all-cedar box of 25.

NAVARETTE
Handmade, with short filler, in Navarette, Dominican Republic.
Wrapper: Indonesia   *Binder: Dom. Rep.*   *Filler: Dom. Rep.*

Shape	Name	Lgth	Ring	Wrapper
Double Corona	Double Corona	7½	50	CM
Long Corona	Cetros	6	44	CM
Corona	Petit Cetros	5½	42	CM
Pyramid	Pyramid	6	54	CM

This short-filler cigar offers a medium-bodied taste with a Sumatran wrapper. You can find it in bundles of 20.

NAVEGANTE
Handmade in San Andres Tuxtla, Mexico.
Wrapper: Mexico   *Binder: Mexico*   *Filler: Mexico*

Shape	Name	Lgth	Ring	Wrapper
Double Corona	Presidente	7½	50	CC-Ma
Double Corona	Churchill	7	50	CC-Ma
Toro	Toro	6	50	CC-Ma
Robusto	Robusto	5	50	CC-Ma

Lonsdale	Lonsdale	6½	42	CC-Ma
Long Corona	Corona	6	42	CC-Ma
Long Corona	Corona Especial	6	44	CC-Ma

Introduced in 1998, this is a medium-to-full-bodied cigar, offered in boxes of 25.

NESTOR 747
Handmade in Danli, Honduras.

Wrapper: Honduras　　　*Binder: Nicaragua*　　　*Filler: Honduras, Nicaragua*

Shape	*Name*	*Lgth*	*Ring*	*Wrapper*
Churchill	747	7⅝	47	CM

This is a full-bodied cigar, developed in 1994, which salutes Nestor Plasencia, one of the world's most prolific cigar makers. His factories in Honduras produce dozens of outstanding brands, including this one, to which he put his name. The 747 is box-pressed, produced in limited quantities, and the plain cedar box understates the quality of the product it presents.

NESTOR 747 SERIES II VINTAGE
Handmade in Danli, Honduras.

Wrapper: Ecuador　　　*Binder: Honduras*　　　*Filler: Honduras, Nicaragua*

Shape	*Name*	*Lgth*	*Ring*	*Wrapper*
Robusto	Robusto	4¾	54	CM-Ma
Toro	Robusto Larga	6	54	CM-Ma
Churchill	747	7⅝	47	CM-Ma

The second generation of the Nestor 747 is the three-shape Vintage line, also a full-bodied cigar. However, this group uses 1989-vintage leaves and is presented in its original rounded shape in cedar cabinets of 50 cigars each (the 747 is also available in a box of 25). Each completed bunch of 50, tied with a silk ribbon, is aged for nine months after rolling to ensure that the aromas and flavors of the bunch have penetrated each of the cigars.

HANDMADE CIGARS: BRAND LISTINGS

NEW YORK, NEW YORK
BY TE-AMO
Handmade in San Andres Tuxtla, Mexico.

Wrapper: Mexico   Binder: Mexico   Filler: Mexico

Shape	Name	Lgth	Ring	Wrapper
Lonsdale	Park Avenue	6⅝	42	CC
Corona	Fifth Avenue	5½	44	CC
Grand Corona	7th Avenue	6½	46	CC
Churchill	Broadway	7¼	48	CC
Toro	Wall Street	6	52	CC
Robusto	La Guardia	5	54	CC

A cigar salute to the Big Apple! Given the widespread popularity of Te-Amo in New York – just look at the number of "Te-Amo" signs above newsstands and tobacco shops – it's little wonder that this specially-blended and banded brand was introduced. Medium in body, these cigars are offered in boxes of 25.

NEXTGENERATION
Handmade in Canca la Piedra, Dominican Republic.
Wrapper: Indonesia, USA/Connecticut

Binder: Dominican Republic   Filler: Dominican Republic

Shape	Name	Lgth	Ring	Wrapper
Robusto	Robusto	5	50	CC-CM
Churchill	Churchill	7	48	CC-CM
Grand Corona	Corona	6	45	CC-CM
Torpedo	Torpedo	6½	52	CC-CM
Lonsdale	Lonsdale	6¼	42	CC-CM
Toro	Almirante	6½	48	CC-CM
Robusto	Vivos I	5	50	CC-Ma
Double Corona	Vivos II	7	50	CC-Ma
	Made with short filler:			

Toro	Monumentos	6½	48	CM

Introduced in 1997, this brand offers a choice of wrappers: Sumatra-grown, with a medium and spicy flavor, or Connecticut, with a mild body. Either way, these are very well made cigars and are offered in four popular sizes in boxes of 25 or in gift boxes of four. The Vivos (seconds) and Monumentos sizes are available in bundles of 25 only.

NICARAGUA SUPREMO
Handmade in Esteli, Nicaragua.

Wrapper: Ecuador　　　　*Binder: Nicaragua*　　　　*Filler: Nicaragua*

Shape	Name	Lgth	Ring	Wrapper
Giant	Presidentes	8½	52	CC
Double Corona	Churchill	7	49	CC
Toro	Toro	6	50	CC
Pyramid	Torpedo No. 1	6½	54	CC
Torpedo	Torpedo No. 2	6½	54	CC
Lonsdale	Corona	6½	42	CC
Robusto	Robusto	4½	50	CC
Small Panatela	Churchill No. 5	4½	30	CC

Introduced in 1997, this is a medium-to-full-bodied cigar presented in beautiful cabinet-style boxes of 25.

1932 SELECTION
Handmade in Miami, Florida USA.

Wrapper: Ecuador　　*Binder: Ecuador*　　*Filler: Dom. Rep., Indonesia, Mexico*

Shape	Name	Lgth	Ring	Wrapper
Robusto	Robusto	5	50	CC
Churchill	Churchill	7	48	CC
Torpedo	Torpedo	6½	54	CC
	Aged Vintage Selection:			

Robusto	Rothchild	4½	50	CC
Long Corona	Corona	6	44	CC
Double Corona	Churchill	7	50	CC

This brand was introduced in 1994 and has a mild-to-medium-bodied taste, featuring a Connecticut-seed wrapper. It is offered in boxes of five and 25. The Aged Vintage Selection is specially treated in wine for a superior and pleasing aroma.

NINETEENTH HOLE SIGNATURE SERIES
Handmade in the Dominican Republic.

Wrapper: Indonesia　　　　*Binder: Dom. Rep.*　　　　*Filler: Dom. Rep.*

Shape	Name	Lgth	Ring	Wrapper
Robusto	Hole in One	5	50	CM
Corona	Par	5½	42	CM
Lonsdale	Birdie	6¾	42	CM
Double Corona	Eagle	7	50	CM
Torpedo	Anniversario	6½	52	CM

Fore! Introduced in 1997, this mild-to-medium-bodied cigar is available with a Sumatra wrapper in bundles of 25.

NIÑO VASQUEZ
Handmade in Miami, Florida, USA.

Wrapper: USA/Connecticut　　　*Binder: Indonesia*　　　*Filler: Dom. Rep., Nicaragua*

Shape	Name	Lgth	Ring	Wrapper
Giant	Presidente	8	52	CM
Double Corona	Churchill	7	50	CM
Toro	Governor	6	48	CM
Corona	Corona	5½	42	CM
Robusto	Robusto	5	48	CM

Torpedo	Torpedo	6¼	54	CM

Now made in Miami, this brand blends four types of four-year-old tobaccos with leaves from four nations, including a genuine Connecticut wrapper. All of the cigars are aged for one year after manufacture and are available in boxes of bundles of 25, or in a sampler pack of six.

NIRVANA
Handmade in Esteli, Nicaragua.

Wrapper: Nicaragua   *Binder: Nicaragua*   *Filler: Nicaragua*

Shape	Name	Lgth	Ring	Wrapper
Robusto	Robusto	5	50	CM
Toro	Lonsdale	6	50	CM
Double Corona	Churchill	7	50	CM

This recently-introduced cigar is a product of the Cubella Cigar Co., is medium-to-full in body and is available in boxes of 25.

NIVELACUSO PRIVATE RESERVE
Handmade in Santiago, Dominican Republic.

Wrapper: Indonesia   *Binder: Dom. Rep.*   *Filler: Dom. Rep.*

Shape	Name	Lgth	Ring	Wrapper
Robusto	Robusto	5	50	CC
Lonsdale	No. 1	7	44	CC
Grand Corona	Grand Corona	6½	46	CC
Giant	Double Corona	8	50	CC

Named for the Cuban factory dating acronym (N=1 through O=0), this brand offers a medium-bodied smoke. Introduced in 1996, it is presented in slide-top cedar boxes of 25.

ÑO
Handmade in Miami, Florida, USA.

Wrapper: Indonesia or Mexico   *Binder: Honduras*   *Filler: Dom. Rep., Nicaragua*

HANDMADE CIGARS: BRAND LISTINGS

Shape	Name	Lgth	Ring	Wrapper
Long Panatela	No. 1	7	38	CM-Ma
Long Corona	No. 2	6	44	CM-Ma
Robusto	No. 3	5	50	CM-Ma
Double Corona	No. 4	7	50	CM-Ma

Another inspiration from Luis Sanchez's La Tradicion Cubana factory, this is a medium-to-full-bodied cigar, whether in the Indonesian, natural-shade wrapper or the Mexican maduro wrapped-version. It is offered in boxes of 25.

NORDING
Handmade in Danli, Honduras.

Wrapper: Ecuador   Binder: Nicaragua   Filler: Dom. Rep., Nicaragua

Shape	Name	Lgth	Ring	Wrapper
Toro	Corona Gorda	6	50	CC
Double Corona	Presidente	7½	52	CC
Lonsdale	Lonsdale	6¾	43	CC
Corona	Corona	5½	43	CC
Robusto	Robusto	4¾	52	CC

One of Denmark's most distinguished craftsmen, Erik Nording has created cigars of expert manufacture, using Cuban-seed Dominican and Nicaraguan filler, Nicaraguan binder and a Connecticut wrapper. The result is a full-bodied smoke that was introduced in 1995, packed with a unique humidification system designed by Nording himself.

NOSTALGIA
Handmade in Danli, Honduras.

Wrapper: Honduras   Binder: Honduras   Filler: Honduras

Shape	Name	Lgth	Ring	Wrapper
Double Corona	Presidente	7½	50	CM
Corona	Corona	5¾	43	CM

Churchill	Churchill	7	48	CM
Robusto	Robusto	5	50	CM
Torpedo	Torpedo	6	54	CM

Introduced in 1997, here is a tribute by Carlos Toraño to his Cuban homeland and memories of growing up among the tobacco fields of the Pinar del Rio. Naturally, this is a full-bodied blend of tobaccos in five of the most popular sizes of all time. You can enjoy them, and the memories, by lighting up one of the beauties, packed in all-cedar cabinets of 25.

OCTAVIO TAVARES
Handmade in Santiago, Dominican Republic.
Wrapper: Cameroon, Indonesia, USA/Connecticut
Binder: Dominican Republic *Filler: Dominican Republic*

Shape	Name	Lgth	Ring	Wrapper
Double Corona	Churchill	7	50	CC-CM-Ma
Torpedo	Torpedos	6	52	CC-CM-Ma
Robusto	Robusto	5½	50	CC-CM-Ma
Churchill	Double Corona	6¾	48	CC-CM-Ma
Perfecto	Bon 'N Petit	4	48	CC-CM

Introduced in 1997, this brand honors the memory of master roller Octavio Tavares, who left Cuba in 1962 and settled in the Dominican Republic. Tobaccos for the first run of these cigars were harvested in 1995 and aged for two years. The final blend offers a mild smoke with Connecticut wrappers, a medium-to-full-bodied flavor with Cameroon wrappers and a full-bodied experience with the Sumatran-grown maduro wrappers.

OH QUE BUENO
Handmade in Las Palmas, the Canary Islands of Spain.
Wrapper: USA/Connecticut *Binder: Indonesia* *Filler: Brazil, Dom.Rep., Spain*

Shape	Name	Lgth	Ring	Wrapper
Churchill	Churchill	7½	48	CC
Corona	Corona	5¼	43	CC

| Toro | Nuncios | 6¼ | 49 | CC |
| Robusto | Robustos | 5¼ | 50 | CC |

Very well constructed, this brand blends tobaccos of five nations to produce a mild-to-medium-bodied smoke, offered in boxes of 25 cigars each or in boxes of 50 for the Churchill and Robustos sizes.

OLD FASHIONED
Handmade in Santiago, Dominican Republic
and Kingston, Jamaica.
Wrapper: Cameroon, USA/Connecticut

Binder: Mexico   Filler: Dominican Republic, Mexico

Shape	Name	Lgth	Ring	Wrapper
Small Panatela	Ascots	4¼	32	CC
Short Panatela	Caviar	4	36	CC
Lonsdale	No. 31	6¾	43	CM
Corona	No. 32	5¾	43	CM
Corona	No. 33	5¼	43	CM
Short Panatela	No. 34	5	38	CM
Slim Panatela	No. 36	6	34	CM
Toro	No. 38	6¼	47	CM
Double Corona	No. 40	7½	49	CM
Robusto	No. 41	5½	49	CM
Robusto	No. 42	4½	49	CM
Slim Panatela	No. 250	6	31	CC
Slim Panatela	No. 350	7	34	CC
Corona	No. 500	5½	42	CC-Ma
Lonsdale	No. 700	6½	42	CC-Ma
Churchill	No. 745	7	45	CC

HANDMADE CIGARS: BRAND LISTINGS

| Double Corona | No. 749 | 7½ | 49 | CC-Ma |
| Cigarillo | Quill | 5 | 28 | CC |

Here are seconds of Macanudo and Partagas, varying from mild to medium-to-full in strength. A great value, they are offered in bundles of 20 or 25.

OLD TRINIDAD XVIII CENTURY
Handmade in Las Palmas, the Canary Islands of Spain.
Wrapper: USA/Connecticut   Binder: Brazil   Filler: Dom. Rep.

Shape	Name	Lgth	Ring	Wrapper
Corona	Corona	5½	42	CC
Robusto	Robusto	5	50	CC
Toro	Toro	6	50	CC
Churchill	Churchill	7	46	CC
Double Corona	Soberano	7½	50	CC

Introduced in 1996, this brand celebrates the Cuban city of Trinidad and offers a mild-to-medium taste, thanks to its Connecticut wrapper, Mata Fina binder and Piloto Cubano filler. It is presented in boxes of 25.

OLIVEROS
Handmade in Santiago, Dominican Republic.
Wrapper: Dominican Republic, Indonesia, USA/Connecticut
Binder: Dominican Republic   Filler: Dominican Republic

Shape	Name	Lgth	Ring	Wrapper
Perfecto	Perfecto	6¼	50	CC-CM
Torpedo	Maestro	6¼	50	CC-CM
Double Corona	Coroneles	7	50	CC-CM
Toro	Toro	5¾	50	CC-CM
Perfecto	Tango	4	50	CM
Lonsdale	Dos Perez	6¾	42	CM
Lonsdale	Mulatos	6¾	42	Stripe

Corona	Reyes	5½	42	CM
Short Panatela	Long Lady	5	36	CM

Oliveros cigars have been produced in one form or another since 1927. The current edition offers either a natural wrapper using Connecticut or Javan leaves. The natural-wrapped cigars are mild-to-medium in body, while the maduro wrapper offers a medium-to-full-bodied taste. The Mulato cigars, with a "barber pole" look, offer a mild taste thanks to the double-wrapper of Connecticut and Javan maduro leaves. All of the shapes are available in sweetened versions, while the Dos Perez and Longlady are available with vanilla flavoring.

OLOR
Handmade in Santiago, Dominican Republic.
Wrapper: Brazil, USA/Connecticut   Binder: Dom. Rep.   Filler: Dom. Rep.

Shape	Name	Lgth	Ring	Wrapper
Double Corona	Cacique	7⅝	54	CC-Ma
Robusto	Rothschild	4½	50	CC-Ma
Corona	Momento	5½	43	CC-Ma
Toro	Paco	6	50	CI-CC-Ma
Long Corona	Lonsdale	6¼	42	CC-Ma
Churchill	Colossos	7¼	48	CC-Ma

This brand is now in national distribution and has won new friends among many cigar enthusiasts. Individually cellophaned and packed in slide-top cedar cabinets, these cigars are produced by the Tabacalera A. Fuente and are an excellent value and a smooth, medium-bodied smoke. The maduro-wrapped version offers a rich flavor, using a Brazilian wrapper.

OLOR VINTAGE
Handmade in Santiago, Dominican Republic.
Wrapper: USA/Connecticut   Binder: Dom. Rep.   Filler: Dom. Rep.

Shape	Name	Lgth	Ring	Wrapper
Double Corona	Presidente	7½	50	CC-Ma
Torpedo	Torpedo	6½	50	CC-Ma

Grand Corona	Suave	6½	46	CC-Ma
Toro	Toro	6	50	CC-Ma
Long Corona	Corona Extra	6	42	CC-Ma
Robusto	Robusto	5	50	CC-Ma

More Olor! This well-kept secret now has a sibling, introduced in 1997. It is even more refined than the standard series and offers a medium-bodied smoke in all-cedar cabinets of 25.

ONE PLUS
Handmade in Navarrete, Dominican Republic.
Wrapper: Indonesia   *Binder: Dom. Rep.*   *Filler: Dom. Rep.*

Shape	Name	Lgth	Ring	Wrapper
Churchill	Churchill	7½	48	CM
Robusto	Robusto	5½	48	CM

Here is a mild-to-medium-bodied brand introduced in 1997, using a specially-aged (four years!) filler and Sumatra wrapper. It is presented in cedar boxes or in bundles of 25.

100 FUEGOS
Handmade in Mexico City, Mexico.
Wrapper: Indonesia   *Binder: Nicaragua*   *Filler: Mexico*

Shape	Name	Lgth	Ring	Wrapper
Long Corona	Corona	6	42	CM
Robusto	Robusto	5	50	CM
Double Corona	Churchill	7½	50	CM
Torpedo	Torpedo	6	52	CM

Introduced in 1996, this is a uniquely presented brand. It comes in a special, slant-front box and is available in a standard series with red bands and a specially-aged "special edition" series with blue bands. In either form, this is a medium-to-full-bodied blend protected in individual cellophane sleeves and packed in the afore-mentioned slant-front cedar boxes of 25.

HANDMADE CIGARS: BRAND LISTINGS

ONYX
Handmade in La Romana, Dominican Republic.
Wrapper: Mexico   Binder: Indonesia   Filler: Dom. Rep., Mexico

Shape	Name	Lgth	Ring	Wrapper
Long Corona	No. 642	6	42	Ma
Grand Corona	No. 646	6⅝	46	Ma
Toro	No. 650	6	50	Ma
Double Corona	No. 750	7½	50	Ma
Giant	No. 852	8	52	Ma

This all-maduro series debuted in 1992 and is hand crafted from the finest tobaccos to be the best in their class. The filler is a Dominican blend of Piloto Cubano and Olor, with some Mexican leaf. A Java leaf is used for the binder, then the cigar is finished with a dark Mexican maduro leaf. The taste is mild with a pleasant spicy note.

OPIUM
Handmade in Santo Domingo, Dominican Republic.
Wrapper: Brazil, Indonesia   Binder: Dom. Rep.   Filler: Dom. Rep.

Shape	Name	Lgth	Ring	Wrapper
Long Corona	Lonsdale	6	44	CM-Ma
Robusto	Robusto	5	50	CM-Ma
Toro	Toro	6	50	CM-Ma
Double Corona	Churchill	7½	50	CM-Ma

This is a mild-to-medium-bodied brand in the Indonesian-wrapped "Red Series" and medium-bodied in the "Maduro Series." Introduced in 1997, it is presented uncellophaned in all-cedar boxes of 25.

OPTIMO CLASICO
Handmade in Santiago, Dominican Republic.
Wrapper: Dom. Rep.   Binder: Dom. Rep.   Filler: Dom. Rep.

Shape	Name	Lgth	Ring	Wrapper

HANDMADE CIGARS: BRAND LISTINGS

Robusto	No. I	4½	50	CM
Long Corona	No. II	6	43	CM
Toro	No. III	6	50	CM
Churchill	No. IV	7	48	CM
Giant	No. V	8	50	CM

Once again, here is an Optimo handmade! Offered in five sizes, this version has a medium body and is offered in fairly-priced bundles of 20.

ORNELAS
Handmade in San Andres Tuxtla, Mexico.

Wrapper: Mexico   *Binder: Mexico*   *Filler: Mexico*

Shape	Name	Lgth	Ring	Wrapper
Long Corona	LTD al Cognac	6¼	42	Ma
Lonsdale	Ornelas No. 1	6¾	44	CC
Long Corona	Ornelas No. 2	6	44	CC
Long Panatela	Ornelas No. 3	7	38	CC
Petit Corona	Ornelas No. 4	5	44	CC
Panatela	Ornelas No. 5	6	38	CC
Short Panatela	Ornelas No. 6	5	38	CC
Double Corona	Churchill	7	49	CC-Ma
Robusto	Robusto	4¾	49	CC-Ma
Grand Corona	Cafetero Grande	6½	46	Ma
Corona Extra	Cafetero Chico	5½	46	Ma
Slim Panatela	Matinee	6	30	CC
Small Panatela	Matinee Lights	4¾	30	CC
Slim Panatela	ABC Extra	7	30	CC
Giant	250 mm	9½	64	CC
Lonsdale	Ornelas No. 1 Flavored	6¾	44	CC

Long Corona	Ornelas No. 2 Flavored	6	44	CC
Long Panatela	Ornelas No. 3 Flavored	7	38	CC
Petit Corona	Ornelas No. 4 Flavored	5	44	CC
Panatela	Ornelas No. 5 Flavored	6	38	CC
Short Panatela	Ornelas No. 6 Flavored	5	38	CC
Slim Panatela	Matinee Flavored	6	30	CC
Small Panatela	Matinee Lights Flavored	4¾	30	CC

Re-introduced in 1995, the Ornelas line continues a 60-year tradition. Each of these handmade cigars is a mild Mexico "puro" with special shapes such as the LTD al Cognac line, featuring cognac-treated wrappers, and the eight shapes of vanilla or chocolate-treated cigars. The huge "250" is one of the largest cigars available anywhere.

ORO DOMINICANO
Handmade in Tamboril, Dominican Republic.
Wrapper: USA/Connecticut   *Binder: Dom. Rep.*   *Filler: Dom. Rep.*

Shape	Name	Lgth	Ring	Wrapper
Toro	No. 1	6½	50	CC-Ma
Robusto	No. 3	5	50	CC-Ma
Long Corona	No. 5	6	42	CC

Introduced in 1998, featuring Piloto Cubano and Olor leaves in the filler, Olor binder and Connecticut or maduro wrappers. Available in three sizes, these are mild to medium-bodied cigars offered in boxes of 25.

ORO 750
Handmade in Santiago, Dominican Republic.
Wrapper: Indonesia   *Binder: Dom. Rep.*   *Filler: Dom. Rep.*

Shape	Name	Lgth	Ring	Wrapper
Churchill	No. 1	7	47	CM
Lonsdale	No. 2	6½	44	CM

Robusto	No. 3	5	50	CM
Toro	No. 4	6⅜	48	CM
Corona	No. 5	5½	42	CM

Here is a recent brand from Savinelli, already one of the most respected names anywhere in pipes, humidors and cigars! This 1997-introduced brand is medium in body and features a dark Sumatra-grown wrapper in boxes of 25.

OROSI
Handmade in Condega, Nicaragua.

Wrapper: Indonesia   *Binder: Nicaragua*   *Filler: Nicaragua*

Shape	Name	Lgth	Ring	Wrapper
Double Corona	Oro 700	7	49	CC
Long Corona	Oro 600	6¼	44	CC
Toro	Oro 650	6	50	CC
Corona	Oro 500	5½	42	CC
Robusto	Oro 550	5	50	CC

This brand debuted in 1996, offering a medium-bodied taste. The blend features an Indonesian-grown wrapper and is offered in individual cellophane sleeves inside all-cedar boxes of 25.

OSCAR
Handmade in Santiago, Dominican Republic.

Wrapper: USA/Connecticut   *Binder: Dom. Rep.*   *Filler: Dom. Rep.*

Shape	Name	Lgth	Ring	Wrapper
Cigarillo	Oscarito	4	20	CC
Short Panatela	Prince	5	30	CC
Long Panatela	No. 100	7	38	CC
Lonsdale	No. 200	7	44	CC
Long Corona	No. 300	6¼	44	CC-Ma
Panatela	No. 400	6	38	CC

Robusto	No. 500	5½	50	CC-Ma
Robusto	No. 600	4½	50	CC-Ma
Pyramid	No. 700	7	54	CC
Petit Corona	No. 800	4	42	CC
Giant	Supreme	8	48	CC
Giant	Don Oscar	9	46	CC

Introduced in October 1988, the Oscar is medium to full-bodied, offering a rich bouquet. The experience is mouth-filling with its smooth draw and the luxurious indulgence of the taste of the Dominican blend with a flawless Connecticut wrapper. Produced by only the most experienced artisans, Oscars are packed uncellophaned in cedar cabinets. A black-as-the-night maduro (actually "oscuro") version, using the finest Connecticut Broadleaf is now available on three shapes.

P & R
Handmade in San Andres Tuxtla, Mexico.

Wrapper: Mexico   Binder: Mexico   Filler: Mexico

Shape	Name	Lgth	Ring	Wrapper
Double Corona	Churchill	7	50	CC
Toro	Toro	6	50	CC
Robusto	Robusto	5	50	CC
Lonsdale	Lonsdale	6½	42	CC
Long Corona	Corona	6	42	CC
Long Corona	Corona Especial	6	44	CC
Cigarillo	Deliciosas	5½	25	CC
Small Panatela	Coronitas	4½	30	CC
Slim Panatela	Victorias	6½	30	CC

This is a series of seconds from two sister brands made in Mexico with all Mexican leaves. It is medium in body and available in 5-packs and boxes of 25.

HANDMADE CIGARS: BRAND LISTINGS

PACO
Handmade, with mixed filler, in Santiago, Dominican Republic.

Wrapper: Indonesia   *Binder: Dom. Rep.*   *Filler: Dom. Rep.*

Shape	Name	Lgth	Ring	Wrapper
Double Corona	Presidente	7½	50	CM
Toro	Toro	6	50	CM
Grand Corona	Lonsdale	6	46	CM
Corona	Corona	5½	42	CM

Introduced in 1998, this mixed-fill, Cuban-Sandwich-style cigar offers a medium body in boxes of 25. The Corona size is also available in flavors: Amaretto, cherry, chocolate, cognac, mint, Pina Colada, rum and vanilla.

PACO DE CUBA
Handmade in Santo Domingo, Dominican Republic.

Wrapper: Indonesia   *Binder: Dom. Rep.*   *Filler: Dom. Rep.*

Shape	Name	Lgth	Ring	Wrapper
Double Corona	Churchill	7	50	CM
Toro	Corona	6	50	CM
Robusto	Robusto	5	50	CM

Introduced in 1997, this is a mild brand offered in your choice of bundles or cedar boxes or plastic cases of 10, 15 or 25 cigars.

PADRINO
Handmade in Esteli, Nicaragua.

Wrapper: Cameroon, Ecuador   *Binder: Dom. Rep.*   *Filler: Honduras, Nicaragua*

Shape	Name	Lgth	Ring	Wrapper
Double Corona	Presidente	7¾	52	CC-CM
Churchill	Churchill	7	48	CC-CM
Robusto	Robusto	5½	50	CC-CM
Toro	Double Corona	6	48	CC-CM

Panatela	Panetela	5½	38	CC-CM

Take your choice of wrapper, the lighter Ecuadorian or the darker Cameroon with a medium-bodied taste. You can find it in boxes of 25.

PADRON

Handmade in Danli, Honduras and Esteli, Nicaragua.

Wrapper: Nicaragua   *Binder: Nicaragua*   *Filler: Nicaragua*

Shape	Name	Lgth	Ring	Wrapper
Giant	Magnum	9	50	Cl-CM-Ma
Giant Corona	Grand Reserve	8	41	Cl-CM-Ma
Double Corona	Executive	7½	50	Cl-CM-Ma
Churchill	Churchill	6⅞	46	Cl-CM-Ma
Lonsdale	Ambassador	6⅞	42	Cl-CM-Ma
Panatela	Panatela	6⅞	36	Cl-CM-Ma
Long Corona	Palmas	6¼	42	Cl-CM-Ma
Corona	Londres	5½	42	Cl-CM-Ma
Panatela	Chicos	5½	36	Cl-CM-Ma
Corona Extra	Delicias	4⅞	46	Cl-CM-Ma
Robusto	2000	5	50	Cl-CM-Ma
Robusto	3000	5½	52	Cl-CM-Ma
	30th Anniversary Series:			
Double Corona	Diplomatico	7	50	CM
Pyramid	Pyramide	6⅞	52	CM
Robusto	Exclusivo	5½	50	CM
Grand Corona	Monarca	6½	46	CM
Lonsdale	Superior	6½	42	CM
Long Corona	Corona	6	42	CM
Corona Extra	Principe	4½	46	CM

Toro	Imperial	6	54	CM

The Padron family began manufacturing cigars by hand in Miami in 1964 using the experience of their Cuban forefathers who began making cigars in 1853. Only Cuban-seed tobaccos are used in the manufacture of this medium-to-full-bodied range from all Nicaraguan tobaccos in factories in Honduras and Nicaragua. The 30th Anniversary Series was introduced to considerable acclaim in 1994.

PAISANOS
Handmade in La Romana, Dominican Republic.

Wrapper: Dom. Rep.   *Binder: Dom. Rep.*   *Filler: Dom. Rep.*

Shape	Name	Lgth	Ring	Wrapper
Corona	No. 1	5½	44	CC
Toro	No. 2	6½	48	CC
Double Corona	No. 3	7½	50	CC
Robusto	No. 4	5	52	CC
Giant	No. 5	8½	52	CC

Here is a 1996-introduced, medium-bodied offering with all Dominican leaves, offered in all-wooden boxes of 25.

PALAIS ROYAL
Handmade in Tamboril, Dominican Republic.

Wrapper: Ecuador   *Binder: Dom. Rep.*   *Filler: Dom. Rep.*

Shape	Name	Lgth	Ring	Wrapper
Double Corona	Churchill	7½	50	CC
Lonsdale	Lonsdale	7	44	CC
Torpedo	Torpedo	6	54	CC
Corona	Corona	5½	44	CC
Robusto	Toro	5	50	CC

First available in 1997, this is a mild-bodied brand offered in cedar boxes of 25 cigars each.

HANDMADE CIGARS: BRAND LISTINGS

PALAIS ROYAL CHATEAUX RESERVE
Handmade in Santiago, Dominican Republic.

Wrapper: Indonesia　　　　*Binder: Dom. Rep.*　　　　*Filler: Dom. Rep.*

Shape	Name	Lgth	Ring	Wrapper
Double Corona	Versailles	7½	50	CM
Lonsdale	El Prado	7	44	CM
Corona	Alhambra	5½	44	CM
Robusto	Kensington	5	50	CM

This brand was introduced in 1998 and has a dark, Sumatra wrapper and a full-bodied taste. You can try it in cedar boxes of 25.

PALMAREJO
Handmade in Villa Gonzalez, Dominican Republic.

Wrapper: Indonesia　　　　*Binder: Dom. Rep.*　　　　*Filler: Dom. Rep.*

Shape	Name	Lgth	Ring	Wrapper
Double Corona	Churchill	7½	50	CM
Long Corona	Corona	6	44	CM
Corona	Petit Corona	5½	42	CM
Toro	Robusto	6	50	CM
Torpedo	Torpedo	6	52	CM
Robusto	Rothschild	4½	50	CM
Pyramid	Pyramid	6½	58	CM

Here is a premium, medium-bodied brand introduced in 1997. It features a Sumatra wrapper and is offered in all-cedar boxes of 25, plus boxes of 3, 5 and 10 in the Corona and Robusto shapes.

PANABANO
Handmade in Chiriqui, Panama.

Wrapper: Panama　　　　*Binder: Panama*　　　　*Filler: Panama*

HANDMADE CIGARS: BRAND LISTINGS

Shape	Name	Lgth	Ring	Wrapper
Double Corona	Churchill	7½	50	CC
Robusto	Robusto	5½	50	CC
Grand Corona	Doble Corona	6	46	CC

This cigar was introduced to the U.S. market in 1997 and offers all-Panamanian, Cuban-seed tobacco for a mild-bodied smoke. The presentation is unique as the brand is offered in cellophane-wrapped octagons of 25 cigars each, in addition to boxes of 10 or 25.

PANAMA JONES
Manufacture and components vary by size; see below.

Shape	Name	Lgth	Ring	Wrapper
	Handmade in Chiriqui, Panama: *(Wrapper: Indonesia; Binder: Panama; Filler: Panama)*			
Churchill	Double Corona	6¾	46	CC
	Handmade in San Andres Tuxtla, Mexico: *(Wrapper: Mexico; Binder: Mexico; Filler: Mexico)*			
Corona	Corona	5½	42	CM-Ma
	Handmade in Santiago, Dominican Republic: *(Wrapper: Dom.Rep.; Binder: Dom.Rep.; Filler: Dom.Rep.)*			
Robusto	Robusto	4¾	50	CC
Lonsdale	Lonsdale	6¾	44	CC

Talk about complicated! Here's a brand with three different blends from factories in three different countries in just four sizes! The Panama-made Double Corona is considered mild-to-medium bodied; the Mexican-made Coronas are medium-bodied and the Dominican-made sizes are also medium-bodied. Introduced in 1997, Panama Jones cigars are modestly priced, so try them all!

PANCHO FLOODS
Handmade in Santiago, Dominican Republic.
Wrapper: USA/Connecticut   Binder: Dom. Rep.   Filler: Dom. Rep., Ecuador

HANDMADE CIGARS: BRAND LISTINGS

Shape	Name	Lgth	Ring	Wrapper
Churchill	Churchill	7	46	CC
Double Corona	Churchill	7	50	CC
Double Corona	Double Corona	7¼	52	CC
Grand Corona	Corona	6½	46	CC
Toro	Toro	6	50	CC
Robusto	Robusto	5	50	CC

This brand was introduced in 1990 and is mild-to-medium in body. It is offered in boxes of 25.

PANTERA
Handmade, with short filler, in Santiago, Dominican Republic.
Wrapper: Dom. Rep.   Binder: Dom. Rep.   Filler: Dom. Rep.

Shape	Name	Lgth	Ring	Wrapper
Robusto	No. 10	5½	50	CC
Corona Extra	No. 20	5½	46	CC
Corona	No. 30	5½	42	CC
Panatela	No. 40	5½	38	CC

This handmade brand is mild in taste and offered in economical bundles of 25 cigars each.

PAPA ARTURO
Handmade in Tamboril, Dominican Republic.
Wrapper: Indonesia, USA/Connecticut   Binder: Dom. Rep.   Filler: Dom. Rep.

Shape	Name	Lgth	Ring	Wrapper
Torpedo	Torpedo	6¾	52	CC-CM
Corona	Petit Corona	5½	42	CC-CM
Lonsdale	Corona	6¾	42	CC-CM
Robusto	Robusto	5	49	CC-CM

HANDMADE CIGARS: BRAND LISTINGS

Double Corona	Churchill	7½	49	CC-CM

Introduced in 1997, this brand is mild-to-medium in strength and is offered in boxes or bundles of 26 (!), except for the Torpedo shape, available in 20s.

PAPA JUANICO
Handmade in Santiago, Dominican Republic.

Wrapper: Indonesia   Binder: Dom. Rep.   Filler: Dom. Rep.

Shape	Name	Lgth	Ring	Wrapper
Toro		6	50	CM
Robusto		4½	50	CM
Corona		5½	42	CM

Although there are no shape names, this is a long-filler, medium-bodied cigar available in modestly-priced bundles or boxes of 25.

PARADISE DESSERT CIGARS
Handmade in Santiago, Dominican Republic.

Wrapper: Indonesia   Binder: Dom. Rep.   Filler: Dom. Rep.

Shape	Name	Lgth	Ring	Wrapper
Short Panatela	Flavors	5	38	CM

This brand is available in Amaretto, Anise, cherry, clove, chocolate, Havana rum, mint and vanilla. Made with long-filler leaves, this is a medium-bodied brand and presented in boxes of 25.

PARADISE ISLAND
Handmade in Miami, Florida, USA.

Wrapper: Ecuador   Binder: Dom. Rep.   Filler: Dom. Rep., Honduras

Shape	Name	Lgth	Ring	Wrapper
Pyramid	Pyramid	7¼	54	CC
Torpedo	Torpedo	6½	54	CC
Double Corona	Double Corona	7¾	50	CC

HANDMADE CIGARS: BRAND LISTINGS

Churchill	Churchill	7	48	CC
Toro	Toro	6	50	CC
Toro	Corona	6	48	CC
Robusto	Robusto	5	50	CC

Now what island could this be referring to? We don't know, but we are aware that this is a mild-to-medium-bodied cigar made in Little Havana. It is offered in boxes or bundles of 25.

PARTAGAS
Handmade in Santiago, Dominican Republic.

Wrapper: Cameroon   *Binder: Mexico*   *Filler: Dom. Rep., Mexico*

Shape	Name		Lgth	Ring	Wrapper
Torpedo	Aristocrat		6	50	CM
Cigarillo	Miniatura		3¾	24	CM
Small Panatela	Puritos		4⅛	32	CM
Panatela	No. 6		6	34	CM
Short Panatela	No. 4		5	38	CM
Robusto	Robusto		4½	49	CM
Corona	No. 2		5¾	43	CM
Robusto	Naturales		5½	50	CM
Grand Corona	Maduro		6¼	48	Ma
Lonsdale	No. 1		6¾	43	CM
Long Corona	Sabroso	(tubed)	5⅞	44	CM
Lonsdale	Humitube	(tubed)	6¾	43	CM
Grand Corona	Almirantes		6¼	47	CM
Lonsdale	8-9-8		6⅞	44	CM
Double Corona	No. 10		7½	49	CM
Double Corona	Fabuloso		7	52	CM
	Limited Reserve series:				

HANDMADE CIGARS: BRAND LISTINGS

Lonsdale	Royale	6¾	43	CM
Grand Corona	Regale	6¼	47	CM
Robusto	Robusto	5½	49	CM
Short Panatela	Epicure	5	38	CM
	150 Signature Series:			
Double Corona	AA	7½	49	CM
Lonsdale	A	6¾	43	CM
Grand Corona	B	6½	47	CM
Robusto	C	5½	49	CM
Short Panatela	D	5	38	CM
Toro	Figurado	6	50	CM
Robusto	Robusto	4½	49	CM
Double Corona	Don Ramon	7	52	CM

This famous brand, originated in 1845, continues to use only the highest quality Cameroon wrappers which, combined with tobaccos from the Dominican Republic and Mexico, gives it a spicy, full flavor. In a salute to the brand's 150th anniversary, the limited edition 150th Signature Series debuted in late 1995. Wrapped in specially-cured, 18-year-old Cameroon tobaccos, these cigars are aged an additional four months and presented in unique, varnished cedar boxes of 25, 50 or 100 cigars.

PARTICULARES
Handmade in Santiago, Dominican Republic.

Wrapper: Ecuador   Binder: Dom. Rep.   Filler: Dom. Rep., Nicaragua

Shape	Name	Lgth	Ring	Wrapper
Slim Panatela	Petit	5½	34	CC
Corona	No. 4	5½	42	CC
Panatela	Panatelas	6⅞	35	CC
Long Corona	Royal Coronas	6¼	43	CC
Robusto	Rothschild	5	50	CC-Ma

HANDMADE CIGARS: BRAND LISTINGS

Lonsdale	Supremos	7	43	CC
Toro	Matador	6	50	CC-Ma
Churchill	Churchills	7	48	CC
Double Corona	Presidentes	7¾	50	CC
Giant	Viajantes	8½	52	CC-Ma

Introduced in the 1980s, the Particulares was originally made in Honduras and, beginning in 1997, is now manufactured in the Dominican Republic. The wrapper is Connecticut-seed from Ecuador and helps to make this a medium-bodied cigar, offered in boxes of 25.

PASEANA
Handmade in Danli, Honduras.

Wrapper: Honduras *Binder: Honduras* *Filler: Honduras, Nicaragua*

Shape	Name	Lgth	Ring	Wrapper
Giant	Presidente	8½	50	CM
Torpedo	Torpedo	7	54	CM
Robusto	Robusto	5	50	CM
Churchill	Churchill	7	48	CM
Toro	Toro	6	50	CM
Long Corona	Cetro	6	44	CM

A limited-production cigar introduced in 1997, this is a medium-bodied brand. It is offered in individual cellophane sleeves and then packed into all-cedar boxes of 25.

PASHA RESERVE COLLECTION
Handmade in Villa Gonzalez, Dominican Republic.

Wrapper: Indonesia *Binder: Dom. Rep.* *Filler: Dom. Rep.*

Shape	Name	Lgth	Ring	Wrapper
Double Corona	Churchill	7½	50	CM
Short Panatela	No. 4	4	36	CM

HANDMADE CIGARS: BRAND LISTINGS

Robusto	No. 5	5	50	CM
Long Corona	No. 6	6	43	CM
Churchill	No. 7	7	48	CM

This brand was introduced in 1998, and offers a medium-to-full body, offered in boxes of 25.

PAUL GARMIRIAN
Handmade in Santiago, Dominican Republic.

Wrapper: USA/Connecticut   Binder: Dom. Rep.   Filler: Dom. Rep.

Shape	Name	Lgth	Ring	Wrapper
Giant	P.G. Celebration	9	50	CC
Double Corona	P.G. Double Corona	7⅝	50	CC
Torpedo	P.G. Belicoso	6¼	52	CC
Churchill	P.G. Churchill	7	48	CC
Long Panatela	P.G. No. 1	7½	38	CC
Grand Corona	P.G. Corona Grande	6½	46	CC
Torpedo	P.G. Belicoso Fino	5½	52	CC
Lonsdale	P.G. Lonsdale	6½	42	CC
Toro	P.G. Connoisseur	6	50	CC
Robusto	P.G. Epicure	5½	50	CC
Robusto	P.G. Robusto	5	50	CC
Robusto	P.G. No. 2	4¾	48	CC
Corona	P.G. Corona	5½	42	CC
Petit Corona	P.G. Petit Corona	5	43	CC
Short Panatela	P.G. Petit Bouquet	4½	38	CC
Petit Corona	P.G. No. 5	4	40	CC
Petit Corona	P.G. Bombones	3½	43	CC
Panatela	P.G. Especial	5¾	38	CC

HANDMADE CIGARS: BRAND LISTINGS

	Artisan's Selection:			
Double Corona	No. 1	7½	50	CC
Toro	No. 2	6	50	CC
Robusto	No. 3	5	50	CC
Robusto	No. 4	5½	52	CC
Robusto	No. 5	5	52	CC
Churchill	No. 6	7	48	CC
Robusto	No. 7	4½	48	CC
Grand Corona	No. 8	6¼	46	CC
Corona	No. 9	5¼	42	CC

"Smooth, subtle, spicy and delicious." That's the response of many smokers who were delighted to enjoy a Dominican-produced cigar which has so many attributes of a high-quality Havana. The characteristics of the P.G. line include a scarce and richly-flavored medium-to-dark reddish-brown Colorado-colored Connecticut Shade wrappers which are the favorite of many connoisseurs. The new Especial shape is specially configured to be of interest to women smokers.

The Artisan's Selection was introduced in 1998 and is an expertly-constructed, mild-to-medium-bodied cigar, with a complex filler blend surrounded by a Connecticut Shade wrapper. It is noteworthy for its consistency and smoothness and is offered in cellophane sleeves inside all-cedar boxes of 25.

PEÑAMIL ORO
Handmade in Tenerife, Canary Islands of Spain.
Wrapper: USA/Connecticut   Binder: Dom. Rep.   Filler: Brazil, Dom. Rep.

Shape	Name	Lgth	Ring	Wrapper
Churchill	No. 25	7⅝	45	CC
Lonsdale	No. 17	6⅞	41	CC
Long Corona	No. 6	6	41	CC
Lonsdale	Gran Reserva	7¼	45	CC

HANDMADE CIGARS: BRAND LISTINGS

Here is a very mild brand with a long history as one of Spain's top brands, offered in a beautifully-decorated box of 25 cigars each.

PEÑAMIL PLATA
Handmade in Tenerife, Canary Islands of Spain.

Wrapper: Indonesia　　　*Binder: Indonesia*　　　*Filler: Brazil, Dom. Rep., Mexico*

Shape	Name	Lgth	Ring	Wrapper
Corona	No. 1	5¼	41	CM
Petit Corona	No. 2	5	40	CM
Cigarillo	No. 3	4¾	29	CM
Cigarillo	Cigarillos	4	21	CM

This "silver" brand features a Sumatra wrapper and Java binder and has a medium-bodied taste. You can enjoy this brand in boxes of five and 25, except for the cigarillos, available in 20s.

PENGUIN
Handmade in Villa Gonzalez, Dominican Republic.
Wrapper: Ecuador, Indonesia and Brazil/Ecuador

Binder: Dominican Republic　　　　　　　　*Filler: Dominican Republic*

Shape	Name	Lgth	Ring	Wrapper
	Deluxe and Supreme Series:			
Double Corona	Emperor	7½	52	CC-CM-Stripe
Torpedo	King	6½	52	CC-CM-Stripe
Lonsdale	Adelie	7	44	CC-CM-Stripe
Toro	Gentoo	6	48	CC-CM-Stripe
Robusto	Gallapagos	5	50	CC-CM-Stripe
	Sabores Series:			
Short Panatela	La Palma	5	38	Stripe
Corona	Petite Corona	5½	42	Stripe
Long Corona	Lonsdale	6	44	Stripe

HANDMADE CIGARS: BRAND LISTINGS

Introduced in 1996, this brand is offered in a variety of wrapper shades – natural-shade leaves from Connecticut seed (grown in Ecuador) and darker wrappers from Sumatra – and in a double wrapped version with wrapper leaves from Brazil and Ecuador. Both the Deluxe (mild-to-medium body) and Supreme (aged, medium body) series are offered in boxes of 25. The Sabores series is mild-to-medium in body and is flavored in your choice of Amaretto, cognac or vanilla, also in boxes of 25.

PERA
Handmade in Esteli, Nicaragua.

Wrapper: Nicaragua   *Binder: Nicaragua*   *Filler: Nicaragua*

Shape	Name	Lgth	Ring	Wrapper
Churchill	Churchill	6¾	48	CM
Corona	Corona	5½	44	CM
Double Corona	Double Corona	7	54	CM
Pyramid	Figurado	7½	52	CM
Robusto	Rothschild	4½	52	CM
Toro	Toro	6¼	50	CM

Created in 1996, this all-Nicaraguan line is medium-bodied, with a touch of spice on the finish. Offered in bundles of 25.

PERIQUE
Handmade in Santiago, Dominican Republic.

Wrapper: Indonesia   *Binder: Dom. Rep.*   *Filler: Dom. Rep., USA/Louisiana*

Shape	Name	Lgth	Ring	Wrapper
Toro	Toro	6	52	CM
Double Corona	Churchill	7½	50	CM
Torpedo	Belicoso	5	50	CM
Corona Grande	Corona Grande	6¼	46	CM
Corona	Corona	5¾	44	CM

HANDMADE CIGARS: BRAND LISTINGS

Introduced in 1997, this is a medium-to-full-bodied brand which utilizes a 1995-vintage Louisiana Perique tobacco leaf in the filler, combined with Indonesian wrapper and a Dominican binder. It is available in boxes of 25.

PETER STOKKEBYE
Handmade in Santiago, Dominican Republic.

Wrapper: USA/Connecticut   *Binder: Proprietary*   *Filler: Dom. Rep.*

Shape	Name	Lgth	Ring	Wrapper
Double Corona	Santa Maria No. 1	7	50	CC
Panatela	Santa Maria No. 2	6¾	38	CC
Corona	Santa Maria No. 3	5½	43	CC

The famous Stokkebye family is now in its eighth generation in the tobacco trade. They were once one of the appointed cigar rollers to Winston Churchill! Their cigars, introduced in 1987, are blended with a delicate balance to simultaneously provide a mild and flavorful smoke.

PETRUS
Handmade in Santa Rosa de Copan, Honduras.

Wrapper: Ecuador   *Binder: Honduras*   *Filler: Honduras*

Shape	Name	Lgth	Ring	Wrapper
Double Corona	Double Corona	7¾	50	CC
Long Panatela	Lord Byron	8	38	CC
Double Corona	Churchill *(tube available)*	7	50	CC
Long Corona	No. II	6¼	44	DC-CC
Toro	No. III	6	50	CC
Panatela	Palma Fina	6	38	CC
Panatela	No. IV	5⅝	38	CC
Corona Extra	Corona Sublime	5½	46	CC
Torpedo	Antonius	5	52	CC
Petit Corona	Gregorius	5	42	CC
Robusto	Rothschild	4¾	50	CC

HANDMADE CIGARS: BRAND LISTINGS

Short Panatela	Chantaco	4¾	35	CC
Small Panatela	Duchess	4½	30	CC

This outstanding line, which debuted in 1989, adds a new panatela shape for 1997 and a double claro wrapper for the No. II size. These natural-wrapped cigars showcase Ecuadorian-grown leaf. Petrus is a mild-to-medium-bodied cigar with dense, spicy aromas and rich flavors.

PETRUS DOMINICANA
Handmade in Tamboril, Dominican Republic.

Wrapper: Gabon *Binder: Dom. Rep.* *Filler: Dom. Rep.*

Shape	Name	Lgth	Ring	Wrapper
Churchill	Churchill	7	48	CM
Robusto	Robusto	5	50	CM
Torpedo	Torpedo	5	54	CM
Long Corona	Lonsdale	6¼	44	CM

The famous Petrus name now adorns a Dominican-made cigar, which debuted in 1998. It is a box-pressed brand with a mild-to-medium and spicy body, offered in boxes of 20.

PETRUS ETIQUETTE ROUGE
Handmade in Danli, Honduras.

Wrapper: Ecuador *Binder: Honduras* *Filler: Dom.Rep., Nicaragua*

Shape	Name	Lgth	Ring	Wrapper
Churchill	RCH 1	7	48	CC
Torpedo	RB 1	7	55	CC
Corona	RCR 1	5¾	44	CC
Robusto	RR 1	5	52	CC

Here is a superior cigar, made in a limited production of 2,000 boxes per shape. Packed in exquisite Caoba wood boxes of 20 cigars, this is a medium-bodied, rich blend created to satisfy the most demanding cigar enthusiast.

HANDMADE CIGARS: BRAND LISTINGS

PETRUS ORO NEGRO
Handmade in Santa Rosa de Copan, Honduras.

Wrapper: Honduras   *Binder: Honduras*   *Filler: Honduras*

Shape	Name	Lgth	Ring	Wrapper
Double Corona	Double Corona	7¾	50	Ma
Double Corona	Churchill	7	50	Ma
Long Corona	No. II	6¼	44	Ma
Toro	No. III	6	50	Ma
Corona Extra	Corona Sublime	5½	46	Ma
Torpedo	Antonius	5	54	Ma
Robusto	Rothschild	4¾	50	Ma

Introduced in 1996, this cigar is wrapped in a superb Honduran maduro wrapper around a blend of all-Honduran-grown tobaccos. This is a medium-bodied smoke available in all-cedar boxes of 25.

PHAT BOYZ
Handmade in Navarrete, Dominican Republic.

Wrapper: Indonesia   *Binder: Dom. Rep.*   *Filler: Dom. Rep.*

Shape	Name	Lgth	Ring	Wrapper
Torpedo	Torpedo	6	54	CM
Giant	Churchill	8½	50	CM

This is a medium-bodied brand which debuted in 1998. It is offered in bundles of 25.

PHEASANT
Handmade in Danli, Honduras.

SIGNATURE SERIES:
Wrapper: Ecuador   *Binder: Mexico*   *Filler: Costa Rica, Honduras, Nicaragua*

MADURO SERIES:
Wrapper: USA/Pennsylvania   *Binder: Mexico*   *Filler: Costa Rica, Honduras, Nicaragua*

HANDMADE CIGARS: BRAND LISTINGS

Shape	Name	Lgth	Ring	Wrapper
	Signature Series:			
Double Corona	Churchill	7½	50	CC
Toro	Toro	6	50	CC
Robusto	Robusto	5¼	54	CC
Lonsdale	Corona	6½	42	CC
	Maduro Series:			
Torpedo	Torpedo	6	50	Ma
Double Corona	Double Corona	7	50	Ma
Robusto	Robusto	4¾	54	Ma
Lonsdale	Gran Corona	6½	44	Ma
Robusto	Rothschild	4½	48	Ma

The Signature Series is a mild-to-medium-bodied brand with a Connecticut-seed wrapper which was introduced in 1995 and complements the outstanding Pheasant line of Spanish leather cigar and smoking accessories. The Maduro Series is new for 1998 and has a medium-bodied taste with a Pennsylvanian leaf wrapper. Each of these styles is offered in elegant boxes of 25.

PHILIPPINE CIGAR COMPANY
Handmade in Manila, the Philippines.

Wrapper: Philippines   *Binder: Philippines*   *Filler: Philippines*

Shape	Name	Lgth	Ring	Wrapper
Double Corona	Double Corona	7½	52	CM
Churchill	Churchill	6¾	47	CM
Lonsdale	Corona Largas	6¾	44	CM
Corona Extra	Rothschild	5½	46	CM
Corona	Corona	5½	42	CM
Robusto	Robusto	5	52	CM

Torpedo	Cortado	5	52	CM
Short Panatela	Half Corona	4	39	CM

This is a medium-bodied cigar with two-year-old tobaccos grown in the Philippines, available in Narra wood boxes of 25.

PHILLIPS & KING GUARDSMEN
Handmade in La Romana, Dominican Republic.

Wrapper: Indonesia   *Binder: Dominican Republic*
Filler: Brazil, Dominican Republic, Mexico

Shape	Name	Lgth	Ring	Wrapper
Giant	No. 1	8	52	CM
Double Corona	No. 2	7½	50	CM
Toro	No. 3	6	50	CM
Robusto	No. 4	4¾	50	CM
Churchill	No. 5	7	48	CM
Corona	No. 6	5½	44	CM
Long Corona	No. 7	6	42	CM
Panatela	No. 8	6	36	CM

The Guardsmen series is the flagship of the famous cigar distribution firm of Phillips & King of Industry, California. It is mild in body, individually wrapped and offered in boxes of 25 cigars each.

PICADURA
Handmade, with mixed filler, in Esteli, Nicaragua.

Wrapper: Cameroon   *Binder: Cameroon*   *Filler: Dom. Rep.*

Shape	Name	Lgth	Ring	Wrapper
Churchill	Cazadores	7½	46	CM
Churchill	Corona	7	46	CM
Long Panatela	Lanceros	7½	38	CM

HANDMADE CIGARS: BRAND LISTINGS

Cigarillo	Pencil	6	28	CM

This mixed-filler brand is available in three sizes, with the Corona, Pencil and Lanceros sizes available in six flavors: Amaretto, Anise, chocolate, cognac, rum and vanilla. All are available in boxes, bundles or glass jar humidors of 25.

PINAR 1958
Handmade in New York, New York, USA.

Wrapper: Cuba   *Binder: Cuba*   *Filler: Cuba, Honduras*

Shape	Name	Lgth	Ring	Wrapper
Robusto	Rothschild	5	50	CM
Churchill	Churchill	7	50	CM
Torpedo	Belicoso	6½	54	CM
Pyramid	Pyramide	6½	52	CM

Miracles do happen . . . like finding 14 bales (4,200 pounds) of 1957 Rosado Corojo leaf grown in the Pinar del Rio region of Cuba, sitting in an old factory building in Trenton, New Jersey. Now this find has been turned into 75,000 cigars at the Puros de Armando Ramos factory in New York. The result is a medium-to-full-bodied blend offered in boxes of 25, available in limited distribution only.

PINNACLE
Handmade in Santiago, Dominican Republic.

Wrapper: Indonesia   *Binder: Dom. Rep.*   *Filler: Dom. Rep.*

Shape	Name	Lgth	Ring	Wrapper
Churchill	Imperial Corona	6¾	46	CC
Robusto	Robusto	5	50	CC
Toro	Corona Gorda	6	50	CC

This brand from the Dominican Republic was introduced in 1996. The medium-bodied taste is complemented by the unusual packaging: each cigar is banded, then presented in an individual foil sleeve, which also bears the brand's band. The finished product is sold in elegant, all-cedar boxes of 25.

HANDMADE CIGARS: BRAND LISTINGS

PINNACLE RESERVE
Handmade in Santiago, Dominican Republic.

Wrapper: Dom. Rep.   Binder: Dom. Rep.   Filler: Dom. Rep.

Shape	Name	Lgth	Ring	Wrapper
Robusto	Rothchild	5	50	CM
Grand Corona	Corona	6½	46	CM
Torpedo	Torpedo	5	50	CM

Aged longer than its sibling above, it is also medium-bodied and offered in elegant boxes of 25 cigars each.

PIO VI
Handmade in Miami, Florida, USA.

Wrapper: Brazil   Binder: Indonesia   Filler: Dom. Rep., Mexico, Nicaragua

Shape	Name	Lgth	Ring	Wrapper
Double Corona	Churchill	7	50	CM
Toro	Doble Corona	6	50	CM
Robusto	Robusto	5	50	CM
Corona	Corona	5½	42	CM
Torpedo	Torpedo	6	54	CM

This brand was introduced in 1994. It features aged filler and a medium-bodied taste of boxes of 25.

PIPERS
Handmade in Dingelstadt, Germany.
Wrapper: Brazil, Indonesia, USA/Connecticut

Binder: Dominican Republic   Filler: Dom. Rep., Honduras, Jamaica

Shape	Name	Lgth	Ring	Wrapper
Robusto	Robusto	5	50	CC-CM
Double Corona	Churchill	6⅞	49	CC-CM

HANDMADE CIGARS: BRAND LISTINGS

This brand was introduced in 1997 and each of the shapes is offered in flavored styles of cherry, plum and vanilla. The cherry line uses a Connecticut wrapper, the plum line has a Brazilian wrapper and the vanilla range has a Sumatra wrapper. The overall strength in mild, however, and the brand is offered in elegant boxes of 10.

PIRATA
Handmade in Santiago, Dominican Republic.

NATURAL SELECTION:

Wrapper: Indonesia   *Binder: Dom. Rep.*   *Filler: Dom. Rep.*

MADURO SELECTION:

Wrapper: Brazil   *Binder: Brazil*   *Filler: Brazil*

Shape	Name	Lgth	Ring	Wrapper
Churchill	Gran Corona	6¾	46	CC-Ma
Giant	President	8	50	CC-Ma
Robusto	Robusto	4½	52	CC-Ma
Toro	Toro	6	50	CC-Ma
Torpedo	Torpedo	6½	52	CC-Ma

This brand achieved wider recognition in 1997 and offers two medium-bodied blends: one that features an Indonesian wrapper with Dominican interior leaves, the other with all-Brazilian tobaccos. In either case, you can enjoy Pirata in boxes of 25.

PLASENCIA
Handmade in Esteli, Nicaragua.

Wrapper: Ecuador   *Binder: Nicaragua*   *Filler: Nicaragua*

Shape	Name	Lgth	Ring	Wrapper
Double Corona	Presidente	7½	50	CC
Torpedo	Torpedo	7	54	CC
Toro	Toro	6	50	CC

Long Corona	Corona Especial	6	44	CC
Robusto	Robusto	4¾	52	CC

Here is a brand that celebrates the famous name of Plasencia — a name revered throughout the cigar world for the manufacture of outstanding cigars. These cigars are outstanding in their own right, with a medium-bodied taste. They are offered in boxes of 25.

PLAYBOY
BY DON DIEGO
Handmade in La Romana, Dominican Republic.

Wrapper: USA/Connecticut   *Binder: Dom. Rep.*   *Filler: Brazil, Dom. Rep.*

Shape	Name		Lgth	Ring	Wrapper
Double Corona	Churchill		7¾	50	CC
Toro	Double Corona		6	52	CC
Churchill	Gran Corona		6¾	48	CC
Robusto	Robusto		5	50	CC
Lonsdale	Lonsdale		6½	42	CC
Toro	C.E.O.	(tubed)	6½	48	CC

Here is the 1996-introduced brand named for the famous magazine and entertainment company, produced in cooperation with Consolidated Cigar Company in its La Romana factory. The blend is medium in body and features a dark shade of Connecticut wrapper. The cigars are presented in elegant wooden boxes of 25, except for the C.E.O., available in 10s.

PLAYERS
Handmade in Tamboril, Dominican Republic.

LEGACY SERIES:

Wrapper: Indonesia   *Binder: Dom. Rep.*   *Filler: Dom. Rep.*

VINTAGE SERIES:

Wrapper: USA/Connecticut   *Binder: Dom. Rep.*   *Filler: Dom. Rep.*

HANDMADE CIGARS: BRAND LISTINGS

Shape	Name	Lgth	Ring	Wrapper
Robusto	Robusto	5	50	CC-CM
Churchill	Churchill	7	46	CC-CM
Long Corona	Lonsdale	6	44	CC-CM
Torpedo	Torpedo	6	52	CC-CM
Petit Corona	Corona	5	42	CC-CM

Introduced in 1998, this is the official cigar of The Players Grill, an NFL-themed restaurant and bar concept developed in association with the marketing arm of the NFL Players Association. The Legacy Series is medium-bodied in flavor, while the Vintage Series is mild-bodied.

PLEASANT PRIVATE STOCK
Handmade in Danli, Honduras.

Wrapper: Honduras　　　　　*Binder: Honduras*　　　　　*Filler: Honduras*

Shape	Name	Lgth	Ring	Wrapper
Corona	No. 544	5½	44	CM
Robusto	No. 530	5	50	CM
Long Corona	No. 643	6	43	CM
Lonsdale	No. 644	6½	44	CM
Lonsdale	No. 744	7	44	CM

Here is a Honduran "puro" which offers five sizes and a full-bodied taste. It is offered in value-priced bundles of 25.

PLEIADES
Handmade in Santiago, Dominican Republic.

Wrapper: Mexico or USA/Connecticut　　　*Binder: Dom. Rep.*　　　*Filler: Dom. Rep.*

Shape	Name	Lgth	Ring	Wrapper
Giant	Aldebaran	8½	50	CC
Giant	Saturne	8	46	CC

HANDMADE CIGARS: BRAND LISTINGS

Giant Corona	Neptune	7½	42	CC
Churchill	Sirius	6⅞	46	CC-Ma
Corona	Orion	5¾	42	CC
Panatela	Uranus	6⅞	34	CC
Corona	Antares	5½	40	CC
Robusto	Pluton	5	50	CC-Ma
Small Panatela	Perseus	5	34	CC
Cigarillo	Mars	5	28	CC
	Machine-made:			
Cigarillo	Mini	3½	24	CC

Pleiades are exquisite cigars imported from the Dominican Republic. They are created by hand using only the finest long-leaf filler and smooth Connecticut Shade wrappers or Mexican maduro wrappers. Depending on the selection from the 11 available shapes, the richness, quality of taste and aroma will vary from mild and light to a bold, full-bodied flavor. The unusual packaging includes not only an all-cedar box, but each is equipped with a mini-humidifier to keep the cigars in perfect condition!

PLEIADES RESERVE PRIVEE
Handmade in Santiago, Dominican Republic.

Wrapper: USA/Connecticut   *Binder: Dom. Rep.*   *Filler: Dom. Rep.*

Shape	Name	Lgth	Ring	Wrapper
Churchill	Sirius	6⅞	46	CC
Robusto	Pluton	5	50	CC

New for 1997, here are glorious examples of the roller's art, using vintage tobaccos from 1991 and 1992 to form beautiful, usually mild-bodied cigars without a hint of harshness. Available only in limited quantities, you can experience them in all-cedar boxes of 16 (Pluton) or 24 (Sirius).

HANDMADE CIGARS: BRAND LISTINGS

PONTALBA
Handmade in Dominican Republic and Nicaragua.

Wrapper: USA/Connecticut   Binder: Dom. Rep.   Filler: Dom. Rep.

Shape	Name	Lgth	Ring	Wrapper
Petit Corona	Club Elites	5	43	CC
Corona	Clintalba	5½	42	CC
Robusto	Robusto	5	50	CC
Toro	Corona Gorda	6	50	CC
Double Corona	Presidente	7¼	50	CC
Torpedo	Torpedo	6½	50	CC
Giant	Private Stock	8¼	50	CC

Produced in factories in two nations, this is a medium-bodied blend which debuted in 1995. You can find it in boxes of 25.

POR LARRAÑAGA
Handmade in La Romana, Dominican Republic.

Wrapper: USA/Connecticut   Binder: Dom. Rep.   Filler: Dom. Rep.

Shape	Name	Lgth	Ring	Wrapper
Lonsdale	Cetros	6⅞	42	CC
Panatela	Delicados	6⅝	36	CC
Double Corona	Fabulosos	7	50	CC
Corona	Nacionales	5½	42	CC
Short Panatela	Petit Cetros en Cedro	5½	38	CC
Pyramid	Pyramides	6	50	CC
Robusto	Robusto	5	50	CC

This is an ancient brand which first saw production in Cuba in 1834! Today's Dominican version is medium-bodied and limited in production. It is generally available only to tobacconists who are members of the Tobacconists' Association of America (TAA) and available in elegant boxes of 10 or 25.

HANDMADE CIGARS: BRAND LISTINGS

POR MATT AMORE
Handmade in Santiago, Dominican Republic.
Wrapper: USA/Connecticut   Binder: Dom. Rep.   Filler: Dom. Rep.

Shape	Name	Lgth	Ring	Wrapper
Double Corona	DJB	7	47	CC
Robusto	Amistad	4½	50	CC
Long Corona	Esperanza	6	43	CC
Toro	MQ	6	50	CC

Known as Por Matamor when introduced in 1996, this is a limited production cigar for the benefit of a discriminating few who appreciate a medium-bodied smoke with excellent construction. These cigars are individually cellophaned and packed in all-cedar boxes of 25.

PORFIRIO
Handmade in Santiago, Dominican Republic.
Wrapper: USA/Connecticut   Binder: Dom. Rep.   Filler: Dom. Rep.

Shape	Name	Lgth	Ring	Wrapper
Corona	Coronas	5½	42	CC
Lonsdale	Lonsdale	6½	42	CC
Robusto	Robusto	5	50	CC
Double Corona	Churchill	7½	50	CC
Giant	Rubi	8½	52	CC

This brand was introduced in 1996, with a mild body and an elegant Connecticut Shade wrapper surrounding Dominican tobaccos. Each cigar is presented in an individual cellophane sleeve and Porfirios are available in cedar cabinets of 25 cigars.

PORT ROYAL
Handmade, with mixed filler, in Ojo de Agua, Honduras.
Wrapper: Indonesia   Binder: Honduras   Filler: Honduras, Nicaragua

HANDMADE CIGARS: BRAND LISTINGS

Shape	Name	Lgth	Ring	Wrapper
Double Corona	Churchill	7	50	CM
Robusto	Robusto	5	50	CM

This mixed-filler brand debuted in 1997. It uses sandwich filler and has a medium-bodied taste, available in bundles of 25.

PORTO BELLO
Handmade in Santiago, Dominican Republic.
Wrapper: USA/Connecticut   *Binder: Mexico*   *Filler: Dom. Rep., Honduras*

Shape	Name	Lgth	Ring	Wrapper
Giant	No. 852	8½	52	CC
Double Corona	No. 750	7½	50	CC
Churchill	No. 646	6⅞	46	CC
Toro	No. 650	6	50	CC
Lonsdale	No. 642	6¾	42	CC
Long Panatela	No. 736	7	36	CC
Long Panatela	No. 738	7½	38	CC
Corona	No. 542	5¾	42	CC
Robusto	No. 450	5	50	CC
Pyramid	Piramide	7	50	CC

Created in 1988, this is an economical, bundled brand which offers a mild taste in a handmade, all long-filler cigar – including a genuine Connecticut Shade wrapper!

PREMIUM DOMINICANA
Handmade in Santiago, Dominican Republic.
Wrapper: Dom. Rep.   *Binder: Dom. Rep.*   *Filler: Dom. Rep.*

Shape	Name	Lgth	Ring	Wrapper
Corona	No. 10	5½	44	CC

HANDMADE CIGARS: BRAND LISTINGS

Robusto	No. 20	5	50	CC
Lonsdale	No. 30	6½	44	CC
Toro	No. 40	6	50	CC
Churchill	No. 50	6¾	48	CC
Double Corona	No. 60	7½	50	CC

Blended in the fabulous Tabacalera A. Fuente a Cia., this is a medium-to-full-bodied cigar introduced in 1998. It is offered in an elegant box of 25.

PRETTY LADY
Handmade, with short filler, in Navarette, Dominican Republic.
Wrapper: USA/Connecticut   Binder: Dom. Rep.   Filler: Dom. Rep.

Shape	Name	Lgth	Ring	Wrapper
Cigarillo	Pretty Lady	6	28	CM

This is a short-filler, mild-bodied, flavored cigar. It is available in Amaretto, Anise, cherry, rum and vanilla flavors in boxes of 10 or bundles of 25.

PRIDE OF COPAN
Handmade in Santa Rosa de Copan, Honduras.
Wrapper: USA/Connecticut   Binder: Honduras   Filler: Honduras

Shape	Name	Lgth	Ring	Wrapper
Double Corona	Pride of Copan No. 1	6¾	50	CC
Long Corona	Pride of Copan No. 2	6	44	CC
Short Panatela	Pride of Copan No. 3	5⅜	38	CC
Panatela	Pride of Copan No. 4	5⅞	35	CC
Slim Panatela	Pride of Copan No. 5	6¼	30	CC
Small Panatela	Pride of Copan No. 6	4¾	30	CC
Cigarillo	Pride of Copan No. 7	4⅛	25	CC

A quality, medium-to-full-bodied cigar with quality construction. That's the story of Pride of Copan, created for those who want quality, consistency and value.

HANDMADE CIGARS: BRAND LISTINGS

PRIDE OF JAMAICA
Handmade in Kingston, Jamaica.

Wrapper: Cameroon, USA/Connecticut　　　　　　　　*Binder: Mexico*
Filler: Dominican Republic, Jamaica, Mexico

Shape	Name	Lgth	Ring	Wrapper
Double Corona	Churchill	7½	49	Ma
Toro	Magnum	6	50	Ma
Lonsdale	Rothschild	6½	42	Ma
Corona	Royal Corona	5½	42	CC-Ma

This famous brand continues to be created daily in Kingston, Jamaica and offered in boxes of 25, 10 or 5 well-made, much-respected cigars. Connecticut Shade wrapper is used for the natural-shade cigars and Cameroon leaf for the maduro cigars to help give the mild, rich flavor for which Pride of Jamaica is so well known.

PRIMERA DE NICARAGUA
Handmade in Ocotal, Nicaragua.

Wrapper: Nicaragua　　　　*Binder: Honduras*　　　*Filler: Honduras, Nicaragua*

Shape	Name	Lgth	Ring	Wrapper
Lonsdale	No. 1	7	44	CM-Ma
Double Corona	Churchill	7	50	CM-Ma
Robusto	Rothschild	5	50	CM-Ma
Toro	Toro	6	50	CM-Ma
Giant	Viajante	8½	52	CM-Ma

Here is a mild-to-medium bodied cigar, produced from all long-filler tobaccos, introduced in 1990. This is one of the first brands to emerge after the civil unrest in Nicaragua and is presented in all-wood boxes of 25.

PRIMO DEL CRISTO
Handmade in Danli, Honduras.

Wrapper: Honduras　　　　　*Binder: Honduras*　　　　　*Filler: Honduras*

HANDMADE CIGARS: BRAND LISTINGS

Shape	Name	Lgth	Ring	Wrapper
Lonsdale	No. 1	7	44	Cl-CC-Ma
Toro	Churchills	7	50	Cl-CC-Ma
Corona	Coronas	6	42	Cl-CC-Ma
Giant	Generals	8½	52	Cl-CC-Ma
Giant	Inmensos	8	54	CC-Ma
Long Panatela	Palmas Extra	7	36	CC
Long Panatela	Palmas Reales	8	36	Cl-CC
Double Corona	Presidentes	7½	50	CC
Petit Corona	Reyes	5¼	44	Cl-CC-Ma
Robusto	Rothschilds	5	50	Cl-CC-Ma
Toro	Toros	6	50	Cl-CC-Ma

These are well-made cigars that are offered in modestly-priced bundles of 25, with a medium-to-heavy body.

PRIMO DEL REY
Handmade in La Romana, Dominican Republic.

Wrapper: Indonesia   Binder: Dom. Rep.   Filler: Dom. Rep.

Shape	Name	Lgth	Ring	Wrapper
Long Corona	Cazadores	6	44	Ma
Lonsdale	Chavon	6½	41	CM
Slim Panatela	Panetela Extras	5⅞	34	CM
Panatela	Reales	6⅛	36	CM
Toro	Churchill	6¼	48	CM
Lonsdale	Seleccion No. 1	6¾	42	CM
Long Corona	Seleccion No. 2	6¼	42	Cl-CM
Panatela	Seleccion No. 3	6¾	36	CM
Corona	Seleccion No. 4	5½	42	Cl-CM-Ma

HANDMADE CIGARS: BRAND LISTINGS

	Machine-made, with short filler:			
Cigarillo	Cortos	4	28	CM

Primo del Rey are first-quality cigars first produced in 1961, offering a mild taste from a unique blend of leaves, notably including a Indonesian wrapper. An excellent value, the entire Primo del Rey series is very well constructed. Please note that some sizes are machine-bunched.

PRIMO DEL REY CLUB SELECTION
Handmade in La Romana, Dominican Republic.

Wrapper: USA/Connecticut   Binder: USA/Pennsylvania
Filler: Costa Rica, Dominican Republic, Indonesia

Shape	Name	Lgth	Ring	Wrapper
Lonsdale	Regals	6¾	44	CM-Ma
Churchill	Aristocratas	6¾	48	CM-Ma
Robusto	Rothchild	4½	50	CM-Ma
Torpedo	Torpedo	6	50	CM-Ma
Giant	Baron	8½	52	CM-Ma

Available once again in 1998, this is a mild blend in five shapes, all with larger ring gauges. It is offered in boxes of 20.

PRINCE BORGHESE
Handmade in Esteli, Nicaragua.

Wrapper: Cameroon   Binder: Cameroon   Filler: Dominican Republic

Shape	Name	Lgth	Ring	Wrapper
Torpedo	Torpedo	7	52	CM
Double Corona	Presidente	7½	50	CM
Double Corona	Churchill	7	50	CM
Toro	Corona Gorda	6	50	CM
Robusto	Robusto	5	50	CM

Churchill	Corona	7	46	CM
Grand Corona	Petite Corona	6	46	CM
Lonsdale	Palma	7	42	CM
Long Panatela	Lanceros	7½	38	CM
Slim Panatela	Panetela	6½	32	CM
Cigarillo	Pencil	6	28	CM

Here is a medium-bodied blend from a five-brand family. It is available in either bundles, boxes or glass jar humidors of 25 each. The Pencil shape is available in six flavors: Amaretto, Anise, chocolate, cognac, rum and vanilla.

PRIVATE STOCK
Handmade in Santiago, Dominican Republic.

Wrapper: USA/Connecticut   Binder: Dom. Rep.   Filler: Dom. Rep.

Shape	Name	Lgth	Ring	Wrapper
Double Corona	Private Stock No. 1	7¾	48	CC
Toro	Private Stock No. 2	6	48	CC
Slim Panatela	Private Stock No. 3	6½	33	CC
Panatela	Private Stock No. 4	5¾	38	CC
Corona	Private Stock No. 5	5¾	43	CC
Corona Extra	Private Stock No. 6	5¼	46	CC
Petit Corona	Private Stock No. 7	4¾	43	CC
Short Panatela	Private Stock No. 8	4⅝	35	CC
Cigarillo	Private Stock No. 9	4⅝	26	CC
Petit Corona	Private Stock No. 10	4	40	CC
Robusto	Private Stock No. 11	4⅝	50	CC

These cigars are manufactured in one of the most exclusive factories in the world. High standards of quality make the Private Stock label an excellent value for cigars with a mild to medium body.

HANDMADE CIGARS: BRAND LISTINGS

PRIZE POINTER
Handmade in Santiago, Dominican Republic.

Wrapper: USA/Connecticut   *Binder: Dom. Rep.*   *Filler: Dom. Rep.*

Shape	Name	Lgth	Ring	Wrapper
Double Corona	Double Corona	7½	49	CC
Corona	Corona	5½	42	CC
Lonsdale	Lonsdale	7	44	CC
Toro	Toro	6½	50	CC

Stop barking! This is no dog, but a full-bodied cigar created in 1997, offered in bundles of 25.

PROFESOR SILA 1934
Handmade in Santiago, Dominican Republic.
Wrapper: USA/Connecticut, Indonesia

Binder: Spain   *Filler: Spain*

Shape	Name		Lgth	Ring	Wrapper
Robusto	Robusto		4⅝	50	CI
Corona Extra	Presidente		5⅜	45	CI
Long Panatela	Principe		7¼	38	CI
Grand Corona	Excellencia		6¼	45	CI
Double Corona	Majestad		7¼	50	CI
Torpedo	Torpedo Reserva		6¼	56	CI
Toro	One Estella	(tubed)	6	50	CI-Ma
Double Corona	Three Estella	(tubed)	7	50	CI-Ma

This factory has been producing cigars since 1934 and, as practice makes perfect, were proud to debut this project in 1996. It offers either a light Connecticut wrapper or an Indonesian maduro wrapper and provides a mild-to-medium-bodied smoke in handy 5-packs or in boxes of 25. You'll recognize it right away with its double band!

HANDMADE CIGARS: BRAND LISTINGS

PROFESOR SILA BABA
Handmade, with short filler, in Santiago, Dominican Republic.

Wrapper: Cameroon, Indonesia   Binder: Dom. Rep.   Filler: Dom. Rep.

Shape	Name	Lgth	Ring	Wrapper
Lonsdale	Baba	6½	42	CI
Cigarillo	Clove	4½	29	CM
Cigarillo	Vanilla	4½	29	CM

This is a mild-bodied, short filler, flavored cigar available in Amaretto, bourbon, coffee, Cognac, rum and vanilla styles. Introduced in 1997, Babas are offered in individual cellophane sleeves in flip-top boxes of 25. There is also a small cigar version, with long filler and a Cameroon wrapper!

PROFESOR SILA NAVEGADOR
Handmade in Santiago, Dominican Republic.

Wrapper: Ecuador   Binder: Dom. Rep.   Filler: Brazil, Indonesia, Spain

Shape	Name	Lgth	Ring	Wrapper
Double Corona	Viajante	7⅝	50	CM
Robusto	Robusto	4¾	48	CM
Grand Corona	No. 1	6¼	47	CM
Corona Extra	No. 3	5½	47	CM
Corona Extra	No. 4	5	47	CM
Panatela	Margarita	5¾	36	CM

Here is a new Profesor Sila line for 1997, made by hand in the Dominican Republic. It features a double band and a medium-bodied flavor thanks to its blend of two-year-aged Olor binder and Cuban-seed filler tobaccos.

PROFESOR SILA SANTA MARIA
Handmade in Santiago, Dominican Republic.

Wrapper: Indonesia   Binder: Dom. Rep.   Filler: Brazil, Dom. Rep., Indonesia

HANDMADE CIGARS: BRAND LISTINGS

Shape	Name	Lgth	Ring	Wrapper
Corona	Ancla	5½	43	CM
Long Corona	Galeon	5⅞	43	CM
Lonsdale	Timon	6¾	43	CM
Grand Corona	Capitan	6¾	45	CM
Grand Corona	Proa	5¾	45	CM
Double Corona	Admiral	7	50	CM
Robusto	Robusto	4⅞	50	CM

New for 1997, the Santa Maria line presents a full-bodied smoke, with a double band and a Sumatra wrapper, offered in boxes of 25 (except for the Robusto, offered in 20s).

PROVIDENCIA
Handmade in Licey, Dominican Republic.

Wrapper: Indonesia   Binder: Dom. Rep.   Filler: Dom. Rep.

Shape	Name	Lgth	Ring	Wrapper
Giant	Presidente	8	50	Ma
Grand Corona	Double Corona	6½	46	Ma
Long Corona	Corona	6	44	Ma
Robusto	Robusto	5	50	Ma

This cigar was introduced in 1997 and the all-maduro range features an Indonesian wrapper combined with Cuban-seed tobaccos grown in the Dominican Republic. The result is a medium-bodied smoke offered in all-cedar boxes of 25.

PUBLIC ENEMY
Handmade in Miami, Florida, USA.

Wrapper: Ecuador   Binder: Nicaragua
                Filler: Dominican Republic, Honduras, Nicaragua

HANDMADE CIGARS: BRAND LISTINGS

Shape	Name	Lgth	Ring	Wrapper
Double Corona	No. 1	7	54	CM
Torpedo	No. 2	6½	54	CM
Toro	No. 3	6	54	CM
Robusto	No. 4	5	54	CM
Giant	Capo	9	54	CM

New for 1998, this is a medium-to-full-bodied blend of 54-ring shapes. Each cigar is offered in cellophane sleeves in cedar-lined, mahogany boxes of 25 cigars each, except for the Capo, offered in 10s.

PUNCH
Handmade in Cofradia, Honduras.

Wrapper: Ecuador, USA/Connecticut   Binder: Honduras
Filler: Dominican Republic, Honduras, Nicaragua

Shape	Name	Lgth	Ring	Wrapper
Giant	Presidents	8½	52	CM-Ma
Churchill	Double Coronas	6¾	48	CM-Ma
Toro	Pitas	6⅛	50	CM-Ma
Long Corona	Punch	6¼	44	CM-Ma
Lonsdale	Lonsdales	6½	43	CM-Ma
Robusto	Rothschilds	4½	50	CM-Ma
Pyramid	Pyramids	6¼	44	CM-Ma
Slim Panatela	Largo Elegantes	7	32	CM-Ma
Corona	Elites	5¼	44	CM-Ma
Petit Corona	London Club	5	40	CM-Ma
Lonsdale	After Dinner	7¼	45	CM-Ma
Cigarillo	Slim Panatellas	4	28	CM-Ma
Corona	Cafe Royal (tubed)	5⅝	44	CM-Ma

Long Corona	Crystals	(glass jar)	6	43	CM-Ma
	Deluxe Series:				
Double Corona	Chateau "L"		7¼	54	CM-Ma
Corona Extra	Chateau "M"		5¾	46	CM-Ma
Grand Corona	Coronas		6¼	45	CM-Ma
Robusto	Corona Gordo		5¼	50	CM-Ma
Lonsdale	Oxford		6½	43	CM-Ma
Toro	Windsor		6⅛	50	CM-Ma
Corona	Royal Coronations	(tubed)	5¼	44	CM-Ma
	Grand Cru Series:				
Toro	Britania		6¼	50	CM
Double Corona	Diademas		7¼	54	CC
Churchill	Monarcas	(tubed)	6¾	48	CM
Giant	Prince Consorts		8½	52	CM
Robusto	Robustos		5¼	50	CM-Ma
Robusto	Superiors		5½	48	CM
Torpedo	No. II		6	50	CM

The world-famous Punch brand is handmade in Honduras since 1969 from Cuban-seed tobaccos grown in Honduras, Nicaragua and the Dominican Republic. This range offers a magnificent, easy smoke with unsurpassed taste and bouquet using Sumatra-seed, Ecuadorian-grown natural wrappers and Connecticut broadleaf for the maduro-wrapped shapes. The Grand Cru series is made from vintage tobaccos aged from 3-5 years under the supervision of Villazon & Co.'s master blenders. Grand Cru cigars are robust in taste, yet sweet with a marvelous bouquet.

PURO PLACER
Handmade in Esteli, Nicaragua.

Wrapper: Indonesia   *Binder: Nicaragua*   *Filler: Nicaragua*

HANDMADE CIGARS: BRAND LISTINGS

Shape	Name	Lgth	Ring	Wrapper
Double Corona	Presidente	7	50	CM
Toro	Grand Corona	6½	48	CM
Toro	Toro	6	50	CM
Long Corona	Lonsdale	6	44	CM
Robusto	Rothchild	5	50	CM

This is a medium-bodied cigar which was introduced in 1997. It features a dark Sumatra-grown wrapper and is offered cellophaned in all-cedar boxes of 25.

PURO VENEZOLANO
Handmade, with short filler, in Guiria Ed. Sucre, Venezuela.
Wrapper: Venezuela　　　　*Binder: Venezuela*　　　　*Filler: Venezuela*

Shape	Name	Lgth	Ring	Wrapper
Robusto	Robusto	5	50	Ma

This is a full-bodied brand, introduced in 1998. It is offered in boxes or bundles of 25 cigars each.

PUROFINO BLUE LABEL
Handmade in Danli, Honduras.
Wrapper: Ecuador　　　*Binder: Mexico*　　　*Filler: Costa Rica, Mexico, Nicaragua*

Shape	Name	Lgth	Ring	Wrapper
Lonsdale	Corona Real	6½	43	CM
Robusto	Robusto Gordo	5¼	52	CM
Double Corona	Churchill	7	50	CM
Pyramid	Piramide	6½	54	CM

Here is a medium-bodied brand introduced in 1995. The wrapper is Sumatra-seed, grown in Ecuador and you can enjoy it in boxes of 20.

HANDMADE CIGARS: BRAND LISTINGS

PUROFINO DOM
Handmade in Danli, Honduras.

Wrapper: USA/Connecticut   Binder: USA/Pennsylvania Filler: Dom.Rep., Nicaragua

Shape	Name	Lgth	Ring	Wrapper
Torpedo	Petit Belicoso	4⅜	50	Ma
Corona	El Fumo	5¼	44	Ma

This unique two-shape brand, introduced in late 1997, offers a curly-top, shaggy-foot corona with a medium-to-full-bodied taste. It is available only in very limited distribution, in boxes of double bundles of 20.

PUROFINO GOLD LABEL
Handmade in Danli, Honduras.

Wrapper: Ecuador   Binder: Nicaragua   Filler: Mexico, Nicaragua

Shape	Name	Lgth	Ring	Wrapper
Lonsdale	Corona Real	6½	43	CC
Robusto	Robusto Gordo	5¼	52	CC
Double Corona	Churchill	7	50	CC
Pyramid	Piramide	6½	54	CC

Here is the medium-to-full-bodied big brother to the Blue Label series, also introduced in 1995. The wrapper is Sumatra-seed, grown in Ecuador and is also offered in boxes of 20.

PUROS 3P
Handmade in Santo Domingo, Dominican Republic.

Wrapper: Indonesia   Binder: Dom. Rep.   Filler: Dom. Rep.

Shape	Name	Lgth	Ring	Wrapper
Panatela	Panatela	5½	38	CM
Long Corona	Corona	6	42	CM
Robusto	Robusto	5	50	CM
Churchill	Churchill	7	48	CM

Double Corona	Presidente	7	50	CM

Made by hand in the Dominican Republic, Puros 3P was introduced in 1998. It is mild in body and is presented in individual cellophane sleeves in boxes of 25.

PUROS DON ABREU
Handmade in Santiago, Dominican Republic.
Wrapper: Indonesia or USA/Connecticut

Binder: Dominican Republic   *Filler: Dominican Republic*

Shape	Name	Lgth	Ring	Wrapper
Toro	Big Toros	6½	50	CC
Grand Corona	Churchill	6½	46	CC
Lonsdale	Coronitas	6½	44	CC
Double Corona	Double Corona	7½	49	CC
Corona Extra	Petit	5	46	CC
Giant	President	8	50	CC
Robusto	Toros	5	50	CC

Introduced in 1996, the Puros Don Abreu line presents a medium-bodied flavor with a Connecticut-grown shade wrapper. It is offered in boxes of 25.

PUROS INDIOS
Handmade in Danli, Honduras.
Wrapper: Ecuador   *Binder: Ecuador*
Filler: Brazil, Dominican Republic, Jamaica, Nicaragua

Shape	Name	Lgth	Ring	Wrapper
Double Corona	Churchill Especial	7¼	53	CM-Ma
Churchill	Presidente	7¼	47	CM-Ma
Churchill	No. 1 Especial	7	48	CM-Ma
Grand Corona	No. 2 Especial	6½	46	CM-Ma
Lonsdale	Nacionales	6½	43	CM-Ma

PURE
Perfection

"Our goal is that every cigar we make be a perfect cigar in its appearance, the way it burns and in flavor - a true work of art."

The Reyes Family
PUROS INDIOS CIGARS

Puros Indios Cigars

Toro	Toro Especial	6	53	CM-Ma
Robusto	Rothschild	5	50	CM-Ma
Corona	No. 4 Especial	5½	44	CM-Ma
Long Panatela	Palmas Real	7	39	CM-Ma
Pyramid	Piramide No. 1	7½	60	CM-Ma
Pyramid	Piramide No. 2	6½	46	CM-Ma
Short Panatela	Petit Perla	5	38	CM-Ma
Short Panatela	No. 5 Especial	5	36	CM-Ma
Perfecto	Victoria	7¼	60	CM-Ma
Perfecto	Gran Victoria	10	60	CM-Ma
Giant	Chief	18	66	CM-Ma

Introduced in 1995, the blending talents of Rolando Reyes are again at work in Puros Indios cigars. Leaves from five nations are blended by hand in Honduras to create a medium-to-full-bodied smoke in a wide variety of sizes, including the 18-inch Chief, one of the longest regular-production cigars marketed anywhere.

PUROS MORGAN
Handmade in San Andres Tuxtla, Mexico.

Wrapper: Mexico   *Binder: Mexico*   *Filler: Mexico*

Shape	Name	Lgth	Ring	Wrapper
Double Corona	Churchill	7¼	50	CM
Long Corona	Morgan No. 1	6	42	CM
Toro	Morgan No. 3	6	50	CM
Robusto	Robusto	5	50	CM

Introduced in 1996, this is a medium-bodied brand of all-Mexican tobacco. It is offered in boxes of five and 25.

HANDMADE CIGARS: BRAND LISTINGS

PUROS NIRVANA
Handmade in Managua, Nicaragua.

Wrapper: Indonesia　　　　*Binder: Costa Rica*　　*Filler: Costa Rica, Nicaragua*

Shape	Name	Lgth	Ring	Wrapper
Double Corona	Churchill	7½	50	CC
Long Corona	Lonsdale	6¼	44	CC
Toro	Corona Gorda	6	50	CC
Robusto	Robusto	5	50	CC

Introduced in 1997, this is a medium-bodied brand with a Sumatra wrapper. It is offered in slide-top, cedar boxes of bundles of 25.

PUROS POLANCO
Handmade in Santiago, Dominican Republic and San Andres Tuxtla, Mexico.

FLAVORED SELECTION, made in Mexico:

Wrapper: Indonesia　　　　*Binder: Mexico*　　　　　　*Filler: Mexico*

VANILLA CIGARILLOS, made in the Dominican Republic:

Wrapper: Indonesia　　　　*Binder: Dom. Rep.*　　　　*Filler: Dom. Rep.*

Shape	Name	Lgth	Ring	Wrapper
	Flavored Selection:			
Lonsdale	Lonsdale	6½	43	CM
	Vanilla Cigarillos:			
Short Panatela	Cigarillos	4⅞	35	CM

Introduced in 1997, this is a medium-bodied, flavored cigar, offered in your choice of Amaretto, rum or vanilla flavors, presented in individual glass tubes in cedar boxes of 20. The cigarillos are available in vanilla only.

PUROS TEJERA
Handmade in Villa Gonzalez, Dominican Republic.

Wrapper: Ecuador or USA/Connecticut　　*Binder: Dom. Rep.*　　　*Filler: Dom. Rep.*

HANDMADE CIGARS: BRAND LISTINGS

Shape	Name	Lgth	Ring	Wrapper
Toro	Toro	6	50	CC
Double Corona	Churchill	7	50	CC
Lonsdale	Corona	6½	44	CC
Corona	Petit Corona	5½	42	CC

Introduced in 1996, this is a mild-to-medium-bodied blend of tobaccos from Connecticut and Cuban-seed leaves grown in the Dominican Republic. You can find it in boxes of 25.

PYRAMID
Handmade in Santiago, Dominican Republic.

Wrapper: Indonesia   Binder: Dom. Rep.   Filler: Dom. Rep.

Shape	Name	Lgth	Ring	Wrapper
Corona	Giza	5½	44	CC
Lonsdale	Chephren	7	44	CC
Robusto	Khufu	5	50	CC
Toro	Mycerinus	6	50	CC
Double Corona	Cheops	7½	50	CC
Torpedo	Great Pyramid	7	50	CC

Introduced in 1997, this brand has shape names that celebrate the Egyptian pyramids of ancient times, the last remaining "wonder" of the ancient world. The blend features a Sumatra wrapper combined with a Dominican Olor binder and Piloto Cubano filler. The strength is medium and the brand is presented in boxes of 25.

QUETZAL
Handmade in La Romana, Dominican Republic.

Wrapper: USA/Connecticut   Binder: Dom. Rep.   Filler: Dom. Rep.

Shape	Name	Lgth	Ring	Wrapper
Giant	No. 1	8	52	CC

HANDMADE CIGARS: BRAND LISTINGS

Toro	No. 2	6	50	CC
Churchill	No. 3	7	48	CC
Lonsdale	No. 4	6¾	44	CC
Long Corona	No. 5	6	42	CC

Introduced in 1997, this brand is made up of Connecticut wrapper and
Dominican interior leaves and offers a mild taste in bundles of 25 cigars each.

QUETZAL
Handmade in Danli, Honduras.

Wrapper: Indonesia *Binder: Honduras* *Filler: Honduras*

Shape	Name	Lgth	Ring	Wrapper
Giant	No. 1	8	50	CM
Double Corona	No. 2	7	52	CM
Churchill	No. 3	6⅞	48	CM
Lonsdale	No. 4	6⅝	44	CM
Long Corona	No. 5	6	42	CM
Robusto	No. 6	4¾	50	CM

This brand debuted in 1997 featuring a Java wrapper and Honduran filler and
binder. It is offered in bundles of 25 cigars each.

QUEVEDO
Handmade in Quayaquil, Ecuador.

Wrapper: Ecuador *Binder: Ecuador* *Filler: Ecuador*

Shape	Name	Lgth	Ring	Wrapper
Double Corona	Churchill	7½	50	CC
Lonsdale	Lonsdale	6½	42	CC
Robusto	Robusto	5½	50	CC
Corona Extra	Toro	5	46	CC
Robusto	Rothchild	4½	50	CC

HANDMADE CIGARS: BRAND LISTINGS

This is a medium-bodied brand with Cuban-seed leaf in the filler, introduced in 1997. It is offered in all-cedar boxes of 25.

QUINTERO
Handmade in Danli, Honduras.

Wrapper: Indonesia   *Binder: Ecuador*   *Filler: Honduras, Nicaragua*

Shape	Name	Lgth	Ring	Wrapper
Double Corona	Doble Corona	7½	49	CM
Toro	Toro	6	50	CM
Robusto	Robusto	5	49	CM
Lonsdale	Lonsdale	6½	42	CM

Named for an old Cuban brand which is still in production, here is a medium-bodied brand with a new look for 1998. It is available in 5 x 5 packing in boxes of 25.

QUINTIN "Q-ORO"
Handmade in the Dominican Republic, Honduras, Mexico, Nicaragua and Miami, Florida, USA.

MIAMI RESERVE:

Wrapper: Ecuador, USA/Connecticut   *Binder: Ecuador*
Filler: Dominican Republic, Honduras, Nicaragua

DOMINICAN REPUBLIC:

Wrapper: Dom. Rep.   *Binder: Dom. Rep.*   *Filler: Dom. Rep.*

HONDURAS:

Wrapper: Ecuador   *Binder: Mexico*   *Filler: Dom. Rep., Nicaragua*

MEXICO:

Wrapper: Mexico   *Binder: Mexico*   *Filler: Mexico*

NICARAGUA:

Wrapper: Nicaragua   *Binder: Nicaragua*   *Filler: Nicaragua*

HANDMADE CIGARS: BRAND LISTINGS

Shape	Name	Lgth	Ring	Wrapper
	Miami Reserve, made in Miami:			
Long Corona	Corona	6	44	CC-CM-Ma
Robusto	Robusto	5	50	CC-CM-Ma
Toro	Epicure	6	50	CC-CM-Ma
Double Corona	Churchill	7	50	CC-CM-Ma
Torpedo	Torpedo	6½	54	CC-CM-Ma
	Dominican Republic, made in Santiago:			
Corona	Corona	5½	42	CM
Robusto	Robusto	5	50	CM
Toro	Toro	6½	52	CM
Double Corona	Churchill	7½	50	CM
Torpedo	Torpedo	6	53	CM
	Honduras, made in Danli:			
Robusto	Robusto	5	50	CM
Toro	Toro Grande	6	50	CM
Lonsdale	Lonsdale	7	44	CM
Double Corona	Imperial	7	50	CM
	Mexico, made in San Andres Tuxtla:			
Robusto	Robusto	4½	50	CM
Toro	Toro	5¾	50	CM
Double Corona	Churchill	6¾	50	CM
	Nicaragua, made in Esteli:			
Robusto	Rothschild	4½	52	CM
Lonsdale	Lonsdale	6½	42	CM
Toro	Double Corona	5⅝	48	CM

HANDMADE CIGARS: BRAND LISTINGS

Double Corona	Churchill	7½	50	CM

Here is an entire family of cigars, all introduced in 1997 and produced in popular sizes in the cigar-making capitals of the world! The Miami Reserve is full-bodied and offers a choice of Ecuador-grown or Connecticut-grown wrappers in natural, English Market Selection, rosado or maduro shades! The Dominican, Mexican and Nicaraguan blends are considered medium-bodied and the Honduran line is mild. All are offered in wood boxes of 25 cigars each.

QUIRANTES
Handmade in Tamboril, Dominican Republic.

Wrapper: Indonesia, USA/Connecticut   Binder: Dom. Rep.   Filler: Dom. Rep.

Shape	Name	Lgth	Ring	Wrapper
Robusto	Robusto	4½	50	CC-Ma
Robusto	Robusto	4¾	50	CC-Ma
Petit Corona	Ricky Ray	5	42	CC-Ma
Cigarillo	Little Ray	5½	28	CC-Ma
Robusto	Corona	5½	50	CC-Ma
Lonsdale	No. 1	6¼	44	CC-Ma
Giant	Magnum	8	54	CC-Ma
Churchill	Lonsdale	6¾	46	CC-Ma
Churchill	Gloria Habana	6¾	48	CC-Ma
Pyramid	Pyramid	6	52	CC-Ma
Torpedo	Torpedo	6½	54	CC-Ma
Long Panatela	Lancero	7½	38	CC-Ma
Double Corona	Churchill	7½	50	CC-Ma

This is a full-bodied cigar from Tamboril, Dominican Republic. It is offered in boxes of 25 (or 20 for the Churchill or Ricky Ray) or bundles of 25, with a choice of Connecticut-grown natural wrappers or Sumatran-grown maduro wrappers.

HANDMADE CIGARS: BRAND LISTINGS

QUO VADIS
Handmade in Esteli, Nicaragua.

Wrapper: Ecuador   Binder: Nicaragua   Filler: Nicaragua

Shape	Name	Lgth	Ring	Wrapper
Double Corona	Churchill	7	50	CC
Lonsdale	Lonsdale	6½	44	CC
Giant	Presidente	8	52	CC
Robusto	Robusto	5	50	CC
Toro	Toro	6	50	CC
Torpedo	Torpedo	6½	54	CC

Here is a 1998-introduced, medium-bodied cigar that you can enjoy either in its natural flavor, or in a version with rum or vanilla flavoring. In either case, the brand is available in value-priced bundles of 20.

RAFAEL
Handmade in Miami, Florida, USA.

Wrapper: Indonesia   Binder: Ecudaor
Filler: Dominican Republic, Honduras, Nicaragua

Shape	Name	Lgth	Ring	Wrapper
Robusto	Robusto	5	50	CM
Torpedo	Torpedo	6	54	CM
Toro	Toro	6	50	CM
Double Corona	Double Corona	7½	50	CM

This is a full-bodied smoke made for limited distribution by Nick's Cigars, developed in 1998. The Rosado-shade wrapper covers the Cuban-seed leaves on the interior and it is offered in boxes of 25.

RAFAEL DE HABANA
Handmade in Esteli, Nicaragua.

Wrapper: Cameroon   Binder: Cameroon   Filler: Dominican Republic

HANDMADE CIGARS: BRAND LISTINGS

Shape	Name	Lgth	Ring	Wrapper
Torpedo	Torpedo	7	52	CM
Double Corona	Presidente	7½	50	CM
Double Corona	Churchill	7	50	CM
Toro	Corona Gorda	6	50	CM
Robusto	Robusto	5	50	CM
Churchill	Corona	7	46	CM
Grand Corona	Petite Corona	6	46	CM
Lonsdale	Palma	7	42	CM
Long Panatela	Lanceros	7½	38	CM
Slim Panatela	Panetela	6½	32	CM
Cigarillo	Pencil	6	28	CM

Here is a medium-to-full-bodied blend from a five-brand family. It is available in either bundles, boxes or glass jar humidors of 25 each. The Pencil shape is available in six flavors: Amaretto, Anise, chocolate, cognac, rum and vanilla.

RAMAR
Handmade in Miami, Florida, USA.
Wrapper: Ecuador, Mexico, USA/Connecticut
Binder: Ecuador or Indonesia   Filler: Dom. Rep., Honduras, Nicaragua

Shape	Name	Lgth	Ring	Wrapper
Robusto	Robusto	5¼	50	CC-CM-Ma
Double Corona	Soberano	7½	50	CC-CM-Ma
Toro	Double Corona	6¼	50	CC-CM-Ma
Churchill	Churchill	7	48	CC-CM-Ma
Lonsdale	Seleccion No. 1	6¾	42	CC-CM-Ma
Long Corona	Seleccion No. 2	6¼	42	CC-CM-Ma
Panatela	Seleccion No. 3	6¾	36	CC-CM-Ma

Corona	Petit Corona	5¾	42	CC-CM-Ma
Giant Corona	Palmas	8	40	CC-CM-Ma
Panatela	Lauren	5¾	36	CC-CM-Ma
Pyramid	Piramides	7	60	CC-CM-Ma
Corona Extra	Adan	5½	46	CC-CM-Ma
Giant	Presidente	8¼	50	CC-CM-Ma

Available since 1977, this cigar is getting wider notice in the 1990s, thanks to its high quality in construction and a mild-to-medium-bodied taste. Three wrapper shades are available: Connecticut tobacco for the lightest, Colorado-Claro wrappers; Ecuadorian leaves for the darker "Cafe" selection and Mexican-grown leaves for the maduro shade.

RAMBLING RIVER
Handmade in San Andres Tuxtla, Mexico.

Wrapper: Mexico   *Binder: Mexico*   *Filler: Mexico*

Shape	Name	Lgth	Ring	Wrapper
Robusto		4¾	50	Ma
Small Panatela		5	32	Ma
Long Corona		6	42	Ma
Toro		6	50	Ma
Panatela		6⅝	35	Ma
Lonsdale		6⅝	42	Ma
Grand Corona		6⅝	46	Ma
Double Corona		6⅞	54	Ma
Double Corona		7½	50	Ma
Giant		8	52	Ma

This brand dates back to the late 1970s and is offered in an all-maduro series. It features all-Mexican tobacco and is medium in body. Although it has no shape names, you can try in boxes of 25!

HANDMADE CIGARS: BRAND LISTINGS

RAMON ALLONES
Handmade in Santiago, Dominican Republic.

Wrapper: Cameroon   *Binder: Mexico*   *Filler: Dom. Rep., Mexico*

Shape	Name		Lgth	Ring	Wrapper
Petit Corona	D		5	42	CM
Lonsdale	B		6½	42	CM
Lonsdale	A		7	45	CM
Double Corona	Redondos		7	49	CM
Lonsdale	Crystals	(tubed)	6¾	42	CM
Lonsdale	Trumps		6¾	43	CM
Robusto	Naturales		5½	50	CM
Small Panatela	Ramonitos		4¼	32	CM

This brand originated in Cuba way back in 1837. The Dominican version is a medium-to-heavy flavored cigar and is manufactured in the same Santiago, Dominican Republic factory which produces famous Partagas cigars. It is exceptionally well made.

RAMONDO
Handmade in Santiago, Dominican Republic.

Wrapper: Dom. Rep.   *Binder: Dom. Rep.*   *Filler: Dom. Rep.*

Shape	Name	Lgth	Ring	Wrapper
Robusto	Robusto	5	50	CC
Toro	Toro	6	50	CC
Corona	Corona	5½	43	CC

New for 1998, this is a product of the famed Tabacalera A. Fuente y Cia. Made by apprentices of the Fuente factory, it has a medium body and is offered in boxes of 25.

RANCHO DOMINICANO
Handmade in Tamboril, Dominican Republic.

Wrapper: Indonesia   *Binder: Dom. Rep.*   *Filler: Dom. Rep.*

HANDMADE CIGARS: BRAND LISTINGS

Shape	Name	Lgth	Ring	Wrapper
Robusto	Robusto	5	50	CM
Long Corona	Coronas Grande	6	44	CM
Toro	Toro	6	50	CM
Churchill	Churchill	7	46	CM
Double Corona	Ranchero	7½	50	CM
Pyramid	Figurado	6	54	CM

This brand was introduced in 1997 and offers a medium body in six sizes. It is offered in boxes of 25.

RASPUTIN
Handmade in Esteli, Nicaragua.

Wrapper: Cameroon   Binder: Cameroon   Filler: Dominican Republic

Shape	Name	Lgth	Ring	Wrapper
Torpedo	Torpedo	7	52	CM
Double Corona	Presidente	7½	50	CM
Double Corona	Churchill	7	50	CM
Toro	Corona Gorda	6	50	CM
Robusto	Robusto	5	50	CM
Churchill	Corona	7	46	CM
Grand Corona	Petite Corona	6	46	CM
Lonsdale	Palma	7	42	CM
Long Panatela	Lanceros	7½	38	CM
Slim Panatela	Panetela	6½	32	CM
Cigarillo	Pencil	6	28	CM

Here is a mild-bodied blend from a five-brand family. It is available in either bundles, boxes or glass jar humidors of 25 each. The Pencil shape is available in six flavors: Amaretto, Anise, chocolate, cognac, rum and vanilla.

HANDMADE CIGARS: BRAND LISTINGS

RASTA RAP
Handmade in Navarette, Dominican Republic.

Wrapper: Indonesia   *Binder: Dom. Rep.*   *Filler: Dom. Rep.*

Shape	Name	Lgth	Ring	Wrapper
Torpedo	Torpedo	6	54	CM
Giant	Churchill	8½	50	CM

This is a medium-bodied brand which debuted in 1998. It is offered in bundles of 25.

RASTAFARI
Handmade in Jamaica.

Wrapper: Gabon   *Binder: Nicaragua*   *Filler: Dom. Rep., Jamaica*

Shape	Name	Lgth	Ring	Wrapper
Perfecto	Afrika	6	60	CM

Accompanied by sensational box artwork, this brand was introduced in 1998. With its unusual Cameroon-seed, Gabon-grown wrapper, this is a medium-bodied, spicy cigar. It is offered in one giant shape in boxes of 20.

RED HEAD
Handmade in Manila, the Philippines.

Wrapper: Indonesia   *Binder: Philippines*   *Filler: Philippines*

Shape	Name	Lgth	Ring	Wrapper
Double Corona		7	52	CM
Churchill		7	47	CM
Robusto		5	52	CM
Petit Corona		5	44	CM
Torpedo		7	52	CM

Although it has no shape names, this is a medium-bodied brand introduced in 1998. It features a Sumatra wrapper and is available in boxes of 25.

HANDMADE CIGARS: BRAND LISTINGS

RARE LION
Handmade in Santiago, Dominican Republic.

Wrapper: Dom. Rep.　　　　*Binder: Dom. Rep.*　　　　*Filler: Dom. Rep.*

Shape	Name	Lgth	Ring	Wrapper
Toro	Mature Toro	6	60	CM
Robusto	Robusto	5½	50	CM
Giant Corona	Lonsdale	7¾	44	CM
Double Corona	Churchill	7	50	CM

Want a fat cigar? How about a long cigar? You can take your choice of styles of these medium-bodied, all-Dominican blends, introduced in 1996. They are available in boxes of 25, except for the Mature Toro, offered in 15s.

REGALOS
Handmade in Danli, Honduras.
Wrapper: Ecuador or Costa Rica

Binder: Dominican Republic　　　　*Filler: Honduras, Nicaragua*

Shape	Name	Lgth	Ring	Wrapper
Long Corona	Lonsdale	6	43	CC
Churchill	Churchill	7	47	CC-Ma
Robusto	Robusto	5	50	CC-Ma
Giant	Presidente	8½	52	CC
Toro	Toro	6	54	CC-Ma
Torpedo	Torpedo	6½	54	CC-Ma
Pyramid	Especial	7½	64	CC

This is a beautiful cigar, well constructed and featuring an Ecuadorian-grown, Sumatra-seed wrapper, or a maduro wrapper from Costa Rica. Introduced in 1996, it is medium-to-full-bodied and offered in individual cellophane sleeves and all-wood boxes of 25.

HANDMADE CIGARS: BRAND LISTINGS

REGATTA
Handmade in Saõ Goncalo de Campos, Brazil.

REGATTA CUBANA:
Wrapper: Nicaragua   Binder: Nicaragua   Filler: Nicaragua

REGATTA NATURAL:
Wrapper: USA/Connecticut   Binder: Brazil   Filler: Brazil

REGATTA MADURA:
Wrapper: Brazil   Binder: Brazil   Filler: Brazil

Shape	Name	Lgth	Ring	Wrapper
Perfecto	Regatta Cubana	6½	52	CM
Toro	Regatta Madura	6	50	CM
Toro	Regatta Natural	6	50	CM

Three styles in three sizes; the Cubana is medium-to-full-bodied, the Madura is full-bodied and the Naturals are medium in body. Look for them in boxes of 25.

REMEDIOS
Handmade in Esteli, Nicaragua.
Wrapper: Mexico, USA/Connecticut   Binder: Mexico   Filler: Dom. Rep., Nicaragua

Shape	Name	Lgth	Ring	Wrapper
Toro	Corona Gorda	6⅛	50	CC-Ma
Double Corona	Clemenceau	7¼	54	CC-Ma
Grand Corona	Corona	5⅝	45	CC-Ma
Toro	Don Victor	6	54	CC-Ma
Robusto	Robusto	4½	50	CC-Ma

Here is a new, super-premium cigar from J-R Tobacco, introduced in 1998, designed to compete with the finest cigars on the market. The combination of Connecticut (natural) or Mexican (maduro) wrapper and Mexican binder complement the blended filler to offer a medium-to-full-bodied smoke. You will find it only in specially-made, all-cedar chests of 40, created to assist in the aging of these cigars when you aren't smoking them!

REPEATER

Handmade, with mixed filler, in Danli, Honduras.

Wrapper: Honduras   *Binder: Honduras*   *Filler: Honduras*

Shape	Name	Lgth	Ring	Wrapper
Corona	Repeater 100	5½	43	CM
Long Corona	Repeater 200	6	43	CM
Lonsdale	Repeater 300	6½	43	CM
Lonsdale	Havana Twist	7	44	CM
Double Corona	Churchill	7	49	CM
Robusto	Robusto	5	50	CM

This brand debuted in the late 1960s and utilizes medium-filler tobacco of all-Honduran origin to produce an enjoyable smoke of medium-to-full body.

REPUBLICA DOMINICANA

Handmade in Santiago, Dominican Republic.

Wrapper: Indonesia   *Binder: Dom. Rep.*   *Filler: Dom. Rep.*

Shape	Name	Lgth	Ring	Wrapper
Pyramid	Pyramid	6¼	52	CM
Churchill	Esplendido	7	48	CM
Grand Corona	Jibarito	6¼	46	CM
Robusto	Robusto	5	48	CM
Long Panatela	No. 1	7½	38	CM
Panatela	No. 2	6¾	38	CM
Panatela	No. 3	6	38	CM

Made by the Montecristi Cigar Factory in the Dominican Republic, this is a full-bodied brand offered in elegant all-cedar boxes of 25.

HANDMADE CIGARS: BRAND LISTINGS

REY ALPHONSO
Handmade, with mixed filler, in Tamboril, Dominican Republic.

Wrapper: Indonesia   Binder: Dom. Rep.   Filler: Dom. Rep.

Shape	Name	Lgth	Ring	Wrapper
Churchill	Churchill	7	48	CM

This is a new brand for 1998, with an Indonesian wrapper. It has a mild-to-medium body and is offered in bundles of 25.

REY DE LOS REYES
Handmade in Santiago, Dominican Republic.

Wrapper: USA/Connecticut   Binder: Dom. Rep.   Filler: Dom. Rep.

Shape	Name	Lgth	Ring	Wrapper
Double Corona	Presidente	7½	50	CC
Churchill	Churchill	7	48	CC
Torpedo	Torpedo	6	50	CC
Torpedo	Petit Belicoso	4½	50	CC
Toro	Toro	6	50	CC
Long Corona	Corona	6	44	CC
Torpedo	Figurado Bala	6	46	CC
Robusto	Bala	4½	48	CC
Panatela	Lanceros	6½	38	CC

This is a full-bodied cigar, introduced in 1998. The "Kings of the Kings" offers a genuine Connecticut wrapper along with Dominican filler and binder and is offered in boxes of 25 cigars each.

REY DE ZABA
Handmade in Santiago, Dominican Republic.

Wrapper: Indonesia   Binder: Dom. Rep.   Filler: Dom. Rep.

HANDMADE CIGARS: BRAND LISTINGS

Shape	Name	Lgth	Ring	Wrapper
Toro	Casadores	6	50	CM
Lonsdale	Lonsdale	6½	42	CM
Robusto	Robusto	5½	50	CM
Long Corona	Churchill	6	44	CM

Introduced in 1995, this full-bodied brand, made with considerable skill in the Dominican Republic, is offered in boxes of 25.

REY DEL MAR
Handmade in Navarette, Dominican Republic.

Wrapper: Indonesia   Binder: Dom. Rep.   Filler: Dom. Rep.

Shape	Name	Lgth	Ring	Wrapper
Panatela	Petit Corona	5⅝	38	CC
Robusto	Robusto	4¾	52	CC
Corona	Corona	5¾	42	CC

Introduced in 1995, this is a medium-to-full-bodied blend of leaves offered in boxes of 25.

REYES & BENECIO
Handmade in Granada, Nicaragua.

Wrapper: Indonesia   Binder: Nicaragua   Filler: Nicaragua

Shape	Name	Lgth	Ring	Wrapper
Torpedo	Volcan	5½	54	CM-Ma
Giant	El Leon	8½	52	CM-Ma
Pyramid	Escudo	7	48	CM-Ma
Double Corona	Gigante	6¾	54	CM-Ma
Churchill	Pistola	7	48	CM-Ma
Toro	Dulce	6	50	CM-Ma

| Robusto | El Canon | 4¾ | 50 | CM-Ma |
| Corona | Bala | 5½ | 42 | CM-Ma |

Introduced in 1996, this is a medium-bodied brand available in both natural and maduro wrapper shades. The Bala shape is also available with vanilla flavoring. It is presented in boxes of 25.

RG SANTIAGO DOMINICAN
Handmade in Santiago, Dominican Republic.
Wrapper: Indonesia or USA/Connecticut

Binder: Dominican Republic   *Filler: Dominican Republic*

Shape	Name	Lgth	Ring	Wrapper
Corona	Corona	5½	43	CC
Robusto	Robusto	5	50	CC
Lonsdale	Lonsdale	6½	43	CC
Toro	Toro	6	50	CC
Double Corona	Churchill	7½	50	CC
Pyramid	Piramide	7	50	CC
Cigarillo	Petit Panatela	5	28	CC
Cigarillo	Purito	4	24	CC

New in 1997, this is a full-bodied cigar that features a choice of delicately-flavored Indonesian or genuine Connecticut wrappers to complement the Dominican-grown binder and fillers.

RIATA
Handmade in Danli, Honduras.
Wrapper: Mexico   *Binder: Mexico*   *Filler: Honduras*

Shape	Name	Lgth	Ring	Wrapper
Panatela	No. 200	6⅞	36	CM
Corona	No. 400	5½	44	CM
Lonsdale	No. 500	6⅝	44	CM

Toro	No. 600	6⅝	54	CM-Ma
Robusto	No. 700	4¾	50	CM-Ma
Toro	No. 800	6¼	50	CM-Ma
Double Corona	No. 900	7½	50	CM-Ma

Now back in circulation after a few years off, this is a full-bodied blend of Riata, with a choice of natural-shade or maduro wrappers. You can enjoy either in bundles of 20.

RICH & FAMOUS
Handmade in Miami, Florida, USA.

Wrapper: Brazil   Binder: Indonesia   Filler: Colombia, Dom. Rep., Indonesia

Shape	Name	Lgth	Ring	Wrapper
Cigarillo	Finos	5	28	CM-Ma
Torpedo	Torpedo	6½	54	CM-Ma
Robusto	Robusto	5	50	CM-Ma
Long Panatela	Lancero	7½	38	CM-Ma
Long Corona	Panetela	6	42	CM-Ma
Double Corona	Churchill	7	50	CM-Ma
Double Corona	Presidente	7½	52	CM-Ma

This is a medium-bodied blend, available only in limited quantities. You don't have to be rich or famous to buy it though, in packs of 25.

RICO HAVANA
Handmade in Danli, Honduras.

Wrapper: Ecuador   Binder: Honduras   Filler: Dom.Rep., Honduras

Shape	Name	Lgth	Ring	Wrapper
Toro	Double Corona	6¼	48	CC-Ma
Double Corona	Churchill	7½	50	CC-Ma
Lonsdale	Plaza	7	44	CC-Ma

Long Corona	Corona	6	42	CC-Ma
Robusto	Duke	4½	50	CC-Ma
Lonsdale	No. 1	6¾	44	CC-Ma
Long Corona	Fuma	6	42	CC-Ma

A favorite since 1939, this medium-bodied blend of Cuban seed, Dominican-grown long-filler tobaccos combines with an Ecuadorian wrapper for great smoking flavor. Rico Havana is available in natural and maduro wrappers.

RICOS DOMINICANOS
Handmade in Santiago, Dominican Republic.
Wrapper: USA/Connecticut   Binder: Dominican Republic
Filler: Brazil, Dominican Republic, Indonesia

Shape	Name	Lgth	Ring	Wrapper
Double Corona	Churchill	7	50	CC-Ma
Toro	Toro	6	50	CC-Ma
Corona	Breva	5½	44	CC-Ma
Lonsdale	Centro Largo	6¾	44	CC-Ma

This brand debuted in 1996 and offers a mild-to-medium bodied taste in either a natural or maduro wrapper. It has a rich aroma and, best of all, is an excellent value.

RICOS DOMINICANOS - ETIQUETA NEGRA
Handmade in Santiago, Dominican Republic.
Wrapper: Ecuador   Binder: Dom. Rep.   Filler: Dom. Rep.

Shape	Name	Lgth	Ring	Wrapper
Torpedo	Figurado	5¾	56	CC
Double Corona	Churchill	7	50	CC
Toro	Toro	6	50	CC
Lonsdale	No. 1	6¾	44	CC
Robusto	Rothschild	5	50	CC

Corona	Breva	5¾	43	CC

Introduced in 1998, this is a medium-to-full-bodied smoke, with a Connecticut-seed wrapper. It is offered in value-priced packs of 20.

RIGOLETTO
Handmade in Santiago, Dominican Republic.

Wrapper: USA/Connecticut   Binder: Dom. Rep.   Filler: Dom. Rep.

Shape	Name	Lgth	Ring	Wrapper
Churchill	Black Magic	7½	46	CC-Ma
Lonsdale	Black Arrow	6¼	44	CC-Ma
Toro	Dominican Lights	6¼	48	CC-Ma

This brand, which debuted in 1905, is made by hand in the Dominican Republic using Connecticut Shade leaves for natural wrappers and Connecticut Broadleaf tobaccos for the maduro style. Medium in body, it's an underrated smoke.

RIO DE CUBA
Handmade, with mixed filler, in Esteli, Nicaragua.

Wrapper: Indonesia   Binder: Indonesia   Filler: Nicaragua

Shape	Name	Lgth	Ring	Wrapper
Churchill	Churchill	7	48	CM
Corona	Corona	5½	43	CM
Lonsdale	Lonsdale	6½	44	CM
Robusto	Robusto	5	50	CM
Toro	Toro	6	48	CM

This is a flavorful, mixed-filler, medium-to-full-bodied cigar. Try it in value-priced bundles of 25.

ROBALI
Handmade in San Jose, Costa Rica.

Wrapper: Ecuador or Indonesia   Binder: Nicaragua   Filler: Costa Rica, Nicaragua

HANDMADE CIGARS: BRAND LISTINGS

Shape	Name	Lgth	Ring	Wrapper
Giant	Viajante	8	52	CC
Churchill	Double Corona	7	46	CC
Lonsdale	Linda	6½	44	CC
Robusto	Robusto	5	50	CC
Toro	Corona	6	50	CC
Corona	Senorita	5½	43	CC
Cigarillo	Cigarello	4½	28	CC

New in 1996, Robali carries on the tradition of Costa Rican cigar making. A mild-to-medium-bodied blend with a Connecticut-seed wrapper, these cigars are offered in boxes or bundles of 25 from the Robali de Centro America, S.A. factory.

ROBLE VIEJO
Handmade in Managua, Nicaragua.

Wrapper: Indonesia   Binder: Mexico   Filler: Costa Rica & Nicaragua

Shape	Name	Lgth	Ring	Wrapper
Robusto	Robusto	5	50	CC
Long Corona	Lonsdale	6	44	CC
Double Corona	Churchill	7	50	CC

Here is the "Old Oak" which presents a Sumatran wrapper and a three-nation interior blend for a medium-bodied experience. An excellent daytime cigar, it is offered in cellophane sleeves in bundles of 25 cigars each.

RODON
Handmade in the Dominican Republic.
Wrapper: Cameroon or USA/Connecticut
Binder: Dominican Republic   Filler: Dominican Republic

Shape	Name	Lgth	Ring	Wrapper
Double Corona	No. 1	7½	50	CC-CM

Robusto	No. 2	4½	50	CC-CM
Long Corona	No. 3	6	44	CC-CM
Corona	No. 4	5½	42	CC-CM
Long Panatela	No. 5	7½	38	CC-CM
Torpedo	No. 6	6	54	CC-CM

This is a mild-to-medium-bodied brand in the Connecticut wrapper and full-bodied in the Cameroon wrapper. Introduced in 1997, it is offered in boxes of five or 25.

RODRIGUEZ & MENENDEZ
Handmade in Tampa, Florida, USA.
Wrapper: Dom. Rep., Ecuador, Indonesia
Binder: Dom. Rep., Honduras, Nicaragua   *Filler: Dom. Rep. Honduras*

Shape	Name	Lgth	Ring	Wrapper
Lonsdale	Fuma	7¼	44	CC-Ma
Lonsdale	Palma	6½	42	CC-Ma
Robusto	Rothschild	4⅞	50	CC-Ma
Churchill	Reyna	7¼	46	CC-Ma
Double Corona	No. 5	7	49	CC-Ma
Churchill	Imperiales	8	47	CC-Ma
Grand Corona	Gran Corona	6	47	CC-Ma
Slim Panatela	Panatela	5½	34	CC
Long Panatela	Panatela Especial Natural	7½	39	CC
Giant	Chula	8½	52	CC-Ma
Corona	Petit Corona	5½	43	CC
Toro	Double Corona	6	50	CC-Ma
Double Corona	Presidente	7¼	50	CC-Ma
Grand Corona	Palma Especial	6¼	45	CC

Churchill	Churchill	7	48	CC-Ma
Torpedo	Torpedo	6½	54	CC
Toro	Toro	6½	50	CC

Well respected since their introduction in 1981, these are medium-bodied cigars in the natural wrappers and full-bodied in maduro. They are produced in a small factory in the famous Tampa suburb of Ybor City.

ROLANDO
Handmade in Santiago, Dominican Republic.
Wrapper: USA/Connecticut   *Binder: Dom. Rep.*   *Filler: Dom. Rep.*

Shape	*Name*	*Lgth*	*Ring*	*Wrapper*
Churchill	No. 2	7½	48	CC
Toro	No. 3	6	50	CC
Long Corona	No. 4	6	43	CC
Robusto	Robusto	4¾	52	CC

Introduced in 1995, meticulously-selected tobaccos and extended aging contribute to the exquisite, mild-to-medium flavor of one of the world's finest cigars. Rolandos are wrapped in the famous Connecticut Shade-grown wrapper, with Dominican filler leaf.

ROLL-X
Handmade in the Dominican Republic and the USA.

ROLL-X BLUE LABEL:
Wrapper: Ecuador and Indonesia   *Binder: Dom. Rep.*   *Filler: Dom. Rep.*

ROLL-X EMERALD LABEL:
Wrapper: Ecuador and Indonesia   *Binder: Mexico*
Filler: Dominican Republic, Mexico, Nicaragua

ROLL-X GOLD LABEL:
Wrapper: Ecuador and Indonesia   *Binder: Dom. Rep. or Mexico*
Filler: Dominican Republic, Mexico, Nicaragua

HANDMADE CIGARS: BRAND LISTINGS

ROLL-X PLATINUM LABEL:

Wrapper: Ecuador and Indonesia   *Binder: Mexico*
Filler: Dominican Republic, Mexico, Nicaragua

ROLL-X RED LABEL:

Wrapper: Ecuador   *Binder: Indonesia*   *Filler: Dom. Rep., Nicaragua*

Shape	Name	Lgth	Ring	Wrapper
	Blue Label, made in Miami, Florida, USA:			
Robusto	Rare & Delicate Robusto	5	50	CC
Long Corona	Rare & Delicate Corona	6	42	CC
	Emerald Label, made in Miami, Florida, USA			
Pyramid	Pyramid	7	58	CC
	Gold Label, made in Miami, Florida, USA:			
Double Corona	Churchill	7	50	CC
Short Panatela	Tahitian Secrets Panatella	5	36	CC
	Platinum Label, made in Miami, Florida, USA:			
Perfecto	Diadema	7	54	CC
	Red Label, made in Santo Domingo, Dominican Republic:			
Toro	Toro	6	50	CC
Giant	Double Corona	8	50	CC
Torpedo	Torpedo	6	54	CC

This complex brand was introduced in 1998. Most of the styles feature a double wrapper of Ecuadorian-grown, Connecticut-seed wrappers rolled over a Sumatra wrapper. The Blue Label is medium-bodied with a hint of Hine "Rare & Delicate" Cognac, which is cured into the Sumatra wrapper leaf. The Emerald Label is medium-bodied and made by hand without molds. The Gold Label has a medium-to-full flavor, but the Tahitian Secrets has a medium-bodied taste tinged with vanilla. The Platinum Label is medium-to-full-bodied, while the 1½-year aged Red Label is medium-bodied and is available only in limited quantities.

HANDMADE CIGARS: BRAND LISTINGS

ROLLER'S CHOICE
Handmade in Santiago, Dominican Republic.

Wrapper: USA/Connecticut   *Binder: Dom. Rep.*   *Filler: Dom. Rep.*

Shape	Name	Lgth	Ring	Wrapper
Double Corona	RC Double Corona	7	50	CC
Long Corona	RC Corona	6	43	CC
Grand Corona	RC Lonsdale	6½	46	CC
Robusto	RC Robusto	5	50	CC
Petit Corona	RC Pequeno	4¼	40	CC
Corona	RC Fino	5½	41	CC
Torpedo	RC Torpedo	5½	56	CC
Toro	RC Toro	6	50	CC
Corona	RC Cetro	5½	43	CC

While not as well known as some other brands, Roller's Choice was introduced in 1992 and is a well-constructed, mild-bodied cigar produced in one of the Dominican Republic's most dependable factories.

ROLY
Handmade in the Dominican Republic and Honduras.

Wrapper: Mexico   *Binder: Dom. Rep.*   *Filler: Dom. Rep.*

Shape	Name	Lgth	Ring	Wrapper
Double Corona	Churchill	7¼	53	CM
Churchill	Presidente	7¼	47	CM
Grand Corona	Corona de Lux	6½	46	CM
Corona Extra	No. 4 Extra	5½	45	CM
Lonsdale	Lonsdale	6½	43	CM
Corona	Remedios	5½	43	CM
Toro	Toro Extra	6	53	CM
Robusto	Rothchild	5	50	CM

Short Panatela	Petit Cetro	5	36	CM
Long Panatela	Long Palma	7	39	CM
Pyramid	Piramide 1	7½	60	CM
Pyramid	Piramide 2	6½	46	CM
	Roly Seconds:			
Double Corona	Churchill	7¼	53	CM
Toro	Cetro	6	53	CM
Grand Corona	No. 2	6½	47	CM
Corona Extra	No. 4	5½	45	CM
Short Panatela	No. 5	5	36	CM
Churchill	Cazadores	7	47	CM
Doo16le Corona	Supers	7½	50	CM
Grand Corona	Fumas	6½	46	CM

Here is a brilliantly constructed cigar, available in a variety of shapes. Medium in body, Roly features a Sumatra-seed wrapper and Dominican binder and filler. Look for it in boxes or bundles of 25. The Seconds are made in Honduras and are offered only in bundles of 25.

ROMANO'S CONNOISSEUR SERIES
Handmade in Tamboril, Dominican Republic.
Wrapper: Indonesia or USA/Connecticut
Binder: Dominican Republic   Filler: Dominican Republic

Shape	Name	Lgth	Ring	Wrapper
Double Corona	Corona Grande	7½	50	CC
Churchill	Churchill	7	46	CC
Panatela	Panatela	6	38	CC
Robusto	Robusto	5	50	CC

HANDMADE CIGARS: BRAND LISTINGS

This is a medium-bodied cigar, with Sumatra wrappers on three sizes and a Connecticut wrapper on the Panatela shape. Introduced in 1997, they are offered in boxes of 25.

ROMANTICOS
Handmade in Villa Gonzalez, Dominican Republic

Wrapper: USA/Connecticut   *Binder: Dom. Rep.*   *Filler: Dom. Rep.*

Shape	Name	Lgth	Ring	Wrapper
Giant	Marc Anthony	8	52	Co
Double Corona	Valentino	7	50	Co
Corona	Cleopatra	5¾	43	Co
Robusto	Eros	5	50	Co
Short Panatela	Venus	5	36	Co
Torpedo	Cyrano	6	52	Co
Torpedo	Casanova	6½	56	Co

Introduced in 1996, this is a rich-flavored, mild-to-medium bodied blend of long-filler tobaccos, offered in individual cellophane sleeves in elegant cedar cabinets of 25. A Vintage Series is also available in the Cleopatra, Eros, Valentino and Casanova shapes, using aged Dominican leaves. Check out the shape names: some of the great lovers and love-gods in history!

ROMEO Y JULIETA
Handmade in Santiago, Dominican Republic.

Wrapper: Indonesia   *Binder: USA/Connecticut*   *Filler: Brazil, Dom. Rep.*

Shape	Name	Lgth	Ring	Wrapper
Giant	Monarcas	8	52	CM
Double Corona	Churchills	7	50	CM
Lonsdale	Presidentes	7	43	CM
Robusto	Rothschilds	5	50	CM-Ma
Lonsdale	Cetros	6½	44	CM-Ma
Long Corona	Palmas	6	43	CM

HANDMADE CIGARS: BRAND LISTINGS

Corona	Coronas	5½	44	CM
Slim Panatela	Delgados	7	32	CM
Panatela	Brevas	5⅝	38	CM
Short Panatela	Panatelas	5¼	35	CM
Small Panatela	Chiquitas	4¼	32	CM
Pyramid	Romeos	6	46	CM

This famous brand originated in Cuba, and this version lives up to its heritage. Made by hand in the Dominican Republic, this line is medium in strength, using tobaccos from many nations to create a complex taste. The shortage of Cameroon wrappers often make these cigars hard to find.

ROMEO Y JULIETA VINTAGE
Handmade in Santiago, Dominican Republic.

Wrapper: USA/Connecticut   *Binder: Mexico*   *Filler: Dom. Rep.*

Shape	Name	Lgth	Ring	Wrapper
Long Corona	I	6	43	CC
Grand Corona	II	6	46	CC
Robusto	III	4½	50	CC
Churchill	IV	7	48	CC
Double Corona	V	7½	50	CC
Pyramid	VI	7	60	CC

This is the ultimate cigar! Made with perfectly fermented tobacco, the wrapper is selected for a natural, oily sheen and silky appearance. The binder is aged Mexican leaf and the filler is superbly blended Cuban seed and long-leaf Dominican tobaccos. Introduced in 1993, this is a finesse cigar, mild with very round flavor and made in extremely limited supply.

ROSA BLANCA RESERVA
Handmade in Esteli, Nicaragua.

Wrapper: Indonesia   *Binder: Nicaragua*   *Filler: Nicaragua*

HANDMADE CIGARS: BRAND LISTINGS

Shape	Name	Lgth	Ring	Wrapper
Corona	Corona	5½	44	CC
Toro	Toro	6	54	CC
Torpedo	Gigante	7	54	CC
Torpedo	Torpedo	5½	56	CC
Churchill	Churchill	7	49	CC

This brand was introduced in 1997 and has a mild-to-medium-bodied flavor. It is offered uncellophaned in cedar boxes of 25.

ROSA CUBA
Handmade, with mixed filler, in Esteli, Nicaragua.
Wrapper: Ecuador   *Binder: Dominican Republic*
Filler: Dominican Republic, Honduras, Nicaragua

Shape	Name	Lgth	Ring	Wrapper
Short Panatela	Angels	4½	38	CC
Corona	Flor de Rosa	5½	44	CC
Toro	Governor	6⅛	50	CC
Robusto	Herencia	4½	52	CC
Churchill	Mille Fleurs	6¾	48	CC
Grand Corona	Media Noche	6½	46	CC
Toro	Ortiz y Laboy	6½	52	CC
Lonsdale	Vargas	6½	44	CC

New for 1996, this line offers a medium-to-full-bodied flavor with a magnificent Ecuador-grown, Sumatra-seed wrapper, in economical bundles of 20.

ROSALONES
Handmade in Esteli, Nicaragua.
Wrapper: Nicaragua   *Binder: Nicaragua*   *Filler: Nicaragua*

HANDMADE CIGARS: BRAND LISTINGS

Shape	Name	Lgth	Ring	Wrapper
Giant	Presidente	8	54	CC-Ma
Giant	Viajante	8½	52	CC-Ma
Double Corona	Presidente Corto	7¼	54	CC-Ma
Double Corona	Viajante Corto	7	52	CC-Ma
Double Corona	Emperador	7¾	50	CC-Ma
Double Corona	Emperador Corto	7½	50	CC-Ma
Churchill	Churchill	6⅞	48	CC-Ma
Churchill	No. 11	7½	46	CC-Ma
Toro	Duke	6	50	CC-Ma
Long Panatela	No. 9	8	38	CC-Ma
Long Panatela	No. 9 Corto	7	38	CC-Ma
Corona Extra	Corona Extra	5½	46	CC-Ma
Robusto	Consul	4½	52	CC-Ma
Lonsdale	No. 1	6⅝	44	CC-Ma
Lonsdale	No. 10	6½	43	CC-Ma
Long Corona	No. 3	6	44	CC-Ma
Corona	Nacional	5½	44	CC-Ma
Panatela	No. 5	6⅞	35	CC-Ma
Long Corona	No. 6	6	41	CC-Ma
Corona	Seleccion B	5½	42	CC-Ma
Slim Panatela	No. 7	7	30	CC-Ma
Panatela	Elegante	6½	38	CC-Ma
Petit Corona	No. 2	4½	42	CC-Ma
Short Panatela	Petits	5½	38	CC-Ma
Slim Panatela	Senoritas	5½	34	CC-Ma
Small Panatela	Piccolino	4⅛	30	CC-Ma

Toro	Corona	5⅝	48	CC-Ma

This line, introduced in 1983, is primarily produced for the Nicaraguan home market, with some distribution reaching the United States. A 27-shape brand, it is a sister to the U.S.-marketed Flor de Nicaragua range. These are mild-bodied cigars, using filler and binder leaf from the Jalapa Valley of Nicaragua, with Nicaraguan wrappers.

ROVANOFF
Handmade in Esteli, Nicaragua.

Wrapper: Indonesia   *Binder: Nicaragua*
Filler: Dominican Republic, Ecuador, Nicaragua

Shape	Name	Lgth	Ring	Wrapper
Giant	Hemingway	8	52	CC
Double Corona	Churchill	7	50	CC-Ma
Robusto	Consul	5	50	CC
Churchill	Presidente	7	46	CC-Ma
Long Corona	Corona	6	44	CC
Torpedo	Torpedo	6	52	CC
Long Panatela	Lanceros	7½	38	CC

Here is a 1997-introduced brand with a medium-bodied flavor, featuring a Cuban-seed, Jalapa Valley-grown wrapper and a blended filler from three nations. It is offered in boxes of 20.

ROYAL DOMINICANA
Handmade in La Romana, Dominican Republic.

Wrapper: Ecuador   *Binder: Mexico*   *Filler: Dom. Rep.*

Shape	Name	Lgth	Ring	Wrapper
Double Corona	Churchill	7¼	50	CC
Grand Corona	Corona	6	46	CC
Corona	Nacional	5½	43	CC

HANDMADE CIGARS: BRAND LISTINGS

| Lonsdale | No. 1 | 6¾ | 43 | CC |
| Panatela | Super Fino | 6 | 35 | CC |

This is a mild-to-medium bodied cigar with a Connecticut wrapper, well-known for its quality construction and reasonable price.

ROYALES
Handmade in Santiago, Dominican Republic.

Wrapper: Indonesia *Binder: Brazil* *Filler: Brazil, Dom. Rep.*

Shape	Name	Lgth	Ring	Wrapper
Giant	No. 1	8	52	CC
Double Corona	No. 2	7½	50	CC
Toro	No. 3	6	50	CC
Robusto	No. 4	5	50	CC
Lonsdale	No. 5	6⅝	44	CC
Long Corona	No. 6	6	42	CC
Panatela	No. 7	6⅞	38	CC

Introduced in 1992, Royales is a careful hand-blend of leaves that produces a mild cigar with a rich bouquet.

ROYAL HONDURAS
Handmade in Danli, Honduras.

Wrapper: Indonesia *Binder: Dom. Rep.* *Filler: Honduras*

Shape	Name	Lgth	Ring	Wrapper
Giant	Czar	8	50	CC
Churchill	Sovereign	7	48	CC
Torpedo	Kings	6⅛	54	CC
Lonsdale	Prince	7	44	CC
Robusto	Majesty	5	50	CC
Corona	Joker	5½	42	CC

HANDMADE CIGARS: BRAND LISTINGS

Pyramid	Princess	5	38	CC
Toro	Knight	6	50	CC

Royal Honduras was introduced in 1996, with a medium-to-full flavor in sizes named after characters in a royal court. All are presented in cedar boxes. The two shaped cigars flare from 42 to 54 ring (Kings) and from 32 to 38 (Princess).

ROYAL JAMAICA
Handmade in La Romana, Dominican Republic
and in Maypen, Jamaica

Wrapper: Indonesia   Binder: Mexico   Filler: Dom. Rep., Indonesia, Jamaica

Shape	Name	Lgth	Ring	Wrapper
Slim Panatela	Buccaneer	5½	30	CM-Ma
Lonsdale	Corona Grande	6½	42	CM-Ma
Giant	Churchill	8	51	CM-Ma
Corona	Corona	5½	40	CM-Ma
Grand Corona	Director No. 1	6	45	CM
Lonsdale	Double Corona	7	45	CM
Slim Panatela	Doubloon	7	30	CM
Slim Panatela	Gaucho	5¼	33	CM
Double Corona	Giant Corona	7½	49	CM
Giant	Goliath	9	64	CM
Giant	Individuales	8½	52	CM
Long Corona	New York Plaza	6	40	CM
Grand Corona	Park Lane *(perfecto tip)*	6	47	CM
Robusto	Robusto	4½	49	CM
Toro	Toro	6	50	CM
Grand Corona	No. 1 Tube *(tubed)*	6	45	CM
Slim Panatela	No. 2 Tube *(tubed)*	6½	34	CM
Giant	No. 10 Downing Street	10	51	CM

LANDMARK TASTE

SINCE 1929

ROYAL JAMAICA

IF THERE WERE A BETTER WAY TO MAKE A CIGAR.
WE'D FIND IT. . .THEN WE'D SMOKE IT.

HANDMADE CIGARS: BRAND LISTINGS

Consistently ranked as one of the tastiest handmade cigars in the world with an abundant variety of shapes and styles, Royal Jamaica is again being made in Jamaica. Transferred to the Dominican Republic in 1988 after Hurricane Gilbert destroyed the factory in Kingston, Consolidated Cigar has opened a new facility in Maypen, Jamaica and production began in late 1996. The filler is predominantly Jamaica-grown tobaccos, with a secret family additive applied during the fermentation process. The Mexican binder combined with the Java wrapper results in a unique, spicy flavor. A dark Mexican maduro wrapper gives that series a rich taste with a hint of sweetness. The Mexican leaf is heated with steam and aged two weeks to result in a deep brown hue.

ROYAL MANNA
Handmade in Santa Rosa de Copan, Honduras.

Wrapper: Ecuador   Binder: Honduras   Filler: Honduras

Shape	Name	Lgth	Ring	Wrapper
Lonsdale	No. 1	7⅛	43	CM
Corona	No. 4	5⅛	42	CM
Panatela	Manchego	6¾	35	CM
Double Corona	Churchill	7½	50	CM
Robusto	Rothschild	4¾	50	CM
Toro	Toro	6	50	CM

This popular brand was introduced in 1972, originally made in the Canary Islands. It is well known for its Connecticut Shade-seed wrapper, excellent construction and a medium-bodied taste.

ROYAL NICARAGUAN
Handmade in Esteli, Nicaragua.

Wrapper: Indonesia   Binder: Nicaragua   Filler: Nicaragua

Shape	Name	Lgth	Ring	Wrapper
Giant	No. 2	8½	52	CC-Ma
Double Corona	No. 8	7	49	CC-Ma
Toro	No. 14	6	50	CC

Lonsdale	No. 16	7	43	CC
Robusto	No. 20	5	50	CC-Ma

This is a medium-bodied cigar with all long-filler tobacco offered in modestly-priced bundles of 25.

ROYCE
Handmade in Danli, Honduras.

Wrapper: Indonesia   *Binder: Ecuador*   *Filler: Dom. Rep., Honduras*

Shape	Name	Lgth	Ring	Wrapper
Robusto	Robustos	5	50	CC-Ma
Lonsdale	Fumas	7	44	CC-Ma
Toro	Coronas	6	50	CC-Ma
Double Corona	Churchills	7	50	CC-Ma

New in 1997, this Honduran-produced brand is medium-to-full in body and only in limited production. Each cigar is protected in an individual cellophane sleeve and packed in all-cedar boxes of 25.

RUBIROSA
Handmade in Santiago, Dominican Republic.
Wrapper: USA/Connecticut (Claro) or Indonesia (Supremo)

Binder: Dominican Republic   *Filler: Dominican Republic*

Shape	Name	Lgth	Ring	Wrapper
	Claro series:			
Double Corona	Maximos	7½	50	CC-Ma
Churchill	Extasis	6⅞	46	CC
Robusto	Polo	5	50	CC-Ma
Long Corona	Caribe	6	44	CC-Ma
Pyramid	Piramide	6½	54	CC
	Supremo series:			

HANDMADE CIGARS: BRAND LISTINGS

Double Corona	Maximos	7½	50	CM
Churchill	Extasis	6⅞	46	CM
Pyramid	Piramide	6½	54	CM
Long Corona	Caribe	6	44	CM
Robusto	Polo	5	50	CM

Named for the famous Dominican playboy Porfirio Rubirosa (1909-65), who charmed, married and befriended many of the most famous and richest women in the world, the Claro line, introduced in 1995, offers a mild taste. The Supremo line, introduced in 1996, offers a mild-to-medium-bodied flavor. Made completely by hand, these cigars are presented in boxes made only of Spanish cedar to enhance the aging process.

RUBY DOOBY
Handmade in Las Palmas, the Canary Islands of Spain.
Wrapper: USA/Connecticut   Binder: Dom. Rep.   Filler: Dom. Rep.

Shape	Name	Lgth	Ring	Wrapper
Perfecto	Small Dooby	4¼	42	CI
Perfecto	Big Dooby	5½	45	CI

You'll know these cigars instantly! Look for the long face of the cigar-smoking dog on them and you'll know these as medium-bodied, 1998-introduced Canary Islands cigars from Marcos Miguel Tobacco Co. The band was designed by the noted artist Ruby Mazur, renowned for his legendary designs including the mouth-and-tongue Rolling Stones logo and many others. The cigars are available in two shapes in boxes of 10 and 25.

RUM RAIDER
Handmade in Miami, Florida, USA.
Wrapper: Indonesia   Binder: Dom. Rep.   Filler: Dom. Rep.

Shape	Name	Lgth	Ring	Wrapper
Robusto	Rum Raider	5	50	CM

HANDMADE CIGARS: BRAND LISTINGS

Here is a thoroughly-soaked, mild-bodied, rum-imbued cigar with a Sumatra wrapper, offered in a large size and available in boxes of 25.

RUM ROYALE
Handmade, with medium filler, in Santiago, Dominican Republic.
Wrapper: Indonesia *Binder: Dom. Rep.* *Filler: Dom. Rep.*

Shape	Name	Lgth	Ring	Wrapper
Long Corona		6	42	CM
Long Corona		6	44	CM

This is a medium-bodied, flavored cigar available in two sizes and introduced in 1996. It utilizes all-Dominican filler and is offered in bundles of 25.

RUSTY'S
Handmade, with short filler, in Esteli, Nicaragua.
Wrapper: Indonesia *Binder: Nicaragua* *Filler: Pipe tobacco*

Shape	Name	Lgth	Ring	Wrapper
Toro	No. 3	6	50	CM
Robusto	No. 5	5	50	CM
Corona	No. 7	5½	42	CM

If you like Peter Stokkebye pipe tobacco, this is the cigar for you! Introduced in 1997, it is mild in body and is offered in either bundles or boxes of 25.

SABANA
Handmade in San Jose, Costa Rica.
Wrapper: Indonesia *Binder: Nicaragua* *Filler: Colombia, Dom. Rep., Nicaragua*

Shape	Name	Lgth	Ring	Wrapper
Robusto	Robusto	5	50	CM
Toro	Toro	6	50	CM
Churchill	Churchill	7	46	CM
Double Corona	Double Corona	7	50	CM

HANDMADE CIGARS: BRAND LISTINGS

Torpedo	Torpedo	7	52	CM

This brand was introduced in 1998 and offers a mild and sweet taste from one of the hottest cigar-producing regions in the world. Sabanas are available in elegant wood boxes of 25.

SABOR A MIAMI
Handmade, with short filler, in Miami, Florida, USA.

Wrapper: Indonesia   *Binder: Indonesia*   *Filler: Dom. Rep.*

Shape	Name	Lgth	Ring	Wrapper
Long Corona	Corona	6	44	CM

This is a flavored, mild-to-medium-bodied brand, offered in Amaretto, cherry, coffee, rum and vanilla. Introduced in 1997, it is offered in boxes of 25.

SABOR CUBANO
Handmade in Miami, Florida, USA.

Wrapper: Cameroon   *Binder: Honduras*   *Filler: Dom. Rep., Nicaragua*

Shape	Name	Lgth	Ring	Wrapper
Torpedo	Small Torpedo	5	54	CM

This brand debuted in 1998 and has a full-bodied taste. It is offered in one size only and presented in all-cedar boxes of 20.

SABOR HABANO
Handmade in Esteli, Nicaragua.

Wrapper: Ecuador   *Binder: Nicaragua*   *Filler: Dom. Rep., Nicaragua*

Shape	Name	Lgth	Ring	Wrapper
Long Corona	Cetro	6	44	CC
Robusto	Rothchild	5	50	CC
Toro	Matador	6	50	CC
Double Corona	Churchill	7	49	CC
Giant	Presidente	8½	50	CC

HANDMADE CIGARS: BRAND LISTINGS

Here is a medium-bodied cigar which matches a Connecticut-seed wrapper grown in Ecuador with a Havana-seed binder from Nicaragua and filler leaves from the Dominican Republic and Nicaragua. Introduced in 1996, Sabor Habano is offered in boxes of 25 cigars each.

SABOR HABANO DOMINICAN RESERVE
Handmade in Tamboril, Dominican Republic.

Wrapper: Nicaragua   *Binder: Dom. Rep.*   *Filler: Dom. Rep., Nicaragua*

Shape	Name	Lgth	Ring	Wrapper
Long Corona	Cetro	6	44	CC
Robusto	Rothchild	5	50	CC
Toro	Matador	6	50	CC
Double Corona	Churchill	7	50	CC

Introduced in 1997, this is a medium-bodied cigar that features a Sumatra-seed wrapper and an Olor binder. It is presented in cellophane sleeves and packed in boxes of 25.

SABROSO
Handmade in Esteli, Nicaragua.

Wrapper: Ecuador   *Binder: Nicaragua*   *Filler: Nicaragua*

Shape	Name	Lgth	Ring	Wrapper
Robusto	Numero Uno	4¾	50	CC
Long Corona	Numero Dos	6	44	CC
Toro	Numero Tres	6	50	CC
Churchill	Numero Cuatro	7	48	CC
Giant	Numero Cinco	8½	52	CC

Introduced in 1996, this value-packed brand from Nicaragua offers a full-bodied taste and an excellent value. Sabroso cigars are packaged in bundles of 25.

HANDMADE CIGARS: BRAND LISTINGS

SACUBA
Handmade, with mixed filler, in Navarette, Dominican Republic.

Wrapper: Indonesia   Binder: Dom. Rep.   Filler: Dom. Rep.

Shape	Name	Lgth	Ring	Wrapper
Petit Corona	Petit Corona	5	43	CM
Long Corona	Cetros	6	44	CM
Toro	Toro	6½	50	CM
Churchill	Churchill	7¼	48	CM

This is a recently-introduced brand with a mild-to-medium body and a shiny Indonesian wrapper. It is presented in boxes of 25.

ST. CHARLES
Handmade in Navarette, Dominican Republic.

Wrapper: Indonesia   Binder: Dom. Rep.   Filler: Dom. Rep.

Shape	Name	Lgth	Ring	Wrapper
Corona	Corona	5½	44	CM
Robusto	Robusto	5	50	CM
Toro	Toro	6	50	CM
Grand Corona	Corona Gorda	6½	46	CM
Double Corona	Churchill	7	50	CM
Torpedo	Torpedo	6¼	52	CM

This is a long-filler flavored brand, accented with brandy for a smooth and flavorful taste. It has a mild-to-medium body and is available in boxes of 25.

ST. GEORGE
Handmade in Tamboril, Dominican Republic.

Wrapper: Indonesia   Binder: Dom. Rep.   Filler: Dom. Rep.

Shape	Name	Lgth	Ring	Wrapper
Giant	Dragonslayer	8	50	CC

HANDMADE CIGARS: BRAND LISTINGS

Churchill	Churchill	7	48	CC
Toro	Ascalon	6½	50	CC
Torpedo	Falchion	6	52	CC
Corona Extra	Chevalier	5½	46	CC
Corona	Coronet	5½	42	CC
Robusto	Chivalry	5	50	CC

Here is a mild-to-medium-bodied smoke offered in cabinets of 25 cigars each. Introduced in 1997, this brand is presented uncellophaned by the Tabacalera La Real.

SAINT LUIS REY
Handmade in Danli, Honduras.

Wrapper: Honduras   *Binder: Honduras*   *Filler: Honduras*

Shape	Name	Lgth	Ring	Wrapper
Torpedo	Torpedo	6	54	CM
Double Corona	Churchill	7	50	CM
Toro	Serie A	6	50	CM
Lonsdale	Lonsdale	6½	44	CM
Double Corona	Double Corona	7½	50	CM

Introduced at *LE CIGAR NOIR - BEVERLY HILLS* on May 1, 1996, this Honduran version of an old Cuban brand was an immediate hit with everyone who tried it. Full-bodied but smooth on the draw, these cigars blend plenty of flavor with a slow-burning cadre of Honduran-grown, Cuban-seed tobaccos for a relaxing smoke. Saint Luis Rey cigars are individually cellophaned and packed in windowed boxes of 25.

SAN VICENTE COLLECTION
Handmade in the Dominican Republic.

Wrapper: Dom. Rep.   *Binder: Honduras*   *Filler: Dom. Rep., Nicaragua*

HANDMADE CIGARS: BRAND LISTINGS

Shape	Name	Lgth	Ring	Wrapper
Pyramid	Petit Pyramid	6	52	CM
Toro	Majestics	6	50	CM
Churchill	Imperial	7¼	46	CM
Corona Extra	Habaneros	5½	46	CM

Celebrating more than 50 years, this respected brand is made by hand in the Dominican Republic. The taste of this blend is mild, with a hint of spice; San Vicente is offered in cedar boxes of 25.

SANTA CLARA "1830"
Handmade in San Andres Tuxtla, Mexico.

Wrapper: Mexico   Binder: Mexico   Filler: Mexico

Shape	Name	Lgth	Ring	Wrapper
Double Corona	I	7½	52	CC-Ma
Toro	II	6½	48	CC-Ma
Lonsdale	III	6⅝	43	CC-Ma
Corona	IV	5	44	CC-Ma
Long Corona	V	6	44	CC-Ma
Toro	VI	6	51	CC-Ma
Cigarillo	VII	5½	25	CC
Slim Panatela	VIII	6	32	CC
Panatela	Premier Tubes (tubed)	6¾	38	CC-Ma
Small Panatela	Quino	4¼	30	CC
Robusto	Robusto	4½	50	CC-Ma
Long Corona	Fiesta	6½	42	Stripe
Giant	Magnum	19	60	CC

This is a medium-bodied cigar of all-Mexican tobacco. The wrapper is a unique Sumatran-seed type, which gives this line a unique flavor in both the natural and maduro shades. The Fiesta features the "barber pole" double wrapper style and

HANDMADE CIGARS: BRAND LISTINGS

the new Magnum can be used as a baseball bat if you're not smoking it. At 19 inches long, it's the biggest standard-production cigar available today.

SANTA CRUZ
Handmade in Las Palmas, the Canary Islands of Spain.

Wrapper: USA/Connecticut   Binder: Indonesia   Filler: Brazil, Dom. Rep., Spain

Shape	Name	Lgth	Ring	Wrapper
Double Corona	Majestad	7½	50	CC
Grand Corona	Excelencia	6½	46	CC
Corona Extra	Presidente	5½	46	CC
Robusto	Robusto	4¾	50	CC

This is a mild-bodied cigar, offered in cellophane sleeves and in four sizes in boxes of 25.

SANTA DAMIANA
Handmade in La Romana, Dominican Republic.

Wrapper: USA/Connecticut   Binder: Dom. Rep.   Filler: Dom. Rep.

Shape	Name	Lgth	Ring	Wrapper
Churchill	Double Corona	6¾	48	CI
Corona Extra	Corona	5½	46	CI
Robusto	Robusto	5	50	CI
Lonsdale	Lonsdale	6½	42	CI
Double Corona	Churchill	7	50	CI
Torpedo	Torpedo	6	50	CI

A beautifully-finished cigar that defines what a "claro" wrapper looks like, Santa Damiana is an elegant, medium-bodied smoke. This brand originated in Cuba and today's Dominican-manufactured cigar was introduced in 1992. It is offered in attractive, slide-top cedar boxes of 25, with new shape names for 1998.

SANTA MARIA
Handmade in David, Panama.

Wrapper: Panama   Binder: Panama   Filler: Mexico, Panama

HANDMADE CIGARS: BRAND LISTINGS

Shape	Name	Lgth	Ring	Wrapper
Grand Corona	Churchills	6½	46	CM
Corona Extra	Generals	5½	46	CM
Slim Panatela	Pricesasa's	6½	30	CM
Panatela	Panatelas	5½	36	CM
Robusto	Robustos	4	46	CM
Grand Corona	Churchill Especials	6½	46	CM

This brand is new for 1998 and offers a medium-bodied taste with a hint of sweetness. It is presented in clamshell-style boxes of 20 or 25.

SANTAMARIA
Handmade in Guiria Ed. Sucre, Venezuela.
Wrapper: USA/Connecticut   *Binder: Venezuela*   *Filler: Venezuela*

Shape	Name	Lgth	Ring	Wrapper
Double Corona	Gigante	7	52	CM
Grand Corona	Elegante	6	46	CM
Robusto	Gordo	5	52	CM
Small Panatela	El Cabito	5	34	CM
Pyramid	Piramide No. 1	6½	54	CM
Pyramid	Piramide No. 2	3½	50	CM
Torpedo	Torpedo	6	52	CM

Here is a mild-to-medium-bodied brand from Venezuela, offered in cellophane sleeves inside all-cedar boxes of 25.

SANTA ROSA
Handmade in Santa Rosa de Copan, Honduras.
Wrapper: Ecuador   *Binder: Honduras*   *Filler: Honduras*

Not satisfied?

Want more?

For more information about
even more cigars, how about

**Perelman's
Pocket Cyclopedia
of
Havana Cigars**

Complete coverage of
Cuban brands, shapes and sizes;
available for $9.95 at your local
smokeshop or by calling
(323) 965-4905.

HANDMADE CIGARS: BRAND LISTINGS

Shape	Name	Lgth	Ring	Wrapper
Corona	No. 4	5½	42	CC-Ma
Long Corona	Cetros	6	42	CC-Ma
Giant	President	8½	50	CC
Double Corona	Churchill	7	49	CC-Ma
Lonsdale	Corona	6½	44	CC-Ma
Lonsdale	Elegante	7	43	CC-Ma
Slim Panatela	Finas	6½	30	CC
Panatela	Largos	6¾	35	CC
Corona Extra	Regulares	5½	46	CC
Robusto	Sancho Panza	4¾	50	CC-Ma
Torpedo	Torpedo	5½	54	CC-Ma
Toro	Toro	6	50	CC-Ma

Introduced in 1985, the Santa Rosa brand is marked by a beautiful new band, along with an expanded set of shapes. Made in the La Flor de Copan factory in Santa Rosa, Honduras, this is a mild brand with a smooth, easy taste that everyone can enjoy. The wrapper is particularly smooth Ecuadorian-grown leaf from Connecticut Shade seeds.

SANTIAGO
Handmade, with mixed filler, in Santiago, Dominican Republic.
Wrapper: Indonesia   Binder: Dom. Rep.   Filler: Dom. Rep.

Shape	Name	Lgth	Ring	Wrapper
Long Corona	Fumas	6	44	CM
Long Corona	Cazadores	6	44	CM
Long Corona	Especiales	6⅜	44	CM
Robusto	Robusto	5	50	CM

This is a medium-bodied blend which features a Sumatra wrapper and is available in value-priced bundles of 25.

HANDMADE CIGARS: BRAND LISTINGS

SANTIAGO DE CUBA
Handmade in Miami, Florida, USA.
Wrapper: Ecuador
Binder: Nicaragua   *Filler: Dominican Republic, Indonesia, Mexico, Nicaragua*

Shape	Name	Lgth	Ring	Wrapper
Churchill	Churchill	7	48	CC-Ma
Corona Extra	Corona	5½	46	CC-Ma
Toro	Double Corona	6	50	CC-Ma
Long Panatela	Lancero	7	38	CC-Ma
Robusto	Robusto	5	50	CC-Ma
Double Corona	Presidente	7½	50	CC-Ma
Torpedo	Torpedo	5¼	52	CC-Ma
Torpedo	Double Torpedo	6¼	52	CC-Ma

Master cigar maker Santiago Cabana has returned with this new brand, which debuted in 1997. It is medium-to-heavy in body and is available in boxes of 25.

SANTIAGO DEL SOL
Handmade in Santiago, Dominican Republic.
Wrapper: Indonesia   *Binder: Dom. Rep.*   *Filler: Dom. Rep.*

Shape	Name	Lgth	Ring	Wrapper
Slim Panatela	Panetela Fina	6	30	CM
Small Panatela	Panetela	5	34	CM
Panatela	Coronita	5½	38	CM
Petit Corona	Little Coronita	5	42	CM

This is a mild, flavored cigar offered in boxes of 25. Available flavors include Amaretto, chocolate and vanilla.

HANDMADE CIGARS: BRAND LISTINGS

SANTIAGO SILK
Handmade in Villa Gonzalez, Dominican Republic.
Wrapper: Ecuador   Binder: Dom. Rep.   Filler: Dom. Rep.

Shape	Name	Lgth	Ring	Wrapper
Robusto	Robusto	4½	50	CC
Lonsdale	Lonsdale	6½	44	CC
Toro	Toro	6	50	CC
Churchill	Churchill	7	48	CC
Giant	Presidente	8	50	CC
Torpedo	Torpedo	6½	52	CC

Here is a new cigar for 1997, with a medium-bodied flavor thanks to its Connecticut-seed wrapper. It is offered in individual cellophane sleeves inside all-cedar boxes of 25.

SAVINELLI EXTREMELY LIMITED RESERVE
Handmade in Santiago, Dominican Republic.
Wrapper: USA/Connecticut   Binder: Dom. Rep.   Filler: Dom. Rep.

Shape	Name	Lgth	Ring	Wrapper
Churchill	No. 1 Churchill	7¼	48	CC
Grand Corona	No. 2 Corona Extra	6⅝	46	CC
Long Corona	No. 3 Lonsdale	6¼	43	CC
Toro	No. 4 Double Corona	6	50	CC
Corona	No. 5 Extraordinaire	5½	44	CC
Robusto	No. 6 Robusto	5	49	CC

"Extremely limited" is the key phrase in the name of this brand. Long famous for their high-quality pipes, the Savinelli tradition of craftsmanship is continued in this limited-distribution line of medium-bodied cigars introduced in 1995.

HANDMADE CIGARS: BRAND LISTINGS

SAVOY
Handmade, with mixed filler, in Quayaquil, Ecuador.

Wrapper: Ecuador *Binder: Ecuador* *Filler: Ecuador, Nicaragua*

Shape	Name	Lgth	Ring	Wrapper
Robusto	Robusto	5	50	CM
Corona	Corona	5½	44	CM
Lonsdale	Cetro	6½	44	CM
Toro	Governor	6	50	CM
Double Corona	Churchill	7	50	CM

This brand debuted in 1998 and is the product of a commitment to quality at a reasonable price. It offers a medium-to-full-bodied taste with a Sumatra-seed wrapper and double binder. You can enjoy it in boxes of 25.

SCHMOKIN
Handmade in Tamboril, Dominican Republic.

Wrapper: Indonesia *Binder: Ecuador* *Filler: Dom. Rep.*

Shape	Name	Lgth	Ring	Wrapper
Torpedo	Torpedo	6¼	52	CM
Pyramid	Pyramid	6	52	CM
Double Corona	Churchill	7	50	CM
Robusto	Robusto	5½	50	CM
Lonsdale	Lonsdale	6½	44	CM
Corona	Petite Corona	5½	44	CM

Here is a Dominican-manufactured cigar that is finished in Kauai in the Hawaiian Islands. It was introduced in 1996 and offers a mild-to-medium-bodied taste in a well-made cigar. It is offered in boxes or bundles of 25.

SCORP
Handmade, with short filler, in Mexico City, Mexico.

Wrapper: Mexico *Binder: Mexico* *Filler: Mexico*

HANDMADE CIGARS: BRAND LISTINGS

Shape	Name	Lgth	Ring	Wrapper
Corona	No. 1	5¼	40	CM
Toro	No. 2	6¼	50	CM

Here is a five-flavor cigar: Guarapo (a traditional Cuban sugar-cane drink), Gold Label Vanilla, Chocolate, rum and Cappuccino, with a light-to-medium body introduced in 1997. The flavor is added through the curing process and the cigars are available in bundles of 25.

SCORPION
Handmade in Santiago, Dominican Republic.

Wrapper: Indonesia   Binder: Nicaragua   Filler: Dom. Rep., Nicaragua

Shape	Name	Lgth	Ring	Wrapper
Robusto	Robusto	5	50	CM

This cigar is packaged in wild, bold graphics, but it is mild in body. It debuted in 1998 and is offered in boxes of 20.

SELECCION ROYALE
BY HOYO DE MONTERREY
Handmade in Cofradia, Honduras.

Wrapper: Ecuador   Binder: Honduras   Filler: Honduras, Nicaragua

Shape	Name	Lgth	Ring	Wrapper
Pyramid	Duque	6⅛	54	CC
Perfecto	Aristocrat	6⅛	54	CC
Pyramid	Condesa	6½	50	CC
Pyramid	Marques	6¼	50	CC

Here are four sensational examples of the cigar maker's art. Introduced in late 1998, these are medium-to-full-bodied cigars which recall the glory days of cigar-making when special shapes were celebrated. Each shape is the handiwork of a single cigar maker, as much as joy to see and touch as to smoke. They are offered in boxes of 20.

HANDMADE CIGARS: BRAND LISTINGS

SELECTO PURO DOMINICANO
Handmade in Villa Gonzalez, Dominican Republic.

Wrapper: Indonesia *Binder: Dom. Rep.* *Filler: Dom. Rep.*

Shape	Name	Lgth	Ring	Wrapper
Giant	Selecto Double Corona	8	50	CM
Long Panatela	Selecto Gran Panatela	7¾	38	CM
Churchill	Selecto Gran Corona	6¾	46	CM
Toro	Selecto Toro	6	50	CM
Corona Extra	Selecto Corona	5½	46	CM
Robusto	Selecto Robusto	5½	52	CM
Churchill	Selecto Churchill	7	48	CM
Torpedo	Selecto Torpedo Gran Reserva	6½	52	CM

Introduced in 1997, this limited-distribution brand features four-year-aged tobaccos grown in the Valle de Yaque of the Dominican Republic, combined with a Sumatran-grown wrapper. It has a medium-to-full-bodied flavor and is offered in boxes of 25 except for the Selecto Double Corona, offered in boxes of ten.

SENOR ARMANDO REYES
Handmade in Granada, Nicaragua.

Wrapper: Indonesia *Binder: Dom. Rep.* *Filler: Dom. Rep.*

Shape	Name	Lgth	Ring	Wrapper
Churchill	Granada	7	48	CM-Ma
Pydamid	Coyotepe	7	48	CM-Ma
Double Corona	Xalteva	7	52	CM-Ma
Torpedo	Triangulo	5½	54	CM-Ma
Giant	Tiburon	8½	52	CM-Ma
Toro	Castillo	6	50	CM-Ma
Robusto	Las Nubes	4½	50	CM-Ma

HANDMADE CIGARS: BRAND LISTINGS

Corona	Xiloa	5½	42	CM-Ma

Here is a medium-bodied brand, introduced in 1996. It is offered in both natural and maduro wrapper shades, available in boxes of 25. The Xiloa shape is available with vanilla flavoring.

SEÑOR CORTO
Handmade, with mixed filler,
in Villa Gonzalez, Dominican Republic.

Wrapper: Indonesia   *Binder: Dom. Rep.*   *Filler: Dom. Rep.*

Shape	Name	Lgth	Ring	Wrapper
Toro	Toro	6	52	CM
Toro	Robusto	6	50	CM
Robusto	Belicoso	5	50	CM
Toro	Hermoso	6	48	CM
Grand Corona	Corona I	6	46	CM
Corona	Corona II	5¾	44	CM
Lonsdale	Lonsdale	6½	42	CM
Slim Panatela	Long Panatela	5¾	30	CM
Small Panatela	Panatela	4¾	30	CM

This medium-bodied cigar became available in 1998 with a Java wrapper. It is offered in individual cellophane sleeves in bundles of 25.

SEÑOR SAN ANDRES
Handmade in San Andres Tuxtula, Mexico.

Wrapper: Mexico   *Binder: Mexico*   *Filler: Mexico*

Shape	Name	Lgth	Ring	Wrapper
Giant	Grand Corona	8	46	CM
Perfecto	Perfecto	7	52	CM
Double Corona	Toro Extra	7½	50	CM

Toro	Churchill	6	48	CM
Lonsdale	Twisted Head	6¼	42	CM
Pyramid	Pyramid	6	48	CM
Torpedo	Torpedo	6	52	CM
Toro	Robusto Extra	6	52	CM
Lonsdale	Lonsdale	6½	42	CM
Slim Panatela	Short Panatela	5½	33	CM
Corona Extra	Corona	4⅞	46	CM
Robusto	Toro	4½	50	CM

Created in 1989 and introduced to the U.S. in 1995, this is a mild-to-medium-bodied brand featuring a Sumatra-seed wrapper. It is offered in cedar gift boxes of 25 as well as in boxes of 10, 5, 3 and 1 in specific shapes.

SEVILLA
Handmade in Tegucigalpa, Honduras.

Wrapper: Ecuador *Binder: Dom. Rep.* *Filler: Dom. Rep., Nicaragua*

Shape	Name	Lgth	Ring	Wrapper
Long Corona	Corona	6	44	CC
Robusto	Robusto	5	50	CC
Toro	Toro	6	50	CC
Churchill	Churchill	7	48	CC
Torpedo	Torpedo	7½	54	CC

Here is a mild brand, introduced in 1997 with a Connecticut-seed wrapper. It is offered in boxes of 25.

SHAMAN
Handmade in Esteli, Nicaragua.

Wrapper: Indonesia   *Binder: Nicaragua*   *Filler: Nicaragua*

HANDMADE CIGARS: BRAND LISTINGS

Shape	Name	Lgth	Ring	Wrapper
Churchill	Churchill	7	48	CM
Toro	Toro	6	50	CM
Lonsdale	Lonsdale	6½	44	CM
Robusto	Robusto	4½	50	CM

Introduced in 1998 and named for the historic helper of mankind with the spirits, Shaman is a full-bodied blend offered in four sizes with a Sumatra wrapper. It is offered in boxes of 25.

SHAMAN RED
Handmade in Esteli, Nicaragua.
Wrapper: Indonesia   Binder: Indonesia   Filler: Nicaragua

Shape	Name	Lgth	Ring	Wrapper
Churchill	Churchill	7	48	CM
Toro	Toro	6	50	CM
Lonsdale	Lonsdale	6½	44	CM
Robusto	Robusto	4½	50	CM

This is a medium-bodied blend introduced in 1998 and offered in boxes of 25.

SIGLO 21
Handmade in Santiago, Dominican Republic.
Wrapper: Ecuador   Binder: Dom. Rep.   Filler: Dom. Rep.

Shape	Name	Lgth	Ring	Wrapper
Robusto	No. 1	4½	50	CC-Ma
Lonsdale	No. 2	6½	44	CC-Ma
Toro	No. 3	6	50	CC-Ma
Churchill	No. 4	7	48	CC-Ma
Giant	No. 5	8	50	CC-Ma
Torpedo	No. 6	6¾	52	CC-Ma

THE **CIGARS**
BLENDED
FOR **AFTER**
DINNER.

Handmade by Swisher International, Inc.

*T*hese are not ordinary cigars. The leaf wrappers have been carefully selected for their pleasant aroma. The long filler for its mild taste and smooth draw. They are cigars made to enhance the finest meal. Santiago Silk, a rich, smooth smoke and Siglo 21, with its mild, delicate finish. Both are handmade in the Dominican Republic.

HANDMADE CIGARS: BRAND LISTINGS

Introduced in 1996 as a salute to the 21st century ("siglo" in Spanish). The cigars are medium-bodied, with excellent draw and a marvelous aroma. It is offered in elegant boxes of 25 cigars each.

SIGNATURE COLLECTION
Handmade in Santiago, Dominican Republic.
Wrapper: Ecuador, USA/Pennsylvania   *Binder: Nicaragua*
Filler: Dominican Republic, Honduras, Nicaragua

Shape	Name		Lgth	Ring	Wrapper
Short Panatela	Coronita	(tubed)	5	38	Co-Ma
Robusto	Robusto	(tubed)	5	50	Co-Ma
Lonsdale	Corona	(tubed)	6½	42	Co-Ma
Double Corona	Churchill	(tubed)	7¼	50	Co-Ma
Torpedo	Torpedo	(tubed)	6½	52	Co-Ma

Introduced in 1994, the Signature Collection by Santiago Cabana cigars are now made in the Dominican Republic. These glass-encased cigars feature an Ecuadorian-grown wrapper in the natural shade and a Pennsylvania wrapper for the maduro wrapped line. The result is a full-bodied cigar with a slow and even burn and a complex bouquet of taste and aroma.

SIGNET
Handmade in La Romana, Dominican Republic.
Wrapper: USA/Connecticut   *Binder: Dom. Rep.*   *Filler: Dom. Rep.*

Shape	Name	Lgth	Ring	Wrapper
Robusto	Bedford	4¾	50	CC
Long Corona	Berkeley	6	42	CC
Churchill	Buckingham	7	48	CC

This brand was introduced in 1996 and is offered only in limited distribution. The brand has a mild, rich taste and is presented in cedar boxes of 25.

HANDMADE CIGARS: BRAND LISTINGS

SILLEM'S
Handmade in Santiago, Dominican Republic.

Wrapper: Ecuador *Binder: Dom. Rep.* *Filler: Dom. Rep.*

Shape	Name	Lgth	Ring	Wrapper
Corona	Las Terrenas	5½	42	CC
Robusto	Levantado	5	50	CC
Toro	Bayahibe	6	50	CC
Double Corona	Samana	7½	50	CC

This brand has been produced intermittently and returns for 1998. It is medium in body and is available in all-cedar boxes of 25.

SINATRA
Handmade in Tamboril, Dominican Republic.

Wrapper: USA/Connecticut *Binder: Dom. Rep.* *Filler: Dom. Rep.*

Shape	Name	Lgth	Ring	Wrapper
Double Corona	Churchill	7	50	CC
Torpedo	Belicoso	6	54	CC
Robusto	Robusto	5	50	CC

Introduced in 1997, this brand is a salute to "Ol' Blue Eyes" who passed away in 1998. Mild in body, this brand is available only in limited distribution and is manufactured under the supervision of Felipe Gregorio. It is offered is elegant boxes of 25.

SMOK-A-CUBA
Handmade in Santiago, Dominican Republic
and Tampa, Florida, USA.

Wrapper: Indonesia *Binder: Dom. Rep.* *Filler: Dom. Rep., Honduras, Mexico*

Shape	Name	Lgth	Ring	Wrapper
	Made in the Dominican Republic:			
Robusto	Rothschilds Ybor	4½	52	CC

HANDMADE CIGARS: BRAND LISTINGS

Double Corona	Corona Gorda	6¾	50	Ma
Double Corona	Don Gaetano	7¼	50	Ma
Toro	Los Toros	6	50	Ma
Churchill	Larabie Court	6¾	46	CC
Corona	Recuerdos de Cuba	5¼	42	CC
Toro	Robusto Grande	6	50	CC
Small Panatela	Los Ninos	4⅛	30	CC
Robusto	1725 East 7th /short filler/	5½	50	CC
	Made in Tampa:			
Panatela	Panatela Fina	6½	38	CC-Ma
Grand Corona	Palma Reserve	6½	46	CC-Ma
Double Corona	Centenario 2086	7¼	50	CC
Churchill	Fumas Grande /mixed filler/	7	46	CC

This new brand for 1997 features a medium-bodied taste, whether made in the Dominican Republic or the USA! The Dominican-made shapes are offered in boxes of 25, while the Tampa-made shapes come in bundles of 25.

SMOKIN' TIGER
Handmade in Woriur, India.

Wrapper: India   *Binder: India*   *Filler: India*

Shape	Name	Lgth	Ring	Wrapper
Grand Corona	Black Tiger	6	46	DC
Cigarillo	Clove Tiger	4¼	28	DC
Cigarillo	Cardamom Tiger	4¼	28	DC
Cigarillo	Senorita	4¼	28	DC

Here is a brand with all-Indian tobacco, available in the U.S. for the first time in 1998. It has a mild body and the cigarillo shape is offered in flavors of Cardamom, Clove and Pineapple. Smokin' Tiger is presented in boxes of 50 except for the Grand Corona shape.

HANDMADE CIGARS: BRAND LISTINGS

SOBERANO
Handmade in Santiago, Dominican Republic.

Wrapper: Indonesia, USA/Connecticut   Binder: Dom. Rep.   Filler: Dom. Rep.

Shape	Name	Lgth	Ring	Wrapper
Double Corona	Churchill	7	50	CC-CM
Toro	Toro	6	50	CC-CM
Robusto	Robusto	5	50	CC-CM
Lonsdale	Lonsdale	6½	44	CC-CM
Corona	Corona	5½	42	CC-CM

This is a mild-to-medium-bodied smoke, offered in box of 25. You can take your choice of either a Connecticut or Sumatra wrapper.

SOCORRO
Handmade in Santiago, Dominican Republic.

Wrapper: Indonesia   Binder: Dom. Rep.   Filler: Dom. Rep.

Shape	Name	Lgth	Ring	Wrapper
Double Corona	Presidente	7¾	50	CM
Double Corona	Churchill	6¾	50	CM
Toro	Toro	6	50	CM
Robusto	Robusto	5	50	CM

New for 1997, this brand combines a Sumatra wrapper with Cuban-seed binder and filler leaves for a medium-bodied taste. It's available in boxes of 10 or 20.

SOLEARES
Handmade in San Jose, Costa Rica.

Wrapper: Indonesia   Binder: Indonesia
Filler: Costa Rica, Mexico, Nicaragua, Panama

Shape	Name	Lgth	Ring	Wrapper
Giant	Imperial	8	52	CM

HANDMADE CIGARS: BRAND LISTINGS

Lonsdale	Lonsdale	7	44	CM
Corona	Corona	5¾	42	CM
Robusto	Robusto	5	50	CM
Petit Corona	Petite Corona	4½	40	CM
Toro	Churchill	6½	48	CM

Introduced at *LE CIGAR NOIR-CHICAGO* in December 1996, this is a well-balanced cigar with a strong finish. It offers a medium-bodied flavor in Cuban-style boxes of 24, slide-top boxes of 10 or five and in bundles of 25.

SOLEARES LIMITED RESERVE
Handmade in San Jose, Costa Rica.

Wrapper: USA/Connecticut   *Binder: Nicaragua*
Filler: Dominican Republic, Mexico, Nicaragua

Shape	Name	Lgth	Ring	Wrapper
Giant	Imperial	8	52	CM
Robusto	Robusto	5	52	CM
Toro	Corona Extra	6	52	CM
Churchill	Churchill	7	48	CM

This special reserve line (introduced in 1997) offers a complex, medium-bodied taste. It is offered available in bundles of 25, boxes of 20 and in cedar hinged boxes of five or 10.

SOLEARES SPECIAL RESERVE
Handmade in San Jose, Costa Rica.

Wrapper: Indonesia   *Binder: Indonesia*   *Filler: Mexico, Nicaragua*

Shape	Name	Lgth	Ring	Wrapper
Giant	Imperial	8	52	CM
Churchill	Double Corona	7¼	46	CM
Robusto	Robusto	5	52	CM
Lonsdale	Gran Corona	6½	44	CM

Churchill	Churchill	7	48	CM

The Special Reserve debuted in 1997 and offers a medium-bodied flavor with a smooth finish thanks to its three-nation blend. It is offered in Cuban-style boxes of 24, bundles of 25 and in smaller boxes of five or 10.

SOLEMNE
Handmade in Quayaquil, Ecuador.

Wrapper: Ecuador   Binder: Indonesia   Filler: Indonesia

Shape	Name	Lgth	Ring	Wrapper
Double Corona	Churchill	7½	50	CM
Robusto	Robusto	4½	50	CM
Lonsdale	Lonsdale	6½	44	CM
Corona Extra	Toro	5	46	CM
Petit Corona	Corona	5	42	CM

This brand debuted in 1997, and offers a mild-bodied taste. It is presented in your choice of boxes of bundle of 25.

SOLO AROMA
Handmade in Santiago, Dominican Republic.

Wrapper: Ecuador   Binder: Dom. Rep.   Filler: Dom. Rep.

Shape	Name	Lgth	Ring	Wrapper
Robusto	Robusto	5	50	CC
Lonsdale	No. 1	6½	44	CC
Toro	Toro	6	50	CC
Churchill	Churchill	7	48	CC
Double Corona	Presidente	7½	50	CC
Giant	Monarch	8	52	CC

Cigar Legends: Juan Sosa

There are people who are born to be athletes, singers, lawyers and teachers. Juan Sosa was born to be in cigars.

Born in the rich fields of the Remedios region of Cuba, Sosa's family farmed tobacco and made their own brand of cigars, A. Vellaneda, in the 1940s. By 1957, there was even a Sosa brand, grown and made in Sancti Spiritus.

All of this changed with the Revolution in 1959 and in 1962, Sosa came to the United States. He parked cars, made deliveries and earned enough to get back into tobacco. Finally, in 1964, he opened a small cigar factory at 471 S.W. 8th Street in Little Havana. Ten years of hard work saw Sosa close his Miami factory and take his mild-bodied Fonseca and Sosa brands to Santiago in the Dominican Republic, producing for export to the U.S.

The cigar boom brought great changes, with Sosa re-opening a Miami plant in 1994 to make Macabi and later Imperio Cubano. In 1995, he joined forces with the Fuente family to make Sosa in their Santiago-based complex and later Macabi and the Sosa Family Selection as well as overseeing the production of Bauza and Montesino.

"I am enjoying life like never before," says Sosa, who has his sons Juan Jr. and Arbi working with him. "We must develop a taste for where the market is, and we are going to cigars with more and more flavor. We are a small business, but we are growing."

The devotion to quality that has made Sosa and his brands a success continues to grow. The natural sweetness found in many of his brands is emblematic of the satisfaction this natural-born tobacco man has found in producing some of the world's finest cigars.

HANDMADE CIGARS: BRAND LISTINGS

This brand was re-introduced in 1998 and offers a mild-to-medium-body. It is offered in bundles of 25. A Connecticut-grown, maduro-wrapped will likely be offered in 1999.

SOSA
Handmade in Santiago, Dominican Republic.
Wrapper: Ecuador, USA/Connecticut

Binder: Dominican Republic   *Filler: Dominican Republic*

Shape	Name	Lgth	Ring	Wrapper
Churchill	Churchill	7	49	CC-Ma
Robusto	Wavell	4¾	50	CC-Ma
Lonsdale	Lonsdale	6½	43	CC-Ma
Corona	Brevas	5½	43	CC-Ma
Pyramid	Piramides	6½	54	CC-Ma
Panatela	Santa Fe	6	35	CC-Ma
Double Corona	Magnums	7½	52	CC-Ma
Toro	Governor	6	50	CC-Ma
Petit Corona	Petit Cetro	4¼	40	CC-Ma

Juan Sosa is well known in the cigar trade for excellent products which are modestly priced. Originally made in Miami in 1964 and then in the Dominican Republic since 1974, this line bears his name and does it proud with a medium bodied-smoke and a choice of an Ecuadorian-grown Sumatra-seed wrapper or, for those who prefer maduro, a well-aged Connecticut Broadleaf. Sosa cigars are cellophaned and presented in slide-top cedar boxes.

SOSA FAMILY SELECTION
Handmade in Santiago, Dominican Republic.
Wrapper: USA/Connecticut   *Binder: Dom. Rep.*   *Filler: Dom. Rep.*

Shape	Name	Lgth	Ring	Wrapper
Lonsdale	No. 1	6¾	43	Co
Toro	No. 2	6¼	54	Co
Corona	No. 3	5¾	44	Co

Petit Corona	No. 4	5	40	Co
Robusto	No. 5	5	50	Co
Panatela	No. 6	6¼	38	Co
Toro	No. 7	6	50	Co
Double Corona	No. 8	6¾	49	Co
Double Corona	No. 9	7¾	52	Co

The Sosa family tradition of fine cigars is carried on in this line, first introduced in 1995. Medium-to-full-bodied in flavor, all of these cigars are round – not pressed – and are presented in elegant cabinet-selection boxes.

SOUTH BEACH
Handmade in Miami, Florida, USA.
Wrapper: Indonesia or USA/Connecticut
Binder: Dominican Republic   *Filler: Dominican Republic, Mexico*

Shape	Name	Lgth	Ring	Wrapper
Cigarillo	Finos	5	28	CC-CM
Torpedo	Torpedo	6½	54	CC-CM
Robusto	Robusto	5	50	CC-CM
Long Panatela	Lancero	7½	38	CC-CM
Long Corona	Panatela	6	42	CC-CM
Double Corona	Churchill	7	50	CC-CM
Double Corona	Presidente	7½	52	CC-CM

This is a mild-bodied brand which salutes Miami's famous South Beach district. It is available in value-priced bundles of 25.

SPANISH HONDURAN RED LABEL
Handmade in Cofradia, Honduras.
Wrapper: Honduras   *Binder: Honduras*   *Filler: Honduras*

HANDMADE CIGARS: BRAND LISTINGS

Shape	Name	Lgth	Ring	Wrapper
Grand Corona	No. 62	5⅝	47	Ma
Toro	No. 49	6	49	CM
Toro	Churchill Round	6	49	CM-Ma
Double Corona	C.L.	7⅜	52	CM
Giant	Emperadore	8½	52	CM-Ma
Double Corona	Magnifico	7¼	54	Cl-CM-Ma
Churchill	Presidente	7½	46	CM
Robusto	Robusto	5¼	50	CM
Long Corona	Super Cetro	6¼	44	CM-Ma

These bundle-packed cigars are medium in body and easy to recognize thanks to the bright red label.

SPEAKEASY
Handmade in Santiago, Dominican Republic and Miami, Florida, USA.

SPEAKEASY CLASSICS:
Wrapper: USA/Connecticut   Binder: Dom. Rep.   Filler: Dom. Rep.

SPEAKEASY GODFATHERS:
Wrapper: Indonesia   Binder: Nicaragua
Filler: Dominican Republic, Ecuador, Honduras

SPEAKEASY UNTOUCHABLES:
Wrapper: Indonesia   Binder: Dom. Rep.   Filler: Dom. Rep.

SPEAKEASY GANGSTERS:
Wrapper: Ecuador   Binder: Nicaragua
Filler: Dominican Republic, Ecuador, Honduras.

Shape	Name	Lgth	Ring	Wrapper
	Speakeasy Classics:			

HANDMADE CIGARS: BRAND LISTINGS

Robusto	Foxes	4¾	50	CC
Robusto	Bugs	5	50	CC
Corona	Legs	5½	42	CC
Torpedo	Untouchables	6½	54	CC
Lonsdale	Bugsys	6¾	44	CC
Double Corona	Machine Guns	7½	50	CC
Giant	Big Bills	8½	52	CC
	Speakeasy Godfathers:			
Churchill	Da Bosses	7	47	CM
Torpedo	Scarfaces	7¼	54	CM
Double Corona	Snorkys	7½	50	CM
Giant	Big Als	8	52	CM
	Speakeasy Untouchables:			
Robusto	Bugs	5	50	CM
Long Corona	Luckys	6	44	CM
Torpedo	Untouchables	6½	54	CM
Double Corona	Machine Guns	7½	50	CM
Giant	Big Bills	8½	52	CM
	Speakeasy Gangsters:			
Robusto	Bugs	5	50	CC
Long Corona	Luckys	6	44	CC
Torpedo	Untouchables	6½	54	CC
Double Corona	Enforcers	7	50	CC

These cigars remember the bad old days of the gangster in Chicago and New York with a series of shapes named for some of the most notorious hoodlums in American history. The Godfathers and Gangsters series are made in Miami and offer a medium-to-full-bodied taste, while the Untouchables and Classics lines

HANDMADE CIGARS: BRAND LISTINGS

are made in the Dominican Republic and provide a medium-bodied flavor. New
for 1997, this line of well-made cigars is presented in individual cellophane
sleeves and packed in boxes of 25.

SPIRIT OF CUBA
Handmade in Danli, Honduras.
Wrapper: Indonesia
Binder: USA/Pennsylvania   Filler: Colombia, Dominican Republic, Nicaragua

Shape	Name	Lgth	Ring	Wrapper
Robusto	Robusto	5	50	CM
Long Corona	Corona	6¼	44	CM
Toro	Double Corona	6	50	CM
Double Corona	Churchill	7	49	CM
Pyramid	Pyramid	6	54	CM

This is a medium-bodied cigar with a Sumatra wrapper, introduced in 1996. It is
offered in boxes of 25.

SPIRIT VALLEY
Handmade in the Jalapa Valley, Nicaragua.
Wrapper: Nicaragua   Binder: Nicaragua   Filler: Nicaragua

Shape	Name	Lgth	Ring	Wrapper
Long Corona	Corona Grande	6	44	CM-Ma
Toro	Toro	6	50	CM-Ma
Giant Corona	Lonsdale	7½	43	CM-Ma
Robusto	Robusto	5	52	CM-Ma
Churchill	Churchill	6⅞	48	CM-Ma

Here is a full-bodied cigar introduced in 1997. All of the leaves are grown in
Nicaragua and you can find this brand with a choice of wrapper shades in boxes
of 25.

HANDMADE CIGARS: BRAND LISTINGS

SPORTSMAN'S RESERVE
Handmade, with medium filler, in Esteli, Nicaragua.

Wrapper: Ecuador   *Binder: Nicaragua*
Filler: Cameroon, Dominican Republic, Honduras, Nicaragua

Shape	Name	Lgth	Ring	Wrapper
Torpedo	The Race	5	54	CC
Torpedo	The Hunt	6	54	CC
Torpedo	The Catch	7	54	CC
Robusto	Crew	5	50	CC

New for 1998, this medium-filler cigar is also medium in body. It is available in bundles of 20.

STEFANO
Handmade in Esteli, Nicaragua.

Wrapper: Ecuador or Indonesia   *Binder: Nicaragua*   *Filler: Nicaragua*

Shape	Name	Lgth	Ring	Wrapper
Pyramid	Pyramid	6½	54	CC-CM
Churchill	Double Corona	7	46	CC-CM
Lonsdale	Lonsdale	6½	44	CC-CM
Robusto	Robusto	5	50	CC-CM
Toro	Corona	6	50	CC-CM
Corona	Senorita	5½	43	CC-CM
	Made with short filler:			
	Picador	Varies		CC-CM

Introduced in 1997, this is a mild-to-medium-bodied cigar. It is presented in individual cellophane sleeves in bundles of 25.

STRELSKY
Handmade in Tamboril, Dominican Republic.

Wrapper: Ecuador, Indonesia   *Binder: Dom. Rep.*   *Filler: Dom. Rep.*

HANDMADE CIGARS: BRAND LISTINGS

Shape	Name	Lgth	Ring	Wrapper
Robusto	Robusto	5	50	CC
Toro	Sophia	6½	50	CC
Double Corona	Ivan	7	50	CC
Double Corona	Czar	7½	50	CC
Grand Corona	Gran Corona	6½	46	CC
Grand Corona	Corona	6	46	CC

Introduced in 1997, this is a mild-bodied brand with a choice of an Ecuadorian or Sumatran wrapper. You can find it mostly on the East Coast in boxes of 25.

STURGIS
Handmade in the Dominican Republic.

Wrapper: Indonesia   Binder: Dom. Rep.   Filler: Dom. Rep.

Shape	Name	Lgth	Ring	Wrapper
Panatela	Bad Boy	6	36	CM
Corona	Fat Boy	5½	42	CM
Lonsdale	Palma	6½	42	CM
Lonsdale	Churchill	6⅞	45	CM
Robusto	Toro	5½	50	CM
Double Corona	Presidente	7½	50	CM

This is a mild-bodied cigar which debuted in 1997. It is offered in boxes of 20 or in bundles of 50.

SUAREZ GRAN RESERVE
Handmade in Santiago, Dominican Republic.
Wrapper: Indonesia or USA/Connecticut

Binder: Dominican Republic   Filler: Dominican Republic

Shape	Name	Lgth	Ring	Wrapper
Robusto	Robusto	5	50	CC-CM

HANDMADE CIGARS: BRAND LISTINGS

Double Corona	Presidente	7½	52	CC-CM
Grand Corona	Royal Corona	6½	46	CC-CM
Long Panatela	Lonsdale	7	36	CC-CM
Torpedo	Torpedo Royale	7	50	CC-CM
Pyramid	Especial No. 1	7	50	CC-CM

Take your choice between the mild-bodied Connecticut wrapper and the medium-bodied Sumatra wrapper in this carefully-produced brand. It is offered in boxes of 25, except for the Torpedo Royale (available in 12s) and the Especial No. 1 (available in 20s).

SUAVE
Handmade in Villa Gonzalez, Dominican Republic.
Wrapper: USA/Connecticut   *Binder: Dom. Rep.*   *Filler: Dom. Rep.*

Shape	Name		Lgth	Ring	Wrapper
Long Corona	Corona	*(tube available)*	6	44	CC
Robusto	Robusto	*(tube available)*	5	50	CC
Double Corona	Churchill	*(tube available)*	7½	50	CC

Introduced in 1996, this brand offers excellent construction and medium body from a blend of a Connecticut wrapper with two-year-old tobaccos from the Cibao Valley, the heart of the Dominican tobacco-growing zone. Suave cigars are presented in individual glass tubes, in boxes of 10, in all-cedar boxes of 25, or in bundles of 25 in individual cellophane sleeves.

SUERDIECK
Made in Cruz des Almas, Brazil.
Wrapper: Brazil   *Binder: Brazil*   *Filler: Brazil*

Shape	Name	Lgth	Ring	Wrapper
	Handmade cigars, made in Brazil:			
Slim Panatela	Brasilia	5½	30	CM
Slim Panatela	Caballeros	6	30	CM

HANDMADE CIGARS: BRAND LISTINGS

Grand Corona	Finos	5¾	46	CM
Petit Corona	Mandarim Pai	5	42	CM
Cigarillo	Nina	6	22	CM
Slim Panatela	Nips	6	32	CM
Slim Panatela	Valencia	6	30	CC
Petit Corona	Viajantes	5	40	CM
	Premium series, handmade in Brazil:			
Corona Extra	Corona Brasil Luxo	5½	45	CM
Corona Extra	Corona Imperial Luxo	5½	45	CC
Corona	Mata Fina Especial	5¼	42	CM
Short Panatela	Panatella Fina	5⅜	36	CM
	Cigarillos, handmade in Brazil of 100% tobacco:			
Cigarillo	Beira Mar Finos	5¼	28	CM
Cigarillo	Copacabana	5	29	CC
	Cigarillos, machine-made in Brazil:			
Cigarillo	Palomitas	3½	32	CM
Cigarillo	Palomitas Classics	3½	32	CM
Cigarillo	Palomitas Cherry	3½	32	CM
Cigarillo	Palomitas Clove	3½	32	CM
Cigarillo	Reynitas	3⅛	22	CC-CM

This well-known brand offers a medium-bodied taste of Brazilian tobacco in both handmade and machine-made shapes, famous since 1892. All use home-grown leaf, although the Corona Imperial, Palomitas, Panatela, Copacabana, Reynitas and Valencia shapes use Sumatran-seed tobaccos grown in Brazil.

SUPER VALUE
Handmade in Bahia, Brazil,
Danli, Honduras and La Romana, Dominican Republic,

HANDMADE CIGARS: BRAND LISTINGS

BRAZIL:

Wrapper: Indonesia *Binder: Brazil* *Filler: Brazil*

DOMINICAN REPUBLIC:

Wrapper: Indonesia *Binder: USA/Pennsylvania* *Filler: Dom. Rep., Indonesia*

HONDURAS:

Wrapper: Indonesia, Mexico *USA/Pennsylvania* *Filler: Mexico*

Shape	Name	Lgth	Ring	Wrapper
	Made in Brazil:			
Lonsdale	Elegante	6½	40	CM
Lonsdale	Escepcionales	7	44	CM
Churchill	Emperadores	7¼	48	CM
Double Corona	Toro	7½	51	CM
	Made in the Dominican Republic:			
Panatela	Panetela	6	36	CM
Long Corona	Lonsdale	6	42	CM
Long Corona	Palma	6⅛	43	CM
Lonsdale	Churchill	6⅝	44	CM
Corona Grande	Corona Grande	6½	46	Ma
	Made in Honduras:			
Lonsdale	Churchill	6⅝	44	Ma
Churchill	Imperial	7	48	CM
Giant	Master	8	52	Ma

This brand is just as it claims: a super value! Take your choice of lines made in Brazil (mild body), the Dominican Republic (Java wrappers for a mild body) or Honduras, with a Java (natural) or Mexican (maduro) wrapper for a mild-to-medium body. You can try it in six-packs.

HANDMADE CIGARS: BRAND LISTINGS

SWEET LADY
Handmade in Santiago, Dominican Republic.
Wrapper: Indonesia or USA/Connecticut

Binder: Dominican Republic   *Filler: Dominican Republic*

Shape	Name	Lgth	Ring	Wrapper
Small Panatela	Petit Panetela	5	30	CC-CM
Cigarillo	Cigarillo	4½	24	CC

This is a mild, flavored cigar introduced in 1998. It is offered in boxes of 25 in a vanilla-flavored version only.

SWEET MILLIONAIRE
Handmade in Santiago, Dominican Republic.
Wrapper: Indonesia   *Binder: Dom. Rep.*   *Filler: Dom. Rep.*

Shape	Name	Lgth	Ring	Wrapper
Small Panatela	Finos Petit	5	30	CM
Panatela	Panetela	6	38	CM
Slim Panatela	Finos Extra	7	30	CM
Robusto	Robusto	5	50	CM
Corona	Corona	5½	42	CM
Double Corona	Churchill	7	50	CM
Long Panatela	Lancero	7	38	CM
Torpedo	Shakespeare	6	44	CM
Long Corona	Hemingway	6	44	CM

This is a flavored cigar, smooth and mild in body. You can find it in boxes of 25 in flavors including Anisette, cognac, mint, pineapple, raspberry, sweet and vanilla.

SWEET SENSATION
Handmade in Tamboril, Dominican Republic.
Wrapper: Indonesia   *Binder: Dom. Rep.*   *Filler: Dom. Rep.*

HANDMADE CIGARS: BRAND LISTINGS

Shape	Name	Lgth	Ring	Wrapper
Short Panatela	Cafe Latte	5	36	CM
Short Panatela	Strawberry Fields	5	36	CM
Short Panatela	Amaretto Nights	5	36	CM
Short Panatela	Vanilla Days	5	36	CM
Short Panatela	Peach Passion	5	36	CM

This flavored brand was introduced in 1998. It offers a mild-to-medium flavor in five-packs and in slide-top boxes of 18 cigars each.

TABACALERA
Handmade in Manila, the Philippines.

Wrapper: Indonesia   *Binder: Philippines*   *Filler: Philippines*

Shape	Name	Lgth	Ring	Wrapper
Long Panatela	Banderilla	7½	35	CM
Corona	Corona	5½	44	CM
Perfecto	Conde de Guell Sr.	7	44	CM
Lonsdale	Corona Largas	7	44	CM
Giant	Corona Largas Especiales	8	47	CM
Pyramid	Cortado	5½	43	CM
Giant	Double Coronas	8½	50	CM
Short Panatela	Half Corona	4	37	CM
Small Panatela	Panatelas	4½	32	CM
Robusto	Robusto	5	50	CM
Torpedo	Pyramid	6	52	CM

The famous history of cigar production in the Philippines is continued with the mild-to-medium-bodied Tabacalera line, which dates to 1881. Using Southeast Asian tobaccos from the Indonesian island of Java for the wrapper, most of the filler and the binder is home-grown from the province of Isabela, on the island of Luzon, also home to the Philippine capital of Manila.

HANDMADE CIGARS: BRAND LISTINGS

TABACON VINTAGE SELECTION
Handmade in Santa Rosa de Copan, Honduras.

Wrapper: Indonesia   Binder: Honduras   Filler: Honduras

Shape	Name	Lgth	Ring	Wrapper
Long Corona	Corona	6¼	44	CC
Robusto	Robusto	5½	50	CC
Torpedo	Belicoso	6	52	CC
Churchill	Churchill	7	48	CC
Double Corona	Double Corona	7¾	50	CC

This is a 1997-introduced cigar with a Sumatra wrapper and a full-bodied flavor. It is offered in boxes of 25.

TABACOS GEORGE
Handmade in Danli, Honduras.

Wrapper: Honduras   Binder: Honduras   Filler: Honduras, Nicaragua

Shape	Name	Lgth	Ring	Wrapper
Double Corona	Churchill	7	50	CM
Toro	Corona	6	50	CM
Long Corona	Double Corona	6¼	44	CM
Lonsdale	No. 1	7	44	CM
Small Panatela	Petit	4½	30	CM
Corona	Petit Cetro	5½	44	CM
Robusto	Robusto	5	50	CM

Introduced in 1996, this is a very well made, medium-to-full-bodied brand, offered in elegant, all-cedar boxes of 25.

TABACOS GRAN COLOMBIA
Handmade in Esteli, Nicaragua and Cumana, Venezuela.

HANDMADE CIGARS: BRAND LISTINGS

NICARAGUAN SELECTION:
Wrapper: Nicaragua   *Binder: Nicaragua*   *Filler: Nicaragua*

VENEZUELAN SELECTION:
Wrapper: Ecuador   *Binder: Venezuela*   *Filler: Venezuela*

Shape	Name	Lgth	Ring	Wrapper
	Nicaraguan Selection:			
Giant	Libertador	8½	52	CM
Double Corona	Angostura	7	52	CM
Robusto	Carabobo	4½	52	CM
Long Corona	Maria Teresa	6	44	CM
	Venezuelan Selection:			
Long Corona	Rubia's	6	40	CC
Long Corona	Duquesa's	6	42	CC
Robusto	Robusto	5	50	CC
Double Corona	Churchill	7	50	CC

There are two blends to choose from: the medium-to-full-bodied Nicaraguan selection and the medium-bodied Venezuelan line with an Ecuadorian wrapper. All of the shapes honor Simon Bolivar, the liberator of much of South America, and are offered in boxes of 25, except for the Libertador and Angostura, offered in 20s.

TABACOS SAN JOSE
Handmade in Esteli, Nicaragua.
Wrapper: Ecuador or USA/Connecticut   *Binder: Dominican Republic*
Filler: Brazil, Dominican Republic, Honduras, Nicaragua

Shape	Name	Lgth	Ring	Wrapper
Corona	Corona	5½	44	Co-CC-Ma
Lonsdale	Lonsdale	6½	42	Co-CC-Ma
Robusto	Robusto	4⅞	50	Co-CC-Ma
Toro	Epicure	6	50	Co-CC-Ma

HANDMADE CIGARS: BRAND LISTINGS

Churchill	Churchill	7	47	Co-CC-Ma
Double Corona	Double Corona	7⅝	50	Co-CC-Ma
Giant	Presidente	8	52	Co-CC-Ma
Torpedo	Torpedo	6½	54	Co-CC-Ma
Torpedo	Gran Torpedo	7½	60	Co-CC-Ma

This brand debuted in 1996, offered in three shades of wrapper: Natural and Rosado, both using an Ecuadorian-grown wrapper, and a maduro shade, utilizing Connecticut leaf. The result is a mild-to-medium bodied taste, offered in all-cedar boxes of 25 (except for the Gran Torpedo, offered in 10s).

TABU
Handmade in Granada, Nicaragua.

CLASSIC SELECTION:
Wrapper: Ecuador   *Binder: Dom. Rep.*   *Filler: Nicaragua*

EMERALD SELECTION:
Wrapper: Indonesia   *Binder: Mexico*   *Filler: Nicaragua*

MADURO SELECTION:
Wrapper: Nicaragua   *Binder: Nicaragua*   *Filler: Nicaragua*

STERLING SELECTION:
Wrapper: Nicaragua   *Binder: Nicaragua*   *Filler: Nicaragua*

Shape	Name	Lgth	Ring	Wrapper
	Classic Selection:			
Robusto	Robusto	5	50	CC
Corona	Corona	5½	43	CC
Toro	Toro	6	50	CC
Lonsdale	Longsdale	6½	43	CC
Double Corona	Churchill	7	50	CC
Torpedo	Torpedo	7	54	CC

Torpedo	Belicoso	5½	54	CC
Toro	Toro Xtra	6	60	CC
Double Corona	Giant	7	60	CC
	Emerald Selection:			
Robusto	Robusto	5	50	CM
Corona	Corona	5½	43	CM
Toro	Toro	6	50	CM
Toro	Toro Xtra	6	60	CM
Double Corona	Churchill	7	50	CM
Torpedo	Torpedo	7	54	CM
Double Corona	Giant	7	60	CM
	Maduro Selection:			
Robusto	Robusto	5	50	Ma
Double Corona	Churchill	7	50	Ma
Torpedo	Torpedo	7	54	Ma
Toro	Toro	6	50	Ma
Toro	Toro Xtra	6	60	Ma
Double Corona	Giant	7	60	Ma
	Sterling Selection:			
Robusto	Robusto	5	50	CC
Double Corona	Churchill	7	49	CC
Toro	Toro	6	50	CC

This brand was introduced in 1997 and offers four choices: the Classic, a medium-bodied blend; Emerald, with a mild body; Maduro, offering a medium body and Sterling, a mild-bodied, short-filler blend. Sampler boxes, as well as cedar boxes of four, up to 25, cigars are available.

HANDMADE CIGARS: BRAND LISTINGS

TAHINO
Handmade in Danli, Honduras.

Wrapper: Indonesia, USA/Connecticut   Binder: Nicaragua   Filler: Dom. Rep.

Shape	Name	Lgth	Ring	Wrapper
Corona	Corona	5½	42	CC-CM
Long Panatela	Lancero	7½	38	CC-CM
Robusto	Robusto	5	50	CC-CM
Toro	Toro	6	50	CC-CM
Churchill	Churchill	7	48	CC-CM
Double Corona	Soberano	7	50	CC-CM

Take a choice of wrappers: Connecticut or Sumatra for this mild-bodied brand, offered first in 1996 and presented in bundles or boxes of 25.

TAINO
BY PROFESOR SILA
Handmade in Santiago, Dominican Republic.

Wrapper: Indonesia   Binder: Dom. Rep.   Filler: Dom. Rep.

Shape	Name	Lgth	Ring	Wrapper
Torpedo	Torpedo	6½	53	Ma
Robusto	Robusto	5	50	Ma
Double Corona	Double Corona	7½	50	Ma

Introduced in 1997, this is a value-priced, all handmade, full-bodied cigar that is a welcome smoke anytime and on any day in yummy maduro wrappers. You'll find it presented in attractive flip-top wooden boxes of 25.

TAMAYO Y PARETO
Handmade in Santiago, Dominican Republic.

Wrapper: Ecuador   Binder: Dom. Rep.   Filler: Dom. Rep.

Shape	Name	Lgth	Ring	Wrapper
Double Corona	Churchill	7½	50	CC

Long Corona	Corona	6	44	CC
Toro	Robusto	6	50	CC
Robusto	Rothschild	4½	50	CC
Toro	Toro	6	52	CC

Introduced in 1997, this is a highly-respected new brand with a mild-to-medium taste in boxes of 25.

TAMBORIL

Handmade in Tamboril, Dominican Republic.

Wrapper: USA/Connecticut, Indonesia   Binder: Dom. Rep.   Filler: Dom. Rep.

Shape	Name		Lgth	Ring	Wrapper
	Connecticut Collection:				
Giant	Double Corona		8	50	CC
Churchill	Churchill		7	47	CC
Churchill	Diablo	*(perfecto tip)*	7	47	CC
Torpedo	Torpedo		6½	54	CC
Corona	Corona		6	44	CC
Robusto	Robusto		5	52	CC
Short Panatela	Cortadito		5	38	CC
	Sumatra Collection:				
Petit Corona	Coronita		4	44	CC
Long Corona	Corona		6	44	CC
Robusto	Robusto		5	52	CC
Churchill	Churchill		7	47	CC
Churchill	Diablo	*(perfecto tip)*	7	47	CC
Torpedo	Torpedo		6½	54	CC

Here is an exhaustingly produced cigar, introduced in 1996, which offers a choice of wrappers. With a Connecticut wrapper, it presents a mild-to-medium-

bodied taste; with a Sumatra wrapper, the taste is medium-to-full-bodied. These
are serious cigars made by serious smokers and presented in boxes of 25.

TAMBORIL CORDOVA COLLECTION
Handmade in Tamboril, Dominican Republic.

Wrapper: Indonesia   *Binder: Dom. Rep.*   *Filler: Dom. Rep.*

Shape	Name		Lgth	Ring	Wrapper
Corona	Corona		5½	44	CC
Panatela	Panatela		6	38	CC
Petit Corona	Short Diablo	(perfecto tip)	4	44	CC
Robusto	Robusto		5	50	CC
Toro	Toro		6	50	CC
Churchill	Churchill		7	47	CC
Long Corona	Pyramid		6	44	CC
Robusto	Robustubo	(tubed)	5½	52	CC

Here is a uniquely-finished cigar . . . with just a hint of cocoa! This is a medium-
bodied smoke, introduced in 1997 and packed in all-cedar boxes of 25.

TAMBORIL FORE
Handmade, with short filler, in Tamboril, Dominican Republic.

Wrapper: Indonesia   *Binder: Dom. Rep.*   *Filler: Dom. Rep.*

Shape	Name		Lgth	Ring	Wrapper
Robusto	Robusto Grande	(tubed)	5½	52	CC

Introduced in 1997, you'll find this Java-wrapped brand in a glass tube inside a
box of 30 cigars, each containing a medium-to-full-bodied, short-filler cigar.

TAMBORIL GOAL
Handmade, with short filler, in Tamboril, Dominican Republic.

Wrapper: USA/Connecticut   *Binder: Dom. Rep.*   *Filler: Dom. Rep.*

HANDMADE CIGARS: BRAND LISTINGS

Shape	Name		Lgth	Ring	Wrapper
Robusto	Robusto Grande	*(tubed)*	5½	52	CC

Introduced in 1997, you'll find this Connecticut-wrapped brand in a glass tube inside a box of 25 cigars with special soccer-themed packaging, each containing a medium-to-full-bodied, short-filler cigar.

TAMPA SWEETHEART
Handmade in Tampa, Florida, USA.

Wrapper: USA/Connecticut   Binder: Dom. Rep.   Filler: Dom. Rep.

Shape	Name	Lgth	Ring	Wrapper
Corona	No. 4	5½	43	CC
Corona	No. 24	5½	42	CC
Small Panatela	No. 32	4	30	CC
Corona Extra	No. 45	5¼	45	CC
Grand Corona	No. 46	6½	46	CC
Unknown!	No. 50	Varies!		CC
Double Corona	No. 54	7⅝	54	CC
Long Panatela	No. 75	7	36	CC
Grand Corona	No. 85	6	47	CC
Lonsdale	No. 100	7	44	CC
Lonsdale	No. 108	6¼	43	CC
Churchill	No. 150	7½	46	CC
Double Corona	No. 156	6⅞	49	CC
Lonsdale	No. 185	6½	43	CC
Lonsdale	No. 270	6¾	44	CC
Short Panatela	No. 380	5	38	CC
Double Corona	No. 490	6⅞	49	CC
Robusto	No. 500	4½	50	CC

Giant	No. 520	8½	52	CC

There are 19 shapes in this mild-bodied, bundled brand made in Tampa. It is available in value-priced bundles of 25 cigars each.

TAMPA TROPICS
Handmade in Tampa, Florida, USA.

Wrapper: Cameroon   *Binder: Dom. Rep.*   *Filler: Dom. Rep., Nicaragua*

Shape	Name	Lgth	Ring	Wrapper
Robusto	Rothschild	5	50	CM
Double Corona	Churchill	7	50	CM
Torpedo	Belicoso	6¼	52	CM

This newest innovation from the Cammarata Cigar Co. of Tampa offers a medium-bodied taste, in boxes of 25.

TATIANA
Handmade in Santiago, Dominican Republic.

Wrapper: Indonesia   *Binder: Dom. Rep.*   *Filler: Dom. Rep.*

Shape	Name	Lgth	Ring	Wrapper
Slim Panatela	Petite	6	30	CM
Slim Panatela	La Vita	5	34	CM
Long Corona	Classic	6	44	CM
Robusto	Bella	5	50	CM
Cigarillo	Miniatures	3½	26	CM

This is a long-filler, medium-bodied, flavored brand, available in either box or bundle of 25. It is offered in chocolate, cinnamon, mint, rum or vanilla.

TATOU
Handmade, with short filler, in Mexico City, Mexico.

Wrapper: Mexico   *Binder: Nicaragua*   *Filler: Dom. Rep., Mexico*

HANDMADE CIGARS: BRAND LISTINGS

Shape	Name	Lgth	Ring	Wrapper
Petit Corona	Amaretto	5	44	CM
Petit Corona	Cherry	5	44	CM
Petit Corona	Coconut	5	44	CM
Petit Corona	Rum	5	44	CM
Petit Corona	Vanilla	5	44	CM
Petit Corona	Mint	5	44	CM
Petit Corona	Cognac	5	44	CM
Petit Corona	Chocolate	5	44	CM
Petit Corona	Hazelnut	5	44	CM
Petit Corona	Coffee	5	44	CM

New for 1997, this is an all-flavored, all-handmade line of corona-sized cigars. Each has a mild taste, with the flavor elements being added after the rolling process has been completed. Tatou cigars are easy on the pocketbook and are presented in boxes of 25.

TE-AMO
Handmade in San Andres Tuxtla, Mexico.

Wrapper: Mexico   *Binder: Mexico*   *Filler: Mexico*

Shape	Name	Lgth	Ring	Wrapper
Lonsdale	No. 1 Relaxation	6⅝	44	CC-CM-Ma
Long Corona	No. 2 Meditation	6	42	CC-CM-Ma
Panatela	No. 3 Torero	6½	35	CC-CM-Ma
Petit Corona	No. 4	5	42	CC-CM-Ma
Cigarillo	No. 5 Picador	7	27	CC-CM-Ma
Giant	No. 6 CEO	8½	52	CM-Ma
Cigarillo	No. 10 Epicure	5	27	CM
Cigarillo	No. 11 Elegante	5¾	27	CC-CM-Ma

Double Corona	No. 14 Churchill	7½	50	CC-CM-Ma
Double Corona	No. 17 Presidente	7	50	CM-Ma
Robusto	No. 18 Torito	4¾	50	CM-Ma
Toro	No. 19 Toro	6	50	CC-CM-Ma
Long Panatela	No. 24 Caballero	7	35	CM
Double Corona	No. 28 Maximo	7	54	CM-Ma
Grand Corona	No. 29 Satisfaction	6	46	CM-Ma
Lonsdale	Celebration (tubed)	6⅝	44	CM
Robusto	Robusto	5½	54	CM-Ma
Torpedo	Figurado	6⅝	50	CM-Ma
Pyramid	Piramides	6¼	50	CM-Ma
Pyramid	Gran Piramides	7¼	54	CM-Ma
Perfecto	Double Perfecto	7	48	CM-Ma
	Made with short filler:			
Cigarillo	No. 26 Intermezzo	4	28	CC
Small Panatela	No. 27 Impulse	5	32	CC
Short Panatela	Pauser	5⅜	35	CC
Small Panatela	Purito	4⅞	30	CC

This very popular brand originated in the 1960s and is a product of the San Andres Valley, where all of the tobaccos for this brand are grown. Considered to be medium in strength, the enthusiast has a choice of natural or maduro wrappers, or can choose many of the shapes in the lighter-wrapped and lighter-bodied Te-Amo Lights.

TE-AMO SEGUNDO
Handmade in San Andres Tuxtla, Mexico.

Wrapper: Mexico   Binder: Mexico   Filler: Mexico

Shape	Name	Lgth	Ring	Wrapper
Panatela	No. 55 Torero	6½	35	CM-Ma

Long Corona	No. 60 Meditation	6	42	CM-Ma
Lonsdale	No. 75 Relaxation	6⅝	44	CM-Ma
Double Corona	No. 90 Presidente	7	50	CM-Ma
Double Corona	No. 110 Churchill	7½	50	CM-Ma
Grand Corona	No. 120 Satisfaction	6	46	CM-Ma
Toro	No. 135 Toro	6	50	CM-Ma

These are just what the name suggests: seconds of the regular Te-Amo line produced with the same San Andres Valley tobaccos. Offered in bundles of 20 cigars each, they are good cigars and an even better value.

TEMPLE HALL
Handmade in Kingston, Jamaica.

Wrapper: USA/Connecticut   *Binder: Mexico*   *Filler: Dom. Rep., Mexico*

Shape	Name	Lgth	Ring	Wrapper
Double Corona	No. 700	7	49	CC
Lonsdale	No. 675	6¾	45	CC
Robusto	No. 550	5½	49	CC
Long Corona	No. 625	6¼	42	CC
Small Panatela	No. 500	5	31	CC
Small Panatela	No. 450	4½	49	Ma
Torpedo	Belicoso	6	50	CC
Lonsdale	Trumps No. 1	6½	42	CC-Ma
Robusto	Trumps No. 2	5½	50	CC
Corona	Trumps No. 3	5½	42	CC-Ma
Double Corona	Trumps No. 4	7½	49	CC

A medium-strength cigar made in Jamaica since 1876, Temple Hall cigars are made and left in a natural, round shape – not pressed. It is an easy-drawing cigar which offers the connoisseur a choice of shapes, and in a few cases, the choice of a natural-shade or maduro-shade wrapper.

Churchills and Double Coronas

These larger shapes are much loved for the full flavor they can deliver. The dimensions of these shapes include:

- Churchill   6¾-7⅞ inches long; 46-48 ring.
- Double Corona   6¾-7¾ inches long; 49-54 ring.

Pictured opposite, from left to right, are:

- **GRAYCLIFF** *Presidente*   *(shape)*
  (Bahamas)   7 x 48   Churchill

- **REGALOS** *Churchill*
  (Honduras)   7 x 47   Churchill

- **PINAR 1958** *Churchill*
  (United States)   7 x 50   Double Corona

- **PUBLIC ENEMY** *No. 1*
  (United States)   7 x 54   Double Corona

- **PETRUS DOMINICANA** *Churchill*
  (Dominican Republic)   7 x 48   Churchill

- **EVIL CLOWN** *Churchill*
  (Dominican Republic) 7¼ x 48   Churchill

- **GRAND NICA** *Churchill*
  (Nicaragua)   7 x 52   Double Corona

HANDMADE CIGARS: BRAND LISTINGS

TEMPTATION
Handmade, with medium filler,
in Villa Gonzalez, Dominican Republic.

Wrapper: Indonesia   Binder: Dom. Rep.   Filler: Dom. Rep.

Shape	Name	Lgth	Ring	Wrapper
Short Panatela	Panatela	5	38	CM
Long Corona	Corona	6	42	CM
Churchill	Churchill	7	48	CM

Introduced in 1997, this is a medium-filler, mild-bodied, flavored cigar. Available in chocolate, mint and vanilla flavors, the tobacco is specially treated in the curing process and not sprayed as in some flavored brands. It is available in cabinets of 25 cigars, in bundles of 25 or in special gift boxes of six cigars each.

TENEGUIA
Handmade, with mixed filler,
in Las Palmas, the Canary Islands of Spain.

Wrapper: Indonesia   Binder: Indonesia   Filler: Dom. Rep., Spain

Shape	Name	Lgth	Ring	Wrapper
Corona	Nuncios	5½	42	CM

This brand was introduced in 1998, with a medium body thanks to its Sumatra wrapper and Java binder. It is offered in boxes of 25.

TENORIO
Handmade in Santiago, Dominican Republic.

Wrapper: Indonesia or USA/Connecticut   Binder: Dom. Rep.   Filler: Dom. Rep.

Shape	Name	Lgth	Ring	Wrapper
Long Corona	Corona	6	44	CC-CM
Robusto	Robusto	5	50	CC-CM
Double Corona	Churchill	7½	50	CC-CM
Panatela	Panatela	6	38	CC-CM

Small Panatela	Privilege	5	30	CC-CM

This line offers a choice of wrapper, both providing a mild-to-medium-bodied taste. The interior of these cigars is all Dominican, with both Cuban-seed and Olor leaves in the bunch. Introduced in 1997, Tenorio is available in 5x5-packed cabinets of 25.

TERCERA GENERACION
Handmade in Cibao, Dominican Republic.

Wrapper: Indonesia   Binder: Dom. Rep.   Filler: Dom. Rep.

Shape	Name	Lgth	Ring	Wrapper
Churchill	Churchill	7	48	CM
Robusto	Robusto	5	48	CM
Corona	Corona	5½	42	CM

This is a mild cigar offered in three sizes. Introduced in 1997, it is offered in boxes of three or 25, or in bundles of 25.

TESORO
Handmade in Santiago, Dominican Republic.

Wrapper: Indonesia   Binder: Dom. Rep.   Filler: Dom. Rep.

Shape	Name	Lgth	Ring	Wrapper
Giant	Conquistador	8½	52	CC-CM-Ma
Double Corona	The Don	7½	50	CC-CM-Ma
Grand Corona	Gorda	6½	46	CC-CM-Ma
Long Corona	Mimosa	6	42	CC-CM-Ma
Robusto	El Plumpo	5	50	CC-CM-Ma
Toro	The Polo	6	50	CC-CM-Ma
Torpedo	Torpedo Fino	6½	50	CC-CM-Ma
Perfecto	Baby Perfecto	4½	44	CC-CM-Ma

HANDMADE CIGARS: BRAND LISTINGS

Introduced in 1997, this is a medium-to-full-bodied cigar, offered in economical bundles of 25 cigars each.

TESOROS DE COPAN
Handmade in Santa Rosa de Copan, Honduras.

Wrapper: Honduras   *Binder: Honduras*   *Filler: Honduras*

Shape	Name	Lgth	Ring	Wrapper
Double Corona	Churchill	7	50	CC
Long Corona	Cetros	6¼	44	CC
Toro	Toros	6	50	CC
Corona Extra	Corona	5¼	46	CC
Robusto	Yumbo	4¾	50	CC

Created in 1993, Tesoros de Copan cigars are much more than simply a mild-to-medium-bodied cigar with Honduran-grown Connecticut-seed wrappers. Part of the proceeds from the sale of these cigars supports the efforts of the La Ruta Maya Foundation, which is dedicated to the conservation of the Central American rain forests and historic preservation of the remains of the Mayans, who originated the use of tobacco many centuries ago.

TEXANA
Handmade in Esteli, Nicaragua.

Wrapper: Nicaragua   *Binder: Nicaragua*   *Filler: Nicaragua*

Shape	Name	Lgth	Ring	Wrapper
Slim Panatela	Elena	5½	34	CM-Ma
Long Corona	La Bonita	6	44	CM-Ma
Toro	Yellow Rose	6	50	CM-Ma
Giant	El Grande	8	54	CM-Ma
Robusto	Sportsman	5½	52	CM-Ma
Double Corona	Player	7	54	CM-Ma

Here is a brand which salutes the work of Robert Wooding Chappell, who grew tobacco in Texas in the middle of the 19th Century. Today's 1997-introduced

HANDMADE CIGARS: BRAND LISTINGS

Texana brand is mild-to-medium-bodied in its natural-shade wrapper and medium-bodied in the maduro wrapper. You can try them in elegant wood boxes of 25.

THIRD MILLENIUM
Handmade in Santiago, Dominican Republic.

Wrapper: Indonesia   *Binder: Indonesia*   *Filler: Dom. Rep.*

Shape	Name	Lgth	Ring	Wrapper
Double Corona	Double Corona	7½	50	CM
Churchill	Preludio I	7	46	CM
Robusto	Preludio II	5½	50	CM
Torpedo	Pyramide	7	56	CM

Hard to find, this is a 1997-introduced cigar which offers full-bodied flavor, presented in varnished all-cedar boxes of 25.

THOMAS HINDS CABINET SELECTION
Handmade in Esteli, Nicaragua.

Wrapper: Nicaragua   *Binder: Nicaragua*   *Filler: Nicaragua*

Shape	Name	Lgth	Ring	Wrapper
Double Corona	Churchill	7	49	CM
Toro	Short Churchill	6	50	CM
Long Corona	Corona Grande	6	44	CM
Robusto	Robusto	5	50	CM
Lonsdale	Lonsdale	7	43	CM
Corona	Corona	5½	42	CM

Here is a creamy, full-bodied brand first introduced in 1997. It offers all Nicaraguan-grown leaves protected in individual cellophane sleeves and packed in cedar boxes of 25.

HANDMADE CIGARS: BRAND LISTINGS

THOMAS HINDS HONDURAN SELECTION
Handmade in Danli, Honduras.

Wrapper: Ecuador *Binder: Honduras* *Filler: Honduras*

Shape	Name	Lgth	Ring	Wrapper
Giant	Presidente	8½	52	CM
Double Corona	Churchill	7	49	CM
Torpedo	Torpedo	6	52	CM
Toro	Short Churchill	6	50	CM
Lonsdale	Supremos	7	43	CM
Robusto	Robusto	5	50	CM
Long Corona	Royal Corona	6	43	CM
Corona	Corona	5½	42	CM

Introduced in the U.S. in 1994, Thomas Hinds Honduran Selection are premium, full-bodied, hand-rolled cigars. The long-leaf filler and double binder are of Honduran origin, while the wrapper is a spicy Ecuadorian leaf. Look for it in cedar boxes of 25.

THOMAS HINDS NICARAGUAN SELECTION
Handmade in Esteli, Nicaragua.

Wrapper: Ecuador *Binder: Nicaragua* *Filler: Nicaragua*

Shape	Name	Lgth	Ring	Wrapper
Torpedo	Torpedo	6	52	CC-Ma
Double Corona	Churchill	7	49	CC-Ma
Lonsdale	Lonsdale Extra	7	43	CC-Ma
Toro	Short Churchill	6	50	CC-Ma
Corona	Corona	5½	42	CC-Ma
Robusto	Robusto	5	50	CC-Ma

First offered in 1995, the Thomas Hinds Nicaraguan Selection showcases filler and binder tobaccos from the Jalapa region of Nicaragua. Easy to smoke thanks

HANDMADE CIGARS: BRAND LISTINGS

to top-quality construction, these cigars are elegantly packaged in handsome all-cedar boxes.

THOMAS HINDS VINTAGE I
Handmade in Esteli, Nicaragua.

Wrapper: Nicaragua   *Binder: Nicaragua*   *Filler: Nicaragua*

Shape	Name	Lgth	Ring	Wrapper
Double Corona	Churchill	7	49	CM
Robusto	Robusto	5	50	CM
Lonsdale	Lonsdale	7	43	CM
Corona	Corona	5½	42	CM

New for 1997, this brand offers a medium-to-full-bodied smoke, but without any harshness. It is presented in individual cellophane sleeves in limited numbers. Once gone, they will not be replenished, but instead a Vintage II will be introduced.

THOMPSON CONSERVA
Handmade in Danli, Honduras.

Wrapper: Indonesia   *Binder: Honduras*   *Filler: Honduras, Nicaragua*

Shape	Name	Lgth	Ring	Wrapper
Churchill	Churchill	7	48	CM
Toro	Toro	6	50	CM
Robusto	Robusto	5	50	CM
Lonsdale	Lonsdale	7	44	CM

This brand was introduced in 1997 and offers a medium-bodied taste from the Tabacos Rancho Jamastram factory. It is available in elegant, hinged-top boxes of 25.

TIA MARTIA
Handmade in Santiago, Dominican Republic.

Wrapper: Honduras   *Binder: Mexico*   *Filler: Dom. Rep., Honduras*

HANDMADE CIGARS: BRAND LISTINGS

Shape	Name	Lgth	Ring	Wrapper
Lonsdale	No. 1	7	44	CM
Petit Corona	No. 4	5	42	CM
Double Corona	Churchill	7½	52	CM
Short Panatela	Petit	5	38	CM
Double Corona	Presidente	7	50	CM
Robusto	Robusto	5	50	CM
Toro	Toro	6	50	CM
Cigarillo	Training Cigars	4	28	CM

Created in 1978, this is a mild-to-medium blend of leaves from three nations, offered in modestly-priced bundles of 25.

TIBURON
Handmade in Danli, Honduras.

Wrapper: Ecuador   Binder: Indonesia
Filler: Dominican Republic, Honduras, Nicaragua

Shape	Name	Lgth	Ring	Wrapper
Slim Panatela	Tiger Shark	6¼	33	CC
Long Corona	Great White	6	42	CC
Corona	Mako	5¼	42	CC

Despite the fierce names of the shapes, these are mild-bodied cigars. They are offered in bundles of 25 cigars each.

TOBACCOS DE MONTERREY
Handmade in Santiago, Dominican Republic.

Wrapper: Indonesia   Binder: Dom. Rep.   Filler: Dom. Rep.

Shape	Name	Lgth	Ring	Wrapper
Corona	Corona	5½	42	CM
Lonsdale	Lonsdale	6½	42	CM

| Double Corona | Churchill | 7½ | 49 | CM |
| Robusto | Robusto | 5 | 50 | CM |

This brand was introduced in 1997 and has a mild, earthy flavor. It is offered in bundles of 25.

TODO EL MUNDO
Handmade in Villa Gonzalez, Dominican Republic.
Wrapper: Brazil, USA/Connecticut   Binder: Dom. Rep.   Filler: Dom. Rep.

Shape	Name	Lgth	Ring	Wrapper
Double Corona	Churchill	7½	50	CC
Toro	Toro	6	52	CC
Grand Corona	Corona	6	46	CC
Corona	Petit Corona	5½	42	CC
Robusto	Rothschild	4½	52	CC
Torpedo	Torpedo	6½	52	CC
	Maduro:			
Torpedo	Torpedo	6½	52	Ma
Toro	Toro	6	50	Ma
Robusto	Robusto	4½	52	Ma
Corona Extra	Elegantes	5½	46	Ma

Here is a 1996 introduction of a cigar whose names means "all over the world" in Spanish. Thanks to its mild-to-medium body and silky Connecticut wrapper, it probably will achieve popularity "todo el mundo." The Brazilian maduro wrapper offers a full-bodied flavor.

TOOTH OF THE DOG
Handmade in Esteli, Nicaragua.
Wrapper: Nicaragua   Binder: Nicaragua   Filler: Nicaragua

HANDMADE CIGARS: BRAND LISTINGS

Shape	Name	Lgth	Ring	Wrapper
Robusto	Robusto	5	52	CM
Double Corona	Double Corona	7	54	CM
Double Corona	Churchill	7	52	CM
Giant	Soberano	8	54	CM

Here is a medium-bodied cigar of all-Nicaraguan origin, offered with an interesting name and an even more interesting box: each holds 25 Tooth of the Dog cigars . . . or is that Teeth of the Dog?

TOPPER CENTENNIAL
Handmade in Santiago, Dominican Republic.

Wrapper: Ecuador   *Binder: Dom. Rep.*   *Filler: Dom. Rep.*

Shape	Name	Lgth	Ring	Wrapper
Double Corona	Churchill	7½	52	CC
Toro	Toro	6	50	CC
Lonsdale	Lonsdale	6¾	43	CC

The Topper Cigar Company was founded in 1896, offering handmade cigars with imported long filler and Connecticut broadleaf wrappers. That tradition is now continued with the Topper Centennial, introduced in 1995. It's a handmade cigar manufactured in the Dominican Republic, providing a medium-bodied smoke, offered in three popular sizes.

TOPPER GRANDE
Handmade in Esteli, Nicaragua.

Wrapper: Indonesia   *Binder: Nicaragua*   *Filler: Nicaragua*

Shape	Name	Lgth	Ring	Wrapper
Double Corona	Churchill	7	50	CM
Toro	Toro	6	50	CM
Robusto	Robusto	4½	50	CM
Lonsdale	Cetro	6½	43	CM

Corona	Corona	5½	43	CM

Here is an outstanding handmade from an American institution among cigar makers which celebrated its 100th anniversary in 1996. This is a medium-to-full bodied smoke, featuring Indonesian wrappers around aged Nicaraguan leaves.

TORAÑO

Handmade in Navarette, Dominican Republic
and Esteli, Nicaragua.

Wrapper: Indonesia

Binder: Dom. Rep. or Nicaragua   *Filler: Dom. Rep. or Nicaragua*

Shape	Name	Lgth	Ring	Wrapper
Robusto	Robusto	5	50	CM
Long Corona	Cetros	6	42	CM
Toro	Toro	6	50	CM
Lonsdale	Lonsdale	7	44	CM
Churchill	Churchill	7	48	CM
Double Corona	Presidente	7½	52	CM

This is a bundled brand, offering a mild-to-medium-bodied taste in either version. The Dominican-made cigars have Dominican-grown binders and fillers, and the Nicaraguan line has Nicaraguan binders and fillers. You can find these value-priced beauties in bundles of 25.

TORCEDOR

Handmade in Esteli, Nicaragua.

Wrapper: Nicaragua   *Binder: Nicaragua*   *Filler: Honduras*

Shape	Name	Lgth	Ring	Wrapper
Lonsdale	No. 1	7	44	CC
Double Corona	Churchill	7	50	CC
Robusto	Robusto	5	50	CC
Toro	Toro	6	50	CC

HANDMADE CIGARS: BRAND LISTINGS

Giant	General	8	52	CC

"Torcedor" means cigar roller in Spanish and this 1996-introduced brand salutes them with a mild blend of long-filler tobaccos from Honduras and Nicaragua.

TORCEDOR GIANTS
Handmade in San Andres Tuxtla, Mexico.

Wrapper: Ecuador, Mexico   Binder: Mexico   Filler: Mexico

Shape	Name	Lgth	Ring	Wrapper
Robusto	Robusto Extra	5	60	CM-Ma
Toro	Super Toro	6½	60	CM-Ma
Giant	Special Churchill	8	60	CM-Ma

Here is a new member of the Torcedor family, introduced in 1997. It features an Ecuadorian-grown wrapper in the natural shade and all-Mexican tobacco in the maduro shade, both with a full-bodied taste. You'll find it in boxes of 25 in your choice of natural or maduro wrapper!

TRABUCOS
Handmade in Tenerife, the Canary Islands of Spain.

Wrapper: USA/Connecticut   Binder: Spain   Filler: Spain

Shape	Name	Lgth	Ring	Wrapper
Petit Corona	Rothschild	5	42	CC

Here is a new brand for 1998, with a medium body in one size only. It is presented in see-through, slide-top cabinets of 25.

TRESADO
Handmade in La Romana, Dominican Republic.

Wrapper: Indonesia   Binder: Dom. Rep.   Filler: Dom. Rep.

Shape	Name	Lgth	Ring	Wrapper
Giant	Seleccion No. 100	8	52	CC
Churchill	Seleccion No. 200	7	48	CC

HANDMADE CIGARS: BRAND LISTINGS

Grand Corona	Seleccion No. 300	6	46	CC
Lonsdale	Seleccion No. 400	6⅝	44	CC
Corona	Seleccion No. 500	5½	42	CC

Tresado provides handmade quality at a value price. Introduced in 1988, the cigar starts with a Dominican blend and binder, then adds a Javan wrapper for a full-bodied yet mild smoke.

TRINIDAD Y HERMANO
Handmade in Santiago, Dominican Republic.

Wrapper: Ecuador   *Binder: Indonesia*   *Filler: Dom. Rep.*

Shape	Name	Lgth	Ring	Wrapper
Corona	Corona	5½	44	CC
Robusto	Robusto	5	50	CC
Long Panatela	Lancero	7¼	36	CC
Double Corona	Churchill	7	50	CC
Pyramid	Piramides	6¼	50	CC

This brand name dates back almost 100 years to when it was produced in Cuba. Introduced once again in 1998, it offers a full-bodied taste, presented in elegant wood boxes of 25 cigars each.

TROPICAL REPUBLIC
Handmade in Santiago, Dominican Republic.

Wrapper: Ecuador   *Binder: Dom. Rep.*   *Filler: Dom. Rep.*

Shape	Name	Lgth	Ring	Wrapper
Double Corona	Churchill	7	50	CC
Robusto	Robusto	5	50	CC
Torpedo	Figurado	4½	48	CC

This brand was introduced in 1997. It has a mild-to-medium-bodied taste and is offered in value-priced packs of 25.

HANDMADE CIGARS: BRAND LISTINGS

TROPICAL TREASURE
Handmade in Tamboril, Dominican Republic.

Wrapper: Indonesia   Binder: Indonesia   Filler: Dom. Rep.

Shape	Name	Lgth	Ring	Wrapper
Petit Corona	Flavored	5	42	CM

Introduced in 1998, this is a mild-bodied, flavored brand available in Almond
Brandy, Cayman Chocolate, cognac, Jamaican Sweets, Pina Colada, spiced
rum, sweet cherry and West Indies Vanilla. You can try them in guaranteed-
fresh, vacuum-sealed cans of 25.

TROPICAL TREATS
BY CARLOS TORAÑO
Handmade in Santiago, Dominican Republic.

Wrapper: Indonesia   Binder: Dom. Rep.   Filler: Dom. Rep.

Shape	Name	Lgth	Ring	Wrapper
Corona Extra	El Niño	5	46	CM
Petit Corona	La Niña	4	40	CM

This is a flavored brand, with long-filler leaves and a mild body. The flavors
include chocolate, rum and vanilla, available in boxes of 25.

TROYA
Handmade in Santiago, Dominican Republic.

Wrapper: Ecuador   Binder: Dom. Rep.   Filler: Dom. Rep.

Shape	Name	Lgth	Ring	Wrapper
Torpedo	No. 81 Torpedo	7	54	CC-Ma
Double Corona	No. 72 Executive	7¾	50	CC-Ma
Churchill	No. 63 Churchill	6⅞	46	CC-Ma
Lonsdale	No. 54 Elegante	7	43	CC-Ma
Long Corona	No. 45 Cetro	6¼	44	CC-Ma
Long Panatela	No. 36 Palma Fina	7	36	CC

HANDMADE CIGARS: BRAND LISTINGS

Corona	No. 27 Corona	5½	42	CC
Robusto	No. 18 Rothchild	4½	50	CC-Ma
	Troya Clasico:			
Double Corona	No. 72 Executive	7¾	50	CC
Corona	No. 27 Corona	5½	42	CC

Troya is a hand-crafted cigar of the highest quality, introduced in 1985. It has a medium body and a consistency in construction and draw that will reward the connoisseur every time. Troyas are offered in boxes of 25 cigars, in natural and maduro wrappers. The Clasico line of two shapes was created in 1991 and is produced only when truly superior leaves are available to create a fuller taste that is now encased in boxes of 20 cigars each. Look for the newer Clasico band, and note that each box produced is sequentially numbered to ensure quality control and exclusivity.

TSAR I
Handmade in Santiago, Dominican Republic.

Wrapper: Indonesia *Binder: Dom. Rep.* *Filler: Dom. Rep.*

Shape	*Name*		*Lgth*	*Ring*	*Wrapper*
Double Corona	Churchill		7½	50	CM
Robusto	Robusto		4¾	50	CM
Grand Corona	Lonsdale		6½	46	CM
Double Corona	Double Corona		6¾	50	CM
Torpedo	Torpedo		6¼	52	CM
Petit Corona	Petit Perfecto	*(perfecto tip)*	4	44	CM
Corona Extra	Intermediate	*(perfecto tip)*	5	46	CM
Toro	Classico	*(perfecto tip)*	6	48	CM

This side of the Tsar brand is mild-to-medium in strength and available in boxes or bundles of 25 or packs of three, except for the three perfecto-tipped sizes. These are offered in groups of eight with 24 to the box, or in bundles of 25 or packs of three.

HANDMADE CIGARS: BRAND LISTINGS

TSAR II
Handmade in Santiago, Dominican Republic.

Wrapper: USA/Connecticut   *Binder: Dom. Rep.*   *Filler: Dom. Rep.*

Shape	Name	Lgth	Ring	Wrapper
Double Corona	Churchill	7½	50	CC
Robusto	Robusto	5½	50	CC
Petit Corona	Lonbusto	4¾	42	CC
Corona	Corona	5½	42	CC
Torpedo	Torpedo	6¼	52	CC

Here is a mild-to-medium range, offered in elegant, clear-topped boxes of 25, or in bundles of 25 or in packs of 3.

TTT TRINIDAD
BY ARTURO FUENTE
Handmade in Santiago, Dominican Republic.

Wrapper: Cameroon   *Binder: Dom. Rep.*   *Filler: Dom. Rep.*

Shape	Name	Lgth	Ring	Wrapper
Robusto	Robusto	5	50	CM
Corona	Corona	5½	44	CM

Introduced in late 1997, this brand is made in limited production by the Tabacalera A. Fuente. It offers a medium-bodied taste with a careful blend of Dominican leaves and a Cameroon wrapper. Elegantly presented in varnished cedar cabinets of 25, it is designed to garner the same respect as its namesake, originally produced in pre-revolutionary Cuba.

TUBANO
Handmade in Santiago, Dominican Republic.

TUBANO GRAND RESERVA:

Wrapper: Cameroon   *Binder: Dom. Rep.*   *Filler: Dom. Rep.*

HANDMADE CIGARS: BRAND LISTINGS

TUBANO PRIVATE COLLECTION:
Wrapper: USA/Connecticut   *Binder: Dom. Rep.*   *Filler: Dom. Rep.*

TUBANO SUAVE:
Wrapper: USA/Connecticut   *Binder: Dom. Rep.*   *Filler: Dom. Rep.*

Shape	Name	Lgth	Ring	Wrapper
	Gran Reserva:			
Double Corona	Churchill	7½	50	CM
Toro	Toro	6	52	CM
Robusto	Rothchild	4½	50	CM
Lonsdale	Corona	6½	44	CM
	Private Collection:			
Double Corona	Churchill	7½	50	CC
Toro	Toro	6	52	CC
Robusto	Rothchild	4½	50	CC
Lonsdale	Corona	6½	44	CC
	Suave:			
Double Corona	Churchill	7½	50	CC
Robusto	Rothchild	4½	50	CC
Lonsdale	Lonsdale	6½	44	CC

This 1997-introduced, three-style brand offers a medium-to-full-bodied taste in the Gran Reserva group, a mild-to-medium flavor in the Private Collection series and a mild flavor in the Suave group. It is available in boxes of 25.

12 STARS

Handmade in Santiago, Dominican Republic.

Wrapper: USA/Connecticut   *Binder: Dom. Rep.*   *Filler: Dom. Rep.*

Shape	Name	Lgth	Ring	Wrapper
Giant	Star 1	8½	50	CC

HANDMADE CIGARS: BRAND LISTINGS

Churchill	Star 2	8	46	CC
Lonsdale	Star 3	7½	42	CC
Churchill	Star 4	6⅞	46	CC
Corona	Star 5	5¾	42	CC
Corona	Star 6	5¾	42	DC
Slim Panatela	Star 7	6⅞	34	CC
Corona	Star 8	5½	40	CC
Robusto	Star 9	5	50	CC
Small Panatela	Star 10	5	34	CC
Cigarillo	Star 11	5	28	CC
Cigarillo	Star 12	5½	28	CC

This is a very high value brand, offering a generally mild-tasting cigar for a price well below its pedigree. Available in bundles of 25, these are among the finest cigars you can buy, penny for penny, thanks to their just slightly imperfect Connecticut wrappers and carefully selected Dominican binder and filler.

U.S.P.A. POLO CIGARS
Handmade in Esteli, Nicaragua.

Wrapper: Nicaragua   Binder: Nicaragua   Filler: Nicaragua

Shape	Name	Lgth	Ring	Wrapper
Churchill	Churchill	7	48	CM

Introduced in 1998, this is the official cigar of the United States Polo Association, this is a mild blend of all-Nicaraguan leaves, offered in a cherry humidor of 36, or boxes or bundles of 25..

ULTIMATE DOMINICAN
Handmade in Santiago, Dominican Republic.

HANDMADE CIGARS: BRAND LISTINGS

	ULTIMATE BUNDLE:				
Wrapper: Indonesia	Binder: Dom. Rep.			Filler: Dom. Rep.	

	ULTIMATE CLASSIC:				
Wrapper: Ecuador	Binder: Dom. Rep.			Filler: Dom. Rep.	

	ULTIMATE GOLD:				
Wrapper: Dom. Rep.	Binder: Dom. Rep.			Filler: Dom. Rep.	

Shape	Name	Lgth	Ring	Wrapper
	Ultimate Bundle:			(long or mixed filler)
Churchill	Churchill	7	48	CM
Grand Corona	Corona Gorda	6	46	CM
Long Corona	Lonsdale	6	42	CM
Robusto	Robusto	5	50	CM
	Ultimate Classic:			
Churchill	Churchill	7	48	CC
Grand Corona	Corona Gorda	6	46	CC
Long Corona	Lonsdale	6	42	CC
Robusto	Robusto	5	50	CC
Petit Corona	Petit Corona	5	40	CC
	Ultimate Gold:			
Churchill	Churchill	7	48	CC
Grand Corona	Corona Gorda	6	46	CC
Long Corona	Lonsdale	6	42	CC
Robusto	Robusto	5	50	CC

You'll find this brand, introduced in 1997, in three different styles. The Classic series offers a mild flavor with an Ecuadorian-grown, Connecticut-seed wrapper. The Gold series is all-Dominican and full-bodied, while the Bundle group has a Sumatra wrapper and a medium-bodied flavor. The Gold and Classic series are available in boxes of 25, while the Bundle group is offered in bundles of 25.

HANDMADE CIGARS: BRAND LISTINGS

UMO V.S.
Handmade in Santo Domingo, Dominican Republic.

Wrapper: Cameroon   Binder: Dom. Rep.   Filler: Dom. Rep.

Shape	Name	Lgth	Ring	Wrapper
Long Corona	Corona	6	44	CM
Grand Corona	Corona Extra	6	46	CM
Churchill	Grand Corona	7	46	CM
Robusto	Robusto	5	50	CM
Double Corona	Churchill	7½	50	CM
Giant	Canon	8½	52	CM
Torpedo	Torpedo	6¾	54	CM
Slim Panatela	Panatella	6½	32	CM
Short Panatela	Petite	3½	38	CM
Perfecto	Shortie	4½	46	CM

This is a medium-to-full-bodied cigar, featuring a Sumatra-seed wrapper. It was introduced in 1996 and is available in boxes of 25 or bundles of 50.

UTOPIA
Handmade in Santiago, Dominican Republic.
Wrapper: Indonesia, USA/Connecticut

Binder: Dominican Republic   Filler: Dominican Republic

Shape	Name	Lgth	Ring	Wrapper
Churchill	Churchill	7	48	CC-Ma
Robusto	Robusto	5½	50	CC-Ma
Toro	Double Corona	6½	48	CC-Ma

Introduced in 1997, this is a mild-bodied brand offered with a choice of a Connecticut-grown, natural-shade wrapper or an Indonesian-grown, maduro wrapper. You can find this cigar in paper-wrapped boxes of 25.

HANDMADE CIGARS: BRAND LISTINGS

V CENTENNIAL
Handmade in Danli, Honduras.

Wrapper: USA/Connecticut   *Binder: Dominican Republic*
Filler: Dominican Republic, Honduras, Nicaragua

Shape	Name	Lgth	Ring	Wrapper
Torpedo	Torpedo	6½	54	CC
Giant	Presidente	8	50	CC
Churchill	Churchill	7	48	CC-Ma
Long Panatela	No. 1	7½	38	CC
Toro	No. 2	6	50	CC-Ma
Lonsdale	Cetros	6¼	44	CC-Ma
Robusto	Robustos	5	50	CC-Ma
Corona	Coronas	5½	42	CC
Perfecto	Perfecto No. 1	4¾	52	CC
Perfecto	Perfecto No. 2	4	51	CC

V Centennial is handmade in Honduras using the finest tobacco from the
Dominican Republic, Nicaragua, Honduras and the United States. Selection and
processing of this cigar began in 1992. It was introduced in November 1993 and
has become one of the top-rated cigars available today. It is considered a
medium-bodied cigar.

V CENTENNIAL 500
Handmade in Santiago, Dominican Republic.

Wrapper: USA/Connecticut   *Binder: Dominican Republic*
Filler: Dominican Republic, Honduras, Mexico, Nicaragua

Shape	Name	Lgth	Ring	Wrapper
Corona	Corona	5½	42	CM
Robusto	Robusto	5	50	CM
Long Corona	Cetro	6¼	44	CM
Toro	No. 2	6	50	CM

HANDMADE CIGARS: BRAND LISTINGS

| Churchill | Churchill | 7 | 48 | CM |
| Torpedo | Torpedo | 6½ | 54 | CM |

A salute to the five centuries since Columbus's voyage to the Caribbean, this is a full-bodied blend of leaves from five nations, available in all-cedar boxes of 20.

V.M. Santana Connecticut Collection
Handmade in Santiago, Dominican Republic.
Wrapper: USA/Connecticut   *Binder: Dom. Rep.*   *Filler: Dom. Rep.*

Shape	Name	Lgth	Ring	Wrapper
Robusto	Robusto	5	50	CC
Long Corona	Lonsdale	6	44	CC
Double Corona	Churchill	7	50	CC
Pyramid	Pyramid	6	54	CC

This brand debuted in 1996, with a mild-to-medium body and a smooth, genuine Connecticut wrapper offered in limited distribution in boxes of 25 cigars each, except for the Pyramid, offered in bundles of 10.

V.M. Santana Sumatra Collection
Handmade in Santiago, Dominican Republic.
Wrapper: Indonesia   *Binder: Dom. Rep.*   *Filler: Dom. Rep.*

Shape	Name	Lgth	Ring	Wrapper
Long Corona	Lonsdale	6	44	CM
Robusto	Robusto	5	50	CM
Double Corona	Churchill	7	50	CM

Mild-to-medium in body but full of flavor, this blend of a Sumatra wrapper with Dominican Olor and Piloto Cubano leaves must be tasted to be appreciated. You'll find these red-labeled beauties in boxes of 25.

VALDEZ
Handmade in San Andres Tuxtla, Mexico.
Wrapper: Mexico   *Binder: Mexico*   *Filler: Mexico*

HANDMADE CIGARS: BRAND LISTINGS

Shape	Name	Lgth	Ring	Wrapper
Robusto	Robusto	5	50	CM
Corona	No. 3	5¾	40	CM
Double Corona	Churchill	7½	50	CM
Lonsdale	Corona Grande	6⅝	42	CM

This brand debuted in 1998. It is medium in body and available in four sizes in boxes of 25.

VALLE DEL SOL
Handmade in San Andres Tuxtla, Mexico.
Wrapper: Mexico   *Binder: Mexico*   *Filler: Mexico*

Shape	Name	Lgth	Ring	Wrapper
Double Corona	Churchill	7½	50	CC
Long Corona	Lonsdale	6¼	42	CC
Robusto	Robusto	5	50	CC
Toro	Corona	6¼	50	CC

New in 1997, this is a medium-bodied, long-filler brand that is offered in boxes of 25.

VAMP
Handmade in Santiago, Dominican Republic.
Wrapper: Indonesia   *Binder: Nicaragua*   *Filler: Dom. Rep., Nicaragua*

Shape	Name	Lgth	Ring	Wrapper
Lonsdale	Corona	6½	42	CM

Introduced in 1998, this is a wildly-packaged cigar that is mild in body and offered in boxes of 20.

VANILLA DELIGHT
Handmade, with medium filler, in Santiago, Dominican Republic.
Wrapper: Indonesia   *Binder: Dom. Rep.*   *Filler: Dom. Rep.*

HANDMADE CIGARS: BRAND LISTINGS

Shape	Name	Lgth	Ring	Wrapper
Long Corona		6	42	CM
Long Corona		6	44	CM

This is a medium-bodied cigar, available in two sizes, that was introduced in 1996. It utilizes all-Dominican filler and is offered in bundles of 25.

VARGAS
Handmade in Las Palmas, the Canary Islands of Spain.
Wrapper: Indonesia   Binder: Indonesia   Filler: Canary Islands

Shape	Name	Lgth	Ring	Wrapper
Churchill	Presidentes	6¾	46	CM
Corona Extra	Senadores	5½	46	CM
Panatela	Diplomaticos	5½	36	CM
Double Corona	Churchill	7½	50	CM
Corona	Capitolios	5⅛	44	CM
Robusto	Robustos	4¾	50	CM
Short Panatela	Cremas	4⅜	39	CM

This is an old brand which was re-introduced in 1996. It is mild in body and has excellent construction of primarily Indonesian leaves, offered in boxes of 25.

VEGA FINA
Handmade in Danli, Honduras.
Wrapper: Indonesia   Binder: Dom. Rep.   Filler: Costa Rica, Honduras, Nicaragua

Shape	Name	Lgth	Ring	Wrapper
Double Corona	Double Corona	7½	49	CM
Lonsdale	Lonsdale	6½	42	CM
Toro	Toro	6	49	CM
Robusto	Robusto	5	49	CM

HANDMADE CIGARS: BRAND LISTINGS

Introduced in 1998, this is a mild, complex brand which includes leaves from five nations. It is value-priced and offered in colorful, paper-wrapped boxes

VEGA VIEJA
Handmade in Santiago, Dominican Republic.
Wrapper: USA/Connecticut or Indonesia

Binder: Dominican Republic   *Filler: Dominican Republic*

Shape	Name	Lgth	Ring	Wrapper
Double Corona	Churchill	7½	50	CC-CM
Robusto	Robusto	5	50	CC-CM
Long Corona	Lonsdale	6	44	CC-CM
Corona	Corona	5½	44	CC-CM
Pyramid	Piramide I	7	50	CC-CM
Pyramid	Piramide II	7½	52	CC-CM
Torpedo	Torpedo I	7	50	CC-CM
Torpedo	Torpedo II	7½	52	CC-CM
Torpedo	Belicaso I	7	50	CC-CM
Torpedo	Belicaso II	7½	52	CC-CM
Toro	Toro	6½	50	CC-CM

This is a mild or mild-to-medium-bodied brand, depending on whether a Connecticut or Sumatra wrapper is chosen. It is available in either a box or bundle of 25 cigars each.

VEGAS CUBANO
Handmade in Esteli, Nicaragua.
Wrapper: Indonesia   *Binder: Nicaragua*   *Filler: Dom. Rep., Nicaragua*

Shape	Name	Lgth	Ring	Wrapper
Robusto	Robusto	5	50	CC
Toro	Churchill	6	48	CC
Double Corona	President	7	50	CC

HANDMADE CIGARS: BRAND LISTINGS

	Hand-molded:			
Double Corona	Churchill	6¾	50	Ma

Here is a full-flavored brand, exquisitely presented in shallow cedar boxes of five cigars, each equipped with a plexiglass window lid. The hand-molded shapes are completely hand pressed and no mold is used, a true challenge to the torcedor!

VENCEDORA NADAL Y NADAL
Handmade in Santiago, Dominican Republic.
Wrapper: Ecuador   *Binder: Dom. Rep.*   *Filler: Dom. Rep.*

Shape	Name	Lgth	Ring	Wrapper
Corona	Coronas	5¾	43	CM
Robusto	Robustos	4¾	52	CM
Toro	Toros	6	50	CM
Long Panatela	Panetelas	7	36	CM
Lonsdale	No. 1	7	43	CM
Churchill	Churchills	7	48	CM
Double Corona	Presidente	7	50	CM

This is a medium-bodied blend introduced in 1997. It features a Sumatra-seed wrapper and is available in all-cedar boxes of 25.

VERACRUZ
Handmade in San Andres Tuxtla, Mexico.
Wrapper: Mexico   *Binder: Mexico*   *Filler: Mexico*

Shape	Name		Lgth	Ring	Wrapper
Small Panatela	Carinas de Veracruz		4⅝	38	CC
Long Corona	Mina de Veracruz	*(tubed)*	6¼	44	CC
Robusto	Corto de Veracruz	*(tubed)*	4⅞	50	CC
Robusto	Corta'o de Veracruz	*(tubed)*	4⅞	50	Ma

HANDMADE CIGARS: BRAND LISTINGS

Torpedo	O.C. de Veracruz	3⅞	47	CC
Torpedo	Marques de Veracruz *(tubed)*	5⅛	46	CC
Lonsdale	Poemas de Veracruz *(tubed)*	6¼	44	Ma
Double Corona	Veracruz Magnum *(tubed)*	7⅞	50	CC-Ma

Created in 1977 and available more widely in 1994, Veracruz ultra-premium cigars are hand-rolled from a selection of choice Mexican tobaccos. Remarkably mild, yet flavorful with hints of honey, spices and coffee, these medium-bodied cigars are guaranteed fresh. In fact, each of the larger-sized cigars are individually encased in glass tubes for air-tight safety.

VICTOR SINCLAIR
Handmade in Santiago, Dominican Republic.
Wrapper: Indonesia, USA/Connecticut
Binder: Dominican Republic   *Filler: Dominican Republic*

Shape	Name	Lgth	Ring	Wrapper
Double Corona	Churchill	7½	50	CC-Ma
Robusto	Robusto No. 1	5½	50	CC-Ma
Robusto	Robusto No. 2	4½	50	CC-Ma
Long Corona	Lonsdale	6	44	CC-Ma
Grand Corona	Corona	6	46	CC-Ma
Pyramid	Pyramid	7	54	CC-Ma

Introduced in 1995, this handmade cigar offers two different shades of wrapper: a natural wrapper grown in Connecticut and a maduro wrapper from Indonesia. The blend is medium in body and offered in boxes of 25, except for the Pyramid, offered in 20s.

VICTOR SINCLAIR GRAND RESERVE
Handmade in Santiago, Dominican Republic.
Wrapper: Indonesia   *Binder: Dom. Rep.*   *Filler: Dom. Rep.*

Shape	Name	Lgth	Ring	Wrapper
Long Panatela	Panatela	7	38	Ma

Corona Extra	Figurado (perfecto tip)	5	46	Ma
Torpedo	Belicoso	5¾	52	Ma
Pyramid	Pyramid	6	54	Ma
Torpedo	Torpedo	5¾	52	Ma

This is a full-bodied, Sumatra-clad cigar introduced in 1997. Available in maduro wrappers only, it is offered in boxes of ten (panatela), 15 (figurado and belicoso) or three (pyramid and torpedo).

VICTOR SINCLAIR VINTAGE SELECT
Handmade in Santiago, Dominican Republic.
Wrapper: Dom. Rep.   *Binder: Dom. Rep.*   *Filler: Dom. Rep.*

Shape	Name	Lgth	Ring	Wrapper
Robusto	Robusto No. 1	4½	50	Ma
Robusto	Robusto No. 2	5½	50	Ma
Long Corona	Corona	6	44	Ma
Churchill	Double Corona	7	48	Ma
Double Corona	Churchill	7½	50	Ma

Here is a full-bodied cigar, introduced in 1996. It is offered in maduro wrapper only with all-Cuban seed binder and filler and presented in cedar boxes of 25

VICTORIA PASHA BOXER
Handmade in Santiago, Dominican Republic.
Wrapper: Indonesia   *Binder: Dom. Rep.*   *Filler: Dom. Rep., Nicaragua*

Shape	Name	Lgth	Ring	Wrapper
Double Corona	Churchill	7	50	CM
Toro	Toro	6	50	CM
Robusto	Robusto	5	50	CM
Petit Corona	Corona	5	42	CM

HANDMADE CIGARS: BRAND LISTINGS

This cigar was introduced in 1998 and is offered in four sizes. It is mild-bodied and available in boxes of 25.

VICTORIA PASHA MATADOR
Handmade in Danli, Honduras.

Wrapper: Ecuador   Binder: Honduras   Filler: Honduras, Nicaragua

Shape	Name	Lgth	Ring	Wrapper
Corona	Corona	5¾	42	CC
Lonsdale	No. 1	7	44	CC
Robusto	Robusto	4¾	54	CC
Toro	Double Corona	6	54	CC
Double Corona	Churchill	7⅝	50	CC
Torpedo	Torpedo	6	52	CC

Introduced in 1998, this is a mild cigar with a hint of spice. Available in six sizes, it is offered in boxes of 25.

VILLA
Handmade in Villa Gonzalez, Dominican Republic.

Wrapper: Indonesia   Binder: Dom. Rep.   Filler: Dom. Rep.

Shape	Name	Lgth	Ring	Wrapper
Double Corona	Churchill	7½	50	CC
Robusto	Rothschild	4½	50	CC
Long Corona	Corona	6	44	CC

New for 1997, this is a very well constructed, medium-bodied cigar presented in all-cedar boxes of 25.

VILLA
Handmade in Santiago, Dominican Republic.

Wrapper: Ecuador   Binder: Dom. Rep.   Filler: Dom. Rep.

HANDMADE CIGARS: BRAND LISTINGS

Shape	Name	Lgth	Ring	Wrapper
Torpedo		6	52	CC
Double Corona		7½	50	CC
Toro		6	50	CC
Robusto		4½	50	CC
Long Corona		6	44	CC
Corona		5½	42	CC

Introduced in 1998, this brand has no shape names, but a medium-to-full-bodied flavor, available in boxes of 25.

VILLA HAVANA
Handmade, with mixed filler, in Santiago, Dominican Republic.
Wrapper: Indonesia   Binder: Indonesia   Filler: Dom. Rep., Indonesia

Shape	Name	Lgth	Ring	Wrapper
Churchill	Churchill	7½	48	CM
Petit Corona	Corona	5	43	CM
Long Corona	Lonsdale	6	44	CM
Robusto	Robusto	4½	50	CM
Toro	Toro	6½	50	CM

This brand is new for 1998 and offers a consistent draw with a medium-bodied taste. You can find it in value-priced bundles of 25.

VILLA LOBOS
Handmade in Santiago, Dominican Republic.
Wrapper: Ecuador   Binder: Dom. Rep.   Filler: Dom. Rep.

Shape	Name	Lgth	Ring	Wrapper
Double Corona	Churchill	7½	50	CC
Robusto	Robusto	5½	50	CC

Grand Corona	Corona Extra	6	46	CC

This brand was introduced in 1996, offering a medium-bodied taste with a Connecticut-seed wrapper. It is presented in cellophane sleeves inside cedar boxes of 25.

VILLAR Y VILLAR
Handmade in Esteli, Nicaragua.

Wrapper: Ecuador   *Binder: Honduras*
Filler: Dominican Republic, Honduras, Nicaragua

Shape	Name		Lgth	Ring	Wrapper
Giant	Bermejos		8½	52	CC
Grand Corona	Cazadores		6½	46	CC
Lonsdale	Figaros		6½	44	CC
Short Panatela	Half Coronas		4½	38	CC
Robusto	Laguitos		4½	52	CC
Pyramid	Pyramides		6¾	52	CC
Corona	Remedios		5½	44	CC
Robusto	Robustos		4½	52	CC
Toro	Toros		6⅛	48	CC
Pyramid	Trumpet		6¾	48	CC
Corona	Crystal	(glass jar)	5⅝	44	CC
Churchill	Valentinos		6¾	48	CC
Double Corona	754s		7	54	CC

The romance of the great days of the Cuban cigar industry are re-kindled immediately by the mere mention of this the name of this storied brand. In 1996, it re-appeared as a modestly-priced, medium-to-heavy-bodied cigar with a Sumatra-seed wrapper grown in Ecuador. Originally offered in bundles, it will be presented in cedar boxes of 20 beginning in late 1997.

HANDMADE CIGARS: BRAND LISTINGS

VINTAGE AGED SELECTION
Handmade in Miami, Florida, USA.

Wrapper: Dom. Rep.   Binder: Dom. Rep.   Filler: Dom. Rep.

Shape	Name	Lgth	Ring	Wrapper
Robusto	Rothchild	4½	50	CM
Long Corona	Corona	6	44	CM
Double Corona	Churchill	7	50	CM

This is a 1994-introduced brand with a mild body, aged for four years in wine to give it a special flavor. It has a Sumatra-seed wrapper grown in the Dominican and is offered in boxes of 25.

VIRTUOSO TORAÑO
Handmade in Danli, Honduras.

Wrapper: Costa Rica, Ecuador   Binder: Honduras
Filler: Costa Rica, Honduras, Nicaragua

Shape	Name	Lgth	Ring	Wrapper
Giant	Presidente	8	52	CC
Toro	Double Corona	6	50	CC-Ma
Robusto	Robusto	4¾	52	CC-Ma
Lonsdale	Lonsdale	7	44	CC
Long Corona	Cetros	6	43	CC

Introduced in 1995, Virtuoso is a long-filler, all hand-made cigar with a Colorado-Claro wrapper of Connecticut-seed origin grown in Ecuador. This and the blend of leaves from three nations in the filler and binder give this line a mild-to-medium body, but with plenty of taste. The maduro-wrapped shapes utilize leaf grown in Costa Rica.

VUELTABAJO
Handmade in Santiago, Dominican Republic.

Wrapper: USA/Connecticut   Binder: Dom. Rep.   Filler: Dom. Rep.

HANDMADE CIGARS: BRAND LISTINGS

Shape	Name	Lgth	Ring	Wrapper
Giant	Gigante	8½	52	CC
Churchill	Churchill	7	48	CC
Robusto	Robusto	4¾	52	CC
Lonsdale	Lonsdale	7	43	CC
Toro	Toros	6	50	CC
Corona	Corona	5¾	42	CC
Pyramid	Pyramid	6¼	54	CC

Introduced in 1994, the Vueltabajo line is fine enough to bear the name of the most legendary tobacco-growing region in the world. Artfully crafted with a smooth Connecticut Shade wrapper, hand-selected Dominican Olor binder and the richest Dominican Piloto Cubano filler, this cigar is mild-to-medium in strength.

W & D
Handmade in Danli, Honduras.

Wrapper: Honduras   *Binder: Honduras*   *Filler: Dom. Rep., Nicaragua*

Shape	Name	Lgth	Ring	Wrapper
Double Corona	Presidente	7½	50	CM
Lonsdale	Cetro	6½	44	CM
Robusto	Corona	5½	50	CM

These are medium-bodied, long-filler cigars offered in bundles of 25, featuring a Connecticut-seed wrapper grown in Honduras.

WALL STREET SMOKES
Handmade in Miami, Florida, USA.
Wrapper: Ecuador, Indonesia, Mexico

Binder: Indonesia   *Filler: Dominican Republic, Nicaragua*

Shape	Name	Lgth	Ring	Wrapper
Torpedo	Torpedo	6½	54	CC-CM-Ma

HANDMADE CIGARS: BRAND LISTINGS

Double Corona	Churchill	7	50	CC-CM-Ma
Robusto	Robusto	5	50	CC-CM-Ma

This is a new brand for 1998, with a choice of wrappers and a medium-to-full body, offered in cedar boxes of 25.

WEST INDIES VANILLA
Handmade, with medium filler, in Jaibon, Dominican Republic.
Wrapper: Indonesia   *Binder: Indonesia*
Filler: Colombia, Dominican Republic, Indonesia

Shape	Name	Lgth	Ring	Wrapper
Short Panatela	Carmelita	4½	36	CM
Petit Corona	Carmela	4½	42	CM
Lonsdale	Grand Carmela	7	42	CM

This is a vanilla-flavored cigar produced by the Caribbean Cigar Company and introduced in 1995. It is handmade, but with medium filler instead of long filler leaves. It has a medium-to-full-bodied taste and is offered in boxes of 25 cigars each.

WILD JAVANOS
Handmade in Java, Indonesia.
Wrapper: Indonesia   *Binder: Indonesia*   *Filler: Indonesia*

Shape	Name	Lgth	Ring	Wrapper
Churchill	Argopuro	7	48	CC
Toro	Indopuro	6½	50	CC
Robusto	Stupa	5	50	CC
Long Corona	Puri	6	42	CC
Toro	Besuki	6	50	CC
Slim Panatela	Gadis	6	30	CC

HANDMADE CIGARS: BRAND LISTINGS

Introduced in 1997 and medium in body, this all-Indonesian cigar is available in
bundles of 25 cigars each.

WORIUR
Handmade in Woriur, India.

Wrapper: Indonesia   *Binder: Indonesia*   *Filler: India*

Shape	Name	Lgth	Ring	Wrapper
Churchill	Churchill	7	48	CM
Grand Corona	Corona Gorda	6	46	CM
Long Corona	Corona	6	42	CM
Toro	Robusto	6	50	CM
Cigarillo	Hamlet Clove	4¼	28	CM

This is the first entry from India in the cigar wars, available in the U.S. in 1998.
There is more than a century of cigar-making tradition in India and this brand
offers a mild taste in boxes of 25, or 50 for the Hamlet Clove cigarillos.

WORLD'S BEST
Handmade in Santiago, Dominican Republic.

Wrapper: Indonesia   *Binder: Dom. Rep.*   *Filler: Dom. Rep.*

Shape	Name	Lgth	Ring	Wrapper
Robusto	Robusto	5	50	CM
Toro	Double Corona	6	50	CM
Double Corona	Churchill	7	50	CM
Toro	Torro	6½	50	CM
Giant Corona	Corona Largo	7¾	44	CM
Giant	Presidente	8	52	CM

This brand debuted in 1998 and features a medium-bodied taste. It is presented
in all-cedar boxes of 25.

HANDMADE CIGARS: BRAND LISTINGS

XCLUSIVO
Handmade in Miami, Florida, USA.
Wrapper: Brazil, Mexico

Binder: Brazil   *Filler: Dominican Republic, Indonesia, Nicaragua*

Shape	Name	Lgth	Ring	Wrapper
Giant	Gigante	8½	52	CM-Ma
Double Corona	Presidente	7¾	52	CM-Ma
Double Corona	Churchill	7	50	CM-Ma
Toro	Toro	6	50	CM-Ma
Robusto	Rothschild	5	50	CM-Ma
Lonsdale	No. 1	7	44	CM-Ma
Long Panatela	Panatela	7	36	CM-Ma
Pyramid	Piramide	6	52	CM-Ma

This line was introduced in 1996 and is available in natural (Sumatra seed) and maduro (Mexican) wrappers. It offers a medium-to-full body and is packed in boxes of 25.

XCUBAN
Handmade in Tamboril, Dominican Republic.
Wrapper: Indonesia   *Binder: Dom. Rep.*   *Filler: Dom. Rep.*

Shape	Name	Lgth	Ring	Wrapper
Lonsdale	Corona	6¼	44	CM-Ma
Robusto	Robusto	5	50	CM-Ma
Toro	Robusto Superior	6	50	CM-Ma
Pyramid	Pyramide	6	48	CM-Ma
Churchill	Churchill	7	48	CM-Ma
Giant	Presidente	8	52	CM-Ma

This is a bundle brand, with a medium body, available in both a natural and maduro-shade wrapper.

HANDMADE CIGARS: BRAND LISTINGS

XILADO
Handmade in Miami, Florida, USA.

Wrapper: Indonesia, Mexico   Binder: Indonesia
Filler: Brazil, Dominican Republic, Indonesia

Shape	Name	Lgth	Ring	Wrapper
Toro	Robusto	6	52	CM-Ma
Giant	Elegante	8	50	CM-Ma
Long Corona	Corona Especial	6	42	CM-Ma
Churchill	Imperial	6¾	46	CM-Ma
Torpedo	Torpedo Clasico	7	54	CM-Ma
Torpedo	Campanita	5	54	CM-Ma
Torpedo	Torpedo	6	54	CM-Ma
Lonsdale	Lancero	7½	40	CM-Ma
Long Panatela	Panatela	7	36	CM-Ma

This line debuted in 1996 and is a full-bodied smoke with excellent construction, offered in individual cellophane sleeves and packed in either wood boxes of 25, upright acrylic cases of 25 or the Torpedo in a plastic four-pack! Take your pick of Sumatra-grown natural wrappers or Mexican-grown maduro wrapped smokes.

XOTICA
Handmade, with mixed filler, in Miami, Florida, USA.

Wrapper: Indonesia   Binder: Indonesia   Filler: Indonesia

Shape	Name	Lgth	Ring	Wrapper
Long Corona	Corona	6	42	CC

Want flavors? Here is a wild brand, new for 1997, mild in body and made with mixed filler accompanied by an Indonesian wrapper. The tobacco is cured prior to rolling and available flavors include (!) Amaretto, black cherry, buttered rum, coconut, Cuban coffee, mango, mint chocolate, Passion Fruit, rum and vanilla. More are on the way!

HANDMADE CIGARS: BRAND LISTINGS

XQUISITO
Handmade in Esteli, Nicaragua.

Wrapper: Indonesia   Binder: Nicaragua   Filler: Nicaragua

Shape	Name	Lgth	Ring	Wrapper
Double Corona	Presidente	7½	52	CM
Churchill	Churchill	7	48	CM
Lonsdale	Lonsdale	6¾	43	CM
Robusto	Gran Rothschild	5½	50	CM

Here is a 1996-introduced cigar, with a Sumatran wrapper and a mild-to-medium body. Available in natural wrapper only, Xquisitos are packed in Spanish Cedar, cabinet-style boxes.

Y2K
Handmade in Navarette, Dominican Republic.

Wrapper: Indonesia   Binder: Dom. Rep.   Filler: Dom. Rep.

Shape	Name	Lgth	Ring	Wrapper
Churchill	Double Corona	6¾	48	CM

Get ready for the new millennium! This celebration of the year 2000 dawned in late 1998, just in time to get ready for New Year's 2000 planning. It is medium in body and offered in packs of three, six and in boxes of 25.

ZALDIVA
Handmade in Esteli, Nicaragua.

Wrapper: Cameroon   Binder: Indonesia   Filler: Dom. Rep.

Shape	Name	Lgth	Ring	Wrapper
Torpedo	Torpedo	7	52	CM
Double Corona	Presidente	7½	50	CM
Double Corona	Churchill	7	50	CM
Toro	Corona Gorda	6	50	CM

Robusto	Robusto	5	50	CM
Churchill	Corona	7	46	CM
Grand Corona	Petite Corona	6	46	CM
Lonsdale	Palma	7	42	CM
Long Panatela	Lanceros	7½	38	CM
Slim Panatela	Panatela	6½	32	CM
Cigarillo	Pencil	6	28	CM

This is a mild cigar, introduced in 1996. The Corona and Pencil sizes are also available in flavored versions including Amaretto, anise, cognac, chocolate, rum and vanilla.

ZAMORA
Handmade in Santo Domingo, Dominican Republic.

Wrapper: Indonesia   *Binder: Dom. Rep.*   *Filler: Dom. Rep.*

Shape	Name	Lgth	Ring	Wrapper
	Gold Label:			
Churchill	Churchill	7	48	CM
Robusto	Robusto	5½	52	CM
	Red Label:			
Robusto	Robusto	5½	52	CM

This brand debuted in 1998 and both sub-brands are medium in body, although the Churchill size is fairly mild. It is presented in cellophane sleeves in all-cedar boxes or bundles of 25.

ZARATE
Handmade in Tampa, Florida, USA.

Wrapper: Ecuador   *Binder: Ecuador*   *Filler: Dom. Rep.*

Shape	Name	Lgth	Ring	Wrapper
Robusto	Rothschild	5	50	CC

HANDMADE CIGARS: BRAND LISTINGS

Churchill	Imperiales	7¾	47	CC
Churchill	Reynas	7½	46	CC
Corona	Petit Corona	5½	42	CC
Giant	Presidente	8	48	CC
Churchill	Churchill	7	46	CC
Long Corona	Nacionales	6¼	43	CC

From the Rodriguez & Menendez factory comes this medium-bodied brand, introduced in 1997. You can enjoy it in boxes of 25.

ZELO DE CUBA
Handmade in Esteli, Nicaragua.

Wrapper: Nicaragua　　　　*Binder: Nicaragua*　　　　*Filler: Nicaragua*

Shape	Name	Lgth	Ring	Wrapper
Double Corona	Churchill	7	50	CM
Toro	Toro	6	50	CM
Robusto	Robusto	5	50	CM
Corona	Corona	5½	42	CM
Lonsdale	Lonsdale	6½	44	CM
Pyramid	Piramid	6	52	CM

Originally introduced in 1997, but now made in Nicaragua in 1998, this is a full-bodied blend of all-Nicaraguan leaves offered in boxes of 25!

ZEPPELIN
Handmade in Santiago, Dominican Republic.

Wrapper: Indonesia　　　　*Binder: Dom. Rep.*　　　　*Filler: Dom. Rep.*

Shape	Name	Lgth	Ring	Wrapper
Giant	Gigante	8½	60	CM
Double Corona	Gordo	7	60	CM

Double Corona	Gran Chuchill	7½	54	CM
Robusto	Gran Robusto	5	54	CM
Toro	Gran Toro	6	54	CM
Toro	Mambo	6	60	CM

Introduced in 1997, this is a mild-to-medium-bodied, not quite as light as the airships that the brand salutes. It is offered in boxes of 20.

ZINO
Handmade in Santa Rosa de Copan, Honduras.

Wrapper: Ecuador *Binder: Honduras* *Filler: Honduras*

Shape	Name		Lgth	Ring	Wrapper
Cigarillo	Princesse		4¼	25	CC
Panatela	Diamonds		5⅝	38	CC
Lonsdale	Tradition		6¼	44	CC
Double Corona	Veritas		7	49	CC
Panatela	Tubos No. 1	*(tubed)*	6¾	35	CC
	Connoisseur Series:				
Double Corona	Connoisseur 100		7½	52	CC
Toro	Connoisseur 200		6½	48	CC
Robusto	Connoisseur 300		5¾	48	CC
	Mouton-Cadet Series:				
Lonsdale	Mouton-Cadet No. 1		6¼	44	CC
Panatela	Mouton-Cadet No. 2		6	35	CC
Panatela	Mouton-Cadet No. 3		5¾	38	CC
Slim Panatela	Mouton-Cadet No. 4		5⅛	30	CC
Petit Corona	Mouton-Cadet No. 5		5	42	CC
Robusto	Mouton-Cadet No. 6		5	50	CC

HANDMADE CIGARS: BRAND LISTINGS

The subtlety of Davidoff combined with the finest Honduran tobaccos and a Connecticut-seed wrapper is expressed in the Zino line. The Mouton-Cadet series was specially selected for Baronne Philippine de Rothschild, offering a rich aroma and a mild taste.

ZIQ
Handmade in San Andres Tuxtula, Mexico.

Wrapper: Mexico   Binder: Mexico   Filler: Mexico

Shape	Name	Lgth	Ring	Wrapper
Perfecto	Perfecto	7	52	Ma
Double Corona	Toro Extra	7¼	50	Ma
Toro	Robusto	6	48	Ma
Lonsdale	Twisted Head	6¼	42	Ma
Churchill	Grand Corona	7	46	Ma
Torpedo	Torpedo	6	52	Ma
Lonsdale	Lonsdale	6½	42	Ma
Pyramid	Pyramid	6	48	Ma
Slim Panatela	Short Panatela	5¼	33	Ma
Robusto	Toro	5	50	Ma

Meaning "tobacco" in the ancient Mayan language, this brand was created in 1989 and debuted in the U.S. in 1995. This is a full-bodied, spicy cigar, offered in boxes of 25, or in packages of 10, 5, 3 or 1 cigar in specific sizes.

4.
MACHINE-MADE CIGARS

This section provides the details on 120 brands of mass-market cigars, generally made by machine for distribution to the widest possible audience in drug stores, supermarkets and, of course, tobacco stores.

Each brand listing includes notes on country of manufacture, shapes, names, lengths, ring gauges and wrapper color *as supplied by the manufacturers and/or distributors of these brands.* Ring gauges for some brands of cigarillos were not available.

Please note that while a cigar may be manufactured in one country, it may contain tobaccos from many nations. All brands utilize short-filler tobaccos unless otherwise noted.

For ease of reference, those brands with at least *one* all-tobacco shape in their line have been grouped together at the front of this section and the remaining brands – those using homogenized (sheet) leaf – follow in alphabetical order in the next grouping.

Although manufacturers have recognized more than 70 shades of wrapper color, six major color classifications are used here. Their abbreviations include:

- ▸ DC = Double Claro: green, also known as "AMS."
- ▸ Cl = Claro: a very light tan color.
- ▸ CC = Colorado Claro: a medium brown common to many cigars on this list.

MACHINE-MADE CIGARS: BRAND LISTINGS

- ▸ Co = Colorado: reddish-brown.
- ▸ CM = Colorado Maduro: dark brown.
- ▸ Ma = Maduro: very dark brown or black (also known as "double Maduro" or "Oscuro.")

Many manufacturers call their wrapper colors "Natural" or "English Market Selection." These colors cover a wide range of browns and we have generally grouped them in the "CC" range. Darker wrappers such as those from the Cameroons show up most often in the "CM" category.

Shape designations are based on our shape chart in section 1.03. Careful readers will note the freedom with which manufacturers attach names of shapes to cigars which do not resemble that shape at all! For easier comparison, all lengths were rounded to the shortest eighth of an inch, although some manufacturers list sizes in 16ths or even 32nds of an inch.

Readers who would like to see their favorite brand listed in the 2000 edition can call or write the compilers as noted after the Table of Contents.

BRANDS WITH ALL-TOBACCO SHAPES

BALMORAL
Machine-made in Duizel, the Netherlands.

Shape	Name	Lgth	Ring	Wrapper
Cigarillo	Shetlands	3⅝	24	CM
Small Panatela	Midlands	4	30	CM
Slim Panatela	Overland	5¼	32	CM

MACHINE-MADE CIGARS: BRAND LISTINGS

This brand was introduced in 1996, offering an all-tobacco cigar with mild-to-medium body and outstanding quality. All of these cigars feature gorgeous Sumatran wrappers, with Java binders and filler blends chosen from premium Brazilian, Javan and Sumatran leaves. The results are outstanding, as is the presentation: an all-cedar box of 10 or 25 cigars or a carton of 10s for the road.

BANCES
Machine-made in Tampa, Florida, USA.

Shape	Name	Lgth	Ring	Wrapper
Robusto	Crowns	5¾	50	Ma
Small Panatela	Demi-Tasse	4	35	CC-Ma
Long Corona	Palmas	6	42	CC-Ma

This respected brand is also a well-known handmade cigar. The machine-made version offers a Sumatra (natural) or Connecticut (maduro) wrapper, Connecticut binder and a blend of tobaccos from three nations in the filler. Only the Crowns shape uses a homogenized binder. You can find Bances in boxes of 25, except for the Demi-Tasse, offered in 50s.

CANDLELIGHT
Machine-made in Dingelstadt, Germany.

Shape	Name	Lgth	Ring	Wrapper
Cigarillo	Mini Sumatra	2⅞	20	CC
Cigarillo	Mini Brazil	2⅞	20	Ma
Small Panatela	Senorita Sumatra	3¾	30	CC
Small Panatela	Senorita Brazil	3¾	30	Ma
Cigarillo	Panatela Sumatra	5¾	20	CC
Cigarillo	Panatela Brazil	5¾	20	Ma
Small Panatela	Corona Slim Sumatra	4	30	CC
Small Panatela	Corona Slim Brazil	4	30	Ma
Short Panatela	Block Corona Sumatra	4¾	38	CC
Short Panatela	Block Corona Brazil	4¾	38	Ma

MACHINE-MADE CIGARS: BRAND LISTINGS

Petit Corona	Aviso		4	43	CC
Cigarillo	Tip	*(tipped)*	4⅛	25	CC

These small cigars are all-tobacco with a mild taste. The two types are puros; all of the tobacco in the Sumatra-named shapes is from Sumatra, likewise with the Brazilian shapes. Candlelights are offered in tins of 10, or boxes of 25 or 50.

CORPS DIPLOMATIQUE
Machine-made in Leuven, Belgium.

Shape	Name	Lgth	Ring	Wrapper
Small Panatela	Panatela	4⅛	33	CC
Corona	After Dinner	5¼	42	CC
Small Panatela	Gouveneur	4½	33	CC
Slim Panatela	International	5¼	34	CC
Corona	Conference	5¼	42	CC

This all-tobacco range of dry-cured cigars offers a mild taste, featuring an Indonesian (Sumatra) wrapper, Java binder and Brazilian and Indonesian filler.

CUBAN CLUB CLASSICS
BY HABANA GOLD
Machine-made in Ireland.

Shape	Name	Lgth	Ring	Wrapper
Corona	Small Corona	5	40	CC-CM
Perfecto	Diablo	3¾	38	CC-CM
Cigarillo	Small Panatela	4¼	26	CC-CM

Introduced in 1998, this is an all-tobacco line that features your choice of an Ecuadorian or Indonesian wrapper and Nicaraguan binder and short filler. The result is a mild smoke, offered in packs of five, eight (Small Panatela only) and ten.

MACHINE-MADE CIGARS: BRAND LISTINGS

DON ANTONIO
Machine-made in Dingelstadt, Germany.

Shape	Name	Lgth	Ring	Wrapper
Slim Panatela	El Gusto Sumatra	6⅛	33	CC
Slim Panatela	El Gusto Brazil	6⅛	33	Ma
Panatela	La Verdad Sumatra	5½	35	CC
Panatela	La Verdad Brazil	5½	35	Ma

This small cigar range was introduced in 1992 and offers either Brazilian or Sumatran wrappers on each shape for a mild-to-medium (Sumatra) or medium-to-full-bodied (Brazil) taste. The binder on all shapes is Indonesian, with filler tobacco from Brazil, the Dominican Republic, Germany, Honduras and Indonesia.

EL CAUTO
Machine-made in Yoe, Pennsylvania, USA.

Shape	Name	Lgth	Ring	Wrapper
Long Corona	Blunt	6	43	CC
Long Corona	Corona Grande	6⅜	44	CC
Grand Corona	Fumas	6⅜	46	CC

This brand includes one all-tobacco style (Corona Grande) and three others which use a sheet binder. El Cautos are offered in either boxes of 50 or bundles of 25.

EL GOZO
Machine-made in Las Palmas, the Canary Islands of Spain.

Shape	Name	Lgth	Ring	Wrapper
Long Corona	Gran Cedro	6	43	CC
Toro	Double Corona	6¼	49	CC
Robusto	Robusto	5¼	50	CC

MACHINE-MADE CIGARS: BRAND LISTINGS

Corona	Corona	5¼	42	CC
Small Panatela	Petit Torpedo	4⅛	33	CC
Cigarillo	Miniatures	3¾	24	CC
Cigarillo	Aromatics	3½	23	CC

This Canary Islands line offers all-tobacco shapes with full body and short filler from the Dominican Republic, Honduras, Indonesia and Germany, offered in boxes of 25. The very small sizes: Petit Torpedo, Miniatures and Aromatics have sheet binders and are offered in boxes of 20, except for the Aromatics, offered in 10s.

EL VERSO
Machine-made in Frankfort, Indiana, USA.

Shape	Name	Lgth	Ring	Wrapper
Grand Corona	Corona Extra	5¾	47	CM
Corona Extra	Bouquet Dark	4¾	45	CM
Panatela	Commodore	6	36	CM
Corona Extra	Bouquet Light Leaf	4¾	45	CI
Cigarillo	Mellow	4¼	29	CI-CM

The sunny graphics on the El Verso box herald a medium-bodied cigar with a Connecticut wrapper, either a Connecticut or sheet wrapper depending on the model, and American and Dominican filler.

EMANELO
Machine-made in Frankfort, Indiana, USA.

Shape	Name	Lgth	Ring	Wrapper
Grand Corona	Gourmet	5¾	47	CC
Long Corona	Executive	6	42	CC
Corona Extra	Premium	5⅛	45	CC
Corona Extra	Classic	4⅝	45	CC

MACHINE-MADE CIGARS: BRAND LISTINGS

Here's the right cigar for the discerning smoker! Introduced in 1997, this is a mild-to-medium-bodied, all-tobacco blend of aged Connecticut broadleaf wrapper, a broadleaf binder and Connecticut and Pennsylvania filler. A very old brand name, Emanelo was much admired by midwestern smokers in the middle of this century.

EVERMORE
Machine-made in Frankfort, Indiana, USA.

Shape	Name	Lgth	Ring	Wrapper
Corona Extra	Original	4⅝	45	Cl-CC-CM
Long Corona	Palma	6	42	Cl-CM
Grand Corona	Corona Grande	5¾	47	Cl-CM

This is an all-tobacco cigar, with a Connecticut leaf wrapper, Connecticut binder and a blend of American and Dominican tobaccos in the filler.

FARNAM DRIVE
Machine-made in Frankfort, Indiana, USA.

Shape	Name	Lgth	Ring	Wrapper
Corona Extra	Original	5⅛	45	CC-CC-Ma

This is an all-tobacco cigar that offers a medium-bodied taste and uses Connecticut leaves for the wrapper and binder and a blend of American and Dominican tobaccos in the filler.

GEORGE BURNS VINTAGE COLLECTION
BY EL PRODUCTO
Machine-made in La Romana, Dominican Republic.

Shape	Name	Lgth	Ring	Wrapper
Double Corona	Churchill	7	50	CC
Grand Corona	Double Corona	6½	46	CC
Long Corona	Lonsdale	6	42	CC

MACHINE-MADE CIGARS: BRAND LISTINGS

| Grand Corona | Monarch | (tubed) | 6½ | 46 | CC |
| Double Corona | Regal | (tubed) | 7 | 50 | CC |

Here is a 1997-introduced tribute to the late George Burns (1896-1996), remembered as a great comedian and as a devoted cigar smoker. These are mild-bodied, all-tobacco cigars, with an Indonesian wrapper, Pennsylvania-grown binder and long and medium filler leaves from the Dominican Republic and Jamaica.

HAVANA BLEND
Machine-made in San Antonio, Texas, USA.

Shape	Name	Lgth	Ring	Wrapper
Short Panatela	Petit Corona	4¾	38	Ma
Cigarillo	Palma Fina	6½	29	Ma
Corona	Coronado	5	43	Ma
Corona	Delicado	5¾	43	Ma
Robusto	Rothschild	5	50	Ma
Lonsdale	Doubloon	6½	42	Ma
Churchill	Churchill	7	47	Ma

This is a medium-bodied blend of 100% tobacco, which includes Cuban tobacco from the 1959 crop, as well as Dominican tobacco, in the filler. The wrapper and binder are both Connecticut Broadleaf and the brand is offered in boxes of either 25 or 50 cigars.

J. CORTES
Machine-made in Moene, Belgium.

Shape	Name	Lgth	Ring	Wrapper
Short Panatela	Casadores	5	38	CC
Cigarillo	Classic	4¼	25	CC
Small Panatela	Club	4½	30	CC
Cigarillo	Grand Luxe	4	25	CC

Cigarillo	Havane		3¾	23	CC
Short Panatela	High Class	*(tubed)*	5	38	CC
Small Panatela	Milord		4¼	30	CC
Cigarillo	Mini		3⅓	19	CC
Short Panatela	Presidency		4⅛	38	CC
Slim Panatela	Slim Corona		5⅛	34	CC
Slim Panatela	Royal Class	*(tubed)*	5¼	30	CC

This Belgian company started making cigars in 1926 and is now the biggest pure-tobacco, dry-cured manufacturer in the world. Each cigar has a Sumatran Deli wrapper, Javan Besuki binder and a blend of Sumatran, Javan and Bahian tobaccos in the filler for a light-spicy but smooth flavor. An excellent choice for morning or afternoon smoking, J. Cortes cigars are available in 12 sizes in elegant "blue" packs, tins and tubes.

JOHN HAY
Machine-made in York, Pennsylvania, USA.

Shape	Name	Lgth	Ring	Wrapper
Robusto	Cadet	5	49	CM
Grand Corona	Diplomat	6	47	CM-Ma
Grand Corona	Pennsylvania Vanilla	6	47	CM

This brand goes back to 1882, when W.W. Stewart actually obtained permission from prominent American statesman John Hay – later Secretary of State – to issue a brand in his honor. The machine-made version is all tobacco, with a Lancaster County, Pennsylvania Broadleaf wrapper, Pennsylvania binder and a medium-filler blend from Connecticut, Maryland and Pennsylvania. This all-American cigar is offered in boxes of 50; be sure to check out the handmade, Dominican-produced version as well. Light one up on the Fourth of July!

JOSE MELENDI
Machine-made in San Antonio, Texas, USA.

Lonsdales, Coronas Extra and Grand Coronas

Here are examples of three larger-sized cigars: the Lonsdale (named for the Earl of Lonsdale), the Corona Extra and the Grand Corona. The dimensions of these shapes include:

- Lonsdale   6½-7¼ inches long; 40-44 ring.
- Giant Corona   7½ inches and more; 42-45 ring.
- Corona Extra   4½-5½ inches long; 45-47 ring.
- Grand Corona   5⅝-6⅝ inches long; 45-47 ring.

Pictured opposite, from left to right, are:

- **DON RENE** *Toro*   *(shape)*
  (United States)   5½ x 46   Corona Extra

- **CROWN ACHIEVEMENT** *Grand Corona*
  (Honduras)   6 x 46   Grand Corona

- **FUNDADORES JAMAICA** *Lonsdale*
  (Jamaica)   6½ x 42   Lonsdale

- **MONTAGUE** *No. 2*
  (Indonesia)   6⅝ x 45   Grand Corona

- **HUGO CASSAR DIAMOND DOMINICAN MYSTIQUE** *Lonsdale*
  (Dominican Republic)   7 x 44   Lonsdale

- **ROYAL JAMAICA** *Tube No. 1*
  (Jamaica)   7 x 45   Grand Corona

MACHINE-MADE CIGARS: BRAND LISTINGS

Shape	Name	Lgth	Ring	Wrapper
Short Panatela	Vega I	5⅜	37	CM
Corona	Vega II	5½	43	CM
Long Corona	Vega III	6	42	CM
Slim Panatela	Vega IV	6½	34	CM
Grand Corona	Vega V	6½	45	CM
Lonsdale	Vega VII	7	45	CM
Slim Panatela	Wild Maduro	6⅞	34	Ma
Robusto	Rothschild Maduro	5	50	Ma

This is a medium-to-full bodied, long-filler blend of 100% tobacco, with a
Cameroon wrapper on the Vega series and Connecticut Broadleaf wrappers on
the maduro styles. The binder is also Connecticut leaf, with the filler composed
of tobaccos from Brazil and the Dominican Republic.

LA EMINENCIA
Machine-made in Tampa, Florida, USA.

Shape	Name	Lgth	Ring	Wrapper
Lonsdale	Churchill Corona	6½	45	CC-Ma
Corona	Brevas	5½	44	CC-Ma
Long Corona	Plazas	6¼	42	CC-Ma
Panatela	Panetelas	6¼	38	CC-Ma

This is a mild-to-medium bodied brand of 100% tobacco, available in two
wrapper shades. The wrappers are Ecuadorian-grown, with a Honduran binder
and long filler from the Dominican Republic, Honduras and Nicaragua. It is
offered is all-cedar boxes of 25.

LA PAZ
Machine-made in Valkenswaard, the Netherlands.

MACHINE-MADE CIGARS: BRAND LISTINGS

Shape	Name		Lgth	Ring	Wrapper
Long Corona	Gran Corona	(tubed)	6	42	CC
Panatela	Especiale		6¼	35	CC
Petit Corona	Corona		5	41	CC
Slim Panatela	Wilde Havana		4⅞	33	CC
Cigarillo	Wilde Cigarillos		4⅛	24	CC

The well-known La Paz brand, made of 100% tobacco, dates back to 1814. It is widely appreciated for the "Wilde" series which has an uncut end that provides a rich aroma from the first moment. Both of the Wilde shapes are full-bodied, while the other shapes offer a mild taste. The wrappers and binders are all Besuki leaf from Indonesia, with filler blends of Brazilian and Indonesian tobacco.

LANCER
Machine-made in San Antonio, Texas, USA.

Shape	Name	Lgth	Ring	Wrapper
Small Panatela	Havana Slims	6¼	29	CM

Here is a cigar made of 100% tobacco, including filler tobacco from the 1958 and 1959 Cuban crops. The wrapper and binder are both genuine Connecticut leaf; Lancers are offered in eight-cigar pocket packs.

LUCKY LADY
Machine-made in Red Lion, Pennsylvania, USA.

Shape	Name		Lgth	Ring	Wrapper
Lonsdale	Corona	(tubed)	6½	43	CM

This new, all-tobacco brand for 1997 offers leaves from the Dominican Republic blended for an enjoyable mild smoke. Bonus: the wrapper and filler are specially imbued with a rich cherry flavor! Available in single units only.

MUNIEMAKER
Machine-made in McSherrystown, Pennsylvania, USA.

MACHINE-MADE CIGARS: BRAND LISTINGS

Shape	Name	Lgth	Ring	Wrapper
Corona Extra	Regular	4½	47	CI-CC-CM
Robusto	Straight	5⅛	48	CC
Grand Corona	Long	6	46	CC
Robusto	Breva 100's	5⅛	48	CC-Ma
Slim Panatela	Panatela 100's	6	33	CC-Ma
Grand Corona	Palma 100's	6	46	CC-Ma
Perfecto	Perfecto 100's	5¼	52	CC-Ma
Corona Extra	Cueto	4⅞	45	CI-CC
Corona Extra	Bouquet Special (tubed)	5⅛	46	CC-Ma
Corona Extra	Judges Cave	4½	47	CI-CC-Ma

F.D. Grave began this line in 1884 with the goal of making "the best possible cigars at prices cigar lovers could afford." Now, F.D. Grave & Sons continues this tradition of all-tobacco, medium-to-full-bodied cigars, featuring Connecticut Broadleaf wrappers and binders around a core of U.S. tobaccos in the filler. The Perfecto 100s and Bouquet Specials are boxed in 25s, while all of the other shapes are available in boxes of 50. Handy packs of four and five cigars each are also available of most sizes.

OLD HERMITAGE
Machine-made in Hartford, Connecticut, USA.

Shape	Name	Lgth	Ring	Wrapper
Corona Extra	Golden Perfecto	5½	45	CI

This brand was created in 1908 and is 100% tobacco. The wrapper and binder are Connecticut broadleaf, with the filler incorporating Brazilian, Dominican and U.S. tobaccos. The shape has a perfecto-style tip and is offered in boxes of 50.

PEDRO IGLESIAS
Machine-made in Tampa, Florida, USA.

MACHINE-MADE CIGARS: BRAND LISTINGS

Shape	Name	Lgth	Ring	Wrapper
Corona Extra	Crowns	5	45	CC-Ma
Long Corona	Regents	6	44	CC-Ma
Lonsdale	Lonsdales	6½	44	CC

This is an all-tobacco brand, featuring a Sumatra wrapper, Connecticut Broadleaf binder and a short-filler blend of tobaccos from three nations. All three shapes are offered in boxes of 50.

PHILLIPS & KING CIGARRENS
Machine-made in Dingelstadt, Germany.

Shape	Name	Lgth	Ring	Wrapper
Small Panatela	No. 1000	4¾	32	CC
Petit Corona	No. 2000	5	40	CC
Corona Extra	No. 3000	4¾	45	CC
Panatela	No. 4000	5½	38	CC

New in the U.S. for 1997, this is a mild, 100% tobacco blend in four popular shapes, each available with a Sumatra-grown wrapper. Look for Cigarrens in boxes of 20, or in easy-to-carry packs of five or 10.

ROSEDALE
Machine-made in Hartford, Connecticut, USA.

Shape	Name	Lgth	Ring	Wrapper
Perfecto	Perfecto	4⅞	48	CM
Corona Extra	Londres	5	46	CM

This brand, made continuously since the 1920s, is a part of the Topper cigar group, made of 100% tobacco. The genuine Connecticut Broadleaf wrapper surrounds a Connecticut binder and filler tobaccos from Brazil, the Dominican Republic and the U.S. Each shape is offered is packs of 5 or boxes of 50.

MACHINE-MADE CIGARS: BRAND LISTINGS

ROYAL HAWAIIAN
Machine-made in Makawao, Hawaii, USA.

Shape	Name		Lgth	Ring	Wrapper
Lonsdale	Long Corona	*(tubed)*	6½	43	CM

This is an all-tobacco brand introduced in 1997 and offering a mild taste in a remarkable cigar which features the flavor of genuine Kona Coffee from Hawaii. The brand features a all-Dominican tobacco and is offered in three-packs.

RUY LOPEZ
Machine-made in Tampa, Florida, USA.

Shape	Name	Lgth	Ring	Wrapper
Panatela	Panetelas	6	38	CC
Grand Corona	Corona Grande	5¾	45	CC
Corona	Vanilla Supreme	6	42	CC

Here is a mild brand, made with 100% tobacco and featuring an Ecuadorian-grown wrapper, Honduran binder and Dominican, Honduran and Nicaraguan tobacco in the filler. Available in bundles of 25, the line also features a flavored shape, the Vanilla Supreme.

SCHIMMELPENNICK V.S.O.P.
Machine-made in Wageningen, the Netherlands.

Shape	Name		Lgth	Ring	Wrapper
Petit Corona	Corona		4¼	41	CM
Corona	Grand Corona		5	41	CM
Small Panatela	Senorita		4	31	CM
Petit Corona	Calendula	*(tubed)*	4⅜	40	CM
Lonsdale	Double Corona		6½	43	CM

Created in 1995, here is a fuller-sized Schimmelpennick cigar for those who enjoy the mild taste of this famous brand, founded in 1924. Named for a famous

MACHINE-MADE CIGARS: BRAND LISTINGS

governor of Holland, Rutger Jan Schimmelpennick (1781-1825), these new sizes feature Sumatra sandleaf wrappers and a Java binder, combined with filler tobaccos from Brazil (Bahia type) and Indonesia (Bezuki). In its first year of distribution, it was named the "Cigar of the Year" in Holland and is offered in boxes of 25.

SWISHER SWEETS
Machine-made in Jacksonville, Florida, USA.

Shape	Name		Lgth	Ring	Wrapper
Petit Corona	Blunt		5	42	CC
Corona	Kings		5½	42	CC
Petit Corona	Perfecto		5	41	CC
Panatela	Slims		5⅜	36	CC
Cigarillo	Coronella		5	27½	CC
Small Panatela	Outlaw		4¾	32	CC
Cigarillo	Cigarillo		4⅜	28½	CC
Cigarillo	Tip Cigarillo	*(tipped)*	4⅞	28	CC
Cigarillo	Wood Tip Cigarillo	*(tipped)*	4⅞	29	CC

Popular? Swisher Sweets are enjoyed everywhere, offering a mild, sweet taste with a manufactured wrapper and binder and a blend of filler tobaccos from four nations. The Outlaw is 100% tobacco and features a Honduran leaf wrapper; the King shape also features a natural leaf wrapper. You can find this brand in thousands of locations, in familiar red five-packs and in boxes of 50.

TOPPER
Machine-made in McSherrystown, Pennsylvania, USA.

Shape	Name	Lgth	Ring	Wrapper
Long Corona	Grande Corona	6	47	CC-Ma
Corona Extra	Breva	5½	46	CC-CM
Perfecto	Old Fashioned	4⅞	44	CC-Ma

MACHINE-MADE CIGARS: BRAND LISTINGS

Corona	Ebony	5½	47	Ma

Since 1896, Topper cigars gave offered a mild, flavorful taste with excellent value. Each of these models is made up of 100% tobacco and is offered in handy packs of 4-5 cigars, or in colorful boxes of 50. All feature genuine USA/Connecticut wrappers and binders and short filler from the Dominican Republic and the United States.

TOPSTONE
Machine-made in Tampa, Florida, USA.

Shape	Name	Lgth	Ring	Wrapper
	Connecticut Broadleaf series:			
Long Corona	Supreme	6	42	CC
Corona Extra	Extra Oscuro	5½	46	Ma
Grand Corona	Grande	5¾	46	CC-Ma
Panatela	Panatela	6	39	CC-Ma
Corona Extra	Bouquet	5½	46	CC-Ma
Corona Extra	Oscuro	5½	46	Ma
Churchill	Directors	7¾	46	CC-Ma

These are well-known, 100% tobacco cigars made in Tampa, Florida and featuring dark-cured Connecticut Broadleaf wrapper and binder and a three-nation short filler blend. The Directors and Supremes are offered in boxes of 25, while the other shapes are available in four-packs or five-packs and in boxes of 50.

TRAVIS CLUB
Machine-made in San Antonio, Texas, USA.

Shape	Name	Lgth	Ring	Wrapper
Double Corona	Churchill	7	50	CC
Grand Corona	Corona Extra	6¼	46	CC
Toro	Toro	6	50	CC

MACHINE-MADE CIGARS: BRAND LISTINGS

Long Corona	Palma	6	43	CC
Perfecto	Perfecto	5¼	52	CC
Robusto	Robusto	5	50	CC

Here is a beautiful cigar which features all-tobacco, all-long-filler construction and a mild-bodied taste. The elegant wrappers are genuine Connecticut Shade, the binders are also Connecticut-grown and the filler is composed of leaves from the Dominican Republic and Brazil. Travis Club Premium cigars are presented in individual cellophane sleeves inside elegant, varnished wooden cabinets.

VASCO DA GAMA
Machine-made in Bunde, Germany.

Shape	Name	Lgth	Ring	Wrapper
Long Corona	Vasco de Gama	6	42	CC

Named for the famed Portugese explorer who was the first to circle the Cape of Good Hope in 1497. The cigar dates from 1816 (!) and is a mild, 100% tobacco blend of Sumatra-seed Indonesian wrappers, with a German binder and Brazilian and Indonesian filler.

WILLEM II
Machine-made in Valkenswaard, the Netherlands.

Shape	Name		Lgth	Ring	Wrapper
Corona	Optimum	(tubed)	5	41	CC

This is a medium-bodied, all-tobacco cigar which dates back to 1916. It features an Indonesian wrapper and binder and Indonesian and Brazilian filler.

WUHRMANN
Machine-made in Rheinfelden, Switzerland.

Shape	Name	Lgth	Ring	Wrapper
Corona	Bahianos	5¼	44	CM
Lonsdale	Big Ben	7	44	CC

MACHINE-MADE CIGARS: BRAND LISTINGS

Corona	El Prado	5¼	44	CC
Petit Corona	Habana Feu	4	44	CC
Corona Extra	Hand Made Sumatra	5	46	CC
Long Corona	Havana Seed	6	44	CC
Robusto	Impulso	5½	52	CC
Short Panatela	La Coronada	4½	36	CC
Petit Corona	Media Corona	4	44	CC
Robusto	Okay Corona (tubed)	5	52	CC
Petit Corona	Rio Santo	4	44	CM
Robusto	San Gonzalo	5	52	CM
Cigarillo	Wuhrillos	4	22	CC

A European favorite since its introduction in 1876, Wuhrmann was introduced to the U.S. market in 1997. These machine-made, mild-to-medium-bodied, all-tobacco cigars feature Brazilian, Sumatra and USA/Connecticut wrappers around Java binders and filler tobaccos from Brazil, the Dominican Republic and Indonesia. Each size is available in boxes of 20, 25, 30 or 50, depending on size.

ZINO
Machine-made in the Netherlands and Switzerland.

Shape	Name	Lgth	Ring	Wrapper
	Made in the Netherlands:			
Cigarillo	Cigarillos Brasil	3½	20	CM
Cigarillo	Panatellas Brasil	5½	22	CM
Cigarillo	Cigarillos Sumatra	3½	20	Co
Cigarillo	Panatellas Sumatra	5½	22	Co
	Made in Switzerland:			
Corona Extra	Grand Classic Brasil	5½	46	CM

Slim Panatela	Relax Brasil	5¾	30	CM
Petit Corona	Classic Brasil	4¾	41	CM
Corona Extra	Grand Classic Sumatra	5½	46	Co
Slim Panatela	Relax Sumatra	5¾	30	Co
Petit Corona	Classic Sumatra	4¾	41	Co

Here are beautifully made, mild cigars which feature Brazilian or Sumatran wrappers, Java binders and Brazilian and Indonesian filler tobaccos, offering outstanding quality and value in all-tobacco cigarillos and small cigars.

BRANDS USING HOMOGENIZED TOBACCO LEAF

ANTONIO Y CLEOPATRA
Machine-made in Cayey, Puerto Rico.

Shape	Name	Lgth	Ring	Wrapper
Cigarillo	Grenadier Whiffs	3⅝	23⅔	CM
Corona	Grenadier Tubos	5⅝	42½	CM
Cigarillo	Grenadier Minis	4½	28	DC-CM
Corona	Grenadier Palma Maduro	5⅝	42½	Ma
Slim Panatela	Grenadiers	6¼	33½	DC-CC-CM
Panatela	Grenadier Panatela	5⅜	35½	DC-CC-CM
Corona	Grenadier Coronas	5⅝	42½	DC-CM
Toro	Grenadier Churchills	5¾	50	CM-Ma
Small Panatela	Grenadier Miniatures	4⅝	31	CC
Corona	Grenadier Presidentes	5⅝	42½	CC

This highly popular brand dates back to 1888. Today, it offers a fairly mild taste with Connecticut Broadleaf (for maduro), Connecticut Shade (some shapes) and Javan (most shapes) wrappers, sheet binders and Cuban-seed filler tobaccos.

MACHINE-MADE CIGARS: BRAND LISTINGS

ARANGO SPORTSMAN
Machine-made in Tampa, Florida, USA.

Shape	Name		Lgth	Ring	Wrapper
Slim Panatela	No. 100		5¾	34	CC-Ma
Lonsdale	No. 200		6¼	42	CC-Ma
Churchill	No. 300		7	46	CC-Ma
Robusto	No. 350		5¾	48	CC-Ma
Churchill	No. 400		7½	48	CC-Ma
Lonsdale	Tubes	*(tubed)*	6½	42	CC-Ma
Cigarillo	Tens		4½	28	CC

Popular since its introduction in 1984, this is a very mild and aromatic cigar, with a touch of vanilla flavoring. It offers an Ecuadorian wrapper, sheet binder and a filler blend of Dominican and Honduran tobaccos. It is offered in boxes of 25, except for No. 100 and Tens, which come in 50s.

AS YOU LIKE IT
Machine-made in Jacksonville, Florida, USA.

Shape	Name	Lgth	Ring	Wrapper
Long Corona	No. 18	6	41	DC-CC-Ma
Petit Corona	No. 22	4½	41	DC-CC
Long Corona	No. 32	6	43	DC-CC
Slim Panatela	No. 35	5¼	33	CC

This popular brand offers a natural leaf wrapper from Ecuador (candela), Connecticut (natural) or Mexico (maduro), combined with a sheet binder and a four-nation blend of tobaccos for a mild taste, presented in boxes of 50.

B-H
Machine-made in Yoe, Pennsylvania, USA.

MACHINE-MADE CIGARS: BRAND LISTINGS

Shape	Name	Lgth	Ring	Wrapper
Lonsdale	Golden Corona	6½	42	CC
Lonsdale	King	6½	42	CC
Long Corona	76	6	42	CC-Ma
Lonsdale	Boston Blunt	6½	44	CC

This is a mild cigar made by the House of Windsor, with a Pennsylvania wrapper, sheet binder and a blend of filler tobaccos. It is offered in wood boxes of 50.

BEN BEY
Machine-made in Frankfort, Indiana, USA.

Shape	Name		Lgth	Ring	Wrapper
Corona	Crystals	(tubed)	5⅝	44	CC

The Crystals are well named, as they are encased in a glass tube. The blend includes a Connecticut leaf wrapper, sheet binder and U.S. and Dominican tobaccos in the filler. Ben Beys are offered upright in specially-made cedar boxes of 50.

BEN FRANKLIN
Machine-made in Cayey, Puerto Rico

Shape	Name	Lgth	Ring	Wrapper
Petit Corona	Perfectos	4⅞	40	CC
Petit Corona	Blunts	5⅛	40	CC

This venerable brand, named for the Revolutionary Era publisher, statesman and the first Postmaster-General of the United States, features a blend of short-filler tobaccos combined with a homogenized wrapper and binder.

BLACK & MILD
Machine-made in King of Prussia, Pennsylvania, USA.

Shape	Name	Lgth	Ring	Wrapper
Small Panatela	Pipe-Tobacco Cigars *(tipped)*	5	30	Ma

Love the smell of pipe tobacco? Here's a cigar for you, with a pipe-tobacco filler and a homogenized wrapper and binder, offered in convenient five-packs.

BLACK HAWK
Machine-made in Frankfort, Indiana, USA.

Shape	Name	Lgth	Ring	Wrapper
Corona Extra	Chief	5⅛	45	CM

The Chief has a medium body and uses a Connecticut leaf wrapper, a sheet binder and a blend of Dominican and U.S. tobaccos in the filler

BUDD SWEET
Machine-made in Wheeling, West Virginia, USA.

Shape	Name	Lgth	Ring	Wrapper
Petit Corona	Perfecto	5	42½	CC
Slim Panatela	Panatela	5¼	34	CC

The Panatela boasts a genuine Connecticut leaf wrapper, sheet binder and U.S. and Dominican tobaccos in the filler for a medium-bodied taste. The Perfecto has the same binder and filler, but uses a homogenized sheet wrapper.

CARIBBEAN ROUNDS
Machine-made in Yoe, Pennsylvania, USA.

Shape	Name	Lgth	Ring	Wrapper
Lonsdale	Casinos	6½	43	Cl-CC-Ma
Short Panatela	Petites	4⅝	36	CC-Ma
Lonsdale	Rounds	7¼	45	CC-Ma
Long Panatela	Royales	6½	36	CC-Ma

MACHINE-MADE CIGARS: BRAND LISTINGS

Available in fairly large sizes for mass-market cigars, this mild-bodied brand offers a natural leaf wrapper, has a sheet binder and a blend of short-filler tobaccos. Most sizes are offered in wood boxes of 50.

CASINO CLUB
Machine-made in San Antonio, Texas.

Shape	Name	Lgth	Ring	Wrapper
Churchill	High Roller	7	47	CC
Robusto	Big Casino	5⅛	52	CC
Long Corona	Roulette	6	43	CC
Corona Extra	Keno	4¾	47	CC

Here is a new cigar from the famous Finck Cigar Company of San Antonio, offering a mild smoke. It features an Indonesian wrapper, sheet binder and filler tobaccos from Brazil and Honduras. You can enjoy them in wood boxes of 50!

CAZADORES
Machine-made in Jacksonville, Florida, USA.

Shape	Name	Lgth	Ring	Wrapper
Long Corona	No. 16	6	40	CC
Long Corona	No. 26	6	40	Ma
Cigarillo	No. 14	4¼	26	CC
Cigarillo	No. 24	4¼	26	Ma

New for 1997 is this mild-tasting, easy-to-draw cigar, available in two-packs or upright boxes of 25. It features a natural leaf wrapper, sheet binder and a blend of cut filler tobaccos. Talk about convenience . . . it comes with a European-style V-cut already made at the top!

CHARLES DENBY
Machine-made in Frankfort, Indiana, USA.

Coronas Group

Here are examples of the corona-sized cigars, one of the most popular on the market. The corona-related shapes in this group include:

- Petit Corona   4-5 inches long; 40-44 ring.
- Corona   5¼-5¾ inches long; 40-44 ring.
- Long Corona   5⅞-6⅜ inches long; 40-44 ring.

Pictured opposite, from left to right:

- **PUROS MORGAN** *No. 2*   *(shape)*
  (Mexico)   5 x 42   Petit Corona

- **CONDAL** *No. 4*
  (Canary Islands)   5⅓ x 43   Corona

- **ESPINOSA CLASSICO** Corona
  (Honduras)   5½ x 44   Corona

- **TTT TRINIDAD** *Corona*
  (Dominican Republic) 5½ x 44   Corona

- **PEÑAMIL ORO** *No. 6*
  (Canary Islands)   6 x 41   Long Corona

- **RODON** *No. 3*
  (Dominican Republic) 6 x 42   Long Corona

- **EVITA** *Corona*
  (Dominican Republic) 6 x 44   Long Corona

- **CUESTA-REY** *No. 95*
  (Dominican Republic) 6¼ x 42   Long Corona

MACHINE-MADE CIGARS: BRAND LISTINGS

Shape	Name	Lgth	Ring	Wrapper
Corona	Invincible	5½	43	Cl

Connecticut wrapper, sheet binders and a blended filler with American and Dominican tobaccos give this brand a medium body.

CHERRY BLEND
Machine-made in King of Prussia, Pennsylvania, USA.

Shape	Name	Lgth	Ring	Wrapper
Small Panatela	Pipe-Tobacco Cigars (tipped)	5	30	Ma

The sweet smell of cherry is the appeal of this pipe-tobacco-filled cigar. Offered in packs of five, it has a homogenized wrapper and binder and a plastic tip for easy smoking.

CHEVERE SMALL CIGARS
Machine-made in Ireland.

Shape	Name	Lgth	Ring	Wrapper
Short Panatela	Half Corona	3¾	36	CM-Ma
Cigarillo	Little Cigarillos	3¼	25	CM-Ma
Small Panatela	Senoritas	3½	30	CM-Ma
Cigarillo	Wilde Cigarillo	3½	27	CM-Ma
Small Panatela	Wilde Havana	3½	30	CM-Ma

These little cigars medium in body and dry-cured, with a choice of Sumatra wrappers or maduro wrappers from Brazil. They are offered in boxes of 25 (Half Corona only) and 50.

CUESTA-REY
Machine-made in Tampa, Florida, USA.

Shape	Name	Lgth	Ring	Wrapper
Small Panatela	No. 120	5	31	CC-Ma

| Long Corona | Palma Supreme | 6¼ | 42 | CC-Ma |
| Slim Panatela | Caravelle | 6¼ | 34 | CC-Ma |

A famous brand in cigars for decades, the machine-made version of Cuesta-Rey offers a mild-to-medium body. It features a Connecticut wrapper, homogenized binder and a blend of short filler tobaccos. All sizes are available in ten-packs; the Palma Supreme and Caravelle sizes are offered in boxes of 50.

CYRILLA
Machine-made in Tampa, Florida, USA.

Shape	Name	Lgth	Ring	Wrapper
Long Corona	Nationals	6	42	CC-Ma
Churchill	Kings	7	46	CC-Ma
Churchill	Senators	7½	48	CC-Ma
Panatela	Slims	6½	36	CC-Ma

These are mild cigars, offered in bundles of 25 cigars each. They feature either an Ecuadorian (natural) wrapper or a Connecticut Broadleaf in the maduro shade, a sheet binder and filler tobaccos from the Dominican and Honduras.

DECISION MADURO
Machine-made in Tampa, Florida, USA.

Shape	Name	Lgth	Ring	Wrapper
Robusto	No. 250	5½	49	Ma
Grand Corona	No. 350	6¼	45	Ma
Corona	No. 450	5	44	Ma
Short Panatela	No. 550	5⅜	37	Ma

This brand has been around since 1935 and today offers a mild to medium smoke at a great value. The all-maduro series features a Connecticut Broadleaf wrapper, with a sheet binder and filler tobaccos from the Dominican Republic. Each size is available in economical bundles of 20.

MACHINE-MADE CIGARS: BRAND LISTINGS

DEXTER LONDRES
Machine-made in Jacksonville, Florida, USA.

Shape	Name	Lgth	Ring	Wrapper
Corona	Dexter Londres	5¼	42	CC

This is a mild cigar, with a natural leaf wrapper, sheet binder and a four-nation filler blend. Dexters are available in handy five-packs and in boxes of 50.

DIRECTORS
Machine-made in Jacksonville, Florida, USA.

Shape	Name	Lgth	Ring	Wrapper
Cigarillo	Cigarillo	4⅜	27½	CM
Cigarillo	Coronella	5	27½	CM
Long Corona	Corona	6	42	CM
Short Panatela	Panatela	5⅜	36	CM

This range offers a mild taste, with a Wisconsin sun-grown wrapper, sheet binder and a blend of chopped filler tobaccos.

DON CESAR
Machine-made in Tampa, Florida, USA.

Shape	Name	Lgth	Ring	Wrapper
Corona	Palma	5⅝	42	CC

Here is a unique, machine-made cigar made from long-filler tobaccos, rather than the cut filler which is more common. The Sumatran wrapper and sheet binder surrounds filler leaves from the Dominican Republic and Honduras.

DRY SLITZ
Machine-made in Wheeling, West Virginia, USA.

Shape	Name	Lgth	Ring	Wrapper
Slim Panatela	Regular	5½	34	CC

MACHINE-MADE CIGARS: BRAND LISTINGS

This is a mild-bodied cigar with a homogenized wrapper, sheet binder and U.S. and Dominican tobaccos in the filler. The head of the cigar is finished with a small hole so that you can light it up without cutting!

DUTCH MASTERS
Machine-made in McAdoo, Pennsylvania, USA and Cayey, Puerto Rico.

Shape	Name	Lgth	Ring	Wrapper
Cigarillo	Cadet Regular	4¾	27½	CC
Cigarillo	Pipearillo	5⅛	27	CM
Petit Corona	Perfecto	4¾	44	CM
Panatela	Panatela	5½	36	CM
Slim Panatela	Elite	6⅛	29½	CM
Corona Extra	Belvedere	4⅞	46½	CM
Corona	President	5⅝	40½	CM
Corona	Corona Deluxe	5¾	43	CM
Corona	Corona Maduro	5¾	43	Ma
Toro	Corona Grande	5¾	50	CM-Ma
	Masters Collection:			
Cigarillo	Cigarillos	4¾	27½	CC
Corona	Palmas	5⅝	42½	CC
Corona	Palmas Maduro	5⅝	42½	Ma
Short Panatela	Panatelas Deluxe	5⅜	35½	CC

Remember the Dutch Masters television commercials of the 1960s, as the actors retired into the brand's trademark portrait at the end? The commercials are history, but the brand continues to do well, offering a mild smoke in both manufactured and natural wrapper styles. All shapes are made in Puerto Rico, except for the Pipearillo. The Corona Deluxe, Elite, Corona Maduro and Corona Grande shapes all feature natural leaf wrappers; all shapes have homogenized binders and a short-filler blend of Cuban-seed tobaccos.

MACHINE-MADE CIGARS: BRAND LISTINGS

1886
Machine-made in Cayey, Puerto Rico.

Shape	Name	Lgth	Ring	Wrapper
Corona	Queens	5⅝	42	CC

This one-shape brand features a Connecticut wrapper, around a sheet binder and a blend of short-filler tobaccos.

EL MACCO
Machine-made in Frankfort, Indiana, USA.

Shape	Name	Lgth	Ring	Wrapper
Corona Extra	Puritano Dark	4¾	45	CM

This brand presents a medium-bodied taste and has a Connecticut leaf wrapper, a sheet binder and a blend of Dominican and U.S. tobacco in the filler.

EL PRODUCTO
Machine-made in Cayey, Puerto Rico.

Shape	Name		Lgth	Ring	Wrapper
Small Panatela	Little Coronas		4⅝	31	CC
Corona	Blunts		5⅝	40½	CC
Petit Corona	Bouquets		4¾	44	CC
Petit Corona	Panatelas		5½	36	CC
Corona Extra	Puritano Finos		4⅞	46½	CC
Corona	Coronas		5¾	43	CC
Robusto	Favoritas		5	48½	CC
Robusto	Escepcionales		5⅛	52½	CC
Corona	Queens	(tubed)	5⅝	42	CC

Introduced in 1916, this was the smoke of choice (in the Queens size) for decades for the late comedian George Burns (1896-1996) and it continues to have many contemporary admirers. The many shapes are primarily clothed in manufactured wrappers; the Escepcionales and Queens feature a natural wrapper. All shapes use homogenized binders.

EL TRELLES
Machine-made in Jacksonville, Florida, USA.

Shape	Name	Lgth	Ring	Wrapper
Long Corona	Bankers	6	43	CC
Corona Extra	Blunt Extra	5¼	45	CC
Long Corona	Club House	6	41	Ma
Long Corona	Kings	6	41	CC
Pyramid	Tryangles Deluxe	5¼	45	CC

This is a very mild cigar, with a natural leaf wrapper from Connecticut (natural) or Mexico (maduro), sheet binder and a four-nation filler blend, available in natural and maduro shades. El Trelles cigars are offered in convenient five-packs and by the box (of 50).

EMERSON
Machine-made in Wheeling, West Virgina, USA.

Shape	Name	Lgth	Ring	Wrapper
Petit Corona	Diplomat	4¾	42½	Cl

American and Dominican filler tobaccos are at the heart of this one-shape brand. It offers a medium body and has a homogenized wrapper and sheet binder.

FLORIDA QUEEN
Machine-made in Wheeling, West Virginia, USA.

Shape	Name	Lgth	Ring	Wrapper
Petit Corona	Florida Queen	5	42½	CC

Here is a medium-bodied cigar, made up of American and Dominican filler tobaccos, a sheet binder and a genuine Connecticut leaf wrapper.

MACHINE-MADE CIGARS: BRAND LISTINGS

GARCIA GRANDE
Machine-made in Tampa, Florida, USA.

Shape	Name	Lgth	Ring	Wrapper
Corona	Corona	5½	42	CC-Ma
Toro	Laguitos	5⅝	48	CC-Ma
Long Corona	Pitas	6	43	CC-Ma

Introduced in 1996, this cigar has a medium body, a Cuban-seed, Nicaraguan-grown wrapper, sheet binder and filler tobaccos from the Dominican Republic, Honduras and Nicaragua. It is an excellent value, offered in bundles.

GARCIA Y VEGA
Machine-made in Dothan, Alabama, USA
and Santiago, Dominican Republic

Shape	Name		Lgth	Ring	Wrapper
Cigarillo	Cigarillos		4¼	27	DC
Cigarillo	Chicos		4¼	27	CC
Cigarillo	Miniatures		4⅝	29	CC
Cigarillo	Whiffs		3¾	23	CC
Cigarillo	Whiffs Gold		3¾	23	CC
Slim Panatela	Tips	(tipped)	5¼	30	CC
Slim Panatela	Bravuras		5⅜	34	CC
Slim Panatela	Panatella Deluxe		5⅜	34	DC
Petit Corona	Senators		4½	41	DC
Petit Corona	Barons		4¾	41	CC
Petit Corona	Bouquets		4⅝	45	CC
Short Panatela	Delgado Panatela		5⅜	34	CC
Panatela	Elegantes		6⅜	34	DC
Panatela	Gallantes		6⅜	34	CC

MACHINE-MADE CIGARS: BRAND LISTINGS

Corona	Presidente		5¾	41	CC
Corona	Napoleons		5¾	41	DC
Corona	English Coronas	(tubed)	5¼	41	CC
Slim Panatela	Granadas	(tubed)	6⅜	34	DC
Slim Panatela	Romeros	(tubed)	6⅜	34	CC
Long Corona	Gran Coronas	(tubed)	6⅛	41	DC
Long Corona	Gran Premios	(tubed)	6⅛	41	CC
Slim Panatela	Crystals No. 100	(tubed)	6⅜	34	CC
Long Corona	Crystals No. 200	(tubed)	6⅛	41	CC
Long Corona	Maduro Crystals	(tubed)	6⅛	41	Ma
Long Corona	Maduro		6⅛	41	Ma

Since 1882, this brand has been a favorite all across the United States, enjoyed more than 300,000 times daily nationwide. The natural leaf wrapper comes from the Cameroon, Connecticut or Mexico and is combined with a sheet binder and a blend of filler tobaccos for the brand's characteristic mild taste. Please note that the Whiffs size offers two flavors: natural and Cavendish. Garcia y Vega cigars are always fresh thanks to in-the-pack pouches or tubes and are offered in packs of 3, 4 or 5 cigars or in boxes of 30, 40 or 50.

GARGOYLE
Machine-made in Frankfort, Indiana, USA.

Shape	Name	Lgth	Ring	Wrapper
Panatela	Lanza	6	38	CI

The cigar is not as ugly as the brand name might imply! It's actually a medium-bodied smoke with a Connecticut wrapper, sheet binder and a blend of American and Dominican filler.

GOLD & MILD
Machine-made in King of Prussia, Pennsylvania, USA.

MACHINE-MADE CIGARS: BRAND LISTINGS

Shape	Name	Lgth	Ring	Wrapper
Small Panatela	Pipe-Tobacco Cigars (tipped)	5	30	CC

The gentle aroma of pipe & tobacco is the appeal of this brand, which features a plastic tip for easy smoking and a homogenized wrapper and binder. It is offered in convenient five-packs.

GOVERNOR
Machine-made in Tampa, Florida, USA.

Shape	Name	Lgth	Ring	Wrapper
Long Corona	Claro	6	42	DC

Here is a modestly-priced, easy-to-smoke cigar with a natural leaf wrapper, homogenized binder and a three-nation blend of filler tobaccos. It is offered in convenient boxes of 50.

HARVESTER
Machine-made in Cayey, Puerto Rico.

Shape	Name	Lgth	Ring	Wrapper
Petit Corona	Perfecto	5	40½	CC
Corona	Record Breaker	5⅝	40½	CC

This brand features a blend of short-filler tobaccos combined with a homogenized wrapper and binder.

HAUPTMANN'S
Machine-made in Frankfort, Indiana, USA.

Shape	Name	Lgth	Ring	Wrapper
Corona Extra	Perfecto	5⅛	45	CI-CM
Corona	Broadleaf	5¼	43	CM
Corona	Corona	5¼	43	CI
Panatela	Panatela	5¾	38	CI-CM

MACHINE-MADE CIGARS: BRAND LISTINGS

This is a medium-bodied smoke, with a genuine Connecticut leaf wrapper, sheet binder and a blend of Dominican and U.S. tobaccos in the filler.

HAV-A-TAMPA
Machine-made in Tampa, Florida, USA.

Shape	Name		Lgth	Ring	Wrapper
Corona	Blunt		5	43	CC
Small Panatela	Cheroot		4¾	31	CC
Cigarillo	Jewel	(tipped)	5	29	CC
Cigarillo	Jewel Sweet	(tipped)	5	29	CC
Cigarillo	Jewel Classic	(tipped)	5	29	CC
Cigarillo	Jewel Black Gold		5	29	Ma
Cigarillo	Jewel Menthol		5	29	CC
Small Panatela	Junior		4½	31	CC
Panatela	Panatela		5½	36	CC
Petit Corona	Perfecto		4¾	43	CC
Petit Corona	Sublime		4¾	43	CC
Cigarillo	Tips Cigarillo	(tipped)	5	28	CC
Cigarillo	Tips	(tipped)	5	28	CC
Cigarillo	Tips Sweet	(tipped)	5	28	CC

This famous brand offers light, mild cigarillos with a manufactured wrapper and binder and a filler blend of Honduran and Dominican tobaccos.

HENRY THE FOURTH
Machine-made in Tampa, Florida, USA.

Shape	Name	Lgth	Ring	Wrapper
Corona	Lydia	5½	43	CM-Ma
Grand Corona	Magnums	5⅝	47	CM-Ma
Long Corona	Mirtas	6	43	CM-Ma

MACHINE-MADE CIGARS: BRAND LISTINGS

Churchill	Principales	7¾	46	CM-Ma

This brand features a Honduran wrapper, sheet binder and a filler mix of Dominican, Honduran and Nicaraguan tobaccos. Medium in strength, you can find it in bundles of 25 cigars each.

HULA GIRL
Machine-made in Kihei, Hawaii, USA.

Shape	Name		Lgth	Ring	Wrapper
Lonsdale	Hula Girl	(tubed)	6½	44	CM

You'll always know the Hula Girl by her distinctive black tube! It contains a Kona Coffee-flavored, machine-made cigar that features an Indonesian wrapper, sheet binder and mixed filler, primarily from the Dominican Republic and Honduras.

IBOLD
Machine-made in Frankfort, Indiana, USA.

Shape	Name	Lgth	Ring	Wrapper
Petit Corona	Blunt	4⅞	44	CI-CM
Petit Corona	Black Pete	4⅞	44	CM
Robusto	Breva	5⅛	51	CI-Ma
Cigarillo	Cigarillo	4¼	29	CI-CM
Panatela	Ideals	5⅞	38	CI-CM
Short Panatela	Slims	5¼	35	CI-CM

Manufactured by the National Cigar Corporation, this brand offers a medium-bodied taste thanks to its Connecticut leaf wrapper, sheet or Connecticut binder - depending on the shape - and the filler blend of U.S. and Dominican leaves.

J-R FAMOUS
Machine-made in Tampa, Florida, USA.

Shape	Name	Lgth	Ring	Wrapper
Toro	Churchill	5¾	50	DC-CM-Ma

Panatela	Delicados	6	39	DC-CM-Ma
Long Corona	Plazas	6	42	DC-CM-Ma
Lonsdale	Presidents	7⅛	44	DC-CM-Ma

This is a medium-bodied, highly popular cigar with a Honduran wrapper, sheet binder and all-Honduran filler. It is an excellent value and offered in boxes of 50.

JON PIEDRO
Machine-made in Yoe, Pennsylvania, USA.

Shape	Name	Lgth	Ring	Wrapper
Lonsdale	Brevas	6½	42	CM
Panatela	Slims	6½	36	CM
Grand Corona	Cazadore	6½	45	CM
Grand Corona	Broadleaf Rounds	6½	46	CM-Ma

This is an old, mild brand, offered in four shapes in boxes of 50. The wrapper is Pennsylvania-grown and a sheet binder is used, along with a blend of filler tobaccos.

KEEP MOVING
Machine-made in Jacksonville, Florida, USA.

Shape	Name	Lgth	Ring	Wrapper
Petit Corona	Goodies	4½	41	CC

This one-size brand has a natural leaf wrapper, sheet binder and blends tobaccos of four nations in the filler. Look for Keep Moving in twin-packs, five-packs and in full boxes of 50.

KING EDWARD
Machine-made in Jacksonville, Florida, USA.

Shape	Name	Lgth	Ring	Wrapper
Corona	Invincible Deluxe	5¾	42	CC

MACHINE-MADE CIGARS: BRAND LISTINGS

Short Panatela	Panatela Deluxe		5¼	38	CC
Long Corona	Corona Deluxe		6	42	CC
Cigarillo	Cigarillo Deluxe		4¼	28½	CC
Petit Corona	Blunt		5	42	CC
Petit Corona	Imperial		5	40	CC
Panatela	Slim		5⅝	36	CC
Cigarillo	Specials		4⅜	28½	CC
Cigarillo	Tip Cigarillo	(tipped)	4⅞	28	CC
Cigarillo	Wood Tip Cigarillo	(tipped)	5½	29	CC
Cigarillo	Little Cigars		4⅜	29	CC

Britain's King Edward VII (1841-1910) is celebrated as the man who, with four words, revised the Victorian prohibition against tobacco soon after his ascension to the throne in 1901: "Gentlemen, you may smoke." This brand still bears his portrait and is now machine-made with a sheet wrapper and binder and a four-nation filler blend. The Deluxe shapes feature a natural leaf wrapper, while the Wood Tip Cigarillo is available in flavored versions of Sweet Cherry and Sweet Vanilla. Widely available in the U.S. and highly popular in England and 60 other countries, King Edward is offered in five-packs and boxes of 50

LA FENDRICH
Machine-made in Frankfort, Indiana, USA.

Shape	Name	Lgth	Ring	Wrapper
Corona Extra	Favorita	5⅛	45	CI
Small Panatela	Buds	4¼	32	CC

La Fendrich cigars have a medium body, with a Connecticut wrapper, American and Dominican filler tobaccos and a sheet binder.

LORD BEACONSFIELD
Machine-made in Tampa, Florida, USA.

MACHINE-MADE CIGARS: BRAND LISTINGS

Shape	Name	Lgth	Ring	Wrapper
Churchill	Rounds	7¼	46	DC-CC-Ma
Slim Panatela	Lords	7	34	DC-CC-Ma
Long Corona	Coronas Superba	6¼	42	DC-CC-Ma
Panatela	Lindas	6½	36	DC-CC-Ma
Corona	Cubanola	5½	44	DC-CC-Ma
Churchill	Directors	7¾	46	Ma

This is a veteran brand with a Sumatra wrapper and a three-nation, short filler blend, combined with a sheet binder for a mild taste. It is offered in boxes of 50 except for the Directors, offered in 25s.

LORD CLINTON
Machine-made in Wheeling, West Virginia, USA.

Shape	Name	Lgth	Ring	Wrapper
Slim Panatela	Panatela	5¼	34	CC
Corona	Perfecto	5	42½	CI

The Panatela has a genuine Connecticut wrapper, sheet binder and a blend of filler tobaccos from the Dominican Republic and the United States. It has a medium-bodied taste. The Perfecto has the same filler tobaccos, but uses a sheet binder and wrapper.

MARSH
Machine-made in Wheeling, West Virginia, USA.

Shape	Name	Lgth	Ring	Wrapper
Slim Panatela	Mountaineer	5½	34	CC-Ma
Panatela	Virginian	5½	37	CC
Panatela	Pioneer	5½	37	CC
Slim Panatela	Old Reliable	5½	33	Ma
Long Panatela	Deluxe	7	34	Ma

MACHINE-MADE CIGARS: BRAND LISTINGS

| Long Panatela | Deluxe II | 7 | 34 | Ma |
| Long Panatela | Olde Style Stogies | 7 | 34 | Ma |

This brand began back in 1840 and continues today as a popular mass-market cigar in many parts of the United States. All of the shapes are mild and all use genuine Connecticut-grown leaves for wrappers and sheet binders. Most of the shapes offer a U.S. and Dominican filler blend, except for the Old Reliable, which incorporates fire-cured Kentucky tobacco in its filler. The Deluxe and Old Style Stogies are finished with a pig-tail head. The heads of the Deluxe II shape are pre-drilled with holes to allow instant ignition without cutting.

MIFLIN'S CHOICE
Machine-made in Wheeling, West Virginia, USA.

Shape	Name		Lgth	Ring	Wrapper
Panatela	Panatela	(tubed)	6⅜	32	CM

This small cigar uses a Cameroon wrapper, sheet binder and a blend of Caribbean tobaccos in the filler.

MOCAMBO
Machine-made in Ireland.

Shape	Name	Lgth	Ring	Wrapper
Short Panatela	Half Corona	3¾	36	CM-Ma
Cigarillo	Little Cigarillos	3¼	25	CM-Ma
Small Panatela	Senoritas	3½	30	CM-Ma
Cigarillo	Slim Panatela	6	27	CM-Ma
Cigarillo	Wilde Cigarillo	3½	27	CM-Ma
Small Panatela	Wilde Havana	3½	30	CM-Ma

These little cigars medium in body and dry-cured, with a choice of Sumatra wrappers or maduro wrappers from Brazil. They are offered in boxes of 25 (Half Corona and Senoritas) and 50.

MACHINE-MADE CIGARS: BRAND LISTINGS

MOYA GUSTO
Machine-made in Tampa, Florida, USA.

Shape	Name	Lgth	Ring	Wrapper
Corona	Deluxe	5⅜	44	CC-Ma
Lonsdale	Fumas	6¼	44	CC-Ma
Panatela	Panatela	6	34	CC

This brand is full-bodied and features an Indonesian wrapper, sheet binder and filler tobaccos from the Dominican Republic. The Deluxe and Panatela shapes are offered in boxes of 50; the others are packaged in bundles of 25.

MR. B
Machine-made in Tampa, Florida, USA.

Shape	Name	Lgth	Ring	Wrapper
Giant Corona	Mr. B	7½	45	DC-CM-Ma

Here is a mild-to-medium-bodied, flavorful cigar which features a Honduran wrapper, sheet binder and Honduran filler tobaccos, offered in bundles of 20.

MURIEL
Machine-made in McAdoo, Pennsylvania, USA and Cayey, Puerto Rico.

Shape	Name	Lgth	Ring	Wrapper
Corona Extra	Magnum	4⅝	46½	CC
Small Panatela	Air Tips Regular *(tipped)*	5	30½	CC
Small Panatela	Air Tips Pipe Aroma *(tipped)*	5	30½	CC
Small Panatela	Air Tips Menthol *(tipped)*	5	30½	CC
Small Panatela	Air Tips Sweet *(tipped)*	5	30½	CC
Small Panatela	Coronella	4⅝	31	CC
Small Panatela	Coronella Pipe Aroma	4⅝	31	CC
Small Panatela	Coronella Sweet	4⅝	31	CC

MACHINE-MADE CIGARS: BRAND LISTINGS

	Muriel Pipe Tobacco Cigars:			
Cigarillo	Black N Cherry	5⅛	27	CM
Cigarillo	Black N Sweet	5⅛	27	CM
	Muriel Sweets Little Cigars:			
Cigarillo	Black & Sweet	3⅞	20	CM
Cigarillo	Sweet & Mild	3⅞	20	CC
Cigarillo	Menthol	3⅞	20	CC

This famous brand features a manufactured wrapper and offer a variety of sizes for every smoker. The Coronella group includes all natural fillers, while the new Pipe Tobacco series includes pipe tobacco filler. All are made in Puerto Rico except for the Sweets, made in Pennsylvania.

NAT CICCO'S
Machine-made in Tampa. Florida, USA and Yoe, Pennsylvania, USA.

Shape	Name	Lgth	Ring	Wrapper
Giant Corona	Churchill Rejects	8	46	DC-CC-Ma
Small Panatela	Jamaican Delights	5	34	CC-Ma
Lonsdale	Jamaican Palmas	6½	43	CC-Ma
Slim Panatela	Jamaican Regales	7⅛	34	CC-Ma
Churchill	Jamaican Rounds	7¼	46	CC-Ma
Long Corona	Plaza	6	42	DC-CC-Ma
Panatela	Rapier	6½	39	DC-CC-Ma
Churchill	Resago Churchill	7	48	CC-Ma
Robusto	Resago Robusto	5	50	CC-Ma
Robusto	Robusto Rejects	5½	49	CC-Ma
	Aromatic and flavored series:			
Panatela	Almond Liquer	6½	39	CC

MACHINE-MADE CIGARS: BRAND LISTINGS

Panatela	Cuban Cafe	6½	39	CC
Long Corona	Plaza Aromatic	6	42	CC

This series is made primarily in Tampa, except for the Aromatic and Flavored group, made in Pennsylvania. Overall, you can expect a mild taste from the Honduran natural leaf wrappers, homogenized binder and a blend of short-filler tobaccos from three nations. Nat Cicco's shapes are offered in boxes of 50.

NATIONAL CIGAR
Machine-made in Frankfort, Indiana, USA.

Shape	Name	Lgth	Ring	Wrapper
Long Corona	Palma	6	42	CI-CM

Made by the National Cigar Corporation, this medium-bodied blend incorporates a Connecticut wrapper, sheet binder and American and Dominican blended filler

ODIN
Machine-made in Wheeling, West Virginia, USA.

Shape	Name	Lgth	Ring	Wrapper
Petit Corona	Viking	4¾	42½	CC

The Odin Viking offers a medium-bodied taste, with tobaccos from the Dominican Republic and the United States in the filler. The wrapper is homogenized tobacco leaf and a sheet binder is used.

OPTIMO
Machine-made in Jacksonville, Florida, USA.

Shape	Name		Lgth	Ring	Wrapper
Panatela	Diplomat		6⅛	33	DC-CC
Long Corona	Admiral		6	41	DC-CC
Slim Panatela	Brigadier	(tubed)	6¼	33	CC-Ma
Corona	Coronas		5¼	42	CC-Ma
Long Corona	Palmas		6	41	Ma

| Slim Panatela | Panatela | 5¼ | 33 | DC-CC |
| Petit Corona | Sports | 4½ | 41 | DC-CC |

This popular brand was, at one time, made of Cuban tobacco, but is today a mass-market favorite. It combines a natural leaf wrapper from Ecuador (candela), Connecticut (natural) or Mexico (maduro), a sheet binder and a four-nation blend in the filler, and is available in twin-packs, five-packs and, of course, full boxes of 50.

PALMA
Machine-made in Yoe, Pennsylvania, USA.

Shape	Name	Lgth	Ring	Wrapper
Lonsdale	Throwouts	6½	43	Cl-CC-Ma

What an undeserving shape name! These are value-priced, machine-made cigars with a natural leaf wrapper, sheet binder and an imported, blended filler. Offered in boxes of 50.

PHILLIES
Machine-made in Selma, Alabama, USA.

Shape	Name	Lgth	Ring	Wrapper
Corona	Perfecto	5¾	43	CC
Long Corona	Titan	6¼	44	CC
Corona	Coronas	5⅜	41	CC
Petit Corona	Blunts	4¾	42	CC
Slim Panatela	Panatella	5½	34	CC
Corona	Sport	5¾	43	CC
Small Panatela	Cheroot	5	32	CC
Slim Panatela	King Cheroot	5½	32	CC
Small Panatela	Mexicali Slim	4⅝	32	CC
Petit Corona	Juniors	5	41	CC
Corona	Sweets	5¾	43	CC

| Cigarillo | Tips | *(tipped)* | 4½ | 28 | CC |
| Cigarillo | Tip Sweet | *(tipped)* | 4½ | 28 | CC |

This well-known brand is constructed with a sheet wrapper and binder, with the filler blend made from Dominican and Honduran tobaccos, to provide its mild-bodied taste.

POLLACK
Machine-made in Wheeling, West Virginia, USA.

Shape	Name	Lgth	Ring	Wrapper
Slim Panatela	Melo Crown Expert	5½	34	Ma
Slim Panatela	Crown Drum	5½	33	Ma

The Crown Drum offers a mild taste with a Connecticut wrapper, sheet binder and U.S. and Dominican filler tobaccos.

R. G. DUN
Machine-made in Wheeling, West Virginia, USA.

Shape	Name	Lgth	Ring	Wrapper
Petit Corona	Admiral	4¾	42½	CC
Petit Corona	Babies	4⅛	42	CC
Slim Panatela	Youngfellow	5¼	34	CC
Corona	Regal Blunt	5¼	43	CC
Corona	Bouquet	5½	42½	CC
Cigarillo	Cigarillo	4¼	29	Cl

This is a medium-bodied cigar made by M. Marsh & Sons. It offers a Connecticut leaf wrapper, has a sheet binder and a blended filler of American and Dominican tobaccos.

RED DOT
Machine-made in Wheeling, West Virginia, USA.

MACHINE-MADE CIGARS: BRAND LISTINGS

Shape	Name	Lgth	Ring	Wrapper
Slim Panatela	Panatela	5¼	34	CC
Corona	Perfecto	5	42½	CC

This brand offers a medium body, with a Connecticut leaf wrapper, sheet binder and a blend of Dominican and flavored American tobaccos in the filler.

RIGOLETTO
Machine-made in Tampa, Florida, USA.

Shape	Name	Lgth	Ring	Wrapper
Long Corona	Londonaire	6¼	43	CC
Corona Extra	Black Jack	5⅜	46	Ma
Long Corona	Natural Coronas	6	42	CC
Long Corona	Palma Grande	6	41	Cl-CC
Slim Panatela	Natural Panatela	5	33	CC
Small Panatela	Wild Dominicans	4¾	34	CC

This is a mild-to-medium brand produced in Tampa. First introduced in 1905, it features a Connecticut Broadleaf or Shade wrapper, a sheet binder and high-quality filler tobaccos from the Dominican Republic.

ROBERT BURNS
Machine-made in Santiago, Dominican Republic and Dothan, Alabama.

Shape	Name		Lgth	Ring	Wrapper
Corona	Black Watch	*(tubed)*	5⅝	41	CC
Cigarillo	Cigarillo		4½	27	CC

The Black Watch model is made in Santiago, the Dominican Republic, with a Connecticut Shade wrapper, sheet binder and a multi-nation blend of filler tobaccos in three-packs and boxes of 30. The famous Cigarillos are made in Dothan, Alabama with sheet wrappers and binders and blended filler, offered in five-packs and boxes of 50.

MACHINE-MADE CIGARS: BRAND LISTINGS

ROI-TAN
Machine-made in Cayey, Puerto Rico.

Shape	Name	Lgth	Ring	Wrapper
Petit Corona	Bankers	5	40½	CI
Corona	Blunts	5⅝	40½	CI
Slim Panatela	Falcons	6¼	33½	CI
Panatela	Panatelas	5½	36	CI
Petit Corona	Perfecto Extras	5	40½	CI

Here is a popular old brand which is now using a manufactured wrapper and binder with short filler tobaccos.

SAN FELICE
Machine-made in Wheeling, West Virginia, USA.

Shape	Name	Lgth	Ring	Wrapper
Petit Corona	Original	4¾	42½	CC

This brand has only one shape, but it's a popular corona thanks to its genuine Connecticut wrapper. The filler is a blend of American and Dominican tobaccos, surrounded by a sheet binder.

SIERRA SWEET
Machine-made in Tampa, Florida, USA.

Shape	Name	Lgth	Ring	Wrapper
Churchill	El Dorado	7¼	46	CC-Ma
Toro	Placer	5¾	48	CC-Ma
Long Corona	Sonora	6¼	42	CC-Ma
Panatela	Renos	6¼	36	CC-Ma
Small Panatela	Tahoes	4¾	30	CC-Ma

Here is a vanilla-flavored brand with a natural leaf wrapper, sheet binder and a blend of short-filler tobaccos. You can have your pick in hand carry-cases of five, eight or 10 cigars.

MACHINE-MADE CIGARS: BRAND LISTINGS

'63 AIR-FLO
Machine-made in Wheeling, West Virginia, USA.

Shape	Name	Lgth	Ring	Wrapper
Petit Corona	Londres	5	42½	CC

One of the most unusual names in cigardom adorns this medium-bodied cigar, which has a sheet wrapper and binder and filler tobaccos from the United States and the Dominican Republic.

SWEET-NUT
Machine-made in Tampa, Florida, USA.

Shape	Name	Lgth	Ring	Wrapper
Slim Panatela	Sweet-Nut	5⅝	30	CC

Introduced in 1997, this is a mild, small cigar with features Dominican-grown filler and homogenized tobacco leaf binder and wrapper.

TAMPA CUB
Machine-made in Wheeling, West Virginia, USA.

Shape	Name	Lgth	Ring	Wrapper
Corona	Straights	5	42½	CC

There is only one shape in this brand, but it offers a medium body with American and Dominican filler tobaccos and a manufactured sheet binder and wrapper.

TAMPA NUGGET
Machine-made in Tampa, Florida, USA.

Shape	Name		Lgth	Ring	Wrapper
Petit Corona	Sublime		4¾	43	CC
Petit Corona	Blunt		5	43	CC
Panatela	Panatela		5½	36	CC
Cigarillo	Tip Regular	(tipped)	5	28	CC

MACHINE-MADE CIGARS: BRAND LISTINGS

Cigarillo	Tip Sweet	(tipped)	5	28	CC
Small Panatela	Juniors		4½	31	CC
Small Panatela	Miniature		4½	31	CC

These "nuggets" incorporate sheet wrappers and binders with a blend of filler tobaccos from the Dominican Republic and Honduras for a mild and flavorful smoke.

TAMPA RESAGOS
Machine-made in Tampa, Florida, USA.

Shape	Name	Lgth	Ring	Wrapper
Corona	Regular	5¼	42	CC
Corona	Sweet	5¼	42	CC

These inexpensive cigars offer a mild taste, with homogenized wrappers and binders and filler tobaccos from the Dominican Republic. A favorite since 1951, Tampa Resagos are offered in bags of 20 cigars each.

TAMPA SWEET
Machine-made in Tampa, Florida, USA.

Shape	Name		Lgth	Ring	Wrapper
Petit Corona	Perfecto		4¾	43	CC
Small Panatela	Cheroot		4¾	31	CC
Cigarillo	Tip Cigarillo	(tipped)	5	28	CC

This three-shape brand features filler tobaccos from Colombia and Italy, surrounded by a homogenized wrapper and binder.

VILLA DE CUBA
Machine-made in Tampa, Florida, USA.

Shape	Name	Lgth	Ring	Wrapper
Corona	Brevas	5¾	44	CC-Ma

MACHINE-MADE CIGARS: BRAND LISTINGS

Long Corona	Majestics	6⅜	43	CC-Ma
Giant Corona	Corona Grande	7¼	45	CC-Ma

Choose a Sumatra or Connecticut Broadleaf (maduro) wrapper in this mild-bodied brand. It has a sheet binder and a three-nation blend of filler tobaccos.

VILLAZON DELUXE
Machine-made in Tampa, Florida, USA.

Shape	Name	Lgth	Ring	Wrapper
Giant Corona	Chairman	7¾	43	CM-Ma
Lonsdale	Cetros	7⅛	44	CM-Ma
Lonsdale	Senators	6¾	44	CM-Ma

Here is a veteran brand which features a Sumatra (natural) or Connecticut (maduro) wrapper, sheet binder and a short-filler blend of tobaccos from three nations. It is offered in boxes of 50 except for the Chairman style, offered in 25s.

VILLAZON DELUXE AROMATICS
Machine-made in Tampa, Florida, USA

Shape	Name	Lgth	Ring	Wrapper
Long Corona	Commodores	6	42	DC-CM-Ma
Slim Panatela	Panatella	5¾	34	DC-CM-Ma

Similar to the regular Villazon Deluxe line, this brand is flavored with vanilla and features a Sumatra wrapper to complement the homogenized binder and three-nation filler blend. It is offered in boxes of 50.

WHITE OWL
Machine-made in Dothan, Alabama, USA.

Shape	Name		Lgth	Ring	Wrapper
Cigarillo	Coronetta		4⅝	29	CC
Short Panatela	Demi-Tip	(tipped)	5⅛	32	CC

MACHINE-MADE CIGARS: BRAND LISTINGS

Cigarillo	Miniatures	4⅝	29	CC
Cigarillo	Miniatures Sweet	4⅝	29	CC
Slim Panatela	Panatela Deluxe	5¼	34	CC
Corona	Invincible	5⅜	41	CC
Corona	New Yorker	5⅝	41	CC
Slim Panatela	Ranger	6⅜	34	CC
Petit Corona	Sports	4¾	41	CC
	White Owl Select:			
Corona	Imperial	5⅝	41	CC
Petit Corona	Regent	4¾	41	CC
Cigarillo	Squire	4⅝	29	CC
Cigarillo	Darts	3¾	23	CC

This brand started way back in 1887. Today, there are two lines: White Owl and White Owl Select. The regular line includes a sheet wrapper and binder around a five-nation blend of filler tobaccos, while the Select line has a Connecticut Shade wrapper and is offered in packs of four or five cigars. The regular line is offered in twin-packs, five-packs, six-packs or in boxes of 50.

WM. ASCOT
Machine-made in Tampa, Florida, USA.

Shape	*Name*	*Lgth*	*Ring*	*Wrapper*
Lonsdale	Palma	6¼	42	DC-CC-Ma
Slim Panatela	Panatela	5¾	34	DC-CC-Ma

This is a very mild cigar, featuring an Ecuadorian wraper, sheet binder and Dominican and Honduran filler tobaccos. The Palma is offered in a variety of wrapper shades in boxes of 25 and the Panatela is available in boxes of 50.

WILLIAM PENN
Machine-made in Dothan, Alabama, USA.

MACHINE-MADE CIGARS: BRAND LISTINGS

Shape	Name		Lgth	Ring	Wrapper
Cigarillo	Willow Tips	(tipped)	5	27	CC
Cigarillo	Willow Tips Sweets	(tipped)	5	27	CC
Cigarillo	Braves		4⅝	29	CC
Corona	Perfecto		5⅜	41	CC
Slim Panatela	Panatela		5¼	34	CC

Introduced in 1924, William Penn cigars offer mild taste thanks to a multi-nation blend of filler tobaccos, surrounded by homogenized wrappers and binders. The brand is offered in twin-packs, five-packs and boxes of 50 in the larger sizes.

WINDSOR & MARK IV
Machine-made in Yoe, Pennsylvania, USA.

Shape	Name	Lgth	Ring	Wrapper
Giant Corona	Imperial	8	43	DC
Lonsdale	Maduro	6½	43	Ma
Lonsdale	Magnate	6½	43	DC
Lonsdale	Palma	6½	43	DC
Slim Panatela	Panatela	6½	34	DC
Petit Corona	Sportsmen	5	43	DC

From the respected House of Windsor comes the Windsor & Mark line, which features natural leaf wrappers, sheet binders and a filler blend of imported, short-filler, tobaccos. Most sizes are available in boxes of 50; the Maduro and Magnate sizes are available in boxes of 25.

WOLF BROS.
Machine-made in Yoe, Pennsylvania, USA.

Shape	Name	Lgth	Ring	Wrapper
Cigarillo	Nippers	4	20	CC
Small Panatela	Rum Crookettes	4½	32	CC

Small Panatela	Sweet Vanilla Crookettes	4½	32	CC
Perfecto	Rum Crooks	5½	42	CC
Perfecto	Sweet Vanilla Crooks	5½	42	CC

These well-known cigars are also produced by the House of Windsor. Most of these shapes offer an imported leaf wrapper, sheet binder and a blend of imported short filler tobaccos. Please note the well-known flavored rum and vanilla shapes.

X-RATED
Machine-made in Tampa, Florida, USA.

Shape	Name	Lgth	Ring	Wrapper
Short Panatela	Honey Pie	5⅜	36	CC

New in 1997, this mild-bodied cigar features filler tobaccos from the Dominican Republic surrounded by homogenized binder and wrapper.

Y.B.
Machine-made in Wheeling, West Virginia, USA.

Shape	Name	Lgth	Ring	Wrapper
Petit Corona	Squires	5	42½	CC

This old brand includes only one size, but it offers a medium body thanks to filler tobaccos from the Dominican Republic and the United States and a sheet binder and wrapper.

Cigarillos, Cheroots and Panatelas

Here are examples of the smallest cigars available on the market today:

- Cigarillos and cheroots — 6 or less inches long with a ring gauge of 29 or less.

- Panatela group, including
  - Small Panatela — 4-5 inches long; 30-34 ring.
  - Slim Panatela — 5 inches and more; 30-34 ring.
  - Short Panatela — 4-5⅜ inches long; 35-39 ring.
  - Panatela — 5½-6⅞ inches long; 35-39 ring.
  - Long Panatela — 7 inches and more; 35-39 ring.

Pictured opposite, from left to right:

		(shape)
CAPTAIN BLACK *Sweet*		
(United States)	3⅞ x 20	Little Cigar
DAVIDOFF *Cigarillo*		
(Denmark)	3½ x 20	Cigarillo
CHRISTIAN OF DENMARK *Long Cigarillo*		
(Denmark)	4 x 20	Cigarillo
PETRI *Toscanelli*		
(United States)	4 x 34	Cheroot
PARODI *Kings*		
(United States)	4½ x 34	Cheroot
EL REY DEL MUNDO *Reynitas*		
(Honduras)	5 x 38	Short Panatela
DON TOMAS SPECIAL EDITION *No. 400*		
(Honduras)	7 x 36	Long Panatela

5.
SMALL CIGARS

This section provides the details on 54 brands of small cigars, generally made by machine for distribution to the widest possible audience in drug stores, supermarkets and, of course, tobacco stores.

For the purposes of this listing, small cigar "brands" are limited to those whose lines are dominated by (i.e., 67 percent or more of the shapes are) cigarillo or cheroot-shaped cigars. In addition, brands in the handmade or mass-market sections that offer the cigarillo shape in their lines include:

Handmade brands (79):

Albero
Alvaro
Andujar
Antelo
Caoba
Carbonell
Chavon
Cibao
Cigar Trader
Corman
Cuba 1800
Davidoff
Don Antonio
Don Diego
Doña Puros
Dos Cubanitos
El Chico

El Guajiro
El Rey del Mundo
El Sabor de Miami
Excalibur
Francisco Pla
Golden Seal
Golden Sun
H. Upmann
Habana Treasure
Hamiltons
Hamiltons Reserve
Hannibal
Havana Nights
Havana Star
Havana Sunrise
Havanilla
Hoyo de Monterrey
Hugo Cassar Private Coll.

SMALL CIGARS: BRAND LISTINGS

Iracema
Jimenez
José Girbés
J-R Ultimate
Juan Clemente
La Flor de Cano
Macanudo
Mendez y Lopez
Montecruz
Morejon y Cuesta
Nat Sherman
Nativo
Old Fashioned
Oscar
P & R
Partagas
Peñamil Plata
Picadura
Pleiades
Pretty Lady
Pride of Copan
Primo del Rey

Prince Borghese
Private Stock
Profesor Sila Baba
Punch
Quirantes
Rafael de Habana
Rasputin
RG Santiago Dominican
Rich & Famous
Robali
Santa Clara 1830
Smokin' Tiger
South Beach
Suerdieck
Sweet Lady
Tatiana
Te-Amo
Tia Martia
12 Stars
Woriur
Zaldiva
Zino

Mass-market brands (31):
Antonio y Cleopatra
Arango Sportsman
Balmoral
Candlelight
Cazadores
Chevere Small Cigars
Cuban Club Classics

Directors
Dutch Masters
El Gozo
El Verso
Garcia y Vega
Hav-A-Tampa
Havana Blend
Ibold

SMALL CIGARS: BRAND LISTINGS

J. Cortes
King Edward
La Paz
Mocambo
Muriel
Phillies
R.G. Dun
Robert Burns

Swisher Sweets
Tampa Nugget
Tampa Sweet
White Owl
William Penn
Wolf Bros.
Wuhrmann
Zino

Each brand listing includes notes on country of manufacture, shapes, names, lengths, ring gauges and wrapper color *as supplied by the manufacturers and/or distributors of these brands.* Ring gauges for some cigarillos were not available.

When comparing and considering cigars listed in this category, it may be worthwhile to remember the standard dimensions of mass-produced cigarettes: almost always 7.9 mm in diameter (20 ring gauge) with lengths of 85 mm (approx. 3¼ inches) or 100 mm (approx. 3⅞ inches).

Please note that while a cigar may be manufactured in one country, it may contain tobaccos from many nations. These cigars utilize short-filler tobaccos unless otherwise noted; a number of brands use homogenized (sheet) leaf for binders and/or filler.

Although manufacturers have recognized more than 70 shades of wrapper color, six major color groupings are used here. Their abbreviations include:

▸ DC = Double Claro: green, also known as "AMS."

SMALL CIGARS: BRAND LISTINGS

- ▸ Cl = Claro: a very light tan color.
- ▸ CC = Colorado Claro: a medium brown common to many cigars on this list.
- ▸ Co = Colorado: reddish-brown.
- ▸ CM = Colorado Maduro: dark brown.
- ▸ Ma = Maduro: very dark brown or black (also known as "double Maduro" or "Oscuro.")

Many manufacturers call their wrapper colors "Natural" or "English Market Selection." These colors cover a wide range of browns and we have generally grouped them in the "CC" range. Darker wrappers such as those from Cameroon show up most often in the "CM" category.

Readers who would like to see their favorite brand listed in the 2000 edition can call or write the compilers as noted after the Table of Contents.

AGIO
Machine-made in Geel, Belgium.

Shape	Name	Lgth	Ring	Wrapper
Cigarillo	Biddies Aroma	3¼	20	CC
Cigarillo	Biddies Brazil	3¼	20	Ma
Cigarillo	Biddies Sumatra	3¼	20	CC
Cigarillo	Mehari's Sumatra	4	23	CC
Cigarillo	Mehari's Brasil	4	23	Ma
Cigarillo	Mehari's Mild & Light	4	23	Cl
Cigarillo	Mehari's Mild & Sweet	4	23	CM
Cigarillo	Mini Mehari's	2⅞	22	CC
Cigarillo	Mini Mehari's Mild & Light	2⅞	22	Cl

SMALL CIGARS: BRAND LISTINGS

Cigarillo	Filter Tip	*(tipped)*	3	21	CC
Cigarillo	Lights		3	21	CC
Small Panatela	Senoritas Red Label		4	31	CC
Small Panatela	Elegant		4⅛	32	CC

Here is one of the famous brands in cigarillos, offering dry-cured cigarillos and small cigars for almost every taste. Most of the shapes use wrapper leaves from Java; the Mini Mehari's Mild & Light and Mehari's Mild & Light use a Connecticut wrapper; the Mehari's Brasil features a Brazilian-grown wrapper; the Biddies Sumatra, Senoritas Red Label and Elegant have Sumatran wrappers; and the Mehari's wrapper is from the Cameroon. All use a sheet binder and a blend of mild tobaccos in the filler.

AL-CAPONE
Machine-made in Germany.

Shape	Name	Lgth	Ring	Wrapper
Cigarillo	Sweets	3¼	28	CC
Cigarillo	Slims	3¼	28	CC
Cigarillo	Pockets	2¾	24	CC

These cigarillos are made by the famous Dannemann firm and are offered in convenient packs of five (Sweets and Slims) and ten (Pockets). The Sweets are flavored with Cognac and the Slims are rum-flavored.

AVANTI
Machine-made in Scranton, Pennsylvania, USA.

Shape	Name	Lgth	Ring	Wrapper
Cheroot	Avanti	4½	34	Ma
Cheroot	Avanti Continental	5¾	34	Ma
Cheroot	Europa	5¾	34	Ma
Cheroot	Ipenema	5¾	34	Ma
Cheroot	Ramrod Deputy	4½	34	Ma

SMALL CIGARS: BRAND LISTINGS

| Cheroot | Ramrod Original | 6½ | 34 | Ma |
| Cheroot | Kentucky Cheroots | 5¾ | 34 | Ma |

Here is an all-tobacco, dry-cured, medium-bodied line of cigars, famous since their introduction in 1972. The ingredients are simple: fire-cured tobaccos from at least three different crop years of the finest farms in Kentucky and Tennessee, all barn-cured for at least four months. The Avanti and Avanti Continental are flavored with Anisette; the Ramrod Deputy and Ramrod Original are Bourbon flavored.

The Europa, introduced in 1994, uses a Kentucky dark-fired wrapper and binder and a blend of Belgian and Italian dark-fired tobacco for the filler.

BABY
Handmade in Villa Gonzalez, Dominican Republic.

Shape	Name	Lgth	Ring	Wrapper
Cigarillo	Natural	4½	28	CM
Cigarillo	Flavored	4½	28	CM

This brand debuted in 1998 and is handmade with an Indonesian wrapper and Dominican binder and filler, It is offered in boxes or bundles of five or 20. The flavors available include Amaretto, Anise, chocolate, cognac, cinnamon, mint and vanilla.

BACKWOODS
Machine-made in Cayey, Puerto Rico.

Shape	Name	Lgth	Ring	Wrapper
Cigarillo	Regular	4⅛	27	CC
Cigarillo	Sweet Aromatic	4⅛	27	CC
Cigarillo	Black & Sweet Aromatic	4⅛	27	Ma

This 100% tobacco brand offers a mild taste but a surprise in its unfinished, "open" end. It has a natural or blackened wrapper, no binder and a blend of short-filler tobaccos. It is presented in foil packs of 8.

SMALL CIGARS: BRAND LISTINGS

BETWEEN THE ACTS
Machine-made in Tampa, Florida, USA.

Shape	Name	Lgth	Ring	Wrapper
Cigarillo	Between the Acts	3⅛	20	CC

Between the acts of your favorite show you can enjoy this mild, flavorful smoke, made up of a sheet wrapper and binder and filler tobaccos from Indonesia and the United States. Offered in packs of 20.

BLACKSTONE
Machine-made in Jacksonville, Florida, USA.

Shape	Name	Lgth	Ring	Wrapper
Cigarillo	Mild	4⅞	28	CC
Cigarillo	Sweet Cherry	4⅞	28	CC

This is a new brand for 1997, with a pipe-tobacco filler surrounded by a homogenized wrapper in two easy-to-enjoy flavors.

CAPITAL
Machine-made in Dingelstadt, Germany.

Shape	Name	Lgth	Ring	Wrapper
Cigarillo	Capital	4½	26	CM

This is an all-tobacco blend of Indonesian-grown leaves, with a mild taste. It is available in boxes of 20.

CAPTAIN BLACK LITTLE CIGARS
Machine-made in Tucker, Georgia, USA.

Shape	Name	Lgth	Ring	Wrapper
Cigarillo	Regular	3⅞	20	CC
Cigarillo	Sweets	3⅞	20	CC

SMALL CIGARS: BRAND LISTINGS

Featuring the famous taste of Captain Black pipe tobacco, these little gems offer a mild taste, with a sheet wrapper and a blend of Indonesian, Philippine and United States tobaccos. Available in packs of 20.

CHRISTIAN OF DENMARK

Machine-made in Denmark.

Shape	*Name*	*Lgth*	*Ring*	*Wrapper*
Cigarillo	Mini Cigarillos	3½	20	CM
Cigarillo	Long Cigarillos	3¾	20	CM
Cigarillo	Light Cigarillos	3½	20	CC

This mild cigarillo is made of dry-cured, 100% tobacco, wrapped in Indonesian leaf (except for the Lights) with Brazilian, Dominican and Indonesian tobacco inside. Christian cigarillos are offered in 20-packs.

DANNEMANN

Machine-made in Germany and Switzerland.

Shape	*Name*	*Lgth*	*Ring*	*Wrapper*
	Made in Germany:			
Cigarillo	Moods	2⅞	20	CC
Cigarillo	Sweets	3⅝	20	CC
Cigarillo	Originale - Brazil	2⅞	20	Ma
Cigarillo	Originale - Sumatra	2⅞	20	CC
Cigarillo	Speciale - Brazil	2⅞	25	Ma
Cigarillo	Speciale - Sumatra	2⅞	25	CC
Cigarillo	Speciale - Lights	2⅞	25	Cl
Cigarillo	Imperial - Brazil	4¼	25	Ma
Cigarillo	Imperial - Sumatra	4¼	25	CC
Cigarillo	Lonja - Brazil	5⅜	25	Ma
Cigarillo	Lonja - Sumatra	5⅜	25	CC

SMALL CIGARS: BRAND LISTINGS

Cigarillo	Menor - Sumatra	3⅞	28	CC
Cigarillo	Pierrot - Brazil	3⅞	28	Ma
	Made in Switzerland:			
Slim Panatela	Lights - Sumatra	6	34	CC
Slim Panatela	Lights - Brazil	6	34	Ma
Corona Extra	Espada - Sumatra	5	45	CC
Corona Extra	Espada - Brazil	5	45	Ma
Cigarillo	Slims - Sumatra	6½	28	CC
Cigarillo	Slims - Brazil	6½	28	Ma

Geraldo Dannemann created this brand in 1873 and today, these famous all-tobacco, dry-cured cigarillos and small cigars feature primarily Sumatran and Brazilian tobaccos and are offered in a dizzying array of packs, tins and boxes of 25 for the small cigars.

DAVIDOFF CIGARILLOS
Machine-made in Denmark and the Netherlands.

Shape	Name	Lgth	Ring	Wrapper
	Made in Ny Kobing, Denmark:			
Cigarillo	Mini Cigarillos	3½	20	CC
Cigarillo	Mini Light	3½	20	Co
Cigarillo	Long Cigarillos	4½	20	CC
	Made in Eersel, the Netherlands:			
Cigarillo	Demi-Tasse	4	22	CC
Cigarillo	Long Panatelas	5½	22	CC

These elegant cigars are all tobacco which use natural leaf and are dry-cured for smoothness. All feature a Sumatra wrapper, Java binder and filler tobaccos from Brazil and Indonesia.

SMALL CIGARS: BRAND LISTINGS

DENOBILI
Machine-made in Scranton, Pennsylvania, USA.

Shape	Name	Lgth	Ring	Wrapper
Cheroot	Popular	3½	34	Ma
Cheroot	Twin Pack	4	34	Ma
Cheroot	Economy	4	34	Ma
Cheroot	Kings	4½	34	Ma
Cheroot	Toscani	6½	34	Ma
Cheroot	Toscani Longs	6½	34	Ma

A wide variety of sizes marks this dry-cured, 100%-tobacco brand, which uses only dark-fired Kentucky and Tennessee tobaccos in its blend. A brand of distinction since 1896, the Denobili range is marked by a mellow, medium-bodied taste.

DUCADOS
Machine-made in Madrid, Spain.

Shape	Name	Lgth	Ring	Wrapper
Cigarillo	Ducados	3	26	CM
Cigarillo	Ducados Extra	3	26	CM
Cigarillo	Ducados Suave	3	26	CM

These cigarillos are fairly mild, thanks to the Sumatran wrapper. A sheet binder is used, along with a blended filler; Ducados are offered in tins of 10 and 20 and in boxes of 50.

DUNHILL SMALL CIGARS
Machine-made in Wageningen, the Netherlands.

Shape	Name	Lgth	Ring	Wrapper
Cigarillo	Miniatures	3¼	26	CC
Cigarillo	Senoritas	3⅞	32	CC

Cigarillo	Panatellas	5½	26	CC
Petit Corona	Grand Corona	5⅛	41	CC
Lonsdale	Double Corona	6½	43	CC

These are elegant cigarillos fully worthy of the revered Dunhill name. Each uses a delicate Sumatra wrapper, Java binder and a combination of Brazilian Bahia and Java fillers to create a mild, flavorful taste. The Senoritas and Pantellas are offered in boxes of five, while the Miniatures are packaged in boxes of 10 cigars each.

DUTCH DELITES
BY VILLIGER
Machine-made in Germany.

Shape	Name	Lgth	Ring	Wrapper
Cigarillo	Light Sumatra	4⅝	20	CC
Cigarillo	Brasil	4⅝	20	CM

The famous Villiger firm offers a choice of wrappers in this cigarillo, available in boxes of 50. The wrappers are from either Sumatra or Brazil, with a sheet binder and a blend of filler tobaccos.

DUTCH TREATS
Machine-made in McAdoo, Pennsylvania, USA.

Shape	Name	Lgth	Ring	Wrapper
Cigarillo	Regular	3⅞	20	CC
Cigarillo	Menthol	3⅞	20	CC
Cigarillo	Pipe Aroma	3⅞	20	CC
Cigarillo	Sweet	3⅞	20	CC
Cigarillo	Ultra Lite	3⅞	20	CC

Here are elegant little cigars, with a homogenized wrapper, no binder and a filler blend of short-filler tobaccos, presented in easy-to-carry packs of 20.

SMALL CIGARS: BRAND LISTINGS

ERIK
Machine-made in Tampa, Florida, USA.

Shape	Name		Lgth	Ring	Wrapper
Cigarillo	Natural	(tipped)	3⅞	21	CM
Cigarillo	Menthol	(tipped)	3⅞	21	CM
Cigarillo	Cherry Flavor	(tipped)	3⅞	21	CM

The familiar Viking-ship logo adorns the ten-pack box of this filter-tipped brand, which features filler tobaccos from the Dominican Republic and the United States with a sheet wrapper and binder.

FLEUR DE SAVANE
Machine-made in France.

Shape	Name	Lgth	Ring	Wrapper
Cigarillo	Petits	3¼	21	CM
Cigarillo	Petits Light	3¼	21	CM
Small Panatela	Wilde Cigares	4¾	31	CM
Cigarillo	Wilde Cigarillos	4	23	CM

Introduced to the United States in 1997, this line features Cameroon wrappers, sheet binders and a blend of Cameroon-grown filler tobaccos. It is offered in packs or 20 or boxes of 50.

G.A. ANDRON
Machine-made in Ireland.

Shape	Name	Lgth	Ring	Wrapper
Cigarillo	Brazil Cigarillo	3	23	CM
Cigarillo	Sumatra Cigarillo	3	23	CC

GOLD SEAL
Machine-made in Indonesia.

SMALL CIGARS: BRAND LISTINGS

Shape	Name	Lgth	Ring	Wrapper
Cigarillo	Cigarillos	3⅝	24	CC
Cigarillo	Senoritas	4⅜	28	CC

This is an all-tobacco, dry-cured series, with a Sumatran wrapper, Javan binder and short filler from Brazil and Caribbean nations.

HAV-A-TAMPA LITTLE CIGARS
Machine-made in Tampa, Florida, USA.

Shape	Name	Lgth	Ring	Wrapper
Cigarillo	Naturale	3⅛	20	CC
Cigarillo	Sweet	3⅛	20	CC

This famous brand offers a little cigar with a sheet wrapper and binder and a blend of filler tobaccos from Honduras and the Dominican Republic.

HENRI WINTERMANS
Machine-made in Eersel, the Netherlands.

Shape	Name	Lgth	Ring	Wrapper
Cigarillo	Cafe Creme	2⅞	28	CC
Cigarillo	Cafe Creme Mini Mild	2⅞	28	CC
Cigarillo	Cafe Creme Mini	2⅞	28	CC
Cigarillo	Cafe Creme Plus Mild	2⅞	28	CC
Cigarillo	Cafe Creme Plus	2⅞	28	CC
Cigarillo	Scooters	3½	28	CC-Ma
Cigarillo	Cafe Noir	2⅞	28	Ma
Cigarillo	Cafe Creme Mild	2⅞	28	CC
Cigarillo	Cafe Creme Tips	3⅞	28	CC
Cigarillo	Slim Panatella	6	26	CC
Cigarillo	Senoritas	4	32	CC

SMALL CIGARS: BRAND LISTINGS

Since its introduction in 1963, this is one of the best-known and most appreciated brands in cigarillos and small cigars. These are mild, dry-cured cigars of high quality, featuring a Java wrapper and homogenized binder, sold in more than 100 countries worldwide.

INDIANA SLIMS
Machine-made in Germany.

Shape	Name	Lgth	Ring	Wrapper
Cigarillo	Indiana Slims	3¼	26	Ma

Despite the American-sounding name, these rum-dipped cigars are made in Germany, dry-cured and offered in packages of 10 cigars each.

LA CORONA
Machine-made in Cayey, Puerto Rico.

Shape	Name	Lgth	Ring	Wrapper
Cigarillo	Whiffs	3⅝	23⅔	Ma
Cigarillo	Whiffs Light	3⅝	23⅔	Cl

The famous La Corona brand continues with the Whiffs series, with the Light style added in 1995. Both sizes offer a natural Connecticut wrapper and sheet binder to complement the blend of short-filler tobaccos.

MADISON
Machine-made in Tampa, Florida, USA.

Shape	Name	Lgth	Ring	Wrapper
Cigarillo	Madison	3⅛	20	CC

The Madison taste is mild, with a filler blend of Indonesian and United States tobaccos, combined with a sheet wrapper and binder, offered in packs of 20.

MARSH
Machine-made in Wheeling, West Virginia, USA.

SMALL CIGARS: BRAND LISTINGS

Shape	Name	Lgth	Ring	Wrapper
Cigarillo	Rough-Cut	4⅜	28	CM
Cigarillo	Cheroot	4⅜	28	CM

Here is a new for 1997 all-tobacco line which features a Pennsylvania-grown (Amish country!) Broadleaf wrapper and a U.S. and Dominican-grown filler blend. You'll find in special six-packs!

MECCARILLOS
Machine-made in France.

Shape	Name	Lgth	Ring	Wrapper
Cigarillo	Filter Cigarillos	3¼	21	CC

New to the U.S. in 1997, this line features a Sumatra wrapper, sheet binder and a blend of filler tobaccos from Brazil and Indonesia. Offered in packs of 20.

MIAMI SUITES
Machine-made in Cayey, Puerto Rico.

Shape	Name	Lgth	Ring	Wrapper
Cigarillo	Amaretto	3⅝	23⅔	CM
Cigarillo	Irish Cream	3⅝	23⅔	CM
Cigarillo	Rum	3⅝	23⅔	CM

Here is a new brand, introduced in 1998. It features a mild taste thanks to its Java wrapper. It has a homogenized binder and highly flavored short filler. It is offered in packs of six.

NATIVO
Machine-made in Mayaguez, Puerto Rico.

Shape	Name	Lgth	Ring	Wrapper
Cigarillo	Jamaican Smalls	4	28	CM
Cigarillo	Cherry	4	28	CM

Cigarillo	Chocolate	4	28	CM
Cigarillo	Vanilla	4	28	CM

This is a uniquely flavored cigar, with a Pennsylvania wrapper, sheet binder and flavored pipe tobacco filler. It is offered in boxes of 50.

NOBEL CIGARS
Machine-made in Eersel, the Netherlands.

Shape	Name	Lgth	Ring	Wrapper
Cigarillo	Petit Sumatra	3½	20	CC
Cigarillo	Petit Brasil	3½	20	CM
Cigarillo	Medium Panatela Sumatra	3½	22	CC
Cigarillo	Grand Panatela Sumatra	5½	28	CC
Cigarillo	Petit Corona	3¾	32	CC
Cigarillo	Petit Lights	3½	20	CC

Introduced in 1988, these elegant cigarillos are dry-cured and made of 100% tobacco, especially Indonesian Sumatran or Brazilian wrappers and Java binders in most sizes.

OMEGA
Machine-made in Tampa, Florida, USA.

Shape	Name		Lgth	Ring	Wrapper
Cigarillo	Omega	(tipped)	3⅜	20	CC
Cigarillo	National Slims 100		3⅞	20	CC
Cigarillo	Cherry Flavor Slims 100		3⅞	20	CC
Cigarillo	Menthol Slims 100		3⅞	20	CC

Here's a mild-bodied smoke in a choice of flavors, with a sheet wrapper and binder and a blend of filler tobaccos from Indonesia and the United States.

SMALL CIGARS: BRAND LISTINGS

ORO DE RENITAS
Machine-made in France.

Shape	Name	Lgth	Ring	Wrapper
Cigarillo	Regular	3½	21	CC
Cigarillo	Light	3½	21	CC
Cigarillo	Aromatic	3½	21	CC

Introduced to the U.S. market for 1997, with a Sumatra wrapper, sheet binder and a mix of Brazilian and Indonesian tobaccos in the filler. It is offered in packs of 20.

PANTER
Machine-made in Geel, Belgium.

Shape	Name	Lgth	Ring	Wrapper
Cigarillo	Sprint	2⅞	21	CC
Cigarillo	Small	2⅞	21	CC
Cigarillo	Lights	2⅞	20	CI
Cigarillo	Silhouette	3⅜	20	CC
Cigarillo	Limbo	3⅞	24	CC
Cigarillo	Mignon	3¾	25	CC
Cigarillo	Mignon de Luxe	3⅜	20	CC
Cigarillo	Tango	3⅞	23	CC
Cigarillo	Vitesse	3¾	23	CC
Cigarillo	Mild Panatellas	5¾	21	CC

A famous brand in cigarillos for many years, the Panter is made by the highly-respected Agio Sigarfabrieken in Holland. The Silhouette, Bijou, Limbo and Panatellas shapes are all-tobacco cigars; the other shapes use a sheet binder. Wrappers come from Java (on Sprint, Small, Mignon and the Panatellas), Sumatra (Silhouette, Bijou and Limbo) and Connecticut (Lights). A new shape, the Mignon Deluxe, features an Ecuadorian wrapper.

SMALL CIGARS: BRAND LISTINGS

PARODI
Machine-made in Scranton, Pennsylvania, USA.

Shape	Name	Lgth	Ring	Wrapper
Cheroot	Ammezzati	3½	34	Ma
Cheroot	Twin Pack	4	34	Ma
Cheroot	Bon Gusto	4	34	Ma
Cheroot	Cello	4	34	Ma
Cheroot	Economy	4	34	Ma
Cheroot	Kings	4½	34	Ma

Here are famous dry-cured, 100% tobacco cigars which use only the finest, dark-fired tobaccos from Kentucky and Tennessee. Highly respected since their introduction in 1913, the blend of leaves always includes not less than three different crop years, which contributes to the medium-bodied flavor which Parodi is famous for.

PEDRONI
Machine-made in Switzerland.

Shape	Name	Lgth	Ring	Wrapper
Cheroot	Classico	3⅝	34	Ma
Cheroot	Anisette	3⅝	34	Ma

These small treats feature dry-cured, dark-fired leaves and are all tobacco; Pedronis are offered in twin-packs and five-packs.

PETRI
Machine-made in Scranton, Pennsylvania, USA.

Shape	Name	Lgth	Ring	Wrapper
Cheroot	AA	3½	34	Ma
Cheroot	Squillo	4	34	Ma
Cheroot	Sigaretto	3½	34	Ma

Cheroot	Sigaretto Kings	4	34	Ma
Cheroot	Toscanelli	4	34	Ma
Cheroot	Toscani	6½	34	Ma

Created in 1906, Petri offers all-tobacco, dry-cured cigars with a medium-bodied taste. The wrapper, binder and filler are all dark-fired Kentucky and Tennessee tobaccos from at least three different crop years.

PHILLIES LITTLE CIGARS
Machine-made in Selma, Alabama, USA.

Shape	Name	Lgth	Ring	Wrapper
Cigarillo	Natural	3⅛	20	CC
Cigarillo	Sweet	3⅛	20	CC

Here are little cigars with the mild taste of the famous Phillies line. The filler tobaccos are a combination of chopped Indonesian and United States leaves, surrounded by a sheet wrapper and binder.

PIPERS
Machine-made in Dingelstadt, Germany.

Shape	Name	Lgth	Ring	Wrapper
Cigarillo	Piper's Mini Vanilla	3	20	CC
Cigarillo	Piper's Mini Cherry	3	20	CM
Cigarillo	Piper's Mini Plum	3	20	Ma
Small Panatela	Piper's Corona Vanilla	4¾	33	CC
Small Panatela	Piper's Corona Cherry	4¾	33	CM
Small Panatela	Piper's Corona Plum	4¾	33	Ma
Cigarillo	Piper's Panatela Vanilla	4½	25	CC
Cigarillo	Piper's Panatela Cherry	4½	25	CM
Cigarillo	Piper's Panatela Plum	4½	25	Ma

SMALL CIGARS: BRAND LISTINGS

This line of cigarillos and small panatelas complements the handmade Charles Fairmorn line. These are all-tobacco, mild cigars available in three flavors and three wrappers: the Vanilla shapes all use Sumatran wrappers, while the Cherry range has Connecticut wrappers and the Plum group uses Brazilian Mata Fina tobacco for its wrappers. All sizes have Dominican binders and a blended Dominican, Nicaraguan and Jamaican filler which are half pipe tobacco and half dry-cured tobaccos.

PRINCE ALBERT
Machine-made in King of Prussia, Pennsylvania, USA.

Shape	Name	Lgth	Ring	Wrapper
Cigarillo	Soft & Sweet Vanilla *(tipped)*	4⅞	20	CM

These tipped cigars are extremely mild and feature an all-pipe tobacco filler, aimed at providing pipe tobacco taste - and aroma - in cigar form.

REGALOS FLAVORILLOS
Handmade in Santiago, Dominican Republic.

Shape	Name	Lgth	Ring	Wrapper
Cigarillo	Vanilla	3⅝	20	CM
Cigarillo	Rum	3⅝	20	CM

This is a handmade brand introduced in 1998. It has Indonesian tobacco throughout with short filler. It is mild-to-medium in body and is offered in a choice of vanilla or rum flavors. It is presented in cellophaned packs of five.

RUSTLERS
Machine-made in McAdoo, Pennsylvania, USA.

Shape	Name	Lgth	Ring	Wrapper
Cigarillo	Black 'n Cherry	3⅞	23	CC
Cigarillo	Menthol	3⅞	23	CC
Cigarillo	Sweets	3⅞	23	CC

SMALL CIGARS: BRAND LISTINGS

This is a machine-made little cigar with a filter tip and a manufactured wrapper, offered in three flavored styles in flip-top boxes of seven cigars each.

ST. REGIS
Machine-made in Tampa, Florida, USA.

Shape	Name	Lgth	Ring	Wrapper
Cigarillo	Regular	3⅞	20	CC
Cigarillo	Menthol	3⅞	20	CC
Cigarillo	Pipe Bouquet	3⅞	20	CC

These little cigars have been around since 1951 and offer a mild taste, featuring a blend of U.S. tobaccos in the filler core. Available in packs of 20.

SCHIMMELPENNICK
Machine-made in Wageningen, the Netherlands.

Shape	Name		Lgth	Ring	Wrapper
Small Panatela	Florina		3⅞	32	CC
Short Panatela	Half Corona		3¾	36	CC
Cigarillo	Nostra		2⅞	20	CC
Cigarillo	Media		3	20	CC
Cigarillo	Media Brazil		3	20	Ma
Cigarillo	Mono		3⅜	22	CC
Cigarillo	Mono Brazil		3⅜	22	Ma
Small Panatela	Vada		3⅞	32	CC
Cigarillo	Mini Tips	(tipped)	4	20	CC
Cigarillo	Duet		5⅝	26	CC
Cigarillo	Duet Brazil		5⅝	24	Ma
Cigarillo	Duet Midi		4¾	26	CC
Cigarillo	Duet Mini		2⅞	26	CC
Cigarillo	Duet Plus		3½	26	CC

Cigarillo	Mini Cigar	2¾	20	CC
Cigarillo	Mini Cigar Milds	2¾	20	CC
Cigarillo	Havana Lights	3	20	CC
Cigarillo	Havana Milds	3	20	CC
Cigarillo	Swing	3	20	CC

One of the great names in cigarillos, enjoyed in more than 130 countries. These carefully-blended small cigars utilize tobaccos of a half-dozen nations to achieve their trademark mild-to-medium body and rich flavor. Highlights of the shapes include Indonesian wrappers on the Half Corona, Media, Mini Tip and Mono; Brazilian and Javan tobaccos in the Florina; a Cameroon wrapper and 12 types of filler tobaccos in the Vada; a combination of Brazilian, Indonesian and Cameroon leaves in the Duet; a Sumatran-seed wrapper grown in Brazil on the Mini, and a Connecticut Shade wrapper on the Mini Mild. The only flavored cigar of the line is the Swing, which offers a surprising taste of mango!

SUERDIECK
Made in Cruz des Almas, Brazil.

Shape	Name	Lgth	Ring	Wrapper
	Handmade, with 100% tobacco:			
Cigarillo	Copacabana	5	29	CC
Cigarillo	Brasilia Petit	3⅛	22	CM
Cigarillo	Beira Mar Finos	5¼	28	CM
	Machine-made, with sheet binders:			
Cigarillo	Palomitas	3½	32	CM
Cigarillo	Reynitas	3⅛	22	CC-CM

The all-tobacco cigarillos are the pride of Brazil, with all home-grown tobaccos used in the blend. The Palomitas shape is available in a classic style plus two flavored styles: cherry and clove.

SUPER VALUE LITTLE CIGARS
Machine-made in McAdoo, Pennsylvania, USA.

SMALL CIGARS: BRAND LISTINGS

Shape	Name	Lgth	Ring	Wrapper
Cigarillo	Cherry	3⅞	20	CC
Cigarillo	Sweet	3⅞	20	CC
Cigarillo	Menthol	3⅞	20	CC
Cigarillo	Ultra Mild	3⅞	20	CC

This brand uses manufactured wrappers and has filter tips. Super Values are offered in packs of 20.

SUPRE SWEETS
Machine-made in McAdoo, Pennsylvania, USA and Cayey, Puerto Rico.

Shape	Name		Lgth	Ring	Wrapper
Cigarillo	Tip Cigarillo	(tipped)	5⅛	27	CM
Cigarillo	Cigarillos		4¾	27½	CM
Petit Corona	Perfectos		4¾	44	CM
Cigarillo	Little Cigars		3⅞	20	CM

The tip Cigarillo and Little Cigars are made in McAdoo, Pennsylvania, while the Perfectos and Cigarillos are produced in Puerto Rico. All styles feature a manufactured wrapper and binder around a short-filler center.

TIJUANA SMALLS
Machine-made in Dothan, Alabama, USA.

Shape	Name		Lgth	Ring	Wrapper
Cigarillo	Aromatic	(tipped)	4¼	21	CC
Cigarillo	Cherry	(tipped)	4¼	21	CC
Cigarillo	Regular	(tipped)	4¼	21	CC

Created in 1968, these mild cigars are tipped and made with sheet wrappers and binders and a blend of filler tobaccos. They are sold only in ten-packs.

SMALL CIGARS: BRAND LISTINGS

TIPARILLO
Machine-made in Dothan, Alabama, USA.

Shape	Name		Lgth	Ring	Wrapper
Cigarillo	Mild Blend	(tipped)	5	27	CC
Cigarillo	Sweet Blend	(tipped)	5	27	CC
Cigarillo	Aromatic	(tipped)	5	27	CC
Cigarillo	Menthol	(tipped)	5	27	CC

These sleek cigars are made with sheet wrapper and binder and a blend of filler tobaccos; all of the sizes feature plastic tips. Tiparillos are offered in five-packs and boxes of 50.

TOBAJARA
Machine-made in Germany.

Shape	Name	Lgth	Ring	Wrapper
Cigarillo	No. 1 Brazil	3¼	20	CM
Cigarillo	No. 2 Brazil	3⅝	26	CM
Cigarillo	Chicos Brazil	5½	28	CM

This is a medium-bodied, dry-cured cigarillo, offered in packs of 20 for the No. 1 and No. 2 models and in five-packs for the Chicos. This brand features a Brazilian wrapper, sheet binder and filler tobacco from Brazil and Indonesia.

TORINO
Machine-made in Scranton, Pennsylvania, USA.

Shape	Name	Lgth	Ring	Wrapper
Cheroot	Twin	4	34	Ma
Cheroot	King	5¾	34	Ma

This blend is 100% tobacco, using only dark-fired Kentucky and Tennessee leaves for a medium-bodied taste . . . but flavored with a touch of vanilla!

SMALL CIGARS: BRAND LISTINGS

VICTORIA
Machine-made in Las Palmas, the Canary Islands of Spain.

Shape	Name	Lgth	Ring	Wrapper
Cigarillo	Mini	3¾	23	CC
Cigarillo	Cortados	3½	27	CC
Cigarillo	No. 5	4⅛	26	CC
Small Panatela	No. 10	4	30	CC
Small Panatela	No. 15	4¼	34	CC
Cigarillo	Coronas Reserve	3¼	20	CC
Cigarillo	Helios Capote Mini Club	4	23	CC

This light-bodied smoke features either a Connecticut wrapper (Cortados, Cigarro, No. 15, Coronas Reserve) or a Sheet wrapper (Mini, No. 10, Capote Mini Club), offered in 10-packs (except for the Coronas Reserve, in 20s).

VILLIGER
Machine-made in Germany and Switzerland.

Shape	Name	Lgth	Ring	Wrapper
Cigarillo	Villiger-Kiel Mild *(tipped)*	6⅝	29	CI
Cigarillo	Villiger-Kiel Brasil *(tipped)*	6⅝	29	CM
Cigarillo	Villiger-Kiel Junior Mild *(tipped)*	4½	25	CI
Cigarillo	Villiger-Kiel Junior Brasil *(tipped)*	4½	25	CM
Short Panatela	Villiger Export	4	36	CC
Short Panatela	Villiger Export Kings	5⅛	36	CC
Cigarillo	Villiger Premium No. 3	6⅛	37	CI
Cigarillo	Villiger Premium No. 6	3¾	23	CI
Short Panatela	Villiger Premium No. 7	4	38	CI

SMALL CIGARS: BRAND LISTINGS

Cigarillo	Villiger Premium No. 10	2¾	22	Cl
Short Panatela	Jewels	3⅞	38	CC
Panatela	Menorca	6⅛	38	CC
Cigarillo	Rillos *(tipped)*	5	29	CC
Culebras	Culebra	7¼	24	Co
	Sweet			
Cigarillo	Braniff No. 2	4⅛	20	Cl
Cigarillo	Braniff No. 3	4⅛	20	CM
Short Panatela	Braniff No. 8	4	38	Cl
Cigarillo	Braniff Cortos Dark	3¼	20	CM
Cigarillo	Braniff Cortos Filter Light	3	20	Cl

This famous brand began in 1888 and continues today as one of the world's most respected producers of cigarillos and small cigars. These models range in body from mild-to-medium to medium, using primarily Indonesian and Brazilian wrappers.

WINCHESTER LITTLE CIGARS
Machine-made in the United States.

Shape	Name	Lgth	Ring	Wrapper
Cigarillo	100s	3⅞	20	CC
Cigarillo	Light 100s	3⅞	20	CC
Cigarillo	Menthol 100s	3⅞	20	CC
Cigarillo	Sweet 100s	3⅞	20	CC
Cigarillo	Kings	3¼	20	CC
Cigarillo	Menthol Kings	3¼	20	CC

6.
INTERNATIONAL MEASUREMENT TABLE

For readers more conversant with cigar lengths in centimeters and ring gauges (diameter) expressed in millimeters, the following table will allow conversion of imperial measures into their metric equivalents.

Length	
In 1/8ths of an inch	Length in cm
2½	6.35
2⅝	6.68
2¾	6.99
2⅞	7.32
3	7.62
3⅛	7.94
3¼	8.25
3⅜	8.57
3½	8.89
3⅝	9.21
3¾	9.52
3⅞	9.84
4	10.16
4⅛	10.48
4¼	10.79
4⅜	11.11
4½	11.43
4⅝	11.75

Ring Gauge/Diameter	
In 1/64ths of an inch	Diameter in mm
20	7.9
21	8.3
22	8.7
23	9.1
24	9.5
25	9.9
26	10.3
27	10.7
28	11.1
29	11.5
30	11.9
31	12.3
32	12.7
33	13.1
34	13.5
35	13.9
36	14.3
37	14.7

MEASUREMENT CONVERSION TABLE

Length	
In 1/8ths of an inch	Length in cm
4¾	12.06
4⅞	12.38
5	12.70
5⅛	13.02
5¼	13.33
5⅜	13.65
5½	13.97
5⅝	14.29
5¾	14.61
5⅞	14.93
6	15.24
6⅛	15.56
6¼	15.87
6⅜	16.19
6½	16.51
6⅝	16.83
6¾	17.14
6⅞	17.46
7	17.78
7⅛	18.10
7¼	18.41
7⅜	18.73
7½	19.05
7⅝	19.37

Ring Gauge/Diameter	
In 1/64ths of an inch	Diameter in mm
38	15.1
39	15.5
40	15.9
41	16.3
42	16.7
43	17.1
44	17.5
45	17.9
46	18.3
47	18.7
48	19.1
49	19.5
50	19.8
51	20.2
52	20.6
53	21.0
54	21.4
55	21.8
56	22.2
57	22.6
58	23.0
59	23.4
60	23.8
61	24.2

MEASUREMENT CONVERSION TABLE

Length	
In 1/8ths of an inch	Length in cm
7¾	19.68
7⅞	20.00
8	20.32
8⅛	20.64
8¼	20.96
8⅜	21.28
8½	21.59
8⅝	21.92
8¾	22.23
8⅞	22.55
9	22.86
9⅛	23.18
9¼	23.50
9⅜	23.82
9½	24.13
9⅝	24.45
9¾	24.76
9⅞	25.08
10	25.40
11	27.94
12	30.48
13	33.02
14	35.56
15	38.10

Ring Gauge/Diameter	
In 1/64ths of an inch	Diameter in mm
62	24.6
63	25.0
64	25.4
65	25.8
66	26.2
67	26.6
68	27.0
69	27.4
70	27.8

7.
REFERENCES

For more information about cigars, these books make excellent and fun reading:

Andriote, John-Manuel, Falk, Andrew E. and Perez, B. Henry. *The Art of Fine Cigars*. New York: Bulfinch Press, 1996.

Bati, Anwer. *The Essential Cigar*. New York: Lorenz Books, 1997.

Bati, Anwer and Chase, Simon. *The Cigar Companion, A Connoisseur's Guide*. 2nd edition. Philadelphia: Running Press, 1995.

Bati, Anwer. *The Cigar Companion, A Connoisseur's Guide*. 3rd edition. Philadelphia: Running Press, 1997.

Cabrera Infante, Guillermo. *Holy Smoke*. Woodstock: The Overlook Press, 1997.

Collins, Phillip. *Cigar Bizarre: an unusual history*. Santa Monica: General Publishing Group, 1997.

Conrad III, Barnaby. *The Cigar*. San Francisco: Chronicle Books, 1996.

Davidoff, Zino with Gilles Lambert. *The Connoisseur's Book of the Cigar*. Trans. Harold Chester. New York: McGraw-Hill Book Co., 1984.

Dunhill, Alfred. *The Gentle Art of Smoking*. London: Max Reinhardt, Ltd., 1978.

REFERENCES

Edmark, Tomima. *Cigar Chic: A Women's Perspective.*
Arlington: Summit Publishing Group, 1995.

Foley, Kevin and Foley, Mary. *Blowing Smoke.* Rocklin: Prima
Publishing, 1997.

Gage, Tad. *The Complete Idiot's Guide to Cigars.* New York: alpha
books, 1997.

Garmirian, Paul B.K. *The Gourmet Guide to Cigars.* 3rd
edition. McLean: Cedar Publications, 1994.

Hacker, Richard Carleton. *The Ultimate Cigar Book.* 2nd
edition. Beverly Hills: Autumngold Publishing, 1996.

Howard, Red. *Cigars.* New York: Todtri Productions Ltd., 1997.

Jeffers, H. Paul and Gordon, Kevin. *The Good Cigar.* New York:
Lyons & Burford, 1996.

Kasper, Rhona. *A Woman's Guide to Cigar Smoking.* New York:
St. Martin's Press, 1998.

Lande, Andrew and Lande, Nathaniel. *The Cigar Connoisseur.*
New York: Clarkson Potter/Publishers, 1997.

LeRoy, Bernard and Szafran, Maurice. *The Illustrated
History of Cigars.* Trans. Lexus Translations Ltd. London:
Harold Starke Publishers, Ltd., 1993

REFERENCES

Millington, Neil. *Cigars*. Edison: Chartwell Books, Inc., 1998.

Resnick, Jane, *International Connoisseur's Guide to Cigars*. New York: Black Dog & Leventhal Publishers. 1996.

Rudman, Theo. *Rudman's Complete Pocket Guide to Cigars 1996*. Cape Town: Good Living Publishing, 1996.

Rudman, Theo. *Rudman's Cigar Buying Guide*. Chicago: Triumph Books, 1997.

Scott, Dale. *How to Select and Enjoy Premium Cigars . . . and Save Money!* 2nd edition. San Diego: Coast Creative Services, 1995.

Seldon, Philip. *The Complete Cigar Book*. New York: Ballantine Books, 1997.

Sherman, Joel with Robert Ivry. *Nat Sherman's A Passion for Cigars*. Kansas City: Andrews and McMeel, 1996.

Stucklin, Mark. *The Cigar Handbook*. London: Quintet Publishing Limited, 1997.

Weiss, Sonia. *The Cigar Enthusiast*. New York: Berkley Publishing Group, 1997.

10.
RING GAUGE GUIDE

Use this handy guide to size up the girth of your cigars.
The illustrated ring sizes correspond to the following
shapes:

Ring: 32-34   Slim and Small Panatelas
       35-39   Panatelas and Long Panatelas
       40-44   Coronas and Lonsdales
       45-47   Coronas Extra and Grand Coronas
       48-50+ Robustos, Toros, Churchills, Double Coronas and
               Giants.

32	33	34	35
●	●	●	●

36	37	38
●	●	●

39	40	41
●	●	●

RING GAUGE GUIDE

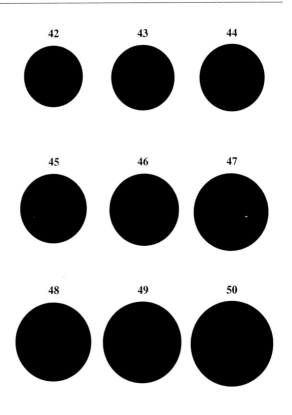

42

43

44

45

46

47

48

49

50

ADDENDUM

Information about these five handmade brands was not available in time to be included in the main brand listings, but are provided here for convenience! Enjoy!

DON KIKO
Handmade in Santiago, Dominican Republic.

Wrapper: Mexico   Binder: Dom. Rep.   Filler: Dom. Rep.

Shape	Name	Lgth	Ring	Wrapper
Double Corona	Churchill	7½	50	CM
Toro	Robusto	6	50	CM
Robusto	Rothchild	4½	50	CM

This is a full-bodied cigar introduced in 1998 by the endlessly inventive cigarmaker Rolando Reyes. It is offered in boxes of 25.

DON SEBASTIAN
Handmade in Santiago, Dominican Republic.

Wrapper: USA/Connecticut   Binder: Indonesia   Filler: Dom. Rep.

Shape	Name		Lgth	Ring	Wrapper
Double Corona	Churchill		7½	49	CC
Lonsdale	Lonsdale		6½	42	CC
Corona	Corona	(tube)	5¾	42	CC
Robusto	Toro		5½	49	CC

This cigar debuted in 1998 and offers a smooth and mild taste. You can find it in boxes of 25 or in convenient packs of six.

LOS REYES ALIADOS
Handmade in Santiago, Dominican Republic.

Wrapper: Cameroon   Binder: Dom. Rep.   Filler: Brazil, Dom. Rep., Nicaragua

ADDENDUM: BRAND LISTINGS

Shape	Name	Lgth	Ring	Wrapper
Pyramid	Piramide	6	52	CM
Churchill	Churchill	7	48	CM
Robusto	Rothschild	5	48	CM
Lonsdale	Corona	6½	44	CM
Torpedo	Figurado	5½	52	CM

Introduced in 1998, this is a full-bodied cigar with a sweet taste and wonderful construction. The four-nation blend is offered in boxes of 25.

REY DE REYES
Handmade in Santiago, Dominican Republic.

Wrapper: Dom. Rep.   *Binder: Dom. Rep.*   *Filler: Dom. Rep.*

Shape	Name	Lgth	Ring	Wrapper
Robusto	Bala	4½	48	CC
Churchill	Churchill	7	48	CC
Long Corona	Corona	6	44	CC
Perfecto	Figurado	6	46	CC
Panatela	Lanceros	6½	38	CC
Torpedo	Petit Belicosos	4½	50	CC
Double Corona	Presidente	7½	50	CC
Toro	Toro	6	50	CC
Torpedo	Torpedo	6	50	CC

Here is the "King of Kings," a medium-bodied cigar that has plenty of flavor with a Connecticut-seed wrapper. You can find it in boxes of 25.

TAKOMA
BY C.A.O.
Hand-rolled in Turkey.

Wrapper: Turkey   *Binder: Netherlands*   *Filler: Turkey*

ADDENDUM: BRAND LISTINGS

Shape	Name	Lgth	Ring	Wrapper
Corona	Takoma	5½	42	CC
Corona	Takoma Special	5½	42	CC

This cigar was introduced in 1997 and offers a full-bodied taste in both styles. It has a spicy flavor and is machine-bunched with the wrapper applied by hand. The filler is made up of Cuban-seed leaves, with the wrapper from Sumatra seed. It is available in packs of five and in boxes of 25.

INDEX
OF ADVERTISERS
AND ILLUSTRATIONS

Page i: Hugo Cassar Cigars
Page ii: Dunhill
Page iii: Diana Silvius
Page iv: La Perla Habana
Page vii: AZ
Page viii: Habano Primero
Page xi: Troya
Page xii: Don Kiko/Los Reyes Aliados/Rey de Reyes
Page 29:   Humi-Pouch
Page 39:   Española   *(see free sampling offer!)*
Page 40:   Size exemplars: Big Cigars – Giants and Double
               Coronas
Page 42:   Stewart-Beckwith humidors
Page 62:   Size exemplars: Figurados – Perfectos, Pyramids and
               Torpedoes
Page 154:   Credo
Page 159:   Pleiades
Page 160:   Size exemplars: Robustos and Toros
Page 173:   Cupido
Page 191:   Dominican Elites
Page 293:   Felipe Gregorio
Page 311:   Fonseca
Page 321:   Barrington House cigars
Page 373:   Hoyo de Monterrey
Page 443:   La Plata
Page 477:   Macanudo
Page 479:   Macarena
Page 507:   Montague
Page 585:   Puros Indios

INDEX OF ILLUSTRATIONS

Page 621:   Royal Jamaica
Page 633:   Santa Rosa
Page 643:   Siglo 21/Santiago Silk
Page 676:   Size exemplars: Churchills and Double Coronas
Page 728:   Size exemplars: Lonsdales, Grand Coronas and Coronas Extra
Page 744:   Size exemplars: Coronas Group
Page 744:   Size exemplars: Cigarillos, Cheroots and Panatelas
Page 818:   Smoke magazine
Page 820:   Roly
IBC: Bering
Back: Zino

NOTES

NOTES

NOTES